DICTIONARY
OF
LABOUR BIOGRAPHY

Volume II

DICTIONARY
OF
LABOUR BIOGRAPHY

Volume II

JOYCE M. BELLAMY
Senior Research Officer, University of Hull

and

JOHN SAVILLE
Professor of Economic and Social History, University of Hull

MACMILLAN

First published 1974 by
THE MACMILLAN PRESS LTD
London and Basingstoke
Associated companies in New York
Dublin Melbourne Johannesburg and Madras

SBN 333 14038 9

Printed in Great Britain by
WESTERN PRINTING SERVICES LTD
Bristol

Contents

Acknowledgements

THE first volume of the Dictionary was assisted with a financial grant from the Institute of Social History, Amsterdam, and we record once again our gratitude to the Institute for help over many years. This second volume and the one that will follow it have been made possible by a substantial grant from the Social Science Research Council. To the members of the Economic and Social History Committee who made the original recommendation and to the Council in general, who supported it, we offer our grateful thanks.

The present volume was completed in MS less than a year after the publication of the first, and we hope that the third will follow just as quickly. Our second volume made such good progress partly because of the increased number of contributors from outside the University of Hull, to whom we are most grateful, but just as much because of the devoted commitment of our own research group. We wish above all to thank Dr David E. Martin, who acted as research assistant for two years and to whose knowledge of bibliographical sources, conscientiousness in application and general helpfulness we are greatly indebted. The second member of our research group to whom we are increasingly beholden is Mrs Margaret 'Espinasse, formerly Reader in English Language in the University of Hull. Mrs 'Espinasse was originally invited to read our entries for construction and style, but her critical appraisal quickly went much beyond her original assignment, and we have come to lean heavily upon her advice and judgement. We have two other part-time research assistants: Mrs Marion Miliband, who has dealt expeditiously and most efficiently with innumerable queries in London libraries and Record Offices, and Mrs Barbara Nield who has performed the same role in Hull.

A research project of this kind must inevitably rely to a considerable extent upon its local library resources, and we are privileged to use the Brynmor Jones Library of the University of Hull, whose rapidly growing research material has been invaluable. To its librarian, Dr Philip Larkin, we are warmly grateful for constant encouragement and sympathetic help; and to his staff, all of whom offer a co-operation that is both skilled and willingly given, we are constantly indebted. We would especially mention Miss Maeve M. Brennan, Miss Wendy P. Mann, Alan Marshall, V. John Morris, Peter Sheldon, Geoffrey D. Weston, and Miss Lila S. Wijayatilake in addition to Norman Higson, late archivist to the East Riding CC and now archivist to Hull University Library.

Outside our own research group and our colleagues at the University of Hull, our greatest obligation is to Dame Margaret Cole, for her continuous interest in the Dictionary and not least for her own contribution to this present volume. The Dictionary was dedicated to her and to the memory of G. D. H. Cole, and we feel a deep sense of gratitude for her steady and helpful support and encouragement. To Dr Robin Page Arnot, too, we continue to be under considerable obligation. As with the first volume, he has read and commented on all the entries on miners' leaders, and we are especially grateful because we know that his help has been given at the expense of his own heavy commitment to his own research and writing. We must add, too, in this context our thanks to Dr A. R. Griffin, of Nottingham University, who has always been most generous in coping with the large number of queries about miners that we have sent him. Among others who have assisted us with comments, suggestions and information on entries in general, we would particularly mention Harold Bing, Edmund and Ruth Frow, Eric Taylor, Martin Upham, Mrs Jill Ward, and also Richard Storey of the Historical Manuscripts Commission. To His Excellency Mr T. A. K. Elliott, British Ambassador, Helsinki, we owe especial thanks for his kindness in supplying a great deal of biographical information on Members of Parliament, some of which we have been able to incorporate in the present volume. We are much indebted to him. We are still relying on work prepared by the following former research assistants (full-time and part-time): Miss Mai Alman (Mrs Allwood), Harry Beeharry, Mrs June Butt, Mrs Valerie Gribbin, Dr Ralph Hayburn, Hugh Inglis, Dr Dorothy Pockley, Bryan Sadler, and Richard Saville. There are, in addition, many individuals who have offered comments on entries, answered our queries or sent information. To all those listed below, we offer our thanks:

Lady Allen of Hurtwood, London; Dr V. L. Allen, Leeds University; Dr B. J. Atkinson, Kent University; R. Bruce Aubry, Bristol; Dr P. S. Bagwell, Central London Polytechnic; Lady Anne Bailey, JP, Cheshunt; Mrs M. Bargrave-Deane, Petersfield; the late A. Barnes, Hull; C. A. Barnwell, Birmingham; H. W. Booth, Hove; Mrs N. Branson, London; Mrs L. Briggs, Rothwell; Lord Brockway, London; Miss J. Brown, Enfield; Miss E. I. Clay, Birstall; G. T. Cottrell, Morley College, London; Mrs R. Dalrymple, Sheffield; A. Deakin, London; B. Dean, Walsall; Councillor J. Donohoe, Blyth; A. Duncan, Newcastle; Mrs J. Dunlop, Wigan; Hon. Lady Alice Egerton, London; Hon. Lady Ruth Egerton, London; Miss M. Fisher, Sheffield; John Foster, Sheffield; the Rt Hon. Tom Fraser, Lanark; Mrs M. Gibb, Cambo, Morpeth; Martin Gilbert, Oxford; Rev. W. Gower, Huddersfield; Mrs M. M. Green, Morley College, London; E. Groves, Hinksford, Brierley Hill; Mrs M. M. Hackett, Birmingham; H. J. Haden, Wordsley, Stourbridge; C. A. Hall, Retford; the 2nd Viscount Hall of Cynon Valley, London; E. Hancock, Lowdham; B. A. Hands, Birmingham; Mrs G. M. A. Harrison, Nottingham; Professor Royden Harrison, Warwick University; Mrs M. Z. Hazell, Birmingham; Dr E. Hinden, London; G. W. Hosgood, Mountain Ash; Mrs J. L. Irvine, Hamilton; A. R. Jones, University of East Anglia; J. C. H. Jones, Pontfadog; Tom Jones, Shotton; S. Knight, *Western Mail*, Cardiff; Hon. Mrs I. Lawson, Chester-le-Street; Lord Leatherland, London; Rev. K. Leech, Canterbury; Dr F. R. Lewis, Hay-on-Wye; G. I. Lewis, University College of Swansea; Mrs M. G. Lindgren, Welwyn Garden City; J. A. Lockwood, Reading; Miss Jane Lockwood, Reading; Edward Longden, Manchester; Councillor Mrs F. M. Longden-Parker, Birmingham; F. Lunn, Wroxall, IOW; Dr A. Mason, Warwick University; Mrs V. Mason, Kenilworth; the late J. A. McHugh, Ellistown; E. Messer, Old Coulsdon; Mrs Lucy Middleton, London; Mrs M. L. Eyles Monk, Barnet; Mrs D. R. North, Reading; F. C. Padley, Reading; Dr E. Palmegiano, New Jersey; N. A. Pease, Limpsfield; Mrs F. E. Percival, Coalville; Dr S. Pierson, Oregon University, USA; Miss G. F. Polley, Croydon; Dr M. L. Kellmer Pringle, London; Lord Robens,

London; D. S. Roberts, Manchester; Rev. M. R. Rostron, Penrhiwceiber; J. Silverman, MP, Birmingham; C. J. Simmons, Birmingham; E. Sitch, Warley; Mrs B. M. Smith, Birmingham; Miss G. Smith, Gawber, near Barnsley; Ald. Dr S. H. Smith, Hessle; P. Strong, Eton College; Mrs A. Swift, Stockport; N. L. Swift, Bath; F. Thickett, Walsall; Miss L. Walvin, Pinxton; Miss G. Webb, JP, London; D. C. Weeks, Harrow; G. Westwood, Birmingham; T. A. Blanco White, QC, London; S. Whittock, Radstock; P. Wildman, Hale; Mrs O. M. Williams, Sanderstead; Mrs A. Wilmot, East Leake; Mrs E. Wyld, Yaddlethorpe, Scunthorpe.

We have used continuously the resources of our public and private libraries and our Record Offices. We are especially grateful to: the British Museum and Colindale Newspaper Library; Goldsmith's Library, London University; R. Garratt, Librarian, Co-operative Union, Manchester; C. G. Allen, Keeper of the MSS, BLPES, LSE; C. E. Makepeace, Local History Librarian, Manchester City Library; E. C. Thompson, House of Commons Library; the Librarian of the *Times*, and Mrs Irene Wagner, Librarian, Labour Party, and her staff. The list of public libraries that follows refers only to work connected with this present volume: Ayr County, Barnsley, Birmingham, Blackpool, Bolton, Bournemouth, Bradford, Brighton, Bristol, Camden, Clitheroe, Denbigh, Derby, Doncaster, Dudley, Durham County, Edinburgh, Enfield, Glasgow, Guildford, Halifax, Hamilton, Ipswich, Kettering, Kingston upon Hull, Lambeth, Leeds, Leicester, Leicestershire County, London: Guildhall, Manchester, Merton, Middlesbrough, Newcastle upon Tyne, Northumberland County, Norwich, Nottingham, Nuneaton, Rothwell, Sheffield, Stirling, Stirling County, Stockport, Sunderland, Swansea, Teesside, Tower Hamlets, Walsall, Waltham Forest, Warwick, Wednesbury, West Bromwich, Wigan, Wolverhampton.

Our thanks are also due to the following archivists and their staffs: G. W. Oxley, Kingston upon Hull County Borough and Dr W. A. L. Seaman, Durham County; to the staffs of the General Register Offices in London, especially I. C. J. Corkindale and R. Wilson, and in Edinburgh, and also to the staffs of the Public Record Office, London and the Scottish Record Office and H.M. Commissary Office, Edinburgh. We should also like to acknowledge the work of two members of the staff of the Royal Commission on Historical Manuscripts for their detailed cataloguing of certain sections of the Labour Party archives, invaluable for students of the labour movement. Much help was also given by the co-operative and trade union movements. To the staffs of the following co-operative organisations and societies we express our appreciation: Co-operative College, Loughborough; Co-operative Party, London; Co-operative Union, Manchester; Oldham Industrial Co-operative Society Ltd and the Scottish Co-operative Women's Guild. To the secretaries and staffs of the following trade unions we are also indebted for help in various ways: Amalgamated Union of Engineering Workers; Birmingham and Midland Sheet Metal Workers' Society; Chainmakers' and Strikers' Association; Iron and Steel Trades Confederation; Manchester Graphical Society; National Union of Mineworkers (especially the following areas: Durham, North Wales, Northumberland, South Wales, Yorkshire); National Union of Railwaymen; Northumberland Miners' Association; Transport and General Workers' Union; Transport Salaried Staffs' Association. We wish to acknowledge further the help given by the following friendly societies and similar organisations: Ancient Order of Foresters, Midland Society, Birmingham; British United Order of Oddfellows; Grand United Order of Oddfellows; Grand United Lodge of England (Free-masons); Independent Order of Oddfellows, Manchester Unity; Northumberland Aged Mineworkers' Homes Association; Province of West Lancashire (Freemasons); and by the following national and local government offices: Home Office, London; Public Trustee, London; the clerks to the Durham CC and Flintshire CC; Glasgow Corporation Town Clerk's Department; and staff at Golders Green Crematorium and Kensal Green Cemetery. We have also received assistance from the following persons and organisations: Chris Cook, Director, LSE Political Papers Project; Fabian Society; Labour Party (Scottish Council); Methodist Archives and Research Centre, London; Salvation Army (Scotland); editor, *Wigan Observer*.

The last group to whom we want to record our thanks are our administrative colleagues at the University of Hull. Mrs J. Naylor, supervisor of the Research Typing Pool, has at all times been most helpful and co-operative and among her staff we should like to mention: Mrs. M. Barker, Miss S. Davies, Miss C. Julian, Miss I. Lindup, Mrs A. Rusling, Miss C. Smith, Miss A. Turgoose and Miss T. Wass. We wish to acknowledge also the typing assistance given by Mrs B. Biggs, Mrs B. Brown and Miss C. Wragg, all of Hull University; and we are especially indebted to Mrs I. Baldwin, departmental secretary of the Department of Economic and Social History, for typing assistance and help in general. Mrs P. Johnson of the Hull University printing staff has provided an excellent photo-copying service. We acknowledge further the assistance in proof-reading given by M. Adams, Mrs M. 'Espinasse, Dr D. E. Martin, Mrs B. Nield, R. Saville, M. Upham and Mrs J. Ward, and in preparing the index by V. J. Morris and G. D. Weston.

We set out in the Introduction to Volume I the general principles upon which the Dictionary was organised, and we have prepared entries for this second volume according to the plans there outlined. By Volume III we shall have completed all the Lib-Lab and Labour Members of Parliament elected before 1914, and extended much further our already large sample of co-operators' and miners' leaders. With this present volume we have begun to work in other areas and movements and with another two volumes we shall have published a large number of entries for the Chartist period, the pre-Chartist radical movement and Christian Socialism. With Volume IV we shall begin completing the entries for all Labour MPs from 1914. As we emphasised in our original Introduction, the plans we have for succeeding volumes do not in any way exclude other types of entries supplied by outside contributors. The number of such contributors to this second volume has exceeded those in Volume I, and we welcome suggestions and offers for future entries. We are especially interested in the personalities of the second and third rank – those who were active at the grass-roots of the movement, and who have remained mostly unknown outside their particular town or region. Finally we wish to repeat another point made in our first Introduction – that our files are at all times open to research workers and to scholars everywhere. Those making inquiries should write in the first instance to Dr Joyce Bellamy, Dictionary of Labour Biography, University of Hull.

University of Hull   J.M.B.
April 1973   J.S.

List of Contributors

Dr Paul Adelman — Senior Lecturer, School of Arts and Languages, Kingston Polytechnic.

Dr R. Page Arnot — London.

Professor Philip S. Bagwell — Central London Polytechnic.

Dr Joyce M. Bellamy — Senior Research Officer, Department of Economic and Social History, Hull University.

Harold F. Bing Esq. — Lecturer, Co-operative College, Stanford Hall, Loughborough.

Dame Margaret Cole — London.

Dr Stephen W. Coltham — Senior Lecturer in History, Department of Adult Education, Keele University.

The late Allan Flanders Esq. — Reader in Industrial Relations, School of Industrial and Business Studies, Warwick University.

Reg Groves Esq. — London.

Dr Brian H. Harrison — Fellow of Corpus Christi College, Oxford.

Professor J. F. C. Harrison — School of English and American Studies, Sussex University.

Dr Ralph H. C. Hayburn — Lecturer, Department of History, Otago University, NZ.

Bernard Jennings Esq. — Head of Liberal Studies Division, Department of Adult Education, Leeds University.

Alan R. Jones Esq. — Senior Administrative Assistant, University of East Anglia, Norwich.

Dr Alan J. Lee — Lecturer, Department of History, Hull University.

Professor Fred M. Leventhal — Associate Professor of History, College of Liberal Arts, Boston University, U.S.A.

Dr Norman McCord — Reader in Economic and Social History, Department of Economics, Newcastle upon Tyne University.

Dr David E. Martin — Lecturer, Department of Economic History, Sheffield University.

Dr Anthony Mason — Lecturer, Centre for the Study of Social History, Warwick University.

Mrs Valerie Mason — Kenilworth.

Neville C. Masterman Esq. — Senior Lecturer, Department of History, University College of Swansea.

Frank Matthews Esq.	Lecturer, Department of History, Stirling University.
Mrs Marion Miliband	Leeds.
Keith Nield Esq.	Lecturer, Department of Economic and Social History, Hull University.
Mrs Barbara Nield	Cottingham, E. Yorkshire.
Frederick C. Padley Esq.	Formerly chief technician, Department of Zoology, Reading University.
Archie Potts Esq.	Principal Lecturer in Economics, Department of Economics, Newcastle upon Tyne Polytechnic.
T. David W. Reid Esq.	Reference Librarian, Stockport Public Library.
Mrs Naomi Reid	Stockport.
Dr Edward Royle	Lecturer, Department of History, York University.
Dr David Rubinstein	Lecturer, Department of Economic and Social History, Hull University.
Bryan H. Sadler Esq.	Lecturer, Department of Economics, Warwick University.
John Salt Esq.	Head of Department of Modern Arts, Sheffield Polytechnic.
Professor John Saville	Department of Economic and Social History, Hull University.
Eric L. Taplin Esq.	Principal Lecturer in Economic History, Department of Social Studies, Liverpool Polytechnic.
Eric Taylor Esq.	Senior Lecturer in Modern History, Wolverhampton Polytechnic.
R. E. Tyson Esq.	Lecturer, Department of Economic History, Aberdeen University.

List of Abbreviations

AEU	Amalgamated Engineering Union
AFL	American Federation of Labor
Anon.	Anonymous
App.	Appendix
ARP	Air Raid Precaution(s)
ASCJ	Amalgamated Society of Carpenters and Joiners
ASE	Amalgamated Society of Engineers
ASLEF	Associated Society of Locomotive Engineers and Firemen
ASLP	Amalgamated Society of Lithographic Printers
ASRS	Amalgamated Society of Railway Servants
BDCRC	Birmingham and District Co-op. Representation Council
Birmingham Cat.	*A Catalogue of the Birmingham Collection* (1918; 1931)
BISAKTA	British Iron, Steel and Kindred Trades Association
BLPES	British Library of Political and Economic Science, LSE
BM	British Museum
Boase	F. Boase, *Modern English Biography* (1892–1921)
BRTTS	British Roll Turners' Trade Society
BSP	British Socialist Party
Bull. Soc. Lab. Hist.	*Bulletin of the Society for the Study of Labour History*
BWL	British Workers' League
Canad. J. Econ. Pol. Sc.	*Canadian Journal of Economic and Political Science*
CB	Companion of the Bath
CBE	Commander of the British Empire
CC	County Council
Cd	Command
Ch.	Chapter
Cmd.	Command
CO	Conscientious Objector
Coll.	Collection
Cont. Rev.	*Contemporary Review*
Co-op.	Co-operative
CP(I)	Communist Party (International)
CPF	Co-operative Productive Federation
CPGB	Communist Party of Great Britain
CRO	County Record Office
CSL	Church Socialist League
Cttee	Committee
CWS	Co-operative Wholesale Society

DLB	*Dictionary of Labour Biography*
DMA	Durham Miners' Association
DNB	*Dictionary of National Biography*
Dod	*Dod's Parliamentary Companion*
EC	Executive Committee
Econ. Hist. Rev.	*Economic History Review*
Econ. J.	*Economic Journal*
Econ. Rev.	*Economic Review*
Edin. Rev.	*Edinburgh Review*
Engl. Hist. Rev.	*English Historical Review*
Engl. Rev.	*English Review*
et al.	*et alia/et alii* (Lat.): and others
Fortn. Rev.	*Fortnightly Review*
GFTU	General Federation of Trade Unions
GSM	Guild of St Matthew
GSO	General Staff Officer
GWR	Great Western Railway
Hist. J.	*Historical Journal*
Hist. Pol. Economy	*History of Political Economy*
HMSO	Her Majesty's Stationery Office
ibid.	*ibidem* (Lat.): in the same place
idem	(Lat.): the same; author as mentioned in previous entry
ILO	International Labour Office/Organisation
ILP	Independent Labour Party
Ind. Rev.	*Independent Review*
Int. J. Ethics	*International Journal of Ethics*
Int. Lab. Rev.	*International Labour Review*
Int. Rev. for Social Hist.	*International Review for Social History*
Int. Rev. Social Hist.	*International Review of Social History*
Int. Soc. Rev.	*International Socialist Review*
IPSU	Industrial and Provident Societies' Union
J.	*Journal*
J. Cont. Hist.	*Journal of Contemporary History*
JDB	Joint District Board
JIC	Joint Industrial Council
J. Mod. Hist.	*Journal of Modern History*
JP	Justice of the Peace
JPE	*Journal of Political Economy*
JRSS	*Journal of the Royal Statistical Society*
KCMG	Knight Commander of St Michael and St George
Kelly	*Kelly's Handbook to the Titled, Landed and Official Classes* (in 1938 only: *Handbook of Distinguished People*)

Lab.	Labour
Lab. Mon.	*Labour Monthly*
LCC	London County Council
LCMF	Lancashire and Cheshire Miners' Federation
LEA	Labour Electoral Association
Lect.	Lecture
Lib-Lab	Liberal-Labour
LMA	Leicestershire Miners' Association
LNER	London and North Eastern Railway
LP	Labour Party
LPD	Labour Publications Department
LRC	Labour Representation Committee
LRL	Labour Representation League
LSE	London School of Economics
LTC	London Trades Council
Macmill. Mag.	*Macmillan's Magazine*
Mag.	*Magazine*
MFGB	Miners' Federation of Great Britain
Misc.	Miscellaneous
MNU	Miners' National Union
Mon. Labor Rev.	*Monthly Labor Review*
Mon. Rev.	*Monthly Review*
MP	Member of Parliament
MS(S)	Manuscript(s)
NAC	National Administrative Council
N. Amer. Rev.	*North American Review*
NAPSS	National Association for the Promotion of Social Science
Nat.	National
Nat. Rev.	*National Review*
NAWU	National Amalgamated Workers' Union
N. Brit. Rev.	*North British Review*
NCA	National Charter Association
NCB	National Coal Board
NCF	No-Conscription Fellowship
NCLC	National Council of Labour Colleges
NCPD	National Committee for the Prevention of Destitution
NCSS	National Council of Social Service
n.d.	no date
NDP	National Democratic Party
NEC	National Executive Committee
NER	North Eastern Railway
New Q. Mag.	*New Quarterly Magazine*
NFBTO	National Federation of Building Trade Operatives
NFGW	National Federation of General Workers
NFRB	New Fabian Research Bureau

NFWW	National Federation of Women Workers
NGL	National Guilds League
NJ	New Jersey
NLP	National Labour Press
NMA	Northumberland Miners' Association
NMCA	Northumberland Miners' Confident Association
n.s.	new series
NUGMW	National Union of General and Municipal Workers
NUM	National Union of Mineworkers
NUPE	National Union of Public Employees
NUR	National Union of Railwaymen
NZ	New Zealand
19th C.	*Nineteenth Century*
OBE	Order of the British Empire
Obit.	Obituary
OEP	*Oxford Economic Papers*
o.s.	old series
OTC	Officers' Training Corps
OUP	Oxford University Press
P	pamphlet
Parl.	Parliamentary
PC	Privy Councillor
PEP	Political and Economic Planning
PKTF	Printing and Kindred Trades' Federation
PL	Public Library
PLP	Parliamentary Labour Party
Pol. Q.	*Political Quarterly*
Pol. Sc. Q.	*Political Science Quarterly*
p. (pp.)	page(s)
PRO	Public Record Office
Proc.	Proceedings
pro tem.	*pro tempore* (Lat.): for the time being
Ps	Psalm
pt	part
Q(s)	Question(s)
QJE	*Quarterly Journal of Economics*
Q. Rev.	*Quarterly Review*
R.C.	Royal Commission
RCA	Railway Clerks' Association
RDC	Rural District Council
repr.	reprinted
Rev.	Reverend
Rev.	*Review*
Rev. of Revs	*Review of Reviews*

RIC	*Review of International Co-operation*
RNVR	Royal Naval Volunteer Reserve
RPC	Revolutionary Policy Committee
Sat. Rev.	*Saturday Review*
S.C.	Select Committee
SCWS	Scottish Co-operative Wholesale Society
SDF	Social Democratic Federation
ser.	series
SFTC	Sheffield Federated Trades Council
SMA	Somerset Miners' Association
Soc. Rev.	*Socialist Review*
Spec.	*Spectator*
SPWMA	Society for Promoting Working Men's Associations
s.v.	*sub voce* (Lat.): under the word
SWMF	South Wales Miners' Federation
TGWU	Transport and General Workers' Union
Trans	*Transactions*
Trans Roy. Hist. Soc.	*Transactions of the Royal Historical Society*
TSSA	Transport Salaried Staffs' Association
TUC	Trades Union Congress
20th C. Q.	*Twentieth Century Quarterly*
UDC	Union of Democratic Control
UM	United Methodist
UNA	United Nations Association
Univ.	University
VFS	Victory for Socialism
WCG	Women's Co-operative Guild
WEA	Workers' Educational Association
Welsh Hist. Rev.	*Welsh History Review*
WFTU	World Federation of Trade Unions
WIR	Workers' International Relief
WRI	War Resisters' International
WSPU	Women's Social and Political Union
WTUL	Women's Trade Union League
WU	Workers' Union
WW	*Who's Who*
WWW	*Who Was Who*
YMA	Yorkshire Miners' Association
YMCA	Young Men's Christian Association
YWCA	Young Women's Christian Association

Notes to Readers

1. Place-names are usually quoted according to contemporary usage relating to the particular entry.
2. Where the amount of a will, estate value or effects is quoted, the particular form used is normally that given in the *Times*, or the records of Somerset House, London, or the Scottish Record Office, Edinburgh. For dates before 1860 the source will usually be the Public Record Office.
3. Under the heading **Sources**, personal information relates to details obtained from relatives, friends or colleagues of the individual in question; biographical information refers to other sources.
4. The place of publication in bibliographical references is London, unless otherwise stated.
5. P indicates a pamphlet whose pagination could not be verified. Where it is known, the number of pages is quoted if under sixty.
6. The *See also* column which follows biographical entries includes names marked with a dagger and these refer to biographies already published in Volume I of the *Dictionary*; those with no marking are included in the present volume, and those with an asterisk refer to entries to be included in later volumes.
7. A consolidated name list of entries in Volumes I and II will be found at the end of this volume before the general index.

List of Bibliographies

The subject bibliographies attached to certain entries are the responsibility of the editors. The entries under which they will be found in Volume I or II are as follows:

ADAIR, John (1872–1950)
MINER

Born 18 November 1872 at Broomside, St Giles, Durham, the son of a miner, John Adair began work in the pits on leaving school. In 1900 he became checkweighman at Littleburn Colliery in Durham. He was then elected successively delegate, secretary and president of the local lodge of the Durham Miners' Association and in 1912 was delegate of the DMA to the Amsterdam Conference of miners. In 1913 he was appointed secretary of the Durham Aged Mineworkers' Homes Association and he held this position until his death. The establishment of the Association was largely the work of Joseph Hopper, and it had opened its first homes in October 1899. It relied on voluntary contributions from all sections of the community but from the earliest days of the Association by far the largest amounts came from the miners themselves [Garside (1971) 291–3].

Adair was much involved in local political and social activities in the county. In 1910 he was elected to the Durham County Council, and served on the Education, Local Government and Old Age Pensions Committees. Between 1918 and 1921 he served on the Durham Board of Guardians; was appointed a County magistrate in 1928 and served for twenty years, including six years as chairman of the Bench; and acted in a number of other capacities, including membership of the board of governors of local grammar schools. He was a keen supporter of Durham's football and cricket clubs.

His main concern in life, apart from his work for the miners, was his religion. He became a Primitive Methodist lay preacher in 1895 and from that time remained a prominent figure in the religious life of the coalfield, preaching regularly and becoming a trustee of several chapels. In 1947 he was awarded the MBE for his political and social work. He died at his Durham home on 28 May 1950, being survived by his wife, a married son and two married daughters. He left effects valued at £1690.

Sources: J. Oxberry, *The Birth of the Movement: a tribute to the memory of* Joseph Hopper [Durham Aged Mineworkers' Homes Association] [1924]; R. F. Wearmouth, *The Social and Political Influence of Methodism in the Twentieth Century* (1957); W. R. Garside, *The Durham Miners 1919–1960* (1971); biographical information: NUM (Durham). OBIT. *Durham Chronicle* and *Durham County Advertiser*, 2 June 1950.

ANTHONY MASON

See also: †Thomas ASHTON, for Mining Trade Unionism 1900–14; †Thomas BURT; †Thomas Henry CANN; *Joseph HOPPER; Peter LEE.

ALLEN, Reginald Clifford (Lord Allen of Hurtwood) (1889–1939)
PACIFIST AND SOCIALIST

Born on 9 May 1889 at Newport, Monmouthshire, Reginald Clifford Allen was the son of Walter Allen, owner of a drapery business and his wife Frances (née Baker), a devout churchwoman. Clifford (the name by which he preferred to be known from his young manhood) was educated first at a Bournemouth preparatory school and then at Berkhamsted School. His mother, a consumptive, died when she was only thirty-five and Clifford inherited her ill-health, suffering from a weak chest throughout his life. He also inherited his mother's missionary zeal and in 1905 entered Bristol University intending to study for the Church. Through the influence of a radically-minded professor, G. H. Leonard, he became interested in social reform and assisted with the work of the University Settlement. He then won a scholarship to Peterhouse, Cambridge, which he entered in 1908 with the intention of completing his studies for Holy Orders. He was still an Anglican and a Conservative, but became converted to a moderate form of Socialism soon after his arrival at Cambridge, where he became a close friend of Rupert Brooke, the poet, and St John Ervine, the playwright, both of them Fabians. Allen himself joined the University Fabian Society and later became its chairman, and was among the small group of Cambridge men who attended the Fabian summer school organised by the Webbs in 1910. Among those who were present were Rupert Brooke, Hugh Dalton and James Strachey. During his Cambridge years Allen was greatly influenced by Goldsworthy Lowes Dickinson, who helped him to lose his Christian faith and become an agnostic; while the main literary influences among contemporary authors seem to have been Bernard Shaw and H. G. Wells.

When he left Cambridge in the summer of 1911 Allen was appointed secretary to a joint committee of the Labour Party and the ILP concerned to promote a Labour daily newspaper. He was by this time resolving his own internal intellectual conflicts between advanced Liberalism and Socialism. He joined the City of London branch of the ILP, and in the autumn of 1911 became secretary of a Fabian Reform Committee, other members of which included Dr Marion Phillips, later chief woman officer of the Labour party, St John Ervine and H. H. Schloesser (later Lord Slesser) [M. Cole, *Fabian Socialism* (1961) 143–4]. A few months later Allen was elected a member of the Fabian executive.

Early in 1912 Allen was among those who convened a national conference of the university Fabian Societies. It met at Manchester on 19 April 1912, established a University Socialist Federation with an initial membership of six hundred, elected Allen as its president, and started publishing the *University Socialist*, edited by Theodore Chaundy. But most of Allen's energies at this time went into building support for the projected *Daily Citizen*. Early in 1912 Labour Newspapers Ltd was established, the first directors of which included J. Ramsay MacDonald, W. C. Anderson, Arthur Henderson, John Hodge and E. R. Pease. The main article of association of the new Company read:

The object for which the Company is established is to establish, print, and publish a newspaper or newspapers and other publications in the interests of and to promote the policy from time to time of the political party known as the Labour party.

Allen's work for the *Daily Citizen*, which first appeared on 8 October 1912, brought him into close working contact with many of the leading personalities of the Labour movement. Among the personal friends he made at this time were Herbert and Mary Wratten, Herbert Morrison and J. S. Middleton, the latter then assistant secretary of the Labour Party. In October 1913 Allen became general manager as well as secretary of Labour Newspapers Ltd, having already shown the flair for organisation that was to be constantly remarked on throughout his career. One immediate and major problem for the *Citizen* was the competition from the *Daily Herald*, which had graduated from a printers' strike sheet in 1911 to a daily paper, first published in April 1912. George Lansbury was the moving force behind the *Herald*, although he did not take over the editorship himself until October 1913; and between the *Herald* and the *Daily Citizen* – the latter representing the official movement – there were bitter recriminations and personal attacks. The *Citizen* was always in financial difficulties, and on 19 May 1916 a board meeting decided that publication must cease immediately.

By this time, however, Allen was already moving well against the main stream of the official Labour movement. On the outbreak of war in August 1914 he took up an uncompromising anti-war position. A lecture he delivered in October 1914 was at once published as a penny pamphlet with the title *Is Germany right and Britain wrong?* – a provocative statement which Margaret Cole notes 'was almost, but not quite, banned from the Fabian bookshop' [(1961) 189]. Capitalism, Allen argued, was the cause of war, and no one side could be blamed more than the other. Both were guilty:

Should then we Socialists have any dealings with this capitalist embroglio? Far from it. Not only should we still condemn all wars, but above all, this war. They say our country is in danger. Of course it is, but whose fault is that? It will be in danger again in fifty years time, if our rulers know they can always win our support by hoisting danger signals. They will never heed our condemnation of their foreign policy if they know that they can always depend upon our support in time of war. We must take what appears an unpatriotic line now so that we may be sure of exercising some influence over future policies. We have to face the only possible outcome of our Socialist faith – I mean the question of non-resistance to armed force.

Towards the end of 1914, together with Fenner Brockway and C. H. Norman, Allen formed the No-Conscription Fellowship. An office just off Fleet Street in London was opened early in 1915, and a national committee established with a young Fabian, Aylmer Rose, as organising secretary. This was the beginning of what it is no exaggeration to describe as Allen's martyrdom in the cause of individual conscience and liberty. The story of the conscientious objectors during the First World War has now been fully documented. Allen was regarded by all of them as a saint and a hero who suffered and endured to the point of destroying his health for the rest of his life. His letters during the war years, published in the volume by Martin Gilbert (1965), were a magnificent tribute to his humanity and sincerity; and on the other side, the prejudiced attitudes of large sections of opinion, including the majority of politicians and public men, towards the conscientious objectors, wrote a black and bitter page in the history of the British people. Everyone who came into contact with Allen marvelled at the spiritual strength in such a frail body. As Bertrand Russell wrote of him in 1917: 'Side by side with his skill and inflexible determination there exists in him a quality almost like that of Saint Francis, a quality of gentleness, of sympathy and understanding.'

The NCF held its first national convention at the Memorial Hall, Farringdon Road, London on 27 November 1915. Allen's presidential address set forth the main lines of their principled opposition to the war. By now the NCF was rapidly developing its organisation throughout the country. Edward Grubb, an elderly Quaker, became treasurer

(and middle-class Quakers were to provide most of the financial backing for the Fellowship), and others who were important in its councils and organisation included Bertrand Russell, Dr Alfred Salter of Bermondsey and Catherine Marshall, whose political experience as parliamentary secretary of the National Union of Women's Suffrage Societies was now put to excellent use in her capacity as political secretary to the NCF, in charge of its important record department. The publications department issued an immense mass of leaflets and pamphlets. In March 1916 the *Weekly Tribunal* was begun and later the *C.O.'s Hansard*.

The Asquith Government introduced the Military Conscription Act on 5 January 1916; and the Derby Tribunals were given the task of assessing appeals for exemption. Allen's first appearance was before the Battersea Tribunal on 14 March 1916; his appeal was held on 10 April just after the second national convention of the NCF, and although he fought an ingenious legal battle, arguing that as chairman of the NCF he was engaged in essential work, his arguments were disallowed. On 11 August 1916 he was arrested, court-martialled and sent to prison. He was twice released and twice imprisoned again, on the last occasion for two years' hard labour: a sentence which brought forth a letter of protest by Bernard Shaw (12 June 1917), who wrote that it was virtually 'a sentence of death by exhaustion, starvation, and close confinement'. Allen had already, on 31 May 1917, in a letter to Lloyd George [Gilbert (1965) 78 ff.] stated his intention to refuse all work in prison. This, as he well appreciated, brought upon him severe additional punishments, and under the strain his health, never good, rapidly deteriorated. The agitation for the release of the absolutists was, however, growing. It was especially associated behind the scenes with the name of Stephen Hobhouse, whose family connections were influential, and Hobhouse and Clifford Allen were released early in December 1917; they were among the first of the 333 absolutists released under the special War Office concession during the following eighteen months [Rae (1970) ch. 10].

From prison Allen went immediately into a nursing home. During his convalescence from what was a desperately sick condition he read widely; and he became generally influenced by the ideas of the Guild Socialists. Towards the end of 1918 he began seriously to renew his political contacts within both the ILP and the Labour Party, and early in 1919 he became a member of the executive of the National Guilds League; a position in which he was expected to use his well-known abilities as a fund-raiser. He took some part in the post-war reshaping of the *Daily Herald*, and he worked also with an advisory committee of the Labour Research Department, whose other members were Margaret Cole, Robin Page Arnot and A. L. Bacharach. But his central political interest in the immediate post-war years was to be the ILP. He was the ILP representative along with Richard Wallhead on the Joint Labour Party–TUC delegation to Russia which left England on 27 April 1920, and which toured the Soviet Union for six weeks. Allen had serious criticisms to make of the Soviet régime, although he was by no means as strongly antipathetic as was Bertrand Russell, another member of the delegation. Allen felt 'profound sympathy' for the sacrifices which had been made during the revolution, although naturally he deprecated the emphasis upon violence. He was taken seriously ill during the visit, and unfortunately most of his notes, including a report of a conversation with Lenin, were lost, but he wrote a short unpublished manuscript which included the interesting comment that:

> Russian Communism, with its principles of common service and social equality may be swept away, and a great centralised bureaucracy substituted, driving a disciplined nation to vast production and perhaps to a new and menacing form of imperialism.

As soon as he had made himself familiar with the internal political situation of the ILP, Allen set himself during the years from 1919 onwards the aim of committing the ILP to a thorough-going programme on mainly Guild Socialist lines. More than anyone else he fully appreciated the new position that the ILP now found itself in with the establishment of the Labour Party on a constituency basis, and he argued strongly that the separate existence of the ILP could only be based on a coherent and clearly defined programme. As he said at the ILP annual conference in April 1920: 'The wider the Labour Party became the more imperative did it become that there should be a nucleus in it which could be represented by the ILP with a programme distinctive from the Labour Party.' To achieve this, Allen won support for an inquiry into both party organisation and party policy. At the next annual conference in 1921 the ILP adopted a programme with a pronounced Guild Socialist bias, and Allen himself was elected party treasurer and from this time entered upon a close collaboration with Ramsay MacDonald.

Allen's election as treasurer was the beginning of his short but enormously important period of influence within the ILP. On assuming the office of treasurer he set about raising much-needed funds and arguing, among other things, for a reconstruction of the *Labour Leader*. The latter changed its name to the *New Leader* in September 1922, and H. N. Brailsford became its editor, thus inaugurating one of the most exciting periods of socialist journalism in the history of the twentieth century. Allen also carried through an elaborate reorganisation of Party Headquarters. He invited Fenner Brockway to join the Head Office staff in December 1922, and he established the Information Department, with Ernest Hunter as secretary and John Paton as national organiser (the latter to be distinguished from the John Paton, a working engineer from Glasgow, who was active in the Guild Socialist movement, and who died early in 1920). Allen reorganised the ILP Summer Schools, encouraged the emergence of the Masses Stage and Film Guild [Brockway, *Inside the Left* (1942) 147 ff.], and most important of all, he began to gather together a group of socialist intellectuals whose efforts culminated in the Living Wage programme, the intellectual stimulus for which came from J. A. Hobson.

Allen became chairman of the ILP at the 1923 annual conference. He was then thirty-four years old. In the general election of December 1923 there were forty-five ILP candidates elected out of a total labour representation of 191; and when MacDonald took office as head of a minority Labour Government, Allen made a series of vigorous pleas for a constructive and dynamic policy. At the ILP conference of Easter 1924 he insisted that it was 'the duty of Socialists as organised in the ILP ... to assist the Government by maintaining a persistent pressure in favour of (1) an increasingly bold use of power for Socialist measures and administration, and (2) a vigorous preparation of Socialist knowledge in readiness for a further appeal to the nation' [Marwick (1964) 86].

The 'Two and a Half International' (the Vienna Union) had reunited with the Second International in May 1923, and Allen became a member of the administrative committee of the new Labour and Socialist International. When, after the formation of the first Labour Government, MacDonald resigned from the executive, Allen took his place. His closest British colleagues in the work of the International at this time were Brailsford, Roden Buxton and Josiah Wedgwood.

The period of Allen's chairmanship of the ILP was one of considerable growth and expansion in its political activities and influence; yet conflicts and tensions were always present within both the national leadership and the party as a whole, and were responsible for Allen's resignation as chairman in October 1925. The background of his resignation has been discussed fully in Brockway (1942) 150 ff., Marwick (1964) 93 ff., and Dowse (1966) 117 ff. Briefly, among the major factors may be noted the hostility of many of the ILP rank and file outside London towards the middle-class intellectuals of the party who became so prominent during Allen's period of influence; the growing political conflict between James Maxton and Allen; and Allen's own state of health. His resignation from the chairmanship of the ILP was really a turning point in Allen's career, for although he continued to regard himself as a Socialist for the rest of his life, his close involvement with Left politics was now at an end. He was never able again to co-operate with those whom he regarded as politically irresponsible and obsessed by the minority mind [Marwick (1964) 104 ff.]. Allen, in fact, never really belonged to the Left; his emotional and intellectual attitudes were always towards a resolution of opposing views, and with his extraordinary charm allied to a very considerable intellectual ability he was often successful in achieving his aims and objectives. One consequence of his break with the Left in the ILP was to bring him even nearer to Ramsay MacDonald, with whom he had always had very close sympathies, and this was to lead him to join forces with MacDonald in the summer crisis of 1931. Before this, however, Allen continued to be active in the affairs of the *Daily Herald* (he was a director from 1925 to 1930) and in this cause he worked closely with Ernest Bevin, particularly during the successful negotiations with Odhams Press in 1929. Allen also devoted much of his time in the late twenties, now that he was removed from direct participation in political matters, to his own personal affairs and in particular to the repair of his own finances.

Although in the late spring and early summer of 1931 Allen had a number of personal discussions with MacDonald on economic affairs, he was never able to convince the latter of the need for positive economic action; and because of his own continued ill-health – he had another breakdown in the summer and during most of August 1931 and was convalescing at the Northumberland home of Sir Charles Trevelyan during the crisis month of August – he was quite out of touch with the day-to-day developments within the Labour camp. When the break came, however, and MacDonald formed his National Government, Allen responded to an appeal for support from MacDonald, and on 7 September 1931 there appeared in the *Manchester Guardian* a letter in defence of MacDonald's action [most of the text will be found in Marwick (1964) 112–14 and Gilbert (1965) 213–14]. The letter, which was long, had been refused publication by the *Daily Herald*. It was later published in an extended booklet version under the title *Labour's Future at Stake*.

Parliament was dissolved on 7 October and the National Government appealed to the country for a mandate. During the election period Allen was urging MacDonald privately to emphasise the need for socialist solutions to the economic problems of Britain, and was at the same time making public declarations (*Times*, 15 Oct 1931) in support of MacDonald's campaign. He accepted MacDonald's offer of a peerage, and the appearance of his name in the New Year's Honours List completed his estrangement from many of his former colleagues and comrades in the Labour movement. Allen, however, was still trying to effect some degree of reconciliation, including the return of Ramsay MacDonald to the Labour Party, but there was never the slightest hope of such an outcome. He first made effective contact with the National Labour Cttee in February 1932, and he became its leading spokesman in Parliament. At this time Allen would seem to have misread the trend of political events in the country at large, and within the Labour movement in particular. He began his association with the National Labour Cttee in the hope of using it as a Socialist pressure group upon MacDonald and the National Government. There was, in fact, never any chance of this strategy succeeding, for MacDonald was now a prisoner of the large Conservative majority in the new House of Commons.

Allen began publishing a fortnightly *Newsletter* from 1 April 1932, using it to provide a forum for the views of progressively-minded people from all parties, and this was the beginning of a coming-together of non-party experts with politicians of the centre which finally resulted in the Next Five Years Group. He resigned from the editorship of the *Newsletter* at the end of July 1932, and was not considered for office by MacDonald during the reconstruction of the National Government in September 1932 – when Snowden, Herbert Samuel and Archibald Sinclair resigned over the tariff issue. MacDonald was now paying much less attention to Allen's views and although it was widely believed that the latter would be brought into the Government as a representative of the National Labour group, he was passed over. It was a considerable setback for one who had gone out on a political limb for MacDonald a year earlier, and who also passionately desired to be active in politics. Allen was distressed by MacDonald's cavalier refusal to treat him with the political confidence which he felt his political experience and position deserved, although his personal relations with MacDonald, it needs to be emphasised, were never of such intimacy that he expected any personal reward for his support. Moreover, political difficulties between Allen and some members of the executive of the National Labour Cttee were increasing during the summer and autumn of 1932, and he resigned from the executive in December 1932 and also from a directorship of News-Letter Ltd.

His resignation from the National Cttee placed Allen firmly in the political wilderness. He was still politically ambitious, but apart from the House of Lords he was now without a platform or organisation. At the end of 1933 he tried to buy a major interest in the *Weekend Review* and turn it into a more popular organ of public opinion, but the scheme failed. His most ambitious, and for a time successful, venture was the Next Five Years Group, the idea of which he first put forward at the 1933 Congress of the National Peace Council at Oxford. The first manifesto, *Liberty and Democratic Leadership*, was published in February 1934, and among its 150 signatures were a number of prominent members of the Labour Party. Signatories to the second public statement issued on 17 May included Roden Buxton, Tom Johnston, A. Conley, chairman of the TUC, and two former chairmen, John Bromley of ASLEF and Arthur Pugh of the Steel Workers. Allen explained what he was trying to do in a letter to Arnold Foster:

Speaking for myself I am as much a thorough-going socialist as ever, but have no intention of hiding my faith under a bushel. But what I do feel sure about is that if I approach non-socialists in the right tone of voice I can get them to endorse what is to all intents and purposes socialism (letter of 17 May 1934) [Gilbert (1965) 294].

It is useful to set against this statement by Allen the comment which Harold Macmillan was to make much later about the most important of all the publications of the Next Five Years Group, called *The Next Five Years*, which was published in July 1935. After remarking that Clifford Allen was 'one of the most remarkable men whom I have known, and one of the most attractive', Macmillan went on to describe his own understanding of what the book, and the Group, were about:

Part 1, on economic policy, was a compromise between Socialists and anti-Socialists; it was a compromise very much to my taste. On looking through it again, it must have seemed at that time to lean rather more to the Left than to the Right, especially as regards the proposals for an increase in public or semi-public control of utilities such as transport, gas, and electricity. My Conservative colleagues and I naturally yielded on some of these questions, in order to meet the many concessions made towards our views on industrial organisation. Nevertheless, on all the other aspects – on the use of money; on expansion; on development; and, above all, on the organisation of economic planning both nationally and locally – the policies of *The Next Five Years* did not differ substantially from those which I had already promoted in my own speeches and writing, and through the organisations with which I was connected. This part of the book might fairly have been described, in political jargon, as a little Left of Centre [*Winds of Change* (1966) 374–5].

The Next Five Years Group was formally inaugurated on 3 February 1935. Allen was chairman, Macmillan and Captain Philip Mumford were joint treasurers, and Barratt Brown, principal of Ruskin College and one of Allen's close personal friends, was secretary. The history of the Group is told in Norman Angell (1951), Lord Salter (1961), Arthur Marwick (1964) and Harold Macmillan (1966).

Allen was a pacifist but a wholehearted supporter of the League of Nations Associa-tion, on whose executive committee he sat from June 1933. He was also a leading figure in the National Peace Council, whose origins went back to 1904. When Canon Dick Sheppard formed the Peace Pledge Union he discussed its aims with Allen, who found himself unable to support it on the ground that while he himself remained a pacifist, reality demanded something more positive than total renunciation of war – an intellectual position which was set out in detail in a speech made to the 1936 Peace Congress, later published as *Peace in our Time*. He had always denounced the Versailles clauses of the Peace Treaty as they applied to Germany, and in the last years of his life, from March 1935, when Hitler repudiated the arms restriction clauses of the Peace Treaty, until Allen's own death in March 1939, he argued for a sympathetic understanding of German claims in Europe. At the end of 1934 he had joined the Anglo-German group which had been formed for the purpose of exploring ways of reducing the tensions between Britain and Germany, and early in 1935 Allen visited Hitler; in September of the same year he was present at the Nuremberg rally of the Nazi party. He reported his visit in the *Spectator*, 25 September 1936. On this and on all similar occasions Allen expounded his ideas and views to members of the British Government and in particular to Lord Halifax, who later became Foreign Secretary to Neville Chamberlain.

In the last years of his life Allen was convinced of two things: first, that the German position was negotiable by men of reason; and second, that he himself might be able to play an important role in the negotiating process. In these last years before the outbreak of war Allen was encouraging what he sincerely felt was only a fair deal for Germany, but at the same time he was profoundly shocked by the anti-Jewish brutalities of the Hitler régime; and on the two occasions he personally met Hitler, in 1935 and 1937, he urged toleration towards those imprisoned and persecuted by the German Government. In particular he strongly championed the cause of a German lawyer, Hans Litten, whose case had been referred to him by Dorothy Buxton [Gilbert (1965) 367 ff.]. On the 27th July 1938 he made a major speech in the House of Lords in which, after re-stating his own record of understanding the German problem, he warned that the continued persecution of the Jews and others would 'bring about an impediment to that peace which we all desire to see established'. His speech ended with an eloquent tribute to the Jewish people.

The agitation of the Sudeten Germans in Czechoslovakia during 1938 evoked a positive response from Allen. He considered that it would be fair to them if they were allowed to join the German Reich; and he advocated this solution both privately and in letters to the *Times*. In August 1938, he visited Czechoslovakia and Germany, and had discussions with Beneš, the Czech President, with Hodža, the Prime Minister, as well as with the leaders of the Sudeten Germans. He also saw Walter Runciman, who was leading the official British mission, and he then went on to Germany, where he had a conversation with Ribbentrop. When he returned to London he discussed his visits with Lord Halifax. Two months later he assessed the part which he played in the negotiations which led to Munich:

> You know that I went to Berlin and Prague during August and had hours of vital negotiation with Ribbentrop, Beneš, Hodža, the Sudeten Germans and all parties both sides of the frontier. It was out of these negotiations that emerged the proposal to use a conference of four powers if a final deadlock occurred. It was a highly controversial technique, but it had the supreme advantage of preventing the actual invasion of Czechoslovakia, stopping a world war and perhaps bringing Germany back into international consultation.
>
> I flew back at once and reported to Halifax and as you all know now the device was the one ultimately employed.
>
> [Allen to Hubert Peet, 8 October 1938 quoted Gilbert (1965) 415–16]

After the Munich Conference, Allen was a vigorous advocate of the correctness of Neville Chamberlain's policy. A long letter to the *Manchester Guardian*, 20 October 1938, was a persuasive argument for his belief that the Munich settlement offered the opportunity for a constructive policy of peace in the coming years.

Allen's health continued to be undermined by the immense strain of the months between August and October, and his tuberculosis worsened steadily in the closing months of 1938. At the end of December he was taken to a Swiss sanitorium at Montana where he died on 3 March 1939; his ashes were scattered on the Lake of Geneva. He was survived by his wife and daughter, and the peerage, lacking a male heir, became extinct. A memorial service conducted by the Bishop of Winchester (Cyril F. Garbett) was held in St Martin-in-the-Fields on 30 March 1939 at which Sir Arthur Salter read the lesson. Allen left an estate valued at £7500 gross, £1230 net.

Clifford Allen, by the verdict of all who met him, was a complex, attractive and fascinating personality. He married Marjory Gill in 1921 and they were quite extraordinarily happy together. His wife, a sister of Colin Gill and cousin of Eric Gill, and herself a skilled landscape architect, later became a regular contributor on gardening and countryside matters to the *Manchester Guardian*. She shared to the full Allen's many interests, and during the last two decades of his life she sustained and encouraged him, and at all times defended him from his critics (for an example of which see the correspondence between Frida Laski and Marjory Allen, in Gilbert (1965) 224–5).

Soon after they settled at Hurtwood House they founded a nursery school for young children in their village; and they enjoyed a common enthusiasm for forward-looking educational schemes and experiments. Allen himself became chairman of the New Schools Association in 1932; and one of the first governors of Kurt Hahn's Gordonstoun School in 1934.

Throughout his life Clifford Allen attracted controversy and argument; and his many detractors have not stilled their criticisms in the years since his death. The biography by Marwick (1964) and the invaluable collection of letters and documents edited and introduced by Gilbert (1965) both provide a reasoned defence of Allen's political career and ideas after the break with the Labour Party. A contrary view was offered by H. N. Brailsford in a remarkable letter to Allen (undated but almost certainly late September or early October 1934) reprinted in Gilbert, 297–9. Allen's death brought a fascinating and revealing collection of letters to his widow (Gilbert, 423–30); of the greatest interest to the students of the 1930s.

Writings: *Is Germany right and Britain wrong?* [1914?] 27 pp.; *Conscription and Conscience: presidential address to the National Convention of the No-Conscription Fellowship November 27 1915* (1916) 15 pp.; *Alternative Service* (repr. from *The Ploughshare*, 1916) 4 pp.; *Why I still resist* [defence made before his 3rd Court-Martial, 25 May 1917] (No–Conscription Fellowship, 1917) 4 pp.; 'Position of British Socialism', *New Statesman 19*, 27 May 1922, 208–209; *Putting Socialism into Practice . . . being an extension of the presidential address to the Independent Labour Party Annual Conference* (1924) 39 pp.; *Socialism and the next Labour Government* [Presidential address ILP conference, 1925] 16 pp.; *The ILP and Revolution* [1925] 15 pp. (repr. from *Soc. Rev. 26* (Oct 1925) 147–60); *Labour's Future at Stake* (1932); *Britain's Political Future: a plea for liberty and leadership* (1934); *Effective Pacifism* (League of Nations Union, no. 368, Apr 1934) 22 pp.; 'Pacifism: then and now', in *We did not fight*, ed. J. Bell (1935); 'Sanctions', *New Statesman and Nation 10*, 12 Oct 1935, 479–80; *Peace in our Time: an appeal to the International Peace Conference of June 16 1936* (1936) 22 pp.; 'Call to Action', *New Statesman and Nation 12*, 4 July 1936, 9; 'Meaning of Nuremberg', *Spec. 157*, 25 Sep 1936, 487; 'Inescapable Facts', *New Statesman and Nation 15*, 26 Mar 1938, 521; 'Lesson of Czechoslovakia', *Spec. 160*, 10 June 1938, 1060.

Sources: (1) MSS: Papers of Lord Allen of Hurtwood, McKissick Library, Univ. of South Carolina, Columbia, U.S.A.; (2) Other: E. R. Pease, *History of the Fabian Society* (1916, repr. with a new Introduction by M. Cole, 1963); *WWW* (1929–40); *DNB* (1931–40); P. Snowden, *An Autobiography* (1934); J. Paton, *Left turn: the autobiography of John Paton* (1936); *Times*, 29 Apr 1939, J. C. Wedgwood, *Memoirs of a Fighting Life* (1940); F. Brockway, *Inside the Left* (1942); F. W. Pethick-Lawrence, *Fate has been kind* (1943); B. Webb, *Our Partnership*, ed. B. Drake and M. I. Cole (1948); M. Cole, *Growing up into Revolution* (1949); N. Angell, *After All* (1951); *Beatrice Webb's Diaries 1912–1924*, ed. M. I. Cole (1952); H. Dalton, *Call back yesterday: memoirs 1887–1931* (1953); C. L. Mowat, *Britain between the Wars* (1955); *Beatrice Webb's Diaries 1924–1932*, ed. M. I. Cole (1956); S. R. Graubard, *British Labour and the Russian Revolution 1917–1924* (1956); R. Bassett, *Nineteen thirty-one: Political Crisis* (1958); G. D. H. Cole, *Socialist Thought: Communism and Social Democracy 1914–1931* (1958); Lord Morrison of Lambeth (Herbert Morrison), *An Autobiography* (1960); M. Cole, *The Story of Fabian Socialism* (1961); Lord Salter, *Memoirs of a Public Servant* (1961); M. Gilbert and R. Gott, *The Appeasers* (1963); A. Marwick, *Clifford Allen: the open conspirator* (1964); Captain L. Hart, *Memoirs*, 2 (1965); M. Gilbert, *Plough my own Furrow: the story of Lord Allen of Hurtwood as told through his writings and correspondence* (1965); A. J. P. Taylor, *English History 1914–1945* (1965); R. E. Dowse, *Left in the Centre: the Independent Labour Party 1893–1940* (1966); H. Macmillan, *Winds of Change 1914–1939* (1966); L. C. B. Seaman, *Post-Victorian Britain 1902–1951* (1966); G. B. Woolven, 'Publications of the Independent Labour Party 1893–1932' (Bibliography for London University Diploma in Librarianship, 1966; copy in Brynmor Jones Library, Hull University); B. Russell, *The Autobiography of Bertrand Russell*, 2 (1968); T. Jones, *Whitehall Diary, 1: 1916–25* (1969); J. Rae, *Conscience and Politics* (Oxford, 1970); M. Cole, *The Life of G. D. H. Cole* (1971); personal information: Lady Allen of

Hurtwood; Martin Gilbert, Oxford. OBIT. *Times*, 4 and 11 Mar 1939.

JOHN SAVILLE

See also: Henry Noel BRAILSFORD;* Charles Roden BUXTON; *George Douglas Howard COLE; †Arthur HENDERSON, for British Labour Party 1914–31;* Frederick William JOWETT, for Independent Labour Party, 1893–1914; †James Ramsay MACDONALD; *James MAXTON, for Independent Labour Party 1914–45; *Ellen WILKINSON.

ALLINSON, John (1812/13–72)
CHARTIST AND RADICAL REFORMER

John Allinson was born in Ireland in 1812 or 1813, but spent his adult life in North West England. With his Irish wife, Jane, he lived in Manchester and Hurst before moving to Stockport, where he worked as a power loom weaver. He first became prominent in the local Chartist movement in the summer of 1842, when the 'Plug Plot' strikes affected the town. Allinson, who was the local delegate to the trades' conference in Manchester, doubted the effectiveness of the strike. He advised his colleagues to return to work before continuing the struggle for the Charter. Nevertheless, in October Allinson was arrested on a conspiracy charge and brought, with fellow-Chartists, for examination at the New Bailey, Manchester. In Stockport, a subscription was raised for his defence, and bail found to secure his release until the trial at the Assizes. Returning home, Allinson then resumed his political activities. He spoke at a meeting held by Thomas Slingsby Duncombe at the Stockport Hall of Science, delivered a lecture on the factory system, and served as a delegate to the Complete Suffrage Conference at Birmingham, in December 1842. Reporting on the proceedings, he advocated union among the Chartists and Complete Suffragists, in support of the Charter. Standing trial at Lancaster, in March 1843, together with Feargus O'Connor and fifty-seven other Chartists, Allinson was acquitted on the grounds of insufficient evidence. He returned home to lecture on the 'Chartist Triumph at Lancaster' and

also, as a Roman Catholic, to join the opposition to the Church of England education clauses in the Factories Bill. In June 1843, Allinson joined the Irish Repeal Association, in the hope of uniting the cause with that of Chartism. He was also involved in the campaign to petition Parliament for the mitigation of sentences passed on Chartist prisoners at Chester and Stafford.

These activities, coupled with his exertions on behalf of the Power Loom Weavers' Union, might have brought John Allinson to a prominent position in the local Chartist movement, had he not found himself at variance with his colleagues on two major issues. Allinson both supported the Anti-Corn Law movement and opposed the leadership of Feargus O'Connor. In October 1843, when already on bad terms with local Chartists because of these views, he was called on by his employer, and agreed to take the platform at an Anti-Corn Law meeting and remonstrate with the Chartists for their opposition. Four months later, Allinson entered into a public discussion with Thomas Clark of the Chartist Executive, in an attempt to prove that Chartist policy was contrary to democratic principles. The *Northern Star* of 24 February 1844 described him as the 'Renegade Allinson', who was 'once of the Irish Repealers, next of the Chartists, then of the Complete Suffrage and now of the Anti-Corn Law League'.

Allinson, who by 1845 had been promoted to overseer by his Anti-Corn Law League employer, maintained his opposition to the Chartists. In 1844, he tried to induce the Irish Repealers to break up a meeting held by O'Connor and George White. He raised objections to the Chartist Land Scheme and supported the Stockport Whigs' Improvement Bill (for which see James TORKINGTON). When John West stood as Chartist candidate at the July 1847 general election, Allinson assisted the Whigs against him. On 31 July, the *Northern Star* described Allinson and Joseph Carter as part of a 'hireling gang' which 'having the purse of the Whig and the press of the League at their command, are using every means to vilify the character of Mr West'.

In 1851 Allinson supported the adoption of an address to Louis Kossuth, who was due to visit Manchester. Two years later he resumed trade union activity, taking a leading part in the formation of the Overlookers' Benevolent Society. This was a friendly society, designed to relieve members in periods of sickness, breakdowns, floods, failures, turn-outs or other contingencies. A member who was out of work might claim the sum of 12s per week, plus 1s per head for every child below the age of thirteen. The founders of the society denied that it was concerned with wage rates.

Allinson, did not, however, abandon the cause of parliamentary reform. In 1858 he proposed petitions to Parliament in support of reform, and in 1866 again advocated the cause of universal suffrage, urging the men of Stockport to put themselves once more in the vanguard of the reform movement. He died at the age of sixty, and was buried in Stockport Cemetery on 2 May 1872.

Sources: (1) MSS: 1851 Census, Stockport, PRO: H.O. 107/2155; Stockport Cemetery records; (2) Other: *Northern Star*, 1842–7; *Stockport Advertiser*, 1842–66; F. O'Connor, *The Trial of Feargus O'Connor* . . . (1843); *Stockport and Cheshire News*, 1866; R. G. Gammage, *History of the Chartist Movement 1837–1854* (1894: repr. with an Introduction by John Saville, New York, 1969); A.R. Schoyen, *The Chartist Challenge* (1958); *Chartist Studies*, ed. Asa Briggs (1959).

Naomi Reid
T. D. W. Reid

See also: George Bradburn; Joseph Carter; Abraham Docker; *Feargus O'Connor; James Torkington.

ANDERSON, William Crawford
(1877–1919)
LABOUR MP

William Anderson was born on 13 February 1877 at Findon, in the parish of Gamrie, Banffshire. In later life he also used the name Crawford, although this does not appear on his birth certificate. His father,

Francis Anderson, was a blacksmith who served the local community of crofters and small farmers, and who in 1868 had married Barbara Cruickshank. Mrs Anderson was a non-conformist and an ardent radical, a woman of wide reading and with a good knowledge of astronomy. She and the local elementary school were responsible for Anderson's education. At the age of sixteen he went to Aberdeen to serve an apprenticeship as a manufacturing chemist. Anderson attended meetings organised by the local branch of the SDF and followed Tom Mann's campaign in the Aberdeen North by-election of May 1896. At another meeting he heard Carrie Martyn give an eloquent and moving speech. Serious-minded and intent on self-improvement, Anderson read extensively: Carlyle and Ruskin were favourites; the novels of Scott, Dickens, Thackeray, Meredith, Hardy and Tolstoi passed through his hands, as did books on politics, history and economics. He regarded Blatchford's *Merrie England*, which he read at about the age of eighteen, as having a particular influence on him, while he was also impressed by some of J. Morrison Davidson's books.

During his years in Aberdeen, however, Anderson did not consider himself to be a Socialist. He advocated land nationalisation, although this was to some extent a reflection of early experiences, for he believed it an injustice that the hard-working crofter, able to gain only a poor living, had to bear the further burden of rent. Many of his attitudes were still based on radicalism and non-conformity, and although he was later to become a free-thinker, as a young man he attended chapel, where he occasionally preached the sermon. Anderson acknowledged the ideas of A. E. Fletcher as being important in his intellectual transition to Socialism. Fletcher at that time was editor of the *New Age*, and ran the journal on Christian Socialist lines. In the 'khaki election' of 1900 Fletcher contested the Camlachie division of Glasgow, being sponsored by the ILP with the support of the Scottish Workers Parliamentary Elections Committee (for which see Bealey and Pelling (1958) App. B). Anderson, who had moved from

Aberdeen to Glasgow, volunteered to assist Fletcher in the campaign on account of the general sympathy he felt for Fletcher's beliefs, and in particular because he was opposed to the Boer War. Before the election was over, Anderson had joined the Glasgow branch of the ILP.

At about the same time Anderson joined the Shop Assistants' Union. He had worked for a short period in a retail grocery store in a poor part of Glasgow before finding employment in his trade of manufacturing chemist. Within three months of joining the local branch of the union he was elected its chairman, and in 1902 he was a delegate to the Shop Assistants' conference at Manchester. In the following year he was appointed as an organiser of the union in the north of England, where he worked to strengthen existing branches and to establish new ones. He was prominent in the agitation of 1907 against the 'radius' clauses which many employers inserted in their managers' contracts. These clauses restricted managers from working within a radius of five or ten miles if they decided to leave the firm or were dismissed. Not only did this stipulation prevent a manager from obtaining employment in his own trade in the town in which he lived, but sometimes also a company with many shops insisted on applying the radius clause in all the towns where it had branches. Some 20,000 managers were involved, and the union, after a nine-month campaign on their behalf, forced most firms to abandon the clauses. In this struggle, as in his other work for the Shop Assistants, Anderson applied great energy and force to the problems before him, and some of the more old-fashioned members of the union became anxious about his radical approach.

Anderson left the Shop Assistants in 1907, partly it would seem because of the misgivings that some officials had about his methods. His departure provided the opportunity for him to concentrate on the political ambitions that had been developing for several years. In 1907 he attended his first ILP conference, held at Derby during Easter; in previous years the conference of the Shop Assistants which met at the same time had claimed his attention. Anderson had already established a reputation as an impressive and persuasive platform speaker, and this he enhanced in the course of his ILP activities. He debated all the political subjects of the day, addressing audiences on such questions as tariff reform, the single tax, national service and land reform; the story is told that on one occasion his listeners were so stimulated that they called for an encore and insisted on Anderson delivering a part of his speech again. His ability to convey a sense of enthusiasm was coupled with a willingness to travel widely throughout the country in order to address meetings; and while still in his early thirties he was one of the best-known and popular leaders of the ILP, regarded by many as the party's rising hope.

In 1908 he was elected to the National Administrative Council of the ILP. Once in the inner councils of the party he was adroit in avoiding too close an involvement with any particular faction. Brockway, who through Anderson's influence became a sub-editor on the *Labour Leader* in 1910, remembered him as an influential member of the NAC who stood midway between Snowden and MacDonald in their quarrels with each other. As a moderating influence, he sought to work with the Labour Party as a whole and smooth over the suspicions with which many trade unionists in particular regarded the ILP. He therefore opposed the ideas set out in *Let Us Reform the Labour Party*, a pamphlet which appeared in 1909, written by J. M. McLachlan with an introduction by Leonard Hall. This pamphlet became known as the 'Green Manifesto', and marked a revolt against the subservience of the Labour Party to the Liberal Government. Those belonging to this faction demanded that MPs who were members of the ILP should vote in the Commons according to the merits of the questions under consideration. Anderson adopted a cautious approach and opposed the rebels, as did the rest of the NAC with the exception of Fred Jowett, who, though not responsible for the 'Green Manifesto', was identified with its ideas. Jowett had been elected chairman of the ILP in 1909, and although it was customary for the chairman of the party to serve for three years, he resigned in 1910; Anderson succeeded him and held the office until 1913.

After ceasing to be an organiser with the Shop Assistants, Anderson appears to have been dependent for an income upon his writing and speaking engagements. He may also have received some financial support from Mary Macarthur whom he had known for some years; they were married by the Rev. R. J. Campbell in September 1911. With the establishment of the *Daily Citizen* Anderson's financial position took a turn for the better. He was chairman of the committee formed in 1911 to organise the setting up of a daily newspaper of the labour movement. Much of the committee's work was done by its secretary, Clifford Allen, who was successful enough in canvassing for funds for a limited company, Labour Newspapers Ltd, to be created early in 1912. Anderson joined the board of directors and acted as its vice-chairman, with MacDonald as chairman. He was also given the post of leader-writer on the new paper at a salary of eight guineas a week. An early problem was the *Daily Herald*, which had a six-month start, and by the time the first issue of the *Daily Citizen* was launched on 8 October 1912 had established itself as a militant and decidedly unofficial voice of labour. The *Daily Citizen* never flourished, but before it finally disappeared in May 1916 Anderson had left the board, resigning in July 1913 along with Arthur Henderson. He explained that he could not accept the decision to give an increased coverage to horse-racing news in the *Daily Citizen* in an attempt to revive its circulation.

In December 1913 he was a speaker at the special conference on the Dublin transport strike called by the parliamentary committee of the TUC. Just as he had maintained a moderate line within the ILP, so also he opposed the dissidents in the trade union movement who demanded more active support for the strikers; and he spoke strongly against the position taken up by Jim Larkin. Anderson seconded a resolution moved by Ben Tillett condemning 'the unfair attacks made by men inside the Trade Union movement upon British Trade Union officials'.

Like most members of the ILP, Anderson adopted an anti-war position in 1914. Shortly after war had been declared the National Council of the ILP met to formulate a manifesto; Anderson read a draft that included the words:

> Out of the darkness and the depth we hail our working-class comrades of every land. Across the roar of guns, we send sympathy and greeting to the German Socialists. They have laboured unceasingly to promote good relations with Britain, as we with Germany. They are no enemies of ours but faithful friends.
>
> In forcing this appalling crime upon the nations, it is the rulers, the diplomats, the militarists who have sealed their doom. In tears and blood and bitterness, the greater Democracy will be born. With steadfast faith we greet the future; our cause is holy and imperishable, and the labour of our hands has not been in vain.
>
> Long live Freedom and Equality! Long live International Socialism!

The Council decided to issue this stirring call rather than the drafts written by Hardie and Bruce Glasier [Brockway (1942) 47]. In August 1914, Anderson was a Labour Party nominee to the War Emergency Workers' National Committee, and he was elected to the executive of the Union of Democratic Control at the inaugural meeting in November 1914.

A few months later, Anderson was successful, at his third attempt, in entering Parliament. On numerous occasions he had campaigned on behalf of other candidates, such as Pete Curran at Jarrow and William Lunn at Holmfirth, and he had contested Hyde, Cheshire, at the general election of 1910, and Keighley in a by-election of 1911. In November 1914 the Labour MP for the Attercliffe division of Sheffield, Joseph Pointer, died and the local party chose Anderson from twelve candidates as their nominee. The operation of the wartime party truce precluded both Liberal and Conservative candidatures, although neither party was happy with the Labour choice.

Another candidate, Col W. L. B. Hirst, who, with the support of Horatio Bottomley, styled himself a business representative for democracy, withdrew from the contest on the last day for nomination (29 December), and Anderson was returned unopposed.

In Parliament he was especially concerned with the consequences of the war for the working class. He spoke frequently on such questions as food supplies (a subject in which he specialised), pensions, working conditions and the operation of the Military Service Act, and acted as a spokesman in the Commons on behalf of the Shop Assistants and the ASE. In 1916 he was a member of a Board of Trade committee appointed to consider the causes of the increase in the cost of living. Like many socialists who opposed the war, he worked for the most part amicably with the pro-war majority within the labour movement. He was chairman of the Labour Party executive in 1915, and he presided at the first national Labour conference to be held after the outbreak of war when it met at Bristol in January 1916.

Anderson's conduct during these years probably enhanced rather than diminished his standing within the labour movement. Glasier, who at times could be a severe critic of colleagues and who had disapproved of Anderson's appointment to the *Daily Citizen*, summed up his opinion of him in February 1915:

Anderson is the most naturally gifted parliamentarian that I know of. He is a born front bench man, and may be Prime Minister yet. He always understands what he speaks about, is always sensible and animated, and never digs too deep to impede his view. He is neither a prophet nor a pioneer; but I have always found him quite open and above-board, friendly and free from plot-hatching. His wife will shove him on should he begin to go slow. What will he do for us? I hardly dare think. He is an opportunist to the core, but not sinisterly so. On the whole I think I would trust him as much as I do MacDonald at any rate. The latter will have to buck up if he wishes to keep his headship of the clan [Thompson (1971) 164–5].

The opportunism to which Glasier referred was exemplified in Anderson's attitude to the war. He concentrated on its impact on working-class living standards, and rather than declare himself against the war as such, when challenged on the point he stated that on humanitarian grounds he was opposed to all wars.

In Parliament it was generally agreed that he added to his reputation as a speaker, addressing the House often and intelligently. He also appeared regularly at meetings in the country; perhaps the most notable speech was the one he made at the Leeds Convention called on 3 June 1917 to welcome the Russian Revolution. Before an enthusiastic gathering, he moved the resolution that local workmen's and soldiers' councils be established to work for peace 'and for the complete political and economic emancipation of international labour' [Graubard (1956) 38]. Some of the other speakers, such as Robert Williams, Sylvia Pankhurst and William Gallacher, regarded the Convention as a first step in a British revolution, but the ardour of most delegates died away as quickly as it had appeared. Anderson's cautious, parliamentary approach reasserted itself and a few weeks later he pointed out that nothing unconstitutional was intended, nor would any councils be formed before permission had been sought from the Government; after this little more was heard of the matter.

The opposition that he had shown to the war bore fruit at the general election of December 1918 when he was overwhelmingly defeated by the Liberal Coalition candidate, T. W. Casey. Despite this setback, he continued to speak on socialist platforms, and after many years of public activity he appeared to enjoy robust health. In February 1919, however, he caught a chill while returning to London from Bradford – he had addressed a large meeting there, the day after attending the NAC in Manchester – influenza developed, and his condition rapidly deteriorated. A particularly virulent influenza epidemic was at its height, and there was difficulty in providing Anderson with proper medical treatment, despite the efforts of Sir Robert Morant, who brought a supply of oxygen to the Andersons' home in Mecklenburgh Square. He died on the morning of 25 February. The news of his death was received by friends and colleagues with deep regret, and many tributes referred not only to his abilities as a speaker and organiser but also to his genial personality and capacity for friendship.

Anderson was cremated at Golders Green on 28 February, when many friends and representatives of several organisations were present. He was survived by Mary Macarthur, whose own work in the labour movement perhaps overshadowed her husband's contribution, and a daughter.

The warmth of Anderson's personal character, his open manner and handsome appearance all served to disarm critics, and enabled him to fill a moderating role in the ILP without attracting bitter comment. His abilities, too, were widely recognised, and not only at the time of his death, but also many years after it, warm tributes were paid to his talents as a politician. Snowden believed that 'No man who knew him intimately would have set a limit to his possibilities. I am sure there was no man in the political life of this country who had such a certain prospect as he of reaching the highest office in the State' [Snowden (1934) 549]; and near the end of his own life Jowett recalled that 'Anderson was not a Hardie, a Smillie or a Maxton, but he had the practical ability and the popular personality which would have made him MacDonald's successor as Labour's leader if he had lived' [Brockway (1946) 185].

Writings: Anderson wrote regularly for the *Labour Leader*; of particular interest among his articles is a series on 'The Independent Labour Party: its meaning, mission, and methods' which appeared between April and July 1912, and 'How I became a Socialist' (25 July 1912), in which he gave some details of his early life; he contributed to other newspapers and journals, notably the *Daily Citizen*, and wrote several pamphlets and articles including: *A Word to the Unattached: a plea for organisation* (Glasgow City Branch of the ILP, [1903?]) 4 pp.; *Tariffs and Toilers* (Hyde?, [1905?]); *The*

Villanies of Adulteration (Eccles branch of ILP, [1906?] 15 pp.; *Servitude of the Shop, and its Abolition* (Nat. Union of Shop Assistants, 1906) 16 pp.; *Parliament and Trade Union History: an argument for political independence* (Hyde, [1907?]) 19 pp.; *The Menace of Monopoly: an argument for public ownership* (City of Manchester ILP branch pamphlet, [1908?]) 16 pp.; *Hang out Our Banners* (repr. from *Labour Leader*, 10 Dec 1909, NLP, 1910) 2 pp.; *Address to ILP Conference, Birmingham, 1911* (NLP, 1911) 14 pp.; *What means this Labour Unrest?* (NLP, [1911?]) 19 pp.; 'The Socialist Movement', *Soc. Rev.* 7 (June 1911) 295–303; 'The Significance of the Labour Unrest', *Soc. Rev.* 8 (Oct 1911) 95–109; (with others) *War Against Poverty* [1912?] 19 pp.; preface to *The Case for the National Minimum* (1913); *Socialism, the Dukes and the Land* [1915?] 12 pp.; *Labour and War Problems* (presidential address to LP Conference, Bristol, 26 Jan 1916, NLP, 1916) 16 pp.; 'The Diplomacy of Labour', *The World*, 12 Mar 1918, 251; *The Profiteers' Parliament* (1918) 7 pp.

Sources: 'The Position of the Independent Labour Party' [interview with Anderson by A. F. Brockway], *Christian Commonwealth* 30 Mar 1910; *Dod* (1915–18); *WWW* (1916–1928); M. A. Hamilton, *Mary Macarthur* (1925); P. Snowden, *An Autobiography* 2 vols (1934); M. A. Hamilton, *Arthur Henderson* (1938); F. Brockway, *Inside the Left* (1942); idem, *Socialism over Sixty Years: the life of Jowett of Bradford* (1946); S. R. Graubard, *British Labour and the Russian Revolution 1917–1924* (Cambridge, Mass., 1956); F. Bealey and H. Pelling, *Labour and Politics, 1900–1906* (1958); A. Marwick, *Clifford Allen: the open conspirator* (1964); R. E. Dowse, *Left in the Centre: the Independent Labour Party 1893–1940* (1966); R. Harrison, 'The War Emergency Workers' National Committee, 1914–1920', in *Essays in Labour History* vol. 2: *1886–1923* ed. A. Briggs and J. Saville (1971); M. Swartz, *The Union of Democratic Control in British Politics during the First World War* (Oxford, 1971); L. Thompson, *The Enthusiasts: a biography of John and Katharine Bruce*

Glasier (1971); personal information: Lord Brockway. OBIT. *Sheffield Independent* and *Times*, 26 Feb 1919; *Labour Leader*, 27 Feb 1919; *Herald*, 1 Mar 1919; *Reynolds News*, 2 Mar 1919; *Shop Assistant*, 9 Mar 1919.

DAVID E. MARTIN

See also: Reginald Clifford ALLEN;* Leonard HALL;* Frederick William JOWETT, for Independent Labour Party, 1893–1914; Mary MACARTHUR; †James Ramsay MACDONALD; *Philip SNOWDEN.

APPLEGARTH, Robert (1834–1924)
TRADE UNION LEADER

Robert Applegarth was born on 26 January 1834 at Hull in the East Riding of Yorkshire. His father, also named Robert, sailed in the Greenland whalers and rose to be the captain of a brig before his death on 7 March 1858 at the age of fifty-five. Apart from a short period at a dame school – to keep him out of mischief – young Robert had no formal education, and at the age of ten he started to make his first contribution to the family income by blacking boots in a shoemaker's shop for two shillings and sixpence a week. After this he became an office boy to a Hull merchant, and then moved to a job in a local joiner's shop, where although not apprenticed, he acquired the basic skills of his trade. In 1852 he moved to Sheffield with his mother, and it was there, a few months later, that she died. Three years later, on 20 August 1855, in the Church of St Mary, Sheffield, Robert Applegarth married Mary Longmoore, the daughter of a farmer. Only weeks after the wedding he left his young bride in order to seek his fortune in America, and but for his wife's frail health, which prevented her from joining him, he might never have returned to England.

America proved to be a rich experience. Applegarth had several jobs ranging from fitting leather on to powder flasks to acting as temporary station master. He saw on one hand the great freedom and opportunities that the continent had to offer, and on the other the horrors of slavery and violence. He read Harriet Beecher Stowe, met Frederick Douglass, the freed slave and orator for emancipation, and became a passionate believer in the abolitionist cause. When he returned to England in 1858 he carried with him three receipts for purchased slaves that were scattered during a fight after a slave sale in St Louis, and which he felt he had a right to keep.

On his return to England Applegarth settled again in Sheffield. On 17 May 1858 he joined the local carpenters' union and soon became president and then secretary. One of his achievements during his period of office was to move the meetings of the union from the public house to a local reading-room. In 1861 he led his union into the Amalgamated Society of Carpenters and Joiners that had been established in June 1860 following the 1859–60 building trades lockout. In August 1862, after a disputed election that had to be settled in the County Court, Applegarth became the ASCJ's second general secretary and moved with his family to 64 York Street, Lambeth. His weekly wage was thirty-three shillings plus a contribution of seven shillings and sixpence towards the rent of his house which also served as the union's headquarters.

For the next nine years Applegarth remained in office, and during that time the membership of the union rose from under 1000 to over 10,000. By the end of 1870 there were 236 branches, including some in America, and 10,178 members; the accumulated funds of the Society amounted to over £17,500. The union that was built under Applegarth's leadership was modelled on the Amalgamated Society of Engineers, and Applegarth acknowledged the ASE's general secretary, William Allan, both as his schoolmaster in trade union affairs and as an important influence in the foundation of the ASCJ. Although individual branches within the Society retained a considerable degree of autonomy, the funds were centralised and efficiently managed. In this way a financially powerful organisation for collective bargaining was built up, and its general secretary soon became experienced in the processes of negotiation, conciliation and arbitration. In addition, in return for the high subscription of one shilling weekly, the Union provided its members with a variety of friendly benefits. The range of these benefits may be judged from the following extract from *A Statistical View and Directory of the Principal Trade and Benefit Societies of London*:

For the year 1869, £5008 16s 4d was expended in sick pay; £8802 18s 10½d was allotted to members out of work, and for travelling expenses; £829 10s 0d was expended in funerals. The whole expenditure amounted to £21,355 15s 2d. The Income was £21,802 13s 7½d; Reserve Fund £17,626 14s 6½d. Sums up to £100 are granted to members rendered incapable of following their employment for life, either from accidents or other causes, and in 1869 the sum of £500 was so devoted.

Various amounts are granted for the relief of members who are in distress, also to their widows and children, and in 1869 the sum of £436 3s 9d was so distributed, and £101 7s 9½d was expended in sending members to situations, and £423 7s 10½d was expended in buying tools for members, and £60 4s 4d was granted for superannuation in weekly sums of 8s, 7s and 5s [*Bee-Hive*, 25 Mar 1871].

During the 1860s and early 1870s Applegarth's activities extended far beyond work directly associated with his own union. He was a member of the London Trades Council and of the emerging 'Junta'. His name featured prominently in the internal politics of the trade union movement in the 1860s, particularly in the disagreements between the Junta and George Potter. Applegarth was active in the agitation which led to the passing of the Master and Servant Act in 1867. He also became deeply involved in many of the working-class movements and other radical, reformist 'causes' of these decades. He was a firm believer in the value of political agitation and involvement, and was therefore an important influence within the London Trades Council at a time when it began to move away from its 'no politics' position. In November 1862, as a member

of the Manhood Suffrage and Vote by Ballot Association, Applegarth wrote an Address to the Trade Unions of the United Kingdom reminding them that by obtaining their political rights they would more effectively secure their legitimate demands as unionists. Applegarth was on the committee responsible for organising Garibaldi's visit to England in 1864; and in the same year he was a member of the LTC deputation that waited on W. E. Gladstone, then Chancellor of the Exchequer, in order to assure him of the Council's support for the Government's Annuities Bill, and to disassociate itself from George Potter's protest against the Bill as an attempt to harm the trade unions by diverting working men's savings away from them and into the coffers of the Exchequer. Applegarth was a prominent member of the Reform League and a member of the executive of the Labour Representation League from the time of its foundation in August 1869. In 1871, he was one of the small group of working-class leaders approached by John Scott Russell in connection with the latter's short-lived proposals for an alliance between Labour leaders and Tory peers in a 'New Social Movement'. It was Applegarth who exposed the 'plot' to the press and thus brought it to a premature end.

Applegarth was a convinced supporter of the North during the American Civil War and of the French Republic during the Franco-Prussian War. While on holiday in France in 1870 he acted as war correspondent for the *New York World*, the *Scotsman*, and the *Sheffield and Rotherham Independent*. He had joined the International Working Men's Association on 1 January 1865, just a few months after its foundation, and the ASCJ became affiliated in June 1867. At the Third Congress in Brussels in June 1868 Applegarth was elected chairman of the General Council, and in the following year he went to the Basle Congress as a delegate from the English section of the movement. The interest of the English working-class leaders in the First International soon declined, but Applegarth remained longer than most of them true to the organisation, which he saw as a movement for promoting international working-class co-operation. Karl Marx, in a number of letters to Engels, had some interesting comments on him. In 1913 Marx's grandson, Jean Longuet, described him as an 'old and respected warrior in our great International army' [J. Longuet to R. Applegarth, 7 Apr 1913, quoted in Humphrey (1913) 125].

But the cause with which Applegarth was most closely associated in the late 1860s and early 1870s was a domestic one, the struggle for the legal recognition of trade unions. In October 1866 the 'Sheffield Outrages' – an outbreak of violence and intimidation among some of the Grinders' Unions in the city – brought to a head a rising tide of anti-union public feeling. On 16 January 1867 the Queen's Bench decision in the case of *Hornby* v. *Close* exposed the accumulated funds of the unions to fraud and embezzlement, by declaring trade unions to be in restraint of trade, and therefore illegal, and not entitled to the protection of the Courts. These events were followed by the announcement, in the Queen's Speech to Parliament on 5 February 1867, of the appointment of a Royal Commission to inquire into and report on the organisation and rules of trade unions.

There were many who hoped that the Commission would lead to the outlawing of trade unions, and there can be little doubt that the revelations of violence and intimidation at Sheffield did great harm to the cause. However, this damage was largely mitigated by the lapse of time (the examination of the Sheffield Outrages was completed by the beginning of August 1867, but the Final Report of the Royal Commission did not appear until March 1869), by the stability and fairness that characterised the activities of the new model unions, and by the integrity of their leaders. Applegarth was the first and most important union witness; he was examined four times and answered 635 questions in all.

Although in his evidence he emphasised the importance of the new model unions in their role as friendly societies, Applegarth did not evade questions bearing upon their activities as trade unions. He did not attempt to deny the existence of their industrial activities, but stressed the moderate and conciliatory policies of his union's governing body. Applegarth admitted that some mild cases of 'rattening' had occurred in the ASCJ, but pointed out that such actions were strongly discouraged. Strikes had occurred, but the executive council never suggested or counselled a strike; furthermore the executive did not automatically sanction the use of union funds in every strike, but carefully examined the circumstances of each, and did in fact refuse to support about one third of the total number of strikes. In cases where it was the union's policy to oppose certain practices, like piecework, Applegarth went to great pains to justify the opposition, at the same time reminding the Commissioners that the union did not go so far as to make it a rule that such practices should not be engaged in by members. The employers' contention that the new model unions were actuarially unsound was also successfully refuted by Applegarth.

As well as providing evidence to the Commission, Applegarth played another important role during the proceedings. As the secretary of the Junta-dominated Conference of Amalgamated Trades, which was called into being on 28 January as a response to the *Hornby* v. *Close* decision, he was permitted to attend the sittings of the Commission as an observer. Between meetings he and one or two others, like George Howell, worked hard in checking the various accusations of the employers and providing information and counter-evidence for the use of the pro-unionist Commissioners Frederic Harrison and Thomas Hughes. This close consultation and collaboration ensured the best possible presentation of the trade union case. Outside the Commission, Applegarth helped to organise many of the public meetings and much of the lobbying that led in 1869 to the enactment of a temporary Bill to protect union funds, and then in 1871 to the Trade Union Act itself. The Act was based very largely on the Minority Report of the Royal Commission signed by Harrison, Hughes and the Earl of Lichfield, and although the value of the legislation was marred by the simultaneous enactment of the Criminal Law Amendment Bill, which effectively outlawed even peaceful picketing, the legality of trade unions had at last been recognised.

The year 1871 saw the dissolution of the Conference of Amalgamated Trades, the beginning of the end of the Junta's influence within the trade union movement, and the disappearance of Applegarth from the national scene after his resignation as general secretary of his union. New men like George Howell and a new, more representative organisation – the Trades Union Congress founded in 1868 – succeeded to the leadership for the second phase of the labour laws agitation, which ended successfully in 1875 with the repeal of the Criminal Law Amendment Act and the passing of the Conspiracy and Protection of Property Act and the Employers and Workmen Act.

The immediate cause of Applegarth's resignation as general secretary of the ASCJ was his appointment in 1871 as a member of the Royal Commission appointed to inquire into the working of the Contagious Diseases Acts. He was the first working man to serve on a Royal Commission, but the honour did not impress certain sections of the ASCJ Executive, who objected to their general secretary's attending meetings of the Commission during office hours. Consequently, in April 1871, Applegarth resigned.

His wife had died on 2 December 1870, and his main concern was to find a job in order to support his young family. (Applegarth's biographer, A. W. Humphrey, records that he had five children to support and although there is no evidence to contradict this, it should be noted that only three children, two sons aged fifteen and four and a daughter aged one year were enumerated in the 1871 Census. A newspaper obituary in 1924, however, mentioned the names of four children still living at that time.) A. J. Mundella offered to find him a place at the Board of Trade, but this was refused. Initially he obtained a part-time post with the Capital and Labour Committee of the Social Science Association, and then for a short time he became secretary to Edward Jenkins, one of the Education League politicians, an author, and sometime MP for Dundee. After this he was appointed a commercial traveller in England for Denayrouze & Co., a French firm that had developed breathing apparatus for use in mine rescue and underwater exploration. Years later the *Times* obituary stated that he 'risked his life many times in demonstrating the use of rescue apparatus in mines'. In 1876 he took out the English patent for the 'Jablochkoff' candle, an electric lighting system invented by a Russian, Paul Jablochkoff, in the Denayrouze laboratories in Paris. Applegarth arranged several lighting demonstrations as well as one or two permanent installations, including one in the machine room of the *Times*. He became the proprietor of the English side of the business in 1880, and in 1886 was elected a Member of the Institute of Electrical Engineers. By 1890 he was a successful small businessman and he moved to Epsom, where he discovered a new pastime in horse riding. In 1898 he moved to Bexley, took up poultry farming, and introduced a new breed of hen from France – the Favorelle. In 1904 he moved to Brighton, where he was made a life member of the Trades Council, and then finally in 1906 to Thornton Heath, Surrey. In 1907 he retired from business.

Applegarth's active concern for reform where he believed it to be necessary continued after 1870. His early business interests gave him first-hand experience of underground work in the mines, and he was a passionate believer in the need to improve safety below ground. In the 1870s he was a member of the Lambeth Vestry, and led a successful campaign to free London's bridges from tolls, and in the 1890s he challenged the Grand Stand Association for the right to gallop without payment on Epsom Downs. Here too he was successful, and the right of free access to the Downs was one of the points in the programme upon which he was elected to the Epsom Local Government Board in 1892. Such an issue was of a temporary nature; of more lasting interest to Applegarth were the causes of co-operation and education.

Applegarth had great faith in the co-operative ideal, which remained with him throughout his life. In the late 1850s, soon after his return to England from America, he had helped to establish the Sheffield Co-operative Society, and during his time as general secretary of the ASCJ the union's monthly reports carried many articles on co-operation. Whenever he moved to a new place he joined the local society. He attended the first national Co-operative Congress (which was held in London in 1869) and was appointed to the organising committee for the 1870 Congress. He was also a member of the first Co-operative Central Board. Two decades later, when he discovered that there was no society in Epsom, he was quick to take steps to remedy the situation.

Universal education was an aim that Applegarth placed above all others as a means of improving the lot of the working class. He had practically no formal education himself, but while in America he had joined a mutual improvement society, and on his return to England one of the first things that he did was to register at the Sheffield Free Library. Even after he became general secretary of the ASCJ he was prepared to expend a portion of his small salary to improve his penmanship. Articles on education as well as on co-operation became a regular feature of the union's monthly reports; and while Applegarth was general secretary, a scheme for technical instruction was launched by the union. It proved successful, and in 1869 Applegarth recorded that he was 'more proud of this than any other work I have had to engage in' [Humphrey (1913) 196 quoting from the ASCJ monthly report for October 1869]. In 1868, after the IWMA Congress in Basle, he spent some time investigating what he regarded as the superior educational system in Switzerland; he reported his findings to W. E. Forster, and published a series of articles in the Bee-Hive, the Sheffield and Rotherham Independent, the Newcastle Daily Chronicle and the Scotsman. Applegarth achieved a certain reputation as an expert on the subject of working-class education. He was a founder member of the National Education League and an eager advocate of compulsory, free and unsectarian education. It was on this platform that he stood as a candidate for the Lambeth School Board in 1870

and only narrowly failed to secure election. Also in 1870, he gave evidence to the Royal Commission on Scientific Instruction and the Advancement of Science, reporting on the progress that was being made in technical education in many parts of the Continent.

After his retirement from business Applegarth initiated in 1909 a new organisation, the National Industrial Education League. It was formally launched at a conference held on 28 February 1911, and its aim was to secure state-financed vocational and technical training for all children immediately after the completion of their elementary education. Applegarth was appointed honorary secretary; but the old man soon withdrew, and the League itself quickly dissolved. He still, however, maintained close contact with the trade union movement. At a dinner in 1914, in honour of his eightieth birthday, the chairman (G. N. Barnes MP), proposing his health, remarked that:

Here was Robert Applegarth, again back in the ranks, not as a big pot, not as an employer as he had been, not as one of the Junta who had got Trade Unionism its legal recognition, but he had come back during the last dozen years taking his part in the work, helping to organise, carrying comfort to the dockers when they were out on strike, and giving his aid and encouragement to any body of men and women whenever he found them. The last part was the best of all, for Robert Applegarth had taken his place in the ranks at 80 years of age exactly where he started [Croydon Advertiser, 31 Jan 1914].

Applegarth, indeed, seems to have retained his radicalism right down to his last years and he always remained lively and interested in the past history and present progress of the labour movement. He wrote, for example, four informative articles in the Newcastle Weekly Chronicle (28 Mar, 4, 11 and 18 Apr 1896) on 'Some Men I Have Known' – full of interest for the historian. (They included, among others, reminiscences of Ernest Jones, Lloyd Jones, J. B. Leno, George Odger.) He was always sympathetic and helpful towards women's trade unionism. In 1917 he declined to be made a Companion of Honour, preferring to remain, as he wrote in his letter of refusal to Lloyd George, 'plain Robert Applegarth' [Labour Party archives and *Westminster Gazette*, 28 Aug 1917]; and at an anniversary dinner of the Woolwich branch of the ASCJ in April 1915, he gave his audience a vigorous warning that while much had been achieved, 'concessions to the workers had been granted very reluctantly, and they had to strengthen their organisations so as not only to keep those concessions, but to get others' [*Pioneer*, 30 Apr 1915].

In politics Applegarth always remained a Liberal. In 1868 he did much to aid the election of A. J. Mundella as MP for Sheffield, securing incidentally the defeat of the unions' arch-enemy, J. A. Roebuck. Although he was a firm believer in the need for direct Labour representation in Parliament he never actually went to the polls himself. In 1870 he was adopted as the working man's candidate for a by-election at Maidstone but withdrew in favour of the official Liberal, Sir John Lubbock. Several approaches were made to him in later years, but he never stood as a parliamentary candidate again.

Applegarth was small in stature – only five feet two inches – but he always appeared to be full of energy. In *Who's Who* he listed his recreations as 'work, more work and still again more'; and George Howell recalled that 'Applegarth was essentially a worker full of energy, almost too full of energy for his build and stature. He never seemed to be tired. . . . As a speaker he was able to hold his own against all comers' [MS Autobiography vol. 1 Howell Coll.]. He had a quick sense of humour and a lawyer's gift for argument and persuasion. He believed in the value of discussion and negotiation, but was never afraid of direct action when the cause justified it. For example, in December 1872 half-a-dozen of the Beckton gas-stokers faced with prosecution for conspiracy were spirited out of the country with Applegarth's help; a year or so earlier a number of *communards* left Paris using his passport [Humphrey (1913) 136, 75].

He was a man who stood firmly for the causes in which he believed, but his activities were not guided by narrowly theoretical principles so much as by a broadly conceived ideal of working-class co-operation and advancement.

Robert Applegarth died on Sunday 13 July 1924. The obituary in the *Croydon Advertiser and Surrey County Reporter* recorded that he had married again and that his second wife predeceased him. He was cremated on 16 July at Norwood Cemetery. At his request there was no religious service, but a secular service was held in the chapel, at which Messrs. A. G. Cameron, E. L. Poulton, Ben Tillett and G. N. Barnes gave addresses. The gross value of his estate was £60.

Writings: Evidence to the R.C. on Trade Unions 1867–69, *First Report* 1867 XXXII Qs 1–302; *Fourth Report* 1867 XXXII Qs 6539–762, 7269–374, 7375–77. (Also published with preface by the ASCJ as *Minutes of Evidence of Mr R. Applegarth, General Secretary of the ASCJ, before the Royal Commission appointed to inquire into Trades' Unions and other Associations. On March 18th, July 9th, July 23rd, and August 1st 1867* (1867); 'Education in Switzerland', eight articles published in the *Bee-Hive* on 19 and 26 Feb; 5, 12, 19, 26 Mar; 2 and 9 Apr 1870; Evidence to R.C. on Scientific Instruction and Advancement of Science 1872 XXV Qs 1937–2043; 'Some Men I have known', *Newcastle Weekly Chronicle Supplement*, 28 Mar and 4, 11, 18 Apr 1896; 'Commemoration of Edward Spencer Beesly', *Positivist Rev.*, 1 Nov 1915, 243–4.

Sources: (1) MSS: Webb trade union collection, LSE; George Howell Collection, Bishopsgate Institute, London; Frederic Harrison papers, LSE; Labour Party archives. (2) Other: *The Bee-Hive* (1861–74) is a most important primary source; E. S. Beesly, *The Amalgamated Society of Carpenters and Joiners . . . . reprinted with appendices from the Fortnightly Review* (1867); *Report of the various proceedings taken by the London Trades Council and* *the Conference of Amalgamated Trades, in reference to the Royal Commission on Trades Unions, and other subjects in connection therewith* (1867) 46 pp.; *Trades Unions Commission: Sheffield Outrages Inquiry* (1867; new edition with an Introduction by S. Pollard, 1971); *Kentish Observer,* 17 Feb 1870; *Bee-Hive,* 5 July 1873 [biography with portrait]; S. and B. Webb, *History of Trade Unionism* (1894); G. Howell, *Labour Legislation, Labour Leaders, Labour Movements* (1902); F. Chandler, *Amalgamated Society of Carpenters and Joiners: history of the Society 1860–1910* (1910); F. Harrison, *Autobiographic Memoirs,* vol. *1: 1831–70;* vol. *2: 1870–1910* (1911); A. W. Humphrey, *A History of Labour Representation* (1912); idem, *Robert Applegarth: trade unionist, educationist, reformer* (1913); *Croydon Advertiser and Surrey County Reporter,* 31 Jan 1914; *Pioneer,* 30 Apr 1915; *Woman Worker* (Feb 1916); *Westminster Gazette,* 28 Aug 1917; C. Richards, *A History of Trades Councils 1860–1875* (1920) 36 pp.; R. W. Postgate, *The Builders' History* [1923]; *WWW* (1916–1928); W. K. Lamb, 'British Labour and Parliament 1865–93' (London PhD, 1933); K. Marx and F. Engels, *Correspondence 1846–1895: a selection* (1934); A Delegate, *Short History of the London Trades Council* (1936); G. Tate, *London Trades Council 1860–1950* (1950); W. H. G. Armytage, *A. J. Mundella, 1825–1897: the Liberal background to the labour movement* (1951); H. W. McCready, 'Frederic Harrison and the British Working-class Movement 1860–1875' (Harvard PhD, 1952); D. Simon, 'Master and Servant' in *Democracy and the Labour Movement,* ed. J. Saville (1954); H. W. McCready, 'British Labour and the Royal Commission on Trade Unions, 1867–1869', *Univ. of Toronto Q.* (1955) 390–409; idem, 'British Labour's Lobby, 1867–1875', *Canad. J. Econ. Pol. Sc.* (1956) 141–160; S. W. Coltham, 'George Potter, and the *Bee-Hive* Newspaper' (Oxford DPhil., 1956); B. C. Roberts, *The Trades Union Congress 1868–1921* (1958); A. Bonner, *British Co-operation* (1961, rev. ed. 1970); S. W. Coltham, 'George Potter, the Junta and the *Bee-Hive', Int. Rev. Social Hist.* (1964) 391–

432, (1965) 23–65; H. Collins and C. Abramsky, *Karl Marx and the British Labour Movement: years of the First International* (1965); A. Briggs, 'Robert Applegarth and the Trade Unions', in A. Briggs, *Victorian People* (1965) 196–204; R. Harrison, *Before the Socialists* (1965). OBIT. *Times,* 14 and 17 July 1924; *Surrey Herald,* 18 July 1924; *Croydon Advertiser and Surrey County Reporter,* 19 July 1924.

ALAN R. JONES

See also: †William ALLAN, for New Model Unionism; *Edward Spencer BEESLY; Henry BROADHURST; Frederic HARRISON; George HOWELL;* Thomas HUGHES; William NEWTON; *George POTTER.

AUCOTT, William (1830–1915)
IRONWORKERS' LEADER

Aucott was born on 20 July 1830 at Hinckley, Leicestershire, the son of a barber who was a Chartist and a Methodist. On account of his father's political and religious connections, Aucott was prevented from attending the local National School, and as this was the only school in his locality he had no formal education. Nevertheless he could read by the age of seven, and thereafter educated himself, as he said, 'by reading and asking questions'. As a boy Aucott worked at home on stocking looms owned by his father until, in 1846, he left Leicestershire for the Black Country. In that year he joined a party of youths recruited by James Talbot, general manager of John Bagnall and Sons, iron manufacturers, Wednesbury, and entered the iron trade as an underhand puddler. At the age of twenty he married Talbot's daughter. She shared her husband's deeply held temperance and religious convictions and was a great source of strength to him throughout their long married life. By the time of his marriage Aucott had become a forehand puddler, a skilled sub-contractor who organised the labour of the underhands and paid their wages, while himself working on a piece-rate basis for the ironmaster. He followed this occupation at various works in the Walsall-Wednesbury area for the next thirty years, and during that time did much to lay the foundations of unionism among the ironworkers. During these years he became a close friend of the Rev. Arthur O'Neill, the Birmingham Baptist Minister and former Chartist. This association and his own family background were the foundations on which were built his political radicalism and his belief in the necessity of discipline and organisation. During the local reform agitation of 1866–7 he was prominent among those pressing the claims of Wednesbury to be a parliamentary division, and thereafter he appeared regularly on the platforms of the Radical-Liberal candidates for the constituency.

The vital year for unionism among the Black Country ironworkers was 1863. Over the previous sixty or seventy years various attempts at organisation had been made, but without lasting success, and puddlers' unions had come and gone. The Black Country during these years was essentially a 'frontier society' and labour generally was restless and reluctant to submit to discipline, whether of employers or unions. This retarded union organisation in all trades, but in the iron industry it was compounded by other factors – the strongly cyclical nature of the industry, the strength of the masters' associations, and division among the ironworkers themselves. In addition to the lateral division arising from the differing functions of puddlers and millmen, the sub-contract system, whereby the income of the sub-contractor depended on maintaining or increasing the output of his underhands while keeping their wages under control, stratified the ironworkers horizontally, and so further weakened the basis of organisation.

In 1863, however, there was established a Millmen's Association, based on West Bromwich, and a new puddlers' union, the Associated Ironworkers of Great Britain, centred on Brierley Hill; and from this time onwards there was a continuing basis of union organisation, however precarious, in the Black Country iron industry. Aucott joined the Associated Ironworkers' union immediately on its formation, and frequently acted as delegate and spokesman for his fellow workers. The Brierley Hill union was wound up in 1868, and thereafter the South Staffordshire district was organised by John Kane's Amalgamated Malleable Ironworkers of Great Britain. Together with Edward Trow, a former Wednesbury furnaceman, Aucott played a major part in establishing Kane's union in South Staffordshire, and in 1874 became its president. By the end of 1872 the Amalgamated Ironworkers had a membership of some 20,000 in 200 branches in the North of England, North and South Staffordshire, Wales and Scotland. This year, 1872, also saw the establishment of the first South Staffordshire Iron Trade Conciliation Board, modelled on the Board established for the North of England by David Dale and John Kane three years earlier. Membership of the South Staffordshire Board consisted of twelve employers chosen by the association and twelve operatives chosen by the union, of whom Aucott and James Capper were the leaders. Its proceedings were deliberately informal, with no permanent machinery, no rules of procedure and no president. A sliding scale was introduced, and where difficulties in its operation arose the Board met to resolve them. The main problem facing the Board was the inability of either side to control those they nominally represented, and it was the union's weakness which led to the breakdown of the Board at the end of 1875. With declining trade, under the so-called 'Derby Scale' of July 1874, covering both the Midlands and North of England, the wages of puddlers reached the 'floor' of 9s 6d per ton, and in July 1875 the employers in both areas gave notice to discontinue the scale as from January 1876. The men's leaders agreed to a five per cent reduction to operate until the end of 1875. In the North of England this was implemented without undue difficulty, but in South Staffordshire a partial strike ensued. Aucott had to admit that the strikers were outside the union and beyond his influence, and the Board was then terminated by mutual agreement.

This setback did not weaken Aucott's conviction that a system of conciliation based on strong organisation was possible, and indeed essential, if the industry was to avoid the damaging strikes he had witnessed as a young man. Together with the leaders of the Ironmasters' Association, Benjamin Hingley and J. P. Hunt, Aucott initiated discussions to devise a new Board, and in March 1876 the South Staffordshire Mill and Forge Wages Board was established. This consisted of twelve employers, and twelve workmen chosen on a works basis and not necessarily union members. The chairman was the current chairman of the Ironmasters' Association and as leader of the operatives Aucott became vice-chairman. There was a paid secretary for each side, James Capper filling this office for the operatives and Daniel Jones for the employers. In addition, there was an independent president from outside the trade to whom any difference which the Board could not resolve was to be referred. He was in fact an arbitrator, and his award in cases of dispute was final. The first president was Joseph Chamberlain, then Mayor of Birmingham.

At this point Aucott's career took a curious turn. In 1877 he left the iron industry, resigned the presidency of the Amalgamated Malleable Ironworkers and the vice-chairmanship of the Mill and Forge Wages Board, and abandoned trade union activity to become superintendent of Wednesbury Corporation Baths. In later years he stated his reason for doing this as disillusionment with the disorganised condition of the ironworkers. During his self-imposed exile he kept in close touch with union affairs, and when in 1887 a series of national conferences of the Malleable Ironworkers' Association was called and the ailing union re-formed as the Associated Iron and Steel Workers of Great Britain, Aucott was elected president of the new union, with Edward Trow as secretary. Within four years the new union had 114 branches and funds of over £5000; and by the time it was absorbed into the British Iron, Steel and Kindred Trades Association (BISAKTA) a year after Aucott's death, funds stood at £39,443 and membership at 9798.

Aucott continued as superintendent of Wednesbury Baths for two years after his election as president of the Associated Iron and Steel Workers. Then, in 1889 James Capper, who had been left partly paralysed by a stroke, resigned from the position of operatives' secretary to what had now become the Midland Iron and Steel Wages Board. Aucott succeeded him and retained the position until his death, combining it until 1912 with the presidency of the Iron and Steel Workers' Association. In this dual capacity he gave evidence before the Royal Commission on Labour of 1892. He also represented the Associated Iron and Steel Workers on parliamentary deputations and at the TUC on many occasions, and in 1895 he was a member of a delegation from the Midland Wages Board which made an extended visit to the Continent to investigate the conditions of iron and steel manufacture in a number of countries. By this time Aucott had become the dominant influence on the operatives' side of the Midland Wages Board. His guidance ensured that the Board was able to maintain consistently harmonious industrial relations within its area, in spite of being beset by the problems of a declining industry; and it became a model for many other conciliation boards in Britain and abroad.

When, in the early years of this century, the transference of the sheet metal iron trade from its traditional Midland location to South Wales necessitated the establishment of the Welsh Sheet Trade Local Committee of the Midland Iron and Steel Wages Board, Aucott became its first operatives' secretary. When he retired from this position in 1907, the chairman of the Board, W. R. Lysaght, presented him with a cheque for £100 in recognition of his services.

Aucott was amongst the first magistrates appointed to the Wednesbury bench, in 1893, but this was his only public office. He was superintendent of the Leabrook Primitive Methodist Sunday School for sixty-two years, and a leading figure in the Sons of Temperance Society which he helped establish in Wednesbury in 1864. In old age he attributed his long life and good health to a régime of rigorous self-discipline and total abstinence, and even when overtaken by infirmity in his last months he remained mentally alert to the end. Shortly before his death he was signatory to an agreement establishing the wages of puddlers at 13s 3d per ton, the highest point reached up to that time.

Aucott died at his home, 10 Rooth Street, Wednesbury, on 27 December 1915. He was survived by one son and one daughter: his wife, after sixty-four years of marriage, had died on 24 February 1915. His remarkable life had spanned over fifty years of trade unionism, from its beginnings until it was assuming something recognisably like its modern form. On 30 December, after a service in the cemetery chapel, he was buried in Wood Green Cemetery, Wednesbury. Aucott's son James trained as a journalist on the *Midland Advertiser* and worked for that newspaper for many years. His daughter, Mrs Wicks, had married an engineer who at the time of Aucott's death was employed at the Wednesbury sewage works. No will has been located at Somerset House.

Sources: Reports of union activities and proceedings of wages boards in *Dudley Herald* and *Midland Advertiser*, 1870–76 and 1889–1915; *Ironworkers' Journal*, 1869–1877 and 1887–1915; *Labour Tribune*, 1886–1894; *Midland Sun*, 15 July 1893 and *West Bromwich Chronicle*, 20 July 1912 [photograph]; evidence before the R.C. on Labour 1892 XXXVI pt I Group A vol. II Qs 14753–844, 15612–54; D. Jones, 'The Midland Iron and Steel Wages Board' in W. J. Ashley, *British Industries* (1903) 38–67; G. C. Allen, *The Economic Development of Birmingham and the Black Country 1860–1927* (1929, repr. 1966); J. Hodge, *Workman's Cottage to Windsor Castle* [1931]; A. J. Odber, 'The Origins of Industrial Peace: the manufactured iron trade of the North of England', *OEP*, *3*, no. 2 (June 1951) 202–20; A. Pugh, *Men of Steel* (1951); A. Fox, 'Industrial Relations in Birmingham and the Black Country 1860–1914' (Oxford BLitt., 1952); J. C. Carr and W. Taplin, *History of the British Steel Industry* (Oxford, 1962); V. L. Allen, 'The Origins of Industrial Conciliation and Arbitration', *Int. Rev. Social Hist.*, 9, pt 2 (1964) 236–54; J. H. Porter, 'Management, Competition and Industrial Relations: the Midlands manufactured iron trade 1873–1914', *Busi-

ness History, 11*, no. 1 (Jan 1969) 37–47; E. Taylor, 'William Aucott – Ironworker and Respectable Radical', *Man and Metal* (Oct 1971) 266–70. OBIT. *Wolverhampton Chronicle*, 29 Dec 1915; *Midland Chronicle*, 31 Dec 1915; *Dudley Herald, Midland Advertiser, Wednesbury Herald* and *West Bromwich Free Press*, 1 Jan 1916 [photographs in all except *Midland Advertiser*]; *Ironworkers' J.* (Jan 1916); OBIT. of Mrs Aucott, *Ironworkers' J.* (Mar 1915).

ERIC TAYLOR

See also: James CAPPER; *John KANE; Thomas PIGGOTT; *Edward TROW.

BAILEY, Sir John (Jack) (1898–1969)
CO-OPERATOR

Born on 1 January 1898 at Miskin, a colliery village adjoining Mountain Ash, Glamorganshire, South Wales, Jack Bailey (by which name he was usually known) was one of six children of a miner, John Bailey, and his wife, Sarah Ann. After an elementary education at Gwyn Ivor School, Miskin, Jack left at the age of twelve to work in a cobbler's shop but he attended evening classes in shorthand and book-keeping. A year later he joined his father, a radically-minded trade unionist and a lay preacher, at the coal face, and worked there until an accident in 1915 compelled him to take a surface job. In 1916 he enlisted in the South Wales Borderers and saw active service in France where he was badly gassed and from the after-effects of this he suffered throughout his life. Like his father he was an accredited Wesleyan lay preacher and had considered entering the Methodist ministry, but decided instead to concentrate on politics. He joined the ILP, read widely, and studied economics through a Ruskin College correspondence course.

When the war ended, he returned to the mines and in 1921 won a South Wales Miners' Federation scholarship to the Central Labour College, London where he studied full-time for two years. Among his contemporaries were Len Williams, Will Owen and Dick Lewis. Nye Bevan, Will Coldrick and Jim Griffiths were students in the previous year.

Bailey fought his first local government election in 1922 in Kensington but was defeated. After completing his course at the Labour College, he returned to South Wales where he was elected to the Mountain Ash Council in 1924, but in the following year, he left South Wales for Yorkshire on his appointment as full-time political secretary of the Bradford branch of the Co-operative Party.

During his years in Bradford he took an active part in the political life of the city and a keen interest in educational affairs. It was during this time that he acquired a broad knowledge of local government organisation through his work on the City Council. From 1928 to 1931 he represented Listerhills ward on the Council and was chairman of the Juvenile Employment Committee, and from 1930 to 1931 he was also deputy chairman of the Education Committee. On the latter he worked with Miriam Lord to establish nursery schools in two areas, and he helped develop special schools for semi-blind and other types of handicapped children. After a two-year break he was re-elected to the Council for Little Horton ward and served until 1936, when he left the city for London. His organising abilities had been recognised when, in that year, he was appointed to the staff of the Co-operative Party as national organiser. Six years later, in 1942, he succeeded S. F. Perry as national secretary of the Party, a position he held until his retirement in 1962.

The Co-operative Party had been established in 1917 in the belief that direct representation of the co-operative movement, both in Parliament and at the local level, was the only effective way for the movement to voice its demands and safeguard its interests. What was not settled at the 1917 Swansea Congress was the relationship with the Labour Party, and this was to provide divisions of opinion within the co-operative movement for many years. What finally emerged from the intensive discussions of the first half of the 1920s was a form of alliance with the Labour Party whereby at the national level there was established a joint committee to consider matters of mutual concern, and at the local level there was provision for Co-operative Parties or Councils to affiliate to divisional Labour Parties. Alfred Barnes moved the resolution to ratify the agreement at the Cheltenham Co-operative Congress in 1927 and on a card vote it was accepted by only 1960 votes to 1843.

Down to the outbreak of the Second World War, political relations between the co-operative movement and the Labour Party operated broadly within the 1927 agreement. There was always, however, a considerable degree of friction on organisational matters, especially at local and regional level; and between 1933 and 1939 further negotiations proved necessary, with few positive results except to indicate the large areas of disagreement as well as of misunderstandings. The coming of war brought some changes. One was the growth in the affiliated strength of the Co-operative Party from local societies, and a second was the representation of the various organisations within the co-operative movement on the National Council of Labour. By 1942, when Jack Bailey took over the position of national secretary of the Co-operative Party, there were a number of urgent problems requiring answers. Lengthy discussions took place during the war years, and in the spring of 1945 there was a joint meeting with the national executive of the Labour Party, the first of a series of further discussions which culminated in a new agreement between the Co-operative and Labour Parties, endorsed by the Brighton conference of the Co-operative Party at Easter 1946 and ratified subsequently by the Co-operative Congress. One of the main items agreed upon was the vexed question of the status and position of Co-operative parliamentary candidates. Henceforth candidates were to be designated 'Co-operative and Labour candidates (and MPs)' and those elected were required to join the Parliamentary Labour Party. The major weakness in all the negotiations and discussions was the lack of agreement on policy issues in contrast with organisational matters; and this lack of policy agreement was to become increasingly noticeable during the years of the Attlee Governments. Once the basic industries had been nationalised, the Labour Government inevitably turned its attention to other sectors of the economy, and it was in certain of these – notably the distributive trades and insurance – that the co-operative movement had important vested interests. The nationalisation of insurance, for example, was a major contentious issue between the National Co-operative Authority and the Labour Party in 1949. Jack Bailey in this, as on all matters of policy, was centrally involved in the negotiations. He argued, for instance, for 'socialisation' rather than nationalisation of insurance, and outlined a plan for a 'self-governing service directly by policy-holders, rather than by State ownership and control. The nation, which consists of a majority of non-policy holders, would organise only at the point at which insurance funds passed into outside investment.' This, he suggested, would be more democratic than nationalisation, because it 'would place insurance directly under the control of the people who insure' [Rhodes (1962) 87–8; Carbery (1969) ch. 12]. The issue of insurance nationalisation was debated again in 1952–3 when Bailey vigorously criticised the pro-nationalisation speeches and writings of Ian Mikardo and James Carmichael.

The election of 1950 sharply reduced the Labour Government's majority and controversial issues such as insurance nationalisation were no longer regarded as practical policies; and after the defeat of 1951 a new period began for the whole movement. By this time Jack Bailey was a major figure in the co-operative movement; he was writing voluminously on all the many economic and political questions relating to the co-operative movement in general; and he was at the centre of the discussions that continued, albeit now at a more leisurely pace, with the Labour Party. Again the main areas of dispute were over policy matters. The 1953 Labour Party statement *Challenge to Britain* evoked widespread criticism from co-operative circles, and Bailey summed up their views in a tart comment in the late summer of 1953, to the effect that 'if there is on both sides a genuine wish to reach an understanding on major policy questions, we already have the machinery to fulfil it. But it must function early in the process of

policy making. Consultation is a farce if it takes place on the eve of publishing a policy statement, when no criticisms can in the slightest degree affect the contents' [*Co-op. News*, 12 Sep 1953]. Policy differences continued, however – over agricultural and marketing policies in particular – and the publication of a new Labour Party policy statement, *Industry and Society*, in 1957 evoked further disagreements in certain parts of its proposals.

The organisational relations between the Labour Party and the Co-operative Party had, by contrast, developed quite smoothly in the years between the 1946 agreement and 1956; but in the latter year a report of a Labour Party sub-committee, under the chairmanship of Harold Wilson, reopened a number of controversial issues. The Wilson sub-committee had been established to inquire into the general structure and organisation of the Labour Party following the defeat of the Party at the general election of 1955; and among its recommendations was a proposal to encourage co-operative societies to affiliate directly to the local Labour Parties. The model to be followed, it was suggested, was that of the Royal Arsenal Co-operative Society which for many years had had a close and intimate association with both the national Labour Party and the London Labour Party. Jack Bailey reacted immediately in vigorous opposition to the recommendation, on the ground that this would mean individual societies affiliating 'would be committed in advance to accepting Labour Party decisions on all questions of major policy, without regard to the views of the Co-operative Union or those of the movement as a whole. That would not do' [*Monthly Letter*, Nov 1955]; and other sections of the movement expressed the same opinion. This was the beginning of a period of quite sharp conflict. In February 1957 the Labour Party's national executive gave notice that it wished to end the 1946 agreement; and it was only in September 1958 that a new agreement was published and subsequently adopted by the various bodies involved. Lord Peddie, who had become chairman of the Co-operative Party in 1957, was, along with Bailey, an important influence during the negotiations. Jack Bailey commented on the new agreement by noting that 'the negotiations ... were protracted and in some respects difficult. . . . In the new Agreement there are provisions which fall below the expectations of either one side or the other. It is, of course, a compromise by which each side makes some concessions to the other. Unless there is goodwill on both sides no agreement will work. If there is goodwill, mutual respect, understanding and tolerance the Agreement will promote our common aims' [Rhodes (1962) 110].

Bailey's contributions to the movement during the long years of his service are difficult to summarise. A great deal of what he achieved involved no formal policy or decision. He did much, for example, to encourage closer contacts between the Co-operative MPs and the business men of the movement [Carbery (1969) 92ff.]; he tried, but was not always successful, to encourage some of the co-operative businessmen to offer themselves as parliamentary candidates; and he continued to be much exercised with the problem of co-operative nominations for parliamentary seats, which involved constant negotiations at the national and local level; and at all times during his general secretaryship he endeavoured to persuade the co-operative trading movement to use the Co-operative Party 'rather than to finance it and ignore it' [Carbery (1969) 256].

Bailey also took an active interest in local Co-operative affairs and was a director of the Enfield Highway Co-operative Society from 1952 and president in the year before his death. After his official retirement from the Party secretaryship at the end of 1962, he continued his association with the movement as a member of the National Federation Negotiating Committee, set up by the Co-operative Congress to consider the amalgamation of the movement's national organisations: the CWS, SCWS, Co-operative Productive Federation and the Co-operative Union. He was also a member for a number of years of the Home Counties Laundry Board and the Metropolitan District Council and District Wages Board. In 1964 he was

president of the national Co-operative Congress. In the following year he was awarded a knighthood, given, according to the official citation, for political and public services in Bradford. Although proud of his association with the Yorkshire city where he acquired much of his political experience, he expressed his personal surprise that no reference was made to his work in subsequent years.

After the move from Bradford he lived at Cheshunt and both he and his wife took a lively part in local politics. At various times Bailey was secretary of the Cheshunt and Waltham Cross Co-operative Party, vice-chairman of the East Herts Labour Party, chairman of governors of Riversmead School, Cheshunt, and chairman of a primary school management committee.

Jack Bailey wrote a great deal on theoretical aspects of the Co-operative movement as well as on its day-to-day affairs. For nearly twenty years, from 1943 to 1962, he edited the Party's *Monthly Newsletter*, wrote a number of books and pamphlets, and lectured at the Co-operative College. In politics, in his years of power in the movement, he became a middle-of-the-road Labourite. He opposed, unsuccessfully as it turned out, the unilateralist resolution at the 1960 Congress of the Co-operative Party; and more generally, nearly always stood against the political Left of the movement. Harold Campbell, who succeeded Bailey in the position of general secretary on 1 January 1963, gave this account of him after his death:

Gentle, at times even diffident, he could nevertheless be bitingly caustic in debate, and particularly so with the written word. He had mastered the art of satire long before I met him, and used it quite devastatingly in dealing with those who had the temerity to challenge him.

He enjoyed writing. It came naturally to him; for he could use words often very skilfully. He had the Welshman's gift of rhetoric and love of philosophic argument. Sometimes his meaning was obscured in subtleties of thought not easy to penetrate; then he could blind you with

BAILEY 29

an enviable clarity of expression that cut like a beam of light through dark places.

Someone once asked him, in my presence, what – if he had not chosen Party politics for a career – he would most like to do. He hesitated – or, at least, paused to gather his thoughts. Then he said if he were not Party Secretary he would like to have been a university teacher in philosophy. In fact, to a large extent, he enjoyed both worlds. He was the Co-operative politician and tactician *par excellence* for 20 years; he was also its theoretician. He was a teacher as well as a polemicist. And he carried off each role with such flair that it was difficult to say which he did better [*Platform* (Feb 1969)].

Jack Bailey married Anne, daughter of Mark Glaser of London, in 1926, and they had a son and two daughters, Anne Bailey shared all her husband's interests and activities, from running soup kitchens for the unemployed to organising a parents–children strike against an antiquated and inadequate school in Cheshunt during the later war years. Lady Bailey is now (1973) a magistrate on the Cheshunt Bench. The son of the family became a surgeon, the elder daughter a teacher after graduating from LSE, and the second daughter a secretary. Jack Bailey died in hospital at Enfield on 18 January 1969 after a short illness and his funeral service was held at Enfield Crematorium. He left an estate valued at £7863.

Writings: 'Co-operative Party', *People's Year Book* (1943) 54–8; *The Co-operative Party: an outline of organisation* (1944); *How the Beveridge Plan will help women* (Manchester, [1945]) 20 pp.; 'Co-operative Party and its Future', *People's Year Book* (1945) 80–2; *Facing the Future together: the Co-operative Labour Agreement explained* (1946) 11 pp.; 'The Party advances', *People's Year Book* (1946) 124–8; *This Your Freedom* (Manchester, 1947) 18 pp.; 'Co-operative Politics now', *People's Year Book* (1947) 73–6; *The Zig Zag "Left": an exposure of Communist tactics* (Manchester, 1948) 24

pp.; 'Britain in Transition – Co-operative View', *People's Year Book* (1948) 92–7; *This One World . . . a Discussion of International Policy* (Manchester, 1948) 24 pp.; *Power for the People* (Manchester, 1949) 20 pp.; 'Co-operators in Parliament', *RIC* 42 (July 1949) 160–3; 'Labour believes', *Monthly Letter* [of the Co-operative Party] (May 1949) [repr. as a pamphlet] [6 pp.]; 'Co-operative Politics in the Life of Britain', *People's Year Book* (1950) 48–53; *A Co-operative Contribution* (1950) 22 pp.; *The Co-operative Movement: obstacle or inspiration?* (Tenth Blandford Memorial Lect: Leicester, 1950) 24 pp.; *Toryism, Road to Chaos* (Manchester, 1951) 23 pp.; *The Co-operative Movement* (Manchester Labour Party Publications Dept Educational Series no. 2, 1952) 30 pp.; *Three Movements – One Purpose* [On the Trade Union and Co-operative Movements and the Labour Party] ([Manchester], 1954) [15] pp.; *The British Co-operative Movement* (1955, rev. ed. 1960); *Co-operation and Modern Socialism* (1957) 16 pp.; *Together we stand* [a commentary on the new agreement between the Co-operative Union Ltd and the Labour Party] (1958) 16 pp.; *Democratic Politics: a co-operative contribution* ([London], 1960) 24 pp.; (with others), *The Co-operative Movement of Poland: an account of a recent visit by a British Co-operative Delegation* (1961) 24 pp.; *Co-operative Politics – the case re-stated* (1962) 22 pp.

Sources: A. M. Carr-Saunders et al., *Consumers' Co-operation in Great Britain* (1938; rev. ed., 1942); G. D. H. Cole, *The British Co-operative Movement in a Socialist Society* (1950); A. Bonner, *British Co-operation* (1961, rev. ed., 1970); G. W. Rhodes, *Co-operative–Labour Relations 1900–1962* (Co-op. College Papers, no. 8: 1962); W. W. Craik, *The Central Labour College 1909–29* (1964); [Bradford] *Telegraph and Argus*, 15 Jan 1964 and 6 Jan 1965; T. F. Carbery, 'An Examination and Evaluation of the Co-operative Party of the Co-operative Union Ltd' (London PhD, 1966); *Kelly* (1966); *WW* (1969); T. F. Carbery, *Consumers in Politics: a history and general review of the Co-operative Party* (Manchester Univ. Press,

1969); S. Pollard, 'The Foundation of the Co-operative Party', ed. A. Briggs and J. Saville, *Essays in Labour History*, vol. 2: *1886–1923* (1971) 185–210; personal information: Lady Anne Bailey, Cheshunt, widow. OBIT. *Telegraph and Argus* [Bradford], *Times* and *Yorkshire Post*, 20 Jan 1969; *Enfield Gazette* and *Enfield Weekly Herald*, 24 Jan 1969; *Co-op. News*, 25 Jan 1969; *Co-op. Rev. 43*, no. 2 (Feb 1969); *Platform*, Feb 1969.

JOYCE BELLAMY
JOHN SAVILLE

See also: †Albert Victor ALEXANDER, for Co-operative Party; †Arnold BONNER, for Co-operation 1945–71; Fred LONGDEN.

BAILEY, William (1851–96)
MINERS' LEADER

William Bailey was born on 29 January 1851, on the island of St Helena in the South Atlantic, where his father served for fourteen years in the British garrison. His father was discharged in 1857 and the family returned to England, settling at Burgate in Suffolk, where William's father had been born. William began work at the age of nine on a farm, but in 1865, when he was fourteen, he went with a cousin to Yorkshire, where he worked at Fence Colliery, Woodhouse Mill, a village ten miles south-east of Sheffield. Six years later he transferred to Beighton in north-east Derbyshire, and then to Norwood Colliery, Killamarsh. It was here in 1875 that he was elected checkweighman, a position he held for ten years.

Following a strike at his colliery in 1884, Bailey was victimised for his support of the strikers and for nearly two years he earned his living as an insurance agent. In 1885 he was election agent for James Haslam, who stood as Liberal-Radical candidate for Chesterfield in a three-cornered contest [Williams (1962) 489–90]. He was by now well known as a forceful advocate of the miners' claims, and in particular he had been vigorous in the agitation to secure amendments to the Coal Regulation Acts of 1860 and 1872 whereby miners could choose checkweighmen from collieries other than their own. This was, in fact, conceded in an amended Act of 1887, and Bailey had the immense satisfaction of knowing that his part in the agitation had been rewarded. Before the Act was passed he had already been invited by the Nottinghamshire Miners' Association first to address a series of open-air meetings at pit-heads, and then to become their agent/secretary from January 1887. It was largely due to Bailey's energy and enthusiasm that membership of the Association rose from about 500 when he first took over to 18,835 in December 1893. He was joined in the latter year by John G. Hancock, who later became general secretary with Bailey acting as agent and financial secretary.

From the early years of the 1880s Bailey played a prominent part in national affairs. By 1883 he was one of four delegates from the South Yorkshire and North Derbyshire Miners' Association to the Nottingham TUC. At the Swansea TUC of 1887 he was the sole delegate of the Nottinghamshire Miners' Association with 1021 members. At Dundee in 1889 he was again sole delegate from his Association, representing 3636 members. He attended the 29–30 January 1889 Leeds conference of the Miners' National Union and was at the inaugural meeting of the MFGB at Newport at the end of November 1889; and it was Bailey who moved the resolution to form the national federation. At the first annual conference of the MFGB (22–24 Jan 1890) his was among the four names who headed the poll for the executive committee [the others being Aspinwall (Lancashire); Ed. Cowey and J. Murray (both of Yorkshire)]; and Bailey served on the executive committee until 1894 and then again in 1896. He was an eloquent speaker and was often called upon to represent the executive committee. He was a delegate from his county union at the famous Rosebery conference of 1893 and was a member of the Conciliation Board, whose establishment (early in 1894) was the main decision of the conference. Bailey made a sharp attack on the independent chairman of the Conciliation Board, Lord Shand, in the early months of the Board's existence, for what Bailey described as leaning too far in the direction of the coalowners. It was a major sensation of the time, and it made him, so Hallam wrote. 'the best-abused man in the country'. The miners of his own county and their executive council passed resolutions expressing 'their unabated confidence' in him. It was otherwise with his colleagues of the MFGB who, after 'a very long discussion' with Bailey on their side of the Conciliation Board passed a vote of censure, as follows:

> That this Board after fully considering the speeches of Mr Bailey and their probable influence in the country desire to express their deep regret at Mr Bailey's conduct and disclaim any responsibility for what has occurred, and we hereby affirm that we are still strongly determined to fight for the principle of a minimum wage, and further we hereby strongly assert that the question of a minimum wage has not yet been determined by Lord Shand, or anybody else, and that this Board accepts Mr Bailey's assurance that he had no intention of casting any reflections upon Mr Pickard or any of the Miners' representatives of the Conciliation Board in the statements he has made [MFGB minutes, 17 Apr 1894].

Throughout his life, Bailey was a man of independent spirit and attitudes. He was an ardent Liberal but he never allowed his political allegiance to obstruct what he felt were the miners' interests. He had been a founder of the Labour Electoral Association in 1886, becoming vice-president in 1890 and president in 1892. In that year, the general election produced an interesting situation in Nottingham West, a constituency which contained nearly all the miners within the boundaries of the city. The sitting member, up for re-election, was Henry Broadhurst, one of the best known Lib-Lab MPs and still secretary of the parliamentary committee of the TUC. Broadhurst was opposed to the MFGB demand for the legislative introduction of the eight-hour day, and Bailey, at the time a Liberal councillor, refused to endorse him, preferring to support the Liberal Unionist, Charles Seely, who, although a coalowner, was willing to support the eight-hour day in principle. Enough

miners followed Bailey's lead to give Seely a majority of 301 over Broadhurst in what was normally a safe Liberal seat [Griffin (1956) 79–80].

Despite ill-health (he was asthmatic) Bailey was also immensely active in local affairs. He was elected a member of the Killamarsh School Board in 1880 and was on the Nottingham Town Council in 1889, 1892 and 1895. He also sat on the Basford Board of Guardians and the Basford RDC. In religion he was a Primitive Methodist and had become a lay preacher at the age of fifteen, and at the time of his death on 26 July 1896 he was still a local preacher of the Nottingham Third Circuit. He had married on 25 December 1871 and there were five children of the marriage. Bailey died when he was only forty-five and he was buried at Old Basford Cemetery on 29 July 1896. He left effects valued at £210.

Sources: Labour Electoral Congress Reports 1888–1893 and 1895: BLPES, LSE; W. Hallam, *Miners' Leaders* (1894) [photograph]; T.R.Threlfall, 'The Political Future of Labour', *19th C. 35* (Feb 1894) 203–16; A. W. Humphrey, *A History of Labour Representation* (1912); H.M.Pelling, 'H. H. Champion: pioneer of labour representation', *Cambridge J. 6*, no. 4 (Jan. 1953) 222–238; A. R. Griffin, *The Miners of Nottinghamshire 1: 1881–1914* (Nottingham, 1956); J. E. Williams, *The Derbyshire Miners* (1962); H. M. Pelling, *Social Geography of British Elections, 1885–1910* (1967); biographical information: Dr R. Page Arnot. OBIT. *Nottingham Daily Guardian*, 28 July 1896.

JOYCE BELLAMY
JOHN SAVILLE

See also: †Benjamin PICKARD, for Mining Trade Unionism, 1880–99.

BATEY, Joseph (1867–1949)
MINERS' LEADER AND LABOUR MP

Joseph Batey was born at West Moor, near Gosforth, Northumberland, on 4 March 1867, the son of Isaac Batey, a coalminer, and his wife Hannah. He was educated at the colliery school in West Moor and the day after his twelfth birthday he began work at West Moor Colliery. After working at three pits in Northumberland he moved to Durham when he was eighteen and started work in one of the two pits at Blaydon Main as a hewer. Sixteen months later he went to St Hilda Colliery, South Shields, one of five mines owned by Harton Coal Company Ltd. There, in 1888, he was elected local president of the union (St Hilda Lodge); in 1891 he became treasurer and in 1896 secretary and checkweighman – a post he held until 1915.

He was first elected to the executive of the Durham Miners' Association in 1901 and continued to serve until 1915 when he was elected agent (joint committee secretary) for the DMA. With W. P. Richardson, elected financial secretary at the same time, he was the first agent to be chosen by an individual ballot vote of members instead of by the lodges as a whole. He now moved to Durham City, giving up all official positions in South Shields. He represented the DMA on the executive of the MFGB in 1917, 1919 and 1922.

In January 1918 Batey, W. Whiteley, W. P. Richardson and T. Trotter joined other Labour supporters in establishing a local Labour Party organisation within the newly-constituted Durham constituency covering fourteen collieries. Their activities prompted similar attempts in other county divisions and it was for one of these, Spennymoor Labour Association, that, in April 1918, Batey was first adopted as Labour candidate. In the general election after the end of the First World War Batey was defeated by Samuel Galbraith, a Lib-Lab Coalitionist and a former agent of the DMA; Batey himself having opposed the continued association of the Labour Party with the Liberals. He stood again for Spennymoor in 1922 and on this occasion secured an overall majority in a three-cornered fight: the Conservative Party candidate was Anthony Eden. His majority was 1267 in a total poll of 17,639. Batey retained this seat at all subsequent elections until his resignation in 1942. In the general election of October 1931 he and Jack Lawson (Chester-le-Street) were the only successful candidates from among the seven miners who contested Durham constituencies.

Before he became an MP, Batey was much involved in local politics. A member of the South Shields Board of Guardians between 1894 and 1915, he was also elected to the Borough Council in 1896 and he continued to serve until he left the town. He was a keen co-operator and in 1906 was president of the South Shields Co-operative Society. In the following year he was appointed JP for the town, the first such Labour appointment to be made in Durham.

Throughout his parliamentary career he defended ably and consistently the interests of his constituents, seeking to make successive Governments aware of the special problems of the Durham mining areas. In February 1927 he expressed great concern for the results of longer working hours, which had come into force after the General Strike of the previous year and which he believed were eroding the social and cultural life in the mining villages. He took up the question of a minimum wage soon after his entry into the House of Commons and it remained one of his principal interests throughout his years in Parliament.

During the twenties he was a constant critic of the Government's inactivity and apparent apathy in the face of mounting unemployment in the mines. In 1926 he advocated their takeover by the Government; in 1931 he urged the removal of royalties without compensation and in an unsuccessful Private Member's Bill in November 1936 he again stressed the necessity of nationalisation. In 1930 he had supported the Mosley Memorandum. During the thirties his interest developed in possible relief schemes, such as the construction of roads and bridges, and the provision of special grants. He spoke frequently on the need to exploit the by-products of coal and to develop oil production in the North East, especially for the Royal Air Force. He continued with others to put the view that shorter hours in the coal industry could do much to help reduce unemployment, if carefully implemented, and he was among those most hostile to the National Government when in 1934 it opposed the recommendations of the International Labour Conference at Geneva for a statutory forty-hour week.

In religion Batey was a Primitive Methodist. He married Martha Irving in 1888 and she predeceased him; they had no children. Batey himself died at his South Shields home on 21 February 1949 and was survived by his brother, John. The funeral took place at South Shields and he was buried in St Cuthbert's Churchyard. J. D. Murray (MP for Spennymoor) represented the Prime Minister, the Northern Group of MPs and the parliamentary miners' group; also represented at the funeral were the Durham Methodist Church, Spennymoor Divisional Labour Party, the County Council and various Durham Miners' organisations. Joseph Batey left an estate of £1749.

Writings: *Durham Miners' Wages. The Present System Condemned* (South Shields, 1904) 26 pp.

Sources: S. V. Bracher, *The Herald Book of Labour Members* (1923); *Labour Who's Who* (1927); *Dod* (1941); W. R. Garside, *The Durham Miners 1919–1960* (1971); R. Page Arnot, *The Miners* vol. 2 (1953); *WWW* (1941–50); R. F. Wearmouth, *The Social and Political Influence of Methodism in the Twentieth Century* (1957); *Hansard*, 1922–42, *passim*. OBIT. *Times*, 22 Feb 1949; *Durham County Advertiser*, 25 Feb 1949.

ANTHONY MASON
BARBARA NIELD

See also: *Clement Richard ATTLEE, for British Labour Party, 1931–51; †Thomas ASHTON, for Mining Trade Unionism, 1900–1914; †Thomas BURT; †Thomas Henry CANN; †Arthur HENDERSON, for British Labour Party, 1914–31; Peter LEE.

BELL, George (1874–1930)
MINER

Born on 18 September at North Seaton Colliery, near Newbiggin, where his father was employed, George Bell was seven years old when his parents moved to West Moor, a hamlet within Longbenton, Northumberland. He attended school there and began work as a 'trapper' at the age of thirteen in Dinnington pit some five miles from Newcastle. He extended his education through night classes and later attended Rutherford College, Newcastle upon Tyne, passing his examinations with honours. It was his ambition to become a mining engineer but he was unable to afford the training, and at the age of twenty-two he went to Burradon, now a part of Longbenton, and remained there, as a working miner, until his death.

His subsequent career is typical of the energetic and politically conscious trade unionist who remained within his local environment all his life. Bell was an active member of the United Methodist Church, serving as steward, trustee, class leader and Sunday school teacher. Between 1904 and 1930 he held office in the Burradon branch of the Northumberland Miners' Association as secretary (for twelve consecutive years) and auditor and served several times on the executive committee of the Association. For many years he represented the Burradon Co-operative Society at the quarterly meetings of the CWS. In local politics he served first on the Camperdown Parish Council and then, from 1912 to 1930, on the Longbenton Urban District Council, of which he was chairman for some years. He served on the Court of Referees and the Board of Assessors and in 1927 was appointed a JP. After the First World War he became for some time chairman of the Wallsend Divisional Labour Party; and among his other activities may be noted his membership of Longbenton District School managers' board; his services as governor of the Newcastle Royal Infirmary and the Eye Infirmary, and as chairman of Burradon and West Moor Nursing Association; and his membership of his local colliery welfare committee. He was married, and was survived by his wife and at least two sons. He died on 1 December 1930 and left effects worth £1010.

Sources: E. Welbourne, *The Miners' Unions*

of *Northumberland and Durham* (Cambridge, 1923). OBIT. *Newcastle J.*, 2 Dec 1930; *NMA* (1930).

ANTHONY MASON

See also: †Thomas ASHTON, for Mining Trade Unionism, 1900–14;* Arthur James COOK, for Mining Trade Unionism, 1915–1926.

BELL, Richard (1859–1930)
TRADE UNION LEADER AND MP

The son of Charles Bell, a stone quarrier, and his wife Ann (née Thomas), Richard, often known as 'Dick' Bell, was born at Penderyn, Brecon, on 27 November 1859. His father's parents had been Scots, who had moved from Lincoln to a farm in Breconshire. Young Richard grew up as a Welshman and became a fluent speaker of the Welsh language. In the early 1860s Charles Bell was involved in an accident in which his brother, who worked beside him at the quarry, was killed. This decided him to take another occupation and he moved with his family to the nearby town of Merthyr Tydfil where he became a policeman. He had the right qualities for the job, eventually being appointed chief of the police staff employed at the Cyfarthfa Iron Works. Charles Bell was a Tory in his views; he believed in authority and unquestioning obedience to his employer, and he tried to instil these notions into young Richard. When he was thirteen, and had received a limited education at church and national schools, Richard started work in the office of the Cyfarthfa Works. His great ambition was to be an engine driver, but his father wished to make him into a clerk, so he had to remain in the office for three years. But as he grew up he reacted against his father's attitudes. He took an outdoor job as a fireman to the boilers of a steel rail mill engine, and when the blacksmiths declared a strike, he refused to obey an order to act as a blackleg. For this he was dismissed by the company and threatened by his father with eviction from the family home. He then worked for about a year at the Dowlais Ironworks before returning to his old employers as a shunter with the locomotives.

In 1876 Bell entered the service of the Great Western Railway Company as a porter and passed through all grades to head goods guard. As head guard he was stationed at Pontypool Road until 1886 when he was transferred to Swansea, and it was at about this time that he became an active member of the Amalgamated Society of Railway Servants, which had been founded late in 1871. Bell soon became assistant secretary of his branch and began to establish a reputation as an energetic worker for trade unionism. At this time the principal issues were not only wages, but also the extremely long hours worked by the railwaymen and the need for more safety precautions. His activities were noticed by his employers, who tried to curb them by transferring him to Carnbrae in Cornwall; but Bell responded by establishing branches of his Society in the district and strengthening the union's organisation. However, he did not remain long at Carnbrae before returning to Swansea to work as a full-time official of the union. In the early 1890s he was appointed organising secretary of the ASRS, taking with him to the post a capacity for hard work, especially where administrative detail was involved. The exact date of this appointment is not certain, although it is in 1892 that his name appears for the first time in the executive minutes of the Society.

An unofficial strike on the North Eastern Railway early in 1897 provided the occasion of Bell's promotion to the general secretaryship of his Society. Edward Harford, who had been general secretary since 1883, took charge of the negotiations, but on the morning he was to sign an arbitration agreement with the North Eastern Railway Company he appeared at the meeting in an intoxicated condition. It was not possible to sign the agreement until a few days later, on 5 April, when Bell, who had taken over from Harford, persuaded the men to agree to the company's proposal and accept Lord James of Hereford as arbitrator. By the award published in August 1897 the Society made a few gains in conditions, but also, more importantly, obtained the NER's recognition of it as a negotiating body. In a letter to

Bell, Lord James thanked him for his assistance and complimented him on his ability as an advocate. Sir George Gibb, manager of the NER, also wrote to Bell expressing his pleasure that the negotiations had been conducted without a trace of bitterness. These letters bear witness to Bell's typical approach: moderate and conciliatory, he had no sympathy for class-war doctrines or even for non-militant socialist ideas.

At the annual general meeting of the ASRS held in October 1897 the delegates passed a motion dismissing Harford as general secretary because of his unsatisfactory conduct during the negotiations with the NER, and Bell was appointed in his place *pro tem*. In June of the following year Bell secured election to the office of general secretary, obtaining about 22,000 votes and a majority of some 8000 over his nearest rival. He now left Wales to live in the Southgate district of London.

Bell assumed office at a time when the union was quickly expanding. Membership had increased rapidly, from 25,000 in 1890 to 86,000 in 1897, and this reflected a more combative attitude among the rank and file. In 1897 an all-grades campaign was launched to obtain improved terms of service for the various classes of railway employees. The majority of companies reacted by adopting a more entrenched position in order to resist the demand for better conditions; they drew up a programme for mutual assistance in the event of industrial action, and declined to acknowledge the union. In the spring of 1898 Bell was involved in two major disputes which had arisen at local level but which had proved costly to the ASRS in terms of strike pay. His answer was to revise the Society's rules to provide for a ballot of the men before any strike action took place. At the same time he worked at the problem of the railway companies' victimisation of the men who had led the grade deputations. The directors of most companies refused to recognise the ASRS as their workmen's negotiating body, but Bell was able to obtain a hearing at the Board of Trade, and during 1898 he provided the Board with many instances of leaders of deputations who had

been dismissed. A lengthy correspondence passed between the companies involved, the Board and the union. Although C. T. Ritchie, the President of the Board of Trade, refused to accept that there had been victimisation, the publicity did have an effect on the directors, and at the annual general meeting of 1899 Bell was able to report that fewer men who were active trade unionists had been dismissed. The problem of non-recognition, however, was to remain for some years.

In July 1899, as a witness before the Royal Commission on Accidents to Railway Servants, Bell went fully into the question of accidents during a lengthy examination. To prepare his evidence he had visited the USA in order to discover how far the American law of 1893 for the fitting of automatic couplers on railway rolling stock reduced accidents to shunters. This careful preparation was also evident during the second all-grades campaign of 1907. He then employed 'two gentlemen from Cambridge' and a staff of clerks to draw up for the ASRS a detailed statistical report which revealed that some 100,000 men employed on British railways were earning less than one pound a week in wages. The detailed material collected was printed as a book, *Report and Census of Wages, Hours of Labour etc.* (1908) – popularly known as the Railwaymen's Charter – and it provided an extraordinarily comprehensive account of wages, hours, overtime, Sunday duties of all the principal grades in the service of the main railway companies. The railway companies were still able to avoid recognising Bell's union, but Lloyd George, the President of the Board of Trade, secured the agreement of both sides to a conciliation scheme in November 1907.

Despite Bell's devotion to Liberal politics the ASRS was to play a prominent part in the events that led to the foundation of the Labour Party. The railwaymen had much to gain from an increased labour representation in parliament. Although by the end of the century the ASRS had become the fifth largest trade union in the country, it had still not secured recognition as the negotiating body from most of the railway companies. Parliament itself was constantly debating railway questions, with the 'railway interest' in the Commons strongly represented, and it was therefore inevitable that among the members and officials of the ASRS the demand for parliamentary action should grow rapidly. Moreover, during the 1890s a number of Socialists had become officials of the ASRS, many of them being appointed because they had been victimised, and Bell was to find himself increasingly at loggerheads with general opinion inside the union, and notably with his executive committee, which consisted not of full-time organisers but of rank and file members. In October 1898 a successful motion at the annual conference called for the election of the general secretary to the House of Commons; and in the following year it was the ASRS's resolution, moved by James Holmes, the West of England organiser, that led to the convening of the first Labour Representation Conference in February 1900. Bell became an MP in the general election of the same year. Following the 1898 resolution he had been adopted as a candidate in a by-election at Rotherham, but he did not fight the seat, on the ground that there was insufficient time to mount a proper campaign. In 1899 the Derby Trades Council selected Bell as its candidate in what was a two-member constituency, and he was elected along with a Liberal. He was not, however, allowed to run as an official Liberal candidate; at the ASRS conference of 1899 a resolution from the Derby branch which would have permitted this was overwhelmingly rejected.

In August 1900 there took place the strike on the Taff Vale railway which was to lead to one of the most famous legal cases in trade union history. Bell was reluctantly drawn into the dispute by the militant Welsh members of his own union on one side and by Ammon Beasley, the litigious general manager of the Taff Vale Railway Company, on the other. The company took vigorous action against the strikers. In the early days of the strike Beasley began importing blacklegs through William Collison's National Free Labour Association. The company took out injunctions against both

Bell and Holmes, the local organiser, and when the issue came before Mr Justice Farwell, the vacation judge sitting in chambers, he not only granted injunctions against the two officials, but against the union itself, whose funds were thereby open to damages. Much of the argument accepted by Mr Justice Farwell rested upon the decision of the 1899 *Lyons* v. *Wilkins* case which had narrowed the limits within which picketing was allowable. When the Taff Vale action was finally taken to the House of Lords, after a reverse judgement had been obtained before the Master of the Rolls, Mr Justice Farwell's decision was upheld. The ASRS was now liable for full damages and in March 1903 a later court agreed upon the sum of £23,000 in settlement of both damages and costs against the union. During the hearing at which these damages were awarded, the judge noted the favourable impression that Bell had made on him, compared with what he regarded as the inexcusable conduct of James Holmes. The latter was unable to get money for his own costs from the ASRS, following a successful injunction from union branches at Liverpool and Accrington restraining such payments. Bell appears to have encouraged these branches to apply for the injunction [Bagwell (1963) 223].

The Taff Vale decision was to influence profoundly the whole trade union movement, and one immediate result was an increase in affiliations to the Labour Representation Committee. Bell's political attitudes and behaviour, however, remained unchanged, and both inside the House of Commons and outside it he was a constant irritant to the supporters of the principle of independent labour representation. Keir Hardie, for example, writing to David Lowe in 1901, described the railwaymen's leader as 'a genial ass' [Lowe (1923) 196]. And later his critics were to regard him with less tolerance.

Bell was not without ability as a parliamentarian and was flexible enough to cooperate with Hardie on occasions, notably in April 1901 when he seconded Hardie's motion calling for the inauguration of a Socialist Commonwealth. But he had none of the radical fervour to be found in the ILP, and he persistently advocated close liaison with the Liberal Party, despite his membership of the executive committee of the LRC and his acceptance of the position of chairman in February 1902. He was also a supporter and for a time vice-chairman of the National Democratic League, a curious hybrid political grouping which for a few years was something of a rival to the ILP. In his support for the League as well as in some of his other exploits, Bell was associated with W.C. Steadman, particularly in a common opposition to the ILP. During a by-election at Norwich in January 1904, to give one instance of Bell's indiscretions, he expressed publicly his regret that the progressive vote would be split by the appearance of a Labour candidate (G. H. Roberts of the ILP) as well as a Liberal, and when the latter was elected Bell telegraphed his congratulations [see J. Ramsay MacDonald, confidential memorandum [on relations between LRC and Richard Bell]: LP Archives].

Bell was a member of the TUC parliamentary committee in 1899 and from 1902 to 1909, and served as chairman of the TUC during 1903–4. In his presidential address at the 1904 Congress he made a vigorous attack upon the Balfour Government for refusing to give any consideration to a Trade Disputes Bill which would have largely remedied the consequences of the Taff Vale decision. He had refused to sign the revised constitution of the LRC in 1903 and he continued his independent way through the remaining years of the Conservative Government. His position in the 1906 general election was singular: he retained the support of the Derby Trades Council and the sponsorship of the ASRS, and was included on the TUC's list of candidates, but the LRC refused both recognition and backing [Bealey and Pelling (1958) 195–7]. Moreover, the Derby Liberals approved of Bell's candidature, and, as in 1900, he was elected for the double-member constituency along with the Liberal, Sir Thomas Roe.

On being returned to the House of Commons Bell continued to collaborate with the Liberal Party and to counter the attacks of his Labour critics; MacDonald, he once said, was 'a Labour member who has never laboured in his life' [Bagwell (1963) 231]. He was increasingly at odds with the two other ASRS MPs, Walter Hudson and George Wardle, and his industrial leadership of the Society was coming under growing criticism. He was still trying by patient and conciliatory methods to persuade the railway companies to recognise the ASRS, and his over-moderate approach was subjected to bitter attack by his membership at branch level. In the all-grades agitation of 1907 he was described by George Askwith as 'a cautious man' who did not go fast enough for his executive [Askwith (1920) 119]. The Liberal press, however, was full of praise for Bell's conciliatory industrial politics and his wholehearted support for the Government. Earlier, in 1905, the Stratford branch had called for an inquiry into Bell's directorships of the King's Cross Publishing Co., the North Wales Quarries and the Co-operative Printing Society; and the growing militancy of the rank-and-file railwaymen in the years after 1906 steadily undermined Bell's credibility within both the Society and the House of Commons. At the annual conference of the ASRS in October 1908 he was attacked for opposing railway nationalisation, which he had previously advocated. By the following year his position had become more untenable. At the annual conference of the ASRS in October 1909 a resolution was moved censuring Bell for his refusal to pursue the ASRS's policies in the Commons, and for his industrial and political conduct in general. Although the motion was defeated, an amendment proposing to relieve Bell of all but his industrial duties was carried; and he offered his resignation as general secretary in December, the same month in which he made public his decision not to contest his Derby seat again. In writing to the secretary of the Derby Labour Association, he gave as his main reason the injunction that had been granted in the Osborne case.

This was the end of Bell's public career on the national stage. His political and industrial influence in the early years of the century, after the momentous Taff Vale decision, had been considerable, and is one more illustration of the tenacity of the Lib-Lab tradition within the British labour movement. He was an extremely capable administrator, reckoned by many to have made the ASRS into one of the best conducted unions in the country, and the attitudes he expressed evoked a considerable working-class response not only among his Derby constituents, but also in the Midlands generally. An indication of the central position that Bell had for many years occupied in the world of railway unionism was the evidence taken before the 1911 Royal Commission on the Railway Conciliation Scheme of 1907. Bell was not a witness before this Commission, but his work was frequently referred to by other witnesses during the course of their evidence.

Early in 1910 Bell accepted a post as an officer in the employment exchanges branch of the Board of Trade, which was later transferred to the Ministry of Labour, where he remained until his retirement, acting after 1920 as a technical adviser. J. H. Thomas, who was to become general secretary of the NUR in 1916, succeeded Bell in the seat at Derby, and J. E. Williams became the general secretary of the ASRS.

In 1897 Bell had been appointed as a JP for Middlesex, and during the First World War he was chairman of the Advisory Committee attached to the military service tribunals both of Southgate and Friern Barnet. While he was general secretary of the ASRS he had visited the United States, Sweden, Austria, Hungary, France and Germany, but declared, 'Nowhere did I find anything that would induce me to favour any country in preference to our own, with all its failings.' For twenty-six years he was a member of the board of directors of the Co-operative Printing Society. In 1922 he was elected as a member of Southgate Urban District Council and was chairman of the Council in 1925–6, retiring in 1929. He sat, too, on a number of other official and voluntary bodies.

Bell died at his home, 19 Derwent Road, Palmers Green, on May Day 1930, after a lengthy illness. The funeral took place on Monday 5 May at Southgate Cemetery, where John Burns and G. N. Barnes, who spoke a graveside tribute, were among the mourners. The funeral service was conducted by the Rev. D. J. Thomas, formerly principal of the Home and Colonial College, Wood Green, and by the Rev. W. L. Hannam, Minister of Bowes Park Wesleyan Church.

Bell was three times married; his last wife survived him, as did his five daughters; of his three sons, one was killed in the Gallipoli campaign, another died on bombing operations in India in 1924, and the third son emigrated to the United States. In his will he left effects to the gross value of £4633.

Writings: Evidence before R.C. on Accidents to Railway Servants 1900 XXVII Qs 2558–3139; *The Taff Vale Case and the Injunction* (1902); *Trade Unionism* (The Social Problem Series no. 3, 1907).

Sources: J. Ramsay MacDonald, Confidential Memorandum 28 Mar 1904 [on relations between LRC and Richard Bell] Labour Party Archives: LP/CAN/06; J. Bardoux, *Silhouettes d'outre-manche* (Paris, 1909); R.C. on Railway Conciliation Scheme of 1907, 1912–13 XLV; W. Collison, *The Apostle of Free Labour* (1913); Lord Askwith, *Industrial Problems and Disputes* (1920); G. W. Alcock, *Fifty Years of Railway Trade Unionism* (1922); D. Lowe, *From Pit to Parliament: the story of the early life of James Keir Hardie* (1923); F. Bealey and H. Pelling, *Labour and Politics 1900–1906* (1958); P. P. Poirier, *The Advent of the Labour Party* (1958); B. C. Roberts, *The Trades Union Congress 1868–1921* (1958); *Dictionary of Welsh Biography* (1959); J. Saville, 'Trade Unions and Free Labour: the background to the Taff Vale decision', in *Essays in Labour History* ed. A. Briggs and J. Saville (1960); P. S. Gupta, 'History of the Amalgamated Society of Railway Servants, 1871–1913' (Oxford DPhil., 1960); P. S. Bagwell, *The Railwaymen: the history of the National Union of Railwaymen* (1963); H. A. Clegg et al., *A History of British Trade Unions since 1889,* *vol. 1: 1889–1910* (Oxford, 1964); H. Pelling, *The Origins of the Labour Party 1880–1900* (2nd ed. Oxford, 1965); P. S. Gupta, 'Railway Trade Unionism in Great Britain, c. 1800–1900' *Econ. Hist. Rev. 19* ser. 2 (1966) 124–53; H. Pelling, *Social Geography of British Elections 1885–1910* (1967); G. Alderman, 'The Railway Companies and the Growth of Trade Unionism in the late Nineteenth and early Twentieth Centuries', *Historical J. 14* (1971) 129–52; biographical information: Dr P. S. Bagwell; Dr Frank R. Lewis. OBIT. *Derby Daily Telegraph*, 2 and 6 May 1930; *Palmers Green and Southall Gazette*, 2 and 9 May 1930; *Daily Herald, South Wales Daily Post, Times* and *Tottenham and Edmonton Weekly Herald*, 2 May, 1930; *Railway Review*, 9 May 1930.

DAVID E. MARTIN

See also: *James Keir HARDIE; Walter HUDSON; †James Ramsay MACDONALD; George James WARDLE.

BONDFIELD, Margaret Grace
(1873–1953)
TRADE UNIONIST, FEMINIST AND FIRST WOMAN CABINET MINISTER

Margaret Bondfield was born on 17 March 1873 at Chard in Somerset. She was the tenth of eleven children of William Bondfield, foreman lace maker, and his wife Ann (née Taylor). Her father was a self-taught man, an active Congregationalist in religion and a radical in politics. He had become a close friend of the Rev. John Gunn – a well-known local preacher and reformer – and together they collaborated in the 1830s to make the Chard Political Union into an active organ of reform propaganda. In the next decade Chard was a lively centre of Chartist activity.

Margaret's family, although large, never experienced deprivation or hunger. She recalled in her autobiography that her father's wages sometimes fell as low as eleven shillings per week, but since he owned their cottage with its large fruit and vegetable garden and also the surrounding fields, the family was always able to feed itself by grow-ing food on the land surrounding its cottage, and even managed at times to supplement its income by selling surplus food. Margaret started her working life at thirteen, as a pupil teacher in the local Chard elementary school where she had been educated. A year later she went to Brighton, where as a child she had already spent some months with an aunt, and where a sister and brother were already living. Margaret took employment as an apprentice shop assistant and experienced the appalling working conditions of the retail trade in those days; with a wage of £25 per annum, a seventy-five-hour week and the indignities of the 'living-in' system. Despite these conditions she managed to read and study, much encouraged by a Mrs Martindale, a Liberal and an advocate of women's rights whose home became a haven for the young girl.

In 1894, having managed to save £5, Margaret moved to London, where she continued to earn her living as a shop assistant. Here her intellectual and political horizons widened rapidly. Her brother Frank worked in the printing trade and was an active trade unionist; she became friendly with the Hicks family where she met, among others, Margaret Gladstone, who was later to marry Ramsay MacDonald; and she joined the Ideal Club – a debating and recreational centre in Tottenham Court Road – where she met a large number of London radicals, including the Webbs and Bernard Shaw. Margaret soon became an active Socialist propagandist. She was at first attracted to the SDF and spoke on the same platforms as Hyndman and Quelch, but according to her own account, written many years later when she had become a respectable figure in the labour movement, she came to reject their emphasis on 'bloody class war' [*A Life's Work* [1949] 48] and moved over to the ILP. No doubt her strong religious faith, which remained with her all her life, influenced her decision. She later joined the Fabian Society.

In the year that she arrived in London she joined the National Union of Shop Assistants, Warehousemen and Clerks; and during the next two years she became extremely active in union affairs, being elected a member of the London District Council and delegate to the national conference, and writing a monthly article for the union journal (founded in 1890 by T. Spencer Jones) under the name of Grace Dare. In 1896 she joined in a two-year investigation of shop workers' conditions, conducted by the Women's Industrial Council. The survey was financed by Mrs Lilian Gilchrist Thompson with money bequeathed by her brother, Sidney Gilchrist Thomas, the metallurgist. The results of the inquiry were widely used by reformers, among them Sir John Lubbock, later Lord Avebury. Lubbock was a Liberal Unionist MP from 1886 to 1900; he showed a continuous interest in the working conditions of shop assistants, and in 1901 it was he who persuaded the House of Lords to set up a Select Committee to inquire into the problems of early closing. Three years later he was largely responsible for the new Shop Hours Act, which Margaret Bondfield and the union vigorously condemned for its failure to insist upon compulsion [Hoffman (1949) 8–10]. In the same year, 1898, that the results of the investigation were made public, Margaret was appointed to the full-time union post of assistant secretary, with John Turner, at that time an anarchist, as organiser; James Macpherson was the general secretary. Together they helped to raise the union membership from under 3000 in 1898 to 7500 in 1900 – an increase that was encouraged by the economic expansion of these years. In 1899 she was delegate from her union to the TUC; the only woman delegate, she moved the vote of thanks to fraternal delegates, in which she spoke of the advantage of fusion between the trade union movement and Socialists, and vigorously supported the ASRS resolution in favour of independent labour representation.

She did not confine her activities to her own union, but was increasingly involved in wider industrial matters as well as in politics. She was associated with the Women's Trade Union League, in which she collaborated for years with the Dilkes and Gertrude Tuckwell. She met Mary Macarthur in 1902, and from then on they were closely linked in their public and private lives. Mrs Hamilton [(1924) 95] wrote of their relationship: 'In the years between 1903 and 1921, the romance of her life – and a very real romance – was her association with Mary Macarthur.' They worked together in the Women's Trade Union League, in the Adult Suffrage Society (founded in 1906), and in the National Federation of Women Workers, the first general union for women, established by Mary Macarthur in 1906. Margaret Bondfield held firm opinions on women's suffrage which sometimes brought her into conflict with other suffragettes. She supported universal not partial suffrage for women, and believed that any Act should also extend the vote to those men who were still disenfranchised under various disabilities. On this her views were broadly those of the Labour Party, but not those of the Women's Labour League, which together with Mrs Ramsay MacDonald and others she helped to found in 1906, to further the education of women in Labour politics. In 1907 she took part in a famous debate on the suffrage question with Miss Teresa Billington-Greig, a prominent member of the Women's Freedom League.

By 1908 her many and varied activities had overtaxed her strength, and she was ordered to take a rest. She gave evidence in this year to the Inquiry into Truck, but she had to resign from her position as assistant secretary to the Shop Assistants' Union. In the meantime, she took up freelance lecturing. Two years later, with her health recovered, she revived her connection with the Women's Industrial Council by helping with their inquiry, under the editorship of Clementina Black, into the work of married women. Miss Bondfield's particular responsibility was the conditions of work in the Yorkshire woollen industry. In the summer of 1910 she went on her first lecture tour of the U.S.A., addressing various kinds of audience on the labour, trade union and adult suffrage movements in Britain. The diary she kept shows her energy, enthusiasm and eagerness to learn. In these years immediately preceding the First World War, she also became more involved in Labour politics. In 1910 and again in 1913 she stood as ILP candidate in the LCC election for Woolwich, but was defeated on both occasions. On the death of Mrs Ramsay MacDonald in 1911 she became organising secretary of the Women's Labour League, and at this time became generally more active within the ILP, contributing frequently to the *Labour Leader* and in 1913 being elected to the National Administrative Council. The greater part of her time, however, seems to have been given to the Women's Co-operative Guild, whose campaigns for a minimum wage and maternity and child welfare schemes she vigorously supported. She helped also to found the Standing Joint Committee of Women's Industrial Organisations, and when domestic servants were included under the Health Insurance Acts, she worked with the Standing Joint Committee to establish an Approved Society.

With the outbreak of war in August 1914 Margaret Bondfield adopted an opposition stand. Like many of her colleagues in the ILP she could not properly be described as a pacifist; but she spoke against the coming war at the famous Trafalgar Square meeting of 1 August 1914, along with Keir Hardie, Arthur Henderson and Mary Macarthur; she signed the ILP manifesto on War Aims, and was later to oppose conscription and support a negotiated peace. She joined the Union of Democratic Control, and the Women's Peace Crusade, and in March 1915, together with Dr Marion Phillips, Mary Longman and Mrs Salter from Britain, attended the Berne conference organised by the Women's International of Socialist and Labour Organisations. There she met delegates from Germany, France, Russia, Poland, Holland, Switzerland and Italy. The conference ended by calling for an immediate peace without annexations, compensation for Belgium and the right of self-determination for all nationalities. In 1917 Miss Bondfield supported the Stockholm peace conference proposal but, like others, she was refused a visa for travel to Sweden. In the following year she was similarly prevented from attending both the AFL conference in the United States and the Hague conference of the Women's International League for Peace and Freedom.

On the home front during the war Margaret Bondfield joined the Central Committee on Women's Employment, the Trade Union Advisory Committee of the Ministry of Munitions, and the important War Emergency Workers' National Committee. When the war ended, she attended the first conference of the ILO in Washington together with Mary Macarthur, and she continued to attend its meetings until 1927, becoming the official UK representative on its governing body in 1924.

One of her first post-war assignments was as member of a joint delegation of the TUC and the Labour Party to the Soviet Union [Hamilton (1924) 128ff]. Clifford Allen and R. C. Wallhead, representing the ILP, also joined the delegation, which was a rather odd assortment of persons, including Ben Turner, A. A. Purcell and Ethel Snowden. The delegation travelled widely in Russia, witnessing conditions of near famine. Margaret was among those who was received by Lenin, and while the majority of the delegation returned convinced that the new Russia was under a dictatorship, the visit undoubtedly helped to stiffen opinion against the Allied military intervention. Margaret referred to her own strong feelings on this issue in her autobiography (p. 224) and when the Council of Action was formed in the early days of August 1920, she joined it as the representative of the National Federation of Women Workers. As with most of her colleagues, however, her opposition to armed intervention against the Soviet state in no way altered her attitude towards the British Communist Party; she opposed the application for affiliation to the Labour Party which it made after the London convention of 31 July–1 August 1920; and Miss Bondfield's hostility to the Communist Party continued for the rest of her life.

Her parliamentary career began with a by-election at Northampton in 1920, and she stood again for the same constituency in the general election of 1922. She was defeated on both occasions. She was, however, successful in the general election of 1923, which gave the Conservative Party the largest number of seats in the Commons, although not an overall majority. The Labour Party took office, and MacDonald offered Margaret Bondfield the position of parliamentary secretary to the Ministry of Labour, with special responsibility for unemployed women workers. Thomas Shaw was her minister, and both had an unhappy time defending the Government's miserable record on unemployment, after its election promises. She headed a delegation sent to Canada in 1924 by the Overseas Settlement Committee and continued to serve on that body until 1929. In the 'Zinoviev letter' election of late October 1924 Margaret lost her seat.

During this first stage of her parliamentary life she continued to be active in her trade union work. Mary Macarthur died on 1 January 1921, and on the same day the National Federation of Women Workers formally merged with the Women Workers' Section of the National Union of General and Municipal Workers; in the same year Margaret Bondfield became the chief women's officer of the NUGMW, and she continued in that position until 1938. She also became chairman of the Standing Joint Committee of Women's Industrial Organisations. In 1923 she was elected the first woman chairman of the TUC, but did not take up the post because of her parliamentary victory at the general election. She was re-elected to the General Council of the TUC in 1925, and was thereby involved in its decision to call the General Strike in May 1926. She also approved the decision to end the strike. On the General Council she generally aligned herself with J. H. Thomas, especially with his anti-Communist position.

In these years after the ending of the First World War her ideas were becoming more conservative. She had rejected in her earliest days in the movement the position of the SDF, and she was against the use of militant tactics in the suffragette movement. A revealing sentence in her autobiography concerning her approach to the Insurance Bills of 1911 goes far to explain those later attitudes for which she was to be much criticised. 'In 1911', she wrote, 'when other people criticised the contributory insurance bill, I thought that it was right that people should pay for it, as they paid for other

things, to realise the seriousness and responsibility of citizenship and to be concerned with the progress of the country, of the whole people and not only of a section' (p. 358). No doubt this helps to explain her opposition to family allowances in the 1920s [Dalton (1953) 184]. She resigned from the National Advisory Committee of the ILP in 1922, although she still occasionally attended New Leader lunches. At the Wallsend by-election of 1926 which followed the resignation of Sir Patrick Hastings, she was returned to Parliament, and in the next year, January 1927, she signed the Blanesburgh Committee Report on Unemployment Insurance. The committee had been set up because of dissatisfaction with supposed frauds under the insurance scheme, and the Report – which rejected all the major proposals made in a joint memorandum submitted by the TUC and the Labour Party – recommended some lowering of benefits and contributions and the abolition of extended benefit; it also somewhat extended the 'genuinely seeking work' clause for applicants. In the autumn of 1927 the Conservative Government introduced an Unemployment Insurance Bill which included the substance of the Blanesburgh Committee's recommendations. There were two other Labour members of the committee – Frank Hodges (ex-secretary of the MFGB and soon to resign as secretary of the International Miners) and A. E. Holmes (Printing and Kindred Trades Federation). The Report aroused considerable hostility in many sections of the Labour movement, and Margaret Bondfield and her two Labour colleagues were vigorously criticised for not having produced a minority statement. But she defended her position tenaciously and successfully before national conferences of the TUC, the Labour Party, her own union, and within the Parliamentary Labour Party. Her acquiescence in the Report's recommendations was given wide publicity during the general election campaign of 1929, when Wal Hannington, Communist leader of the National Unemployed Workers' Movement, stood against her, and made her the main target of his attack. She was, however, easily elected with a majority of 7105 in a total poll of 40,543 and Hannington came bottom of the poll with 744 votes.

In the second minority Labour Government of 1929, MacDonald appointed her Minister of Labour. This earned her the distinction of being the first woman Cabinet Minister and Privy Councillor. She found herself in one of the most difficult positions in the Government. Unemployment moved sharply upward during the closing months of 1929 and throughout 1930, and Margaret Bondfield became increasingly unpopular among her own people on two main counts. One was the Government's handling of unemployment. At the outset of her term of office she had persuaded the Treasury to increase the contribution to the Unemployment Insurance Fund – this was greeted, however, with reminders that the Party had promised work or full maintenance – and in November 1929 some rates were slightly increased; but the biggest innovation, after considerable back-bench and trade union pressure, was the elimination of the 'genuinely seeking work' clause which had aroused such anger among the movement. The Bill, however, still did not satisfy the left wing of the ILP, and Maxton and others introduced a number of amendments condemning its 'omissions'. Towards the end of the Government's period of office the 'Anomalies' [Unemployment Insurance No. 3] Bill of July 1931 was introduced to end what were regarded as growing abuses in the benefits system; in the Bill certain classes of the unemployed, mostly married women were deprived of benefit altogether. The Bill carried into effect most of the recommendations of the Holman Gregory Commission, the establishment of which in December 1930 had resulted in estrangement between Margaret Bondfield and the General Council of the TUC. Skidelsky writes of her 'monumental tactlessness' [Skidelsky (1970) 293ff]. The 'Anomalies' Bill was again vigorously attacked by Maxton and other back benchers, but without success, and it passed on to the Statute Book.

The other main ground for attack upon her was her acceptance of the financial caution, indeed conservatism, of Philip Snowden and the Treasury. Again, her orthodox financial approach to the unemployment problem was bitterly resented, both on the Labour back benches and outside Westminster. Hugh Dalton [(1953) 301] has a scathing comment on the political innocence and economic naïvety of the leading members of the MacDonald Government:

> Still less was it sensible to try to balance the unemployment fund. Clearly this should show a deficit in years of heavy, and a surplus in years of light, unemployment. But Labour Ministers had been talking awful nonsense on this subject for some time. Miss Bondfield had frequently said that it was 'dishonest' to borrow for the unemployment fund. The official who taught her to use this epithet in this context should have been sent away on a very long leave ... Ministers, including the Big Five, were all humbugged by their advisers into believing that this fund could only borrow from the Post Office.

At least Miss Bondfield tried to solve some of the problems of the unemployment fund by proposing more comprehensive legislation; but the continued growth in the unemployment figures, and the continued inability of the Labour Government to offer any constructive proposals, large or small, made all other problems appear of relatively minor importance. When the crisis came in August 1931, Margaret Bondfield voted with the majority in the Cabinet in favour of the economies in public expenditure, including reductions in unemployment benefits. She stayed with the Labour Party when Ramsay MacDonald formed the National Government, and like most of her colleagues lost her seat at the general election which followed. She was defeated again in 1935. She stood again for election to the General Council of the TUC but was unsuccessful. In 1938 she retired from full-time trade union work, and visited the U.S.A. and Canada on a lecture tour. During the Second World War she helped to organise voluntary services for civilian evacuation. She became vice-chairman of the National Council for Social Service, contributed to its well-known volume, *Our Towns*, and helped to found the Women's Group on Public Welfare. She was also active in the YWCA. During the early years of the war (1941–3) she undertook several lecture tours of Canada and the United States on behalf of the British Information Services. She published her autobiography in 1949.

Throughout her life Margaret Bondfield was a teetotaller and a deeply religious person. Her most productive years were before the First World War, when her work for women's trade unionism was of great importance. The close association with Mary Macarthur was obviously of major significance in her life at this period. The years after 1918, although she achieved high office in the Labour movement, and in government, were much less successful. Her continued shift to the Right in labour politics sharply narrowed her vision, and like all her senior colleagues in the 1929 Government her intellectual equipment for the political and economic problems of this period of crisis and depression was wholly inadequate. During the second Labour Government she became extremely unpopular with many sections of the Labour movement, and especially with the Left; but there was an earlier Margaret Bondfield whose enthusiasm and idealism charmed and impressed her contemporaries. Mary Agnes Hamilton's book of 1924 is hagiography, but Margaret Bondfield was unquestionably more attractive as well as more constructive in the first twenty years of her public life than she later became. At the time of her resignation from the Shop Assistants' Union in 1908, Margaret Llewelyn Davies wrote to Mary Macarthur:

Being away at Guildford on Guild work today, I am unable to be present at the gathering to do honour to our dear friend Margaret Bondfield. But I cannot let the occasion pass without sending her my love, congratulations and admiration. No workers in any movement ever had a colleague who was more single-minded, generous, and loyal. She is in many ways the type of what all Labour women should be – unflinchingly staunch to her cause, fair to her opponents, radiating good will to all [*A Life's Work* [1949] 81].

She had been given an honorary LL.D.

by Bristol University in 1929 and the Freedom of Chard in 1930, and she was made a Companion of Honour in 1948. She died on 16 June 1953 at the age of eighty. Her funeral was at Golders Green Crematorium on 22 June, and a memorial service was held on 9 July 1953 at St Margaret's, Westminster, where C. R. Attlee gave the address. She left £6063 in her will.

Writings: 'Conditions under which Shop Assistants work', *Econ. J.* 9 (1899) 277–86; 'Jean' [a serial by Grace Dare], *Shop Assistant* (July 1899); *Sex Equality versus Adult Suffrage* (verbatim report of debate held on 3 December 1907 with Teresa Billington-Greig) [Women's Freedom League] (1908) 29 pp.; 'What Shop Workers want from Parliament', *Women's Trade Union Rev.* (July 1908); Evidence before R. C. on Truck 1908 LIX Qs 13093–545; *Socialism for Shop Assistants* (Pass on Pamphlets no. 10, 1909) 15 pp.; 'Human Documents', *Women's Industrial News* (July 1909); 'Tribute to Mrs J. R. MacDonald', *Lab. Leader*, 15 Sep 1911; 'Shop Workers and the Vote' in *People's Suffrage Federation Pamphlet* (1911); (with others), *War against Poverty* [Standing Committee of the ILP and Fabian Society, [1912?]) 20 pp.; *The National Care of Maternity* (Women's Co-operative Guild, 1914) and *New Statesman*, 16 May 1914 (special supplement); 'Sentenced to Life', *Woman Worker*, 1 Jan 1916; 'The Future of Women in Industry', *Labour Year Book* (1916) 253–79; 'Women as Domestic Workers' in M. Phillips, *Women and the Labour Party* (1918) 66–73; 'Some Lessons of the British Health Insurance Act', *American Labor Legislation Rev.* 9 (June 1919) 202–3; 'Recollections of working with Mary Macarthur', *Woman Worker* (Feb 1921); 'Women and Unemployment', *Labour Mag. 1*, no. 9 (Jan 1923) 399–400; 'Women's Trade Unions' in *The Woman's Year Book 1923–1924* ed. G. E. Gates (1923); 'Women Workers in British Industry' in *British Labour speaks* ed. and arranged R. W. Houghe (New York, 1924); 'In the Days of my Youth', *T.P.'s and Cassell's Weekly*, 12 Jan 1924; 'Great Britain's responsibility' in appendix to *Labour and* *the League of Nations* (League of Nations, 1927); 'Can the Strike be replaced?', *World Tomorrow*, 10 Mar 1927, 105–6; 'Women in Industry in Great Britain', *American Federationist 34* (May 1927) 567–70; 'Public Opinion; Women in Industry', ibid., (July 1927) 836–8; 'Women within the Trade Union', ibid., (Nov 1927) 1340–2; *The Meaning of Trade* (Self and Society Booklets, no. 9, 1928) 32 pp.; 'Unemployment Insurance in Great Britain', *American Labor Legislation Rev. 20* (Sep 1930) 237–48; (with others), *Unemployment* (New York, 1930); 'America's Approach to Job Insurance', *American Labor Legislation Rev. 23* (Sep 1933) 121–2; 'Effect of New Forms of Power upon the Lives of Workers', *Proc. National Conference of Social Work* (Columbia Univ. Press, New York, 1938) 29–43; *Why Labour fights* [London?, 1941]; Preface to NCSS, Women's Group on Public Welfare, *Our Towns, a close-up: a study made in 1939–42* (1943, 2nd ed. 1944); *A Life's Work* [autobiography] [1949]. Margaret Bondfield was a regular contributor to *The Woman Worker*, founded and edited by Mary Macarthur.

Sources: B. Drake, *Women in Trade Unions* (1921); M.A. Hamilton, *Margaret Bondfield* [with portrait] (1924); H. Tracey, 'Miss Margaret Bondfield: the first woman in the Ministry' in *The Book of the Labour Party, 3* [1925] 259–63; *Labour Who's Who* (1927); *Potted Biographies: a dictionary of anti-national biography*, 4th ed. (1931); Struwelpeter, Jnr, 'Miss Bondfield to Mr Snowden' [poem], *Saturday Rev. 151*, 21 Feb 1931, 255; P. Snowden, *Autobiography* 2 vols (1934); H. M. L. Swanwick, *I have been young* (1935); M. A. Hamilton, *Arthur Henderson* (1938); NUGMW, *Fifty Years* (1939); C. F. Brand, *British Labour's Rise to Power* (Stanford, 1941); M. A. Hamilton, *Remembering my Good Friends* (1944); A. F. Brockway, *Socialism over Sixty Years: the life of Jowett of Bradford 1864–1944* (1946); J. R. Clynes, 'The Rt Hon. Margaret Bondfield, C. H.', in *The British Labour Party*, ed. H. Tracey, *3* (1948) 239–41; G. D. H. Cole, *A History of the Labour Party from 1914* (1948); P. C. Hoffman, *They also serve:*

the story of the shop worker (1949); F. Williams, *Fifty Years March: the rise of the Labour Party* [1949]; *WWW* (1951–60); H. Dalton, *Call back Yesterday: memoirs 1887–1931* (1953); C. L. Mowat, *Britain between the Wars* (1955); H. Dalton, *The Fateful Years; memoirs 1931–1945* (1957); *Beatrice Webb's Diaries 1924–32*, ed. M. Cole (1956); R. W. Lyman, *The First Labour Government 1924* (1957); R. Bassett, *Nineteen Thirty One: political crisis* (1958) H. S. Morrison, *Herbert Morrison: an autobiography* (1960); M. Foot, *Aneurin Bevan: a biography 1: 1897–1945* (1962); H. A. Clegg, *General Union in a Changing Society: a short history of the National Union of General and Municipal Workers 1889–1964* (1964); R. J. A. Skidelsky, *Politicians and the Slump: the Labour Government of 1929–1931* (1967, Penguin, 1970). OBIT. *Manchester Guardian*, 18 June 1953; *Times*, 19 June 1953; *Labour Party Report* (1953); *TUC Report* (1953). The editors wish to express their gratitude for an early draft on Margaret Bondfield by Mr Bryan H. Sadler, Univ. of Warwick.

MARION MILIBAND

See also: †Arthur HENDERSON, for British Labour Party, 1914–31; Mary MACARTHUR; †James Ramsay MACDONALD.

BRADBURN, George (1795–1862)
CHARTIST

Born in 1795 in Prescot, Lancashire, George Bradburn spent most of his life in Stockport, Cheshire, where he worked as a boot and shoe maker. His wife, Martha, was a spinner. During his youth, he was probably associated with the Deists of the town, but after he joined the Temperance Society in the mid-1830s he turned to Christianity. His obituary in the *Stockport Advertiser* was to place great emphasis upon this change of heart:

When Mr Bradburn first joined the Temperance Society, nearly 27 years since, he was wallowing in the depths of Infidelity; but Teetotalism was the means, in the hand of God, of bringing him to the feet of Jesus and placing his hope on the Rock of Ages.

The denomination to which he adhered was not mentioned.

By 1840, Bradburn was prominent in the local Chartist movement. He was elected chairman at a meeting addressed by John Collins of Birmingham, and also at a local branch meeting called to devise means of supporting the Chartist prisoners' families. In April 1841, he was nominated to the General Council of the National Charter Association, a position which he retained in September of that year. Bradburn again returned to the role of local chairman in February 1842, when James Leach and John Doyle of Manchester arrived in the town. On 10 March, he presided when Feargus O'Connor addressed the Stockport Chartists. Still acting as chairman of the Stockport Association, Bradburn took part in the campaign to memorialise the Government for the relief of the poor, as Stockport was especially hard hit by the 1842 depression in the cotton trade. Like the majority of the local Chartists, he turned in 1846 to opposition to the Whigs' Improvement Bill (for which see James TORKINGTON). Bradburn's son, William, was a member of the Stockport Chartist Youths' Association, and was nominated by them to the General Council of the NCA in January 1841.

Bradburn had, however, turned against his former Chartist colleagues by 1852. In May of that year, he took the chair at an election meeting in support of the parliamentary Liberal candidates, J.B. Smith and James Kershaw. James Williams, later elected to the executive of the 1854 'Labour Parliament', took up the cause of Chartism from an adjacent cart. The outcome was that a Liberal supporter named Boon accused Williams of being a 'Tory tool', who had received £5 and wine from that party at the recent municipal election. Williams challenged his opponent to prove the charges at an open inquiry. On the appointed evening, each of the antagonists had his own chairman, with Bradburn acting for Boon. The large attendance of Kershaw's workpeople assured a Liberal victory. In June 1852, Bradburn also campaigned against John West of Macclesfield, the Chartist candidate in the general election.

It was therefore not as a Chartist, but as a teetotaller, that Bradburn was last remembered. He died on 9 February 1862 in Stockport Workhouse aged sixty-six, and at his funeral over seventy sympathisers of the Temperance Movement joined in procession to pay their last respects. No will has been located.

Sources: (1) MSS: 1861 Census, Stockport, PRO: R.G.9 2569; Stockport Cemetery records; (2) Other: *Northern Star*, 1840–1847; *Stockport Advertiser*, 1842–52; R. G. Gammage, *History of the Chartist Movement 1837–54* (1894: repr. with an Introduction by John Saville, New York, 1969); A. R. Schoyen, *The Chartist Challenge* (1958); *Chartist Studies*, ed. Asa Briggs (1959). OBIT. *Stockport Advertiser*, 21 Feb 1862.

NAOMI REID
T. D. W. REID

See also: John ALLINSON; Joseph CARTER; Abraham DOCKER; *Feargus O'CONNOR; James TORKINGTON.

BRAILSFORD, Henry Noel
(1873–1958)
AUTHOR AND JOURNALIST

Henry Noel Brailsford was born at Mirfield in Yorkshire on 25 December 1873, the only son of the Rev. Edward John Brailsford (1841–1921) and Clara Pooley (1843–1944). During his early years the family lived mainly in Scotland, where his father, a graduate of Didsbury College and a prominent Wesleyan minister, was posted to congregations in Edinburgh, Greenock, Blairgowrie, and Glasgow. After schooling at George Watson's College (1883–5) and at Dundee High School (1885–91), Brailsford received a scholarship to attend Glasgow University, where he studied classics and philosophy under Gilbert Murray, Edward Caird (later Master of Balliol), and A. C. Bradley. The most brilliant of a promising undergraduate generation which included John Buchan, Robert Horne and A. H. Charteris, he received numerous prizes for academic distinction, founded the University Fabian Society, and was a frequent contributor to the Glasgow University Magazine.

After taking his M.A. in 1894 with first-class honours in logic and moral philosophy and a second class in Latin and Greek, he studied for two terms as an unattached student at Oxford, followed by a term in Berlin. He returned to Glasgow in 1895-6 as Assistant to the Professor of Logic and Metaphysics, Robert Adamson (the father of Mary Agnes Hamilton), teaching logic to women undergraduates at Queen Margaret College. When his appointment was terminated after one year, he applied for a position as an assistant lecturer at the University College of North Wales, but failed to obtain it. Abandoning the idea of an academic career, Brailsford turned to journalism, becoming sub-editor of the *Scots Pictorial* in March 1897. The position offered too little scope for his literary talents, and within a few weeks he resigned to enlist in the Philhellenic Legion, a volunteer army fighting alongside the Greeks in their struggle against Turkish oppression. Although his initial enthusiasm for the Greek cause, inspired in part by his classical training, was dispelled, he saw combat in the disastrous campaign in Thessaly in the spring of 1897 and was wounded in action. He returned to Scotland to pick up the pieces of his career and to recount his experiences in his first book and only novel, *The Broom of the War-God*, which was published in 1898. On the recommendation of Professor Adamson, C. P. Scott sent Brailsford to Crete and Macedonia to report on the military situation for the *Manchester Guardian*; this was the first of many foreign assignments for the *Guardian* and other newspapers. He returned in 1899 by way of Paris, where he covered the Dreyfus affair and came to know Jaurès and Clemenceau. Although he continued to write for the *Guardian* intermittently, it did not have a permanent position vacant at the time, so Brailsford moved to London and was employed as a leader-writer for the *Morning Leader*. From 1899 to 1909 he served successively as principal leader-writer for the *Morning Leader*, the *Echo*, the *Tribune*, and the *Daily News*. In addition, he wrote regularly for the *Speaker* until its demise, and for the *Nation* during the editorship of H. W. Massingham from 1907 to 1922. His leaders and articles dealt primarily with foreign and imperial affairs, and he quickly established himself as an authority on Russia, Egypt, and the Balkans.

In London he became involved in radical politics and befriended foreign exiles and revolutionaries who congregated in England during these years. As a prominent member of the Balkan Committee, he was selected to lead a relief mission to Macedonia in 1903, where he distributed food and medical assistance in Ochrida and Monastir and reported on the situation for the *Guardian*. His first-hand knowledge provided the basis for his second book, *Macedonia*, which appeared in 1906 and became the standard work on the subject. Brailsford was also a member of the Friends of Russian Freedom and was acquainted with Kropotkin, Miliukov, and Theodore Rothstein. In October 1904 he was approached by Russian friends seeking English passports to enable exiles to return to Russia in disguise. Although he was assured that the passports secured would not be used to commit acts of violence, they fell into the hands of terrorists, one of whom was blown up by his own bomb in a St Petersburg hotel. After an official Russian protest was lodged, Brailsford was brought to trial in July 1905, convicted, and fined £100. Two years later he was asked to help in raising £500 to enable Social Democratic party delegates, including Lenin and Trotsky, to return home from their London conference. With the help of George Lansbury, he prevailed upon the soap manufacturer Joseph Fels to lend the money.

After his youthful rebellion against the Methodism and Liberalism of his upbringing, Brailsford considered himself a Socialist, although more under the influence of Shelley and the English Radical tradition than of Marx. It was not until 1907, however, that he joined the ILP, having found the Fabian attitude towards the Boer War unpalatable. Although he had long admired Keir Hardie, he waited until he was certain that the ILP did not disdain middle-class intellectuals employed by Liberal newspapers. Throughout the next few years he was deeply committed to the women's suffrage campaign. Sympathetic to the WSPU and associated with the Pankhursts and the Pethick-Lawrences, he sought to reconcile the militants in the movement and the parliamentary supporters of votes for women. From 1910 to 1912 he served as secretary of the Conciliation Committee, which attempted to sponsor enfranchising legislation, and was a member of the Men's League for Women's Suffrage. In 1910 he was adopted as a women's suffrage parliamentary candidate for South Salford in opposition to Hilaire Belloc, but stood down when a pro-suffrage Liberal was nominated. His protest against the forcible feeding of women prisoners led Brailsford to resign from the *Daily News* in 1909 after its editor, A. G. Gardiner, refused to repudiate the government's policy.

Having removed himself from the pressures and financial rewards of daily journalism, Brailsford turned increasingly to books, although he continued to write weekly foreign affairs articles for the *Nation* and more occasionally for the *Guardian*. In 1911 he published a collection of his essays entitled *Adventures in Prose*, and two years later *Shelley, Godwin and Their Circle* appeared in the Home University Library. In 1913 he was appointed a member of the Carnegie Commission of Enquiry on the origins of the Balkan wars and was one of the authors of its report.

In the years before the First World War Brailsford was an outspoken critic of British foreign and imperial policy. He championed Egyptian nationalism, a cause that he shared with his friend Wilfrid Scawen Blunt, and was an enthusiastic supporter of Russian constitutionalism. His hatred of Tsarist tyranny led him to denounce the Anglo-Russian *entente*, which he felt would undermine the possibility of liberal change and encourage Russian expansionism in Persia. Under the influence of the writings of J. A. Hobson, he began to identify economic imperialism and the military rivalry of the great powers as the causes of war. These ideas were given their fullest expression in

his celebrated work *The War of Steel and Gold* (1914), which immediately became a textbook for those on the Left who were trying during and after the war to formulate a Socialist foreign policy. Brailsford opposed British participation in the war, blaming the alliance system and Russian ambitions for its outbreak. His wartime pamphlets *The Origins of the Great War* (1914) and *Belgium and 'The Scrap of Paper'* (1915) – the latter confiscated by the War Office – refuted the myth of exclusive German guilt.

From the outset of the war he was involved in the Union of Democratic Control and endorsed its goal of a negotiated peace and general post-war disarmament. He advocated the satisfaction of German economic grievances as the only means of eradicating the forces of militarism which had precipitated the conflict. In addition, Brailsford became the outstanding proponent of international government during the war, calling for a league of nations with full responsibility for trade, overseas investment, and the distribution of raw materials, as well as with military power to enforce its decisions. These ideas were embodied in his influential book *A League of Nations* (1917), which commanded wide attention in England and in America, where its readers included President Wilson. It was in these years that Brailsford began to write a weekly column on international affairs (which he continued until 1922) for Lansbury's *Herald*, and to serve (until 1946) as a London correspondent for the American *New Republic*.

After his defeat as Labour candidate for the Montrose Burghs in 1918, he toured the war-torn capitals of Central Europe, and his eye-witness accounts of the starvation and economic devastation were incorporated into two books, *Across the Blockade* (1919) and *After the Peace* (1920). He was one of the foremost critics of the Versailles treaty, which he felt defied the professed principles of national self-determination and the need for economic reconstruction. Throughout the 1920s he warned that unless the vindictive policy of the Allied Powers were reversed and Germany permitted to recover, peace would remain in jeopardy. In the summer of 1920 Brailsford became one of the first Western journalists to tour the Soviet Union. Travelling alone, unhindered by the protocol inhibiting the Labour delegation earlier that year, he was able to interview Trotsky and other officials and to spend several weeks in Vladimir, the first foreigner to visit the region since 1914. His impressions of the Soviet experiment were generally favourable, and he was encouraged by the economic and educational strides made since the revolution. He was, however, disturbed by the persistence of Bolshevik terror, which he felt might undo the achievements of the régime. He described his Russian experiences in *The Russian Workers' Republic* (1921) and in *How the Soviets Work* (New York, 1927), published after a second visit in 1927. His understanding of foreign affairs also made him a valued participant in the deliberations of the Labour Party's Advisory Committee on International Questions from 1918 to 1922.

In 1922 Clifford Allen secured Brailsford's appointment as editor of the *New Leader*, the reconstituted weekly newspaper of the ILP. Under his editorship it acquired a unique international reputation, being regarded by many as the finest Socialist journal of its time. The *New Leader* sought to overcome the traditional parochialism of the labour press by balancing politics with the arts, the class struggle with cultural enrichment. Although designed as a mass paper, it provided serious and exhaustive analyses of world affairs and of economic problems in an attempt to educate as well as to entertain. Its contributors included writers as eminent as E. M. Forster, Bernard Shaw, and H. G. Wells, and artists like Gwen Raverat and Clare Leighton. The steady rise in its circulation, which ultimately exceeded that of any other weekly review of the period, helped to reduce, but did not eliminate, a continuing deficit, and in 1926 (Clifford Allen having resigned in autumn 1925) the ILP leaders decided to dismiss Brailsford and reorganise the *New Leader* as a less expensive and less intellectual journal.

During his years as editor he had written much of the paper's content, using it as a platform from which to promote his ideas about the revision of the peace treaties, re-

conciliation with the Soviet Union, and the Living Wage. Popularised in the *New Leader* and in Brailsford's own *Socialism for To-day* (1925), the Living Wage concept derived from J. A. Hobson's ideas regarding underconsumption, and aimed at the increase of mass purchasing power through the establishment of the wage levels needed for a civilised standard of life, supplemented by family allowances. These proposals were presented to the ILP in a report drawn up by Brailsford, Hobson, E. F. Wise, and Arthur Creech Jones, and were enthusiastically endorsed at the 1926 annual conference. Their subsequent rejection by the Labour Party embittered its relations with the ILP, foreshadowing the split which led to disaffiliation in 1932. Brailsford also served on an ILP committee which devised the agricultural policy adopted in 1924.

In the 1920s Brailsford maintained close links with European Socialists, many of whom later regarded him as a trusted mediator in internecine disputes in the period of exile during the Second World War. He attended the international conferences in Berne in 1919, in Vienna in 1921, and in Hamburg in 1923, at which he came to know Otto Bauer, Friedrich Adler, and Léon Blum. His writings were read on the Continent, his articles appearing in the Viennese *Arbeiter Zeitung* and in *Der deutsche Volkswirt*. In 1928 Brailsford visited the United States for the first time, and delivered a course of lectures at the New School for Social Research. He returned to America for five additional trips between 1929 and 1941, lecturing and meeting politicians and journalists like Alvin Johnson and Walter Lippmann. He was a familiar figure in American intellectual circules, known for his articles in the *New Republic*, the *Baltimore Sun*, and the *World Tomorrow*. Long a champion of colonial independence, Brailsford toured India in 1930, later describing it in a stirring denunciation of British imperialism, *Rebel India* (1931).

Despite his dismissal as editor, Brailsford continued as principal writer for the *New Leader* until he broke with the ILP in 1932. The termination of his editorial duties left more time for writing, travel, and political activity. In *Olives of Endless Age* (1928) and *Property or Peace?* (1934) he elaborated his views on internationalism and the relation of capitalism to war. Although his goals were revolutionary, he remained committed to democratic Socialism and to the parliamentary system in the face of totalitarian threats. Profoundly critical of MacDonald and the cautious reformism of the two Labour Governments, he nonetheless refused to follow the ILP when it resolved to disaffiliate, thus terminating a twenty-five-year bond. Along with E. F. Wise, he helped to organise ILP dissidents in the Socialist League in 1932 and continued throughout the decade to be identified with Sir Stafford Cripps's campaign to prod the Labour Party in more radical directions. While his passion for liberty made him immune to the appeal of Communism, he was a strong advocate of unity on the Left, notwithstanding official Labour hostility to all united front proposals. In January 1937, along with Cripps, Fenner Brockway, James Maxton, and Harry Pollitt, he signed the Unity Manifesto against Fascism, Reaction, and War. In the same year he was one of the founders of *Tribune*, but personal and political disagreements led him to withdraw from its board after the first year.

When his association with the *New Leader* ended, Brailsford began two of his most fruitful journalistic partnerships. Sydney Elliott asked him to write a weekly foreign affairs column for *Reynolds News*, and Kingsley Martin invited him to join the staff of the *New Statesman* as chief leader-writer. During the next fifteen years he devoted most of his energies to these two weeklies, although he continued to produce books like *Voltaire* (1935), his personal favourite among his works, and *Why Capitalism Means War* (1938), a reinterpretation of themes articulated earlier in *The War of Steel and Gold*. Brailsford was one of the first English Socialists to interpret the advent of Hitler in his pamphlet *The Nazi Terror* (1933), just as he had predicted the resurgence of German militarism ever since Versailles. Although revolted by Nazi methods and by the prospect of British concessions to Hitler,

he could not forsake long-held convictions about the wisdom of revising the injustices perpetrated in the post-war settlement. He continued to urge disarmament and the reinforcement of international government in the hope that the satisfaction of German grievances would either eliminate Hitler or mitigate the danger. The outbreak of civil war in Spain, however, convinced Brailsford that Nazi aggression must be countered by a military alliance of anti-Fascist powers. In the autumn of 1938 he parted company with many of his colleagues on the Left, as he already had in his condemnation of the Russian purge trials. His stinging attacks on the British concessions at Munich, which appeared in *Reynolds*, made one of the strongest indictments of Chamberlain's policy to appear in the press at the time.

In the 1930s Brailsford's articles were mainly focused on India, Spain, and the Soviet Union. During the Round Table Conference of 1931 he had become acquainted with Gandhi and Nehru, both of whom cherished his friendship. He continually criticised the National Government for its reluctance to concede autonomy, and in the press and on the platform he sought to arouse public sentiment in favour of Indian freedom. The Spanish Civil War, more than any other issue during his lifetime, appealed to Brailsford's romantic and libertarian instincts. Although in his mid-sixties, he was dissuaded only with the greatest difficulty from enlisting in the International Brigade. Assured that he could better aid the Republican cause with his pen, he vividly documented the heroism of the Loyalists and the duplicity of the European powers. In addition, he served as chairman of the Labour–Spain Committee, which attempted to mobilise rank-and-file support in the movement and to persuade the NEC of the Labour Party to challenge official Government policy towards Spain more vociferously. He also raised money for the International Brigade and for Spanish relief, recruited volunteers to fight in Spain, and assisted refugees. Throughout the 1920s and 1930s Brailsford was a critical admirer of the Soviet régime, and his writings tended to underscore the accomplishments of Russian

Communism. Nonetheless, he was never deceived about the lack of political and intellectual freedom in Russia, a factor which always qualified his approval. While refusing to condone Stalinist repression, he held that an alliance with the Soviet Union, as the leading Socialist power, was a prerequisite to a victorious struggle against Fascism. The 1933 engineers' trial created a rift in his close relations with Ivan Maisky, but it was his candour at the time of the purge trials that outraged not only the leaders of the CPGB, but also much of the Left-wing press in England. No other Socialist writer with Brailsford's reputation spoke out as forcefully or as consistently as he did from 1936 to 1938, chiefly in his weekly *Reynolds* column but also in articles in the *New Statesman*. Moreover, he tried to intercede, without success, on behalf of Christian Rakovsky, the convicted Russian diplomat. He denounced the use of extorted confessions and questioned the guilt of men like Radek and Tukhachevsky, whom he had known personally.

During the Second World War Brailsford helped Kingsley Martin to edit the *New Statesman* with a considerably reduced staff, and broadcast regularly in the Overseas Service. Although he offered himself as a stretcher-bearer, he was rejected for reasons of age, but he registered as a Local Defence Volunteer and took his turn as a fire-fighter in Hampstead. He continued to write extensively: *Democracy for India* (1939) for the Fabian Society, *From England to America* (1940), a plea for American entry into the war, and *Subject India* (1943) for the Left Book Club. He befriended many German and Austrian refugees, protesting against their internment and assisting several of them to find homes or to secure passage to America. His contacts with the German resistance movement and his affinity with German culture led him to refute Lord Vansittart's condemnation of the 'black record'. *Our Settlement with Germany* (1944), which was accorded a chilly reception, argued the case for a magnanimous peace that would ensure her inclusion in a revitalised European community. In 1944 Brailsford was awarded an honorary LL.D.

by Glasgow University, fifty years after completing his undergraduate work.

Despite his failing health – he had undergone two cataract operations and was suffering from an angina condition – Brailsford undertook several strenuous foreign trips after the war. At the end of 1945 *Reynolds* sent him to India to observe the provincial elections. As a friend of Gandhi and Nehru, as well as of Lord Pethick-Lawrence, he functioned effectively as an intermediary between the British and Indian camps. In 1947 he was invited to lecture at a writers' conference and at universities in Germany, and at the end of 1950 was one of the first Englishmen to be asked to visit Yugoslavia after Tito's breach with the Soviet Union. Upon his return from India, he retired from the *New Statesman* and from *Reynolds* and devoted his energies to research for what was to be his *magnum opus*, a history of the Leveller movement. A continuing deterioration of his health curtailed his activities after 1951, and during the remaining years of his life he was virtually an invalid. His final work, *The Levellers and the English Revolution*, although incomplete at his death, was edited by Christopher Hill and published posthumously in 1961.

In 1898 Brailsford married Jane Esdon Malloch, a fellow student at Glasgow University and the daughter of a Scottish cotton spinner. Jane Brailsford, who died in 1937, studied at Somerville College, accompanied her husband to Macedonia in 1903, where she worked in a hospital in Ochrida, and later achieved notoriety as a suffragette. The marriage was not a success, and the Brailsfords separated shortly after the First World War. He later found much happiness in the companionship of the artist Clare Leighton. In 1944 Brailsford married Evamaria Perlmann Jarvis, the daughter of a German doctor. He had no children. His only sister, Mabel Richmond Brailsford (1875–1970) was an accomplished writer and translator, whose works included biographies of William Penn and of the Wesley brothers. Brailsford died of a stroke on 23 March 1958, at West London Hospital. At his funeral five days later at Golders Green Crematorium Lord Pethick-Lawrence delivered the eulogy. He was survived by his wife and he left estate valued at £693.

Brailsford was widely recognised as one of the greatest journalists of his generation and as one of the outstanding socialist political writers of the century. Reserved and shy in personal relations, he was admired for his disinterestedness and intellectual integrity. Throughout a literary career that spanned more than half a century he was animated by a hatred of oppression and exploitation in any form. Sensitive to human suffering, he placed his pen at the service of numerous causes for which he received little reward. A champion of sex equality, colonial freedom, and international conciliation, Brailsford was a man of unswerving principle, maintaining his convictions with little regard to their popularity. A master of lucid, epigrammatic prose, he had an enormous capacity for indignation, which infused his best writing. His works remain compelling not only for their passion and consistency, but for the formidable knowledge of world affairs and of literature that they reflect. At the end of his life a testimonial volume was gathered from among his many admirers, and its foreword contained the following tribute:

In the hearts of many he sowed a burning hatred of imperialism and all its crimes. He seemed to combine freedom and Socialism in a wonderful alchemy. More than any other writer of the century he took what was best in the Liberal and Radical tradition of England and used it for the purpose of preparing the revolutionary future ... His imaginative sympathy made him the inspired spokesman of people in many distant lands, and in speaking their thoughts he performed a matchless service to his own country too.

Writings: The most important of Brailsford's books and pamphlets are: *The Broom of the War-God* (1898); *Some Irish Problems* (1903) 44 pp.; *Macedonia* (1906); *The 'Conciliation' Bill: an explanation and defence* [1910] 16 pp.; *Adventures in Prose: a volume of essays and sketches* (1911); *The Fruits of Our Russian Alliance* (1912); *Shelley, God-*

win, and Their Circle (1913); *The War of Steel and Gold* (1914); *The Origins of the Great War* (UDC Pamphlet, no. 4: 1914) 22 pp.; *Belgium and 'The Scrap of Paper'* (ILP Labour and War Pamphlets, no. 10: 1915) 16 pp.; 'The Organization of Peace' in *Towards a Lasting Settlement*, ed. C. R. Buxton (1915) 149–76; *Turkey and the Roads of the East* (UDC Pamphlet, no. 18: 1916) 23 pp.; *A League of Nations* (1917); *Poland and the League of Nations* (1917) 27 pp.; *A Share in Your Motherland and Other Articles* [1918] 49 pp.; (with K. D. Courtney) *Equal Pay and the Family: a proposal for the national endowment of motherhood* (1918); *The Covenant of Peace: an essay on the League of Nations* (1918) 32 pp.; *Across the Blockade* (1919); *After the Peace* (1920); *The Russian Workers' Republic* (1921); *Socialism for Today* (1925); (with J. A. Hobson, A. Creech Jones and E. F. Wise) *The Living Wage* (1926) 55 pp.; *Families and Incomes: the case for children's allowances* [1926] 16 pp.; *How the Soviets Work* (New York, 1927); *Olives of Endless Age* (1928); *Rebel India* (1931); *If We Want Peace* (New Fabian Research Bureau Day to Day Pamphlet, no. 11: 1932) 57 pp.; 'A Socialist Foreign Policy' in *Problems of a Socialist Government* (1933) 252–86; *The Nazi Terror: a record* (Socialist League Pamphlet: 1933) 9 pp.; *Property or Peace?* (1934); *Voltaire* (1935); *India in Chains* (Socialist League Pamphlet: [1935]) 11 pp.; *Spain's Challenge to Labour* (Socialist League Pamphlet: [1936]) 12 pp.; *Towards a New League* (New Statesman Pamphlet: 1936); *Why Capitalism Means War* (New People's Library, vol. 14: 1938); *Democracy for India* (Fabian Society Tract: 1939) 15 pp.; *From England to America* (New York, 1940); *America Our Ally* (Victory Books, no. 11: 1940); *The Federal Idea* [1940?] 16 pp.; *All Souls' Day: an essay in understanding* [1942] 8 pp.; *Subject India* (Left Book Club, 1943); *Our Settlement with Germany* (1944); *Making Germany Pay?: the reparations problem* (National Peace Council Peace Aims Pamphlet, no. 23: 1944) 8 pp.; *Germans and Nazis: a reply to 'Black Record'* (Commonwealth Popular Library, no. 2: [1944]) 16 pp.; 'Socialism and Empire' in *Fabian Colonial Essays*, ed. R. Hinden (1945) 19–35; *The Life-Work of J.A.Hobson* (L. T. Hobhouse Memorial Trust Lecture, no. 17: 1948) 29 pp.; (with H. S. L. Polak and Lord Pethick-Lawrence) *Mahatma Gandhi* (1949) 95–224; *The Levellers and the English Revolution*, ed. C. Hill (1961).

Sources: (1) MSS: Allen of Hurtwood papers, McKissick Library, University of South Carolina; Noel-Buxton papers, Redpath Library, McGill University; Sir Stafford Cripps papers, Nuffield College; Millicent G. Fawcett papers, Manchester Central Library; Labour Party Advisory Committee on International Questions Coll., Transport House, London; Kingsley Martin papers, University of Sussex Library; Gilbert Murray papers, Bodleian Library; Henry W. Nevinson diaries, Bodleian Library; Bertrand Russell archives, Mills Memorial Library, McMaster University; *Manchester Guardian* editorial correspondence, University of Manchester Library; UDC records, Brynmor Jones Library, Hull University. (2) Secondary: *Labour Leader*, 28 Sep 1922; *The Patriot*, 29 Dec 1927; *DNB* (1951–60); W. S. Blunt, *My Diaries* (1921); H. W. Nevinson, *Changes and Chances* (1923); *More Changes More Chances* (1925); H. M. Swanwick, *I have been young* (1935); J. Paton, *Left Turn!* (1936); A. F. Brockway, *Inside the Left* (1942); M. A. Hamilton, *Remembering My Good Friends* (1944); J. Braunthal, *In Search of the Millennium* (1945); R. Postgate, *The Life of George Lansbury* (1951); M. Anderson, *Noel Buxton: a life* (1952); H. R. Winkler, *The League of Nations Movement in Great Britain, 1914–1919* (New Brunswick, NJ, 1952); S. R. Graubard, *British Labour and the Russian Revolution, 1917–1924* (Cambridge, Mass., 1956); A. J. P. Taylor, *The Trouble Makers: dissent over foreign policy, 1792–1939* (1958); M. Foot, *Aneurin Bevan: a biography* (1962); H. Hanak, *Great Britain and Austria-Hungary during the First World War* (1962); E. Hyams, *The New Statesman: the history of the first fifty years, 1913–1963* (1963); M. Gilbert, *Plough My Own Furrow: the story of Lord Allen of Hurtwood as told through his writings and correspondence* (1965); J. A.

Smith, *John Buchan* (1965); R. E. Dowse, *Left in the Centre: the Independent Labour Party 1893–1940* (1966); K. Martin *Editor* (1968); R. Churchill, *Winston S. Churchill*, Companion vol. 2 pt 3 (1969); *The Political Diaries of C. P. Scott, 1911–1928*, ed. T. Wilson (1970); D. Ayerst, *Guardian: biography of a newspaper* (1971); M. Swartz, *The Union of Democratic Control in British Politics during the First World War* (1971); B. Pimlott, 'The Socialist League: Intellectuals and the Labour Left in the 1930s', *J. Cont. Hist.* 6, no. 3 (1971) 12–38; S. E. Koss, *Fleet Street Radical: A. G. Gardiner and the Daily News* (1973). Obit. *Times* and *Manchester Guardian* and *New York Times*, 24 Mar 1958; *Tribune*, 28 Mar 1958; *New Statesman*, 29 Mar 1958.

F. M. Leventhal

See also: †John Atkinson Hobson; *James Maxton; *Edmund Dene Morel.

BRANSON, Clive Ali Chimmo (1907–44)
ARTIST AND COMMUNIST

Clive Ali Chimmo Branson was born in Ahmednagar, India, on 8 September 1907. His father was Lionel Hugh Branson, a British officer in the Indian Army and at that time a subaltern in the 110th Mahratta Light Infantry. His mother was Emily Winifred (née Chimmo). She had spent part of her youth in China, since she was the daughter of the manager of the Hong Kong and Shanghai Bank. The baby was christened Clive after Robert Clive of India, and Ali after Alphonse de Bourbon and Orléans, who had been a friend of the father's at Heidelberg College. The baby was the eldest of three brothers.

He was two years old when he was brought back to England; at seven he went as a boarder to St Hugh's preparatory school at Bickley, and at thirteen became a day boy at Bedford Public School. He showed talent for drawing, was good at his work, liked cricket. He won a *Daily Mail* shooting competition for boys, was in the OTC and captain of the school shooting eight. As a good mixer, he was chosen in 1925 to go to the Duke of York's holiday camp at which public school boys mingled with boys from poor homes.

Branson passed his matriculation examination and finished at Bedford in the summer of 1925, just before he was eighteen. He had been accepted for a career in the Hong Kong and Shanghai Bank, and as part of his training started work in an insurance office. He disliked this, and asked his parents to let him go to art school; after the head of the Slade School of Art, Professor Tonks, had said that his drawings showed talent, he was allowed to enter the Slade in January 1926. When the General Strike took place in May 1926 he believed that the nation was in danger and volunteered as a special constable. He was sent to patrol a 'quiet' area in South Kensington, saw nothing of the strike, and spent several days sitting on a doorstep reading *Paradise Lost*. He worked hard at the Slade, winning second prize in the 1927 Summer Competition, and finished there at the end of that year. Among his friends and contemporaries were William Coldstream and Claud Rogers.

For the next four years he was absorbed in his painting. Unlike most of his artist friends he had no financial problem, since his maternal grandmother had left him with a private income from a trust fund. He lived for some time in Little Goodge Street near the Tottenham Court Road; later in Earls Court; later he moved to a studio in Chelsea. He was a realist painter, and his paintings, like those of some of his friends, showed at this time the influence of Sickert. He spent much of his time in Lyons teashops drawing the customers, and in railway stations drawing the waiting passengers. Like nearly all young painters he had great difficulty in getting his paintings exhibited, and was pleased when two were accepted for the Summer Exhibition of the Royal Academy in 1931, although he held the Academy in some contempt.

During his Slade years and after, the attitudes instilled into him by his upbringing began to be discarded. He began reading in a serious and concentrated way. Books which he found important he annotated copiously both in the margins and on slips

pasted in. Shakespeare (the three-volume Everyman edition) was treated in this way. Branson was reading it during 1929, and as his wife observes, it is clear from some of the notes that he was questioning almost everything he had been brought up to believe. Formerly rather religious, he became very critical of the church. Always interested in military theory, he began to question the purposes for which armies are used, and in particular the underlying purpose of the British Empire which had been so much a part of his background. He began to buy and read radical books and socialist books. Among them were Wells's *Outline of History*, Henry George's *Progress and Poverty*, Winwood Reade's *Martyrdom of Man*, and Shaw's *Intelligent Woman's Guide to Socialism*. The first of these, Wells's *Outline*, which he finished in December 1930, came as a revelation. He annotated it methodically, starting with the introduction, where he underlined the sentence which observed that people were taught history 'in nationalist blinkers ignoring every country but their own', and ending with the last page, where he wrote: 'Wells is certainly on the right track in his sketch of Utopia and undoubtedly there must be the overthrow of Imperialism but what he seems to have forgotten to state is what is to happen when the final overthrow is completed.' With the rest of his note this shows that Socialism was not yet part of Branson's intellectual equipment and belief; yet only four months later he was a convinced and conscious Socialist. We do not know what influences promoted this rapid development, but he must at least have read other books on Socialism besides Shaw's *Guide*. At all events he had become convinced that war, oppression and poverty were the products of the capitalist system.

He put this view, along with many others, to Noreen Browne, whom he met in the last week of April 1931. At their first meeting, she recalls, they discussed Russia, the position of the artist in society, the position of women, religion and war. Noreen Browne was a student of music. Her parents had died when she was eight, and she had been brought up by her grandparents who were 'well-to-do, but old-fashioned by the standards of the time'. She was twenty-one, Branson twenty-three. They were married on 1 June 1931. When the August 1931 crisis came, with the defection of Ramsay Mac-Donald, and the crushing Labour defeat in the subsequent general election, Branson decided he could no longer stand aside from the political struggle. Since he knew hardly anyone who was active in the Socialist movement, he wrote to Sir Stafford Cripps, whose speeches he had read, asking him if there was any way in which he could help in an unpaid capacity. Cripps arranged for him to become secretary to Morgan Jones, Labour MP for the Welsh mining constituency of Caerphilly. Simultaneously, both the Bransons joined the Chelsea branch of the Independent Labour Party, in which the leading personalities were two well-known pacifists, Alan Skinner and his wife.

By this time Branson had become convinced that the capitalist system was not only wicked but doomed. Moreover, he had begun to believe that the Russian revolution offered the chief hope for the future of mankind. He rapidly became absorbed in his work for Morgan Jones and for the time being gave up painting. He devoted himself to constituency correspondence, did research and prepared briefs for Morgan Jones's speeches, and accompanied him to weekend conferences. But he rapidly became disillusioned with the approach of the Labour Opposition in Parliament, and, moreover, began to feel that much of what went on in the House was irrelevant to the situation. He disagreed with Morgan Jones on many matters. For example when a brief was needed for a debate on India on 24 March 1932, he prepared an indictment of British imperialism which Morgan Jones refused to use; he wanted criticism of the British administration rather than a challenge to their right to be there at all. Branson was now studying Lenin's works for the first time. It seemed to him that events were moving steadily towards a Second World War which might possibly be averted, but only by revolution. He was filled with a sense of urgency, and believing it necessary to break with what he considered the class collaboration and reformist line of the Labour Party

which had led up to the Ramsay MacDonald débâcle, he resigned from his position with Morgan Jones in the spring of 1932.

Meanwhile he had become secretary of the Chelsea Branch of the ILP. He began to attend meetings called by the Revolutionary Policy Committee of the ILP led by Jack Gaster and Dr C. K. Cullen; for some months the RPC's bulletin to its supporters was despatched from the Branson home in Burnsall Street, Chelsea, where a room had been converted into an office with typewriter and duplicating machine. Branson attended the Blackpool ILP annual conference at Easter 1932, as delegate from his branch, and voted in favour of a motion for the disaffiliation of the ILP from the Labour Party. The motion was lost on that occasion.

As secretary of the Chelsea Branch, Branson was concerned that the membership included very few industrial workers. He suggested that an intensive canvass of working-class families was needed and that for this purpose the branch should get out its own cyclostyled street paper. The branch members agreed.

This street paper made its appearance under the title of *Revolt*. It began as a weekly duplicated sheet sold for a halfpenny; later it was enlarged and appeared, less frequently, for a penny. The team who sold it consisted of Branson and his wife, and three others, all in their early twenties, who turned up night after night to discuss its contents. Branson wrote it all, or nearly all, and put it on stencils; Friday nights were spent in running it off; weekends in selling it. Sales rose to 400, mainly readers in the working-class blocks of flats built by charitable trusts – the Sutton Dwellings, the Lewis Dwellings, the Guinness Trust Buildings – and also in the streets round Lots Road power station. *Revolt* was intended as an organising medium, so a ledger was kept in which every scrap of conversation with the readers was entered, together with information about their jobs, their experiences of the means test and so on. The ledger grew into a 'social survey' full of entries like: 'Granny's gone to hospital', or 'Printer lives here. Wife says she makes steak and kidney pudding – a man needs something to line his stomach.'

The first member of the CP whom the Bransons met told them that *Revolt* was not a Leninist but an anarchist paper. On the other hand, the older members of the ILP branch objected to such articles as one which praised the Soviet Red Army. Branson believed it was the duty of Socialists to support the Soviet Union, which was to him the first workers' state, struggling up out of centuries of backwardness and surrounded by hostile capitalist powers. He had for some time been thinking of joining the Communist Party, which seemed to him the only party trying to apply the principles of Marxism. Moreover he was attracted by the existence of the Communist International, which he thought was trying to unite the workers of the world in the struggle for liberation. In August 1932 he and his wife and two out of the three members of the *Revolt* team left the ILP and joined the Communist Party. The Party asked them to continue running *Revolt* as a Communist paper. This was done; none of the readers raised any objection, and the Communist branch provided some extra canvassers to help with the work. In the late summer and autumn, *Revolt* promoted a campaign to get rid of an insanitary public lavatory the smell of which was causing much discontent in the Sutton dwellings. Branson persuaded the tenants to form a committee to run the campaign, which ended in success. The tenants were delighted with their victory, and formed an association. It was Branson's first experience of getting people into action.

During this period and for the next few years, Branson was studying intensively, systematically building up his knowledge and understanding of Marxist theory. He methodically compiled notes on economics, history, philosophy and the science of revolution, as well as on current political questions. His reading embraced not only politics and economics but aesthetics and, to some extent, scientific and technical developments.

Early in 1933 a Marx Commemoration Committee was set up on the initiative of the Labour Research Department and Martin Lawrence, the publishers, to mark the occasion of the fiftieth anniversary of the death of Karl Marx. The committee

comprised well-known trade unionists and veteran Socialists belonging to the Labour Party (like Alexander Gossip, general secretary of the Furnishing Trades Association, and Harry Adams, chairman of the London District Committee of the Building Trade Workers), or the Communist Party (like Tom Mann, Harry Pollitt and Joe Scott of the Amalgamated Engineering Union). The Labour Research Department was represented by its secretary W. E. [*sic*] Williams; Emile Burns and R. P. Arnot (members of the Executive Committee) and Martin Lawrence Ltd by Ralph Fox, soon to die in battle for Republican Spain [Rothstein (1966) 73].

A conference called by the committee decided 'that the best memorial . . . would be a Marxist Library and workers' school and educational centre' [*Lab. Research*, Apr 1933]. Branson offered to provide the money for a permanent building (Marx House was purchased in the name of Noreen Branson) and a fund was opened with him in charge. A suitable building was found at 37a Clerkenwell Green which was opened in October 1933 as the Marx Memorial Library and Workers' School.

The Bransons' daughter was born on 10 March 1933; they named her Rosa, after Rosa Luxemburg. Branson wanted to leave Chelsea and live in a working-class borough, so in June 1933 they moved to Tramway Avenue, Edmonton, where houses were being bought on mortgage by better-paid industrial workers. The inhabitants of the estate had formed a ratepayers' association, the chairman of which (Sid Chivers) was a member of the London busmen's rank and file movement; Branson became the association's secretary soon after he arrived.

In July 1933 Branson offered his help to the strike committee of the Firestone Tyre Company in Brentford, where 900 unorganised workers had come out spontaneously against speed-up. He edited and ran off a duplicated bulletin on behalf of the strike committee during the four weeks for which the strike lasted.

Towards the end of 1933 he established and helped to run a bookshop for left-wing literature in Tottenham. It sold socialist literature of every kind, with other 'serious' reading such as the Thinker's Library, and some second-hand fiction – Jack London's novels had a good sale. The shop was opened late in 1933 and continued until the end of 1934. Although it was combined with a modest little café at the back (intended as a meeting place where left-wing people could congregate), and although there were a number of voluntary helpers, it made no money. In the autumn of 1934 Branson was asked to help in the preparation of Marxist education syllabuses, study courses and speakers' notes at the Communist Party headquarters at 16 King Street. He was associated with this work for several years. It was a long journey from Edmonton to King Street, and late in 1934 the Bransons moved to Battersea.

Branson was increasingly concerned at what he believed to be the Communist Party's failure to direct its work sufficiently towards industrial workers, and towards the factories. He got George Renshaw (formerly prominent in the Minority Movement) to speak to a group of railwaymen from Nine Elms at his home; the group grew into a regular discussion circle. He got the same thing going with a group of building workers, and with one or two engineering groups. He became an NCLC lecturer, giving lectures to trade union branches on Marxist economics, working-class history and Socialist theory. The date when Branson began to lecture for the NCLC is not quite certain, but it could not have been before the second half of 1935 and was probably early in 1936. The area organiser was George Phippen. Branson's lectures were popular and he received numerous bookings, not just for individual or occasional lectures but often for courses of six or more, since the local branch officials found that his lectures promoted better attendances than pure business meetings. In this way he became widely known in the trade union movement in South London.

In 1936 when Franco's rising against the Spanish Republican Government took place and it became clear that fascist Italy and Germany were involved on Franco's side, Branson helped to initiate the Battersea Aid Spain Committee, a big affair in which all sections of the Battersea labour movement participated. In the spring of 1937 he volunteered to go and fight in Spain with the International Brigade. However, he was asked to postpone going to Spain in order to help the Communist Party with volunteers to the Brigade. It should be remembered that in early 1937 it was made illegal in all the non-intervention countries to volunteer or to get others to volunteer. Nevertheless in the end there were over 2000 British volunteers, and Branson's job was to interview them, get them accommodation if they came up from the provinces, see that they had boots, give them all necessary instructions, and escort them in groups as far as Paris, mainly on weekend tickets. Since this work was illegal it had to be kept away from King Street and from his own house. Towards the end of 1937 he realised that the police were watching his movements, so the work was passed over to someone else, and early in 1938 he left for Spain himself.

He was some weeks at the Brigade training base at Albacete, and was sent into action in March 1938. It was the time of the big Franco offensive into the Aragon with the aid of Italian troops; the Republican troops were in continuous retreat – there were not enough rifles to go round – and the Italians drove straight through, leaving confusion on either side. Branson, like many others, found himself cut off. The roads were crammed with refugees who were being bombed and machine-gunned from the air, so he took to the hills, and managed over several days to work his way back to headquarters, where he found that he had been reported as missing.

After a few days' rest he and others were formed up as part of the Major Attlee company of the British Battalion and were sent up to the front again. On 3 April 1938, most of the company, including over a hundred British, were surprised, surrounded and captured. The company was disarmed and was marched in triumph through lines of heavily-equipped and jeering Italians.

They were taken to San Gregorio Military Academy at Saragossa, where foreign correspondents were invited to interview them. In the *News Chronicle* Branson was reported as saying that he had come to help the Spanish people against an invasion by Germany and Italy: 'What we lacked was equipment and we met an army with everything under the sun. Enthusiasm cannot fight that.'

The prisoners were then sent to a big prison at San Pedro de Cardena. In this prison were many hundreds, including Brigaders of all nationalities. It was very cold, and Branson and his companions slept on a concrete floor, at first without blankets. Many had dysentery, and there was no proper sanitation, and very little food. The prisoners' fingerprints were taken by the German Gestapo. The Spanish guards beat up the prisoners, though on the whole they left the British alone; captured German anti-fascists from the Thaelmann battalion suffered most. One of his comrades wrote of this period in Clive's history: 'In any difficult time, Clive was always cheery, putting forward what we should do, and helping to educate others in order to use the time usefully. He was one of the most popular and most respected among the British prisoners' [quoted by H. Pollitt in his Introduction to Branson's *British Soldier in India* (1944)].

In July Branson, along with a hundred other British prisoners, was transferred to an Italian concentration camp at Palencia. Conditions there were much better; they did light work in the fields and the Italian guards treated them reasonably well. The Italian Commandante asked Branson to paint a series of pictures of the camp for him to take home to Italy. He procured the only paints to be had in Burgos – two blues and a yellow – and Branson did six paintings, two large ones which the Commandante kept and four small ones which Branson managed to hand over to the British consul when the latter was at last permitted to visit the prisoners; the consul sent them through the post to Branson's wife, together with about fifty drawings of heads of prisoners and some poems. Some of the poems written in Spain were later published in *New Writing* and *Poetry and the People*.

In November 1938, through the mediation of the International Red Cross, a hundred British prisoners were exchanged for a hundred Italian prisoners in the hands of the Spanish Republican Government, and Branson was one of those who got home. After Christmas 1938, when the rest of the International Brigaders came home he organised a speaking tour of Brigaders; they raised £5000 for Spanish relief.

The next few months saw the defeat of everything which British anti-fascists had been struggling for. In February 1939 the Spanish Republican Government was finally defeated; in March Hitler occupied the whole of Czechoslovakia. Branson was convinced that Chamberlain's policy (non-intervention in Spain, the Munich agreement, etc.) was designed to encourage Hitler to fight the Soviet Union. He saw the Russo-German non-aggression pact of August 1939 as an attempt by the Soviet Union to avoid Chamberlain's trap. And when, in September 1939, the British Government declared war on Germany, he found it impossible to believe that Chamberlain could be engaged in an anti-fascist struggle. He accepted the analysis made by Dimitrov, the secretary of the Communist International, that it was an imperialist war embarked on by Britain and France after the failure of their anti-Soviet plans. This view of the war seemed initially to be reinforced by the tendency of British statesmen to talk as though the war was a continuation of the First World War, which all Communists and most Socialists had long since characterised as imperialist. Months of 'phoney war', and the sending of volunteers to Finland, seemed further to confirm it.

Early in 1940 Branson got a temporary job as painter's labourer, decorating the interior of a West End club. He made friends with the waiters and kitchen staff and persuaded some of them to join a union. At weekends he spoke at open air meetings, and in the summer of 1940 was arrested for a speech on Clapham Common. He was fined £5 and bound over for twelve months.

Branson had painted only intermittently since 1932. He had returned to it in 1937 and a series of landscapes had been taken by the Lefèvre Gallery, but he had had to stop when he went to Spain. After the blitz started in the autumn of 1940, he turned again to painting because, as he said, 'It may be my last chance'. His subjects were working-class people in Battersea streets and the impact of air-raids. Later, some of these paintings were exhibited by the Artists' International Association. His call-up came in January 1941, just after all the windows in his home had been blown out.

He was sent to the 54th Training Regiment of the Royal Armoured Corps at Perham Down Camp near Andover. Shortly after getting there he was given his first stripe, and became a squad instructor; in April 1941 he got his second stripe. He was anxious to make himself technically proficient, but he also managed to do a little painting when he was off duty.

When Germany attacked the Soviet Union in June 1941, he believed that this denoted a change in the character of the war; this was the guarantee that it could become a genuinely anti-fascist war. In any case he thought it absolutely crucial for the future of the world working-class movement that the Soviet Union should win. With some reluctance he came to the conclusion that the war must be supported. 'My whole being revolts against war and I found myself much more wholehearted in opposing the war than I do now in urging more drastic prosecution of the war', he said in a letter dated 8 July 1941.

That month Branson was asked to give a lecture on the International Brigade. His lecture was divided into seven main heads: (1) political training and morale, (2) selection of leaders, (3) discipline, (4) political commissars, (5) how the prisoners organised in the concentration camp, (6) the relation of the IB to the peasantry, (7) internationalism and anti-fascism. He wrote home describing this event: 'About fifty turned up including the Squadron Leaders, the S. Sergeant Major and two sub-lieutenants and a host of sergeants. I gave a chatty kind of lecture – non-political i.e. I didn't specifically mention Karl Marx, although I raised very sharply the questions of officers, spit and

polish, type of training, men's meetings etc. It was a tremendous success. I was congratulated by everyone and was immediately booked for another lecture – probably on Cromwell's Army (the same points will be made again – men's meetings etc).' However, while he was preparing his lecture on Cromwell's Army, an order came down from the Southern Command that he was not to lecture again on any subject anywhere. He had already been invited to do his lecture on the International Brigade at Tidworth, but this had to be cancelled too.

In October he was suddenly transferred to the 57th Training Regiment at Warminster – 'the reason is known to everyone here as political', he said in a letter home. There he was put on a gunnery course, and met an old friend, Stephen Swingler, who became a Labour MP in 1945 and died in 1969. In January 1942 Branson was selected for a gunnery instructor's course, but before this began he was suddenly transferred (again, he gathered, for political reasons) to the 52nd Training Regiment at Bovington Camp near Wool in Dorset.

Shortly afterwards he was told he was going overseas. He left in March 1942 and was on a troopship for about six weeks, reaching India in May 1942. During the voyage he gave his talk on the International Brigade eight times to different units, and a special one to officers. On this last he wrote home:

There was a good turn-up and I took great care with my notes. I explained among other things, in great detail and point by point, the work of political commissars – the right of political organisation to check up on the work of senior ranks, political training of men, etc. etc. At the end the senior officer thanked me for an interesting talk and then added that "the work of the political commissars is done by the officers in HM Army and so the post would be superfluous" ... For interest sake I have been asking fellows if their unit has had a lecture on the peoples and politics of our destination. Two so far have said yes. One, a talk by a Sergeant Major, who had been there, dealt mainly with prisons and brothels; the second, a talk by an OC unit, dealt with all the religious castes but no mention of real politics. So you see how the duties of political commissars are carried out!

On arrival in India Clive Branson was stationed with the British Cavalry Regiment at Gulunche, near Poona. He spent less than twenty-one months in India, from May 1942 to about January 1944. In this comparatively short time he became deeply interested in the country and the people, and eager to learn all he could about them. He was always modest about his own capabilities. In August 1942 for example, he wrote: 'Tonight on orders I am detailed for an escort duty to a place some hundreds of miles from here. It will take several days so I should see a lot of India – only I'm afraid as a spectator and a very ignorant one at that, but I shall use my eyes.' And later in the same month: 'One thing I have learnt out here more than anything else is that life in England, and therefore one's outlook towards people and the world, is hopelessly divorced from the rest of humanity. When this war is over we must go to China, come back to India as civilian friends. This all sounds rather unpractical I know, and it probably is, but it just lets you know that my stay abroad this time is not having the effect of making me want to settle down at home after the war, but to see and learn more, much, much more.' The beauty and strangeness of the Indian scene, the depth and contrasts of colour made him long to paint; the violent contrast of native and British, penury and comfort, moved and enraged him. In May 1942 he wrote: 'Although I have only been in India a little time there is one problem which hits you in the face – the life of the peasantry; and in Bombay, the housing. But Oh, what a people this is for painting.' Painting he had to postpone till April 1943, but he began at once to get to understand the political and social scene. He learned partly from newspapers and journals: the Times of India is mentioned so frequently in his letters as to suggest that he saw it almost daily; he also makes occasional reference to other Indian papers, including

People's War, the organ of the CPI, and to English journals such as the New Statesman and Labour Monthly; also to the Indo-Soviet Journal and Soviet War News. And one of the things he most looked forward to when he was going on leave to Bombay was visiting the bookshops. On the first day of his first leave there he wrote: 'I have bought a number of excellent books.' Some of the books he bought on various leaves were political or sociological, such as Mehta and Patwardan's The Communal Triangle in India; some were on Indian literature or Indian art, such as P. E. N.'s Indo-Anglian Literature, Mulk-Raj Anand's The Hindu View of Art. He also discovered that Anand's Coolie was banned, along with the Penguin Problem of India by K. S. Shelvankar, and R. Palme Dutt's India Today.

Even more important than reading about India was getting to know as many Indians as possible. This was not difficult for a person of Branson's sincerity, warmth and sensitivity. On his first leave in Bombay he managed to contact Indian Communist Party circles (the Indian Party was semi-legal, though with many hundreds of members in prison) and also to make other Indian friends and to meet Congress supporters. From then, much of his free time was spent in the company of Indian friends. It was a great relief from army life to be able to discuss not only social and political conditions but also music, literature and art. 'July 25th 1943 . . . On my last day in Bombay I went round to some friends where among lots of interesting talk (1) I gave an outline of the history of the Labour Movement in England with special reference to the basic meaning of "I'm a Labour Man"; (2) I met the [Censored] who has just been to S. India, including Madras, and he talked to me for over an hour on things in S. India; and (3) in the evening an Indian lady, the wife of one of my friends, played music on an Indian mandolin-like instrument and we had a long discussion on types of Indian music as well as on the traditional cultural forms – musical (vocal) epic recitation – so loved by the Indian peasantry – forms into which the new poets are putting new content.'

In March 1943 Branson was posted to the gunnery wing in Ahmednagar (his birthplace) and in April he was able to find an Indian art master there, at whose house he could work. He became a close friend of this teacher, Kelkar, and of his family, whom he drew and painted – some sketches and a study for a painting of this household are reproduced in the volume of his letters, *British Soldier in India* (1944). In October 1943, when Branson was posted back to his unit near Calcutta, 'the whole family wept', as his friend told him; they gave him presents, including a painting of Kelkar's, and had his photograph taken, so that the children 'will always know of their good Kaka (uncle), a real friend of India'. Branson's affectionate relations with this family seem to have been characteristic. *British Soldier in India* ends with a touching tribute from some of Clive's Indian friends written to Mrs Branson: 'we came close enough to know and feel the man that he was, and the valuable friend of the Indian people that he always had been . . . Our sense of personal loss is further deepened by the feeling that our people in particular is poorer for the death of Clive Branson.'

Certainly, Branson's letters constantly show his profound sympathy with the Indian people, and his anger and distress at their condition. His analysis of the political situation led him to believe that the oppressive and reactionary behaviour of the British Government and of the wealthy class of Indians too, was imperilling victory in the Japanese war: the imprisonment of the Congress leaders was mistaken both because nothing could be done without Congress and because the absence of the leadership meant that Japanese agents and undercover supporters of the Japanese could mislead the people into strikes and sabotage which were advantageous only to the enemy, and which those arrested as responsible – Congress and CPI members – had been endeavouring to prevent.

Branson was especially appalled, as any eyewitness must have been, by the famine in Bengal. His letters speak with angry disgust of 'the hoarders, the big grain merchants, the landlords and the bureaucrats *who have*

engineered the famine' (his italics). One description written in October 1943 is full of sharp detail:

The last part of my journey was like a nightmare. The endless view of plains, crops, and small stations, turned almost suddenly into one long trail of starving people. Men, women, children, babies, looked up into the passing carriage in their last hope for food. These people were not just hungry – this was *famine*. When we stopped, children swarmed round the carriage windows, repeating, hopelessly, 'Bukskish sahib' – with the monotony of a damaged gramophone. Others sat on the ground, just waiting. I saw women – almost fleshless skeletons, their clothes grey with dust from wandering, with expressionless faces, not *walking*, but foot steadying foot, as though not knowing where they went. As we pulled towards Calcutta, for *miles*, little children naked, with inflated bellies stuck on stick-like legs, held up empty tins towards us. They were children still – they laughed and waved as we went by. Behind them one could see the brilliant fiendish green of the new crop.

In January 1944 Clive Branson's unit went into action. By now a troop sergeant in the 25th Dragoons, Royal Armoured Corps, he was killed on the Arakan Front in Burma during the fighting for the Ngandedank Pass on 25 February 1944, at the age of thirty-six. He was survived by his wife and daughter, and left an estate valued at £6985.

Clive Branson was one of the first of the many intellectuals who joined the Communist Party in the 1930s. He was somewhat unusual in that he seems to have found his own way to Socialism, without much help from his contemporaries; and apart from Bernard Shaw's *Intelligent Woman's Guide to Socialism* the books that first awakened him to some at least of the social realities of capitalism were also somewhat unusual. Like the overwhelming majority of the Communist intellectuals of his generation, he had no serious doubts about Soviet policy during the 1930s, and he accepted, for example, the official explanation of the

Moscow trials. Branson's career in the Communist Party may be taken as an archetype of the history of many young middle-class intellectuals who, reacting passionately to the economic waste of capitalism at home and the rise of Fascism abroad, rejected the British Labour Party as impossibly cautious and compromising, and allied themselves to the militant working-class movement. Branson was utterly devoted to the causes he believed in, and his courage and idealism shine through the years of the last decade of his life.

After his death the British Communist Party published extracts from his letters together with some drawings in the form of a book entitled *British Soldier in India*. It came out in October 1944, was listed by the *Sunday Express* of 29 October as one of the 'books most in demand last week', and was published also in India and in the United States. A translation into Marathi was being planned in 1972, the twenty-fifth anniversary of Indian independence. Sean O'Casey reviewed it in the *Daily Worker* (21 Oct 1944) and H. N. Brailsford in the *New Statesman* (25 Nov 1944):

> He was an artist who had the talent and courage to see. He was also a devoted Communist who started with none of the legends about our Empire which cloud the eyes of the average Englishman who lands for the first time in Bombay. The result is that he saw the poverty of the Indian masses and the incompetence of our rule with a vividness and an anger that give this book a unique value. His letters were written in haste with no thought of publication . . . None the less, by the sureness of their vision and their skill in rendering things seen and felt, they convey more of the essential truth about India than a dozen of the pretentious volumes the experts write.

Writings: *Poems* [privately printed] (1932); 'The Red Air Force', *Cambridge Left*, 2 no. 1 (Autumn 1934) 29; 'San Pedro', *New Writing*, n.s. no. 2 (1939) 53; 'To the German Prisoner and the Nightingale in San Pedro', *Poetry and the People*, no. 11 (May 1939) 6–7; 'The Asturian Miners', ibid., 7; 'The International', ibid., no. 17 (Feb 1940) 18; 'May First', ibid., no. 18 (May 1940) 2–3 [All the above are poems]; *British Soldier in India: the letters of Clive Branson* (1944). The untitled poem on p. 113 of *British Soldier in India* was reprinted in the anthology of War Poets 1939–45, *The Terrible Rain*, ed. B. Gardner (1966) 167.

Sources: F. Pitcairn, *Reporter in Spain* (1936); A. Hutt, *The Post-war History of the British Working Class* (1937); W. Rust, *Britons in Spain. The history of the XVth International Brigade* (1939); *Daily Worker*, 21 Oct 1944; *New Statesman*, 25 Nov 1944; P. Toynbee, *Friends Apart: a memoir of Esmond Romilly and Jasper Ridley in the thirties* (1954); C. L. Mowat, *Britain between the Wars* (1955); N. Wood, *Communism and British Intellectuals* (1959); H. S. Thomas, *The Spanish Civil War* (1962, rev. ed. 1965); P. Lowbridge, 'The Spanish Civil War', in *The Review* (the thirties – a special number) no. 11–12 [1964] 42–50; A. Rothstein, *A House in Clerkenwell Green* (1966, 2nd ed. Marx Memorial Library, 1972); H. Francis, 'Welsh Miners and the Spanish Civil War', *J. of Cont. Hist.* 5, no. 3 (1970) 177–91.

NOTE: Mrs Noreen Branson provided a detailed sketch of Clive Branson's life, from which this entry has been largely produced, although she must not be held responsible for any errors of fact or evaluation. The editors wish to express their appreciation for her generous help and co-operation.

JOHN SAVILLE

See also: *Christopher CAUDWELL; *John CORNFORD; *Ralph Fox; *Harry POLLITT.

BROADHURST, Henry (1840–1911)
TRADE UNIONIST AND LIB-LAB MP

Henry Broadhurst was born in the village of Littlemore, near Oxford, on 13 April 1840, the son of Thomas and Sarah Broadhurst, and the youngest of twelve children. His father, like most of his forebears, was a stonemason, and a staunch chapelgoer; and his son remained a loyal, though unsectarian, member of the Methodist Church throughout his life. Though his father's wages were no more than a pound a week, the family added to its resources by pig-rearing and raising fruit and vegetables, and thus lived in a state of rude plenty. Young Henry was sent to a local private school at a fee of sixpence a week, the only formal education he received. At the age of twelve he began work in the blacksmith's shop, but soon left to serve his apprenticeship under his father at Oxford where (like Hardy's Jude) he worked on the colleges and churches and, as he tells us, developed a lifelong love for the University city.

After serving his time as a stonemason, the trade depression of the later 1850s forced him to leave Oxford, and for many months he became a typical 'tramping artisan', intermittently working in the south of England and London, and finally spending some time in Norwich. In the winter of 1858-9 he was again 'on the tramp' for a long period, obtaining help from local branches of the masons' union, but living in desperate conditions in his search for work; at one point he tried to join the Army, but was rejected as not tall enough. In 1859 he returned to Norwich, where he obtained permanent employment at his trade, and settled down for the next six years. There he married Eliza, a seamstress, daughter of William Olley, of Norwich; and since the couple were never to have any children of their own, they adopted Eliza's niece into the family. This niece married a Wesleyan minister, W. H. Hopkinson, who subsequently wrote a life of Broadhurst (unpublished).

In 1865 Broadhurst moved to London, where he obtained work on the new government offices and Houses of Parliament, and the whole family settled down in a house at Brixton. The next few years, with the growth of working-class militancy and the agitation over the Reform Bill, were a period of intense political excitement in the capital; and Broadhurst, as a member of the Reform League, supported most of the radical movements of the time. For instance, he gives a vivid account in his memoirs of the famous Hyde Park incident of July 1866 (at which he was present); part of the background of the events which led in 1867 to the Second Reform Act, by which the Conservative Government granted the vote to most urban industrial workers. In 1872 there was a flare-up in the London building trade over pay and hours of work, which led to an employers' lock-out; and Broadhurst's growing powers of leadership and oratory led to his being elected chief spokesman for the workmen. After successful negotiation with the employers he was able to secure an extra halfpenny an hour for the men and reductions in the working week.

This was a turning point in Broadhurst's life. He gave up working at his trade - for ever, as it turned out - to become a full-time official in the Stonemasons' Union. There he worked actively over the next few years in settling local disputes, and reorganising his union's structure on 'new model' lines: with a powerful central executive in London, and social benefits for the members. He also became the Stonemasons' delegate to the TUC, and was elected a member of its parliamentary committee. He was described by a local journalist who heard him at the 1874 Sheffield Congress as 'a fine outspoken Committee man, with a bluff independent manner, and a loud sounding voice' [W. H. Hopkinson, MS. life of Broadhurst, p. 24].

The parliamentary committee of the TUC had been set up in 1871 'to watch all legislative measures directly affecting the question of labour', and 'to initiate whenever necessary such legislative action as Congress may direct or as the exigencies of the time and circumstances may demand'. In fact, after 1871 most of its energies were directed towards destroying the Liberal Government's Criminal Law Amendment Act, which imposed severe restraints on peaceful picketing, and towards amending the harshness of the Master and Servant laws, which made breach of contract a criminal offence for working men. As a member of the parliamentary committee Broadhurst worked with George Howell, its secretary, and other leading trade unionists and their sympathisers, in the powerful nation-wide campaign directed against the 'labour laws'. In particular, in

1872 he took the lead in the agitation organised on behalf of the London Gas Stokers who had been imprisoned for twelve months for breach of contract. Partly as a result of this pressure the men were eventually released after four months. Three years later, Disraeli's Government repealed the Criminal Law Amendment Act, thus legalising peaceful picketing, and then passed the Employers and Workmen Act, which made breach of contract an ordinary civil offence for both workmen and employers. With the passing of this legislation, it seemed as if the trade union movement had at last triumphantly secured all its aims as far as the legal status of its members was concerned; and George Howell, believing that the work of the parliamentary committee was therefore accomplished, resigned as secretary. The TUC of 1875, less sanguine, elected Henry Broadhurst in his place. The 'Broadhurst Era' in British trade union history had begun.

For the next ten years at least, it was Henry Broadhurst's image of trade unionism that exercised an almost undisputed sway within the movement. It was an image which owed most to the ethos of mid-Victorian craft unionism, and especially the tactics and assumptions of those shrewd hard-headed union leaders who had led their members successfully through to the legal triumphs of the 1870s. In this respect Broadhurst was very much the successor of George Howell. Like Howell, he believed that the major tasks of the movement had now been accomplished: under the umbrella of legal security the trade unions could go their own way, free from interference by or dependence upon the state. For Broadhurst then, after the heroic struggles of the 1860s and early 1870s, the task was one of consolidation: quiet persistent pressure on Parliament for the removal of the remaining impediments which stood in the way of complete civil equality for working men, and the improvement of existing labour legislation. This was almost the limit of his ambition. And what seemed to justify his cautious policy was the fact that his assumption of the secretaryship of the parliamentary committee coincided with the onset of the 'Great Depression' which brought long periods of unemployment for many trade unionists during the later years of the nineteenth century. Economic depression was, as always, reflected in declining membership: whereas in the peak year of 1874 more than a million trade unionists had been affiliated to the TUC, by the end of the following year this was down by half. Declining membership meant also declining revenue, which acted as a brake on militant action; and, as the Webbs have emphasised, increasing sectionalism within the movement as a whole. During his fifteen years of power, therefore, Broadhurst's ambition was to retain what had been won and keep the movement together until better times returned, at the same time pushing for important if minor legislative reforms.

The first bill he drafted as secretary was for abolishing property qualifications in local government, and this was taken up by A. J. Mundella and became law in 1878. At the same time he was concerned with promoting the parliamentary programme of the Trades Union Congress, in particular the extension of the 1875 Employers and Workmen Act, an improved Factory Act, a Merchant Shipping Bill and an Employers' Liability Bill. All this parliamentary lobbying could obviously be done much more easily from within the House of Commons itself; and in the 1870s Broadhurst was already concerned with those wider political movements which would eventually lead to his election as a member of parliament in 1880. In 1873 he had become secretary of the Labour Representation League, which aimed at putting up working men at general elections; and in the contest of 1874 his own name was put forward as a last-minute candidate for the borough of Chipping Wycombe, Bucks – where he was hopelessly defeated. During the election campaign of that year he expressed his views on labour and politics in a letter to John Bright (who had indicated his disapproval of working-class candidates) in which he asserted ' . . . it has never been our desire or intention to harass the great Liberal party of which we shall ever remain a section'. This attitude – from which he never wavered throughout his career – became more apparent after the virtual collapse of the LRL which followed the election of 1874, an election which in any case brought only two working men into the House of Commons. Broadhurst's identification with the Liberal Party was strengthened by his pugnacious leadership of the workmen's committee of the Eastern Question Association, which brought him in 1876 under the personal spell of Mr Gladstone, for whom he developed a lifelong devotion. By this time he had built up a reputation as one of the best platform speakers for the Liberal cause; and in 1880 he was adopted as the Liberal candidate for Stoke and elected with a handsome majority.

Throughout his career in the House of Commons – which spanned almost the whole period up to 1906 – he appears to have been a popular and effective member; and after his election in 1880 he was helped enormously in the heavy burden of his dual role, as MP and trade union official, by the unpaid services and personal devotion of his secretary, Mr Maxwell. His main role in the House was, of course, as a spokesman for the Labour cause, but on topics like land reform and the franchise he was clearly identified with the radical wing of the Liberal Party. In the field of labour legislation his most important achievement was his strong support for an Employers' Liability Bill on which he made his successful maiden speech and which became law in 1881. Though the act did not satisfy the trade unions, since it still retained the doctrine of 'common employment', it did recognise the employer's responsibility for insuring his workers against industrial accidents. Its major weakness, however, was the escape clause by which employers could 'contract out' and persuade their workmen to do the same. Other minor reforms which Broadhurst secured were: the appointment of working men as Justices of the Peace in 1885, and a 'fair wages' clause in government contracts; but his Bill to ban the work of girls under fourteen in the Midlands nail and chain-making industries failed. This failure is significant: it shows that Broadhurst's legislative successes were largely due

to the coincidence of his proposals with Liberal policy, and indeed not very much was done for labour in the course of the next ten years.

As the outstanding Liberal trade unionist in Parliament Broadhurst was offered an Assistant Factory Inspectorship by Harcourt, the Home Secretary, and later an Inspectorship of Canal Boats, both of which he refused in order to continue his trade union work. This meant (as he points out with some unctuousness in his memoirs) a real financial sacrifice, since his salary as secretary to the parliamentary committee of the TUC was only £150 p.a., later raised to £200. He did, however, suggest the name of another trade unionist for the first inspectorship, and indeed while the Liberals were in power he was usually consulted unofficially over similar appointments.

In 1884 he was made a member of the R.C. on the Housing of the Working Classes, partly perhaps because of his particular interest in leasehold enfranchisement, on which he published a book in 1885 in collaboration with Sir Robert Reid (Lord Loreburn). As a result of the parliamentary Redistribution Act of that year, he abandoned his Stoke constituency, and was returned in the subsequent general election for the Bordesley division of Birmingham. When Gladstone formed his third Ministry in 1886, Broadhurst was appointed undersecretary at the Home Office – mainly as a personal reward by the Prime Minister for his earlier services to the Eastern Question Association. He was the first working man to be appointed to a Ministerial post. The one significant event of his period of office was the unemployed demonstrations in London, with which he showed scant sympathy. But he was in power for only five months, for after the defeat of Gladstone's Home Rule Bill in that same year, the Unionists won a massive victory at the polls. Broadhurst himself was elected as a Gladstonian for West Nottingham – since Birmingham was now a Unionist stronghold – and in 1887 resumed the post of secretary to the parliamentary committee which he had relinquished while he was a member of the Liberal Government.

But Broadhurst's position within the trade union movement now had to be vindicated. For in the later 1880s, faced with the profound problems of persistent unemployment, technological change and demarcation disputes, and the appalling conditions of the unskilled workers, the complacent *laissez faire* attitudes of the trade union 'old gang' seemed increasingly intolerable – especially to the Socialists, whose influence was increasing. 'A kind of deadly stupor covered them', wrote Tom Mann and Ben Tillett, two of their bitterest critics, 'and they really seemed to be dying of inanition' [T. Mann and B. Tillett (1890) 4]. Nor did their representatives in Parliament, led by Henry Broadhurst, show any greater understanding of the developing aspirations of labour; they were content to be, in Engels's scornful phrase, the 'tail of the Great Liberal Party'. Beatrice Webb, who was present at the Congress of 1889, described Broadhurst as: 'A commonplace person: hard-working no doubt, but a middle-class philistine to the backbone: appealing to the practical shrewdness and high-flown, but mediocre, sentiments of the comfortably-off workingman. His view of women is typical of his other views: he lives in platitudes and commonplaces' [*Our Partnership* (1948) 22]. This was perhaps unfair. But certainly Broadhurst's unconstructive attitude towards the problem of unemployment, his refusal to help over inter-union disputes, his personal commitments to the Liberal Party, and, above all, his obstinate opposition to the legal enforcement of the Eight Hour Day – the symbol of the 'new unionism' – made him the representative of everything the Socialists detested in the 'old unionism'. Nor was it only the Socialists who were critical: even leaders of the craft unions were not entirely unaffected by the winds of change blowing in the 1880s which were already shaking the once solid opposition to the principle of state intervention in industrial matters. Between 1885 and 1887, for example, the three presidential speeches at the TUC's annual conferences all spoke out in favour of the Eight Hour Day and land nationalisation, and criticised the capitalist system. Moreover, there was growing sympathy for the idea of increased labour representation in the House of Commons, and this led to the setting up of the Labour Electoral Committee in 1886 (though this soon became a Liberal appanage), as well as to attempts at fostering closer relations with the Labour International.

It was at the Swansea TUC of 1887 that these growing discontents erupted. Following Kill Bevan's belligerently anti-capitalist presidential speech, Keir Hardie (representing the Ayrshire miners) called for the Eight Hour Day, and later delivered a blistering personal attack on Henry Broadhurst for following the Liberal rather than the Labour line. But Broadhurst easily countered Hardie's outbursts by appealing to the deep-rooted instincts of loyalty among the delegates and his own record of service to the movement, even while reaffirming his own support for independence in industrial matters. It was clear that Hardie's personal attack was bitterly resented by many of the delegates, and for the next three years Hardie and his friends – even when joined by Mann and Burns for the Engineers – made few converts at the TUC. At the 1889 Congress Hardie again took up the cudgels against Broadhurst by moving an amendment asserting his unfitness for the office of secretary to the parliamentary committee, on the grounds that he had given electoral support to bad Liberal employers and accepted money from the Liberal Party, as well as holding shares in the firm of Brunner, Mond and Co. Once again Broadhurst paraded his rectitude before the Congress:

I have refused subscriptions, I have refused friendly aid, I have refused all approaches in years past when they were made to make friends in the Congress, and if today you discharge me from my position – I shall leave your service with clean hands. I shall leave your reputation untarnished and unblemished.

He spoke for an hour and sat down to terrific applause, and Hardie's amendment was lost by 177 votes to eleven. But in all this Broadhurst was protesting rather too much: for he had received money from the Liberal

Party for propaganda and electioneering, and, as he did not deny, he *did* hold shares in Brunner, Mond. Nevertheless, the temper of the majority of the delegates was seen in their rejection of the Eight Hour Day motion, and their singular lack of enthusiasm for the achievements of the unskilled workers – notably the dockers – in the East End of London that very summer.

On the other hand, the resolution in favour of the Eight Hour Day for miners *was* passed. This is significant. For (as Dr Duffy has argued) the real struggle for the Eight Hour Day was being fought at union level; and faced with the grim realities of depression and unemployment, the rank-and-file were now ahead of their leaders. By the end of 1889 many craft unions, such as the spinners, the carpenters, and even the masons – Broadhurst's own union – were in favour. Hence the battle was half won even before the famous Liverpool Congress of 1890, and the new unionists there could afford to be more moderate. Congress in fact passed the resolution in favour of the Eight Hour Day by thirty-eight votes; and, in addition, three new men, including John Burns, were voted on to the parliamentary committee. Following this *volte face*, Broadhurst submitted his resignation as secretary, ostensibly on grounds of ill-health, and was succeeded by Charles Fenwick.

As the events of the next few years clearly showed, the Socialists' victory in 1890 was very much a pyrrhic one; yet it is difficult not to see Broadhurst's resignation in 1890 as marking something of a turning point in British trade union history. Despite the bitter and intensely personal attacks upon him by the new unionists during his last years of power, Henry Broadhurst was a powerful and impressive trade union leader; and even the Webbs (who disliked him) paid tribute to his 'skilful guidance and indefatigable activity', a verdict endorsed by historians like Henry Pelling and B. C. Roberts. Within the limits of the narrow aims he set himself he was remarkably successful: by 1890 organised trade unionism was fully accepted by the country, and the Liberal 'alliance' seemed to have paid off in terms of status, prestige and legislation.

Moreover, the movement had been kept united during a period of economic depression and union sectionalism, and membership had again begun to creep up in the 1880s to reach a record figure of nearly a million and a half at the end of the decade. It was on the basis of these solid achievements that the British trade union movement could face the new problems that beset it in the age of the employers' counter-attack and Taff Vale.

In 1890, when Henry Broadhurst resigned as secretary of the parliamentary committee, he was only fifty; but as far as the labour movement was concerned his career was virtually over. In 1895, owing to a change in the TUC's rules, he even lost his seat at Congress. Yet, despite his loss of office, he was still harried by his Labour opponents. In 1892 he was defeated at West Nottingham by Colonel Sir C. Seely, a coalowner, owing to the defection of the miners' vote due to his opposition to the miners' Eight Hour Day, which Seely publicly supported [Pelling (1967) 208]. In the following year he lost a by-election at Grimsby as a result (so he believed) of the hostility of the ILP and the personal campaign directed against him by the *Labour Elector*. At a by-election in 1894, however, he was safely returned for one of the Leicester seats, which he retained until 1906 when, partly owing to disappointment at not being offered a post by the new Liberal Government, he retired. During these years he sat as the leading member of the small group of Lib-Labs in the House, sticking closely to the Gladstonian line on all the great issues of the day. The only important public service he performed during this quiet period was as a member of the R.C. on the Aged Poor (1892–1895), to which he submitted a Minority Report (written apparently by Sidney Webb) advocating Old Age Pensions.

In 1890, mainly because of bad health (he suffered from diabetes) he had given up residence in London and retired to Cromer on the Norfolk coast. There he became closely associated with his adopted county, and was made an alderman and Justice of the Peace of Norfolk. He had developed a passion for golf in his middle years, and was one of the founders of Tooting Common, Royal Cromer and Sheringham clubs. He died at Cromer on 11 October 1911 and was buried at Overstrand. His wife, to whom he had been married for more than fifty years, had died six years earlier. He left an estate valued at £7046.

Writings: 'The Enfranchisement of Urban Leaseholders', *Fortn. Rev. 41* o.s. *35* n.s. (Mar 1884) 344–53; 'The Ideas of the New Voters', ibid., *43* o.s. 37 n.s. (Feb 1885) 149–155; 'Leasehold Enfranchisement', *19th C. 17* (June 1885) 1064–71; (with Sir R. Reid) *Leasehold Enfranchisement* (1885); *Henry Broadhurst, M.P. The Story of his Life from a Stonemason's Bench to the Treasury Bench* (1901); 'Labour Representation Thirty Years Ago', *General Federation of Trade Unions* (Mar 1903) 15–19.

Sources: (1) MSS: Henry Broadhurst Coll. and unpublished Life of Henry Broadhurst by W. H. Hopkinson, LSE; Minute Book, Labour Representation League, LSE; Misc. references, Howell Coll., Bishopsgate Institute. (2) Other: *Bee-Hive*, 1867–78; *TUC Reports*, 1887–90; T. Mann and B. Tillett, *The 'New' Trades Unionism* (1890); G. Howell, *Trade Unionism New and Old* (1891); idem, *Labour Legislation, Labour Movements and Labour Leaders*, 2 vols (2nd ed. 1905); W. J. Davis, *The British Trades Union Congress: history and recollections*, 2 vols (1910–16); *DNB* (1901–11) [by J. Ramsay MacDonald]; J. H. Linforth, *Leaves from an Agent's Diary: being some reminiscences of thirty years' work as a Liberal Agent* (1911) 138–47; S. & B. Webb, *History of Trade Unionism* (2nd ed., 1920); G. D. H. Cole, 'Some Notes on British Trade Unionism in the Third Quarter of the Nineteenth Century', *Int. Rev. for Social Hist. 2* (1937) 1–27; idem, *British Working Class Politics 1832–1914* (1941); B. Webb, *Our Partnership*, ed. B. Drake and M. Cole (1948); H. Pelling, *The Origins of the Labour Party 1880–1900* (1954, 2nd ed. 1965); B. C. Roberts, *The Trades Union Congress 1868–1921* (1958); A. E. P. Duffy, 'New Unionism in Britain 1889–1890: a reappraisal', *Econ. Hist. Rev. 14* (1961–2) 306–

319; H. Pelling, *A History of British Trade Unionism* (1963); H. A. Clegg et al., *A History of British Trade Unions since 1889 1: 1889–1910* (Oxford, 1964); H. Pelling, *Social Geography of British Elections 1885–1910* (1967); A. E. P. Duffy, 'The Eight Hours Day Movement in Britain, 1886–1893', pts 1 and 2, *Manchester School, 36* (1968) 203–22; 345–63; F. M. Leventhal, *Respectable Radical: George Howell and Victorian working class politics* (1971). OBIT. *Times*, 12 Oct 1911; *Norfolk Chronicle*, 14 Oct 1911; *Reynolds's Newspaper*, 15 Oct 1911. The editors wish to express their gratitude for an early draft on Henry Broadhurst by Dr Eugenia Palmegiano, St Peters College, Jersey City, New Jersey.

PAUL ADELMAN

See also: †William ALLAN, and for New Model Unionism; George HOWELL.

BROWN, Herbert Runham (1879–1949)
PACIFIST; SECRETARY AND CHAIRMAN OF WAR RESISTERS' INTERNATIONAL

Herbert Runham Brown was born at Redhill, Surrey, on 27 June 1879, the son of Frederick William Brown, a fancy stationer, and his wife Mary (née Cunningham). Herbert's father was also a Congregationalist Sunday School superintendent and his grandfather was a minister of religion. Herbert Brown showed no particular ability and left school at fifteen to be apprenticed to the building trade. Here, however, his skill as a craftsman and his genius for establishing human relationships soon showed themselves. At the end of his apprenticeship, while still only nineteen, he became manager of a small building concern, and a year later founded his own business. With his brother Eric, he later formed the firm of Runham Brown Brothers, which became well known and highly respected in northeast London. He remained actively engaged in the building trade till his death. His attitude to his employees was shown when he kept them all on the payroll at the expense of his own income during the depression of the early 1930s even though there was often insufficient work.

Runham Brown's pacifism dated from his early adolescence. At fourteen he wrote a paper on the incompatibility of war and Christianity. When Britain entered the Boer War he at once felt bound to oppose it. His first public speech, made in 1900, was a denunciation of the British concentration camps in South Africa. By the time the First World War broke out, he moved away from orthodox Christianity towards Humanism, but he remained an uncompromising pacifist. In 1915 he joined the No Conscription Fellowship which had just been formed by Clifford Allen and Fenner Brockway. He became chairman of the Enfield branch of the NCF (he was by this time married and living in Enfield), and this brought him for the first time into conflict with the law. In 1916 a Mr Beavis brought him a letter from his son, H. Stuart Beavis, who had just been court-martialled and sentenced to death in France, along with twenty-nine other conscientious objectors, for disobeying military orders. In an effort to save his friends, Runham Brown had the letter printed and circulated to MPs and local clergy and residents and the sentences were commuted to ten years' penal servitude. But he was prosecuted under the Defence of the Realm Act for prejudicing recruiting and the discipline of the Forces and sentenced to a fine of £30 or two months' imprisonment.

In the summer of 1916, shortly after the coming into force of the second Military Service Act, which conscripted married men, Runham Brown appeared before the local Military Service Tribunal as a conscientious objector. Three members of the Tribunal were for granting him absolute exemption and four were against. The result was the offer of non-combatant military service. The Appeal Tribunal withdrew even this concession, and in due course he was called up, arrested, and court-martialled. Like many more he served three successive sentences of hard labour, and was released only in April 1919, after two and a half years' imprisonment.

While in prison he underwent some trying ordeals such as being put in a strait-jacket and douched with cold water, but they failed to break his spirit. For a long time he edited the manuscript magazine which was secretly written and circulated among COs in Wandsworth Prison. In his prison cell, he became convinced that there must be many in other countries making the same radical anti-war stand as himself, and he had a vision of their all being united after the war in one world-wide family.

On discharge from prison, he at once became active again in the pacifist movement, and was largely responsible for organising the final convention of the No Conscription Fellowship, held in London in November 1919. Shortly afterwards when the No More War Movement was established he became a member of its national committee, and continued to serve in this capacity till it merged with the Peace Pledge Union in 1936. Shortly after forming the Peace Pledge Union in 1934, Canon Dick Sheppard had invited him to become one of its sponsors. Brown also served in the Pacifist Research Bureau which was set up to continue one aspect of the work of the No More War Movement.

In 1921 Runham Brown visited Germany to contact the No More War Movement's sister organisation in that country, 'Nie Wieder Krieg'. From this first contact the War Resisters' International was to grow. A few months later, representatives of these two organisations and of similar bodies in France and Holland met at Bilthoven in Holland, and founded an international organisation named Paco (the Esperanto word for Peace). Two years later the name was changed to War Resisters' International, and the headquarters was transferred to England, actually to Runham Brown's home in Enfield; and from then until his death he continued to direct it, first as secretary and then as chairman. The whole of his leisure time for nearly thirty years was devoted to this task.

Though without knowledge of any other language than English, Runham Brown had a notable capacity for establishing friendship with all sorts and conditions of people, and a genius for organising without dominating. He gathered around him, inspired by his own enthusiasm, a band of voluntary translators who assisted him in the rapidly growing correspondence of the International. Under his guidance it became a world-wide organisation with members in eighty-four countries, discovering and assisting men who were refusing military and war service for reasons of religious, moral or political conviction. In the later 1930s he succeeded in helping some 400 people to escape from Nazi Germany to start new lives in Britain or elsewhere; in this work he won the sympathetic co-operation of officials of the British Home Office. His success in rescuing refugees from Continental tyrannies won him the name of 'Pimpernel' Brown. During the Second World War he was instrumental in the purchase of a farm in Essex (called Lansbury Gate Farm after George Lansbury, one-time chairman of the War Resisters' International) for the employment of English pacifists allocated to agricultural work as an alternative to military service. After the war the farm was sold and the money was used to buy a house (known as Lansbury House) for the headquarters of the War Resisters' International. Until then the office had been in Runham Brown's home, continually encroaching on the accommodation available for his own family, despite the additional storey which he built to store the International's archives.

In 1903 Runham Brown married Edith Miller, to whom he had become engaged at the age of sixteen and whose death in 1947 was a blow from which he never really recovered. They had two daughters. Joyce, the elder, trained as a secretary and worked in that capacity for some years; when her mother became an invalid she took over the housekeeping. The younger daughter, Eileen, was a professional photographer, and had a studio in Barnet where she used 'Runham' as her business name. All the family were united in the work to which Runham Brown was devoted and joined in extending hospitality to the many refugees who arrived, often without notice, on their doorstep. Some years after her father's death, the elder daughter took on the treasurership of the War Resisters' International.

In the early years of his adult life, Brown had been an active supporter of the ILP and of the Union of Democratic Control. It was from about 1923 when he became secretary of the War Resisters' International, that the anti-war movement totally absorbed all his spare-time activities. He remained however a nominal member of the ILP for many years.

After a long illness, Runham Brown died early in the morning of 19 December 1949 and was cremated at Golders Green Crematorium on 22 December. Many prominent members of the Peace Movement were present, and moving tributes were paid to his long life of service to his ideals. A meeting was also held at St Ermin's Hall, Westminster, on 26 February 1950 to honour his memory and was attended by war resisters of many nationalities. He left an estate valued at £13,257.

Writings: 'Die Internationale der Kriegsdienstgegner' [The WRI], translated from the English by Martha Steinitz in *Gewalt und Gewaltlosigkeit* [Violence and Non-Violence] ed. F. Kobler (Rotapfel Verlag, Zurich and Leipzig, 1928; repr. Garland Library of War and Peace, New York, 1972); *Cutting Ice*, [a brief survey of war resistance and the International] (Enfield, 1930); *Western Samoa: imprisonment, deportation and shooting* (Enfield, 1930) 16 pp.; *Spain: a challenge to pacifism* [Enfield, 1936?] 12 pp.; *The War Resisters' International: principle, policy and practice* (Enfield, 1936) 8 pp.; *Why Hitler?* (Enfield, [193–]) 19 pp.; *What is the WRI?* (Enfield, [1939?]) 4 pp.; *The War Resisters' International in War Time* (Enfield, [194–]). He also wrote editorials and articles in the *Bulletin* of the WRI (later the *War Resister*) in the years between 1923 and 1949.

Sources: *N.C.F. 1914–1919* [souvenir publication] (1919); J. W. Graham, *Conscription and Conscience* (1922); *Peace News*, 6 Aug 1948; S. Morrison, *I renounce War* (1962); personal information: Miss Joyce Brown, London, daughter. OBIT. *Peace News*, 30 Dec 1949; *War Resister* no. 57 (spring 1950).

H. F. BING

See also: Reginald Clifford ALLEN.

BRUFF, Frank Herbert (1869–1931)
CO-OPERATOR

The son of Henry Bruff, a cooper, and his wife Maria (née Thompson), F. H. Bruff was born on 12 September 1869 at 14 Court, Navigation Street, Birmingham. He was educated at Christ Church Schools, Birmingham, and entered the printing trade; in 1891–2 he was a bronze medallist and honours-man (typography) of the City and Guilds of London Institute. From 1902 to 1919 he held the post of superintendent and lecturer in typography at the Birmingham Municipal Technical School.

While a young man, he became associated with the co-operative movement. In 1895 he was appointed to the district committee of the Co-operative Union, upon which he served until 1920 (acting as secretary from 1913 to 1920). He was a member of the board of the Birmingham Industrial Co-operative Society from 1897 to 1906. In 1902 he founded the firm of Birmingham Printers Ltd which operated on co-partnership principles; he managed the company upon this basis until his death. Bruff was a member of the reception committee that welcomed delegates to the 1916 Trades Union Congress in Birmingham; a special souvenir handbook was printed by his firm, which undertook much work on behalf of the local labour movement.

Although his interests were almost exclusively at a local level, they found expression in several directions. He officiated as the independent chairman of the Birmingham Joint Industrial Council of Master and Operative Bakers in 1918–19. In 1920 his name was put forward by the Birmingham and District Co-operative Representation Council as that of a suitable person to sit as a magistrate. The proposal was accepted, and he was appointed as a JP and sat on the Birmingham bench until a few months before his death when ill-health forced him to retire. He belonged to the King's Norton Lodge of Freemasons, and for many years was connected with St Stephen's Church, Selly Park.

Bruff died at his home in Eastern Road, Selly Park, on 23 February 1931, and was survived by his wife, five sons and two daughters. The funeral took place on 26 February with a service at St Stephen's Church. In his will he left effects valued at £1073.

Writings: *Birmingham: a handbook to the 38th annual Co-operative Congress* (Manchester, 1906).

Sources: *Cornish's Birmingham Year Book* (1927); Anon., *History of the Birmingham Co-operative Society Limited 1881–1931* (Birmingham, 1931). OBIT. *Birmingham Mail*, 23 Feb 1931; *Birmingham Post*, 24 Feb 1931.

DAVID E. MARTIN

See also: Arthur EADES; †Benjamin JONES, for Co-operative Production.

BURNETT, John (1842–1914)
TRADE UNIONIST AND CIVIL SERVANT

Burnett was born on 21 June 1842 at Alnwick, Northumberland, and educated at the Duke of Northumberland's charity school there. Orphaned at the age of twelve, he moved to live with an uncle on Tyneside, and for two years worked as an errand boy, before being apprenticed in a local engineering works. He attended evening classes in Newcastle, and became a member of the town's Mechanics Institute, taking a leading part in its debating activities.

By the early 1860s he had clearly emerged as one of the leaders of the skilled labour groups on Tyneside. He was prominent in the agitation for the Saturday half-holiday in 1864, and subsequently in the parliamentary reform movement in the years preceding the 1867 Act. This activity brought him into close contact with Joseph Cowen, Jun., an association of considerable significance for his later career.

Perhaps his greatest service to labour was the part he played in the agitation for a reduction in the standard working week. In 1866 he was a leading member of a deputation of engineering workers who unsuccessfully sought to persuade Charles Mark Palmer to concede a fifty-seven hour week instead of the prevailing sixty-one hours. Burnett later moved to Armstrong's Elswick works, where his personal prestige among his fellow-workers remained high.

With the trade revival of the early 1870s, pressure from the workers for concessions mounted, and now their demand was for a fifty-four hour standard week or for the 'nine hours day' for the five main working days. At Sunderland a short strike led by Andrew Gourley, an old associate of Burnett's, succeeded in imposing the fifty-four hour week in the engineering works on Wearside. The struggle on Tyneside, however, was more strenuous and more prolonged. The men's Nine Hours League – a name pregnant with memories of free trade and reform agitations – led by a committee on which Burnett was the most important moving spirit, organised a strike which lasted from May till October 1871 and ended in a clear-cut victory for the men. This was the more notable in that the employers' resistance was determined; Sir William Armstrong and most of his fellow-employers in the Tyneside engineering works were resolved to resist the men's claim to determine working hours. It is clear, however, that the associated employers played their hand extremely badly, alienating uncommitted public opinion by their harshness and intransigence, to the benefit of the Nine Hours League.

In contrast, the quality of the men's leadership was superb, continuously proffering a picture of sweet reasonableness which succeeded beyond any doubt in undermining the employers' public image and enlisting powerful support for the strikers. Well before the end of the long strike, the engineering employers were being severely criticised in the national and local press, and the Nine Hours League was able to raise some £20,000 to support its members and their dependants. Joseph Cowen's energetic help was a considerable asset, both in financial terms and in the steady support given to the strike by his *Newcastle Chronicle*. The success of the strike was in part due to the relative ease with which many of the workers involved were able to find alternative employment during the strike; only a a small minority of

the strikers were union members, with a claim on union funds, and the employers' failure to persuade other employers to refuse work to Tyneside strikers may have been decisive. On the other hand, the strike committee obtained substantial aid from other working-class groups, notably from the miners of the North-East coalfield. For this subvention there were two reasons: Burnett's conception of working-class activity was very much in tune with the beliefs of such miners' leaders as Thomas Burt, while in addition there was a substantial overlap between the Tyneside engineering workers and some of the skilled tradesmen employed in the pits.

The skill of the leadership was clearly evinced in the reaction of the men to the employers' attempt to break the strike by the importation of blacklegs, including foreign workers from Europe. Burnett was delegated to contact the International Association of Working Men (the First International) as a result of which James Cohn, the secretary of the Danish section, was sent to Belgium to dissuade workers from coming to Britain. For this he was expelled from Belgium and he then went to Tyneside where, according to Burnett's own account 'by the manner in which he induced foreigners to leave Newcastle he was of great service to the cause'. In general, the strike's leaders appeared as conspicuous advocates of law-abiding restraints while in practice the blacklegs appeared unescorted in public at their peril. In this, as in many other ways, the leaders of the Nine Hours League demonstrated nineteenth century working-class leadership at its most skilful, and this is the more notable in that the conduct of the strike did not depend on formal trade union organisation. The principal leaders seem all to have been trade unionists, but the overwhelming majority of their followers were not; the position of the leaders did not derive from trade union office, but rather represented a genuine personal prestige recognised on the shop floor level.

After five months the solidarity of the men, and the considerable outside sympathy and support which they enjoyed, coupled with the employers' loss of business, brought

Armstrong and his associates to surrender on the hours issue. The victory of the Tyneside engineering workers went further than this, however, for the long strike had aroused very widespread interest. Engineering employers elsewhere were immediately forced to make the same concession, and naturally the Northumberland miners' union was quick off the mark in obtaining it likewise for the skilled workshop men in its own ranks. The 1871 strike marked an important stage in the agitation for reduced hours, and remained a significant victory for workers faced with intransigent employers.

After the victory it was clearly inexpedient for Burnett to return to the Elswick works, and for some time Cowen provided him with employment on the *Chronicle*. Then in 1875 Burnett succeeded William Allan, after the latter's death in October 1874, as general secretary to the Amalgamated Society of Engineers. He also took Allan's place as treasurer of the parliamentary committee of the TUC. Burnett had never been a man of violence, as his conduct during the Nine Hours Movement made abundantly clear; but his militant record during the early years of the 1870s undoubtedly contributed much to his election as the engineers' general secretary. He came to this important position, however, at a time when new problems were demanding radical solutions, partly in the matter of the union's structure and organisation, partly in response to economic and technical change. Burnett, like Allan before him, was overburdened with the administrative pressures of a highly centralised organisation, and despite his undoubted personal ability as well as his devotion to the purposes of his union, he failed to match the challenge of the new period. The 'shortcomings of the Society's structure and policy', wrote the historian of the ASE, were 'partially concealed by his personal brilliance' [Jefferys [1945] 111]. As Burnett himself wrote in his last report before he resigned office in 1886: 'Policies and practices that suited the conditions of things forty years ago cannot do so now; and instead of clinging in blind tenacity to traditions, we must remodel the Society where such is required' [ASE, *Annual Report* (1886)].

Burnett played his part at the national level of the union movement, although his decade of office covered a defensive period in its history. In 1883 he was one of a three-man delegation from the parliamentary committee (the other two being A. W. Bailey, of the Amalgamated Society of Tailors, and Henry Broadhurst) to a Paris meeting of trade unionists, and their report was presented to the 1884 TUC. He was soon, however, to leave the trade union movement. The events which were to bring to an end Burnett's career as a trade union leader stemmed from the three-day Industrial Remuneration Conference in January 1885, and the aftermath of debate in the House of Commons.

It had long been recognised that the British Government was exceedingly ill-served in the matter of statistical information, especially with regard to labour questions; and there was a growing pressure, from the late 1870s on, to improve both the collection and the processing of economic and social data. The discussions of the Industrial Remuneration Conference were full of references to the problem and Charles Bradlaugh was especially active in pressing the point upon those who sat on the ministerial benches in the House of Commons. In the spring of 1886 John Burnett was appointed the first Labour Correspondent to the Board of Trade [Davidson (1972) 228ff]. The President of the Board of Trade, who had much to do with his appointment, was A. J. Mundella (who had watched with sympathy Burnett's leadership of the 1871 strike).

It was a small beginning to the solution of the problem, since Burnett was the only new senior appointment. In his opinions and attitudes at this time, he was a typical example of the leaders of the craft unions. The Webbs [*Industrial Democracy* (1897) 1, 160] quoted him as saying frequently: 'A trade society without friendly benefits, is like a standing army. It is a constant menace to peace.' We have a detailed account of Burnett's views just at the time he left the trade union movement from a long essay that was published in 1886, in a volume that arose directly out of the Industrial

Remuneration Conference. The Conference had been made possible by the donation of one thousand pounds from an Edinburgh businessman who remained anonymous (the name was revealed in 1911 by Frederic Harrison in his *Autobiographic Memoirs 2* (1911) 296–7); and since a large part of the money was in fact returned to the donor, it was decided to use it as a subsidy for a series of lectures in Edinburgh, Glasgow and Dundee, during the summer months of 1886, and then to publish the lectures in book form, edited by James Oliphant. Burnett's contribution, from which the extract below is taken, was entitled 'Trade Unions as a Means of Improving the Conditions of Labour':

I have now reached a point [Burnett wrote] where I may fitly sum up the propositions I claim to have established:—

1. The condition of the working classes can never be materially improved except by the action of that portion of the community itself working in a united and disciplined manner.

2. The condition of the workers never was improved until after the era of Trade Unions; and all their improvement, whether in wages or better conditions of working, has gone on step by step with the extension and adoption of Trade Union principles.

3. During the early part of the present century, which may be taken as a fair illustration of what the state of the working classes would be without organisation, the wealth of this country enormously increased, but its possession was shared by a very small section of the community, while the poverty of the masses was intense.

4. Employers are seldom known to raise wages or shorten hours of their own accord, and combination among the workmen was found to be the only means whereby pressure could be brought to bear upon them to effect either object.

5. Since the establishment of Trade Unions we have seen a more equal distribution of the wealth of the country, and a greater participation by the workers in the fruit of their labour.

6. By their means such alterations have been effected in the law of the land as have placed labour on an equality with capital in the eye of the law; also the enactment of laws for the protection of the health and life of the workman in the workshop, and for securing him compensation for accident if such laws are neglected.

7. To the action of Trade Unions are also due the adoption of arbitration, conciliation, and sliding scales, as a means of settling disputes by reason instead of force.

8. The shortening of the hours of labour, which has given to the working man increased opportunities for mental development and recreation; the fruits of which, though already evident in a higher standard of technical knowledge, and a longer average duration of life, can only be fairly seen after the lapse of a generation or two. And,—

9. By the disbursement of their funds for friendly purposes they have reduced and prevented pauperism, and rendered their members the most peaceful and contented portion of the toiling population

I have here advanced no speculative arguments nor mere abstract opinions. This is simply a record of work done, and upon that I rest the claim of the Unions to consideration, respect, and support.

Even now, with but half their number enrolled as unionists, our workmen have achieved vast moral and material victories; and if the other half, which not only stands aloof but fights on the other side, will but join the organisations of their trades, further progress will be made. Recent disturbances in this and other countries show very clearly that unorganised labour is most dangerous to social order. No stronger barrier to social revolution exists than those which have been erected by the Unions. Their providence and foresight have enabled them to combat social forces which would otherwise have been too strong for them, and thus they have been saved from the desperation and misery which regard revolt and death as a means of relief from slavery. Capitalists should remember this, should be less rancorous in their hatred and persecution of unionists, and should instead encourage their growth and development.

Finally, and briefly, in what way may Unions make progress in the future? The extension of boards of conciliation and arbitration, and of joint committees of masters and men, seems to me to be gradually leading up to a modern type of the ancient guild. The board of green cloth is becoming more and more the scene of the peaceful councils of conflicting interests which are yet felt to be identical, and in the spirit of the old guilds decisions are arrived at and acted upon which are for the good of the trade at large. The cultivation and development of the modern guild on these lines should be a task reciprocally undertaken by unions of masters and of men.

In his early years at the Board of Trade Burnett produced two useful, and highly topical, accounts of the sweating system in East London (1887) and Leeds (1888); but the Labour Department for the first few years of its existence had a restricted life, mainly because of obstruction from the Treasury. Burnett was seconded as joint secretary to the Royal Commission on Labour (1892–4) but it was only with the formation of a Labour Department with Hubert Llewellyn Smith as the first Labour Commissioner that labour questions began to receive the detailed attention that was required. Burnett was appointed Chief Labour Correspondent in a now much enlarged department. His main work until his retirement was the preparation of reports and the compilation of statistical data on strikes, industrial disputes and trade unionism generally; although after the passing of the Conciliation Bill in 1896 some part of his time was taken up with arbitration matters. In this latter work he seems to have been conspicuously successful. He retired from government service in 1907, at the age of sixty-five, but still continued to act as conciliator and arbitrator in disputes. After the passing of the Trade Boards Act in 1909

he became one of the appointed members of the Tailoring Board and continued to serve up to the time of his death. His work in the Labour Department inevitably involved close contacts with his former colleagues in the trade union movement, and after his retirement he seems to have continued to identify himself with the movement.

His death in London on 30 January 1914 brought many tributes to the liberality of his views, and the fairness and straightforwardness of his conduct in industrial questions. His wife Jean and his children Andrew, Lily and Margaret survived him, and he left an estate with net personalty of £5472. He was buried at Nunhead Cemetery.

Writings: *Nine Hours Movement. A History of the Engineers' Strike in Newcastle and Gateshead* (Newcastle, 1872); ASE, *Monthly Reports*, 1875–86; 'Trade Unions as a Means of improving the Condition of Labour', in *The Claims of Labour*, ed. J. Oliphant (Edinburgh, 1886) 7–39; *Report to the Board of Trade on the Sweating System at the East End of London* 1887 LXXXIX; *Report to the Board of Trade on the Sweating System in Leeds* 1888 LXXXVI; 'The Boycott as an Element in Trade Disputes', *Econ. J. 1* (1891) 163–73. Burnett was responsible for the Reports on Trade Unions as Labour Correspondent to the Board of Trade and later, as Chief Labour Correspondent from the first – in 1887 – until his fifteenth in 1906 when he retired. The reports were comprehensive, and some contained comparative data. One of the most important was the twelfth (1900 LXXXIII) which included statistics of all trade union membership for the years 1892–8, together with financial data for the 100 principal unions.

Sources: (1) MSS: Lab 2 series, PRO; A. J. Mundella papers, Sheffield University; Graham Wallas papers and Webb Coll., LSE; Sir H. Llewellyn Smith papers. (2) Other: *Industrial Remuneration Conference. The Report of the Proceedings* (1885; repr. with an Introduction by John Saville, New York, 1968); C. Bradlaugh, 'Labor Statistics: their utility to employers and employed',

Our Corner 7, 1 Mar 1886, 129–33; D. F. Schloss, 'The Reorganisation of our Labour Dept', *JRSS* 56 (1893) 44–70; S. and B. Webb, *History of Trade Unionism* (1894); idem, *Industrial Democracy*, 2 vols (1897); H. Llewellyn Smith, *The Board of Trade* (1928); J. B. Jefferys, *The Story of the Engineers* [1945]; W. H. G. Armytage, *A. J. Mundella 1825–97* (1951); L. A. Clarke, 'The Liberal Party and Collectivism 1886–1906' (Cambridge MLitt., 1957); J. A. M. Caldwell, 'The Genesis of the Ministry of Labour', *Public Administration* 37 (1959) 371–82; H. A. Clegg et al., *A History of British Trade Unions since 1889, 1: 1889–1910* (Oxford, 1964); E. Allen, J. F. Clarke, N. McCord and D. J. Rowe, *The North East Engineers' Strike of 1871* (Newcastle, 1971); R. Davidson, 'Sir Hubert Llewellyn Smith and Labour Policy 1886–1916 (Cambridge PhD, 1971); idem, 'Llewellyn Smith, the Labour Department and Government Growth 1886–1909', in *Studies in the Growth of Nineteenth-Century Government*, ed. G. Sutherland (1972) 227–62. OBIT. *Times*, 2 Feb 1914; *Newcastle Daily Chronicle*, 3 Feb 1914; *Wandsworth Borough News*, 6 Feb 1914; *Newcastle Weekly Chronicle*, 7, 14 and 21 Feb 1914.

NORMAN MCCORD
JOHN SAVILLE

See also: †William ALLAN and for New Model Unionism; Henry BROADHURST; †Thomas BURT; †Joseph COWEN; Frederic HARRISON.

BYRON, Anne Isabella, Lady Noel
(1792–1860)
PHILANTHROPIST AND SOCIAL REFORMER

Much of the life of Lady Byron lies outside the scope of entries for a Dictionary of Labour Biography. Born on 17 May 1792, at Elemore Hall, Durham, Anne Isabella was the only child of Sir Ralph and Lady Milbanke Noel and spent her earlier years between the family homes of Halnaby Hall in Yorkshire and at Seaham Harbour in Durham. She married Lord Byron, the poet, on 2 January 1815 and they separated early in 1816. The deed of separation was signed by her on 22 April 1816. There was one child of the marriage. On leaving her husband, Lady Byron re-entered her father's family, occupying herself with her daughter's education, and becoming increasingly interested in social questions. She became a close friend of Dr William King, of Brighton, one of the pioneers of the co-operative movement in Britain, and for a short time King was tutor to her daughter. It is probable that she helped financially with the publication of Dr King's journal, the *Co-operator* (1 May 1828–1 August 1830). Lady Byron met Robert Owen in 1829 but found him vain and presumptuous, and at no time was she ever influenced by his social ideas. Lady Byron was deeply religious, and her philanthropy stemmed from her Christian beliefs. She gave an annual subscription to the Sunday and evening school opened by the Manchester and Salford Association for the Spread of Co-operative Knowledge, and although she continued to offer financial help to the educational efforts of the young co-operative movement, she was hostile to the growing militancy, both political and anti-religious, of the leading Owenite co-operators in the early 1930s.

The main educational influence upon Lady Byron would seem to have been Philipp Emanuel von Fellenberg, whose patrician background was similar to her own, and with whose general attitudes she found herself in broad agreement. They both intensely disliked revolutionary France and, despite their progressive educational aims and policies, they were both opposed to radical social change. Lady Byron visited Fellenberg at Hofwyl first in 1828, and was especially impressed with Jacob Wehrli's teaching in the Poor School. This trained vagrant children, mostly in agricultural and craft pursuits, with a minimum of formal education. It was Fellenberg's and Wehrli's ideas which encouraged Lady Byron to sponsor the industrial and agricultural school at Ealing Grove in 1834. [See Appendix IV in E. C. Mayne (1929) for an interesting essay by Lady Byron on the 'History of Industrial Schools'.] E. T. Craig, who had been secretary to the Ralahine community, was in charge of Ealing Grove. Craig himself visited Hofwyl before the school was opened, and in any case had developed many of his ideas on education during his three years at Ralahine. The school, which occupied four acres of grounds soon attracted many notable visitors. The curricula and teaching methods were a mixture of Craig's own ideas and borrowings from Fellenberg, Pestalozzi and Owen; corporal punishment was abolished; much of the work of the school was in the hands of a committee elected monthly by the pupils themselves; gardening and other manual labour was an essential part of the school's life; there was no sectarian religious instruction. Craig himself left Ealing Grove at the end of 1835, but the basic features of his system remained. There are lively contemporary accounts by W. C. Woodbridge, the American educationalist, and by B. F. Duppa. Lady Byron continued her direct interest in the school until 1848, when she handed over control to the organising master. The most useful modern summary of Ealing Grove is in Stewart and McCann (1967).

Lady Byron's encouragement and support to individual reformers and to reforming movements is still insufficiently documented. Among those she helped was Rowland Detrosier; she was for many years a vigorous supporter of the allotments system; and in the 1850s, mainly through a close friendship with Mary Carpenter, she became especially interested in the problems of juvenile delinquency. When Miss Carpenter established a reformatory for boys at Bristol in 1852, the house was furnished by Lady Byron; two years later she bought the Red House at Bristol and placed it at the disposal of Miss Carpenter to use as a reformatory for girls. She was also a close friend and confidante of the Rev. Frederick Robertson, a young Church of England clergyman interested in social reform, and incumbent of Trinity Chapel, Brighton from 1847 to his early death in 1853 at the age of thirty-seven. Robertson was associated with the formation in 1848 of a Working Man's Institute in Brighton which provided reading facilities for about 1100 members. Evening classes were inaugurated a few years later and held in a room provided by Lady Byron, who was

residing in the town. On leaving Brighton, she arranged for the premises to be used by the members for the remainder of the lease. Other examples of her benevolence included financial assistance to some unemployed Spitalfields weavers who were organising themselves on co-operative lines [Brown (1944) 27] and, when she was living in Leicestershire, an interest in 'tenants' schools, game laws and manifold projects for the benefit and happiness of others' [Macpherson (1878) 209]. In the last decade of her life she became a close friend of Barbara Bodichon, the educational reformer. One of Lady Byron's last public acts before she died was a subscription to the Garibaldi fund. Like a number of the reformers of her day she was for many years passionately interested in phrenology.

Lady Byron died on 16 May 1860 in London and was buried in Kensal Green Cemetery where her name is also on the Reformers' Memorial. This memorial was erected by Joseph William Corfield (1809–1888), a member of the South Place Institute, London to remind the British people of those 'men and women who have generously given their time and means to improve the conditions and enlarge the happiness of all classes of society'. Forty-nine names were originally engraved on two sides of the monument, a further twenty-five names were added on the third side by Corfield's daughter, Emma, in 1907, and eleven more have been engraved on its base. Brief records of seventy-four of the personalities whose names are included on the memorial are given in W. H. Brown, *Pathfinders...*(1925). G. K. Chesterton commemorated the cemetery, and possibly the Reformers' Memorial in his poem 'The Rolling English Road', the last two lines of which read:

But there is good news yet to hear and fine
  things to be seen,
Before we go to Paradise by way of Kensal
  Green.

Lady Byron's grave had, however, been forgotten with the passage of time but when, in 1972, the description of it given in Mayne (1929) was presented personally to the cemetery authorities, a search of the records then indicated its location in the old part of the cemetery. It was completely overgrown by bracken and ivy, but when this was cleared, a remarkably well-preserved stone was revealed, clearly inscribed with Lady Byron's name and dates of birth and death.

Lady Byron left an estate valued between £60,000 and £70,000. Besides legacies to her family and personal friends she also left bequests to a number of those friends with whom she had been associated in her work for social reform. Included among these bequests was £1000 to Mary Carpenter and £300 to Dr William King, of Brighton, with the request that it might be used by his daughter for the publication of extracts from his mss. She also left £300 to an American who was sympathetic towards the rights of coloured people, and £100 each to three clergymen of whose parishes she was the patron in Leicestershire, to provide comforts for their poor parishioners.

Writings: *Lady Byron's Reply to her Lord's Farewell with referential notes to the lines in Lord Byron's poem, particularly alluded to by her Ladyship* (1825) 16 pp.; *Remarks occasioned by Mr Moore's notices of Lord Byron's Life* [1830] 15 pp.; *A Letter to Thomas Moore Esq., occasioned by his Notices of the Life of the Late . . . Lord Byron* [1830] 19 pp.; *What De Fellenberg has done for Education* (1839); 'Educational Institutions of Emanuel De Fellenberg by his son, W. De Fellenberg', communicated by Lady Noel Byron, *NAPSS* (1858) 323–35.

Sources: Anon., *The Education for the Peasantry in England: what it is and what it ought to be with a . . . detailed account of the establishment of M. de Fellenberg at Hofwyl in Switzerland* (1834); Anon., 'Manual Labor School for the Working Classes, at Ealing in England', *Am. Annals of Education and Instruction* 6 (Feb 1836) 75–84; B. F. Duppa, 'Industrial Schools for the Peasantry', in Central Society of Education, *First Publication* (1837) 172–213; Anon., 'Schools for the Industrious Classes, or the Present State of Education among the Working People of England', in Central Society of Education, *Second Publication* (1838) 339–407; 'Lady Noel Byron', in *Our Exemplars: poor and rich*, ed. M. D. Hill (1861) 338–42; S. A. Brooke, *Life and Letters of the Rev. F. W. Robertson* 2 vols (1865, repr. in one vol. 1872); H. Martineau, 'Lady Noel Byron', *Biographical Sketches* (2nd ed. 1869) 316–25; H. B. Stowe, 'The True Story of Lady Byron's Life', *MacMill. Mag.*, 20 (Sep 1869) 377–96; G. Macpherson, *Memoirs of the Life of Anna Jameson* (1878); F. Arnold, *Robertson of Brighton* (1886); A. Ross, 'Reminiscences of Lady Byron', *19th C.* (May 1899) 821–32; *DNB* 3 [s. v. Lord Byron]; G. J. Holyoake, *History of Co-operation* (1906); F. Smith, *The Life and Work of Sir James Kay-Shuttleworth* (1923); W. H. Brown, *Pathfinders . . . Brief Records of Seventy-four Adventurers . . . whose Names are inscribed on the Reformers' Memorial, Kensal Green, London* (Manchester, 1925) 47 pp.; idem, *A Century of London Co-operation* [1928]; E. C. Mayne, *The Life and Letters of Anne Isabella, Lady Noel Byron* (1929); W. H. Brown, *Brighton's Co-operative Advance, 1828–1938: with the jubilee history of the Brighton Equitable Co-operative Society Ltd 1888–1938* (Manchester, [1938]); T. W. Mercer, *Co-operation's Prophet: the life and letters of Dr William King of Brighton* (Manchester, 1947); H. Burton, *Barbara Bodichon, 1827–1891* (1949); S. Pollard, *Dr William King of Ipswich* (Co-operative College Papers, no. 6: 1959); W. H. G. Armytage, *Heavens Below* (1961); A. Bonner, *British Co-operation* (Manchester, 1961; revised edition, 1970); R. G. Garnett, 'E. T. Craig: Communitarian, Educator, Phrenologist', *Vocational Aspect of Secondary and Further Education*, no. 31 (Summer, 1963) 135–50; W. A. C. Stewart and W. P. McCann, *The Educational Innovators* (1967); J. F. C. Harrison, *Robert Owen and the Owenites in Britain and America* (1969). Obit. *Times*, 18 May 1860. The editors are indebted to Mr H. F. Bing for an earlier draft of this biography.

JOYCE BELLAMY
JOHN SAVILLE

See also: †Edward Thomas CRAIG; †William KING; *Robert OWEN; †William PARE.

CAIRNS, John (1859–1923)
MINERS' LEADER AND LABOUR MP

Born on 31 May 1859 at Choppington, Northumberland, he was one of the youngest of a large family whose mother died when John Cairns was a small boy. He attended a colliery school, and when twelve or thirteen years of age began work in the pit at Choppington. Later he attended evening classes, becoming especially interested in political economy, and while still in his teens he became secretary of the Choppington Mechanics' Association. He moved to Bedlington, in the same county, in his late youth, and again became involved in trade union work. In November 1892 he was one of six elected to the joint committee of the Northumberland coal trade. This was the joint Committee of the Northumberland Coal Owners' Association and the Northumberland Miners' Mutual Confident Association set up in 1873. The object of the joint committee was 'to discuss all questions (except such as may be termed County questions, or questions affecting the general trade) relating to matters of wages, practices of working, or any other subject which may arise from time to time at any particular colliery, and which shall be referred to the consideration of the Committee by the parties concerned. The Committee shall discuss all disputes and hear evidence, and their decision shall be final.' The chairman was re-elected in May of each year. Whereas only a few cases came up before the Board of Conciliation for the Coal Trade of Northumberland, the joint committee settled a growing number of cases without a stoppage. In 1905, for example, 105 cases were adjudicated without resort to a strike.

By the time he was appointed to the joint committee Cairns was already a leading personality in the Northumberland coalfield. He attended, for the Miners' National Union, the fourth Miners' International Congress at Brussels in May 1893. The Congress began with the now well-established statement of the need for the legal eight-hour day. William Bailey of Nottingham moved (seconded by a Frenchman)

'that this Congress affirm the principle of a legal eight hours' day from bank to bank, and advises all nationalities to obtain the same'. The delegates from the north-east coalfields of England were at this time the most vigorous opponents of the eight-hour principle; and an (unsuccessful) amendment was moved by Hugh Boyle and seconded by John Cairns:

that this conference, recognising the great diversity in the natural conditions existing in the several nations represented, is of opinion that it is inadvisable to delegate to Parliament or legislative body the power or right to fix the hours adults shall labour in mines, but would strongly urge every nation and districts to embrace every opportunity afforded them to reduce their working hours as far as may be practicable without injuring themselves.

In July 1906 Cairns was appointed financial secretary of the Northumberland Miners' Mutual Confident Association. He was now also secretary to the joint committee and he held both these positions until he died. On Hugh Boyle's death in 1907 he also took over the presidency of the Northumberland Aged Mineworkers' Homes Association. It was a cause very dear to him.

Cairns was something of a radical in his younger days, and he supported the principle of an independent party of Labour earlier than did the majority of the miners' leaders in the north-east. When Thomas Burt retired from the Morpeth parliamentary constituency, Cairns was selected to replace him, and in the general election of 1918, against four other candidates, he won with a majority of 537. The actual figures given in the table on page 80 reveal the varieties of political expression at the 'coupon election', so-called because of the letter signed by Lloyd George and Bonar Law certifying that the recipient was a true supporter of the Government.

At the succeeding election of 1922, with Liberal and Conservative opponents, his majority was 5019. In his 1918 election address he had supported the Labour programme, including nationalisation of certain industries and the capital levy.

(1918) MORPETH (Electorate 39,773)	
Cairns, John (Labour)	7677
Thornborough, F.C. (Coalition Liberal)	7140
Meares, C. H. (Unionist)	4320
Newton, Capt. G. (Independent)	2729
Allison, Maj. T. M. (National Democratic Party)	511
Labour majority	537

Like many leading trade unionists of the period, Cairns was also much involved in local affairs. For many years he served as a Poor Law Guardian; was an active co-operator and treasurer of the Bedlington Co-operative Society until 1906; and was on the house committee of the Royal Victoria Infirmary. He became a Primitive Methodist early in his life and was much in demand as a local preacher. In 1918 he was awarded the OBE for his part in recruiting drives during the First World War. He was a JP for Newcastle upon Tyne.

He married Annie Dixon in 1901 and his wife and two sons and one daughter survived him at his sudden and unexpected death on 23 May 1923. Among those who spoke at the graveside was Stephen Walsh, MP, representing the MFGB. Cairns left effects valued at £1507.

Writings: *Money* (n.d.); *Economics of Industry* (n.d.).

Sources: *Blyth News*, 30 Dec 1918; *WWW* (1916–28); *Dod* (1922); E. Welbourne, *The Miners' Unions of Northumberland and Durham* (Cambridge, 1923); R. Page Arnot, *The Miners* (1949); R. F. Wearmouth, *Methodism and the Struggle of the Working Classes, 1850–1900* (1954); R. Gregory, *The Miners and British Politics, 1906–1914* (1968); biographical information: Dr R. Page Arnot; Dr A. Mason. OBIT. *Times* and *Newcastle J.*, 24 May 1923; NMA, *Monthly Circular* (1923).

See also: †Thomas ASHTON, for Mining Trade Unionism, 1900–14; †Thomas Henry CANN; †Benjamin PICKARD, for Mining Trade Unionism, 1880–99; †Arthur HENDERSON, for British Labour Party, 1914–31; William STRAKER; †John WILSON (1837–1915).

JOHN SAVILLE

CAPPER, James (1829–1895)
IRONWORKERS' LEADER

James Capper was born in 1829, probably in South Staffordshire. Nothing is known of his parental background, or of his early life, except that he began work at the age of eight in the Toll End ironworks, Tipton, where he eventually became an underhand puddler. As a young man he spent six years in the United States, but in 1862 he returned to this country, apparently disillusioned, and found work as a forehand puddler at the Patent Shaft and Axletree Company, Wednesbury.

By this time the ironworkers of South Staffordshire were beginning to move towards the establishment of lasting organisation. Hitherto this had been checked by three main factors – the strongly cyclical nature of the iron trade; the strength of the masters' association; and the divisions among the ironworkers which resulted from two features of the organisation of production in the finished iron trade. The first of these was the sub-contract system. Under this system the ironmaster furnished the plant and raw materials, but actual production was carried on by sub-contractors, or forehands. The ironmaster dealt only with his sub-contractors and it was their responsibility to employ such further labour as they needed. The men and youths so employed were the underhands and were controlled absolutely by the sub-contractors. These were paid by the ironmaster on a piece rate basis, but they paid their underhands day wages. In order to earn the highest possible income, therefore, the sub-contractors had to maintain or increase the output of their team while keeping wages under control. This system obviously gave the forehands considerable scope for exploitation, but the custom of the trade was usually strong enough to prevent this. By this custom the day wages of underhands moved up and down with variations in sub-contractors' piece rates, so that when the sub-contractors obtained an increase per ton they usually raised underhands' day wages and lowered them when tonnage rates fell. The system did, however, mean that the skilled fore-hands were the key figures in the trade, and support or want of support from the under-hands was quite irrelevant in any contest with the owners; so that organisation, where it developed, was confined almost exclu-sively to the sub-contractors. The result was a very shallowly-rooted kind of trade union-ism, and through the first half of the nine-teenth century organisation among Black Country ironworkers rose and declined. Walter Williams, secretary of the South Staffordshire and East Worcestershire Iron-masters' Association told the Royal Com-mission on Trade Unions in 1867 that the then existing unions were the third set he had known.

The second feature of the organisation of the finished iron trade retarding the growth of unionism was the lateral division between sub-contractors. After being refined by the puddler the pig was hammered into the form required in the mills and forges by the shingler before being converted into sheets, plates, rods or bars by the roller, millman and furnaceman. These latter employed large teams of between ten and twenty underhands and regarded themselves as the aristocracy of the iron trade. The greater standing and self-conscious dignity of these larger sub-contractors *vis-à-vis* the puddlers was a constant source of friction between the two groups, and so further weakened the basis of organisation. The puddlers were traditionally the most mili-tant of the ironworkers, since the uniformity of the puddling process enabled them to feel a sense of common interest to a greater degree than other sub-contractors, and since they were the worst paid group in the trade. Their solidarity was, however, weakened by two factors: the scope offered by the sub-contract system for owners or managers to

play off one puddler against another, par-ticularly in the allocation of work at slack times; and the practice of management, in the event of a prolonged strike, of putting the more experienced underhands on to puddling, thus leaving some puddlers with-out work when the strike was over.

These obstacles to combination among the puddlers of the Black Country were only finally overcome in 1863, when the Associated Ironworkers of Great Britain took its rise from a dispute over the method of wage fixing in the South Staffordshire iron trade. This centred on the Thorney-croft scale of the South Staffordshire Iron-masters' Association. Under this scale pud-dlers' wages varied by 1s per ton for every variation of £1 per ton in the 'declared' price of the 'marked bars' of high-quality iron produced by leading firms of the Iron-masters' Association. Millmen's earnings were also tied to this scale by the custom of varying their rates by 10 per cent for every 1s per ton variation in the rates paid to puddlers. Though this unofficial sliding scale had fairly general application through-out the South Staffordshire iron trade, its operation was far from smooth, and through the 1840s and 1850s the ironworkers' resent-ment of it resulted in frequent strikes and lockouts. Then early in 1863, as trade re-vived following a prolonged depression, an agitation developed among the puddlers for an increase of 1s per ton on puddling rates. Since there was no change in declared prices at this time, the masters resisted the men's claim, and the puddlers responded by establishing the Associated Ironworkers of Great Britain. Together with William Aucott and Thomas Piggott, Capper was among the first 'to unfurl the flag of union-ism' at this time and for the next twenty-five years he remained a leading figure among the ironworkers of the Black Country.

The Associated Ironworkers' union met with considerable initial success among the Black Country puddlers, but there was no accession of support from the millmen, who formed their own union, the Staffordshire Millmen's Association, based in West Brom-wich. The long-standing differences between puddlers and millmen precluded any successful co-operation between the two unions, and throughout the five years of their existence relations varied between the suspicious and the openly hostile.

Of more significance in the longer term were relations between the Associated Ironworkers and John Kane's National Association of Ironworkers, established in 1862, with headquarters at Gateshead. From the outset these were never easy, and a series of misunderstandings between the two associations quickly widened mutual suspicion into an open breach. After the failure of the South Staffordshire men to support Kane's union during the Leeds lockout of 1864, the National Association withdrew its support from the North Staffordshire strikers in 1865, leaving the Associated Ironworkers to carry the burden alone. Then in 1866, any hope of co-operation between the two unions was finally destroyed when Kane apparently agreed that if the northern ironmasters would sever their connections with the ironmasters of other districts, the National Association would abandon all attempts to co-operate with the Associated Ironworkers. Kane later maintained that this agreement was a fabrication by the ironmasters, designed to drive a wedge between the two unions, and if this was in fact the case it succeeded admirably. Suspicion between the northern and southern unions now hardened into open hostility, and in 1867 the headquarters of the National Association was moved temporarily to Walsall in an attempt to establish itself in South Staffordshire. The attempt was not successful, but it was a divisive influence among the Black Country ironworkers and together with the return of depression to the iron trade it brought about the collapse of the Associated Ironworkers of Great Britain in 1868. The Staffordshire Millmen's Association also broke up in the same year.

By this time Capper had become well known locally as a fervent advocate of Gladstonian Liberalism. His influence with the ironworkers was an important factor in securing the return of the Gladstonian candidate, Alexander Brogden, in the first contest for the new Wednesbury constituency at the 1868 general election; and thereafter his forceful speeches in support of Brogden and his successor, the Hon. Philip Stanhope, were a feature of succeeding election campaigns in Wednesbury. Capper was a committed secularist and land reformer, and a convinced supporter of Home Rule for Ireland. All three elements in his political attitudes were revealed in one of his last public speeches, in April 1887, when he suggested that a suitable epitaph for all the Irish who had died of starvation might be:

Here lie
Toiling fathers, mothers and children of
Ireland,
starved to death by
the Imperial Government of England
in the
Nineteenth Century, with the aid of the
Episcopal Church.
[*Ironworkers J.*, June 1887]

The return of prosperity to the South Staffordshire iron trade in the last months of 1869 ushered in the great boom of the early 1870s. As the boom moved to its peak, the relationship between iron prices and wages embodied in the Thorneycroft scale broke down, and there was a long period of confusion on the question of wage fixing until a series of conferences between masters and men in 1871 and 1872 resulted in the establishment of a new sliding scale, administered by an *ad hoc* Board of Conciliation.

Capper took a leading part in these conferences. His commitment to the twin principles of sliding scale and conciliation derived from recognition of the ironmasters' determination to preserve the customary price-wage relationship. Hitherto this had only operated automatically in a downwards direction – in rising markets, pressure and agitation had been required to secure the corresponding advance in wages. Capper's objective was to ensure the same rigid correspondence when prices moved upwards as when they fell and so to avoid the uncertainty and hardship which resulted from the invariably unsuccessful attempt to resist reductions, and the need to agitate and possibly strike to secure wage increases.

There was a persistent element of opposition to this view among a section of Black Country ironworkers, who could see only the undesirable effects of fluctuating wage levels. But with William Aucott's support Capper's view prevailed, and sliding scales operating within a system of conciliation remained the basis of wage fixing in the South Staffordshire iron trade up to 1914 and beyond.

The great boom and the success of the conciliation movement brought a resurgence of trade unionism among Black Country ironworkers in the early 1870s. The ailing National Association of Ironworkers had been reorganised as the Amalgamated Malleable Ironworkers in 1868, with John Kane as general secretary, and by the early months of 1872 had recruited a considerable number of members in South Staffordshire. This prompted Capper to call for a national conference of ironworkers 'to take into consideration the present position and future prospects of all Ironworkers and to make a united effort to bring the whole within the pale of one great union'. This conference was duly held in Sheffield during Whit week 1872, and it was quickly agreed that the Amalgamated Malleable Ironworkers should be developed into a national association, embracing all iron-working districts, while the delegates agreed on behalf of their constituents to accept the recently revised rules of the union. The question whether to appoint district agents proved much more contentious. The opposition to such appointments was led by Edward Trow, a former Wednesbury furnaceman now living and working in the north of England, and currently the vice-president of the union. With John Kane's support it was resolved that agents should be appointed in all districts where membership of the union reached 2000. But Trow remained unconvinced, and their differences on this question marked the beginning of mutual suspicion and mistrust between Capper and Trow which persisted until Capper's retirement from trade union activity sixteen years later.

The progress of the great boom pushed membership of the Amalgamated Malleable Ironworkers in the Black Country to about 10,000 in August 1872. In accordance with the resolution of the Sheffield conference Capper was appointed agent for the Midland Counties with effect from 1 September 1872. Twelve months later he was presented with a gold watch with an Albert guard, and a purse of £77 to mark his services to trade unionism in the Black Country. By this time the boom had passed its peak, and as depression returned to the iron trade throughout 1874 and 1875 union membership collapsed as spectacularly as it had grown only two years earlier. This in turn was a main factor in the break-up of the Conciliation Board in the autumn of 1875. The end of an experimental joint sliding scale with the North of England in July 1875 saw the South Staffordshire ironmasters try to introduce a new scale with a lower wages basis, and against the advice of Capper and Aucott the ironworkers resisted with strike action. With union membership in the Black Country area standing at less than 1500 and the ironworkers 'so disorganised and dissatisfied that we cannot give any pledge on their behalf', Capper and William Aucott withdrew from the Conciliation Board and it broke up.

In spite of this failure Capper's belief in the absolute necessity for conciliation machinery in the iron trade remained undiminished, and he played a major part in getting the Board reconstituted in the spring of 1876 as the South Staffordshire Mill and Forge Wages Board. Its former *ad hoc* procedures were placed on a firmer formal basis; and its composition now included an independent president who would act as arbitrator at such times as a sliding scale was not in operation, and a paid secretary for each side, with Capper filling this office for the operatives. Another important change involved the membership of the operatives' side of the Board. Formerly this had been chosen on a union basis, but with the Amalgamated Malleable Ironworkers now in decline the owners were able to insist that in the new Board it should be on a works basis.

The new Board ran into difficulties when no agreement could be reached on the basis for a sliding scale, and until July 1880 wage adjustments remained in the hands of the president. Reductions amounting to 20 per cent were imposed in 1876 and 1878, and together with the reductions that had occurred in 1874 and 1875 this meant that by 1879 ironworkers' wages in the Black Country were $57\frac{1}{2}$ per cent lower than at the peak of 1873. This however provided Capper and the other ironworkers' leaders on the Wages Board with a positive argument for its retention, namely that if the Board was abandoned in the depths of depression the men would have suffered all the drawbacks and gained none of the advantages of its operation. Stirrings of discontent against the Board were notably absent at this time.

The successive wage reductions also had the effect of eliminating any remaining union influences in South Staffordshire. By the early months of 1877 the Amalgamated Malleable Ironworkers could claim only just over 100 compliance members in the Black Country districts and shortly afterwards Capper himself ceased to be a member. His union contributions ended in February 1877 when the lodge of which he was a member broke up, and when his term of office as agent expired in May his failure to renew his subscriptions meant that his membership automatically lapsed. By this time Edward Trow had succeeded John Kane (who died on 21 March 1876) as secretary of the Amalgamated Malleable Ironworkers, and the antagonism between Trow and Capper, which dated from the Sheffield conference of five years earlier, was probably a main factor in Capper's decision not to renew his union membership.

The decline of unionism had important consequences for the Wages Board. The absence of effective organisation on the men's side undermined its representative character, and consequently the authority it exercised was always uncertain. This was dramatically revealed in the summer of 1883, when successive wage reductions provoked a violent reaction from the ironworkers. Inspired by a dissident group in the West Bromwich area, some 15,000 ironworkers struck work in protest at the reductions. The accompanying violence and intimidation resulted in fourteen arrests and there was widespread condemnation of the Wages Board and Capper's leadership. Capper condemned the strike as 'unjustifiable and dishonourable', and courageously reiterated the advantages of the Board and his intention of carrying through its decisions. With the owners also standing firm the strike quickly collapsed, but the incident was indicative of the Board's weakness.

Recognition of this weakness, and of the fact that lack of organisation on their side was a main cause of it, resulted in the Black Country ironworkers extending a cautious welcome to proposals for the reorganisation and strengthening of the Amalgamated Malleable Ironworkers, and this was eventually put in hand in 1887. In April Capper and William Aucott led the South Staffordshire delegation to a three-day conference in Manchester, where the union was reformed as the Associated Iron and Steel Workers of Great Britain. The main difficulty in the reorganisation was the question of control of union funds. Edward Trow was the chief spokesman for those in favour of centralisation, while Capper led those who preferred 'the principle of local self government'. Eventually a compromise solution, involving joint control by local trustees and the General Council of the new union, was agreed, and the new union safely launched. As a gesture to the Black Country men Trow proposed that he and Capper should be joint secretaries of the new organisation; but this proposal was never put into practice, and it appears that Capper only joined the Associated Iron and Steel Workers in order to preserve his position as operatives' secretary to the Wages Board.

Union reorganisation was accompanied by parallel efforts to strengthen the Wages Board, and it was reorganised in the early months of 1888 as the Midland Iron and Steel Wages Board. In the new Board, operatives' representation was again on a works rather than a union basis, and with initial recruitment to the Associated Iron and Steel Workers proceeding only slowly in the Black Country a recurrence of the former situation, where the absence of union organisation had been a main factor undermining the authority and effectiveness of the old Board, was clearly possible.

Accordingly it was agreed between representatives of the union and operative members of the Wages Board that none but compliance members of the union should be elected to serve on the Board. It was only in face of this development that Capper joined a union lodge.

The latent conflict between Capper and Trow was finally resolved in an unfortunate way. In the summer of 1888 Capper suffered a stroke which left him partly paralysed, and at the end of the year he resigned his position on the Wages Board, to be succeeded by William Aucott. In spite of worsening paralysis Capper's courage and great physical strength kept him alive for a further six years. During this time he and his family were supported by an allowance of £12 10s per quarter from the Midland Wages Board. His friend and former colleague, William Aucott, appears to have neglected him in these last years. Capper died at his home in Bloxwich Road, Walsall, on 29 December 1895, survived by his wife and five sons. He was buried in Walsall Old Cemetery on 2 January 1896. No will has been located.

In many ways Capper was an archetypal figure among Black Country working-class leaders of the last quarter of the nineteenth century. In his insularity, his implicit faith in sliding scales and conciliation machinery, and his strong commitment to Gladstonian Liberalism, he was fully representative of the main stream of working-class attitudes in this area at this time, attitudes which go a long way towards explaining the uncertain progress of trade unionism and the Labour Party in South Staffordshire in the period to 1914 and beyond.

Sources: Reports of union activities and proceedings of wages boards in *Dudley Herald*, *Midland Advertiser* and *Wolverhampton Chronicle*, 1870–88; *Ironworkers' J.* 1869–88; *Labour Tribune*, 1886–8; D. Jones, 'The Midland Iron and Steel Wages Board' in W. J. Ashley, *British Industries* (1903) 38–67; G. C. Allen, *The Economic Development of Birmingham and the Black Country 1860–1927* (1929, repr. 1966); A. Pugh, *Men of Steel* (1951); A. Fox, 'Industrial Relations in Birmingham and the Black Country 1860–1914' (Oxford BLitt., 1952); J. C. Carr and W. Taplin, *History of the British Steel Industry* (Oxford, 1962); J. H. Porter, 'Management Competition and Industrial Relations: the Midlands manufactured iron trade 1873–1914', *Business History*, 11, no. 1 (Jan 1969) 37–47; E. Taylor, 'The Origins and Early Years of the Midland Wages Board', *Man and Metal*, 49, no. 4 (Apr 1972). OBIT. *Wolverhampton Express and Star*, 31 Dec 1895; *Wolverhampton Chronicle*, 1 and 8 Jan 1896; *Midland Advertiser*, *Midland Sun*, *Walsall Advertiser*, *Walsall Observer*, 4 Jan 1896.

ERIC TAYLOR

See also: William AUCOTT; *Samuel HARRIS; *John KANE; Thomas PIGGOTT; *Edward TROW.

CARPENTER, Edward (1844–1929)
SOCIALIST AND AUTHOR

Edward Carpenter was born in Brighton on 29 August 1844. He was the second son of Charles and Sophia Wilson Carpenter; there were subsequently eight further children. In his youth a naval officer, Charles Carpenter became a Chancery lawyer in the 1820s. He practised at the Bar for over fifteen years, retiring when he inherited a considerable fortune from his own father, an admiral of the Napoleonic period. For nearly forty years thereafter Charles Carpenter lived the life of a *rentier*, managing his substantial investments, chiefly in British and American railway companies.

The Carpenter family was respectable. The head of it was a successful man of business and a magistrate first of the Brighton and later of the Hove bench. There were never fewer than three servants in the fashionable house in Brunswick Square. For most of the year 1857 the whole family, accompanied by two servants, went to live in Versailles, where Edward and his brother Alfred attended the Lycée Hoche. The three Carpenter sons were destined respectively for the Indian Civil Service, the Church and the Navy: the daughters were brought up in that state of cultured idleness thought to fit them for the marriage market. Two of them at least subsequently married into the gentry or lesser nobility.

In this conventional atmosphere Edward Carpenter gradually became aware of his own homosexuality. The resulting tensions were a major determinant of the pattern of Carpenter's life and attitudes. From adolescence until his late twenties, however, he submitted to the norms and acquiesced in the values of his domestic and class environment. After spending some time in Germany, he went up to Trinity Hall, Cambridge, with the intention of becoming a minister of the Anglican Church. He studied mathematics chiefly, and was very successful throughout his Cambridge career. By 1870 he had graduated as Tenth Wrangler and won a Cambridge literary prize for a heavily Ruskinian essay, 'The Religious Influence of Art', published in that year. He was ordained deacon of the Church of England and accepted a clerical fellowship at Trinity Hall which had fallen vacant as the result of Leslie Stephen's resignation. His first curacy was at St Edward's, Cambridge; the second incumbent for whom he worked was F. D. Maurice, whose Broad Church metaphysics puzzled Carpenter.

In the early 1870s a profound psychological crisis jeopardised an apparently stable and successful way of life. His was not the religious crisis of conscience which led others of his generation to set at risk security and career; but, as a homosexual, Carpenter's sense of social and cultural estrangement in Cambridge deepened and became intolerable. This caused him to attack indiscriminately the social values and intellectual aspirations of Cambridge. 'I had come to feel,' he wrote later, 'that the so-called intellectual life of the University was . . . a fraud and a weariness. These everlasting discussions of theories which never came anywhere near actual life, this cheap philosophising and ornamental cleverness . . . all impressed me with a sense of utter emptiness . . . and as I had seemed to see already the vacuity and falsity of society life at Brighton, so in another form I seemed to see the same thing here' [My Days and Dreams (1916) 72]. In 1873 Carpenter took the first steps towards

resigning his fellowship by relinquishing his orders.

At Cambridge Carpenter had been deeply absorbed in the poetry of the English romantics – indeed, his volume of poems entitled Narcissus (privately printed in 1873) was too closely imitative of them, and proved a failure. Under the influence of W. K. Clifford he read Mazzini and dabbled with armchair republicanism. But by far the greatest influence upon him was the work of Walt Whitman, which became easily available in England in the late 1860s. In Whitman's Leaves of Grass and Democratic Vistas Carpenter found intimations of a solution to personal problems, as well as an undeveloped theory of populism which served as the rationale for a complete break with his former life. Under Whitman's influence he determined to '. . . throw in [his] lot with the mass-people'. In 1874 he gave his first series of lectures on science and on music for the Oxford and Cambridge University Extension Movement; and he was among the first extension lecturers in the industrial towns of Yorkshire and the North Midlands.

The extension movement itself was quickly captured by the provincial middle class which organised and financed it locally. But it still provided Carpenter with his first experience of the social effects of urban industrialisation. At first this was an aesthetic shock without political dimension. It took seven or eight years more for Carpenter's vigorous revulsion from middle-class life and industrial ugliness to assume a political character. A lengthy visit to Whitman in America in 1877, when Carpenter also met Emerson and Wendell Holmes among others, simply confirmed his overwhelming admiration for Whitman and his work.

The early years of the 1880s were the period of Carpenter's most rapid personal emancipation. He left extension lecturing and, after some part-time experiment with rural life and continuous manual work, he bought Millthorpe, three fields comprising seven acres, in the Derbyshire hills south of Sheffield. His knowledge of the Ruskinian experiment at St George's Farm nearby at Totley gave him confidence and encouragement. For a time St George's Farm was managed by W. H. Riley, former editor of the *International Herald*, who was known to Carpenter chiefly through his utopian political work in Bristol and Sheffield in the late 1870s. In 1883 Carpenter confirmed his decision to retire to Millthorpe by building a house there which he paid for out of £6000 inherited in the previous year as his share of his father's estate. He was determined to begin market gardening and to continue creative writing. Shortly before his final move to Millthorpe, Carpenter completed and published the first part of *Towards Democracy*.

This long free verse poem had been conceived over the extension years of the 1870s and early 1880s. At first it had little sale and was reviewed only in the most hostile manner; the *Saturday Review* attacked it as an example of dangerous but 'cultivated' Socialism. *Towards Democracy*, relying for its form upon Whitman's *Leaves of Grass*, was mystical and radical, transcendental and sensuous; at once the vehicle of Carpenter's successful sublimation of guilt, and a violent, if unsystematic, assault upon existing class and property relationships, which Carpenter believed responsible for his own failures of personal adjustment. More broadly, its thesis was that spontaneity of social and personal behaviour, the freeing of sex from a damaging morality of constraint, would create conditions in which the individual might regain a sense of personal wholeness and social community. A central prop of Carpenter's intellectual position, which owed much to Carlyle, was his conviction that individuals, their consciousness transformed, would restructure and revolutionise social relationships through their spontaneous actions. This commonplace argument was clothed in powerful, millenarian language, and pleaded frankly for a complete sexual emancipation.

Havelock Ellis described the poem as 'Whitman and water', but, subsequently recognising in it certain themes of Hindu philosophy, he revised his opinion and claimed that it was an important religious text. *Towards Democracy* was full of separate statements and intuitions, some of which

Carpenter took up again in the three further parts of the poem, which was finally completed in 1902. The success of the book increased with time. From a sale of some seven hundred copies in its first seven years, *Towards Democracy* reached its thirtieth thousand in 1921. In terms of popularity, it mattered less that *Towards Democracy* was expressed in prophetic and mystical language than that its basis was an idealist attack on Mammon and hypocrisy, on the ethics of the cash-nexus and a middle-class morality of repression.

Besides *Towards Democracy*, Carpenter published two much smaller pieces in 1883, both of which went further to establish him as a radical in the narrow circles of organised Socialism in London. The first was an essay entitled 'Desirable Mansions' which appeared in *Progress* in June, and which attacked the rich by characterising them as the victims of convention and prejudice, their consciousness invaded and controlled by acquisitiveness and class platitude. The second essay, 'Modern Money-Lending and the Meaning of Dividends', made much less impact although it demonstrated that Carpenter appreciated the argument from surplus value, learned by him from Hyndman's *England for All*. This last essay was printed in Manchester by John Heywood, in whose small publishing firm Carpenter had an interest, as he had later in the Manchester Labour Press.

By this time Carpenter had links with two areas of activity which were more or less political in character. These were, first, the small but growing circle around Hyndman and the Social Democratic Federation; and second, the Fellowship of the New Life, to which Carpenter fled in the face of uncongenial political choices in the winter of 1884. Unable to accept without a break the isolation of Millthorpe, he had begun to make frequent trips to London and to attend the meetings of the SDF. He put up the initial £300 which launched *Justice*, and, with William Morris, met its running deficits for the first year. But despite growing commitment Carpenter acknowledged that he had little talent for the exigencies of day-to-day politics. When the SDF executive council split in December 1884 [Thompson (1955) 384–421] he found himself opposed to William Morris, for whom he had a great admiration, and in support of Hyndman, for whom he had little. The experience drove him increasingly out of active Socialist politics and into the Fellowship of the New Life.

The Socialism of the Fellowship was ethical rather than practical. It sprang from an idealist philosophy with no conception of political agency. The Fellowship provided a politics for the apolitical: its interests were dispersed so widely between spiritualism and psychology, sex reform and communitarian anarchism that a number of activists broke away to form the Fabian Society. For Carpenter in 1885, however, the Fellowship provided an agreeable intellectual milieu. *Towards Democracy* had some currency among its members, and at Fellowship meetings he made the acquaintance of Havelock Ellis, Olive Schreiner and Henry Salt among others. Many of these friendships were lasting and of great importance to Carpenter throughout his life. These were the most interesting figures of the literary intellectual circle in which Carpenter increasingly moved after the middle of the 1880s.

Outside London Carpenter turned more towards local political agitation. He gave his special support to the Bristol Socialists. Carpenter's contacts in Bristol, made originally through W. H. Riley, continued with Robert Weare, Robert Sharland, Ramsay MacDonald and Katharine Conway (later Katharine Bruce Glasier). The peculiar development of organised Socialism in the city also had Carpenter's approval. Formed from the 'pioneer class' of the Bristol Radical Reform Association, the Bristol branch of the SDF survived the schism of December 1884 only to withdraw from the Federation during the scandal of the 'Tory gold' allegations in the elections of the following year. The Bristol Socialists retained an independence from London which appealed to Carpenter, and which he tried to incorporate in a new group, the Sheffield Socialist Society. Carpenter was a founder of this society in 1886, the year in which he published

England Arise. Largely following Morris's Socialist League in declared policy, the Society took up the cause of the unemployed in Sheffield, organising meetings and demonstrations in the late 1880s and early 1890s. A number of small community projects, such as the 'Commonwealth Café' set up by the Socialists in a slum area of the city, ultimately came to very little; although Kropotkin, William Morris and Annie Besant, all of whom spoke in Sheffield at Carpenter's invitation at this time, attracted very large audiences.

The Society itself was never more than a small group, predominantly of working men, and under Carpenter's guidance it avoided scrupulously the sectarian conflicts of the London groups. In fact only specific *causes célèbres* drew Carpenter back into intensive agitation in London. He was prominent both in the committee organised to assist the Walsall anarchists after their imprisonment in 1892, and also in the Free Press Defence Committee set up after what amounted to police attempts in 1898 to censor Havelock Ellis's *Studies in the Psychology of Sex*. But major figures in London came to recognise and to regret Carpenter's shortcomings. Sidney Webb described Carpenter's position, and that of the Sheffield Socialists, 'as tending towards a "Ruskinian Socialism", not free from influences akin to those emanating from Thoreau on the one hand, and from Tolstoi on the other' [*Socialism in England* (1890) 42]. Bernard Shaw, in reference to Carpenter's sandal-making and market gardening, described him as the 'Noble Savage', and in a piece written for a volume which Carpenter himself edited referred disparagingly to '... carpenterings and illusions', and to the dangers of drawing back from an active political contribution. Even William Morris, momentarily captivated by life at Millthorpe, concluded nevertheless that it would be 'dastardly to desert' the cause.

These opinions notwithstanding, Carpenter was a major Socialist propagandist in the twenty years after 1885. Year after year he lectured as many as ten or a dozen times a month to Socialist, trades union, ethical society and Labour Church audiences in major towns all over England and Scotland.

His subjects for these lectures often re-appeared in printed form especially, in the 1880s, in two very popular volumes of essays: *England's Ideal* (1887) and *Civilisation: its cause and cure* (1889). In these years were built the foundations of a popularity among the movement's rank and file which lasted into the years of the First World War. In the 1890s especially, Carpenter sometimes drew as many as two thousand people to a Sunday meeting of a Labour Church or to a lecture in the Sheffield Hall of Science or some other large hall, usually in a provincial town. In Glasgow, for example, in the early years of the twentieth century Carpenter was almost as prominent and well known as Robert Blatchford, a man who often corresponded with Carpenter in this period. Among the provincial, if not the metropolitan, leaders of the movement, too, Carpenter enjoyed a substantial popularity – as a writer with men like Fred Jowett in Bradford; as a confidant and adviser to Bruce Glasier, and to Alf Mattison, and briefly to Tom Maguire in Leeds. For a time Millthorpe became a place of pilgrimage for the West Riding Labour movement as it was to become for food faddists, vegetarians and anti-vivisectionists as Carpenter took up these interests. Only occasionally was Carpenter's reputation in the movement tarnished. When he came out publicly in favour of the Syndicalists in 1912 he earned the disappointed and fiercely hostile criticism of Bruce Glasier and other former friends in the Independent Labour Party. And his failure wholeheartedly to condemn the First World War in the same unequivocal terms that he had used to condemn British actions before and during the Boer War, lost him considerable standing, especially among the pacifists. The reputation of his nephew, Captain (later Vice-Admiral) Carpenter, hero of the assault on Zeebrugge in 1916 and a temporary focus for the eulogies of the jingo press, did little to lesson hostility towards Carpenter's equivocation about the war. As a member of the Union of Democratic Control, however, Carpenter was one of the few people to whom Siegfried Sassoon felt able to turn during the period of his attempt to make public his sense of the futility of the war and of the criminality of its conduct.

As early as 1890 there is evidence to show that Carpenter's intellectual work increasingly competed with his political work and lecturing. In that year he visited Ceylon and sat at the feet of a Hindu guru, an experience for which he subsequently claimed the deepest effects. And not only his writing, but also activities more closely associated with Millthorpe and its locality, came to preoccupy him. In 1889 and 1890 he spent a great deal of time in helping Cecil Reddie to set up a private progressive school for boys. Originally the school was to have been located near to Millthorpe, and Carpenter was to have taken a considerable part in its management. The two soon quarrelled, however, and Carpenter withdrew leaving Reddie to put into practice at Abbotsholme, near Uttoxeter, his sometimes bizarre educational ideas. But it was in Carpenter's writings especially that certain political and intellectual ambiguities became more exposed; notably his belief in individual emancipation through spontaneity and mystical experience as the basis of the coming Socialist millennium. The range of his books, while it continued to include specific themes of reform as in *Prisons, Police and Punishment* (1905) and *Towards Industrial Freedom* (1917), concentrated increasingly upon esoteric philosophy in *The Art of Creation* (1904) and *The Drama of Love and Death* (1912), upon sex psychology and upon questions of social evolution. While his reputation in the labour movement grew, and his books sold in thousands, the arguments by which Carpenter sustained his own conception of Socialism became increasingly remote from the mainstreams of Socialist theory in England.

On matters of sex and sexual psychology Carpenter closely followed Havelock Ellis; the two men quoted each other's work with approval, and later on both of them were founder members of the British Society for the Study of Sex Psychology. Carpenter supplied material for Ellis's *Studies in the Psychology of Sex*. In his theory of social evolution Carpenter tried to demonstrate that men and societies evolve, chiefly as the result of unconscious impulse and biological drive, to a point where 'higher consciousness' and mutual aid should take over from politics and the struggle for power. He called this the theory of 'exfoliation' and based it primarily upon Lamarckian biology. It was an attempt to account simultaneously for biological, cultural and social evolution. But – in this almost alone in the labour movement except for Kropotkin – Carpenter used his theory of exfoliation consciously to combat the excesses of the tide of Social Darwinism in England in the late nineteenth and early twentieth centuries. It was in this connection that Carpenter's ideas had much in common with Kropotkin's conceptions of anarchy and mutual aid.

With his interests in the non-rational elements of human motivation and behaviour, it is not surprising that some of Carpenter's books found a considerable audience in Germany, where such questions were more central to intellectual debate than they were in Britain at this time. *Love's Coming of Age* (1896) was a volume of essays by Carpenter on 'sex questions' which was published in German in 1902. Eventually it ran to three large editions and Karl Federn, the translator, claimed that it sold more than forty thousand copies. Federn went on to translate *Civilisation: its cause and cure* and *The Art of Creation*. The four parts of *Towards Democracy* were published separately in Germany between 1903 and 1909, and *The Intermediate Sex* and *England's Ideal* were each published in one German edition in the few years before the outbreak of war in 1914. As Karl Federn proudly acknowledged, his translations of Carpenter's work enjoyed a success in Germany at least the equivalent of that of any other modern foreign author.

Nor was Carpenter's success overseas confined to Germany. In the period from 1900 to 1914, various books and pamphlets were translated into French, Italian, Dutch, Russian, Norwegian, Bulgarian, Spanish and Japanese. His attack on positivism in science in a pamphlet entitled *Modern Science: a criticism* (1885) was published with an introduction by Tolstoi which increased still further its considerable international market after 1908. In America all of Carpenter's

books were published; most ran to several editions; some of them were pirated and mutilated as well.

America and Germany were the most important areas of his overseas influence; and in Germany in particular, the very intellectual preoccupations which detached him from the Socialists in Britain made him an intellectually central figure to certain movements for a time. Indeed, it might be supposed that a substantial reputation abroad before 1914, a prominent place in the Labour movement in Britain, and a range of books which covered social and sex reform, psychology, philosophy, art and international relations would have kept alive a continuing interest in Carpenter. But even before his death in 1929, he had become a forgotten figure. A glowing address signed by the whole Labour Cabinet on the occasion of his eightieth birthday in 1924 seemed an empty gesture, for Carpenter himself felt as though he had outlived his intellectual milieu. 'What is to be done?' he wrote to a friend in 1927, 'Though I have written on the Cure of Civilisation generally I grieve to say I have no panacea for the present mass of human ills, & sometimes certainly they seem intolerable.'

By the end of the First World War, Carpenter's once substantial influence in the Labour movement had all but vanished. And certainly the basis of that influence is hard to discover in the corpus of Carpenter's published work, in specific statements made at certain times or in the general coherence of his theories. Probably his most tangible and permanent contributions, at least to progressive thought, were indirect. First, as an early advocate of techniques of birth control, especially as a partial solution to chronic poverty, Carpenter earned the admiration of Emma Goldmann, Marie Stopes and Margaret Sanger, all of whom corresponded with him at one time or another. And to the women's movement in general Carpenter gave his support – more as a speaker on public platforms than in print – although when pressed by Mrs Despard in the autumn of 1910 he contributed to *The Vote*, the paper of the Women's Freedom League.

Secondly, for the better part of forty years

Carpenter lived at Millthorpe a life more or less openly homosexual. George Merrill was his constant companion throughout these years. In publications after 1890 Carpenter broached questions of sex in general, and homosexuality in particular, with an unparalleled frankness, for, where Havelock Ellis investigated and published in a scientific way, Carpenter was a populariser and accordingly ran the greater risk. In this connection Carpenter's writing was intended less as a contribution to knowledge in an academic sense, and more as a contribution to the knowledge of individuals: it was an act of persuasion and propaganda. Yet from the 1880s Carpenter succeeded where others, including Oscar Wilde, had failed. He managed to combine with a life partly lived as a public figure his unconcealed homosexuality; and while the social influence of this prolonged act of propaganda by deed cannot be evaluated accurately, it can only be supposed that it was considerable. In matters of sex and sexuality Carpenter was unquestionably one of the earliest contributors to the wholesale reconsideration of these questions in the present century. It was his books on sex reform alone that continued to sell, even in paperback in the 1950s. Although they now seem antiquated and coy, they survived Carpenter's literary and political reputations by well over two decades.

Edward Carpenter died on 28 January 1929, aged eighty-four. Against his own wishes, frequently expressed in life, he was given a Christian burial at Mount Cemetery, Guildford, the town to which he had moved from Millthorpe with George Merrill in 1922. The Edward Carpenter International Memorial Fellowship, set up in 1931, enjoyed a series of greatly successful annual meetings in the Cordwell Valley in Derbyshire in the 1930s. But after a continuous decline in numbers in the years following the Second World War, the Fellowship was wound up in 1962. Of the substantial inheritance of 1883, Edward Carpenter left £5214 gross, £4152 net, with Millthorpe heavily mortgaged.

Writings: *A Bibliography of Edward Carpenter* (Sheffield City Libraries, 1949). This catalogue, virtually complete up to the date of publication, lists all books, articles and mss, by and about Carpenter held in Sheffield City Library, together with many references to material held in other libraries. The following list includes only the first editions of Carpenter's major writings: *Towards Democracy* (1883); *England's Ideal, and Other Papers on Social Subjects* (1887); *Civilization: its cause and cure, and other essays* (1889); *From Adam's Peak to Elephanta: sketches in Ceylon and India* (1892); *Woman, and her Place in a Free Society* (Manchester, 1894); *Marriage in Free Society* (Manchester, 1894); *Homogenic Love, and its Place in a Free Society* (Manchester, 1894; for private circulation only); *Sex-love, and its Place in a Free Society* (Manchester, 1894); *Love's Coming of Age: a series of papers on the relations of the sexes* (Manchester, 1896); Editor of *Forecasts of the Coming Century, by a Decade of Writers*, (Manchester, 1897); *Angels' Wings: a series of essays on art and its relation to life* (1898); Editor of *Iolans: an anthology of friendship*, (1902); *The Art of Creation: essays on the self and its powers* (1904); *Prisons, Police and Punishment: an enquiry into the causes and treatment of crime and criminals* (1905); *Days with Walt Whitman; with some Notes on his Life and Work* (1906); *The Village and the Landlord* (Fabian Tract no. 136, 1907); *Sketches from Life in Town and Country, and some Verses* (1908); *The Intermediate Sex: a Study of some Transitional Types of Men and Women* (1908); *The Drama of Love and Death: a study of human evolution and transfiguration* (1912); *Intermediate Types among Primitive Folk: a study in social evolution* (1914); *The Healing of Nations, and the Hidden Sources of their Strife* (1915); *My Days and Dreams: being autobiographical notes* (1916); *Never Again!: a protest and a warning addressed to the peoples of Europe* (1916); *Towards Industrial Freedom* (1917); *Pagan and Christian Creeds: their origin and meaning* (1920); *Some Friends of Walt Whitman: a study in sex psychology* (The British Society for the Study of Sex-Psychology, Publication no. 13, 1924); (with G. Barnefield [G. C. Barnard]), *The Psychology of the Poet Shelley* (1925).

Sources: (1) MSS. The chief manuscript sources are (i) Carpenter Coll. Held at Sheffield City Library, the Carpenter Coll. is an extensive archive of printed and ms material by and about Carpenter including large files of correspondence for the period 1870 to 1929. It includes a large section of Carpenter's working library, and a substantial collection of personal and other papers deposited there in 1958 by Gilbert Beith, one of Carpenter's three executors. A master copy of *A Bibliography of Edward Carpenter*, available only in the Department of Local History, contains some additional material as well as a detailed reference guide to the collection itself; (ii) Alf Mattison Coll., Brotherton Library, Leeds University. Other relevant ms material may be found in the Labour Party archives; in the letters and documents by and about William Morris, Add. MSS, BM; the business archives of George Allen and Unwin Ltd. [see B. E. Maidment, 'Author and Publisher – John Ruskin and George Allen, 1890–1900', *Business Archives*, no. 36 (June 1972) 31] and an early ms version of Carpenter's autobiography, John Rylands Library, Manchester.

(2) Biographies: T. Swan, *Edward Carpenter: the man and his message* (Manchester, 1901); E. Crosby, *Edward Carpenter, Poet and Prophet* (1905); E. M. O. Ellis, *Three Modern Seers: James Hinton, Nietzsche, Edward Carpenter* (1910); M. Senard, *Edward Carpenter et sa philosophie* (Paris, 1914); E. Lewis, *Edward Carpenter: an exposition and an appreciation* (1915); M. Sime, *Edward Carpenter: his ideas and ideals* (1916); *Edward Carpenter: in appreciation*, ed. G. Beith (1931).

(3) Other: S. Webb, *Socialism in England* (1890); H. H. Ellis, *Studies in the Psychology of Sex*, vol. 1 (1897); R. Gardner, *In the Heart of Democracy* [1908]; M. D. O'Brien, *Socialism and Infamy; the Homogenic or Comrade Love exposed: an open letter in plain words for a socialist prophet, to Edward Carpenter* (Sheffield, 1909); H. S. Salt, *Seventy Years among Savages* (1921); *DNB* (1922–30); S. Bryher, *An Account of the Labour and Socialist Movement in Bristol* (Bristol, 1929–31); H. S. Salt, *Company*

I have kept (1930); G. Elton, *England arise!: a study of the pioneering days of the labour movement* (1931); I. Clephane, *Towards Sex Freedom* (1935); H. H. Ellis, *My Life* (1940); A. F. Brockway, *Socialism over Sixty Years* (1946); *The Letters of William Morris to his Family and Friends*, ed. P. Henderson (1950); E. M. Forster, *Two Cheers for Democracy* (1951); D. L. Hobman, *Olive Schreiner: her friends and times* (1955); E. P. Thompson, *William Morris: romantic to revolutionary* (1955); A. C. Marshall, *Havelock Ellis* (1959); *Surrey Advertiser*, 9 and 23 Sep 1961; T. Eagleton, 'Edward Carpenter', *Tribune*, 18 Mar 1966; R. Croft-Cooke, *Feasting with Panthers: a new consideration of some later Victorian writers* (1967); T. Eagleton, *Shakespeare and Society: critical studies in Shakespearian drama* (1967); S. L. Hynes, *The Edwardian Turn of Mind* (Princeton NJ, 1968); T. Eagleton, 'Nature and Spirit: a study of Edward Carpenter in his intellectual context' (Cambridge PhD, 1969); S. Pierson, 'Edward Carpenter, Prophet of a Socialist Millennium', *Victorian Studies 13*, no. 3 (Mar 1970) 301–18; *Sexual Heretics: male homosexuality in English literature from 1850 to 1900: an anthology*, selected with an Introduction by B. Reade (1970); T. d'Arch Smith, *Love in Earnest: some notes on the lives and writings of English 'Uranian' poets from 1889 to 1930* (1970); D. K. Baruah, 'Edward Carpenter and the Early Sheffield Socialists', *Trans Hunter Archaeological Society 10*, pt. 1 (1971) 54–62; E. Delavenay, *D. H. Lawrence and Edward Carpenter: a study in Edwardian transition* (1971); L. V. Thompson, *The Enthusiasts: a biography of John and Katharine Bruce Glasier* (1971). OBIT. *Sheffield Daily Independent*, *Sheffield Daily Telegraph* and *Times*, 29 June 1929.

NOTE: The editors are indebted to Dr Stanley Pierson, Head of the Department of History, College of Liberal Arts, Univ. of Oregon, U.S.A. for a biographical sketch of Carpenter.

KEITH NIELD

See also: *Bruce GLASIER; *Henry Mayers HYNDMAN; *William MORRIS; *William

Harrison RILEY; *Henry Stephens SALT; *Olive SCHREINER; *Robert SHARLAND; Sidney WEBB.

CARTER, Joseph (1818–61)
CHARTIST

Born in 1818 in Bury, Lancashire, Joseph Carter spent his adult life in nearby Stockport. Both he and his wife, Jane, a native of Stockport, were weavers. His participation in the Chartist movement began in 1839, when he became involved in the local campaign to raise support for John Frost and other Chartist exiles. Although never achieving national status, Carter was a prominent figure in the Stockport Charter Association. Between 1840 and 1844 he was frequently elected chairman and, in 1841, sub-secretary; and in April 1842 he represented his locality at the County Delegate Meeting in Macclesfield. When, in August 1843, the county organisation set up a finance committee to collect expenses for a conference delegate, he was again chosen to serve. He then attended the Convention at the Carpenters' Hall, Manchester, in April 1844.

Like most of his colleagues, Carter was a staunch supporter of Feargus O'Connor. He joined in the protest against O'Connor's treatment in York Gaol, and opposed the attempt by Lovett and Collins to take over the Chartist leadership in 1841. He campaigned against the Anti-Corn Law League, playing a leading role in Chartist attempts to take over local meetings. In April 1844, as chairman of a meeting addressed by O'Connor and George White, Carter was instructed to issue a formal challenge to Richard Cobden to meet O'Connor at Stockport in open discussion on corn law repeal. In spite of two letters from Carter and a challenge from O'Connor himself, the confrontation did not occur until August, in Northampton.

Carter himself avoided conflict with the authorities, although during the Plug Riots of 1842 he was a prominent local advocate of continuing the strike until the Charter was obtained. When the Stockport Chartists' leaders, James Mitchell and Charles Davies, were sentenced to eighteen months'

imprisonment in August 1839, on a charge of conspiracy, Carter had helped to provide for their families, and had taken the chair at a demonstration organised to celebrate their release in 1841. After the wave of arrests in the autumn of 1842, Carter even approached the Anti-Corn Law League for assistance with Chartist prisoners' legal expenses.

In June 1843 his Chartist activities were linked to his support for the Irish Repealers. In an attempt to bring about a rapprochement between the two groups, Carter and two fellow Chartists, John Allinson and Thomas Clark (who was later a member of the National Executive), paid their 3s subscriptions to become members of the Repeal Association. The scheme was apparently short-lived, for O'Connor, who had recently supported an alliance, changed his mind and advised Chartists against membership. Besides his Chartist and Repeal activities, Carter also took part in the bid in May 1842 to obtain government relief for the poor, and opposed the Anglican education clauses in the Factories Bill, which was before Parliament in April 1843. In December 1843 he proposed a collection to secure the release of Richard Oastler from prison.

After 1844 Carter disappeared from the local political scene, to re-emerge in December 1846 as a supporter of the Municipal Improvement Bill, the Stockport Manorial Tolls and Bridges Bill. Since this was the work of the Whig Corporation, it was opposed by most Chartists, many of whom formed a Working Men's Ratepayers' Association. Among the members of that body were Abraham Docker, James Torkington and George Bradburn. Carter's alienation from his former Chartist colleagues became complete at the general election in July 1847, when he assisted the Whigs against John West of Macclesfield, the Chartist candidate. Some indication of the cause – or perhaps the effect – of these actions may be found in the fact that by 1851 Carter was no longer a weaver but an overlooker. Between 1855 and 1857 he again changed his occupation, to that of beer seller. He died on 7 July 1861 at 22 John

Street, Brinnington, Cheshire, aged forty-three, leaving his widow to continue running the beer shop. No will has been located.

Sources: (1) MSS: 1841 Census, Stockport, PRO: H.O. 107/108; 1851 Census, Stockport, PRO: H.O. 107/2157; 1861 Census, Stockport, PRO: R.G.9 2570; (2) Other: *Post Office Directory of Cheshire* (1857); *Slater's Royal National Commercial Directory of Manchester and Liverpool and the principal manufacturing towns in Lancashire . . .* (Manchester, 1858); *Slater's Royal National Commercial Directory of Lancashire . . .* (Manchester, 1865); *Register of Burials in the Parish of Portwood in the County of Chester*, 1861 (Stockport Reference Library); *Northern Star*, 1839–47; *Stockport Advertiser*, 1841–8; F. O'Connor, *The Trial of Feargus O'Connor . . .* (1843); R. G. Gammage, *History of the Chartist Movement 1837–54* (1894: repr. with an Introduction by John Saville, New York, 1969); A. R. Schoyen, *The Chartist Challenge* (1958); *Chartist Studies*, ed. Asa Briggs (1959).

NAOMI REID
T.D.W.REID

See also: John ALLINSON; George BRADBURN; Abraham DOCKER; *Feargus O'CONNOR; James TORKINGTON.

CLARKE, William (1852–1901)
FABIAN AND JOURNALIST

Born on 22 November 1852 at William Street, Heigham, Norwich, to John Scott Clarke, a warehouseman from Peebles, and his wife Mary Ann Pigg, an Englishwoman, William attended the King Edward VI Commercial School in Norwich until his father, then a sales representative for the firm of Gurteens of Haverhill, moved to Cambridge in 1866. After two or three years in a private school he became a clerk at W. Eaden Lilley and Co., of Market Street, Cambridge, where he found life so tedious that he persuaded his father to let him become a non-collegiate student at the University in 1872. Soon he was a leading member of the non-collegiate debating society

founded by Stopford Brooke, and there formed a lasting friendship with Herbert Burrows. He was a teetotaller and won a prize essay competition in the temperance newspaper, the *Alliance News*; while he had begun regular writing for the provincial press, including leaders for the *Cambridge Independent*. Having transferred from the Natural Science Tripos to the new Historical Tripos, he gained a second class degree in 1876.

He was a voracious reader, with a strong memory, and gravitated easily into the world of journalism and lecturing, contributing to the monthly reviews and speaking for the National Reform Union and the Liberation Society. In 1877 he moved to London and started to write for the evening papers the *Star* and the *Echo*, as well as for a number of British and American reviews. A frequenter of London Positivist circles, he also acted for a time as secretary to the Bedford Chapel Debating Society, founded in Bloomsbury by Stopford Brooke, where he would have encountered Graham Wallas, Bernard Shaw, and Michael Davitt. Among his close friends were Burrows, and the journalists Clement Shorter and H. W. Massingham. Massingham noted that 'he seems to have been building up friendships with the great from his cradle', but he does not appear to have gained much personal influence in this way [Shorter (1927) 42].

He had developed an early and passionate interest in the United States, and made the first of many visits there in 1881–2, supporting himself by lecturing and corresponding with some English provincial newspapers. On his return he became the English correspondent of the *Boston Advertiser* and the *Springfield Republican*, and a regular contributor to the *New England Magazine* and the *Outlook* (New York). His interest in the development of modern capitalism was stimulated by an article by the American radical H. D. Lloyd, 'Making Bread Dear' (*North American Rev.*, Aug 1883), which Clarke reviewed enthusiastically in the *Cambridge Independent* (29 Sep 1883). On his next visit to America he met Lloyd and began a firm and important friendship. Another of Lloyd's articles, 'The Lords of Industry' (*North American Rev.*, June 1884), virtually clinched his decision to move from the Fellowship of the New Life into the Fabian Society in that year. He had been among the first members of Thomas Davidson's Fellowship, formed in 1882, which was a humanist, ethicist group who read Goethe, Carlyle, Emerson and James Hinton. Ethicist ideas were to remain an important ingredient of Clarke's thinking, but he belonged to 'the politically minded rationalists of the group' [Jupp (1918) 77] (who included men like Edward Pease, Hubert Bland and Ramsay MacDonald), and with them he withdrew in 1884 to the splinter Fabian Society.

He did not, however, become an official member of the Society until February 1886. Two years later he joined the executive committee, and in 1889 he contributed the article on the 'Industrial' basis of Socialism to *Fabian Essays*. While he had remained active in other London radical circles, lecturing for J. C. Foulger's Progressive Association and the London Ethical Society, it was his Fabian essay which really established him as a leading British radical. In time it came to be acknowledged as the most perceptive and relevant of all the essays. He traced the development of modern capitalism from pre-industrial society, through the Free Trade era which had witnessed the triumph of the capitalist over the landlord class, to the world-wide expansion of industrial nations on a basis of tariffs and trusts, so dramatically manifested in the United States. This development, he argued, was 'inevitable', and contained within itself the seeds of its own destruction. He was perhaps one of the first to perceive that the increasing separation of the roles of the capitalist (or *rentier*) and manager would make the former obsolete, and would mean the passing of large sectors of industry into public ownership. The alternative to this socialisation would be, as in America, the increasing power of the monopolies. The question was whether 'to submit to trusts or give up capitalists'. The best policy would be to absorb and administer already monopolised industries, but 'human stupidity' would lead to a compromise policy of taxation and public control. Either

way the inevitable end was Socialism. When society was educated and organised as an industrial democracy 'the class struggle [will] be ended' and replaced by a Whitmanesque vision of 'the practical, peaceful life, the people's life'. The analysis owed much to Lloyd's work, and not a little to Marx, although references to the *Communist Manifesto* were excised from the published version of what had originally been a lecture [McBriar (1962) 62–3]. Elsewhere Clarke had stressed that it was the unconscious drift towards Socialism through the extension of state intervention, particularly in the case of Irish land reform, rather than the activities of the trade unions, whose 'task is now mainly accomplished', that would be the most important factor in the future [*Political Science Quarterly* (1888) 549–71].

In August 1890 he was recruited as a leader writer and literary contributor to the *Daily Chronicle*, shortly to be followed there by his friend Massingham. For the next nine years he wrote many hundreds of leaders and many reviews, and while he was on the paper the *Chronicle*, which also called upon Graham Wallas, became an important Fabian mouthpiece. The work, however, made it difficult for Clarke to participate fully in the activities of the Fabian Society, and he resigned from the executive in April 1891, after having played a major part in the famous Lancashire campaign of the previous year. In 1894 he was made a joint trustee of the Hutchinson Bequest, and joined the administrative committee of the LSE which the Webbs had used the Bequest to found. In 1897, however, Clarke withdrew from the Society altogether. For some time he had been unhappy about the Fabians, for whom 'there was a danger of falling into mere wire-pulling and making of political deals' [*New England Mag.* (1894) 94]. Furthermore his own belief in democracy and hatred of imperialism found little sympathy among the leaders of the Society.

His later articles in the *Contemporary Review* and the *New England Magazine* revealed the pervasive humanist influence of Ruskin, Morris, Whitman, Mazzini, and especially Emerson, and his earlier Christianity became more of a social aesthetic, an attack upon the tawdry commercialism of industrial society, 'the perpetual domination of business', and the gloomy evils of urban life. He had no sympathy with the 'old liberals', or for Gladstone, despite a notably restrained obituary he wrote of the latter in the *Daily Chronicle* [20 May 1898; repr. in Burrows and Hobson (1908) 281–5]. Instead, a 'new liberalism' would be a limited collectivism, leaving open to individual decision the qualitative aspects of life, and relieving man of the burden of mechanical toil. These aims were shared by some of his friends in the National Liberal Club, and in 1894 they organised themselves into an intellectual pressure group known as the Rainbow Circle. In 1896 they started the *Progressive Review*, with Herbert Samuel, Richard Stapley and J. A. Hobson among the directors, Clarke as editor, helped by Hobson, and Ramsay MacDonald as secretary. It survived barely a year owing to internal dissension. Clarke and Hobson clashed with Samuel over imperialism: MacDonald proved an erratic and irritating secretary; and Clarke, troubled by severe and recurrent bouts of influenza, found it all too much.

He had by this time travelled extensively in Europe and America as a journalist, and as a delegate to a meeting of the Second International in Paris in 1889, and to Lloyd's International Labour Congress in Chicago in 1893. In that year he lost some of his money in the Liberator Building Society crash; and his mother died. He had always disliked city life, and he took this opportunity to seek a country refuge, renting the small rectory at Greenstead in Essex, a choice which may have reflected his growing interest in architecture. He continued to rent rooms in London, while his sisters kept house for him at Greenstead.

His journalistic work continued to expand, and by the late 1890s he had become a leader writer for the *Spectator* and the *Economist*, and a regular contributor to the *Manchester Guardian*. In 1899 Frank Lloyd, proprietor of the *Daily Chronicle* had indicated to Massingham, who had been editor since 1895, that he did not wish

his paper to criticise the Government over the Boer War, and Massingham, Clarke, Harold Spender, and Vaughan Nash of the editorial staff resigned as a result. There is some evidence that Clarke may have become C. P. Scott's private secretary for a time, but his main employment continued to be journalism.

Growing steadily more pessimistic about the future of an imperialist England, he joined the League Against Aggression and Militarism in 1900; this was a group of leading anti-war Liberals, which included J. L. Hammond, F. W. Hirst, R. Spence Watson, C. P. Scott, and Lloyd George [Hirst (1947) 199–200]. Clarke's analysis of the political situation was shared by many of the anti-imperialist 'new liberals', but it was not given as forceful an expression until some years later with Hobson's *Imperialism* (1902) and Hobhouse's *Democracy and Reaction* (1904). Clarke was inclined to be far more pessimistic than his fellow radicals. There was a tendency, he thought, for modern industrial nations to become oligarchic, and perhaps nowhere more so than in England where the people were inherently anti-democratic. Despite her Empire, England was destined to lose her economic lead in the world in competition with the strong young economies of Germany and the United States. As she was an urban country, she would not follow the road to a 'peasant democracy such as one finds in France, Switzerland, Denmark or Sweden'. Instead, she would become the Anglo-Saxon's pleasure ground, a recreational area for the successful industrialists of America and Australasia, for she could supply wealth and service, and it was her immense servile class which would obstruct any move towards democracy [*Cont. Rev. 78* (1899) 44–58].

This pessimism, which increasingly tempered Clarke's underlying Emersonian idealism, was in part the result of a certain misanthropic moroseness which accompanied his continued ill-health. In the late 1890s this was diagnosed as diabetes. His condition improved after treatment, but while accompanying Herbert Burrows, J. A. Hobson and the Rev. A. Lilley on a walking tour of the Balkans, he died on 8 May 1901.

He was buried in the military cemetery at Mostar in Hercegovina. He left effects to the value of £3272, and a portion of his library was given to the National Liberal Club, together with a portrait of him by Felix Moscheles. He never married.

Personal and political circumstances had contributed at the end to give an impression of despair, not uncommon, if less intense, among radicals of the time. His early prognosis of the inevitability of Socialism, and his 'faith in ideas and in the growing capacity of the common people to absorb and to apply ideas in reasonably working out the progress of the commonwealth [which] forms the moral foundation of democracy' [quoted in Burrows and Hobson (1908) xxviii], were submerged in a disenchantment born of an inability to suffer either fools or knaves gladly, and of an impatience with the methods of 'gradualism'.

Writings: *Essays selected from the writings . . . of Joseph Mazzini*, edited and with an Introduction by Clarke (1887); 'The Industrial Basis of Socialism', in *Fabian Essays*, ed. G. B. Shaw (1889; 6th ed. with an Introduction by Asa Briggs, 1962) and also included in *William Clarke, a Collection of his Writings*, ed. H. Burrows and J. A. Hobson (1908) 3–23; *Political Orations from Wentworth to Macaulay*, edited and with an Introduction by Clarke (1889); *Walt Whitman* (1892); An essay on the Fabian Society, in *Fabian Essays*, ed. G. B. Shaw with an Introduction by E. Bellamy (Boston, 1894); 'Emerson', in *Prophets of the Century*, ed. A. C. Rickett (1898).

His early journalism may be found in the *British Quarterly Review*, the *Cambridge Independent Press*, the *Echo* [London], and the *Star* [London]. Later he contributed to *Cassell's Magazine, Commonwealth, Contemporary Review, Daily Chronicle, Economist, English Illustrated Magazine, Manchester Guardian, Progressive Review, Reynolds News, Speaker,* and *Spectator*. He also contributed to the following American journals, the *Boston Advertiser, Chicago Tribune, Christian Reporter* [Boston], *New England Magazine, North American Review, Outlook* [New York], *Political Science*

Quarterly, and the *Springfield Republican*. Some other important articles are also collected in *William Clarke*, ed. H. Burrows and J. A. Hobson (1908). Articles of particular interest which are not included in this collection are: 'The Spoils System in American Politics', *Cont. Rev. 40* (1881) 633–50; 'The Power of Monopolies', *Cambridge Independent Press*, 29 Sep 1883; 'The Influence of Socialism upon English Politics', *Pol. Sc. Q. 3* (1888) 549–71; 'William Ewart Gladstone', *New England Mag. 2* (1890) 122–34; 'William Morris', ibid., *3* (1891) 740–9; 'Carlyle and Ruskin and Their Influence on English Social Thought', ibid., *4* (1893) 473–88; 'The Old Order Changeth', *Outlook*, 31 Mar 1894; 'Life of the London Working Classes', *New England Mag. 10* (1894) 572–84; 'The Fabian Society', ibid., *10* (1894) 89–99; 'The British Independent Labour Movement', *Outlook*, 30 June 1894; 'The Present Mood of England', *New England Mag. 16* (1897) 690–6; 'The Decline in English Liberalism', *Pol. Sc. Q. 16* (1901) 450–62.

Sources: (1) MSS: Viscount Samuel papers, House of Lords; J. Ramsay MacDonald papers, PRO; H. D. Lloyd Coll., Wisconsin State Historical Society and on microfilm at LSE; T. Davidson papers, Yale University Library; C. P. Scott papers, The Guardian Office, Manchester. (2) *Ethical Society Annual Reports* (1886–91); *Encyclopaedia of Social Reform*, ed. W. D. P. Bliss (New York, 1897); *Labour Annual* (1897); E. R. Pease, *History of the Fabian Society* (1916; repr. 1963); L. P. Jacks, *Life and Letters of Stopford Brooke* (1917); W. Jupp, *Wayfarings* (1918); *H.W.M.* ed. H. J. Massingham (1925); C. K. Shorter, *C.K.S. An Autobiography* (1927); A. C. Rickett, *I look back* (1933); The Economist, *The Economist 1843–1943: a centenary volume* (1944); J. A. Venn, *Alumni Cantabrigiensis*, pt 2 vol. 3 (Cambridge, 1944); F. W. Hirst, *In the Golden Days* (1947); H. M. Pelling, *America and the British Left* (1956); J. Bowle, *Viscount Samuel* (1957); L. A. Clark, 'The Liberal Party and Collectivism 1886–1906' (Cambridge MLitt., 1957); H. Ausubel, *In Hard Times: reformers among the late*

98 CLARKE

Victorians (1960); B. Semmel, *Imperialism and Social Reform: English Social-Imperial Thought 1895–1914* (1960); M. Cole, *The Story of Fabian Socialism* (1961); A. M. McBriar, *Fabian Socialism and English Politics 1884–1918* (Cambridge, 1962); C. M. Destler, *Henry Demarest Lloyd and the Empire of Reform* (Philadelphia, 1963); Bernard Shaw, *Collected Letters 1874–1897*, ed. Dan H. Laurence (1965); W. S. Smith, *The London Heretics 1870–1914* (1967); B. Porter, *Critics of Empire* (1968); E. J. Hobsbawm, 'The Lesser Fabians', in *The Luddites and Other Essays*, ed. L. M. Munby (1971); Bernard Shaw, *Collected Letters 1898–1910*, ed. Dan H. Laurence (1972). OBIT. *Daily Chronicle*, 9 May 1901; *Manchester Guardian*, 10 May 1901; *Economist* and *Spectator*, 11 May 1901; *Cambridge Independent Press*, 17 May 1901; *Fabian News*, 11 (June 1901).

ALAN J. LEE

See also: *Herbert BURROWS; †John Atkinson HOBSON; †James Ramsay MACDONALD.

COMBE, Abram (1785?–1827)
OWENITE

Abram Combe was born in Edinburgh in 1785 (the usual date given for his birth, although the *DNB* entry for George Combe, who was an elder brother, gives the latter's date of birth as 1788). Abram was one of seventeen children of George Comb (as he spelt it), a brewer, and his wife Marion Newton. The parents brought their children up according to strict Calvinist principles, and both Abram and his brother George later said that this gave them a gloomy impression of religion and made their boyhood unhappy. It may also have led them to the progressive views which they adopted in adult life. George Combe, Writer to the Signet, was the son-in-law of Mrs Siddons and a friend of George Eliot and of George Hogarth, who was later to become Dickens's father-in-law. He was a phrenologist, a disciple of Spurzheim. He wrote a number of books including *Elements of Phrenology* (1824), *Essay on the Constitution of Man* (1828), which was still selling at the rate of 2500 copies a year in 1843, and was translated into Polish, and several works on education. Abram's younger brother Andrew was even more distinguished. After taking his diploma as a surgeon in Edinburgh he went to Paris for advanced medical work: he studied anatomy, and under Spurzheim's influence paid particular attention to the brain. After he returned to Edinburgh he joined his brother George and others in establishing the *Phrenological Journal*. Andrew Combe published a number of books on medical and socio-medical subjects, and in 1838 he was appointed physician extraordinary to the queen in Scotland. He died of lung tuberculosis in 1847.

Abram Combe was educated at the High School, Edinburgh, and then apprenticed to a tanner; on the completion of his apprenticeship he went to London. Two years later he started a tannery in Glasgow, but in 1807 returned to Edinburgh and set up his business there. Until 1820 his interests were those of a typical manufacturer and merchant; he was hard working and self-centred. But in October of that year he visited New Lanark with his brother George and was introduced to Robert Owen. He was deeply impressed with what he saw, especially the infant school, and by what Owen said. He began to study Owen's writings and rapidly became an enthusiastic convert. To his friends it appeared that the changes in his character resulting from his adoption of the New View of Society were similar to a religious conversion. Previously he had been a severe satirist of the faults of others, and had championed the pursuit of self-interest as man's first duty. Now he spoke of universal benevolence and justice, showed compassion for others' weaknesses, and gave up animal food, fermented liquor and the theatre.

Combe's Owenite activities began in the autumn of 1821, with the foundation of the Edinburgh Practical Society. This was promoted by a group of Scottish followers of Owen, including Donald Macdonald, a captain in the Royal Engineers, and Archibald J. Hamilton, the laird of Dalzell. The members of the Practical Society, which included at one time about five hundred families, 'opened a co-operative store, met regularly in the evenings for mutual instruction, dancing and social intercourse generally, and instituted a school for their children on the New Lanark model' [Podmore, 2 (1906) 357]. Captain Macdonald was in charge of the school. The Society lasted for not more than a year, and Combe then tried a small-scale community in his own tanyard. He built dormitories and a kitchen for his labourers, and promised a share of the profits to those who would join the community; but the venture soon collapsed. His last and most ambitious experiment was the establishment of an Owenite community at Orbiston, Lanarkshire, on an estate of 291 acres some nine miles east of Glasgow.

Orbiston 'was the first communal experiment on British soil with a view to emancipating the working class through a transformation of the economic system' [Garnett (1972) 65]. Robert Owen had already purchased a large part of the Motherwell estate from General John Hamilton (A. J. Hamilton's father) and the General sold to Abram Combe, as trustee of the new community, part of the remaining estate at Orbiston, which was one mile west of the Motherwell site. A joint-stock company was established, with clearly defined articles of agreement for both proprietors and tenants, and building operations began on 18 March 1825. After the launching of the scheme A. J. Hamilton did not play a very active part in its affairs and it was Abram Combe who was its leading spirit. He edited the community's journal, the *Orbiston Register*, the first number of which was published on 11 October 1825; and it was Combe who gave its name to the community: 'The First Society of Adherents to Divine Revelation.' The name puzzled and irritated both friends and enemies. Combe himself never claimed supernatural inspiration and he did not quote scripture, but he exhibited many characteristics of the millennial mentality: belief in the imminence of a great and fundamental change in society, a dogmatic reduction of all issues to simple absolute alternatives, and the circumvention of logical difficulties by faith in divine certainty. Combe expounded his Owenite views in several tracts and

books, the two most important being the *Metaphorical Sketches of the Old and New Systems* (1823) and *Observations on the Old and New Views* (1823).

The domestic history of Orbiston has been described in detail in a number of texts including Podmore (1906); Cullen (1910); Harrison (1969); Garnett (1972). The community was basically agricultural – Owen's arguments for 'spade husbandry' being generally accepted – but it also had a flourishing iron foundry which encouraged the development of other trades such as printing and weaving. Community life was begun in April 1826 and continued until December 1827, and at one time there were over three hundred persons in residence. The community had its full share of the usual problems that always beset communitarian experiments, but it was the illness and death of Abram Combe on 11 August 1827 which precipitated the crisis in which the community was already finding itself. When the mortgagees began to press for payment in the autumn of 1827 William Combe, Abram's youngest brother who had been associated with him in his Owenite community, assumed management of it after his brother's death. He ordered the members to leave, and the first British Owenite community came to an end. Alexander Campbell and William Sheddon, who had accepted personal liability for certain of the debts outstanding, were imprisoned in Hamilton Gaol at the instance of certain of the creditors. William Combe emigrated to America in 1828 where he managed a brewery in Albany, New York, and later in Jersey City.

There was much criticism at the time by Owenites of the organisation and arrangements of the community, but Orbiston was nevertheless a considerable influence upon contemporary social thinking. The buildings at Orbiston were soon pulled down, and their materials used for new houses in nearby villages. Combe's inventory was registered at Edinburgh in May 1829, and the value of his estate was given as £1488 12s 7d, with the following note inserted after the total:

He was possessed of 10 shares of £200

each in the Orbiston Company in Lanarkshire which at his death were and still are of no value as the proprietors lost all their capital and must make further advances to pay the company's debts. He acted as trustee for said company and at his decease the balance of £508 5s 4d appears due to him on his account by the company but from the state of the company's affairs the executors do not consider this claim as of any value . . .

Writings: *An Address to the Conductors of the Periodical Press* (Edinburgh, 1823); *Metaphorical Sketches of the Old and the New Systems* (Edinburgh, 1823); *Observations on the Old and New Views* (Edinburgh, 1823); *A Proposal for commencing the Experiment of Mr Owen's System* [first published in the *Edinburgh Observer*, 31 Jan 1824; repr. in the *Orbiston Register*, 2, 19–32 (14 Feb, 14 Mar 1827)]; *The Religious Creed of the New System* (Edinburgh, 1824); *The Sphere for Joint-Stock Companies* (Edinburgh, 1825); [Anon.], *The New Court, No. 1* (n.p., 1825); *Life and Dying Testimony of Abram Combe*, ed. A. Campbell (1844).

Sources: (1) MSS: George Combe papers, Nat. Library of Scotland, Edinburgh; Hamilton papers, Motherwell PL, Scotland; (2) Other: *The Register for the First Society of Adherents to Divine Revelation at Orbiston*, 2 vols (Edinburgh, 1825–7) [especially 19 Sep 1827, pp. 65–71]; J. M. Morgan, *Hampden in the Nineteenth Century* (1834); F. Podmore, *Robert Owen: a biography* (1906); A. Cullen, *Adventures in Socialism* (1910); A. C. Grant, 'George Combe and his Circle' (Edinburgh PhD, 1960); F. L. P. Knight, 'Owenite Socialism in the Period 1817–1840' (Manchester MA, 1965); J. F. C. Harrison, *Robert Owen and the Owenites in Britain and America* (1969); R. G. Garnett, *Co-operation and the Owenite Socialist Community in Britain 1825–45* (1972): biographical information: Scottish Record Office, Edinburgh.

J. F. C. HARRISON

See also: †George MUDIE; *Robert OWEN

COOK, Cecily Mary (1887/90?–1962)
CO-OPERATOR AND SOCIALIST

Cecily Cook was the daughter of Alfred Graves but her exact date of birth has not been traced. When she married Herbert G. N. Cook, a clerk to a Distress Committee, at Camberwell Register Office on 6 November 1909, however, she gave her age as twenty-two, although at the time of her death fifty-three years later her age was quoted as seventy-two. Of her early life nothing is known apart from the fact that she experienced poverty as a young working girl and from her early days she was always a keen trade unionist. Among her first interests was the struggle for women's suffrage and she played an active part in this campaign between 1911 and 1913. She once recalled how she 'held a policeman at bay on her front doorstep while a colleague he had come to arrest escaped by the back door' [*Co-op. News*, 21 July 1962].

After the First World War Mrs Cook took part in the political side of the Labour movement and on several occasions acted as agent for Labour candidates. At the general elections of 1922 and 1923 she was chief woman worker for Clement Attlee when he won and held the Limehouse Division of Stepney for Labour. As a Women's Co-operative Guild nominee she fought a seat on the LCC at Wandsworth in 1925. Between 1924 and 1932 Cecily Cook was in the information and research department of the ILP and her duties included the preparation of weekly notes for speakers, memoranda for the use of MPs, the writing of the column 'Propaganda Points' for the *New Leader* and other articles. She left the ILP in 1932 when the Party severed its relationship with the Labour Party.

It was for her service to the Women's Co-operative Guild, however, that Mrs Cook is particularly remembered. She joined the Earlsfield branch (London) in the early 1920s and served as the branch's second president. She later moved to the St Marylebone branch where she held the offices of president and secretary. In 1933 she joined the head office staff of the Guild where until 1938 she worked as confidential clerk to the general secretary. She served as secretary of the Guild Standing Orders Committee, was minute secretary of the central committee and prepared many notes for speakers. In 1940 she succeeded Miss Rose Simpson as general secretary of the Guild, a position she held until 1953. In January 1948 Mrs Cook was awarded the OBE, an honour which she regarded as recognition of the public service undertaken by guildswomen generally.

When the presidency of the International Co-operative Women's Guild became vacant in 1951, Mrs Cook was invited to become president. After considerable hesitation she agreed. Although she had no knowledge of foreign languages, she made an excellent president and henceforth the ICWG became her first love. This was closely followed by another absorbing interest, the Women's Council, a non-political and non-sectarian organisation with headquarters in London which had developed from the Women's Advisory Council on Indian Affairs founded in 1932. Its aims were the promotion amongst British women and women's organisations of an interest in and knowledge of Asian countries, especially in the spheres of social and family welfare and the position of women. Cecily Cook joined in 1952. Just before her death she undertook the leadership of the Women's Council work among Asian students in London in which, although over seventy, she showed a remarkable understanding of the problems and aspirations of the young. She also became a member of the Winifred Cullis Committee of the British-American Associates, whose purpose was to choose women from Britain to lecture in the U.S.A. and Canada.

Her husband died fairly early in their marriage (her only son had died when he was about 19) and Cecily Cook lived for many years with Arthur Thomas Hogg although they never formally married. Hogg had been a conscientious objector in the First World War, a member of the ILP and was an artist by profession. Mrs Cook had a caravan in the corner of a field on the outskirts of London. She enjoyed gardening, was a great lover of poetry, had a repertoire of character sketches, and a passion for archaeology. In mid-June 1962 she collapsed after returning from a Guild Congress and was taken to Whittington Hospital where she died on 28 June 1962 at the age of seventy-two. She was cremated. Probate of her will, valued at £503, was granted to Arthur Hogg, who himself died fairly soon after Cecily.

Writings: Articles in the *New Leader* and the *Bulletin* of the ICWG etc.

Sources: *Co-op. News*, 18 May 1940; personal information: The Hon. Lady Ruth Egerton, J. Gaster and Mrs Lucy Middleton, all of London; Miss G. F. Polley, Croydon. OBIT. *Co-op. News*, 7 and 21 July 1962; *Times*, 13 July 1962 [by the Hon. Lady Ruth Egerton, president of The Women's Council]; *RIC* 55 no. 9 (Sep 1962) [by the secretary, Miss G. F. Polley].

JOYCE BELLAMY
H. F. BING

See also: †Miss Margaret Llewelyn DAVIES; †Miss Alice Honora ENFIELD; *James MAXTON, for Independent Labour Party 1915–32.

COOPER, George (1824–95)
TRADE UNIONIST AND RADICAL

George Cooper was born on 24 January 1824, in Stockport, Cheshire. His father, James, was a newsagent and billposter, who also had a stall on the market and acted as money-taker at a theatre. George began work at the age of six, with a local twine maker. He later became a weaver and a tenter.

In 1847, while employed as a weaver, he played a leading part in the campaign against the 'loom tax'. This tax of 6d per loom was introduced by Messrs Kershaw, Leese and Co., on the ground that operatives had been enabled to increase their earnings through the introduction of new improved looms. Since James Kershaw was also standing as a parliamentary candidate for the borough, the issue became prominent in the political as well as the industrial field. It may well have been the approach of a general election which persuaded the firm to abandon the tax in July. As economic depression became increasingly prevalent in the town, Cooper took part in a plan to stage a strike in the cotton district, presumably to bring the plight of the operatives to the notice of the Board of Guardians: he was a delegate to the meeting at Bolton which decided upon strike action; but the plan was never in fact put into action. Instead, Cooper acted as secretary to a committee representing the unemployed, and formed part of a deputation to the borough magistrates, urging the adoption of some scheme to alleviate distress.

He continued his activities on behalf of the power-loom weavers in 1848, when the manufacturers made a successful attempt to reduce wages by ten per cent. By 1848, the Ten Hours Factory Act was being evaded by many Stockport millowners, the first among them being Cooper's employer, Mr Stewart. Cooper, then secretary of the weavers' union, was instrumental in preparing a memorial to the Queen, outlining the hardships imposed by the relay system. The campaign in Stockport for an effective Ten Hours Act continued into 1853, with Cooper still playing a leading role. The existing acts were still being violated in the town and neighbourhood, and the operatives therefore pressed for further legislation which would restrict the operating time of the moving power in all factories to ten hours per day during the first five days of the week, and to seven and a half hours on Saturdays.

As a result of his activities, Cooper was dismissed by Stewart in 1848, and was unable to find work as a weaver elsewhere in Stockport. With loans of 4s each from two of his friends, he rented a cottage near to his home, and set up a small shop, whose trade he supplemented by going round country wakes and fairs with a basket of nuts and a turning board. He eventually expanded his business by taking over the public house opposite, together with two houses, and became a prosperous shopkeeper. In the winter of 1852–3, he was approached by a deputation of operatives, who wanted him to lead a campaign for the return of the ten per cent by which wages had been reduced in 1848. Cooper realised that he would incur severe financial loss by such a move, but nevertheless agreed. On 9 June 1853, this Ten Percent. campaign culminated in a strike, which

lasted until 1 August, and ended in a victory for the operatives. George Cooper later claimed to have played no part in the decision to strike, asserting that individual shop meetings had passed their own resolutions, and that, in his own words, he had then 'assumed the head of affairs with the object of successfully engineering it'. He refused, however, to handle any financial matters. In order to popularise the movement he composed rhymes and ballads, which became widely known in the locality, and was prepared to enter into public debate on behalf of the strikers. Once the Stockport victory had been won, Cooper visited Blackburn and Preston, on both occasions advising against any further strike action.

After being presented with a gold watch and purse for his services, Cooper decided to take a sea voyage, before once again going into business in Stockport. This voyage, however, resulted in his going to live in Toronto and setting up in business there. But when in 1855 his wife died of heart disease, he decided to go to the United States. In 1856 he was in the state of Maine, where he remained until the latter part of 1858. By this time, he was contemplating a return to England, and decided that, en route, he would go to Philadelphia to see an old Stockport friend, Sandy Challenger. Challenger had been prominent among the Ashton Chartists during the 'Plug Plot' of 1842, and later, in Stockport, had been associated with Cooper in the Ten Percent. agitation of 1848. The reunion in America was not to be, for Cooper discovered that his old friend was dead. Cooper remained in Philadelphia until the outbreak of the American Civil War, when, because he detested slavery of every kind, he enlisted in the Philadelphia Merchant Troop of Cavalry. After enrolment, they were sent to Washington, but soon became the first Volunteer Cavalry to cross the Potomac into Virgina. Cooper's company, with eleven others, was formed into a regiment known first as Colonel Young's Kentucky Light Cavalry, then as the 3rd Pennsylvania Cavalry. His first engagement took place at Kelly's Ford, in the Rappahannock. Cooper acted as a war correspondent (so he stated in an interview not long before his death – *Cheshire County News*, 30 Mar 1894), and was wounded on the forehead while near General Grant's tent.

In 1865 he returned to Stockport, at first helping his brother Alexander with his work of bellringing and billposting, and attending some parliamentary reform meetings in 1867. He became landlord of a hotel but gave it up in 1882, when he was apparently feeling the effects of advancing age. He then 'picked up a living as best I could', which at first involved posing as a model for Art School students. (At least one portrait of him still survives.) In 1888 he applied to the American Government for a pension, which was granted in 1890. After Cooper had enjoyed his new income for only three months, the United States passed a Bill declaring that aliens drawing such pensions must spend the money in the U.S.A. Cooper was thus obliged to relinquish his income, but in 1893 was provided with a similar allowance, paid out of his own pocket by W. Mather, Liberal MP for the Gorton Division of South East Lancashire. After a long period of bad health, including a serious throat infection, Cooper died on 14 March 1895. He was twice married, but left no children. His effects were valued at £30.

Sources: (1) MSS: Hurst MSS, vol. 4: Stockport Reference Library; (2) Other: *Stockport Advertiser*, 1847–54, 1867; Alfred [Samuel H. G. Kydd], *The History of the Factory Movement*, 2 vols (1857, repr. in one vol. New York, 1966); *Cheshire County News*, 1894–5; E. L. Hutchins and A. Harrison, *A History of Factory Legislation* (1903, 3rd ed. 1926, repr. 1966); *Stockport Photographic Society Record Section*, 1915: Stockport Reference Library; C. Driver, *Tory Radical: the life of Richard Oastler* (Oxford, 1946); J. T. Ward, *The Factory Movement 1830–1855* (1962); personal information: Mrs A. Swift, Stockport, a great-grand-daughter of Cooper's brother, Thomas. OBIT. *Cheshire County News*, 15 Mar 1895.

NAOMI REID
T. D. W. REID

See also: Joseph CARTER; James TORKINGTON.

COOPER, Robert (1819–68)
OWENITE AND SECULARIST

Robert Cooper was born at Barton upon Irwell, near Manchester, on 29 December 1819. His father, a fervent admirer of Paine, Cartwright, Cobbett and Hunt, had moved from Yorkshire to Manchester during the Napoleonic Wars to avoid persecution for refusing to join the volunteers, or the militia, or provide a substitute for the latter. Cooper's father was present at Peterloo, escaping from being cut down by the cavalry by defending himself with a stout stick, afterwards kept as an heirloom in the family. As a noted freethinker he used to gather friends at his house on Sunday evenings to read and discuss Paine's *Age of Reason* and *Rights of Man* and other radical pamphlets and newspapers, and young Cooper, who was occasionally asked to read aloud while still a boy, was thus educated in the ways of ultra-radicalism.

At the age of twelve Robert became a clerk with a Manchester firm, and two years later, when he was fourteen, he began to teach at the Co-operative School, George Street, Salford. The conductor of the school was Charles Bury, with James Rigby and Joseph Smith among his assistants. Salford in the early 1830s was a vigorous centre of Owenite activity. Although Cooper does not mention him in his autobiographical articles, he presumably knew Rowland Detrosier, whose lectures at the New Mechanics' Institution were making a very considerable impact on the young Owenite radicals. Cooper also taught further classes at the Secular school, Bywaters Rooms, Peter St, among the patrons of which was Joseph Brotherton, MP. In 1835 the Salford Owenites built the 'Social Institution', the first of its kind in the country. Cooper later described the building:

The windows were of stained glass, the floors carpeted, and the platform neat and elegant, ornamented with mottoes in gilt mouldings. Altogether it bore an aspect of comfort and respectability, such as I never saw before or since in connection with an almost purely working-class movement.

It was at this time that Robert Owen came to lecture in the Social Institution, and Cooper became a total believer. 'It determined my future career', he wrote later, 'To the day of his death I revered him as a father, and he treated me as a son.' Cooper was not yet seventeen, but from this first meeting with Owen he accepted the role of propagandist and lecturer in the Owenite cause. He devoted his Sundays, and many nights, to lecturing in towns and villages in Lancashire and Yorkshire. Some of his lectures were published, including one on *Original Sin* in 1838 and *The Holy Scriptures Analyzed* in 1839. This latter pamphlet was among those denounced by the Bishop of Exeter early in 1840 in the House of Lords when he made his hysterical attack upon the Owenite 'infidels'.

When Robert Cooper entered actively into the Owenite movement it was in the last main phase of its life, after the collapse of the Grand National Consolidated Trades Union and the demise of the *Pioneer* and the *Crisis*. From the second half of the thirties Owenism was to be increasingly identified with attacks upon orthodox religion and an explicit rejection of politics. There were certain exceptions among the Owenites, especially among the rank and file, for whom Owenism and Chartism were not incompatible movements; but for the majority of the Socialists, as the Owenites were now universally called, political activities were a diversion from their aims and purposes. Cooper himself, until the last decade of his life, concentrated all his energies upon secularist writing and lecturing within an Owenite framework of reference.

His growing prominence as a Socialist led to his dismissal by his employers. He was now twenty-one and for the next six years was employed full time as an Owenite social missionary [J. F. C. Harrison (1969) 216 ff.]. He went first to Hull, for a few months in 1841, and then to Newcastle and Sunderland. In 1842 he moved to Scotland, and settled in Edinburgh, where he attended Professor Wilson's and Sir William Hamilton's lectures at the University. He himself lectured in many towns and villages, and during the riotous summer and autumn of 1842 was mostly in Dundee and Glasgow. His main argument to the unemployed was not to join the military (recruitment was being vigorously pursued) but to demand home colonisation as the way to solve the crisis. He returned to England in 1843, and held posts in Derby and Stockport before going back to Edinburgh in May 1845; but when the Edinburgh Social Institution closed down in the following year, he found himself out of a job. He then went south to Huddersfield, where he was a part-time lecturer at the Hall of Science, while he earned his living as a clerk once again. He was, however, soon persuaded by Robert Owen to come to London, and for the next few years he lectured on freethought and Owenism in both the metropolis and the provinces. In 1852, with G. J. Holyoake, he was a founder of Secularism, which for Cooper at any rate was understood as a revival of Owenism; and he played a large part in the spread of the new movement among his old followers in the North of England. In 1854 he started a monthly periodical, the *London Investigator*, in which he advocated militant freethought. The new journal was established mainly because Cooper, and others, were becoming dissatisfied with Holyoake's *Reasoner*, which, as Cooper wrote, 'had declined in vigour and boldness, its pages being filled with Mr Holyoake's proceedings to the almost entire exclusion of his co-workers'. Cooper edited the *Investigator* for three years; it was then continued for a further year before Charles Bradlaugh took it over, only to suspend publication when he and Joseph Barker began the *National Reformer* in 1860.

Cooper remained faithful to Owenite ideas in the 1850s. He was a founder of the Social Reform League, one of the last Owenite organizations, in 1850, and assisted Robert Owen thereafter as the old man grew feebler. He was present with Owen, for example, at the first conference of the National Association for the Promotion of Social Science, held in Birmingham in 1857, and he read out Owen's last three major public speeches at St Martin's Hall, London, in May 1858. By this time Cooper's own health was deteriorating, and he returned to his native Manchester shortly before Robert Owen's death in November 1858.

The last decade of Cooper's life saw him begin to take an active part, for the first time, as far as his health would allow, in radical politics. In the twelve chapters of his autobiographical sketch published in the *National Reformer* there was no direct mention of political activities until he came, in his narrative, to the concluding chapter, which dealt with the early 1860s. He has an interesting comment in an earlier chapter which illuminates the meaning for him of working-class progress. 'Eighteen hundred and forty-six', he wrote,

witnessed the dissolution of the organisation of English Socialism. This was mainly owing to the failure of the premature experiment at Harmony Hall, Hants. Begun hurriedly, without due preparation, and continued without matured plans and adequate capital, disruption was the necessary result. But though the *organisation* of this memorable movement dissolved, its principles still live. They are silently growing under new auspices, and manifesting new phases. Secular education, free libraries, public recreation grounds, Sunday excursions, public baths and wash-houses, cheap lectures, free museums, restriction of the hours of labour, co-operative stores, social science associations, &c., are some of the many Social innovations directly traceable to an agitation, the initiation of which is due to Robert Owen [*National Reformer*, 5 July 1868].

In the early sixties he became an executive member of the Union and Emancipation Society, whose purpose, in his own words, was 'to protest against the efforts of the English aristocracy and moneyed classes, to force the government to recognize the late Southern Confederacy'. But the most interesting political development of these early years of the sixties was Cooper's involvement in the agitation for the franchise. With his brother, J. R. Cooper, and others, he helped to found The Manchester Working Men's Parliamentary Reform Association. The organisation was similar to one formed

earlier in Leeds [Gillespie (1927) 238 ff.]. Robert Cooper became president of the Manchester Association, his brother, secretary, and their political aims were broadly the achievement of a common platform for both middle and working class on the franchise question. Robert wrote a long and fascinating letter to Joseph Cowen (28 July 1862) urging compromise on the old Chartist demand of nothing short of complete manhood suffrage, in order to accommodate the middle-class reformers. The nub of his argument is quoted below:

Experience has demonstrated that the middle class – whether justly or unjustly is not now the question – exercise, in the present political scale, a determining power in settling national concerns. If they and the aristocracy unite, they beat the people, – if they and the people combine, they defeat the aristocracy, and the *latter* are the natural enemies of popular power. Is it not worthwhile, therefore, to make some sacrifice to secure the help of that class which would give the preponderance in the political scale in favour of popular interest? It may not be that the middle class would go for manhood suffrage – I know they would not *as a class*, but the more advanced portion, if we earnestly sought their support, would go just so far, that a liberal majority would be secured in almost every borough in the kingdom. And would not such a House of Commons be likely at the just favourable opportunity, to grant a *further* extension of the suffrage, until, by degrees, a House of Commons would be returned that would pass a Manhood Suffrage Bill? On the other hand, if we take a position at first so advanced as to repel the Middle Class, we at once strengthened the hands of the common enemy – the aristocracy, who will concede nothing to the people unless sustained by the commercial community.

It was an old debate within the working-class movement. Cooper took a prominent part in reform conferences in Leeds and London, and his Manchester Association was a prime mover in the summoning of a further reform conference in Manchester, in the Free Trade Hall, on 19 and 20 April 1864. This was to be the inaugural meeting of the National Reform Union, whose draft constitution was prepared by Cooper himself. The political basis of the Reform Union was a rating suffrage instead of manhood suffrage. George Wilson, former chairman of the Anti-Corn Law League, became president (proposed by Cooper) and Cooper himself became for a time honorary secretary until a paid agent was employed. In December 1866 he represented the Reform Union at a major demonstration in London in December 1866.

He would, no doubt, have continued to play a part in the franchise movement, but his health broke down. He had been suffering from bronchitis since the mid-1850s and his health seriously worsened in the closing months of 1866. By then he was a poor man, dependent financially upon his two sons. In 1856 his supporters had presented him at Halifax with a testimonial of £345, and in the same year a legacy from a rich friend, Samuel Fletcher, ought to have made him financially independent for the rest of his life. But for various reasons, which he explains at length in his autobiographical sketch [*National Reformer*, 19 and 26 July 1868], there was no money left from the bequest by 1862, and he lived on what he earned until the last two years of his life. He died on 3 May 1868 at his home in Moss Side, Manchester, leaving a wife, whom he had married about 1839, and several children. No will has been located. Robert's autobiographical recollections began to be published in the *National Reformer* on 14 June 1868.

Writings: *A Lecture on Original Sin, delivered in the Social Institution, Great George Street, Salford* (1838) 16 pp.; *A Contrast between the New Moral World and the Old Immoral World: a lecture delivered in the Social Institution, Salford* (1838) 16 pp.; *The Holy Scriptures Analyzed, or Extracts from the Bible, shewing its Contradictions, Absurdities, and Immoralities* (1839) 64 pp.; *Death-Bed Repentance; its fallacy and absurdity when applied as a test of the truth of opinion; with authentic particulars of the last moments of Distinguished Free-Thinkers. A Lecture by Robert Cooper* (1840), fifth ed. with additions (1852), 16 pp.; *Christianity a Failure! A lecture intended to have been delivered in the Golden Lion, Long Room, Sunderland, on Friday Evening, November 19, 1841, but was prevented by the interference of the magistrates of the town* (1841); *Two Lectures on Free Agency versus Orthodoxy* (1845); *The Infidel's Text Book, being the substance of Thirteen Lectures on the Bible* (1846) [revised as *The Bible and Its Evidences; ... inquiry into the Divine Origin of the Old and New Testament* (1858)]; *The Immortality of the Soul, Religiously and Philosophically considered* (1852); *A Popular Development of Atheism; being a reply to Mr Knight's 'Atheism Renounced': a lecture delivered in the Literary Institution, John Street, Fitzroy Square, London* (1853) 16 pp.; *Brewin Grant Refuted. Lectures to the Working Classes on Christianity and Secularism; being a review of the arguments of the Rev. B. Grant and Rev. J. H. Hinton* (1853) 44 pp.; *London Investigator*, edited, 3 vols, monthly, Apr 1854–Mar 1857; *A Reply to Thomas Cooper's Recent Lectures on God and a Future State ... delivered in the Literary Institution, John Street, Fitzroy Square, London, Sunday, March 23, 1856* (1856) 16 pp.

Sources: Cooper's autobiography, written during his last illness in March 1868, was printed in the *National Reformer*, 14 June –26 July 1868. There is also a fragment of autobiography in the *London Investigator*, May 1855. Scattered references appear elsewhere in these periodicals and also in the *New Moral World* (1834–45) and the *Reasoner* (1846–61). Cooper's mature political views are set out in a letter to Joseph Cowen, jr, 28 July 1862. Cowen Papers, C.1738, Newcastle Public Library. See also occasional letters in the Owen and Holyoake Collections, Co-operative Union, Manchester. Brief entries appear in J. M. Wheeler, *A Biographical Dictionary of Freethinkers of all Ages and Nations* (1889) and J. McCabe, *A Biographical Dictionary of Modern Rationalists* (1920). See also: F. E. Gillespie,

Labor and Politics in England, 1850–1867 (Duke Univ. Press, 1927); J. M. Robertson, *A History of Freethought in the Nineteenth Century* (1929); J. Eros, 'The Rise of Organised Freethought in mid-Victorian England', *Sociological Rev.* (July 1954) 98–118; F. B. Smith, 'The Atheist Mission, 1840–1900' in *Ideas and Institutions of Victorian Britain* ed. R. Robson (1967); J. F. C. Harrison, *Robert Owen and the Owenites in Britain and America* (1969); E. Royle, *Radical Politics, 1790–1900, Religion and Unbelief* (1971).

EDWARD ROYLE
JOHN SAVILLE

See also: †George Jacob HOLYOAKE; *Robert OWEN.

COULTHARD, Samuel (1853–1931)
MINER AND TRADE UNIONIST

Born on 8 August 1853 at Coxhoe, County Durham, the son of George Coulthard, a miner who went as overman at Seghill Colliery, Northumberland, in 1864. Samuel began work in the mines at the age of ten and most of his education was obtained at evening classes. He went through all the grades of colliery work and rose to be deputy overman at Seghill, a position he occupied for many years. He was active in the Northumberland Deputy Overman's Association holding a number of part-time positions, and in 1907 he was elected full-time secretary, retaining the office until March 1931, a few months before his death.

In his early years he was a well-known Radical, was associated with the co-operative movement and also with the Oddfellows and the Independent Order of Good Templars. Both in Seghill and in Newcastle (where he moved on being appointed a full-time official) he was active in the United Methodist Connexion, and he served as Sunday school teacher and lay preacher for over half a century. He was also an assiduous Sunday hospital visitor at the Royal Victoria Infirmary in Newcastle, and for many years was a member of its house committee. He was elected a member of the first committee of the Northumberland Aged Miners' Homes Association in May 1900, and in August 1930 he became its chairman; he held this office until his death the following year.

He married Mary Ann Taylor, the daughter of a miner, in 1875; and he died on 13 May 1931, leaving his widow, two sons and three daughters. One son had become a United Methodist minister, the other a teacher. Following a service in Sandyford U. M. Church he was buried in St Andrew's Cemetery. He left effects valued at £671.

Sources: *The Northumberland Aged Mineworkers' Homes Association Jubilee Souvenir 1900–1950* (Newcastle, [1950]); R. F. Wearmouth, *The Social and Political Influence of Methodism in the Twentieth Century* (1957); OBIT. *Newcastle J.* 14 May 1931; NMA, *Monthly Circular* (1931).

ANTHONY MASON

See also: John BATEY; Harry HUTCHINGS; George Edward MIDDLETON; William WEIR.

CROOKS, William (1852–1921)
LABOUR MP

Will Crooks was born on 6 April 1852 at Shirbutt Street, Poplar, the third of seven children of a ship's stoker. His early years were spent in deep poverty, especially after his father lost an arm at work and was reduced to odd jobs, such as that of a watchman. His mother tried to raise the family's income by taking in sewing, a poorly-paid and sweated form of labour, while at the age of eight Will began to earn sixpence a week as a milkman's boy. In one period when the Crooks family was unable to maintain itself, the mother asked for parish relief but after allowing bread and a small amount of money for a time the Guardians decided against further outdoor relief and offered the workhouse. This led to a period in which Will was separated from his family, and although Mrs Crooks was soon able to earn enough to reunite them, his experience of the harsh conditions of workhouse life made a lasting mark on his character. His mother had had to move to a cheaper room in Poplar High Street, and as this was next to the workhouse casual ward, Will was still familiar with the lot of the pauper. On one occasion, in the winter of 1866, he witnessed a bread riot by the poor who attacked the baker's waggon at the workhouse gates. In later life Crooks paid tribute to the exceptional character of his mother who struggled to raise her family decently. She insisted that Will should attend the local Congregational Sunday school, and a day school where the fees were one penny per week. Later, at some sacrifice to the family income, she had Will apprenticed to a cooper. For a time he had worked as a grocer's errand boy, for two shillings a week, and at eleven he became a blacksmith's labourer. Although by the time he was fourteen this latter job was bringing in six shillings, Mrs Crooks wanted her son to have a trade, and it was decided that he should work in a cooper's yard although the weekly wage was only half a crown.

In December 1871 Crooks married Matilda South, the daughter of a shipwright, and with the full wages of a journeyman cooper his fortunes seemed to be improving. As an apprentice he had discussed political and social questions with a fellow workman of advanced vews, and had conceived a great admiration for John Bright. When the men in his yard had a dispute over inferior materials and excessive overtime Crooks was their natural spokesman. This led to victimisation. He was dismissed from his job and the word was put around that he was an agitator, which meant that no other employer would take him on. There then followed a period 'on the tramp', that is, walking the country in search of work and supported by small sums from fellow-craftsmen in the towns where no job was available. At Liverpool Crooks was able to get work, and he sent for his wife to join him with their child, a daughter. This was in 1876. But soon after, the child died, and with his wife also ill he decided to return with her to London. After another spell of unemployment he tramped to Liverpool again, where occasional jobs came his way, before he resolved to find work back in London. Going outside his own trade, he became a casual labourer on the docks, where he saw

at first hand the daily struggle of men to obtain work, and its demoralising effects. By a fortunate chance he again obtained work as a cooper, and with the reassurance that regular employment gave, was able to take an active interest in the affairs of the labour movement.

In the 1880s Crooks gradually became well known in the East of London. He was an eloquent speaker, who, with a homely turn of phrase and an anecdote from everyday life, was able to win the sympathy of his audience. In his speeches he always emphasised that he too was a working man and that this was a source of pride. Crooks spoke regularly at Sunday morning meetings outside the East India Dock gates, touching on social questions as well as the day-to-day problems of the London working class. A teetotaller and non-smoker, he could reproach his listeners for their drinking habits without incurring the hostility or indifference aroused by many temperance speakers. At these meetings, which became known as 'Crooks's College', a number of campaigns were originated, including those for a free public library, a footway tunnel under the Thames, and the operation of the Poor Law on more humane principles. When the dock strike of 1889 broke out, Crooks helped to lead it, although during the day he was working at his own trade. The strain occasioned by these efforts led after the strike was over to a serious illness, during which he spent three months in hospital.

After his recovery he resumed employment and an active part in public life. He joined the Fabian Society in January 1891, and although not typical of the Society's middle-class and intellectually-disposed membership, he did share its gradualist approach to social and political reform. One outcome of 'Crooks's College' was the formation of the Poplar Labour Electoral Committee, which later became known as the Poplar Labour League. The League included representatives of the London Trades Council and a number of trade unions, including Crooks's own union, the coopers, as well as the dockers, gasworkers, plumbers and engine drivers, and it was committed to the policy of labour representation. Towards this end members of the League established a Will Crooks Wages Fund early in the 1890s which made it possible for Crooks to give up his job and devote all his energies to public work. At first he was paid £3 a week, later £3 10s and then £4. In addition to the subscriptions paid by several trade unions, a number of individual admirers assisted Crooks, including both Liberal and Conservative MPs. The Fund was his only source of income, but offers of better-paid posts he refused, as he believed he could do more good in public work.

In one of its first efforts the League met with success when Crooks was elected to the London County Council in 1892. While his election address stressed his desire to represent the working class, he stood jointly with Sir John MacDougall, a Progressive, against two Moderate candidates. The Progressive Party at this time, though broadly Liberal, drew support from many sources, and not until after 1906 was it generally identified with the Liberal Party [Ensor (1936) 296]. On the Council Crooks joined the small group of about a dozen Labour members and was active in pressing for the sort of reforms that had been debated at 'Crooks's College'. He sat as a member of the LCC until 1910, and though working closely with the Progressives, he turned down their suggestion that he should become the Council's vice-chairman. In 1901, a Coronation year, Crooks was proud to be elected as mayor of Poplar. He was London's first Labour mayor, and his success in filling the office was generally acknowledged.

A few months after his election to the LCC he was elected to the Poplar Board of Guardians, and began to campaign for improved workhouse conditions. George Lansbury, too, had become a Guardian in 1892, and he and Crooks were associated with the policy that became known as 'Poplarism', in which an attempt was made to operate the poor law on a more humane basis, with an emphasis upon rehabilitation. Critics of this policy contended that the abandonment of the old principle of deterrence would encourage pauperism, and matters came to a head in 1906 when the Local

Government Board ordered an inquiry into the administration of the Poplar Union. There were some grounds for disquiet, and Beatrice Webb, herself an opponent of the existing Poor Law, was unhappy with the management of the Poplar Board of Guardians. On 19 March 1906 she attended a meeting at which the Guardians allotted contracts for the year. 'The procedure', she wrote,

was utterly reckless. The tenders were opened at the meeting, the names and prices read out; and then, without any kind of report of a committee or by officials, straight away voted on. Usually the same person as heretofore was taken, nearly always a local man – it was not always the lowest tender, and the prices were, in all cases, full, in some cases obviously excessive . . . 'Give Bow a chance' was one of the relevant considerations urged successfully in favour of a change in the contractor. Will Crooks sat in the chair and did nothing to check the recklessness. Even Lansbury, by constitution a thorough-going sentimentalist, and with no other experience of public affairs, protested, and was clearly ashamed of the procedure [B. Webb (1948) 337].

Allegations were also made that the workhouse had been dishonestly managed and James Davy, the Local Government Board chief inspector, made a determined attempt to bring to light evidence of corruption as well as to show the mistaken nature of the Guardians' policy. Crooks, who had been chairman of the Board of Guardians since 1897, and Lansbury appeared before the inquiry, and although both were subjected to a searching examination, they were exonerated of any dishonesty by Davy's report, which only found evidence of minor irregularities by some of the workhouse officials. Despite this, sections of the press had during the course of the inquiry made great issue of the abuses alleged to have been common in Poplar, and this harmed the efforts of Poor Law reformers in other London boroughs. But in Poplar Crooks and Lansbury, who refused to be deflected from their policy of reform, held a number of public meetings to state their case. In the borough and council elections that followed, Poplar was notable for the support given to Progressive and Labour candidates against the trend in other parts of London. Nevertheless, Crooks decided to resign as chairman of the Guardians, as he felt he could no longer give sufficient time to the office.

Crooks's duties as an MP had been partly responsible for his failure to keep in close contact with the Poplar Union. As an LRC candidate he had been elected to the Commons in March 1903 in a by-election at Woolwich, a constituency on the south bank of the Thames some two miles below Poplar. Just as he had been happy to work with Liberals in his election to the LCC, so in this campaign Crooks welcomed assistance from local Liberals and the support of the *Daily News*, which opened an election fund. His candidature was also backed by the local branch of the National Democratic League. After a soundly-organised and well-financed campaign, he was returned with a majority of over 3000 in a straight fight with a Conservative. The seat had previously been Conservative-held, but, although it gave a considerable fillip to the cause of Labour representation, Crook's victory did not win the unqualified approval of Socialists, who contended that he had been too closely identified with the Liberals, in terms of both the help he received and the platform upon which the election was fought. Nor did he, in many respects, reflect the vigour of the labour movement in Woolwich [Thompson (1967) 255].

In the Commons he proved to be a conscientious MP, and was especially active in raising the unemployment question, but he dismayed Keir Hardie by the sympathy he evinced for Liberalism. He had made the free trade issue the dominant feature of his election campaign and the reforms he supported were those of radical Liberals rather than advanced Socialists. The views he expressed were those he had arrived at during his association with London Progressivism, and the newer ideas of Socialism and independent Labour representation made little impact upon him. In the Norwich by-election of January 1904 Crooks refused to speak on

behalf of G. H. Roberts of the ILP. Like Richard Bell, he argued that rather than split the Progressive vote, the Liberal candidate, Louis Tillett, should be supported. In Parliament he attacked destitution and advocated old age pensions, but his efforts to relieve unemployment were perhaps his main contribution in those years. He was a firm supporter of the 1905 Unemployed Workmen Bill, which some trade unionists disliked, and carried the campaign outside the Commons in November 1905 when he and Lansbury helped to lead a demonstration of six thousand women who marched to the offices of the Local Government Board in Whitehall to petition Balfour for relief measures.

Crooks was returned for Woolwich at the general election of 1906 with a comfortable majority; his platform had included the issues of free trade and Chinese Labour. He remained a member of the Fabian Society, and received some financial support from its parliamentary fund until the payment of MPs in 1911 [Cole (1961) 130]. In the general election held in January 1910 he lost his seat, regaining it narrowly in December of that year. But his best days had passed before he entered the Commons. He suffered a long illness in 1904, having overworked himself in campaigning on behalf of the unemployed. His poor state of health was the reason for a voyage to Canada, Australia and New Zealand; and his inability to return to Woolwich until the eve of the poll in January 1910 probably contributed to his defeat. With some other Labour MPs, as well as a number of Liberals and Conservatives, he supported the Labour Disputes Bill of 1911 which was designed to curtail strikes. The Bill was unpopular with many sections of the labour movement and its sponsors were subjected to a good deal of criticism.

With the outbreak of war Crooks entered upon a new phase of activity. At the beginning of the century he had been known as a 'pro-Boer' and an outspoken opponent of the South African War; he had then tried to bring out the Fabian Society against the war. But in 1914 he had no doubt about the righteousness of the war against Germany. He took a firmly patriotic line, creating parliamentary history by leading the Commons in the singing of the national anthem in September 1914. During the first fifteen months of hostilities he travelled over 50,000 miles as a pro-war speaker and often addressed some thirty meetings in a week. He produced a pamphlet, written in his simple style, *The British Workman Defends His Home*, which justified the war effort; it was translated into French and Italian. Crooks also became associated with the British Workers' National League, and was a signatory to its manifesto [*Times*, 2 May 1916]. On 1 January 1916 he was created a Privy Councillor.

Later that year Crooks had to undergo an operation, and during his illness he was visited in hospital by King George V. In June 1917 his health suffered a further deterioration when he witnessed the aftermath of the bombing of a school in Poplar. After this time he could no longer deliver lectures or speeches, and he never really recovered from the shock. He continued to sit as an MP, being unopposed in the 1918 general election, and appeared for the last time, almost blind and deaf, during the 1920 session of Parliament. In February 1921 he resigned his seat. Ramsay MacDonald contested Woolwich in the by-election held in March, but was defeated by the Coalition Conservative.

Many of the reformist traditions of the British labour movement are exemplified by Crooks's career. He had little interest in the theoretical basis of Socialism, and it was from a religious humanitarianism that he derived most of his ideals. If ideological problems arose, such as the question of working with other political groups, his response was calmly to ignore them and to act in the way he believed to be the most sensible. Though he had witnessed deep poverty and had been put out of work because of his opinions, he did not advocate the overthrow of society as a means of changing it. A monarchist and respecter of the constitution, he believed that conditions could be improved through established procedures. In religion a Congregationalist, he was also an advocate of temperance and a strong opponent of gambling. Among the

books that had influenced him he mentioned the Bible, *Pilgrim's Progress*, Charles Kingsley's *Alton Locke* and Ruskin's *Unto This Last* – a selection of reading matter common to several Labour MPs in the 1906 Parliament [*Review of Reviews* (1906) 572–573]. Born and raised in the working class, he spoke their language and could judge exactly how to address an East End audience on the virtues of self-improvement. His figure with its burly frame and full beard was familiar and was greeted with affection in Poplar, where he lived in a small terraced house until the end of his life. He was also popular with individuals from other social classes, and had an ingenuous pride in the friendships he had formed with the famous. These influences helped, perhaps, to mellow Crooks's views, although there was no suggestion that his financial affairs were conducted, as he always insisted, with anything but absolute probity. He was open about the sources of his modest income, never being a person of wealth – in his will he left only £1863 gross. Shortly before his death a Will Crooks Testimonial Fund was established; Asquith and Balfour acted as patrons, and subscriptions to the value of about £3000 were received, but too late for Crooks to derive any benefit from it.

Crooks died in Poplar Infirmary on 5 June 1921. The death of his first wife, who bore him two sons and five daughters, had occurred in 1892. He married Elizabeth Lake, a nurse, in 1893 and she, and six of his children survived him. Large numbers attended his funeral on 9 June, when after a service at All Saints Church he was buried in Tower Hamlets Cemetery, Bow. In his address, the Bishop of Stepney (Henry Mosley) recalled that exactly twenty years earlier he had first met Crooks who told him: 'I am Mayor of Poplar; you have just been made Rector; we must shake hands, for both of us alike are servants of the people.'

Writings: *Dividend; what it is, and how it is made* ... (Manchester, 1885) 4 pp.; *Education in Connection with Co-operation: a paper read at the Congress held at Oldham, Whitsuntide, 1885* (Manchester, [1885]) 7 pp.; (with others) *Addresses delivered at the*

Twenty-sixth Annual Co-operative Congress, held at Sunderland . . . 1894 (Manchester, [1894]) 29 pp.; 'Cask-Making' in *Workers on their Industries*, ed. F. W. Galton (1896) 115–26; *Poor Law and Pensions . . .* (1901) 12 pp.; *Percy Alden . . . ; his public & civic life*, with an Introduction by Will Reason [1903] [14 pp.]; 'The Prospects and Programme of the Labour Party' *Nat. Rev. 46* (Dec 1905) 621–32; *An Address on the Unemployed Problem . . .* (Political Committee of the National Liberal Club [1905]) 14 pp.; *Working Men and Gambling* (Social Tracts for the Times, no. 1 [1906]) 15 pp.; (with others) *Social Ideals* (n.d. [1909?]); 'Piety at Home', in *Labour and Religion*, ed. W. A. Hammond (1910); *A Living Wage for All* [1911?] 11 pp.; (with others) *The Gospel of Labour* (1912); *The British Workman Defends His Home* (1917) 12 pp.; Evidence before the S.C. of the House of Lords on the Infant Life Protection Bill, 1896 X Qs 1319–416; Departmental Committee of the Local Government Board on Poor Law Schools 1896 XLIII Qs 12409–642; Departmental Committee on Vagrancy 1906 CIII Qs 5324–503; Inquiry into the Poplar Union Cd 3274 (1906) 316–72.

Sources: 'How I got on, no. 5: Mr Will Crooks, M.P.', *Pearson's Weekly*, 22 Feb 1906; W. T. Stead, 'The Labour Party and the Books that helped to make it', *Review of Reviews 33* (June 1906) 572–3; G. Haw, *From Workhouse to Westminster: the life story of Will Crooks, M.P.* (1908); *DNB* (1912–1921) by G. D. H. C.[ole]; G. Lansbury, *My Life* (1928); R. C. K. Ensor, *England 1870–1914* (Oxford, 1936); E. M. Hayes, *Up from an Orange Box* (1947); B. Webb, *Our Partnership* (1948); R. Postgate, *The Life of George Lansbury* (1951); F. Bealey and H. Pelling, *Labour and Politics 1900–1906* (1958); P. P. Poirier, *The Advent of the Labour Party* (1958); Margaret Cole, *The Story of Fabian Socialism* (1961); A. M. McBriar, *Fabian Socialism and English Politics 1884–1918* (Cambridge, 1962); H. A. Clegg et al., *A History of British Trade Unions since 1889* vol 1: *1889–1910* (Oxford, 1964); P. Thompson, *Socialists, Liberals and Labour: the struggle for London 1885–1914*

(1967); R. Douglas, 'The National Democratic League and the British Workers' League', *Hist. J. 15*, no. 3 (1972) 533–52; J. O. Stubbs, 'Lord Milner and Patriotic Labour, 1914–1918', *Engl. Hist. Rev. 87*, no. 345 (Oct 1972) 717–54. OBIT. *Daily Chronicle, Evening News, Star* and *Times*, 6 June 1921; *Daily Herald*, 6, 7 and 10 June 1921; *East End News*, 7 and 11 June 1921; *Walthamstow Guardian*, 10 June 1921; *East London Observer*, 11 June 1921; *Reynolds's Newspaper*, 12 June 1921 [by C. W. Bowerman]; *Labour Party Report* (1921).

DAVID E. MARTIN

See also: George LANSBURY, for British Labour Party, 1900–13.

DEAKIN, Arthur (1890–1955)
TRADE UNION LEADER

Arthur Deakin was born on 11 November 1890 at Sutton Coldfield, Warwickshire, the son of Annie Deakin, a domestic servant. The copy of his birth certificate lodged at Somerset House does not state his father's name, and there are still one or two matters about Deakin's youth that remain obscure. V. L. Allen, who made a close study of Deakin's career, writes that he was the son of a cobbler and that it was in the atmosphere of a cobbler's shop that he spent the first ten years of his life [Allen (1957) 3]. At the age of thirteen Deakin left school and was employed as a butcher's assistant for two years until he moved to South Wales with his mother, who then remarried. Another version suggests that Deakin's father died when Deakin was ten years old and that his mother, marrying again, took him in 1901 to Merthyr Tydfil. What is certain is that Mrs Deakin was on very friendly terms with the family of Arthur Horner's sister's husband. The family, Joe and Mrs Harding, lived at Dowlais, and Mrs Deakin – with presumably young Arthur – used to visit the Hardings regularly. This explains the reference to Arthur Deakin in Horner's autobiography, *Incorrigible Rebel* (1960) 183–4, although Horner was incorrect in describing Deakin as an orphan boy. In South Wales Deakin obtained his first job as a labourer in the Dowlais works of Guest, Keen and Nettlefold, where he worked long hours for a wage of four shillings a week. Becoming friendly with a manager at the works, he was trained in roll-turning, and when this manager moved to a steel works at Blaenavon, Deakin went with him, staying until the manager died. During this period he began attending the Primitive Methodist Chapel and became a teetotaller.

In 1910 he moved to Shotton in North Wales and secured a job as a roll-turner at the works of John Summers and Sons Ltd. It was here that he met Jack George, an active trade unionist. Deakin had earlier belonged to the National Union of Gas Workers and General Labourers, and had heard the MP for Merthyr, Keir Hardie, and other Labour speakers at factory-gate meetings. Against this background he formulated his ideas and in addition to the instruction of political meetings, he supplemented his elementary education by reading and study at night school, but it was not until he met George that he took his first steps on the ladder of trade union officialdom. In 1914 he married George's sister, Annie.

For a short time after arriving in Shotton Deakin belonged to the Amalgamated Society of Engineers as well as the British Roll Turners' Trade Society. He transferred from the ASE to the Dock, Wharf, Riverside and General Workers' Union in 1911, though he kept up his membership of the BRTTS, for which he was acting general secretary during part of 1919; but he left the Society in that same year. During the First World War Deakin was an active lay member of the Dock, Wharf, Riverside and General Workers' Union, and he was appointed as a full-time organiser in 1919. When in 1922 the Dockers' Union became part of the TGWU, he became assistant district secretary for the North Wales area of the new union, and held the post for ten years. He was based on Shotton, and it was in this period that he also became active in local government. In 1919 he was elected an alderman of the Flintshire County Council; six years later he was elected county councillor for the Shotton (West Saltney) division. He was appointed vice-chairman of the

County Council in 1930 and chairman in March 1932. He had become a JP for Flintshire in October 1923.

In June 1932 he moved to London as national secretary of the General Workers' trade group of the TGWU. Deakin's great administrative ability and the patience and skill which he employed as a negotiator were noted by Ernest Bevin, the general secretary and father figure of the union. In 1935 Deakin became the union's assistant general secretary and developed a close working relationship and friendship with Bevin. Bevin and Walter Citrine dominated the TUC during the 1930s and their support was always thrown against the Left, whether industrial or political, and behind the orthodox Labour leadership. In their own union, Bevin and Deakin fought a vigorous and successful fight against the Communists and their allies. The most notable battleground was in the London busmen's section of the union, where from 1932 the Rank and File movement had maintained attacks on official union policy and had in effect become an organisation within the TGWU, with its own constitution, elected officers, committee and journal, the *Busmen's Punch*. It had wide support from London busmen, and its activities culminated in the 'Coronation Strike' which lasted from 1 to 26 May 1937. Although Bevin was aware that the Central London Area Bus Committee was controlled by Communists and Communist sympathisers, he allowed the General Executive Council of his union to give it plenary powers to withdraw labour. It has been argued that the union leadership allowed the Central Bus Committee to take over the strike in order to reveal its true position; but in any case on 26 May the executive reasserted its authority by withdrawing plenary powers and instructing Bevin to enter into negotiations with the London Passenger Transport Board.

Subsequently the union's delegate conference declared that an end had to be put to Rank and File and similar organisations within the union, and a number of busmen's leaders were expelled or suspended from holding office. A breakaway union was then formed, with some assistance from W. J.

Brown of the Civil Service Union, who believed the busmen had a good case and blamed the leaders of the TGWU for the outcome of an 'appallingly badly handled' strike [Brown (1943) 199]. This new organisation, the National Passenger Workers' Union was, however, non-Communist. The Communist attempt to control certain sections of the TGWU had been blocked, and no doubt Bevin's forceful methods in dealing with the CP provided Deakin with an object lesson which would be borne in mind when he took charge of the union. Deakin himself was secretary of the committee – made up of eight members of the Executive – which was appointed to inquire into the conduct of the members of the Central Bus Section. The committee produced a unanimous report and Deakin presented it at the Biennial Delegate Conference at Torquay in July 1937. The report recommended that the busmen's Rank and File movement should be declared a subversive organisation, and that three members (A. F. Papworth, W. Payne and J. W. (Bill) Jones) should be expelled from the union, and that four others be debarred from holding office for varying periods [Bullock (1960) 613]. The committee's report was accepted by 291 votes to 51.

On the question of rearmament in the 1930s, Deakin argued that as the trade union movement had accepted the principle of rearmament, it must co-operate in ensuring that production went on. This was the argument employed by him before the 1938 Congress at Blackpool, but at the same time he insisted that it was an industrial question; political aspects such as the attempt to link rearmament with the Spanish Civil War, must, he insisted, be left to the political wing of the movement.

Bevin joined the Coalition Government in May 1940 as Minister of Labour and National Service, although Deakin had advised him to demand a higher position, one of at least the same standing as the posts filled by Morrison and Dalton [Bullock (1960) 652]. This appointment led to Deakin's becoming acting general secretary of the TGWU and his election to the General Council of the TUC.

Because of the close relationship Bevin had established with Deakin he was still able to exercise an influence within the union while he was a member of the Government, although there is no evidence that he directly interfered in its affairs. By this time Deakin's attitudes were similar to Bevin's and were to remain so; Deakin endeavoured to follow his master's footsteps, and appropriately, on Bevin's death in 1951, acted as his executor.

During the war Deakin sat as a member of the War Transport Council and the Committee to advise the Government Production Executive, but while supporting the war effort, he would not neglect what he considered to be the interests of his union. In matters relating to inter-union demarcation he was especially insistent. He intensified a dispute with the Chemical Workers' Union to the extent of excluding them from the National Joint Industrial Council; and he resisted NUPE's attempts to join the Midland JICs until at the Trade Union Congress of 1942 Bryn Roberts, general secretary of NUPE, successfully applied pressure in order to secure his union's representation. On the ground that they would be taken into consideration during wage negotiations, Deakin opposed family allowances, and he also spoke against wartime attempts to secure nationalisation or workers' control or participation in the engineering and mining industries, arguing that private enterprise had proved highly successful. However, at the 1942 Labour Party Conference he moved a resolution urging the co-ordination of all forms of transport during the war and full public ownership after the restoration of peacetime conditions.

His opinions on the war effort were often contentious. He was hostile to the demand that a second front should be opened in Europe to divert German pressure from the Russian front: the question was one that should be left in the hands of the Government, he told delegates at the 1942 congress of the TUC. In the following year while attending the conference of the Swedish Transport Workers' Union, he discussed with the Finnish representative, M. Vuori, the possibility that Finland might make a separate peace with the Allies. When criticised for this conduct on the ground that peace initiatives should be left to the Government and not attempted by private individuals, Deakin replied that there was nothing unreasonable in trade unionists discussing together matters of common concern.

When in 1945 Bevin became Foreign Secretary in the Labour Government, Deakin continued as acting general secretary of the TGWU. Later that year Deakin had a substantial majority over his five rivals for the general secretaryship of the union, and he officially replaced Bevin on the latter's retirement in March 1946. An unusual note of disagreement had been struck between the two men when Deakin had been rebuked by Bevin for his suggestion that, rather than be content with the Foreign Office, Bevin should challenge Attlee for the party leadership. According to Hugh Dalton, Deakin had been incited to approach Bevin by Harold Laski, who was canvassing for Bevin as Prime Minister, with Herbert Morrison as his deputy [Dalton (1957) 467].

In the TUC, Deakin, Lawther, Williamson and Sir Lincoln Edwards took effective control. Deakin, the dominant personality, was the ruler of the TUC, and, as Francis Williams has said, exercised on the General Council an influence in many ways greater than Bevin's – perhaps because he had no Citrine to match him. Believing that the Labour Party was but the political wing of the trade union movement, Deakin intervened continually as would-be king-maker and keeper of its conscience, while denying the right of politicians to intervene in industrial issues. Openly contemptuous of politicians, he declared on several occasions that nothing would induce him to go to 'that place'—the House of Commons. He continued, however, to give his loyalty and respect to Bevin, which meant that the Labour Government of which Bevin was a member received Deakin's full support. An early instance of this occurred in the dock strike of autumn 1945, when Deakin accused the Trotskyists of the Revolutionary Communist Party of fomenting and spreading the strike amongst the dock workers.

In 1946 Deakin succeeded Lord Citrine as president of the World Federation of Trade Unions and was soon in conflict with Communist elements that opposed Marshall Aid. At Paris in 1948 he denounced the WFTU as an instrument for the furtherance of Soviet policy and led the British, Dutch and American delegates from the meeting hall. Deakin then played a leading part in the foundation of the International Confederation of Free Trade Unions with a view to furthering the European Recovery Programme (Marshall Aid).

In regard to wages Deakin initially held that restraint would be unnecessary if there were price controls in the post-war period. But frequent visits to Europe during 1946 and 1947 created a fear of inflation, and in 1948 he was converted to belief in the necessity of wage restraint, a view he held until his death, despite the steady increase in prices and the wage claims of smaller unions—forces that tended to weaken the position of the General Council. Deakin believed that the administration of wage restraint was the responsibility of the unions and not of the Government. He continued to preach wage restraint after the establishment of the Conservative Government in 1951, and had a friendly working relationship with Sir Walter Monckton who became Churchill's Minister of Labour [Allen (1957) 150]. Except in his opposition to the denationalisation of road haulage, his tone towards the Government was conciliatory, partly because he believed it improper to oppose politically a government that had been democratically elected.

However, Deakin's hostility towards Communist trade unionists was implacable: in 1949 he had helped promote the TUC's anti-Communist policy statement *Defend Democracy*, and in the same year his own union proscribed Communists from office. Deakin fought the Labour Left and the Communists with great relish: Francis Williams described him on the platform as 'square, solid, short legs pugnaciously astride, often red in the face with passion' as he denounced opponents [*New Statesman*, 7 May 1955]. At the 1954 Trade Union Congress, for example, he castigated Communists as 'college rabbits suffering from myxomatosis who blindly stagger from one indiscretion to another'; and as a fraternal delegate to the 1952 Labour Party Conference he told the Bevanites 'to abandon their vituperation and carping criticism which appears regularly in the *Tribune*'. Although Deakin was opposed to any legislative action against Communists, it is probable that because he encouraged his union and others to exclude them from office, there was less industrial unrest than might otherwise have been expected in a period of austerity and inflation.

Deakin believed that the role of the trade unions was to work within the economic system, not to replace it, a belief which he demonstrated at the Labour Party Conference of 1953 when, despite his membership of the General Council, he opposed the TUC-approved 'Plan for Engineering'. This advocated the nationalisation of parts of the engineering industry and, amid uproar, Deakin described it as 'a mumbo-jumbo of meaningless words and phrases ... the worst abortion ever conceived in the mind of man'. Private enterprise in engineering, he went on to argue, was efficient and had done 'a fine job of work'.

In the affairs of the Labour Party Deakin supported Morrison against Greenwood for the post of treasurer in 1953 until he realised that Greenwood's sympathy vote would defeat Morrison. In 1954 he dropped his support for Morrison, agreeing with Lawther that Gaitskell was the best anti-Bevanite candidate. On the controversial issue of German rearmament he supported the orthodox members of the Labour Party against the large minority who opposed it. After the Commons 'H-bomb' debate of 1955, Deakin unsuccessfully canvassed the NEC of the Labour Party for Aneurin Bevan's expulsion. In the same year, the TGWU was able to give increased support to the Executive against the Bevanites by the device of retroactively paying higher affiliation fees – 1954 affiliation fees were paid in 1955 – thus giving Deakin a bigger block vote at the 1955 Labour Party Conference.

In 1951–2 Deakin was president of the TUC. He was awarded the CBE in 1943, became a Companion of Honour in 1949 and was created a member of the Privy Council – an unusual honour – in 1954; but he twice refused a knighthood. He sat on a number of public bodies during his career, including the Institute of Transport; the European Recovery Plan Trade Union Advisory Committee; the advisory committees of the Ministries of Reconstruction and Production; the advisory panel, Ministry of Materials; National Advisory Council, Ministry of Labour and the British Transport Joint Consultative Council; and he was a member of the executive council for a National Memorial for King George VI. He was a director of the *Daily Herald*.

Deakin collapsed and died of coronary thrombosis on May Day 1955, while addressing a rally at the Corn Exchange, Leicester. His speech dealt with the recent settlement reached by ASLEF which prevented a threatened railway strike. Deakin was due to retire in October 1955, and although he had been in poor health for a number of years, he let it be known that he was not looking forward to retirement.

For many years the most powerful and best-known trade union leader in Britain, Deakin was dedicated to his work. His supporters believed that by working with governments and opposing the left-wing of the labour movement, Deakin was pursuing a policy of political responsibility. Those subjected to his attacks sometimes suggested that he was used by other right-wing politicians and trade unionists for their own ends; Arthur Horner, for example, expressed his opinion that Deakin did not realise 'what it was all about'. Horner had known Deakin since childhood, and despite Horner's Communism, they remained close friends. It was generally agreed that however ruthless Deakin may have been in public, in private his manner was friendly and genial. Deakin was once described as having a majority mind, and his approach to problems was not that of an intellectual; although, while delighting in the exercise of authority, he could be skilful in negotiation and conciliation. Critics also accused him of being out of touch with the union membership. Certainly all the major disputes which took place during his period as general secretary were unofficial and opposed by him, and this was largely the result of his belief in the absolute sanctity of agreements and procedure and in the righteousness of the union's position. Dissidents, in Deakin's eyes, were subversive trouble-makers or were ignorant of the complexities of trade union organisation. Disputes involving London busmen in the late 1940s and the dockers in 1952 showed that he was prepared to back his beliefs even at the cost of losing members. His belief in wage restraint extended to his own union; TGWU officials were not well paid, despite the problems presented by a steadily growing membership, and Deakin refused to accept increases in his own salary. Financial rewards were of secondary importance to him in his work, as is indicated by the relatively modest size of the estate which he left – £8382 (gross). His succesor as general secretary of the TGWU was Arthur Tiffin, who in turn was succeeded by Frank Cousins.

Deakin was survived by his wife (who died in 1970) and their two sons, Arthur, who was born in 1918 and became an executive with a publishing corporation, and Aubrey, born in 1915, who became a schoolteacher. Arthur Deakin's funeral took place on 5 May at Golders Green crematorium; the Rev. Dr Leslie Weatherhead officiated and Sir Vincent Tewson gave an address. Mr and Mrs Attlee were among the mourners. A memorial service was held at St Martin-in-the-Fields on 16 May.

Writings: the Union journal, *TGWU Record*, was the main vehicle for Deakin's views; he also wrote: 'Critics are Wrong on Five Counts', *Labour*, 11 (Sep 1948) 11–13; 'The International Trade Union Movement', *International Affairs*, 26 (April 1950) 167–171; foreword to C. H. Sharpley, *The Great Delusion: the autobiography of an ex-Communist leader* (1952) and to J. Goldstein, *The Government of British Trade Unions* (1952).

Sources: TUC and Labour Party conference reports; A. Hutt, *The Post-War History of the British Working Class* (1937); W. J. Brown, *So Far . . .* , (1943); G. D. H. Cole, *A History of the Labour Party from 1914* (1948); H. A. Clegg, *Labour Relations in London Transport* (Oxford, 1950); *DNB*

(1951–60) [by V. L. Allen]; *WWW* (1951–1960); W. W. Craik, *Bryn Roberts and the National Union of Public Employees* (1955); V. L. Allen, *Trade Union Leadership: based on a study of Arthur Deakin* (1957) does not claim to be a biography but discusses Deakin's career sympathetically and in some detail; H. Dalton, *The Fateful Years: memoirs 1934–1945* (1957); L. Hunter, *The Road to Brighton Pier* (1959); V. L. Allen, *Trade Unions and the Labour Party since 1945* (1960); A. Bullock, *Life and Times of Ernest Bevin*, vol. 1: *1881–1940* (1960); A. Horner, *Incorrigible Rebel* (1960); B. Roberts, *The Price of TUC Leadership* (1961); M. Foot, *Aneurin Bevan*, vol. 1: *1897–1945* (1962); E. Shinwell, *The Labour Story* (1963); H. Pelling, *A Short History of British Trade Unionism* (1963); P. Duff, *Left, Left, Left: a personal account of six protest campaigns 1945–65* (1971); personal information: Arthur Deakin, London, son, Tom Jones, Sholton. OBIT. *Leicester Evening Mail* and *Times*, 2 May 1955; *Spectator*, 6 May 1955; *New Statesman*, 7 May 1955 [by Francis Williams]; *TGWU Record* (June 1955).

DAVID E. MARTIN
BRYAN SADLER

See also: *Ernest BEVIN; *Clement Richard ATTLEE, for British Labour Party, 1931–51.

DEAN, Frederick James (1868–1941)
MINERS' AGENT

Frederick Dean was born on 5 November 1868 at Walsall, the second son of Benjamin Dean and his wife Mary Ann (née Cousins). At the time of Frederick's birth his father was a working miner and followed this occupation until 1887, when he established the Pelsall Miners' Association and became its first agent. His organising ability and flair for public speaking, combined with his personal integrity, quickly won him a considerable local reputation, and he later became a national figure as one of the early leaders of the MFGB [*DLB 1* (1972) 100–1].

Frederick was educated at the Butts School, Walsall and then served an apprenticeship as a horse-collar maker in the town, which was then a main centre of the leather trade. On completing his apprenticeship he left Walsall to follow his trade in Manchester, where he met and married Mary Emma Senior. Their two daughters were born in Manchester, but by 1900 Dean and his young family had returned to live in Rushall, near Walsall, and his son Benjamin, named after his grandfather, was born there in May of that year. He now became an active member of Rushall Congregational Church, being a chorister for many years. Dean's return to the Walsall area was occasioned by the death of Samuel, his elder brother. Samuel had been a lifelong invalid, and in order to support him their father had established a small tobacconist's business, which, since his father was in poor health, Frederick now took over. He also helped his father in his work as the Pelsall Miners' agent, and when his father died in 1910 Frederick was elected to succeed him. His 556 votes made him a clear winner over ten other candidates who between them polled 647 votes.

By this time the Pelsall district had developed into one of the strongest of the smaller miners' associations in the country. In his last annual report, Benjamin Dean had recorded: 'As an association we stand as one of the strongest, and have in hand almost as much money per head of membership as any other trade association in the country.' The success of the Pelsall Association contrasted sharply with the declining fortunes of the miners' associations in the Black Country, immediately to the south, where because of flooding and wasteful exploitation the decline of the coalmining industry was well advanced. Output had fallen from a peak of over ten million tons per year in 1865 to about three million tons in 1913, and this was inevitably reflected in mining trade unionism. The Pelsall district, however, lies within the Cannock section of the South Staffordshire coalfield to the north of the Great Bentley Fault which marks the northern edge of the Black Country and effectively divides the South Staffordshire coalfield into two parts. The Cannock section was developed later than the Black Country section, so that it continued to expand into the 1920s, and by 1913 over two-thirds of the 30,000 miners employed in

South Staffordshire and Worcestershire were working in the Cannock division, and its output was more than twice that of the Black Country section of the coalfield.

The prosperity based upon this continuing expansion enabled the Pelsall Association to withstand successfully the consequences of the two great national stoppages which occurred during Dean's agency – the strike over the individual minimum wage in 1912 and the three-month lockout of 1921 – and when he resigned the agency in 1923, because of ill-health, he handed over the Association in good order to his successor, John Blakemore.

As well as taking over the leadership of the Pelsall miners from his father, Dean had also in 1910 inherited his position as a leader of Lib-Labourism in Walsall and the district. By this time the position of Lib-Labs in general, and those who were miners' leaders in particular, was being made increasingly difficult by the rise of the Labour Party and the decision of the MFGB in 1908 to affiliate to it. Dean came to exemplify these difficulties. While still a member of the Liberal Party he was among the MFGB delegation to the Labour Party Conference in 1912, and later in the same year unsuccessfully contested Bridge Ward as an independent Labour candidate at the Walsall Town Council elections. He was subsequently elected to Rushall Parish Council as a Liberal but finally broke with the Liberal Party after the Lloyd George split in 1916, and thereafter represented the Labour Party. The precise dates of Dean's service on the Rushall Parish Council are not known, the records having been lost or destroyed, but it seems that he was first elected to the Council at some time between the end of 1912 and the outbreak of the First World War and that he resigned his seat soon after the first onset of illness in 1923. During the years following 1916 he was regularly among the MFGB representatives at the annual conferences of both the TUC and the Labour Party, and in 1922 he was the Midland Federation representative on the Executive Council of the MFGB.

After his retirement from the Pelsall miners' agency Dean's health got progressively worse. In 1924 he resigned his position as the Walsall Wood representative on the Walsall Board of Guardians which he had held since 1912. Then in 1925 he suffered the first of a series of strokes which eventually left him paralysed and bedridden. Nevertheless he retained until his death his position as a Staffordshire County magistrate, to which he had been appointed in 1917, though he resigned the presidency of the Rushall bench in 1931.

During his last years his condition made him almost totally dependent on his wife, who as well as nursing him ran the wholesale and retail tobacconist's business which Dean had bought in 1926 to support himself and his family. To avoid confusion with the firm of B. Dean & Co. established by his father and taken over by his brother William in 1910, Dean continued to trade under the name of the previous owner, H. S. Farrington & Co.

Dean died at his home in Lichfield Road, Rushall, on 24 April 1941, and was buried in the churchyard of Rushall Parish Church on 26 April. He was survived by his wife, to whom he left an estate of £2161, and three children.

Two of Dean's brothers also made notable contributions to the civic and commercial life of Walsall and district. William remained a lifelong Liberal and was a Walsall alderman for many years, becoming mayor in 1932; he carried on the business of B. Dean & Co. until his death in 1958. Wilfred, who was the proprietor of the Leamore Currying Co., also remained a Liberal and represented the party on the Rushall Parish Council and Staffordshire County Council for many years, as well as being an Aldridge magistrate. He died in 1952. The third surviving brother, Arthur, was a partner in the Walsall printing firm of Ballinger and Dean. Frederick Dean's son, Benjamin, attended Queen Mary's School, Walsall. On leaving school he joined his uncle Wilfred in the Leamore Currying Co. and worked there until 1940. During the war years he worked at the Walsall aircraft firm of Helliwell & Co. and then in 1946 took over the running of H. S. Farrington & Co. from his mother.

Sources: Reports of Pelsall Miners' Association activities, and political activities, *Walsall Observer, Walsall Red Book*, 1910–1938, *Wolverhampton Chronicle*, 1910–1924; R. Page Arnot, *The Miners: years of struggle* (1953); G. C. Allen, *The Industrial Development of Birmingham and the Black Country 1860–1927* (1929, rev. ed. 1966); K. J. Dean, 'Parliamentary Elections and Party Organisations in Walsall 1906–45' (Birmingham MA, 1969); idem, *Town and Westminster: a political history of Walsall from 1906–1945* (Walsall, 1972); personal information: Benjamin Dean, Walsall, son (by interview March 1972). OBIT. *Walsall Observer* and *Walsall Times*, 26 Apr 1941.

ERIC TAYLOR

See also: *John BLAKEMORE; †Benjamin DEAN; *Isaac ECCLESTONE; *William SMITH.

DOCKER, Abraham (1788/91?–1857)
CHARTIST

Abraham Docker was born in Almondbury, near Huddersfield, Yorkshire. The date of his birth is difficult to ascertain, since his ages as given on census returns do not tally with other evidence. Docker was described as being fifty years of age in the 1841 Census, and sixty-one in 1851. When he gave evidence before the 1833 Factories Inquiry Commission, his age was then given as forty, but when he died in 1857, he was said to be sixty-nine. It is quite conceivable that Docker himself was unsure of his date of birth, a not uncommon phenomenon among his generation of operatives. By the age of eight, at all events, he was living in Stockport, Cheshire, and working as a scavenger in a cotton mill. He was later employed at piecing and feeding cards, until he was big enough to become a spinner. Docker then worked in several Stockport mills as either a spinner or a stretcher until January 1833, when poor health obliged him to leave the cotton industry. He next became a baker. Later in life, he also worked as an agricultural labourer and a 'chair bottomer'.

As a cotton operative, Docker became involved in trade union activities, including the major strike which affected Stockport in

1829. The strike began in January, when operatives refused to submit to the wage reductions (averaging about 10 per cent) which were proposed by the millowners. The spinners, weavers and dressers who turned out were supported by subscriptions from local inhabitants, and from trade unions in surrounding towns. Some of this money they gave to colleagues in other branches of the cotton trade who were unemployed as a result of the strike. The antagonism of the strikers towards the masters, aggravated by social distress, was then increased still further by the introduction of blackleg labour. In April, over a hundred weavers from Lancashire arrived in the town, many bringing with them large families. Some employers even built cottages for these immigrants, and rewards of £10 were offered for the conviction of anyone who committed offences against them. In these circumstances, the strike became increasingly violent, with attacks against the 'knobsticks' which included vitriol-throwing. In May 1829, Docker was arrested on a charge of throwing vitriol over the face and chest of George Philips, a Scot who was continuing to work at Garside's mill. Despite his own plea of 'not guilty' and the alibi provided by his brother John, Docker was sent for trial at Quarter Sessions. Meanwhile he was required to find his own bail of £50, and two sureties of £25 each. The trial took place at Knutsford in July. After an eight-hour investigation Docker was found not guilty and discharged. He assured the jury that 'if he knew who had committed so diabolical a crime, he would be the first to give evidence thereof'.

In 1832, William Longson of Stockport, giving evidence to the Sadler Committee, (M. T. Sadler was MP for Aldborough, E. Yorks., at the time), quoted Docker's wage rates as proof of a decline in wages since 1810, despite increased production. In 1810, Docker had worked a stretcher, which spun 400 lb of boving, and he had been paid at the rate of 1s 3½d per score. The amount of boving had increased over the years, from 600 lb in 1811 to 850 lb in 1813, and 1000 lb in 1823, but Docker's wage rate per score had shown a marked decline: in 1811

he had received only 10d per score, which then fell to 9d in 1813 and 7½d in 1823. In 1810, moreover, if Docker's pay at the end of the week had not amounted to 26s, that sum had always been made up to him.

Docker himself gave evidence in favour of a Ten Hours Bill to the 1833 Factories Inquiry Commission. He described his own childhood in the mills, how as a piecer he had been affected by the dust and become sickly and weak. He also spoke of a fourteen-year-old boy, who had once worked with him as a piecer; he had been crippled within two years. Other children had also been in poor health, and were commonly beaten in all the mills at which Docker had worked. Parents, he maintained, were evading Hobhouse's Act, in order to keep their children in work. Abraham Docker's concern for the health of factory children may well have been affected by the case of his own son, whom he had frequently been obliged to carry on his back to the mill, where the nine-year-old boy worked as a scavenger. His son's health had declined, but Docker's ambition to put him to another trade had never been fulfilled, for the boy was drowned at the age of twelve.

The hostility of the manufacturers to the operatives' political activities was also revealed by Docker, who had frequently sat on the operatives' committees, and attended all their public meetings. On the previous occasion when a Ten Hours Bill had been before the Commons, masters had sent petitions through the mills, which the men were obliged to sign, stating that they were content with a twelve-hour day. A meeting had been called in the Bull's Head, in Stockport Market Place, to which hundreds of men flocked. Although under duress they had signed the employers' petitions, they now signed in support of a Ten Hours Bill. Docker himself had collected money for Sadler's expenses, and was most anxious to see legislation which placed a restriction on the operating time of the moving power in factories.

During the struggle for the 1832 Reform Bill, Docker was active in the Stockport Political Union. After such a career, it was perhaps fitting that he became one of the founder members of the local Chartist movement. He helped to elect delegates to the first National Convention, and to devise a scheme for local collection of the National Rent. When the Stockport Association's leaders, James Mitchell and Charles Davies, were imprisoned in 1839, he proposed the formation of a committee to organise collections for their families and for legal expenses. However, Docker also urged caution in local political activities. He opposed any commitment of the Chartist vote in the 1839 municipal elections, on the ground that this might lead to the dismissal of Chartists, who were expected to vote for Whig or Tory masters. In December 1840, Docker became chairman of the local Committee for the Restoration of Frost, Williams and Jones, the Chartists who had been transported for their part in the Newport *émeute*.

During the 1840s Docker's activities were chiefly aimed at exerting or increasing Chartist influence upon municipal politics. In 1841 he objected to any town improvements which would place an increased burden upon poorer ratepayers. At meetings to select Overseers of the Poor and the Board of Surveyors in 1841, 1845 and 1846, Docker and his fellow Chartists supported their own nominees, objecting in particular to the high salaries of local officials. When in 1846 the Corporation prepared a Municipal Improvement Bill [for which see James Torkington], Docker took part in the ratepayers' organisation formed to oppose it. The Whigs, who had held power in the town since 1836, and were to continue to do so until 1848, were seen as attempting to remove the ratepayers' control over the Corporation's expenditure. The opposition thus attracted both Chartists, like Docker, James Torkington and George Bradburn, and Tories. Although the Bill was lost at its Third Reading in the Commons, its opponents had to prepare to meet the threat of further attempts at legislation, and so the Chartist/Tory Alliance remained, and an association was formed which eventually became known as the Working Men's Ratepayers' Association. Docker was elected to its central committee in September 1846, and formed part of a deputation to the

town's MPs. In 1847, seeking grounds on which to oppose the Corporation's purchase of the water works, Docker carried out a survey on water supplies to firms in the borough. He continued his campaign for economy and retrenchment, criticising the incomes of local officials, and calling for fixed salaries as opposed to fees.

Docker remained in the Chartist movement in the years of decline after 1848. Divisions within the movement were becoming serious during the spring and summer of 1850. Early in the year Harney and his supporters had won a majority on the new provisional executive elected by a London Metropolitan Conference, and in the summer Feargus O'Connor and his faithful ally, Thomas Clark, lost further ground when the composition of the national executive shifted to Harney and those who accepted the new emphasis upon social rights. There was opposition to the new executive, however, from Stockport. James Williams, who was later to achieve prominence in the 'Labour Parliament' of 1854, expressed the views of the majority of Stockport Chartists in a letter to the *Northern Star* of 19 October. He complained that the London conference had been undemocratic; that Lancashire and Yorkshire, in which the mass support for Chartism lay, had not been adequately consulted; and that the executive had not been elected by universal suffrage. The Stockport Chartists were therefore making their protest by supporting the Manchester Conference called by Feargus O'Connor for January 1851.

In this controversy with the Provisional Executive, one man apparently stood apart from his colleagues in Stockport – Abraham Docker. No hint of discord emerged from reports of meetings, but in a letter to the *Stockport Advertiser* of 6 February 1851, Docker explained the situation: he had resigned from the local Chartist Association on 11 December 1850,

. . . because I thought I had paid my money long enough to a set of men who could not afford any one of their subscribers a good word if they would not succumb to their dictation . . .

Docker's political arguments were never expressed but, being an essentially practical man, he may well have been influenced in his decision less by ideological considerations than by the failure of his colleagues to respect his right to dissent. He had proceeded to send his subscriptions directly to the Executive in Southampton Street, London, whereupon he found himself to be the only paid-up member in Stockport. The other Chartists had apparently withheld their money as well as their allegiance from the Executive. In his letter, Docker had called for unanimity among the Chartists in seeking the emancipation of their country, and had signed himself 'A consistent Member of the National Chartist Association of Stockport'. But the Stockport Chartists now displayed posters in shop windows, insinuating that Docker had been discharged from the local Association, and stating that any receipt of funds by him would be fraudulent.

Thus ended Docker's Chartist activity and, it would seem, his political career. He continued to live in Newbridge Lane, Stockport, with his second wife, Martha, and a daughter Ann, who worked as a cotton trimmer and spinner. When he died at his home on 13 February 1857 his occupation was given as a chair bottomer. He was buried on the 15th in the parish of Portwood. No will has been located.

Sources: (1) MSS: Stockport Marriage Registers vol. 10 (1810–12), Cheshire CRO; 1841 Census Stockport, PRO H.O. 107/114; 1851 Census Stockport, PRO H.O. 107/2157; Register of Burials in the Parish of Portwood in the County of Chester (1857), Stockport Reference Library. (2) Other: *Handbill on the 1829 strike in Stockport*, Stockport Reference Library; *Stockport Advertiser*, 1829–51; *Northern Star*, 1838–51; *North Cheshire Reformer*, 1839; S.C. on Children, Mills and Factories [Sadler Committee] 1831–2 XV; Employment of Children in Factories Commission of Inquiry 1833 XX [for Docker's evidence see D.2 Lancashire District pp. 9–15]. (3) Secondary: Alfred [Samuel H. G. Kydd], *The History of the Factory Movement*, 2 vols

(1857, repr. in one vol. New York, 1966); R. G. Gammage, *History of the Chartist Movement* (1894; repr. with an Introduction by John Saville, New York, 1969); E. L. Hutchins and A. Harrison, *A History of Factory Legislation* (1903, 3rd ed. 1926, repr. 1966); C. Driver, *Tory Radical: the life of Richard Oastler* (Oxford, 1946); A. R. Schoyen, *The Chartist Challenge* (1958); J. T. Ward, *The Factory Movement 1830–1855* (1962).

T. D. W. REID
NAOMI REID

See also: John ALLINSON; George BRADBURN; Joseph CARTER; *Feargus O'CONNOR; James TORKINGTON.

DUNCAN, Andrew (1898–1965)
CO-OPERATOR AND LABOUR PARTY WORKER

Andrew Duncan was born in the Govan district of Glasgow on 15 November 1898, the son of Edward Duncan and his wife Helen (née McFadyen). His father, who died when Andrew was only eighteen months old, was a foreman at the SCWS boot factory at Shieldhall. Andrew worked as a ship's plater until unemployment in the shipyards around 1930 led to his becoming an agent for the Co-operative Insurance Society. He served as part-time secretary to the Education Committee of the Kinning Park Society (later Glasgow South) and then as Secretary of the Board of Management of that Society for four years. During the early war years he represented his Society on the directorate of the United Co-operative Bakery Society.

It was on the political side of the Co-operative movement that Duncan was most active. He was appointed to the staff of the Co-operative Party as Scottish Organiser in January 1943, succeeding Duncan Howie who had held the post since the movement entered politics in 1917. For the first six years Duncan was responsible for the whole of Scotland together with Northumberland, Cumberland, Durham and the North Riding of Yorkshire. Thereafter an increase in the Party's staff enabled him to devote all his time to his native land. He inaugurated the

Scottish Party Summer School at Newbattle Abbey in 1949 which after a few years was transferred to St Andrews University. It is said that it was his spirit and personality which gave a very special quality to this school.

Duncan was much appreciated in the co-operative movement, where he was an extremely popular figure at annual conferences and congresses, at week-end and summer schools. He was seemingly tireless in addressing meetings, interviewing society boards and organising membership and election campaigns. His relations with labour and trade union officials were also very cordial. A frequent speaker at joint rallies, he was well known in almost every Scottish constituency, and at the Scottish Labour Party Conference his annual speech as fraternal delegate was always well received. On reaching retiring age he left the position of party organiser in October 1963. During the twenty years he held this post, he worked devotedly to strengthen the political wing of the movement and was sometimes outspoken in his opposition to those who wished to build up only the commercial side of the movement. He was something of an agnostic in religious matters, and had pacifist leanings: in the Second World War he did not support the official Labour policy of active participation in the war effort.

After retirement he contested the Knightswood ward, and was elected as a Labour member of the Glasgow City Council in May 1964. He had, however, been suffering from ill-health for some time, and at the election was able to appear only at an eve-of-the-poll meeting. Duncan's career in local government politics was only a brief one; he died on 21 January 1965, in the Victoria Infirmary, Glasgow, aged sixty-six. He was cremated at Craigton on 25 January, when many leading co-operators from all parts of the movement were present. In 1919 he had married Helen Love, who with two married sons and a married daughter survived him.

Sources: *Co-op. Party Monthly Letter* (Nov 1963); T. F. Carbery, *Consumers in Politics: a history and general review of the Co-operative Party* (Manchester, 1969); per-sonal information: Andrew Duncan, Newcastle upon Tyne, son. OBIT. *Glasgow Herald*, 23 Jan 1965; *Co-op. News* and *Scottish Co-operator*, 30 Jan 1965; *Co-op. Party Monthly Letter* (Feb 1965).

H. F. BING

See also: †Albert Victor ALEXANDER, for Co-operative Party; †Arnold BONNER, for Co-operation, 1945–70; †William MAXWELL, for Scottish Co-operation.

DUNCAN, Charles (1865–1933)
TRADE UNION LEADER AND LABOUR MP

Charles Duncan was born on 8 June 1865 at 93 Stockton Street, Middlesbrough, the son of a ship's pilot, Alexander Duncan, and his wife Jane Dobson. His father earned good wages, but as the family lived in a working-class area, young Charles quickly became familiar with the conditions of the manual labourer. As he himself said in a short account of his life, 'I longed to do something to better them'. He continued:

I remember I was particularly impressed by the misery and degradation caused by drink, and, at an early age, became, and have remained, a total abstainer. My teetotalism has, I am sure, greately helped me in life, and given me influence among working men, for they respect a teetotaller, and like to think that their interests are being looked after by one who may be relied upon to keep a clear head [*Pearson's Weekly*, 15 Feb 1906].

Duncan was educated at a local Church school, where according to his own account he was 'distinguished chiefly for his fighting propensities'; but his father's means enabled him to stay till he was sixteen and he had a good education. On leaving school he wanted to be a ship's engineer, but after two or three voyages to France he settled for a career on shore and was apprenticed at the Tees-side Iron and Engine Works, Middlesbrough. For some years he worked at the Elswick Ordnance Factory, Newcastle upon Tyne, where he became a member of the Amalgamated Society of Engineers in about 1888. He acted as the union's district secretary, and retained his membership of the ASE (after 1920 the AEU) for the remainder of his life. At the age of twenty-two he was converted to Socialism after hearing Tom Mann and Jack Williams lecture in Newcastle. Although impressed by their arguments, he studied both sides of the question by reading the writings of Auberon Herbert and other individualists before committing himself to a socialist position. In the early 1890s, during a period of unemployment, he helped to organise a relief fund and soup kitchen. This brought him into public notice, and he was elected to the Board of Guardians. Six months later he became a member of the Middlesbrough Town Council, on which he sat from 1895 to 1900. At this time he belonged to the ILP. He joined the National Democratic League and in 1902 was reported as being on its executive committee.

An energetic and ambitious young man, Duncan accepted in 1898 Tom Mann's invitation to become an official of the Workers' Union, which was launched in May of that year. He had known Mann for some years, and although his trade union experience had been confined to working among skilled engineers, he appears to have had no hesitation in undertaking the organisation of unskilled workers. He became full-time president and general organiser, and in a period of buoyant economic conditions the union began to recruit members despite the taxing problems of dealing with a shifting and heterogeneous labour force. Towards the end of 1900, Tom Chambers resigned as general secretary and Duncan took over the post, with Robert Morley of Halifax moving into the presidency. In 1901 Mann, who was described as the union's vice-president, sailed for New Zealand, leaving Duncan as the dominant figure.

The new century saw a period of depression in the economy which brought a decline in the union's membership. Duncan responded with a period of retrenchment. He closed the union's office, and from his home struggled to gain solvency, paying attention to the financial rather than the numerical strength of the union. In its earliest stage, the union's leaders had explicitly rejected the provision of friendly benefits on the grounds that such activities inhibited vigorous action on the industrial front. Duncan reversed this policy by instituting schemes for funeral and sickness benefits, arguing that fewer members would lapse if they had a financial interest in the union. He succeeded in stabilising the union's financial affairs and after about four years began to expand by appointing new organisers and covering a wider area. For the first time membership rose above 5000, with recruits from a wide range of occupations.

In 1906 Duncan entered Parliament as the representative for Barrow-in-Furness. Neither Hardie nor MacDonald had been favourably impressed by him, and they had hoped to allow the Liberal a straight fight at Barrow in return for a clear run for a Labour candidate elsewhere. But Duncan, sponsored by the ASE, secured LRC approval and was elected with a majority of 1772 over the previous Conservative MP. In his election campaign he declared himself to be the same type of Socialist as John Burns, and he received official Liberal support [Poirier (1958) 253].

His response to Stead's questionnaire on the books that had influenced him shows that when he became an MP he was fairly well-read: Carlyle, Ruskin, Burns, Blatchford and the Webbs were among the writers he mentioned, and his reply also has a flavour of the self-improvement that was then common within the labour movement:

My advice to all men is to have books of your own. Public libraries are very good, but private libraries are very much better, as you thus command the pick of the world's brains as your close friends and advisers as well as teachers . . . The unread man has a narrow outlook, and easily goes astray; he is the sport of political tricksters and the tool for all knaves. The brain is a wonderful garden; but its cultivation requires assiduous attention, and the harvest is simply astounding [*Review of Reviews* (1906) 573].

The harvest in this case, however, did not include success in Parliament. The House of

Commons was not the medium in which Duncan operated most effectively. Though by no means a failure, he made no particular mark, apart from serving for a time as a Labour Whip and being noted for his sartorial elegance. In the general elections of 1910 he defeated the Conservative candidate with majorities of 1006 and 520 respectively.

During the industrial unrest of 1910–14 the Workers' Union underwent a rapid expansion in membership. Numbers rose from about 5000 in 1910 to over 140,000 in 1914. Duncan employed the extra income brought in by this upsurge to establish the union on a more solid basis and to expand his staff in order to increase recruitment further. In this work he showed great flair for publicity, and the advertisements he placed in the *Daily Citizen* and elsewhere were remarked upon for their striking qualities. While new members were drawn from many industries, the union made a particular impact among agricultural workers and the less skilled in the engineering trades. In 1910 Mann had returned from Australia, and, still holding the post of vice-president, helped as a speaker at meetings of the union. His militant ideas were not, however, put into practice; Duncan firmly retained control of union policy and continued in the moderate approach born of a decade of difficult survival.

In 1914 Duncan showed himself to be a strong supporter of the war. He began to appear on recruiting platforms, and later supported conscription. He was appointed to the labour supply committee, the munitions advisory committee and the national industrial council – all parts of the government bureaucracy designed to direct labour into the war effort. In 1916 he signed the manifesto of the British Workers' National League. Lloyd George sent Duncan and three other delegates to the United States where they addressed numerous mass meetings on the importance of American aid in defeating Germany; the other three were J. Butterworth, D. L. Mosses and W. A. Appleton [*Times*, 14 Feb 1918].

Duncan and John Beard (who had replaced Morley as president of the union at the end of 1913) were associated with the British Workers' League, which voiced a nationalistic pro-war policy. They resigned when the League decided to oppose certain Labour candidates in parliamentary elections. This did not save Duncan from defeat in the general election of December 1918. Ironically, when it was generally anti-war candidates that polled badly, militants in Barrow, mostly from the engineering trades, induced the local Labour Party to withhold support from Duncan, and he was narrowly beaten in a straight fight with a Conservative. He was still anxious to return to Parliament, as he thought his status as an MP useful to him in conducting the financial affairs of the union. In February and November 1920 he contested the Wrekin division of Shropshire, being defeated on both occasions by candidates who were supported by Horatio Bottomley. From 1920 to 1922 he was a member of the executive committee of the Labour Party. At the 1922 general election he was returned by a large majority as MP for Clay Cross, a Derbyshire mining constituency. Though he did not visit the constituency very often, he held the seat until his death, when he was succeeded in it by Arthur Henderson.

The war had witnessed a further increase in the numbers belonging to the Workers' Union; women had been recruited in large numbers, and developments in the engineering and munitions trades had also created opportunities for expansion. By the time of the formation of the National Amalgamated Workers' Union in 1919, membership was approaching the half million mark and the union was the largest in the country. The NAWU had been established to facilitate a proposed amalgamation with two other unions, but conditions did not turn out to be suitable for a further period of growth. After 1920 the union suffered a decline which the activities of Duncan and other officials only served to hasten.

In 1920, in an attempt to prevent the large turnover of membership, the union executive introduced a generous benefit scheme. It proved to be too liberal, and in 1921, with the onset of economic depression, the funds of the union began to evaporate rapidly. Membership fell to 250,000, thus further reducing income, and in 1922 the loss of another 100,000 members contributed to a deficit of £30,000 in that year. Duncan responded as he had done twenty years earlier with an economy drive, although Beard modified this course by arguing that greater efforts should be made in recruitment. There was a slight recovery from 1923 to 1925, but the General Strike (which brought out approximately forty per cent of the union's membership) was a heavy drain on funds. To avoid bankruptcy the union negotiated for absorption into the TGWU, which came about in 1929 when the membership of the Workers' Union had fallen below 100,000.

The difficulties of the 1920s were increased by some of the union's officials, whose dealings showed, if not outright dishonesty, then a certain financial unscrupulousness. In 1925 Duncan and Beard came into conflict with their executive council over the expenses claimed by its members. After a bitter wrangle, four of the six EC members were removed, but one of these, Neil Maclean, who was MP for Govan, issued a series of circulars bringing countercharges. Maclean accused Duncan and others of misusing union funds. Among the issues raised was the £3500 spent in financing Duncan's candidatures for the Wrekin in 1920 – a sum almost twice the legal limit. The charge was not denied by Duncan, but the new EC decided to expel Maclean for contravening a rule against the distribution of unofficial circulars [Hyman (1971) 141].

Despite the odour of corruption that emanated from these proceedings, Duncan appears to have remained secure in his position as general secretary. The government of the union was such that power was concentrated in the hands of the leadership, and rank-and-file pressure, even had it existed, could not easily make itself felt through the union's structure. The undemocratic organisation of the union was probably largely due to the considerable turnover of membership, which left the permanent officials in a strong position. The absorption of the WU into the TGWU which took place in 1929 did not deprive Duncan of employment. He became secretary of the Workers' Union group within the TGWU, a post largely created for him, to keep him in office until his retirement. During these years he was designated a parliamentary representative of the TGWU. As well as being an active trade unionist and MP, Duncan was a lifelong co-operator, and served as president of the Willesden Co-operative Society. In 1919 he had been made a JP for Middlesex.

Duncan died in Manor House Hospital, Hampstead, on 6 July 1933, after a long illness. He had married Lydia Copeland in 1890; his wife survived him and he left effects valued at £3883. His services to the labour movement were commemorated by the unveiling of a plaque in Transport House on 26 April 1935; at this ceremony tribute was paid to Duncan's qualities by George Lansbury, Arthur Henderson and John Beard.

Writings: articles in the Workers' Union *Record*, Annual Reports and circulars; some account of his early years is given in a short article, 'How I got on', *Pearson's Weekly*, 15 Feb 1906.

Sources: (1) MSS: Labour Party archives: LRC; (2) Other: W. T. Stead, 'The Labour Party and the Books that helped to make it', *Review of Reviews 33* (June 1906) 568–582; S. V. Bracher, *The Herald Book of Labour Members* (1923); *Dod* (1907, 1932); *WWW* (1929–40); P. P. Poirier, *The Advent of the Labour Party* (1958); J. E. Williams, *The Derbyshire Miners* (1962); R. Hyman, *The Workers' Union* (Oxford, 1971); R. Douglas, 'The National Democratic League and the British Workers' League, *Hist. J. 15*, no. 3 (1972) 533–52; J. O. Stubbs, 'Lord Milner and Patriotic Labour, 1914–1918', *Engl. Hist. Rev. 87*, no. 345 (Oct 1972) 717–54; biographical information: His Excellency Mr T. K. A. Elliott, Helsinki. OBIT. *Daily Herald* and *Times*, 7 July 1933; *Derbyshire Times*, 9 July 1933; *Labour Party Report* (1933); *TUC Report* (1933).

DAVID E. MARTIN

See also: *John BEARD; †Arthur HENDERson, for British Labour Party, 1914–31; George LANSBURY, for British Labour Party, 1900–13; *Tom MANN; *Samuel MORLEY.

DUNNING, Thomas Joseph (1799–1873)
TRADE UNIONIST AND BOOKBINDERS' LEADER

Born in Southwark, London, on 12 January 1799, Dunning was apprenticed as a bookbinder in 1813; and at the end of his apprenticeship, in 1820, he joined his local Journeymen Bookbinders' Lodge. His abilities soon became recognised for in 1826 he was reported as a member of an audit committee of No. 5 lodge, set up to inquire into a case of fraud by a former secretary. Dunning appears to have had no formal education but he was noted throughout his long trade union career for a rational, lucid style of argument in speech and in writing. Although his authorship cannot be wholly certain, his first publication was probably the anonymous forty-page pamphlet, *The Reply of the Journeymen Bookbinders, to remarks on a Memorial addressed to their Employers* [Howe and Child (1952) 107–8].

The decade of the 1830s witnessed a series of running fights between the London bookbinders and their employers, culminating in the eight-months' strike which began in January 1839. Dunning resigned from the committee in March, on the ground that the intransigence of its members had prevented a possible settlement, but he was one of the negotiators who brought the strike to an end in August. The long struggle had greatly weakened the finances of the London lodges (of which there were three at this time) and in May 1840 it was decided to bring them together to form the London Consolidated Society of Bookbinders – sometimes referred to as the London Consolidated Lodge – and at the same time to stop meeting in public houses. Dunning who had campaigned vigorously on this last matter, was elected secretary, and this was the beginning of over thirty years' service in that position.

His position for the next ten years was by no means secure, but he survived the many attacks upon his administration and policies. He was an extraordinarily effective debater,

an excellent administrator, a personality of considerable force: as the Webbs summed him up, 'one of the ablest Trade Unionists of his time'. The internal strife of the 1840s came to a head during a major confrontation between the Society and Watkin's bindery where most of the binding of the British and Foreign Bible Society was done. The strike also exacerbated the tensions within the Bookbinders' Society itself and after its conclusion the Finishers' Association, a minority group, were required to sign a written statement repudiating their divisive activities; a demand whch Dunning later admitted was an error – 'it was too much like signing "a document"' [*Trades Societies and Strikes* (1860) 103]. This was, however, the beginning of a period of consolidation for the London Bookbinders and Dunning's position thereafter was never seriously challenged.

For the next two decades Dunning remained one of the oustanding leaders of London trade unionism; and his views reflected many of the attitudes of the skilled workers of these middle years of the century. In October 1850 he founded and edited the *Bookbinders' Trade Circular*, one of the most successful of the new trade union journals. It its columns he propounded a theory of Trade Unionism, from which, as the Webbs commented, 'McCulloch himself would scarcely have dissented' – a statement which, however, is not wholly fair to Dunning. The most elaborate exposition of his principles was in the well-publicised *Trades' Unions and Strikes: their philosophy and intention*, published by himself in 1860 on behalf of his Society after commercial firms had refused to consider it. In this fifty-two page booklet Dunning began by accepting that 'it is by the principle of exchange that all the transactions of civilised life are carried on, by which indeed, civilised society exists and is held together' (p. 3). He then proceeded to define the fundamental bases of exchange: Labour, Capital, Individual Property and Security. Dunning fully accepted the market determination of wages as the result of the operation of demand and supply, but it was at this point that he began to argue the case for trade unionism. He agreed that there were two extreme situations in which trade unions could not expect to influence the bargaining situation: when the supply of labour permanently exceeds its demand, 'nothing can prevent the reduction of wages; and, conversely, when the demand for it permanently much exceeds its supply, nothing can prevent their rise' (p. 6). It was in the middle ground between these two extreme points that the necessity for trade unions arose, and it was here that the combination of workmen was crucial in order 'to put themselves on something like an equality in the bargain for the sale of their labour with their employers' (p. 7).

Some part of his argument was a confutation of the ideas of Adam Black, MP, whose attack in 1859–60 upon the basic principles of trade unionism evoked a vigorous response from the working-class movement [see also William Newton]. Dunning set out carefully and patiently the practices, procedures and policies of trade unions as they then existed. He emphasised the reasonableness of their approach, the difficulties they always experienced in obtaining a fair hearing, their abhorrence of violence, their acceptance of the strike as a measure of last resort. He was, however, quite firm and unyielding on the necessity of combination, both to improve the bargaining power of the workers and to offset the 'predatory instinct' (p. 43) on the side of employers, of which he gave many examples. His whole argument was a theory of bargaining power for skilled workers, and Dunning implicitly assumed throughout his essay that little, if anything, could be done for those – the unskilled – who found themselves in a permanently overstocked labour market. He concluded that his essay had showed 'that Trade Unions are necessary to secure to the workmen a free, and sonsequently fair, exchange for his labour, which, from a disadvantage inherent in his position, he is unable otherwise to obtain'. His final paragraph, given below, opens with words which have been much quoted and which sum up many of the attitudes of his contemporaries:

We have before said that the true state of employer and employed is that of amity, and that they are the truest friends, each of the other – for each derives his revenue from the other. And the fact is, notwithstanding all that has been written to the contrary in the "Quarterly" and "Edinburgh" Reviews, and from them down to the humblest writer who has added his little spark to the general blaze – that this state is for the most part their actual condition. Under no other circumstances could the trade and manufacturers of the country have so greatly prospered and extended. It should, therefore, be the duty of both to prevent this harmony being interrupted. Each should consider this state their true relation, and consider its interruption the greatest of calamities (p. 52).

Dunning's pamphlet was reprinted by the Bookbinders' Society in 1873, and in its day it achieved considerable prominence. In the fifth (1862) edition of his *Principles* John Stuart Mill added a footnote warmly commending the tract to his readers and adding that while there were some opinions in it with which he did not agree there were 'many sound arguments, and an instructive exposure of the common fallacies of opponents' [vol. 2 Book 5, chapter 10, p. 542]. A few years earlier than the publication of his pamphlet, Dunning had given evidence on behalf of his Society before the Select Committee on Conciliation of 1856. He favoured the establishment of a tribunal which would, on the application of one side or the other, decide whether arbitration should take place or not. If arbitration was to take place – before a different tribunal from the first – Dunning made it clear that he would accept the arbitrators' decision as binding on the parties involved; and to this position – broadly similar to that held by William Newton – he adhered to the end of his life. What Dunning always insisted upon, however, was that trade unions must at all times retain the clear and specific functions he had elaborated in the 1860 pamphlet; and he deplored any signs of their degeneration into mere benefit societies. In January 1866, for example, he published in the *Bookbinders' Trade Circular*, an article severely critical of the ASE and of William Allan's policy of concentrating on the benefit side of the union, writing in undoubtedly exaggerated terms that the ASE:

> is now as incapable to engage in a strike as the Hearts of Oak, the Foresters or any other extensive benefit society . . . The Amalgamated Engineers, as a trade society, has ceased to exist.

In his early days as an active trade unionist Dunning had been sent by his Society in 1838 to represent them on the committee of trade delegates appointed to oppose the attack on the unions which followed the conviction of the Glasgow cotton-spinners [Webb (1894) 153 ff.; Schoyen (1958) 23 ff.]. This brought Dunning into contact with William Lovett, among other London Chartist leaders, and Dunning was further involved with the *Charter*, edited by William Carpenter, to which he contributed a large number of articles on political economy, many of the arguments being those he later used in the 1860 pamphlet on *Trades' Unions*. In 1864 he won first prize in an essay competition – 'On the Advantages and Disadvantages of Trade Combinations' – sponsored by the *Newcastle Chronicle*.

In his years as a leader of London unionism Dunning's political attitudes again seem to have been what historians have come to accept as typical of the middle decades of the century. He supported the movement for the extension of the franchise in the 1860s and became a foundation member of George Potter's London Working Men's Association in 1866. Dunning supported Potter throughout the latter's quarrel with the Junta. A letter to the *Bee-Hive* from Dunning (7 Oct 1865) referred to his opposition to the leaders of the London Trades Council for their 'desire to control and to dominate over everything and everybody'. Dunning was a vigorous advocate of the revision of the labour laws in the late sixties and again supported Potter against the Conference of Amalgamated Trades. In 1869 he was a signatory to the Prospectus of the Labour Representation League, and was a member of its first executive committee. On one important political issue – the

American Civil War – Dunning adopted a most interesting position.

It has now become accepted, since the work of Royden Harrison, that the British working-class movement was by no means as pro-North, especially in the early years of the Civil War, as was formerly believed; and Dunning was among those 'whom hatred of the North made friends to the Confederacy' [Harrison (1965) 42]. Dunning attacked what he believed to be the hypocrisy of the North towards the slave issue; he declared himself to have no confidence in President Lincoln 'either as an opponent to slavery or as a friend to the Negro' [*Bookbinders' Trade Circular*, 2 Mar 1864]; and perhaps most important of all, Dunning was hostile to the alliance which working-class supporters of the Federal cause were forming with middle-class radicals of the John Bright school. Dunning had been one of the earliest supporters of the *Bee-Hive*; his Society was among its largest shareholders, and as Coltham (1960) and Royden Harrison (1965) have described in detail, the bitter passions which the Civil War aroused were argued and debated at length in its columns. Dunning was not alone in his opposition to the Federal cause; J. B. Leno, Thomas Vize and Alexander Campbell were among those similarly opposed to the pro-Northern support which Beesly in particular was encouraging.

He disputed again with Beesly at the time of the Paris Commune. Beesly and Frederic Harrison were writing in enthusiastic support of the Commune in the *Bee-Hive* and the *Fortnightly Review* respectively, and it was in answer to Beesly's earlier letters (from 25 March on) that Dunning wrote a long reply in the *Bee-Hive* of 8 April 1871. After noting that he had 'a great respect' for Beesly and that his motives were undoubtedly of the 'purest', Dunning characterised Beesly as 'too innocent' to understand what was really happening in Paris. What had scandalised Dunning was the attack upon property – the appropriation of rent 'at the expense of the landlords' – and this, Dunning explained, was wholly contrary to the fundamental laws of exchange and could only lead to 'the law of barbarism, or of savage life'. Dunning ended his letter:

I should be glad to disbelieve the evident tendency to anarchy in Paris; and I hope, even now, if it be not past hoping for, that the confiscation of rent decreed by the Paris Commune may be reversed. If, however, these things go on they will tell their own tale, though the English newspapers, 'whose malice', Professor BEESLY tells us, 'is only exceeded by their ignorance', are entirely silent on the matter, which tale must in the end be that of anarchy, disaster and ruin.

It is reasonable to assume that Dunning had held classical-liberal views on property in general, and on land in particular, all his adult life. In a letter to the *Bee-Hive* (23 Oct 1869), at a time when the land question was being vigorously debated, Dunning wrote that while he accepted the demand for the revision of the land laws – in respect of primogeniture and entail – and thereby a more equal division of the land-holdings, he was wholly against any form of nationalisation. That, he argued, would contravene the freedom of exchange which he once again emphasised was for him the basis of civilised society.

In 1869, on his seventieth birthday Dunning was the guest of honour at a dinner in London. George Potter was in the chair. The testimonial with which Dunning was presented bore the following inscription:

This testimonial is presented to Mr Dunning for his indefatigable devotion to the interests and prosperity of the bookbinding trade, and for his zealous efforts to improve and elevate the social position of the working classes universally. His untiring capacity in every good work, his extensive knowledge of the laws that govern labour and capital, together with his energetic illustration and enforcement of those principles – both in his official and in his literary capacity – have been recognised by all classes as conducting much to the general welfare of society.

Dunning continued in office as secretary of the Bookbinders' Society until 1871, when on 8 June he was involved in a street accident (he was knocked down by a light trap) and had to spend eight weeks in hospital. He was discharged with paralysis of the left leg, resigned from his union position, and was given a pension of £1 per week. He still, however, edited the *Bookbinders' Trade Circular* for nearly two more years, until the summer of 1873. His health was now rapidly deteriorating, and he died at his home at 65 Napier Street, Hoxton, on 23 December 1873. Almost the last act of his life was correcting the proofs of the reprint of his 1860 pamphlet on *Trades' Unions and Strikes*. He left effects of under £100 to his wife, Susannah, and was buried in Abney Park Cemetery.

Dunning was a quiet scholarly man, interested in music, painting and photography. He had a good bass voice and could play the organ and the violin. He took great interest in a class of blind persons, conducted by a Mr Thomas Ireland. Dunning went occasionally to read to them and he wrote a quite widely circulated pamphlet on the *Best Mode of Relieving the Blind,* which ran to four editions.

In the London trade union world Dunning was a quiet but impressive figure. He was always prepared to use the 'no politics' rule in union affairs, but like so many of his contemporaries he was not consistent. The outstanding instance in his case was probably his objection in 1864 to the London Trades Council's becoming directly involved in support of the Federal cause in the American Civil War. He himself seems to have maintained a continuous interest in political affairs, and on the franchise issue and the legal position of trade unions, was fully prepared to involve unions in the agitation and campaigns. It is probable that his independent, rather conservative attitudes on some issues restricted his general influence in the trade union movement, although he seems deliberately not to have sought publicity. He rarely, for example, appeared on public platforms. Some sixty or seventy people only followed his funeral cortège and this may be compared with the impressive demonstration on the occasion of William Allan's death which took place some nine months later; although part of the reasons for the difference must lie in the relative importance of the unions they each served. Dunning's career is, however, worth more attention than it has usually been given. Although he was more intelligent and lively than the majority of his trade union colleagues, his attitudes and policies were in most respects typical of those building the trade union movement in the decades which followed the decline of Chartism. Much of the general approach of these years may be summed up in the words which Dunning himself used on the title-page of *The Bookbinders' Trade Circular*: 'United to Support, but Not Combined to Injure'.

Writings: Dunning wrote most editorials and much other material in the *Bookbinders' Trade Circular*, 1850–73. He contributed many articles and letters to the *Bee-Hive* during 1861 to 1871, among them the following: 'The London Bookbinders' Strike', 20 Dec 1862 (letter); 'America – National Character and Religion of the South', 28 Mar 1863; 'Trades Societies and Working Men's Clubs', 28 Mar 1863 (letter); 'National Character of the Federal States', 16 May, 13 June and 11 July 1863; 'The Land Question', 23 Oct 1869 (letter); 'The Commune in Paris', 8 Apr 1871. Among his other writings may be noted: articles on political economy in the *Charter*, Jan–Dec 1839 [written as letters to the Editor]; evidence before S.C. on Conciliation 1856 XIII Qs 2147–240; 'Some Account of the London Consolidated Society of Bookbinders' in NAPSS, *Trades' Societies and Strikes* [1860] 93–104; *Trades' Unions and Strikes: their philosophy and intention* (1860) 52 pp.; 'How Calumny is propagated', *Industrial Mag.* 1, no. 1 (1862) 26–32.

Sources: (1) MSS: Thomas Dunning's scrap book (letters, leaflets, press cuttings, etc.), London Bookbinders' Branch, National Union of Printing, Bookbinding and paper Workers. (2) Other: Biographical sketch in *Bee-Hive*, 8 Nov 1873 repr. in *Bee-Hive Portrait Gallery*, 2 (1874); S. and B. Webb, *History of Trade Unionism* (1894); E. D. Adams, *Great Britain and the American Civil War* (New York, 1925); F. E. Gillespie, *Labor and Politics in England 1850–1867* (Duke Univ. Press, 1927); K. Marx and F. Engels, *Correspondence 1846–1895* (1934) *passim*; E. Howe and J. Child, *The Society of London Bookbinders* (1952); H. Pelling, *America and the British Left* (1956); R. Harrison, 'British Labour and the Confederacy', *Int. Rev. Social Hist.* 2, pt. 1 (1957) 78–105; A. R. Schoyen, *The Chartist Challenge* (1958); C. J. Bundock, *The National Union of Printing, Bookbinding and Paper Workers* (1959); S. Coltham, 'The *Bee-Hive* Newspaper: its origin and early struggles' in *Essays in Labour History*, ed. A. Briggs and J. Saville (1960) 174–204; R. Harrison, 'Professor Beesly and the Working Class Movement', ibid., 205–41; S. Coltham, 'George Potter, the Junta and the *Bee-Hive*', *Int. Rev. Social Hist.* 9, pt 3 (1964) 391–432 and 10, pt 1 (1965) 1–65; R. Harrison, *Before the Socialists* (1965); F. M. Leventhal, *Respectable Radical: George Howell and Victorian Working Class Politics* (1971). Obit. *Bookbinders' Trade Circular*, 25 Feb 1874.

STEPHEN COLTHAM
JOHN SAVILLE

See also: Robert APPLEGARTH; William NEWTON; *George POTTER.

EADES, Arthur (1863–1933)
TRADE UNIONIST AND CO-OPERATOR

Arthur Eades was born on 17 December 1863 in Grove Road West, Enfield, Middlesex. Alexander Eades, his father, who was a barrel borer at a gun factory, died while Arthur was still a child, leaving his wife Betsey with five children to bring up. Mrs Eades then moved to Emily Street in the Highgate district of Birmingham where, at the age of eight, Arthur began work as a half-timer. Later he joined the trade he was to follow in adult life and became apprenticed to a cabinet-maker.

In 1888 he entered the Alliance Cabinet-Makers' Society and within six months of taking out membership was made president of his branch. In 1896 he became its secretary and held this post for several years. Eades took a leading part in the work of a joint committee of the trade that was agitating for a wage increase; in 1890 he was elected president of this body, which was able to obtain an eight per cent advance in wages and higher overtime rates. At about the same time he became associated with the Birmingham Trades Council. He was chairman of one of its committees which raised a substantial sum for relief among coalminers in the 1893 strike, and in the same year he was elected vice-president of the Council. Two years later he became its president and in 1898 was elected to the secretaryship. Eades was also actively interested in the question of provision for the aged: along with J. V. Stevens, another prominent member of the Trades Council, he led an organising committee which, with financial support from George Cadbury, called a conference in March 1899 to hear Charles Booth put forward his proposals for old age pensions. The delegates who attended this conference represented some 350,000 members of trade and friendly societies in the Midlands. Two months later, in May 1899, the National Committee of Organised Labour on Old Age Pensions held its first meeting, and Stevens was appointed chairman; he occupied this office until 1902 (when he was succeeded by G. N. Barnes), although it was Frederick Rogers, the paid secretary, who was the committee's driving force.

In the municipal elections of 1893 Eades had stood unsuccessfully as an independent labour candidate for St Martin's ward. He also failed to gain a seat on the Birmingham School Board in 1896 when he was a Trades Council nominee. The following year, however, he stood as an Independent and was elected; later he served on the School Board's successor, the Education Committee. Education was one of his main interests. He used his standing in the local labour movement to promote an Industrial Polytechnic Exhibition, held in 1901 with the object of raising funds to provide scholarships to Birmingham University for working-class students. As secretary of a joint committee of trade, friendly and co-operative societies, he did much to organise this scheme, which was keenly supported by the Trades Council, whose president, Joseph Millington, also took an active part. Subsequently, Eades became a life-governor of Birmingham University; he was at that time the only working man to sit on the University's board of governors.

In 1901 he was trade union candidate for the Deritend ward of the City Council and in his campaign emphasised the Council's negligent treatment of the housing question; but he was defeated. Although as Trades Council secretary he signed, jointly with J. R. MacDonald, a letter convening a meeting of the Birmingham Trades Council and the Labour Representation Committee in July 1901, he was not in sympathy with the ideas of many of his colleagues. In 1903 he resigned and was replaced as secretary by a young socialist, J. E. Berry. Eades's influence on the Trades Council further waned as he became attracted by Joseph Chamberlain's tariff reform campaign, so much so that in the 1904 municipal elections the Council repudiated his candidature.

Eades was also an active co-operator. He was the first chairman of the Birmingham Printers, a co-operative established by F. H. Bruff in 1902, and for several years he sat on the committee of the Birmingham Co-operative Society. He took an especial interest in promoting the educational facilities provided by the co-operative movement.

As a young man he was noted as an expert marksman; having joined the Birmingham Volunteers in 1892, he won many prizes for the accuracy of his rifle-shooting. In later life Eades became a Quaker and was a regular attender at the Friends' Institute, where he was an adult scholar. Although he remained a delegate to the Trades Council, with which he was associated for some forty years, in later life he appears to have played only a small part in local labour politics. He died on 3 November 1933 at his home in Ombersley Road, Balsall Heath, aged sixty-nine. The funeral took place at Brandwood End Cemetery on 7 November when the service was conducted, by Barrow Cadbury and others, according to the usages of the Society of Friends. Eades was twice married, and he left a widow and three sons. His effects were valued at £297.

Writings: (with W. A. Dalley) *Souvenir of the Forty-eighth Annual Trade Union Congress* (Birmingham, 1916).

Sources: J. Corbett, *The Birmingham Trades Council 1866–1966* (1966). OBIT. *Birmingham Despatch* and *Birmingham Mail*, 6 Nov 1933; *Birmingham News*, 11 Nov 1933; *Birmingham Gazette*, 4 Dec 1933.

DAVID E. MARTIN

See also: Frank Herbert BRUFF; Joseph MILLINGTON; †Frederick ROGERS: John Valentine STEVENS.

FALLOWS, John Arthur (1864–1935)
CLERGYMAN, SOCIALIST COUNCILLOR AND JOURNALIST

Fallows was born at Gough Road, Edgbaston, on 22 December 1864 into a prosperous middle-class family which had had a long association with Birmingham. His great-grandfather was a solicitor, and his grandfather an architect and surveyor of high reputation. His father, Thomas Stratton Fallows, followed the profession of auctioneer, and married Jane, daughter of Ald. J. C. Wynn, who belonged to another well-known local family. Thomas Fallows was a Conservative member of the City Council from 1881, became an alderman, and in 1894 was mayor of Birmingham.

J. A. Fallows, who was the only son, was educated at Rugby School and Queen's College, Oxford, where he gained honours in the second class in Classical Moderations (1884), Greats and Law (1887) and History (1888). He was vice-president of his college debating society, took a keen interest in the university settlement movement, and was a local secretary of the Guild of St Matthew (the Christian Socialist organisation founded in 1877 by Stewart Headlam). These latter interests brought him into contact with a number of clergymen who directed his strong conviction of the need for greater social justice towards the acceptance of Socialist ideas. In 1890, having decided to enter the Church, he began work in the parish of St Andrew's, Stockwell, and soon after became curate at St Mary's, Huntingdon. At about this time, his father offered to purchase for him the advowson of the living of Solihull, but he refused, as his beliefs were undergoing further changes. He had been ordained in 1891, but in 1894 he renounced Holy Orders, resigned his curacy, and adopted the Unitarian faith. After preaching in a number of churches, he became a minister in Guildford.

In 1898 Fallows returned to Birmingham, where for the next few years he took an active part in Socialist politics. He frequently contributed to newspapers and magazines on various social questions, and as secretary of the Birmingham Socialist Centre he worked to gather converts from both Gladstonian liberalism and the unique local influence exerted by Joseph Chamberlain. Fallows pursued similar aims as secretary to the Birmingham Labour Church, a post (presumably unpaid) to which he was appointed in 1899. The Birmingham Labour Church had been founded in 1893, and its members were expected to adhere 'to the moral and economic laws that may be adduced from the Fatherhood of God *or* the Brotherhood of Man'. Its membership increased in the last year of the century, and its finances were improved through a substantial contribution by Fallows [Summers (1958) 336]; in 1900 it claimed a membership of a hundred and an average attendance of eighty at its Sunday evening services. Members of the Church were often active in other parts of the Labour movement, notably in the formation of the Birmingham Labour Representation Committee in 1901.

Besides acting as secretary of the Socialist Centre and the Labour Church, Fallows wrote and issued numerous leaflets on social problems, and was editor of the *Pioneer*, a magazine for Midland Socialists which appeared for twenty numbers between June 1899 and February 1902. As a member of the ILP, he was a delegate to the 1902 conference of the Labour Representation Committee, which met in Birmingham. He served for a time on the King's Norton

Board of Guardians, and as a councillor for Bordesley ward from 1902 to 1905. He was the first candidate to win a seat on the City Council with an explicitly socialist programme, but after serving for three years he was heavily defeated by a Liberal Unionist.

Shortly after, Fallows again left Birmingham, and the last thirty years of his life appear to have been spent quietly in retirement in Bournemouth. He died at his home there after a lengthy illness on 6 August 1935, and left an estate to the gross value of £66,285. Nothing has been discovered about his years in Bournemouth, and the Public Trustee administered his estate. There was a High Court action which attempted to render invalid the last will and testament governing the distribution of the estate, but the office of the Public Trustee is evidently not permitted to reveal any details of the action or its outcome, except that probate was granted to the Public Trustee in 1938.

Writings: *A Visit to Hell. Dedicated to W. H.* (Oxford, 1886); Birmingham Public Library holds a collection of leaflets and pamphlets by Fallows including the following: *Facts for Birmingham: the housing of the poor* (Midland Socialist Pamphlets no. 1, Birmingham Socialist Centre, 1899) 16 pp.; *Moral Teaching in the Board Schools* (Birmingham, 1900) 7 pp.; *Education and the Local Authorities* (Birmingham, 1901) 8 pp.; a collection of leaflets issued by Fallows with Midland Socialist Pamphlets [1902–5]; (with Fred Hughes) *The Housing Question in Birmingham* [1905] 4 pp.; *Three Years in the Birmingham City Council* [1905] 4 pp.; *A Cycling Tour in Denmark* (Birmingham, [1912]) 19 pp.; *An Introduction to the study of the French Revolution* (1914); (with H. T. Wilkins) *English Educational Endowments* (WEA, 1917); Editor of *Realistic Aphorisms and Purple Patches* [a collection of quotations] (1922); Editor of *Critical Aphorisms* [a collection of quotations] (1927); *The Story of German and English Relations* (NLP, n.d.) 11 pp.

Sources: A. T. Michell, *Rugby School Register* vol. 3 (Rugby, 1904); Birmingham

Cat.; A. Briggs, *History of Birmingham* vol. 2: *1865–1938* (1952); K. S. Inglis, 'The Labour Church Movement', *Int. Rev. Social Hist. 3* (1958) 445–60; D. F. Summers, 'The Labour Church and Allied Movements of the late 19th and early 20th centuries', (Edinburgh PhD), 1958); R. B. Rose, 'Protestant Nonconformity' *Victoria History of the Counties of England: A History of the County of Warwick* vol. 7: *The City of Birmingham* ed. W. B. Stephens (1964); biographical information: The Public Trustee, London. OBIT. *Birmingham Post*, 9 Aug 1935; *Birmingham Gazette*, 10 Aug 1935.

DAVID E. MARTIN

See also: Eldred HALLAS; Stewart Duckworth HEADLAM; John Valentine STEVENS.

FOX, Thomas (Tom) (1860–1934)
TRADE UNION LEADER

Tom Fox was born at Stalybridge in 1860 and educated at St Peter's School, Stalybridge and later at the evening classes of a local Mechanics' Institute. As a boy, he worked as a half-timer in a cotton mill for a wage of 1s 6d a week, but poor health forced him to give up this job and he became a shop assistant. Shop work was not to his taste, however, and at the age of twenty-one he enlisted in the King's Liverpool Regiment. He served in the Army for eight years, mostly in India and Burma, and nearly lost his life in the Burmese War of 1885–7. While fighting against the Dacoits, he was severely wounded in the chest by a rifle bullet fired from close range; fortunately a metal plate on his straps broke the force of the bullet, and, after three months in hospital, he was able to return to the field. Before leaving the Army he was wounded on two other occasions, and was awarded three service medals.

Retiring from the Army with the rank of sergeant, he took employment first as a general labourer in an ironworks, and later in a boilermakers' shop. Dissatisfied with the low wages paid for strenuous labour, he turned to trade unionism. In about 1892 he joined the organisation known as the Lancashire and Adjacent Counties' Labour Amalgamation, a union that had undertaken the task of organising unskilled and casual labour in the district. Its secretary was Leonard Hall. Fox was elected to the executive committee, and in 1894 succeeded Hall in the secretaryship, a position he retained until 1916. The name of the union was changed in the mid-1890s to the British Labour Amalgamation, and it was finally absorbed into what became the National Union of General and Municipal Workers in 1924. During the period of Fox's leadership, the membership and financial resources of the union increased substantially, an advance was secured in the wages of engineers' labourers, and the working conditions of other sections of the union's membership were improved. During the 1890s Fox also became known in the political as well as the industrial wing of the local labour movement. He joined the ILP shortly after its formation, and he was one of many who were influenced by Robert Blatchford.

From 1901, Fox served on the executive committee of the Manchester and Salford Trades and Labour Council as a delegate from the British Labour Amalgamation. Many new branches were being formed, with Manchester and Salford as areas of strong union activity. After 1902, Fox's branch was known as the Manchester Central Branch, for which he also acted as secretary. In addition, in 1906 and 1907 he was secretary of the newly-formed Salford No. 1 Branch of the Amalgamation.

In 1906, in A. A. Purcell's first year as president of the Manchester and Salford Trades and Labour Council, Fox succeeded G. D. Kelley as its secretary, a post he held until he was elected vice-president in 1910. He was president from 1911 to 1913, and from 1916 to 1922 acted as treasurer, again during Purcell's years as president of the Trades Council. From 1909 onwards, Fox was a Trades Council representative on the Co-operative Union Ltd, and also on the Lancashire and Cheshire Federation of Trades and Labour Councils, of which body he was secretary in 1911 and 1912. In 1910 he sat on the executive committee of the national Labour Party as a representative of

trades councils. He was also a member of the advisory committee on Labour Exchanges.

Fox was nominated by the Trades Council in February 1904 as a Labour candidate for the Bradford ward of the Manchester City Council. He was successful by a majority of 906, and retained his seat until he became an alderman in 1919. In 1905 he moved a resolution that was adopted by the Council, which secured for all able-bodied labourers employed by the Corporation a minimum wage of 25s a week. Four years later, when there was much unemployment and distress in the city, he succeeded in persuading the Council to pass a resolution authorising a loan of £50,000 for local relief works. He was an early, persistent and powerful supporter of the women's suffrage movement.

In 1914 Fox was elected to the chairmanship of the Labour Party, and presided at the Glasgow conference of that year. During the First World War, as befitted an old soldier, he was active in encouraging young men to join the armed forces. In 1916 he became a director of the Manchester Ship Canal Co. He was elected an alderman in 1919, and in the same year accepted the City Council's invitation to become Lord Mayor, the first Labour Mayor to hold office in Manchester. One of the things for which his year of office was remembered was his attempt to provide employment for ex-servicemen. Towards the end of his term of office, he intervened in the 'Datum Line' coal strike by interviewing Evan Williams of the coal-owners and Frank Hodges, the miners' secretary, and, with the help of the Lord Mayor of London, induced Lloyd George to call the two sides together again [*Manchester Guardian*, 25 Oct 1920].

As a member of the City Council, Fox was interested in a number of municipal problems, and in particular was associated with the work of the Parks Committee, of which he was chairman for many years. It was to this work that he devoted much of his energy after 1920. During his chairmanship many important developments were carried out, especially in the provision of facilities for games: cricket and football pitches, bowling greens and tennis courts (the lack of which he had felt greatly in his own youth) increased rapidly in number, and several new parks and open spaces were acquired.

After several months of illness, Fox died at his home in Telfer Road, Longsight, Manchester, on 10 August 1934, at the age of seventy-three. He had been a practising Catholic and a Requiem Mass was held at St Edward's Roman Catholic Church, Rusholme, on 13 August before the burial at St Philip's Park Cemetery. At the funeral service were representatives from every part of the civic life of Manchester, and from numerous political, industrial and social organisations with which he had been associated. Fox was survived by his wife (he had married a Miss Platt of Stalybridge in 1918), three sons and one daughter. In his will he left effects to the value of £1938.

Sources: (1) MSS: Labour Party archives: LRC; (2) Other: Manchester and Salford Trades Council, *Annual Reports* (1901–22); L. Bather, 'A History of Manchester and Salford Trades Council' (Manchester PhD, 1956). OBIT. *Manchester Evening Chronicle*, 10 Aug 1934; *Daily Dispatch*, 11 and 14 Aug 1934; *Manchester Guardian*, 11 and 14 Aug 1934; *Times*, 11 Aug 1934.

RALPH HAYBURN

See also: *William Leonard HALL; George Davy KELLEY; †Albert Arthur PURCELL.

GIBBS, Charles (1843–1909)
TRADE UNIONIST

Born on 12 August 1843 at Dorking, Surrey, Charles Gibbs grew up in the Dorking area where as a boy he was a friend and playmate of W. G. Grace. He was, as he put it, 'partly educated' at various Church schools before entering the bakery trade at the age of fourteen. His hours of work were from 4 a.m. to 7 p.m., and he frequently worked in flooded cellars, so that he and his fellow workers had to stand in tubs to keep themselves dry. At the age of twenty he entered the specialised and more remunerative confectionery branch of the trade, studying for a time under Franc Atella, the famous chef to the Reform Club. At the

same age he joined the Associated Operative Bakers' and Confectioners' Union, of which he remained an active member for the rest of his life. In 1872 he took part in the big demonstration in Hyde Park against night work in the baking trade, and thereafter remained an ardent campaigner against night work and insanitary conditions in bakeries. Gibbs himself never again worked at night after the Hyde Park demonstration. At this time he was working for a wholesale confectioner in Mortlake, where his foreman persuaded him to join the Forum Club in Fleet Street, which was a meeting place for radicals and advanced thinkers. Gibbs regularly walked six miles from his home to attend its meetings, and his own progressive thinking stemmed from the ideas he first heard there.

This thinking was translated into practical action when he moved to West Bromwich in 1880, to join Messrs Couse as head confectioner, a position he filled with distinction for twenty-eight years; in 1889 he was awarded the certificate of merit of the National Association of Master Bakers and Confectioners, and two years later he was elected one of the judges at the Bakers' Exhibition in London. As Secretary of the Birmingham District Associated Operative Bakers' and Confectioners' Union Gibbs did much to build up the organisation of the union and improve the desperate working conditions of bakers in the Birmingham area. He also represented the union at the TUC on a number of occasions. In 1885 he became the representative of the Bakers' and Confectioners' Union on the Birmingham Trades Council, and seven years later he took a leading part in establishing the West Bromwich Trades Council. He was elected its first president in 1897 and combined membership of the two Councils with that of the Bakers' and Confectioners' Union until his death. Under his presidency the West Bromwich Council, though never strong numerically or financially, did much valuable work as a pressure group in what remained largely a non-union town until the great Workers' Union strike of 1913.

In politics Gibbs was for much of his adult life a Radical Liberal and on a number of occasions campaigned actively for Liberal candidiates in West Bromwich, but gradually became disillusioned with the Liberal Party's reluctance to embrace collectivist social and economic ideas. Accordingly he joined the Independent Labour Party soon after its foundation, and so became, with Harry Brockhouse, the pioneer of Socialism in West Bromwich. In 1895 he was elected to the West Bromwich School Board as the representative of the Trades Council, remaining a member until the dissolution of the Board under the Education Act of 1902. This, however, was his only political office. He was many times canvassed to contest seats on the town council but always declined, in the belief that the immediate practical ends he sought could be better obtained as the leader of a group standing outside the party struggle than as a lone voice in the council chamber. In both his early conversion to Socialism and his scepticism about the value of political office Gibbs was an untypical figure among Black Country labour leaders of the pre-1914 period. In other ways, too, he was unusual. The nature of his occupation and the relatively comfortable circumstances arising from his distinction in it, the exercise of influence through a Trades Council, and Gibbs's southern background, all marked him off from the usual pattern and provided the basis of a detachment and vision that was not always to be found among his contemporaries; he was, for instance, the only labour figure in the Black Country to be a member of the Peace Arbitration League. His achievements cannot adequately be measured in the precise terms of wage negotiations successfully carried through, of offices held, or of gains in union membership. Gibbs's distinctive contribution to the labour movement, like that of Joseph Deakin, was as a teacher of others, who found their inspiration in his idealism.

He was dogged by poor health in his last years, but remained active until about six months before his death, when illness finally confined him to his home. He died at his home, 117 Beeches Road, West Bromwich, on 27 July 1909, survived by a large family, mostly grown up and married. Following a service at St Philip's Church he was buried in West Bromwich Cemetery on 29 July. No will has been located.

Sources: Reports of union and trades council activities in *Birmingham Daily Post*, *Birmingham Weekly Post*, *West Bromwich Chronicle*, *West Bromwich Free Press*, 1880–1909; *West Bromwich Chronicle*, 13 Aug 1897 [photograph when Gibbs was president of West Bromwich Trades Council]; J. Corbett, *The Birmingham Trades Council 1866–1966* (1966); R. Hyman, *The Workers' Union* (Oxford, 1971). OBIT. *West Bromwich Chronicle* and *West Bromwich Free Press*, 30 July 1909; *West Bromwich Free Press*, 13 Aug 1909 [an appreciation].

ERIC TAYLOR

See also: *Henry BROCKHOUSE; *Joseph Thomas DEAKIN.

GILL, Alfred Henry (1856–1914)
TRADE UNION LEADER AND LABOUR MP

The son of John Gill, a cotton spinner, and his wife Mary Stott, A. H. Gill was born on 3 December 1856 at 36 Oldham Road, Rochdale. His father, who was treasurer of the Rochdale Operative Spinners' Association for many years, believed in thrift (a principle he inculcated into his son); by careful saving John Gill was able to open a newspaper shop, which gave Alfred at the age of seven his first job – delivering newspapers and selling them in the street. At ten he began work as a half-time little piecer in a cotton mill, becoming a full-timer after three years when he left St Mary's School, Balderstone. In 1879 he moved to the nearby town of Oldham, where he worked for eight years as a cotton spinner at the Moss Lane Spinning Co., Heyside. During this period he was active in the co-operative movement; he was elected to the education committee of the Crompton Co-operative Society, of which he later became a director, and, in 1885, chairman.

Though Gill's formal education had been limited, he continued to improve himself in a manner typical of the self-help philosophy among many working men. His advancement was closely associated with the system of work relationship then operating in the Lancashire cotton industry. A complicated list of piecework rates formed the basis of wage assessment, and the ability to apply it was the most important single part of the work of the permanent official. It demanded a special type of union officer, which the Webbs described:

> For although the lists are elaborately worked out in detail – the Bolton Spinning List, for instance, comprising eighty-five pages closely filled with figures – the intricacy of the calculations is such as to be beyond the comprehension not only of the ordinary operative or manufacturer, but even of the investigating mathematician without a very minute knowledge of the technical detail. Yet the week's earnings of every one of the tens of thousands of operatives are computed by an exact and often separate calculation under these lists. And when an alteration of the list is in question, the standard wage of a whole district may depend upon the quickness and accuracy with which the operatives' negotiator apprehends the precise effect of each projected change in any of the numerous factors in the calculation. It will be obvious that for work of this nature the successful organiser or "born orator" was frequently quite unfit. There grew up therefore, both among the weavers and the spinners, a system of selection of new secretaries by competitive examination, which has gradually been perfected as the examiners – that is, the existing officials – have themselves become more skilled [*History of Trade Unionism* (1894) 293–294; also *Industrial Democracy* (1897) 196–9, 312–13, for the competitive examination and duties of the officials].

This system gave Gill his opportunity, and as he has left a short account, it is worth reproducing in his own words his rise to the post of trade union official:

> On Jubilee Day, 1887 – no wonder the date is fixed firmly in my memory – I left Oldham to take up a better position, although still as an operative cotton spinner, at Pendlebury, near Manchester.

> Pendlebury was a small place compared with Oldham, and I found time hang rather heavily upon my hands.

> So, although I was over thirty years of age, I attended scientific and technological evening classes, and applied myself diligently to study with a view to improving my position in life.

> This, I think, bespeaks a certain amount of determination on my part, for it is no light matter for a grown man to live laborious days and studious nights – to paraphrase the well-known line.

> However, my industry had its reward. In 1896 the post of assistant-secretary to the Bolton and District Operative Spinners' Assocation fell vacant, and, one of fifteen candidates, I competed for it.

> After a stiff examination extending over two days, I was fortunate to be one of the first three, and on the voting taking place was successful in obtaining the appointment.

> Eight months later I became general secretary, a position I have held ever since [*Pearson's Weekly*, 22 Mar 1906].

In Bolton, Gill became a respected figure in progressive politics; in addition to his trade union work, he represented the Trades Council on the Bolton Technical Education Committee, and, from 1899 onwards, sat on the magistrate's bench. He was also a member of the Bolton and Manchester Chambers of Commerce, and a director of the British Cotton Growing Association; he served on the committee of the United Textile Factory Workers' Association for about fifteen years. He was noted for his skill as an organiser and his ability in settling disputes without resorting to strike action.

In 1903, sponsored by the Cotton Spinners, Gill was adopted as Bolton's LRC candidate, and in the general election of 1906 he contested the double-member constituency with George Harwood (Liberal) and G. J. Goschen (Conservative). Harwood was elected with a few hundred more votes than Gill, but Gill had a comfortable majority over Goschen. The arrangement between the local Liberal and Labour Parties by which each secured a seat was an amicable one, and it continued to operate in the elections of 1910 when on both occasions Gill was returned with Harwood.

Gill's chief interest in Parliament was in the operation of the Workmen's Compensation Act. He campaigned persistently from the back benches to end the many anomalies in the working of the Act (see, for his ideas, a major speech: *Hansard*, 20 May 1914); and on 25 June 1914, just before his death, he introduced an amending Bill. He also introduced a Bill to reduce the hours worked in the cotton trade from fifty-three to forty-eight a week by means of a sliding scale. At the time of his death he was vice-chairman of the Parliamentary Labour Party.

As a leader of the cotton spinners he became involved in the wider trade union movement: he was a member of the parliamentary committee of the TUC from 1903 to 1907 and again in 1913–14. At the 1907 Trades Union Congress, held in Bath, he occupied the presidential chair, and as a fraternal delegate of the TUC he visited the United States to attend the conference of the American Federation of Labour. During this visit Gill gave evidence before the New York State Commission on the operation of the workmen's compensation law in England. Like many of the Labour MPs he combined his trade union work with his House of Commons duties, and held the general secretaryship of the Bolton Operative Spinners' Association until his death.

In religion Gill was a Wesleyan Methodist and was closely connected with the Lower-place United Methodist Church and Sunday School. He had joined the Band of Hope at the age of twelve, of which he became secretary. He became a member of the Improvement Class and was a total abstainer. In June 1913 he suffered a heart attack, and after a period of slow recovery, he again fell ill in July 1914. He died at his Bolton home on 27 August 1914, aged fifty-seven. His funeral took place on 31 August at Halliwell Road Wesleyan Church; he was buried in the nonconformist part of Heaton Cemetery. His wife, Sarah Ellen Greenwood, one son and four daughters survived him, and he left effects to the value of £3750.

Writings: 'The Organisation of Labour as a political force', *Trans. Manchester Statistical Society* (1904–5).

Sources: *WWW* (1897–1916); 'How I got on', *Pearson's Weekly*, 22 Mar 1906; *Dod* (1907–14); B. C. Roberts, *The Trades Union Congress 1868–1921* (1958); E. Hopwood, *A History of the Lancashire Cotton Industry and the Amalgamated Weavers' Association* (Manchester, 1969); P. F. Clarke, *Lancashire and the New Liberalism* (Cambridge, 1971). OBIT. *Bolton Evening News*, 27 Aug 1914; *Bolton Journal and Guardian, Manchester Guardian* and *Times*, 28 Aug 1914; *Cotton Factory Times*, 28 Aug and 4 Sep 1914; *Rochdale Observer*, 29 Aug 1914.

DAVID E. MARTIN

See also: George LANSBURY, for British Labour Party, 1900–13.

GROVES, William Henry (1876–1933)
TRADE UNIONIST

Born on 21 April 1876 at Level Street, Brierley Hill, Staffordshire, William Henry Groves was the second son of William Groves, an ironworker employed at the Earl of Dudley's Round Oak Iron and Steel Works, and his wife Mary Ann (née Jeavons). At the age of thirteen he joined his father and elder brother in the Round Oak Works, where he was employed, first as a jib crane driver and then as a melting shop operative, for the whole of his working life. In turn he was joined by two younger brothers, one of whom was later killed in an accident in the works. At the age of twenty-two he married Agnes Baker and they set up house for a time in High Street, Holly Hall, before moving to Ivanhoe Street, Scott's Green, Dudley, where they then lived for most of their married life. Groves was an Anglican, and while living in Dudley worshipped regularly at St Luke's Church.

As a young man Groves took a keen interest in the welfare activities fostered by Lord Dudley at the Round Oak Works. He became vice-chairman of the Hospital Committee, and the first chairman of the Sports

Club. In this latter capacity he was largely responsible for raising the funds required for the layout and equipment of the excellent Round Oak Sports and Social Club. A keen bowls player and a good cricketer, he was captain of the Round Oak Works cricket team for a number of years, having previously played for Brierley Hill Cricket Club. He always spent his annual holiday in Rhyl, and for many years organised a visiting eleven to play Rhyl Cricket Club during their annual cricket festival.

Groves's interest in the welfare of his fellow workers led to an involvement in trade unionism, and he became an active member of the Associated Iron and Steel Workers of Great Britain, formed in 1887 under the presidency of William Aucott, who had been one of the main driving forces behind trade unionism in the industry since the establishment of the Associated Ironworkers of Great Britain at Brierley Hill in 1863. When on 1 January 1917 the Associated Iron and Steel Workers joined with John Hodge's Steel Smelters' Union and the National Steelworkers' Association to form the British Iron Steel and Kindred Trades Association (BISAKTA) within the Iron and Steel Trades Confederation, Groves was quick to recognise the value of this development in reducing the number of unions in the industry and establishing a unified organisation which could speak for the great majority of workers in the iron and steel trades. He had been president of the Round Oak branch of the Associated Iron and Steel Workers since 1914, and he now threw his considerable energy and organising ability behind the new organisation. He became the first president of the Round Oak branch of BISAKTA and held this position until about a year before his death. He also held at various times the offices of district auditor, divisional president, and area president, and from 1923 to 1925 he was a member of BISAKTA's national executive committee; he represented BISAKTA on a number of occasions at both the TUC and the annual conferences of the Labour Party.

On 24 September 1932, when failing health had forced him to relinquish all union and other offices, he was presented with a cheque and an illuminated address in recognition of his many services to the union. His reply on that occasion, as well as indicating something of his good sense and personal modesty, also revealed a great deal about his industrial attitudes. The tendency towards conciliation and co-operation with management was particularly strong among Black Country iron and steel workers by virtue of their long experience, dating back to 1872, of resolving disputes through a succession of Wages Boards, and Groves's remarks made it clear that he stood firmly in this tradition. He said:

I have always played for my side, and my side has always been the men's side. I have played for my side to win, but I have never forgotten there are two sides, and each side has the right, providing it keeps within the laws and regulations of the game, to play the game to win. The other side have as much right to play the game for themselves as we have the right to play the game for ourselves. Our associations at Round Oak have been of the pleasantest character and I have a high regard for all the directors and departmental managers at the works . . . The steel trade has been under a cloud of depression for the past twelve years. There are signs, very faint perhaps, that the depression is going to lift, and I sincerely hope it will do so in the near future and that the management at Round Oak and the members of the Iron and Steel Trades Confederation will march forward to a new era of prosperity. Again I thank you all very much for your kindness. My last words to you my fellow workers are these: Get inside your Confederation, give it your loyalty, and give the works management your co-operation in furthering the interests and welfare of the industry [*Stourbridge County Express*, 1 Oct 1932].

In addition to his work for his own union, Groves was a prominent member of many local committees concerned with trade union and labour matters. He was an assessor of the Court of Referees, a member of the Dudley Borough Advisory Committee, and in 1925 he was appointed a Dudley magistrate.

In the last years of his life he returned to live in Brierley Hill, became president of the Brierley Hill Trades and Labour Council, and his organising ability was a main factor in its successes on the Brierley Hill Urban District Council. He represented the Brierley Hill Trades Council on the Divisional Council of the Labour Party.

For much of his adult life Groves was a member of the Conservative Party, and frequently campaigned for Sir Arthur Griffith-Boscawen, the Conservative MP for Dudley (December 1910 to 1921). However, Groves gradually became disillusioned with the Conservative Party's failure to deal effectively with social and economic problems, and in 1920 he changed his allegiance and thereafter was closely associated with Charles Sitch, Labour MP for Kingswinford from 1918 to 1931. It was a measure of Groves's personality that his change of political allegiance was made without leaving any legacy of malice or bitterness. During the long illness that preceded his death, A. S. Todd, the Conservative MP for Kingswinford, was a frequent caller at his home, and on one occasion he was visited by the Earl of Dudley.

Groves died at his home in John Street, Brockmoor, Brierley Hill, on 19 April 1933, just two days before his fifty-seventh birthday. He was survived by his wife and one son, Edgar, who had followed his father into the Round Oak Works on leaving school, so taking the family's record of service at the works to a total of more than 200 years. On 22 April, following a service at Brierley Hill Parish Church, Groves was buried in the churchyard. He left effects valued at £508.

Sources: Reports of union and political activities in *County Advertiser* [for Staffordshire and Worcestershire], *County Herald* [for Staffordshire and Worcestershire], *Dudley Herald* and *Stourbridge County Express*, 1900–32, *Ironworkers' J.*, 1900–17; *J. of the Iron and Steel Trades Confederation*, 1917–1923; *Man and Metal*, 1923–32; J. Hodge, *From Workman's Cottage to Windsor Castle* [1931]; *Stourbridge County Express* and *County Advertiser and Herald* [for Staffordshire and Worcestershire], 1 Oct 1932; A.

Pugh, *Men of Steel* (1951); J. C. Carr and W. Taplin, *History of the British Steel Industry* (Oxford, 1962); personal information: E. Groves, Hinksford, Brierley Hill, son. OBIT. *County Advertiser and Herald* [for Staffordshire and Worcestershire], *Dudley Herald*, and *Stourbridge County Express*, 22 Apr 1933; *Man and Metal* (June 1933) [photographs with each obituary].

ERIC TAYLOR

See also: William AUCOTT; *John HODGE; Charles SITCH.

HACKETT, Thomas (1869–1950)
CO-OPERATOR AND LABOUR COUNCILLOR

Tom Hackett was born on 14 June 1869 in Crawford Street, Smethwick. His father, also named Thomas, started work at the age of six as an agricultural labourer, and later became a groom to the firm of Nettlefold and Chamberlain (subsequently Guest, Keen and Nettlefolds); he married Catherine Risdon of Exeter, and Tom was the eldest son of a family of seven sons and a daughter. The children, who all rose to responsible positions, were educated at Dudley Road Board School, and Tom, who left school at thirteen, later attended Corbett Street Evening School.

At the age of ten Hackett had begun to earn his living as a newsboy, and he took his first full-time job in the engineers' fitting shop at Nettlefold's. During the ten years he worked at Nettlefold's he learned the trade of engineering. In November 1892 he took a post with Cadbury Bros, the chocolate manufacturers, whom he joined for a wage of 31s – just one shilling a week more than his previous job had paid. At Cadbury's he soon began to make his mark and worked his way up to senior management. He used to boast that he had worked on the highest stack and in the deepest cellar at Bournville, and in every hour of the twenty-four. In 1901 he was made night foreman, and in October 1906 he was promoted to works foreman, a position he held continuously until he retired in 1932.

Hackett showed much of that combination of entrepreneurial skill and paternalism that was characteristic of the Cadbury family. He was noted for the enormous energy and enthusiasm with which he undertook his work and the deep interest he had in the welfare of the factory personnel. He largely organised the Works Council, established after the publication of the Whitley Report in 1917: he helped to draft its constitution, set up committees to represent the workers, and for twelve years was chairman of the Men's Rules and Discipline Committee.

Like the Cadburys he was active in public affairs. In 1913 he was elected to the Birmingham City Council as the Labour representative of the Rotton Park ward. He was proposed for the aldermanic bench in 1920, only to be defeated by a single vote. Several years later, in November 1932, he was elected for Northfield ward, and was made an alderman in 1941. Having served as a councillor and alderman for a total of twenty-four years, he failed to secure re-election in 1949 when the Conservatives came into the council with a majority.

In the First World War Hackett was a conscientious objector, although too old to be eligible for conscription. Opponents raised his anti-war beliefs into an issue when he contested the King's Norton division of Birmingham in the 1918 general election. He was one of two candidates sponsored by the Birmingham and District Co-operative Representation Council (and endorsed by the Labour Party), and in a three-cornered contest he was runner-up to the Coalition Conservative, Sir H. Austin. The BDCRC subsequently became known as the Birmingham Co-operative Party, and Hackett was its chairman from 1919 to 1923.

He was a dedicated co-operator, giving much of his time outside Cadburys to the movement. In 1892 he had joined the Ten Acres and Stirchley Co-operative Society, and was appointed as a director two years later at the age of twenty-four. Apart from a break of twelve months, he was president of the society from 1923 to 1946, and he served continuously on its education committee from 1905 to 1946. Education was one of his keenest interests: he sat on the central education committee of the Co-operative Union, and for many years he was a WEA

tutor and a member of the joint board of Birmingham University and the WEA. He took an active part in the work of the Selly Oak group of colleges, particularly Fircroft Adult School, which he served as president. He was also a governor of the Birmingham Blue Coat School. His characteristic vitality was evident in his lecturing and teaching; co-operation, trade unionism, local government and religion were the subjects upon which he spoke most often. He invariably refused to accept a fee.

During the economic depression of the inter-war years Hackett helped to establish the Brynmawr and Clydach Valley Industries (Public Utility Society) Ltd. Organised as a co-operative production society, this body aimed at bringing new jobs to parts of South Wales that were particularly hard hit by unemployment; and Hackett acted as its chairman up to 1939. He was also well known as a local magistrate (he was a Birmingham JP from 1929 until his death) and as a Methodist lay preacher.

After retirement he continued to live in the factory village of Bournville, where he was regarded with lasting affection. He died on 9 May 1950, aged eighty. In 1892 he had married Elizabeth James, and was survived by his wife, three sons and two daughters. One son became a garage proprietor, another a farmer, and the third a civil servant; the daughters both worked as secretaries at Cadbury's before their marriages. Hackett's funeral took place on 12 May and a memorial service was held on 19 May in the George Cadbury Hall. In his will he left effects to the value of £20,942.

Sources: Anon., *History of the Birmingham Co-operative Society Limited 1881–1931* (Birmingham, 1931); *Bournville Works Magazine 31* (Feb 1933) 33–6, 50; *Cornish's Birmingham Year Book* (1938–9); personal information: Mrs Margaret M. Hackett, daughter-in-law and G. Westwood, son-in-law, both of Birmingham. OBIT. *Birmingham Mail*, 10 May 1950; *Birmingham Post*, 11 May 1950; *Co-op. News*, 20 May 1950; *Bournville Works Magazine 48* (June 1950) 168–70, 172–3.

DAVID E. MARTIN

See also: †Albert Victor ALEXANDER, for Co-operative Party; †Fred HALL, for Co-operative Education.

HADFIELD, Charles (1821–84)
TRADE UNIONIST AND JOURNALIST

Born in Glossop, Derbyshire, in 1821, of unknown parents, Charles Hadfield entered the painting trade. While still a young man he went to Manchester and became secretary of the House Painters' Society. In Manchester he set about educating himself, at 5s 0d per quarter, at the Mechanics' Institute in Cooper Street, where he won prizes for some of his essays. He read a great deal, and developed a good memory and a facility for quotation in ordinary conversation. These interests led him to submit some verses to the *Manchester Examiner and Times* which were duly published. His first opportunity in journalism was provided for him by Joseph Johnson, and for a number of years he became a regular contributor to the *Examiner and Times*. He was a radical in politics and attracted to Feargus O'Connor and Chartism. In the late 1850s his articles advocated such causes as a free art gallery and public baths and washhouses, and he was active in the movement which secured for the Manchester building trades the Saturday half-holiday which had long been enjoyed by other classes of workers, and in other industrial matters.

In 1861 he co-operated with another housepainter, William Macdonald, a relative of the poet and novelist George Macdonald, in the founding of the Labour Journal Company Ltd. They proposed to raise a capital of £100 in 400 five shilling shares, one shilling to be paid on allotment and one shilling a week for four months, thus making it possible for working men to become shareholders. The scheme was announced in a new paper called *Weekly Wages*, a monthly publication issued for August, September and October 1861. Its price was one penny, and it was printed by the *Manchester Guardian* printer, William Evans, and published by the famous Manchester publisher Abel Heywood. It was 'intended to be an organ representative of the interests of all workmen receiving "weekly wages" ', and it was thought that at least one tenth of the workers in the Manchester area and the trades unions would support it. A 40,000 printing was said to have been projected, but prudence prevailed and only 4000 or so were printed of the first number. The circulation is not known, but it was found that it was impossible to continue after the third issue. At that time the Labour Journal Company had issued about seventy single shares, and £5 worth each to the House Painters' Society and another building trades society. The tone of the paper had been moderate enough to win the praise of Thomas Hughes, and it was claimed that 'it will not seek to prolong a war with capital; the day of such weak impolicy is past. It will aim to enter into an alliance with it.'

Hadfield was by this time moving into the ambit of Joseph Cowen's Northern Reform Union, for which he soon became a lecturing agent. When *Weekly Wages* collapsed he became a member of the staff of Cowen's *Newcastle Chronicle*. After only a brief period in the North East, however, he returned to Manchester as manager of the commercial department of the *Manchester Examiner and Times*. A series of articles contributed to the new *Manchester City News* in 1866, and that paper's want of an experienced journalist, secured for him the editorship, at £5 a week. He replaced the previous editor in September 1866. He was unable to make the paper a success in a time of poor trade, and in September 1868 he was asked to resign, which he did in October with three months' notice. Evidently he tried to find another job, but by December he was still unsuccessful, and began to plead with the directors to retain him, at a salary reduced first by £25 a year, then by 50 per cent, and then even as a contributor at £2 a week. The directors refused and he left at the end of December 1868.

As a full-time journalist he seems to have become less politically active, and after a period on the *Glasgow Herald* he became editor of the *Warrington Examiner* and other associated papers in the Cheshire area, before finally taking the editorship of the *Salford Weekly News.* He continued in this post until 1883, and died at Stretford on 4 June 1884. His earlier radicalism seems to have been moderated in later years, as he lost contact with his trade society and improved his economic position as a journalist, and his status as an editor. He had been brought up as a Roman Catholic, but he left the Church in his early manhood, and did not formally attach himself to any other Christian community. Of his family, nothing is known. No will has been found.

Sources: (1) MSS: Minute book of *Manchester City News,* Manchester PL; (2) Other: *Manchester City News,* 25 May 1878; unidentified cuttings in Manchester PL; T. Hughes, 'To Mr Cobden and other Public Men in Search of Work', *Macmill. Mag.* (Sept 1861) 329–35. OBIT. *Manchester Guardian,* 9 June 1884; *Salford Weekly News,* 14 June 1884.

ALLAN J. LEE

See also: *Feargus O'Connor; †Joseph Cowen.

HALL, Fred (1855–1933)
MINERS' LEADER, LIB-LAB AND THEN LABOUR MP

Born on 23 September 1855 at Oldbury, Worcestershire, on the borders of Staffordshire, Fred Hall started work at nine years of age as a trapper boy at a Staffordshire colliery and went to Yorkshire when he was fifteen to work at Aldwarke Main Colliery, Parkgate, near Rotherham, owned by John Brown and Co. Ltd. He took a prominent part in trade union affairs and was elected secretary of the Aldwarke Main Lodge of the Yorkshire Miners' Association in 1878 and in the following year became a checkweighman at Aldwarke Colliery. He was a delegate to the first annual conference of the Miners' Federation of Great Britain in January 1890, where he was elected one of the two auditors so that his name appears together with Thomas Ashton, secretary, on the first annual balance sheet. In 1898 he was appointed treasurer of the YMA and in

1904 succeeded William Parrott as agent of the Association; from 1904 to 1907 he represented the Yorkshire miners on the MFGB executive.

Hall was a close associate of Ben Pickard and like most of the late-nineteenth-century miners' leaders in Yorkshire and the North-East he was a fervent Liberal in politics. In March 1904 the YMA recommended that five more parliamentary candidates should be selected in readiness for any vacancy that might occur in the future. Hall was one of the five selected and he was chosen as prospective candidate by the Osgoldcross miners in the summer of 1905. The local Liberal Association had already invited a coal owner to consider the seat, and a bitter fight was in the making when William Parrott, MP for Normanton, suddenly died in November 1905. The miners' choice as his successor became an indication of the relative strength of the Lib-Labs and the ILP (whose nominee was Herbert Smith). Fred Hall won the vote, much to the relief of the local Liberals and he won the seat both at the by-election in November 1905 and at the general election of 1906, at which he continued to stand as a Lib-Lab [Gregory (1968) 107 ff.]. The trend within the MFGB towards affiliation to the Labour Party went against Fred Hall's Liberal grain, and he was firmly against the move. At the annual conference in 1908 of the MFGB at which it was finally decided to make formal application for admission to the Labour Party, it was moved – unsuccessfully – by James Haslam from Derbyshire and seconded by Fred Hall 'that in view of the fact that the number of votes against joining the Labour Representation Committee together with the number of members of the Federation who did not vote at all, far exceeds the number in favour of changing; this Conference is of opinion that another ballot should be taken, and that nothing less than a two-thirds membership vote be permitted to finally settle this question'.

Hall did not decline to sign the Labour Party constitution, and he continued to serve Normanton in the Labour interest from 1910 until his death. He relinquished his appointment as agent of the YMA in 1918 when it was ruled that miners' representatives in the House of Commons could not hold official posts in the Association. In 1919 he was made a junior Whip and in the same year was nominated a member of the House of Commons Committee of Selection. Among his principal interests was workmen's compensation and he was one of three Labour members of the Holman Gregory Committee which reported in 1920 on compensation law reform. In the Labour Government of 1924 he was a junior Lord of the Treasury.

Apart from his work for the miners and his parliamentary duties, he was much concerned with local government affairs, being the chairman of the Rawmarsh School Board for nine years, a member of the Rawmarsh Urban District Council for twenty years, also serving as chairman, and a member of the West Riding County Council for twenty-five years. He also served as a West Riding JP for a quarter of a century. His interests extended to the co-operative and friendly society movements: he was a member of the Barnsley Co-operative Society and in 1880 joined the Mundella's Pride Lodge, No. 148 of the British United Order of Oddfellows. He held various offices in the Order and was Grand Master in 1891. He was also a member of the committee of the Yorkshire Society for the Encouragement of Humane Treatment and Kindness to Pit Ponies, and a year or so before his death he had presided at a special supper in Barnsley given to pony drivers.

In religion he was a Methodist, having joined the United Methodist Church about 1880. He married in 1878 and there was a family of four sons and a daughter. Hall was much liked and respected, in his home town and at Westminster. He was regarded by his constituents as a very 'approachable' man, one whom you could 'chat with', as someone was reported to have said after Hall's death. He died at his Barnsley home on 18 April 1933 and following a service in the Blucher Street Methodist Church, he was buried at Rawmarsh Cemetery. His wife had predeceased him by a few years, but he was survived by his family, all of whom were married. He left an estate worth

£2,740. Hall was suceeded as Labour MP for Normanton by Tom Smith, formerly MP for Pontefract.

Sources: British United Order of Oddfellows, *Quarterly Mag.* (Sept 1891) 420; *Labour Record and Review* (Dec 1905); *Dod* (1918) and (1932); Departmental Committee on Workmen's Compensation Cmd 812 (1922); S. V. Bracher, *The Herald Book of Labour Members* (1923); *Labour Who's Who* (1927); *WWW* (1929–40); F. Bealey and H. Pelling, *Labour and Politics 1900–1906* (1958); R. Gregory, *The Miners and British Politics 1906–1914* (Oxford, 1968); biographical information: Barnsley Public Library; P. Wildman, British United Order of Oddfellows, Hale. OBIT. *Times*, 19 Apr 1933; *Barnsley Chronicle* and *Barnsley Independent*, 22 Apr 1933; *Labour Party Report* (1933); *TUC Report* (1933).
JOYCE BELLAMY
JOHN SAVILLE

See also: †Thomas ASHTON, for Mining Trade Unionism, 1900–14; †Benjamin PICKARD, for Mining Trade Unionism, 1880–99.

HALL, George Henry (1st Viscount Hall of Cynon Valley) (1881–1965)
MINER AND LABOUR MINISTER

Born on 31 December 1881 at Penrhiwceiber, near Mountain Ash, Glamorgan, he was one of eight children of a colliery ostler, George Hall, and his wife Ann. George attended the local elementary school but was only eight when his father died, leaving a family whose eldest child was a daughter of fifteen. In his spare time George sold home-made soft drinks to assist the family budget, and on 1 January 1894, when he was twelve, he began work at the Penrikyber Colliery, near Mountain Ash. His mother, a deeply religious woman, was unable to read, but enjoyed listening to readings from the Bible by her children, who were encouraged to be regular Church attenders. George Hall remained a practising Anglican throughout his life.

In 1902, when he was twenty-one, he was

involved in a serious accident. The cables of the pit cage in which he was travelling broke, and the cage ricocheted from side to side of the shaft until it crashed on the pit-bottom. Hall's right leg was severely broken, his left leg less so, and he spent the next thirteen months confined to bed. The local vicar, the Rev. J. R. Jones of St Winifred's Church, became an increasingly frequent visitor, and their discussions at first centred upon religious matters, to the point where Hall was seriously considering entering the Church. But the vicar was also a radical, and in the end, when he had fully recovered from his accident, Hall turned towards politics. In 1908 he was elected the first Labour member for the Penrhiwceiber ward of the Mountain Ash Urban District Council, and in 1911 he was chosen from thirteen candidates to be a checkweighman at Penrikyber Colliery, in the Rhondda No. 1 district of the SWMF. Mountain Ash was in the Aberdare part of the Merthyr Tydfil parliamentary constituency, which since 1868 had been represented by two MPs, both of whom were Liberals until 1900. But the main occupation of the district was mining, and events during the 1890s – especially the 1898 lock-out – radicalised an important minority of the local miners. The ILP was also becoming an important political factor in the area [Arnot (1967) 47 ff.]. Consequently, in the election of 1900 when Keir Hardie stood as an independent Labour candidate he was elected, along with the Liberal, D. A. Thomas. George Hall could not fail to have been influenced by both the lock-out and the 1900 election; and at the three subsequent elections in 1906 and January and December of 1910, he is known to have vigorously supported Hardie.

By 1910 Hall had become chairman of the Merthyr Tydfil Labour Party and in 1916 he was elected chairman of his own Urban District Council, having particularly occupied himself on the Council with educational issues. Thus by the outbreak of the First World War he had had considerable experience both in trade union affairs – in addition to his position as checkweighman he was treasurer of his colliery lodge for some dozen years – and in local Labour

politics. What his more precise views were, however, it is difficult to determine. These were the years of rising militancy in the South Wales coalfield with strong syndicalist attitudes among many of the younger leaders; but what position Hall took towards, for example, *The Miners' Next Step*, and its demands, is unknown. He was an excellent speaker – the words flowed from him – and the strength of his local standing was revealed when the local lodges balloted in July 1920 for a miners' candidate for the Aberdare district of the Merthyr Tydfil constituency. (His political speeches were always in English, for he had only limited conversational Welsh; and he always sought help in the writing of the Welsh section of his election addresses.) Hall had a majority over the combined vote of the other two candidates and he contested, and won the seat in the general election of November 1922. The sitting member was C. B. Stanton, a former militant, who had turned jingoist during the First World War and who had won Aberdare in 1918 on the National Democratic Party ticket with a majority of over 16,000. George Hall was returned in 1922 with a majority over Stanton of 5217, and he was to represent the constituency for the next twenty-four years, with increased majorities in all the three elections in the twenties, and with two unopposed returns in 1931 and 1935.

He remained on the back benches until after the general election of 1929, when Ramsay MacDonald appointed him Civil Lord of the Admiralty. The appointment involved responsibility for the Admiralty's industrial employees, and Hall was judged by his contemporaries to have been a competent administrator. He also interested himself, as befitted a miner, in the distillation of oil from coal for use by the Navy; but the resignation of the Labour Government in August 1931 brought the experiments to an end.

There was never any likelihood that Hall would follow MacDonald, and he became a member of the greatly reduced Parliamentary Labour Party after the general election in the autumn of 1931. Throughout the 1930s he was an orthodox member of the

Labour Party, and at no time did he feel impelled to join any of the dissident groups or movements. Never an aggressive personality, he became increasingly moderate during his long service as an MP, and from the 1930s he belonged firmly to the right wing of the Party. When the Churchill Government was formed in the spring of 1940 he was appointed Under-Secretary of State for the Colonies. One of his first duties was to pilot through the Commons the Colonial Welfare and Development Bill. Always a believer in studying his task at first hand, he visited all the main islands in the West Indies and discussed affairs with local industrial, political and trade union leaders. When this tour ended he visited the U.S.A. with suggestions for suitable sites for American naval bases in the Caribbean. He hoped to see a new, enlightened outlook on colonial trusteeship when the war ended. After only two years in office he became, in February 1942, financial secretary to the Admiralty, much to the regret of a number of Labour members. Arthur Creech Jones, at the time a backbencher and much to the political left of Hall, wrote an interesting letter to him, deploring the change:

You have a good record of achievement and I am angry that in the midst of this important work for the social and economic development of the colonies you have been taken away. These are important formative years – your knowledge of labour, of poverty, of popular movements and your sympathy with the oppressed and your love of freedom – all these qualities are desperately important. And now Labour has no spokesman there. We have surrendered every point touching overseas – Foreign Office, Dominions and Colonies. It really is too bad. I just want you to know of my appreciation and gratitude for your comradeship and attention in your office [8 Feb 1942].

In 1942 also Hall was made a Privy Councillor, and in 1943 he was sent as one of the British representatives to a Bermuda conference on refugees and the reconstruction of enemy-occupied territories. In the same year he was moved from the Admiralty to become Under-Secretary of State for Foreign Affairs and in this position naturally came into close contact with Anthony Eden, the Foreign Secretary, with whom he developed an intimate friendship.

When the Labour Government took office after the general election of 1945, Hall first entered the Cabinet as Secretary of State for the Colonies. Creech Jones was his Under-Secretary. Hall soon began to initiate proposals for far-reaching reforms including some relating to inter-territorial organisation in East Africa and colonial development and welfare which were issued in December 1945. But, once again, Hall was prevented from continuing his work in the Colonial Office when, in 1946, he was reluctantly prevailed upon by Prime Minister Attlee to accept a peerage – on the ground that the Lords were desperately short of experienced Labour spokesmen – and he became Viscount Hall of Cynon Valley, the first ex-coalminer to sit in the Upper House. In October of the same year he was appointed First Lord of the Admiralty, and in 1947 he became deputy-leader of the House of Lords; both these positions he continued to hold until his retirement in 1951.

Hall always maintained very close links with his native Wales. He was a JP for Glamorgan and Deputy Lieutenant of the County. He served as chairman of the Welsh Youth Committee in 1939, was a governor of Cardiff University College, and received honorary degrees from the Universities of Birmingham and Wales. He maintained an especial interest in educational questions, and in 1944, when his constituents presented him with a testimonial for £2000 in recognition of his twenty-two years in Parliament, he donated all of it to found language scholarships which enabled grammar school children from the Aberdare valley to visit European countries.

In his retirement, he divided his time between his local Welsh interests and business. He had always been concerned with the need for the development of new industries in the Welsh mining valleys, and in 1937 encouraged the establishment of Aberdare Cables Ltd at a time of severe unemployment in the area. He became a director of this new cable company (later Aberdare Holdings Ltd), an appointment which brought some criticism at the time from sections of the local labour movement. During the middle 1950s he acted for some years as consultant to International Combustion (Holdings) Ltd (involved in nuclear power station construction), and was also on the board of South Wales Switchgear Ltd. From 1954 to 1962 he was chairman of Gwent and West of England Enterprises.

He was twice married: first in 1910 to Margaret Jones, a local girl who died in 1941 and by whom he had two sons; and secondly, to Alice M. Walker, in 1964. His eldest son, William George (Leonard) qualified as a surgeon, and after service in the Royal Navy joined the Powell Duffryn group in 1945 as medical adviser. Then from 1950 he began a new career as an investment adviser, and in 1969 was appointed by the Labour Government as first chairman of the Post Office Corporation. With the victory of the Conservative Party in the summer of 1970, Leonard Hall, who had succeeded to the title on his father's death, was dismissed from office by the new Government in November of that year, an act which aroused considerable controversy at the time. The second son, Bruce, a law student, was killed in 1942 on active service as an RNVR officer in HMS *Bedfordshire*.

George Hall died in Leicester on 8 November 1965 and was cremated after a service at All Saints, Blaby. A memorial service was held at his home church, St Winifred's, Penrhiwceiber, on 12 November, after which his ashes were buried in his native valley. He was survived by his wife and son, and he left an estate valued at £30,659.

Writings: 'The Co-ordination and Extension of the Social Insurance Services' [typescript 193–]; preface to J. E. Morgan, *A Village Workers Council – and what it accomplished* (Celtic Press, Pontypridd, n.d.).

Sources: We are grateful to the 2nd Viscount Hall for the loan of family papers, some of which have been copied and deposited in the Brynmor Jones Library, Hull University. The papers mainly comprise newspaper cuttings, correspondence and photographs. We also acknowledge the biographical information supplied by Lord Leatherland, and the assistance given by G. W. Hosgood, Clerk of Mountain Ash Urban District Council, the Rev. M. R. Rostron, Penrhiwceiber, and D. C. Weeks, Aberdare Holdings Ltd. Other sources: S. V. Bracher, *The Herald Book of Labour Members* (1923); *Empire Digest, 3,* no. 11 (Aug 1946); G. D. H. Cole, *History of the Labour Party from 1914* (1948); R. Page Arnot, *The Miners: years of struggle* (1953); C. L. Mowat, *Britain between the Wars* (1955); *WW* (1955); *Dod* (1964). Obit. *Times* and *Western Mail*, 9 Nov 1965; *Aberdare Leader*, 20 Nov 1965; *Labour Party Report* (1966).

JOYCE BELLAMY
JOHN SAVILLE

See also: *Clement Richard ATTLEE, for British Labour Party, 1931–51; †Arthur HENDERSON, for British Labour Party, 1914–1931; George LANSBURY, for British Labour Party 1900–13; †Charles Butt STANTON.

HALL, Joseph Arthur (Joe) (1887–1964)
MINERS' LEADER

'Joe' Hall, as he was called for much of his life, was born on 26 July 1887 at Lundhill, Wombwell, in South Yorkshire. He was the third youngest of eleven children; his mother, Emma Jane Brittain, had lost her first husband after bearing him three children, and then married Charles Hall, a colliery banksman, by whom she had a further eight children. Hall remembered his mother as a woman of great physical and mental strength who in addition to her own household chores went out to do washing and paperhanging in order to supplement the family income. She insisted that her children attend the local Methodist Sunday school, and it was here that Hall became a boy preacher. His formal education had been scanty; at three years of age he went to the Hemingfield Church of England School where he remained until the age of eleven years and nine months when he obtained his leaving certificate and got his first job.

Hall first began work at Darfield Main Colliery, some three miles from his home. He gave his age as twelve, and was signed on as an underground worker at a wage of 1s 3d per day, although in fact he was three months short of the legal starting age. His first task was carrying lamps to replace those at the coal face that had burned out, but after a few weeks he became a pony driver and was put in charge of a pony named 'Gladstone'. Most of his weekly spending money of a shilling went on books, including *The Pilgrim's Progress*, the works of Shakespeare and poetry; at Sunday school and Band of Hope meetings he recited poems such as 'The Deserted Village' and the 'Elegy in a Country Churchyard'. On reaching the age of thirteen he was taken on at Cortonwood Colliery, a pit nearer to his home, and worked there until 1904, when the pit was temporarily closed down after an underground fire. Hall obtained work at another colliery as a trammer, a job that involved moving empty tubs to the coal face and returning full tubs back to the loading point. The trammer (a Yorkshire term) was usually paid by the coal face worker at a rate only a little above that of the ordinary day-wage worker. Hall regarded the trammer's job as a harder task than hewing coal, and he rebelled against what he described as a 'vicious system' which encouraged bitterness between workers. When, at the age of twenty, he became a collier working his own stall, he paid his trammer the same money as himself. This was at Cortonwood, to which he had returned on its reopening, after a short spell at Wombwell Main Pit.

Hall joined the Cortonwood branch committee of the Yorkshire Miners in 1907, and three years later, at the age of twenty-three, he was elected as a delegate of the Yorkshire Miners' Association. In July 1915 he went to London as a delegate to a special conference called to appeal for the greatest possible output of coal. Among the speakers were Robert Smillie and Lloyd George, and Hall, who was greatly impressed by the oratory of the Minister of Munitions, re-

ported back to his colliery on the need for both management and men to pull their fullest weight. In 1916 he was elected as secretary of the Cortonwood branch, which had some 2000 members; in the following year Hall took another step up the ladder of trade union officialdom when he was elected as checkweighman. He continued to act as branch secretary, representing miners who had grievances against the colliery company and for so doing, Hall believed, he was victimised. The employers maintained that it was improper for a checkweighman to intervene in disputes, and in November 1922 they successfully applied to the Rotherham magistrates for his removal from the position. Evidence against Hall was given by some members of his branch as well as by the colliery management. The income from his remaining position of branch secretary was less than a pound a week, but he was eligible for election as the Miners' Safety Inspector, and this position he also filled until January 1925, when he obtained a post as a permanent official of the YMA, succeeding the Rev. John Hoskin as financial secretary.

At that time the YMA had over 160,000 members, each paying a contribution of a shilling a week; but because of the 1921 strike it had only limited financial assets. Thus in the nine-month stoppage of 1926, the available funds were equivalent to only three weeks' strike pay. Though Hall believed that with the collapse of the General Strike the miners should also end their struggle, he was active in organising meetings and distributing assistance to miners' families. He also fully supported the leadership of A. J. Cook and Herbert Smith; both were close friends of Hall's and he had a high opinion of their abilities. By the time the men returned to work, the YMA had lost 60,000 members and had incurred a large debt which had to be paid off, and it was not until 1930 that he could report that the financial situation had been restored.

In 1930 he became a member of the executive committee of the MFGB, on which he served continuously until 1952. One of Hall's principal concerns was to make the lives of underground workers less dangerous. He was present at many mining disasters, often organising rescue operations and leading teams to search for trapped men. After the Gresford Pit disaster of 1934 in which 265 men and boys were killed, the MFGB nominated Hall and Peter Lee to serve on the official Court of Inquiry. The Gresford disaster was the worst in mining for over twenty years [Arnot (1961) 131–43]. The Court of Inquiry had two assessors, John Brass and the MFGB president, Joseph Jones; and the North Wales and Border Counties Mineworkers' Association engaged Sir Stafford Cripps, Geoffrey Wilson and Arthur Henderson (junior) as their legal representatives. Stafford Cripps claimed no expenses or fee, while his junior barristers took only travelling and out-of-pocket expenses. The Inquiry lasted two years, mainly because it was months before any of the affected parts of the pit could be examined, although the fatal areas themselves were never explored. Evidence was provided to show that numerous breaches of the regulations had occurred, and that fear of losing their jobs caused many miners to accept what they knew to be dangerous conditions. Cripps's concluding speech took over three days to deliver and ran to nearly 150,000 words; a summary was later published as a pamphlet. Hall spoke more briefly in the closing stages, and he was followed by Hartley Shawcross, representing the owners. The Report of the Inquiry was debated for six hours in the House of Commons on 23 February 1937. One consequence of the Gresford disaster was the establishment in December 1935 of a Royal Commission on Safety in Mines, to which Hall gave evidence. The rough notes of his ms autobiography contain a number of gruesome accounts of pit rescue operations in which he was involved. On one occasion he was in Prague at a Miners' International Conference when news was received of a major disaster at Wharncliffe Woodmoor on 6 August 1936 where fifty-eight men and boys were killed. He wrote of his experiences:

The destruction was even worse than any I had seen then, and will say it now, as bad as any I have witnessed. The first victim I found was without head and legs, in fact his legs were found like covering wood over a bar support, his trunk was found inside a truck, he was a Deputy and his detonator bag was still round his body. Woodmoor provided more brutal damage to humans than any other disaster I have experienced, yet even in these circumstances in roads where full blast had not been evident, we found in one case nine men laid as if all had fallen together. Their bodies only a few feet from each other, indicating to me the valiant struggle they had made to escape their cruel end. Only 300 yards from safety but that was denied them.

Hall made a number of official visits to other countries. The Trades Union Congress of 1932 elected him as a delegate to the American Federation of Labor Convention held at Washington in 1933. While in the United States he spoke on the same platform as Franklin Roosevelt at the unveiling of a monument to Samuel Gompers. In 1937 Hall was a member of a seven-man delegation of the MFGB to the USSR, which toured mining areas and met Alexei Stakhanov, at that time a Russian miner famous internationally for his productivity records. The delegation, however, was unable to agree on a report of the visit: Joseph Jones, the MFGB president, was determinedly anti-Russian, while Arthur Horner and Will Lawther were sympathetic to the Soviet Union. There were three delegates on one side and three on the other, with Hall, whom they called 'the balance of power', between them [Horner (1960) 161].

In 1937 the campaign against the breakaway union of George Spencer, focused especially on the mining village of Harworth, reached its climax. Hall was among many who vigorously denounced Spencerism, comparing the struggle with that which was currently being waged in Spain. With the death of Herbert Smith in 1938, Hall succeeded, in the following year, to the presidency of the YMA, and held the post until his retirement in 1952. In 1942 he was a member of the National Joint Consultative Committee Sub-Committee which formulated amendments to the Government's White Paper on the Coal Industry. In the same year, when the White Paper had received Parliamentary approval, Hall was appointed as workmen's representative on the regional Coal Board for South and West Yorkshire. At the 1943 Blackpool conference of the MFGB the Yorkshire district's resolution on nationalisation of the mines was accepted; it was moved by E. Hough and seconded by Joe Hall.

As president of the YMA, Hall took a middle-of-the-road position. He could be outspoken in expressing the miners' case, as, for instance, when he issued a public statement replying to critics of absenteeism. To the annoyance of some right-wing members of the NUM, he was on good terms with a number of Communists and was a personal friend of Abe Moffat. But he was not a revolutionary; politically, he supported the Labour Party, and from 1920 until his death sat as a Labour councillor on the Wombwell Urban District Council, of which he was seven times chairman. He was twice offered parliamentary constituencies, but on both occasions preferred to continue as a trade union official. During the Second World War he used his influence to support the war effort, and on one occasion accused the Trotskyist *Socialist Appeal* of 'subversive and pro-Nazi' views when it printed a series of articles by Jock Haston on industrial disputes in the Yorkshire coalfield. The Workers' International League, to which Haston belonged, issued a four-page open letter to the YMA, attacking Hall, above the signature of E. (Ted) Grant, the editor of *Socialist Appeal*.

In 1949 Hall made another official visit abroad, this time to Calgary as a fraternal delegate to the Canadian TUC. In addition to his interest in local government he was for many years a magistrate, being appointed in 1932 for the West Riding of Yorkshire, and a school governor. He received the OBE in 1946. After his retirement from the YMA he acted as chief welfare officer for the north-eastern division of the National Coal Board until 1958. By religion Hall was a Methodist; as a young man he had been known as a temperance advocate and a lay-preacher on the Wes-

leyan Reform Circuit, but after 1922 he discontinued preaching. In 1927 Hall had been knocked down by a car and severely injured – for a year or more he went on crutches and sticks – but in the end he apparently made a complete recovery.

He died at his Wombwell home on 28 May 1964 and was cremated at Ardsley on 2 June. In 1911 he had married Lily, daughter of Albert Pigott, a miner, and had a son, who became a National Coal Board purchasing officer, and a daughter; his wife and children survived him. Hall left effects to the value of £23,042.

Sources: (1) MSS: autobiographical notes in possession of Mr C. A. Hall, Retford, son; (2) Secondary: *Gresford Disaster: Report of the Speech by Sir Stafford Cripps, K.C. at the Government Inquiry into the Causes of the Disaster, April 15th, 16th and 17th, 1936* (MFGB, 1936) 44 pp.; *The Harworth Colliery Strike: a report to the executive committee of the National Council for Civil Liberties* (March 1937) 16 pp.; Evidence before the R.C. on Safety in Coal Mines, vol. III 1936–8 Non-Parl. Qs 27876–28268; E. Grant, *An Open Letter to the Yorkshire Miners' Association: our answer to the slanders of the president, Mr Joseph Hall* (1942) 4 pp.; N. Dennis et al., *Coal is our life: an analysis of a Yorkshire mining community* (1956); A. Horner, *Incorrigible Rebel* (1960); R. Page Arnot, *The Miners in Crisis and War* (1961); A. Moffat, *My Life with the Miners* (1965); biographical information: NUM, Barnsley; personal information: C. A. Hall, Retford, son. OBIT. *Barnsley Chronicle* and *Times*, 30 May 1964; *Labour Party Report* (1964).

DAVID E. MARTIN

See also: *Arthur James COOK, for Mining Trade Unionism, 1915–26; *Arthur HORNER; Peter LEE, for Mining Trade Unionism, 1927–44; Herbert SMITH.

HALL, Thomas George (1858–1938)
TRADE UNIONIST AND CO-OPERATOR

Born in Hull on 13 July 1858, the son of William Henry Hall, a stationary engine driver, Thomas Hall was educated at St Peter's National School, Drypool, and became a joiner by trade. He was an active trade unionist all his life, becoming a local organiser for the Amalgamated Society of Woodworkers and then district delegate, and he had a long association with the Hull Trades Council, of which he became president in 1899 in succession to W. G. Millington. Hall played a leading role in the victory achieved by the Hull building workers against an employers' lock-out in 1899, when the latter attempted to use blackleg labour on a large scale, provided by the 'Free Labour' organisations of both Graeme Hunter and William Collison.

Hall was also active in local politics. He first contested a seat on the local council early in 1894; he was unsuccessful, but later in the same year he was elected on the platform of the Progressive Party. This group had been formed mainly on the initiative of the Trades Council and was made up of leading members of the Trades Council together with a few left-wing Liberals. Hall was a founder member of the Progressive Party, being present at the first public meeting when its policies were formulated: these included the municipalisation of monopolies, free technical education and the 'righteous treatment of labour'. The growth of socialist ideas within the Trades Council led to increasing tensions among their members elected to the city council, although voting was not yet disciplined; but after the Conservative members on the city council had coalesced to form the Municipal Reform Party in 1907, it was decided, in 1911, that Labour members should also vote as a group. Following this decision, Hall left the group and joined the Conservatives. He continued to represent South Newington ward until 1929, having become an alderman in 1915, but he was displaced by the new Labour majority in 1929. He had been Lord Mayor in 1919, becoming a JP in the same year. Between 1920 and 1922 he served as Conservative agent for the Central Hull parliamentary constituency.

Hall, with A. J. Boynton, was one of the early members of the Hull Co-operative Society, having joined the management committee in 1898. He served for some thirty years on the committee, was vice-president during the First World War and early post-war years and retired under the age rule in 1929.

He contributed much to the civic life of Hull. For thirty-five years he was a governor of Hymers College and for some years he was president of the Hull Musical Union. He was a member of the Hull Lodge of Freemasons. He was married twice: to Elizabeth Cockerill in 1885 and to Rebecca Osborne in 1907. He died at his Hull home on 3 April 1938, and following a service at St Columba's Church, he was cremated. No record of a will has been located.

Sources: *First Annual Yearbook of the Hull Trades and Labour Council* (1903); W. Collison, *The Apostle of Free Labour: the life of William Collison founder and general secretary of the National Free Labour Association* (1913); S. Marshall, *Co-operative Development in Kingston upon Hull and District* (Manchester, 1951); John Saville, 'Trade Unions and Free Labour: the background to the Taff Vale decision', in *Essays in Labour History*, ed. A. Briggs and J. Saville (1960) 317–50; R. Brown, 'The Labour Movement in Hull, 1870–1900 with Special Reference to New Unionism' (Hull MSc (Econ), 1966); idem, 'The Temperton v. Russell Case (1893): the beginning of the legal offensive against the unions', *Bull. of Economic Research, 23* no. 1 (May 1971) 50–66; personal information: A. Barnes, Hull and East Riding Co-op. Soc. Ltd.; Ald. S. Smith, MA, LL.D, Hessle. Obit. [Hull] *Daily Mail*, 4 Apr 1938, *Hull Times*, 9 Apr 1938.

JOHN SAVILLE

See also: †Arthur John BOYNTON; †William Henry BROWN, for Retail Co-operation 1900–45.

HALLAS, Eldred (1870–1926)
TRADE UNION LEADER AND LABOUR MP

Eldred Hallas was born on 23 February 1870 in Elm Street, Stainland, in the West Riding of Yorkshire, the son of Edward

Hallas and his wife Sarah (née Barrett). His father, who worked in the woollen trade, had been a Chartist, and Eldred, too, adopted radical ideas. Although his formal education was limited to elementary school and evening classes, he was able to obtain employment as a lecturer and journalist. In 1906 he moved to Birmingham to take up a post at the Ethical Church. He worked to build up Labour support in the King's Heath area, and appeared regularly on ILP platforms, and as a speaker at the Birmingham Labour Church. On one occasion he took part in a public debate in which he opposed co-operation as a means of political advancement. Hallas became quite a prolific writer in the years before the First World War. Mostly he published political pamphlets but he wrote at least one novel, *Josie* (1914), and two or three longer tracts of a philosophic-political nature, of which *The Upward Way: from fire-mist to the common-good* (1914) was a typical example.

In 1911 he contested the Duddeston and Nechells ward as a Labour candidate, and was elected to the City Council, upon which he served until 1919. He was Neville Chamberlain's strongest ally in supporting the promotion of the Birmingham Municipal Bank, and on his retirement from the Council he remained on the Bank Committee, as a co-opted member, until his death. With the outbreak of war in 1914 Hallas adopted an ultra-patriotic line. A capable public speaker, he frequently addressed recruiting meetings on the need to defeat German militarism. In 1916 he became chairman of the Birmingham branch of the British Workers' National League, an organisation that called on the working class to support the war fully. He became estranged from Labour politics for a time, and worked with W. J. Davis to set up a Trade Union Industrial Trades Council for Birmingham. This body, formed for a brief period in 1918, claimed to be non-political, and had similar aims to the National Trade Union Labour Party, which was anti-socialist and favoured a continuation of the wartime political truce.

In the general election of December 1918 Hallas contested the Duddeston division of Birmingham as the National Democratic Party candidate. He received Conservative support and was elected by a substantial majority over a Liberal opponent. Fifteen members of the NDP were returned to Parliament, but the party was short-lived and Hallas was one of its earliest defectors. In 1919 he declared that the NDP was not acting in the way he had expected and rejoined the Labour Party. Though he offered to resign, his election committee endorsed his change of allegiance. Hallas did not find the operation of the Commons to his liking, and in October 1920 announced that he did not intend to seek re-election; accustomed to the pragmatism of local politics, he found that in Parliament 'custom and precedent going back to Queen Anne, rest like a dead-weight on the shoulders of those who want to "deliver the goods"'. In the 1922 general election his former seat was easily won by the Conservative candidate.

On leaving Parliament, Hallas returned to the Birmingham trade union movement. He had founded the Birmingham and District Municipal Employees' Association in 1910; it operated until 1915, when it became part of the gas workers' society, which in turn amalgamated in 1921 with the National Union of General and Municipal Workers. From 1922 until his death he was an official of the NUGMW, and president of its Birmingham and Western District branch. One of his last public actions was to join, in May 1926, a General Trade Union Emergency Committee which had been formed to organise the General Strike in Birmingham. By this time he was a sick man, and at the end of May he entered a nursing home for treatment. He failed to recover from an operation, and died on 13 June 1926, aged fifty-six. The funeral took place at Brandwood End Cemetery on 16 June, when many representatives of the local labour movement were present at a service conducted by the Rev. S. Wood of Wythall Baptist Chapel. Hallas had married Clara Bottomley in 1892; his wife, a son and a daughter survived him. In his will he left effects to the value of £3081.

Writings: *The Higher Life* (Keighley, 1902);

It can see as well as hear (Birmingham Ethical and Psychical Society, pamphlet no. 2, 1906) 16 pp.; *Theohumanism* (Birmingham [1906?]) 45 pp; *Is Socialism possible?* (King's Heath branch ILP, 1908) 15 pp.; *The Land Problem: State ownership as true solution even with monetary loss* (Birmingham, [1914]) 11 pp.; *The Science of Goodness* (Birmingham, [1914]) 15 pp. [Repr. from the *Worcestershire & Staffordshire County Express*]; *The Upward Way: from fire-mist to the common-good* (Birmingham [1914]); *Josie* [a novel] (Birmingham, 1914); *The Religion of Democracy* (Birmingham [1914?]) 16 pp. [Repr. from the *Birmingham Weekly Mercury*]; *Labour and the War* (1915) n.p.; *Nationalism* (Birmingham [1915]) 12 pp.; *The International* (Birmingham branch of the Socialist National Defence Committee [1915?]) 12 pp.; *A German Soldier writes to his Father* (1918) 12 pp.; *Social Evolution in English History* (Birmingham [1922]); *Morality and Social Reform* [Birmingham, n.d.] 14 pp.

Sources: *WWW* (1916–28); Birmingham PL, *A Catalogue of the Birmingham Collection* (1918) supplement 1918–31 (1931); *Dod* (1919–22); *Cornish's Birmingham Year Book* (1922); A. Briggs, *History of Birmingham* vol. 2: *1865–1938* (1952); J. Corbett, *The Birmingham Trades Council 1866–1966* (1966); R. Douglas, 'The National Democratic Party and the British Workers' League', *Hist. J. 15*, no. 3 (1972) 533–52; J. O. Stubbs, 'Lord Milner and Patriotic Labour, 1914–1918', *Engl. Hist. Rev. 87*, no. 345 (Oct 1972) 717–54. OBIT. *Birmingham Gazette* and *Birmingham Post*, 14 June 1926; *Birmingham Despatch* and *Birmingham Mail*, 16 June 1926.

DAVID E. MARTIN

See also: John Arthur FALLOWS; John Valentine STEVENS.

HALSTEAD, Robert (1858–1930)
CO-OPERATOR AND EDUCATIONALIST

Robert Halstead was born on 19 May 1858 at Ramsden Wood, Walsden, near Todmorden, the son of Robert Halstead, a power loom weaver. He was left an orphan, and started work at the age of eight as a half-time doffer in a cotton spinning mill. He later graduated to cotton weaving. As a youth he attended evening classes run by the Working Men's Club and Institute, and when Oxford began to provide extension lectures in the upper Calder Valley, in the late eighties, he became one of the most dedicated local students. He attended courses in both Todmorden and Hebden Bridge, distinguished himself in the examinations, and won a succession of essay prizes which took him to most of the extension summer meetings held in the eighteen-nineties.

In the early nineties Halstead became a four-loom weaver for the Hebden Bridge Fustian Co-operative Manufacturing Society. This was founded in 1870 by a group of fustian cutters, some of them ex-Chartists, who had been influenced by the Christian Socialist advocacy of co-operative production. The work of the society expanded and diversified to include every process from yarn doubling, through weaving, dyeing and cutting, to the manufacture of fustian clothing. At one stage in the society's development there was a serious danger that non-working shareholders would turn it into an ordinary joint-stock company, but capital was eventually restricted to a return of five per cent with a limit of £100 on individual shareholding. The basic principle, as explained by Joseph Greenwood, one of the founders and for many years the manager of the society, was 'that labour ought to hire capital, pay it its wages, and make it the first charge on the profits at current rates only'. Effective control was in the hands of the member co-operative societies, over a hundred in number, and the workers, who owned about thirty per cent of the capital. After the payment of the five per cent dividend on capital, the disposable profit was divided into bonuses on wages, members' purchases and non-members' purchases at rates of 1s, 1s, and 6d in the pound in good years, and less, *pro rata*, in poor ones. The workers numbered 54 in 1874, 85 in 1880, 260 in 1890 and 356 in 1900. By the 1890s it was, by local standards, a large-scale enterprise.

The 'Fustian Co-op.' came to occupy a similar place in the world of productive co-operation to that of the Rochdale Pioneers in the consumer field. When the International Co-operative Congress met at Manchester in 1902, the delegates were taken in pilgrimage to Hebden Bridge. Their Belgian spokesman said that they had come to hail the solution of the class war (this was over-optimistic) and to salute 'the birthplace of productive co-operation' (this was inaccurate). But the activists of the Fustian Society who were drawn from both management and workers, played a leading part in the Co-operative Productive Federation (founded in 1882) and the Labour Association for the promotion of Labour Co-partnership, founded in 1884 following the Co-operative Congress at Derby, and later known as the Labour Co-partnership Association.

Robert Halstead became well known as an advocate of co-operative production, co-operative education and university extension. He lectured frequently to co-operative gatherings in Yorkshire and Lancashire, and wrote for the co-operative press, extension journals and other periodicals, including the *Economic Review*, the influential quarterly of the Christian Social Union. He gave evidence, on behalf of the Co-operative Union, to the Royal Commission on Secondary Education (1894–7). He was a natural choice to serve on the special committee on co-operative education appointed by the Co-operative Congress in 1896. In the following year the Fustian Society organised a conference which established a Lancashire and Yorkshire Centre of the Labour Co-partnership Association, of which Halstead became secretary. He was instrumental in the creation of a special co-operative wing to the extension summer meetings. All these activities were carried on in his spare time, after he had put in a fifty-hour week in the fustian mill.

Halstead was an eloquent advocate of a set of views shared by most of the 'Fustian Co-op.' activists. In matters of economic organisation they were equally opposed to the capitalist system and to state socialism. Halstead and his associates also had periodic skirmishes with other sections of the co-operative movement, particularly the CWS, which were criticised by the 'productives' for not practising profit-sharing with their employees.

Halstead's criticisms of the capitalist system were set out in two articles in the *Economic Review*. The first, on 'The Stress of Competition from a Workman's Point of View', appeared in January 1894. 'Beginning work at such an early age,' he wrote, he could 'testify to the evil effects of child labour upon himself as to health, education and moral life'. It would, however, be difficult to raise the age of children's employment without increasing family poverty, as long as 'the exacting customer and fortune-building capitalism insist on labour being paid on the lowest possible scale'. The strain on the workers was increasing through the speeding-up of machinery and the adulteration of materials, e.g. the excessive sizing of cotton. It was unfair to blame, and useless to preach to, individual masters, as they were themselves in the grip of a demoralising system. Halstead criticised the flow of books about 'fortunes made in business', which enticed the more able and energetic members of the working class away from the task of raising the material and moral level of their fellows to a search for private gain 'where their influence and worth is used only so far as they create fresh capital to be employed mainly for squeezing still larger fortunes out of us'. The workers should not too readily be blamed if they sought relief from hard work, unhealthy conditions, poor wages and insecurity, in drink.

Halstead warned his readers that 'the struggle between unearned privilege and unremunerated toil is but in its initial stage'. The 'gathering resentment' of the workers could, 'unless the labour movement is conducted with the utmost caution', lead to 'industrial paralysis and social disorder'. Trade unions had grown up as an essential defensive shield, but should take up a more positive role through an alliance with productive co-operation. In asking for the support of the Christian Social Union, he pointed to the danger that the toleration of a fundamentally immoral system would destroy the traditional religious faith of the workers.

Halstead developed his views in a second article in the *Economic Review*, in July 1895, entitled 'Some Thoughts of a Workman concerning the Plea for a Living Wage'. He defined a 'living wage' as one which would keep a man physically and mentally fit to be a good worker and a good citizen, 'and which will supply him with a reasonable satisfaction of the best aspirations and instincts common to humanity'. The level of income required was not fixed for all time, but would have to be revised upwards to take account of such factors as the increased strain caused by the speeding up of machinery, and also of rising aspirations as expressed in the desire for books, musical instruments and better clothes. Widespread literacy had allowed the workers to learn more about the way of life of the comfortable classes: 'the journals of fashion ... are fast obliterating some extreme social distinctions, to the scandal of those who think that manners and quality of costume should be standing institutions for keeping the poor in their places.' Despite falling prices and the benefits of co-operation, many families in the textile districts could achieve the conventional standard of comfort of their class only if two or more wages were coming in. Halstead suggested a system of family allowances, carefully planned so as not to encourage idleness or excessively large families, to allow mothers to stay at home while their children were young. His other proposals were a progressive income tax, the taxation of luxury goods, free education – as far as the university for 'exceptional students'; and, for his fellow workers, temperance, trade unions, and co-operation, especially co-operative production. He did not demand the equalisation of manual wages and professional incomes, but warned that the workers, who were as important a national resource as capital and business skill, would not indefinitely tolerate inequality of opportunity and unfair shares, would not always 'sharpen the sickles for those who reap the golden grain'.

'Co-operation and Socialism' was a theme frequently discussed at co-operative gatherings in the Calder Valley. Halstead rejected vehemently all forms of 'central-ised' or 'doctrinaire' Socialism. The most vigorous expression of this view appeared in an article in *Commonwealth*, another journal of the Christian Social Union, in 1899. It was written in reply to a review by Henry Macrosty of Henry Demarest Lloyd's book on *Labor Co-partnership*. Macrosty wrote disparagingly about producer co-operatives, including Hebden Bridge Fustian Society, commenting that 'Mrs Webb long ago exposed the character of many of the societies run by working-men capitalists'. In her book *The Co-operative Movement* (1891) 144–6, Beatrice Webb laid great stress on the fact that workers in the Fustian Society could not act as directors. But worker-shareholders voted in the election of directors and had a voice at general meetings; one of the pioneer band of fustian cutters was manager; and from time to time men 'stepped down' from the board of directors to become full-time workers for the society). Halstead defended societies such as the 'Fustian Co-op.', as genuine partnerships, which gave the workers a share in responsibility and organising enterprise as well as in profits. The system 'depends largely for initiation on a high level of character in the rank and file, and fosters and further elevates it by the bracing need of exercise'. Halstead rejected with scornful eloquence the Socialist alternative:

I have to confess that the idea of a well-drilled, well-conditioned, wage-earning labour population such as Mr Macrosty wants in order to stifle the craving for the bracing incentive of Labour Co-partnership is to me morally repulsive. Unless we workers can realise that the best part of the Industrial Democracy is, like the Kingdom of Heaven, within us to be worked into outward realisation, there seems to be very little heaven for us ... or very little democracy except an exchange from capitalistic to official domination at the top, with the same disinherited wage-earners at the bottom, eating such messes of pottage as the Jacobs of a centralised collectivism can find it in their hearts or in their power to give us [*Commonwealth* (Mar 1899) 76].

Halstead advocated the development of co-partnership in capitalist as well as co-operative enterprises. As secretary of the Lancashire and Yorkshire Centre of the Labour Co-partnership Association, he organised the Leeds Industrial Conference in March 1899. Thomas Burt MP presided over a distinguished gathering, including the Bishop of Rochester, Earl Grey, leading local employers, and Ben Turner and other trade union leaders. Papers were read, on Industrial Conciliation and Arbitration by Sir David Dale, and on Labour Co-partnership by Dr James Bonar. Halstead's own report of the proceedings concluded with this paragraph:

> There was present at the meeting a vigorous, though not a numerous body of socialists, who at various stages of the proceedings expressed their dissent from some of the speeches. But the meeting as a whole was in cordial sympathy with its purpose, and cannot fail to have a considerable educational effect.

In the followng year Robert Halstead read a paper at the British Association meeting on 'Wages in Co-partnership Establishments'. He produced figures which showed that workers in these enterprises worked on average two hours a week less than those in comparable employment outside, for better wages and a labour bonus averaging five to six per cent. The co-partnership enterprises had in the previous year made a profit of 13 per cent on their capital.

The urge to preach, as well as to practise, the principles of productive co-operation, and conviction that success in this field depended upon the moral character of the workers, made the Fustian Society enthusiastic for adult education. It was probably the only co-operative society to devote almost the whole of its educational funds to the support of university extension work. Halstead gave a good deal of thought both to the role of adult education as an agent of social change and to possible ways of 'bringing a scheme of comprehensive University teaching within reach of the toiling millions'. He was greatly influenced by what he saw as the ability, integrity and enthusiasm of the university extension lecturers, such as Hudson Shaw and Cosmo Gordon Lang, who came to Hebden Bridge and Todmorden. The impression was reinforced by his visits to summer meetings at Oxford and Cambridge: 'In respect of the blending of all classes in a democracy of common intellectual interests these gatherings succeed in a more marked degree than I have seen anywhere else.' A Calder Valley contingent could regularly be found taking part in debates and special events arranged for co-operators at the summer meetings, and Halstead himself lectured on some of these occasions. Halstead looked to the universities to

> educate men and women of high and low degree for larger and more intelligent public service . . . The great drawback to the working man at the present time is that he is largely at the mercy of political tacticians and extravagant socialists for his knowledge of history . . . If it be possible we want access to a knowledge of all the truth without reference to any other consideration than a right discharge of political duties in the largest sense of the word. We need contact with men whose great work is to impart knowledge from sources as uncontaminated as anything that is human can be . . . For the supply of this knowledge . . . it would be difficult to turn to any organisation as well qualified as University Extension . . . [*Oxford Univ. Extension Gazette* (May 1893) 109].

The benefits of a spread of workers' education would accrue not only in the long run through the promotion of peaceful social change, but immediately in the form of intellectual compensation for the 'so many kicks and so few half-pence' of working-class life.

> . . . Fortunately for the poor, the highest pleasures of life are not inseparably connected with material possessions. Wealth of intellect has other laws of distribution than material riches, and those who are poor in worldly goods need not succumb to the greater curse of poverty of ideas . . . [ibid.].

In his consideration of possible ways of bringing the universities and the workers together, Halstead anticipated much of the thinking which led in the following decade to the founding of the Workers' Educational Association. He envisaged a scheme involving a greatly increased provision of extension courses, so as to offer in each area both a choice of subjects and an opportunity for continuous and progressive study in each subject, supported financially by county councils and school boards. Co-operative funds could then be redirected to the provision of special libraries for extension students, and the energies of local extension organisers released for the task of running permanent student associations. These would in turn evangelise the workers, particularly those already made receptive to the call through membership of co-operative societies, mutual improvement societies, working men's clubs and Sunday Schools.

When Albert Mansbridge began the process of forming the WEA in 1903, Halstead offered his full support. The pamphlet which was used to launch the movement contained three articles by Mansbridge and a fourth in which Halstead argued, *inter alia*, that the best hope for mobilising trade union support lay in an approach to the Trades Councils. Halstead read a paper at the inaugural conference of the WEA at Oxford in 1903, and served on the executive committee of the association for several years.

In the meantime, Halstead had, in 1900, moved to Leicester to succeed Thomas Blandford as full-time secretary of the Co-operative Productive Federation. In his early years in this post he interpreted his role as an evangelical one, writing pamphlets and making lecture tours to spread the productive gospel. In 1904 a joint propaganda scheme was formulated with the Labour Co-partnership Association. About 1910, however, Halstead's health began to fail, and he had to confine himself to routine clerical labours which were uncongenial to a man with his particular gifts. The CPF appointed J. J. Worley as propaganda agent to take over the field work. Halstead's later years with the CPF were neither happy nor productive. The work of the Federation office came to be dominated by a centralised invoicing service operated for member societies, the business of which exceeded £400,000 a year by 1919. Halstead found himself, to his dismay, paid less than the finance officer who was his nominal subordinate. When Worley returned from military service to resume his position as propaganda agent, he too was paid a higher salary than Halstead. The latter, according to his friend W. Henry Brown (who wrote his obituary notice in the *Co-op. News*) 'steadily slowed down and evidenced the illness that has made him such a pathetic figure in the last sad years'. At the end of 1921 Halstead retired, receiving a gratuity of £400 but no pension. He was succeeded by Worley.

Halstead picked up his pen again to argue the case for his vision of industrial democracy, but poor health prevented him from making much use of his retirement. He died on 11 October 1930 in Bristol, and was buried in Kingswood Parish Church. He was survived by his wife Martha Ann and left effects valued at £760 gross, £440 net.

W. H. Brown recalled that he had first met Robert Halstead in the Hebden Bridge fustian mill in the classic pose of the workman-scholar with a book (Ruskin's *Crown of Wild Olives*) propped open so that he could read it in the intervals of attending to his looms. In his obituary article, Brown argued that Halstead should never have undertaken the job of secretary of the CPF, which compelled him to devote to office routine 'the visionary nature that was meant for propaganda amongst small groups and guilds'. Whether or not Brown was right on this point, there is no doubt that Halstead's importance lies less in his achievements as an organiser and more in his consistent advocacy of a particular path towards the development of an educated industrial democracy.

Writings: 'University Extension and Popular Audiences', *Oxford University Extension Gazette*, (Feb 1893) 59–60; 'Working Men and University Extension', ibid., (May 1893) 1708–10; 'The Stress of Competition from the Workman's Point of View', *Econ. Rev.*

4 (Jan 1894) 43–58; Reports and impressions of summer meetings in *University Extension J.* Oct 1894, Oct 1898, Dec 1900 and *University Extension Bull.*, no. 45 Michaelmas, 1922; (with S. Fielding), 'University Extension and County Council Grants' *Oxford University Extension Gazette* (Feb 1894) 58–9; Evidence, with F. Peaker of Co-op. Union Educational Cttee before R.C. on Secondary Education 1895 XLVI Qs 16, 212–408 and a separate note submitted to the Commission by Halstead on 'Teaching Political Economy to Working Men'; 'Some Thoughts of a Workman concerning the Plea for a Living Wage', *Econ. Rev.* 5 (July 1895) 350–69; *Co-operative Production viewed in the Light of some First Principles* (Manchester, 1895) 8 pp.; 'Education from a Working Man's Standpoint', *University Extension J.* (Jan 1897) 54–5; 'A Co-operative Wing of the Summer Meeting', ibid., (May 1897) 119–20; 'Practical Co-operation', *Econ. Rev.* 8 (Oct 1898) 446–62; 'Labour Co-partnership', *Commonwealth* 4, no. 3 (Mar 1899) 75–6; 'Report on the Leeds Industrial Conference', *Econ. Rev.* 9 (July 1899) 374–7; 'Variations of Wages in some Co-partnership Workshops, with some Comparisons with Non-co-operative Industries', in British Association for the Advancement of Science, *Report of the seventieth meeting* (1900) 849–50 [Repr. Labour Co-partnership Association, (1903) 16 pp.]; 'An Alliance with Co-operation and Trade Unions', *University Extension J.* (Apr 1903) 100–1; *Co-partnership and the Store Movement* [1909?] 11 pp.; *The Producer's Place in Society* (Manchester, 1921) 48 pp.; *History of Walsall Locks and Cart Gear Ltd 1873–1923* (Birmingham, 1924); *Thomas Blandford: hero and martyr of Co-partnership* (repr. from the *Co-operative Official* (Manchester, 1925) 15 pp.

Sources: (1) MSS: Minutes of Co-operative Productive Federation and Minute Book of the Lancashire and Yorkshire Centre of the Labour Co-partnership Association, CPF records, ref. DCF, Brynmor Jones Library, University of Hull. (2) *Co-op. Congress Reports*; *Co-op. News*; *Labour Co-partnership*; J. Greenwood, *The Story of the Formation of the Hebden Bridge Fustian Manufacturing Society Ltd* (Manchester, [1889]) 23 pp.; B. Webb, *The Co-operative Movement in Great Britain* (1891); H. D. Lloyd, *Labor Co-partnership: notes on a visit to co-operative workshops, factories and farms in Gt Britain and Ireland* (1898); A. Mansbridge, *An Adventure in Working-Class Education: being the story of the Workers' Educational Association 1903–1915* (1920); W. H. Draper, *University Extension 1873–1923* (Cambridge, 1923); G. D. H. Cole, *A Century of Co-operation* (Manchester, [1945?]); R. Peers, *Adult Education: a comparative study* (1958); J. F. C. Harrison, *Learning and Living 1790–1960: a study in the history of the English Adult Education Movement* (1961). OBIT. *Co-op. News*, 18 Oct 1930.

BERNARD JENNINGS

See also: †Thomas BLANDFORD; †William Henry BROWN; †Edward Owen GREENING, for Co-partnership; *Joseph GREENWOOD; †Fred HALL, for Co-operative Education; †Benjamin JONES, for Co-operative production; †Joseph James WORLEY.

HANCOCK, John George (1857–1940)
MINERS' LEADER AND LIB-LAB MP

Born on 15 October 1857 at Pinxton, Derbyshire, a colliery village on the border of Nottinghamshire, John Hancock was the son of Joseph Hancock, a miner, who was a leading member of the Derbyshire and Notts Miners' Association (1863–78) and a founder-member of the Notts Miners' Association (1881). John Hancock was educated at village schools, beginning work in the local colliery at the age of ten and going underground at thirteen. He was elected a checkweighman when in his early twenties and was the leading figure in the formation of a local miners' lodge which later, although within the county boundary of Derbyshire, was affiliated to the Nottinghamshire Miners' Association. Wages in Notts were higher for men working in the 'top hard' seam than in Derbyshire [J. E. Williams (1962) 369], and most of the border mines which elected to belong to the Notts Miners' Association did so for this reason.

At the first Miners' Demonstration held in Nottinghamshire in 1884, Hancock moved the opening resolution on the extension of the franchise to workers outside the towns. He was elected assistant secretary and agent of the Notts Miners' Association in 1892, and acted for a time as general secretary until Aaron Stewart took over this office in 1897. Hancock succeeded William Bailey as agent and financial secretary in 1896, and served as a full-time official of the Notts Miners' Association until 1927. He represented the Nottinghamshire miners on the MFGB executive for thirteen terms during the years 1895 to 1926; and in 1907 he gave evidence before the R.C. on Mines. Hancock's brother, Gervase, was also active in the Notts Miners' Association and was secretary of the Bentinck branch.

Hancock was a Gladstonian Liberal in politics, a Methodist by religion and an active temperance worker. He was a member of the 'Wharf', the name given to the United Methodist Free Church in Pinxton, and served the denomination as a local preacher for over fifty years. He was also involved in a wide range of other local activities: he served on the Pinxton School Board and the Basford and Nottingham Boards of Guardians and was a Liberal member of the Nottingham City Council 1904–9. In 1906 he was made a JP for the county. He entered the House of Commons in 1909 following a by-election in the Mid-Derbyshire constituency. The MFGB had already affiliated to the Labour Party, and before the election Hancock had informed the executive of the MFGB that he intended to sign the Labour Party constitution. The MFGB thereupon endorsed his candidature, and a few days later he was officially adopted as a Labour candidate – being the first miner to stand in that capacity since the MFGB's affiliation. Having thus secured Labour endorsement Hancock then assured the Mid-Derbyshire Liberal Association that his personal views remained Liberal; and during the election, in which he was vigorously supported by Sir Arthur Markham, the coalowner Liberal MP for Mansfield, he continued to employ the Liberal election agent and ignore the Labour Party. Hancock

retained the seat in the two general elections of 1910. The local Labour movement became increasingly exasperated at his stubborn adherence to a Lib-Lab position and after a number of attempts to repudiate him, the Labour Whip was withdrawn in October 1914. This meant that since Hancock was now not even a nominal member of the Labour Party, he forfeited the £100 a year parliamentary allowance, plus election expenses, which miner MPs drew from the MFGB Political Fund. Despite this, Hancock still enjoyed the confidence of the majority of miners in his constituency as well as the support of the Notts Miners' Association. The Council of the latter were vigorous in their condemnation of anti-war attitudes in general after August 1914, and in 1915 there was an attempt, led by Hancock and seconded by G. A. Spencer, to break away politically from the MFGB. The move was frustrated largely because of a protest campaign led by Herbert Booth, a left-wing member of the ILP who had recently returned from the Central Labour College, and W. Askew of Newstead. In 1916 Hancock became a vice-president of the British Workers' National League, a jingoistic organisation formed in 1916 to combat pacificism, and he later supported National Democratic Party candidates in opposition to the Labour Party. In the 1918 general election Hancock was elected unopposed for the Belper Division as a Liberal; although issued with the Coalition 'coupon', he repudiated it. He held the seat at the 1922 general election but was defeated in a three-cornered contest in 1923.

The war had greatly radicalised political opinion in the Nottinghamshire coalfield, and Hancock found himself subject to growing criticism. He had never been a successful public figure in the miners' world, having rather a businessman's attitude to administration; but as a backroom organiser he was hardworking and efficient. There was a serious attempt to remove him from office in May 1920 – the votes on the Council were thirteen against Hancock and twenty-five in his favour – and in 1921 the staffing committee decided to downgrade him from secretary to agent. (In the early days the agent was the senior official and the secretary the junior; after about 1916 the term agent was used for officials without a special functional title.) G. A. Spencer became general secretary and F. B. Varley financial secretary. Hancock remained strongly opposed to the political activities of the Association and particularly to the national campaign for nationalisation.

The most dramatic event in the history of the Nottinghamshire miners during the 1920s was the emergence of the Industrial Union, a breakaway from the MFGB which was vigorously supported in Nottinghamshire by the colliery owners. The Union came into existence in the final period of the miners' lock-out in 1926. Hancock did not join George Spencer immediately, although his general political and industrial attitudes were more or less identical, but in 1927 the Notts Miners' Association, because of financial stringency, decided to retire two of their agents. Hancock, who was already in his 70th year, was not unreasonably selected to go; and after losing his appointment with the Association, he was presented with a parting gift of £100. This was in lieu of a pension after a lifetime's service and Hancock felt he had been deprived of his pension by the militants who had dissipated in strike and lock-out pay money he had helped to accumulate with much difficulty. George Spencer persuaded Hancock to become treasurer of his Industrial Union immediately on leaving the Notts Association (this was mainly because Spencer was not entirely certain of the probity of some of his colleagues whereas Hancock was personally honest in the old-fashioned sense); and he remained an official of the Union for ten years. The fusion between Spencer's Union and the Notts Miners' Association on 1 September 1937 included a clause to the effect that Hancock could, if he wished, take up the position of agent with the new Federated Union; but he decided at last to retire.

He had married in 1882 Mary, daughter of Thos. Hoten of Pinxton and had four sons and a daughter. The eldest son became a manager of the Gelding Colliery but left to join a motor engineering concern; the youngest son was also at the same colliery until he retired; another son became a poultry farmer and the fourth a works chemist; of the daughter's career nothing is known. Hancock died on 19 July 1940 in his eighty-third year at his Sherwood home, and was buried in Redhill Cemetery. His wife and family survived him, and he left an estate valued at £1380.

Sources: Evidence before R.C. on Mines vol. III 1908 XX Qs 20216A–20770; *Dod* (1922); *WWW* (1929–40); R. Page Arnot, *The Miners*, vols 1 and 2 (1949 and 1953); A. R. Griffin, *The Miners of Nottinghamshire 1 : 1881–1914* (Nottingham, 1956) and *2 : 1914–44* (1962); J. E. Williams, *The Derbyshire Miners* (1962); H. A. Clegg et al., *A History of British Trade Unions since 1889: 1889–1910* (1964); H. Pelling, *Social Geography of British Elections 1885–1910* (1967); R. Gregory, *The Miners and British Politics 1906–1914* (Oxford, 1968); A. R. Griffin, *Mining in the East Midlands, 1550–1947* (1971); biographical information: Dr R. Page Arnot; Dr A. R. Griffin; personal information: E. Hancock Esq., Lowdham, near Nottingham, nephew; Miss L. Walvin, Pinxton. OBIT. *Nottingham Guardian*, and *Nottingham J.*, 20 July 1940; *Times*, 22 July 1940.

JOHN SAVILLE

See also: †Thomas ASHTON, for Mining Trade Unionism 1900–14; William BAILEY; *Arthur James COOK, for Mining Trade Unionism, 1915–26; Peter LEE, for Mining Trade Unionism, 1927–44; †Benjamin PICKARD, for Mining Trade Unionism, 1880–1899; †George Alfred SPENCER; Frank Bradley VARLEY.

HANDS, Thomas (1858–1938)
TRADE UNIONIST

Thomas Hands was born in the Aston district of Birmingham on 6 July 1858, the son of Charles Hands, a journeyman brasscaster, and his wife, Elizabeth Hood. His uncle, William Hands, was a silversmith and while still a young boy Thomas worked for him, being hidden in the attic when the factory inspector paid a visit. Consequently, he received little formal education although he did attend a night school for instruction in elementary science. At the age of fourteen he was apprenticed to his uncle and after seven years became qualified as a silversmith in 1879.

While still a young man he began to take part in public affairs. In 1878–9 he was secretary of the Birmingham branch of the National Anti-Vaccination Society and from 1882 to 1892 was active in the North Birmingham Liberal Association, serving for a short period as vice-president of the St George's ward branch of the Association. He broke with the Liberals in the 1890s, and regarded himself as a Socialist in politics after 1894. In later years he joined the Labour Party and assisted in the work of the Birmingham Trades Council.

He worked as a journeyman silversmith until 1909 when he became secretary of the Birmingham Silver and Electro-plate Operatives' Society. In 1914 he was appointed district secretary of the National Union of Gold, Silver and Allied Trades, a post he held until his retirement in 1927. On a number of occasions he was approached to stand for Parliament, but he always declined.

His other activities included acting as a trustee of the Ebenezer Sick Society and as an arbitrator of the Cannon Street Provident Sick Society. For many years he was a delegate to the Birmingham Hospital Saturday Fund. In 1911 he was appointed a magistrate for Birmingham. During the First World War he held the post of assistant secretary to the Aston Prince of Wales Fund and was a member of the local Munitions Tribunal. From its inception until 1919 he sat on the Birmingham Insurance Committee, and for a number of years before 1927 he belonged to the Greater Birmingham Employment Committee and the King's Roll Committee.

Hands was a spiritualist in his religious beliefs and acted as secretary of the Birmingham Spiritualist Union from 1899 to 1904. He died in hospital on 25 July 1938, aged eighty, and after a service at his son's home was buried at Lodge Hill Cemetery, Birmingham. In 1887 he had married Mary Louisa Shaw, who predeceased him. His eldest son was reported missing after the Battle of the Somme, 1 July 1916, but Hands was survived by a married daughter, who emigrated to Canada, and a son, who worked as a time and motion engineer.

Sources: *Cornish's Birmingham Year Book* (1938–9); personal information: B. A. Hands, Birmingham, son. OBIT. *Birmingham Gazette* and *Birmingham Post*, 26 July 1938.
DAVID E. MARTIN

See also: John Valentine STEVENS.

HARRISON, Frederic (1831–1923)
POSITIVIST, RADICAL REFORMER, JURIST, HISTORIAN

Born in London on 18 October 1831, Frederic Harrison was the eldest, but not the first born, child of Frederick and Jane Harrison (Jane was an Irishwoman, a daughter of Alexander Brice, of Belfast). His father was trained as an architect, but became a prosperous stockbroker. Frederic was born in Euston Square, but his childhood was spent in Muswell Hill, then a beautiful and peaceful village [*Memoirs 1* (1911) 2]; when he was nearly nine the family moved to a house designed by his father, 22 Oxford Square, Hyde Park; and from 1860 to 1870 his London home was 10 Lancaster Gate. The Harrisons also had a country home, Sutton Place near Guildford, of which Frederic wrote a charming account in *Annals of an Old Manor House* (1893). At the age of eleven, Frederic went to King's College School which he left as second in the school in 1849. From school Harrison went to Wadham College, Oxford, and there he was contemporary with E. S. Beesly and J. H. Bridges. Harrison was placed in the second class in Classical Moderations in 1852, but in the following year obtained a first in *Lit. Hum.*, J. M. Wilson, Mark Pattison and Jowett being the examiners. In 1854 Harrison was elected a Fellow of Wadham, a position he held until his marriage in 1870; and many years later, in 1899, he was elected an Honorary Fellow.

Harrison went to Oxford a High Churchman, sympathetic to neo-Catholicism. His college tutor was Richard Congreve, and it was under Congreve's influence that Harrison advanced towards an acceptance of the Positivism of Auguste Comte – more rapidly than Beesly, more slowly than Bridges; although according to Harrison's own testimony, none of the three adopted the positivist creed until several years after they had left Oxford. In 1855 Harrison began to read law, in Lincoln's Inn, and was called to the Bar in 1858.

Harrison and Beesly, who were to develop a very close working relationship, were strongly at odds with society during the 1850s without, however, achieving any coherent critique. 'What a vile system it is where you and I can't get a morning paper to print our remarks on politics', Harrison wrote to Beesly in 1859. The only political figure for whom they had any respect was John Bright; but Harrison was already coming to distrust orthodox political economy, and Bright was never going to step outside the boundaries of a *laissez-faire*, manufacturer's way of thinking. It was the Carlyle of *Past and Present* and *Chartism* to whom Harrison was responding emotionally in the 1850s, and Ruskin's essays in the *Cornhill Magazine* in 1860 (published as *Unto this Last* in 1862) produced in him the same sense of outrage at the gospel of Mammon that he had accepted from the earlier writings of Carlyle. These native influences helped to make Comte's own attack on the political economy of his day much more congenial, as Harrison wrote in his diary in May 1861: 'nothing can ever be done in England in the way of great social improvement until the cruel jargon of economists is discredited' [*Autobiographic Memoirs 1*, 252–3].

The context of this comment was the struggle of the building workers during the 'Payment by the Hour' dispute of 1861–2. According to his *Memoirs*, Harrison had already resolved, in 1861, to obtain 'knowledge of the Working Classes . . . and witness by personal inquiry the sufferings and necessities which weigh upon them' [1, 248]; and in supporting the building workers he found himself in association with the Christian Socialists Tom Hughes and J. M. F.

Ludlow as well as with his fellow Positivists, Beesly and Godfrey Lushington. The Christian Socialists he knew already, for he had been lecturing at the Working Men's College since 1859; but he found the students too genteel, and he was contemptuous of F. D. Maurice's intellectual position. Harrison's involvement with the building workers was an important turning-point in his political life; and from that time until the mid-1870s he was a prolific contributor to labour weeklies and radical monthlies. Compared with Beesley he was somewhat less radical and class-conscious in his politics, and his main interest in the 1860s remained within the trade union movement: he became recognised as the leading middle-class advocate of trade unionism before the British public. His intellectual defence of the unions was founded on an acceptance of Comte's critique of 'vulgar' political economy – above all of its refusal to recognize the interrelationships of all social phenomena – and it was the dogma especially of the wages fund theory upon which Harrison centred much of his criticism. In a famous article in the first volume of the *Fortnightly Review* (1865) – a radical journal which published many of his articles – he wrote:

So far from the rate of wages invariably falling or rising with the 'wages-fund', or any other fund, or, indeed, anything at all, it is often in particular occupations, over long courses of years absolutely fixed . . . So far from fluctuations in the rate of wages being the rule, the rule is rather that it is stationary. So far from attempts to affect the rate of wages artificially being hopeless, it hardly ever varies in the principal trades from any other causes [p. 97].

For Harrison, the trade union movement was about much more than just a wages question. Trade unions were the embodiment of the highest aspirations of working people, and they represented working-class democracy in action. Although it was Beesly who first spoke out in defence of unionism against the rising tide of hostile opinion which followed the Sheffield Outrages [Royden Harrison (1965) 278 ff.], it was Frederic Harrison who became a member of the

Royal Commission on Trade Unions. The story behind Harrison's appointment is interesting. A LWMA deputation headed by Potter had an appointment on 8 February 1867 with the Home Secretary to draw his attention to the unsatisfactory position that the unions were placed in after the *Hornby v. Close* decision. The announcement of the appointment of the Royal Commission in the Queen's speech on 5 February 1867 gave the deputation an unexpected opportunity to press its views on the subject. Potter requested that a working man be placed on the Commission, or, failing that, some 'gentleman ... well known to the working classes as possessing a practical knowledge of the working of Trades Unions, and in whom they might feel confidence'. Spencer Walpole, the Home Secretary, rejected the first alternative but accepted the second, and from a list submitted by Robert Hartwell selected Harrison's name. The names of the Commissioners were announced immediately, and Harrison knew nothing of the appointment until he read about it in *The Times*. There is no doubt that Connolly, Potter et al. would have preferred a Labour Leader on the Commission, and several strongly worded articles appeared in the *Bee-Hive* criticising the composition of the Commission. The same can be said for the Junta, who made determined efforts to get a working man appointed, without success. Potter's importance in the appointment of Harrison therefore lies in his being at the right place at the right time with a suggestion that, although perhaps not fully meeting either his own wishes or those of the trade union movement as a whole, was acceptable to the Home Secretary. In the end Harrison's appointment proved to be vastly more satisfactory from the unions' point of view than the appointment of a trade union representative would have been.

The Royal Commission began its inquiries in an atmosphere that was strikingly hostile to the union movement. Harrison was in close touch with Beesly throughout the Commission's proceedings, and among the trade unionists Robert Applegarth was invaluable in his advice and help. Harrison prepared union witnesses by telling them in advance what questions would be asked, rescued them from difficult situations during their cross-examination, and frequently asked leading questions to enable them to give prepared answers. During the work on the Report, Harrison and Tom Hughes chipped away at the draft prepared by James Booth, and succeeded in getting a Majority Report accepted that was considerably more favourable to the unions than the original draft. Even so, it would seem that from the outset neither Harrison nor Hughes had any intention of signing it.

It was Harrison's remarkable ingenuity which formulated the privileged legal status for the unions set out in the Minority Report, which he signed together with Hughes and the Earl of Lichfield. Harrison's propositions for the amendment of the law were: first, that the legality of combination should be recognised once and for all, and that persons so combining should not be liable for indictment for conspiracy unless their actions would be criminal if committed by a single person. Second, that the common law doctrine of restraint of trade in its application to trade associations should be repealed. The Minority argued that simply because an association had rules in restraint of trade this should not alter its basic legality, although they accepted that such rules and regulations should not be enforceable in a court of law. The importance of this second point was that it would give the unions a recognisable legal status but it would not subject them to judicial interference in their internal affairs. Restraint of trade was to be no bar to legality, but it was to be a bar to undue interference from a profession that had proved itself to be hostile to trade unionism. Third, that all legislation dealing specifically with the activities of employers or workmen should be repealed so as to render all offences punishable under the general criminal law only. Should it prove necessary to provide any additional protection for person or property, this should be achieved by amendment of the general law and not by the enactment of special penalties.

Finally, Harrison proposed that trade unions should receive full and positive protection for their funds and other property. By depositing their rules with the Registrar of Friendly Societies, unions would, provided that those rules did not disclose criminal intent or object, receive a certificate under the Friendly Societies Act, giving them power to appoint trustees and enabling them to benefit from summary remedies against fraud and embezzlement. The certificate was renewable annually by the Registrar provided that the unions' accounts were in order. The unions, because they were in restraint of trade, would not be able to use the courts to enforce rules or contracts, but equally they would 'not be capable of being sued as a corporate body, or of being dissolved, or otherwise wound up by the courts'. Nor would they be accountable to their members 'in respect of any rule, agreement, resolution, or act of the society'.

The Minority Report's recommendations were clearly for legalization on the most favourable terms for the unions. The exceptional statutory legislation and the vague common law doctrines of conspiracy and restraint of trade were to be repealed in so far as they affected the unions adversely, while full legal protection was to be extended to union funds. At the same time the unions were not to be subjected to judicial interference in their internal affairs. Harrison appended to the Minority Report a detailed summary of the objects and aims of trade unions as revealed in the evidence submitted to the Commission; and at the beginning of 1869 he drafted a comprehensive Bill embodying all the legislative proposals of the Minority Report. The history of subsequent developments in trade union legislation is well known [Webb (1894) 258 ff.; McCready (1954-5 and 1956); Roberts (1958) ch. 2; Royden Harrison (1965) 278 ff.]; the Positivists' contribution to the final victory of 1875 being considerable.

Harrison did not stand aside from political activity, broadly defined, but like his Comtist friends he refused any formal position in the radical and working-class movements. In 1865, for example, he was offered, but declined, the editorship of the Bee-Hive and the Commonwealth. His strength, like that of Beesly, was in advocacy. Harrison

was a vigorous supporter of the Polish and Italian National Liberation movements; a violent opponent of imperialist methods in Asia and Africa; at one with Beesly in the latter's campaign in the columns of the Bee-Hive in support of the Federal cause in the American Civil War; an active member of the Jamaica Committee in 1866, and author of Martial Law: Six Letters to the Daily News, later published as Jamaica Papers No. 5 in 1867 [Semmel (1962) 129]. He became a vice-president of the Reform League in 1866, and contributed an essay on 'England and France' to International Policy (1866) and a further essay in foreign policy to Questions for a Reformed Parliament (1867). In the 1860s Harrison and Beesly were working towards an alliance between the masses and an intellectual élite which would provide the country with an intelligent, non-sectarian and 'class-less' leadership on a national plane. Their hopes culminated in the 1867 Reform Act and the subsequent general election.

The most dramatic period of the Positivists' ultra-radical phase – except for Beesly's famous Exeter Hall speech of 2 July 1867 – was their campaign for the recognition of the French Republic in 1870, and above all, their defence of the Paris Commune in 1871. They were, of course, ardent Francophiles. From the beginning of the Franco-Prussian War, Beesly and Harrison demanded armed intervention by Britain on behalf of France, and many of the radical Left among the London working men went with them; but it was the Paris Commune, following the defeat of France, which gave rise to major divisions within radical opinion and largely separated off the Positivists from their working-class allies.

Harrison in the Fortnightly Review and Beesly in the Bee-Hive both eloquently defended the Commune against an increasingly hostile British public. The Commune, Harrison wrote to John Morley, was 'perhaps the most striking event (as yet) of the nineteenth century' (22 Mar 1871). In the first of his two articles in the Fortnightly Review (May 1871) he first disclaimed the role of mere apologist but then proceeded to a vigorous statement of his position. He began by summarising the five principal aims of the Commune. The first was the acceptance of the Republic, involving the recognition that government was 'a responsible public duty' free from dependence on social origins or social class. The Commune repudiated, and this was its second main principle, 'the dogma of universal suffrage'. It had long been known in France, as elsewhere, that under the organised system of electioneering small minorities had learnt the art of manipulating the mass of the voters. It followed, thirdly, that the Commune was correct in asserting the principle of direct instead of indirect government. The old representative assembly was a sham, a mere 'talking parliament'; and the working men had shown their political sagacity in substituting a simple executive council – 'a committee for action' – in place of the parliament of 'rhetoricians and intriguers'. 'Government', he continued,

by the parliamentary system, is government without real responsibility, without efficiency and without simplicity. All these are lost in the meshes of divided authority and personal rivalries. Government, in a word, breaks down under the tangle of machinery which it has to work. What we need is, as the Commune proclaims, a responsibility of the governing body, real, direct, and personal, the greatest simplicity of authority, and the utmost supervision of opinion.

The fourth principle of the Communards was the abolition of 'that curse of modern society – the standing army'; and the fifth was the rejection of the traditionally fostered belief that only the leisured classes were fit to govern, and the application of the principle that workmen can carry through the function of government with energy and efficiency. There were many minor objectives, which naturally arose out of these basic ideas: the establishment of a secular, free, state educational system, the complete separation of church and state, 'the transformation of the police from a political engine into a civic protection'; and so on. Harrison ended this remarkable article with a notable prophecy:

As a political and violent remedy of profound social disorders, the Revolution of the Commune is abortive, and must fail. These disorders need a true education, a new morality, and an organised religion of social duty. But as a political solution of a profound political disorder, the oppression of the cities by the rural suffrage, the cause of the Commune has triumphed, however cruel the reaction it may suffer. Their great political programme is effectually founded in France; is sufficiently suggested to Europe; and the bloody vengeance of the Monarchists will not blot it out for the memory of the future.

His second article 'The Fall of the Commune' in the 1 August 1871 issue of the *Fortnightly Review* further developed his defence. He vigorously attacked both the French and English press for their mendacity and invention, wrote bitterly and vehemently on the part which the Catholic Church had played in the butchery practised on the people of Paris, and vigorously indicted 'the friends of Order throughout Europe' for the delight with which they received the news of the Commune's downfall. It was a passionate plea for humanity; a call for social change and social reorganisation; a recognition that in the future there was a clear choice to be made. He ended his article: 'The *status quo* is impossible. The alternative is Communism or Positivism.'

Harrison's defence of the Commune, which he followed by great and generous exertions on behalf of communard refugees in Britain, was partly the reason why Beesly and he were excluded from the deliberations of the TUC parliamentary committee during 1871–2. They had both continued to be intensely involved with the evolution of the labour legislation of 1871, and its aftermath, and they sharply attacked the attempts by George Howell and Alexander Macdonald in the summer of 1872 to negotiate an amending bill to the Criminal Law Amendment Act [Royden Harrison (1965) 290 ff.; Leventhal (1971) 154 ff.]. They both played a part in the 1875 legislation which, *inter alia*, repealed the obnoxious clauses relating to picketing, and Harrison in particular continued his association with the leaders of the trades, being a frequent attender at the annual meetings until the 1880s. He was, of course, never a Socialist, and by comparison with those involved with the early socialist movement he was now beginning to appear somewhat conservative in ideas and attitudes. It was the political situation, not Harrison, that was changing. At the Nottingham Congress of 1883, the delegates denied him the right to speak against land nationalisation: and his contribution to the Industrial Remuneration Conference met with sharp criticism from both the land reformers and the Socialists. Yet in spite of his deepening distrust of the growing movement of socialist ideas and ideals, Harrison as a good Comtist never ceased his opposition to imperialist expansion. The indignation which had poured from him at the bombing of Kagoshima in 1863 continued unabated. He continued to protest at the growing number of frontier incidents and wars in the last half-century before 1914, and not least during the Boer War. Among the imperialist atrocities he protested against were the Afghan wars of 1879–80; the bombardment of Alexandria in 1882 and the subsequent occupation of Egypt; the Boer War 'engineered by a conspiracy of financiers and ambitious politicians' [Memoirs, 2, 126] and the policy of destruction and internment which followed as its aftermath. Foreign affairs in general became a major preoccupation of the last half-century of his life. He took an unpopular stand in the Eastern crisis of 1876–8, opposing the Gladstonian policy of driving the Turks out of Europe; became a member of the short-lived Anti-Aggression League in 1882; and was made president of the pro-Turkish Eastern Question Association in 1910, in succession to James Bryce. In European affairs Harrison was always vigorously anti-German after the Prussian victory of 1870–1, and adopted an extreme position during the First World War, in 1915 publishing The German Peril, about half of which was a recapitulation of his former warnings about German imperialism. France and Holland were the two countries which he especially loved. He was special correspondent of the Times in France in 1876 and on several later occasions, and represented Lord Salisbury at the ceremony of Installation of Queen Wilhelmina at The Hague in 1898.

In addition to all these social and political activities Frederic Harrison was a considerable intellectual and literary figure. He was an original member of the Metaphysical Society. He was personally acquainted with almost all the outstanding Victorian personalities, poets and novelists as well as historians and politicians, and his friends were too many to be even enumerated here. But one friendship may be singled out since it is of particular literary interest. Harrison twice found himself acting as legal mentor to George Eliot in regard to a novel of hers ['Reminiscences of George Eliot' in Memories and Thoughts (1906) 146 ff.; letters: Haight 4 (9 Jan to 1 June 1866) and 6 (30 Dec 1874 to 18 June 1875)]. She consulted him first on her difficulties with what he calls the 'intricate legal imbroglio' on which the story of Felix Holt turns, and in consequence of his advice and suggestions she 'recast her plot' [Memories and Thoughts, 148]. In their fairly lengthy correspondence over Felix Holt, Harrison appears as the perfect adviser – warmly interested, patient and lucid. He 'read large portions of the book in MS. and in proof', and gave her information for every part which deals in legal matters, from the complex settlement of the Transome estate to the trial of Felix and the memorial to the Home Secretary. In regard to the Transome settlement he wrote for her the imaginary opinion of 'the Attorney General and the first Conveyancer of the day' (the day, that is, in which the novel is set, the 1830s), and was delighted when she inserted it in the book verbatim (in ch. 35). 'I shall have the satisfaction', he wrote to her on 26 May 1866, 'of thinking to myself that I have written one little sentence which will be immortal and will be embodied in the literature of England.'

George Eliot also consulted him over a later novel, Daniel Deronda. There are nine letters from her inquiring about points of law, but no replies from Harrison. Some of the questions he answered *viva voce*, others in letters apparently not now extant. It is therefore difficult to assess her debt to him in this case; but the terms of lively gratitude used in two of her letters (9 and 15 June 1875) suggest that it was not inconsiderable.

Besides his political and sociological articles – which are very numerous, and notably well informed on his very various subjects – his literary and historical writings cover a quite extraordinary range; they show him as a shrewd and perceptive critic of literature and a good historian with an intimate and specialised knowledge of certain periods. He published a monograph on Cromwell in 1888; a biography of William the Silent in 1897; a short life of Ruskin in 1902; and a biography of Chatham in 1905. In 1892 he edited the *New Calendar of Great Men*, biographies of the 558 great men of all ages and nations who appeared in the Positivist Calendar; and in 1895 he published his *Studies in Early Victorian Literature*. His writing has striking virtues which are rare in combination but are all invariably present: marked intellectual and organising power, great energy, and total clarity. With all these qualities, Harrison was in addition a wit and a polemical satirist.

He was Rede lecturer at Cambridge in 1900 (on Byzantine history in the early Middle Ages, a subject he specialised in and one which provided the material for his romantic novel *Theophano, A Crusade of the Tenth Century*, published in 1904); Washington lecturer in Chicago in 1901; and Herbert Spencer lecturer at Oxford in 1905. He received honorary degrees from Oxford, Cambridge and Aberdeen.

Harrison's profession was, however, the law. In 1877 he had been appointed professor of Jurisprudence, International and Constitutional Law for the Council of Legal Education, and he regularly lectured in the Middle Temple Hall from 1877 to 1889. Earlier, in 1869 he was made secretary to the R.C. for Digesting the Law – a Commission which did not, however, for reasons of internal dissensions, last long. Among other legal work, he was a member of the committee appointed by Lord Chancellor Halsbury to continue the Reports on State Trials from 1820. The idea originated with Harrison himself, and he served for thirteen years, from 1885 to 1898, both on the main committee and on the working sub-committee. Eight volumes were published, most of them, Harrison notes in his *Memoirs*, being read in proof by himself.

Harrison stood for Parliament once only, in spite of many requests, and this was for the University of London constituency in 1886 as a home-ruler against a Liberal Unionist. He was easily defeated. His public offices were relatively unimportant although Harrison brought to them his usual liveliness and fertility in ideas. In February 1889 he was nominated an alderman of the newly constituted LCC; he served for five years, and from 1892 was chairman of the Improvements Committee which, *inter alia*, initiated the Kingsway and Aldwych development. When he went to live at Elm Hill, Hawkhurst, in 1902 he was appointed a magistrate for Kent, and sat on the Bench at Cranbrook and Maidstone. His *Memoirs* [2, 244 ff.] offer an incisive commentary on the role and the place of the magistracy in rural areas.

Harrison wrote in his autobiography that the Positivist movement was 'the constant occupation of my mind and the real business of my life' [*Memoirs*, 2, 251]; but this is not the place to describe his strictly Positivist activities in any detail. In the famous split in the movement in 1878–9, when Congreve announced his secession from Pierre Lafitte, Harrison, together with Beesly, stayed with the latter, and when Newton Hall was opened in 1881 Harrison took a full share in its work. He was president of the Positivist Society from 1890 until 1904 and for over twenty years he lectured regularly on Sundays. His annual New Year's address, which he delivered for at least a decade, became an occasion in the intellectual life of London.

In 1912 Harrison moved to Bath, a town of which he became very fond, describing it as a home of culture, good fellowship, and ease. In November 1921 the city conferred on him her honorary freedom. He had married in 1870 Ethel Harrison, a cousin who shared all his tastes, sympathies and enthusiasms. She died in June 1916. One of the sons of the marriage, an officer in the Leicestershire Regiment, died of wounds in 1915; and three sons and one daughter survived him when he himself died on 14 January 1923, in his ninety-second year. He left an estate with a net value of £32,486.

Both the *Times* and the *Manchester Guardian* devoted several columns to their excellent obituary notices. 'Few men of our time', wrote the *Manchester Guardian*,

have done more work than Harrison. Still fewer men with a like multiplicity of other labours on their hands have carried on, not only without payment but at heavy and continuous expense, a work so arduous and in some respects so thankless as that of Positivism. He was a sterling Englishman, strenuous, robust, virile to a fault: indefatigable in the cause of his evangel, but singularly free from the intolerance of the missionary: happily blending the intellectual catholicity and the logical definiteness of France with the practical shrewdness and initiative which the world agrees to attribute to the 'Anglo-Saxon'.

No less remarkable was the tribute paid to Harrison by Sir Frederick Pollock, who emphasised the contribution that Harrison's legal training and historical scholarship made to his general writing. 'Indeed', Pollock said,

if I had to name one single essay as an example of Harrison's true temper and best workmanship, it would be just his survey of the thirteenth century, which he rightly, and with fulness of knowledge rivalled only by Bryce among our countrymen, celebrated as the culminating period of the Middle Ages, when creative and constructive work was at its best. So far as I can judge, the exactness of his account is not less remarkable than its compass . . . As to another of Harrison's studies in history, the paper on King Alfred contributed to a millenary celebration volume, and supplemented by a discourse on Alfred's writings, I can bear witness to its accuracy and good judgment with some confidence, having myself gone over the

same ground on the same occasion. Here one may note that to Frederic Harrison, as a true humanist, it did not matter whether a great man lived a hundred or a thousand years ago. . . . [Pollock ended his address]: Others have spoken and will speak of Frederic Harrison in other aspects. But our testimony surely converges on this, perhaps the best that anyone can desire to have said of himself: Here is a man it was good to know [*Engl. Rev.* (May 1923) 411–13].

Writings: The *Autobiographic Memoirs*, 2 vols (1911), apart from being indispensable for the detailed biography of Frederic Harrison, contain a full bibliography of books, pamphlets and articles in monthly and quarterly journals down to 1911. See also Harrison's *Memories and Thoughts: men – books – cities – art* (1906). An extensive list of his contributions to the Labour press is included in Roydon Harrison, 'The Activity and Influence of the English Positivists upon Labour Movements, 1859–1885' (Oxford DPhil., 1955). The two main phases of Harrison's labour journalism may be distinguished as follows:

(i) 1863–7, during which period he contributed twenty-six articles to the *Bee-Hive* as well as thirteen to the *Commonwealth* (between 3 Feb 1866 and 5 Jan 1867). In the latter he first openly appeared as a Positivist: 'A Comtist's reply to an English Radical', 19 May 1866; and 'A Last Word about Comte', 2 June 1866. The *Bee-Hive* articles included a series on Poland: 21 Mar, 2 May and 27 June 1863; 'The Burning of Kagoshima', 13 Feb 1864; and several contributions to the Reform agitation: 1 July 1865; 21 Apr, 23 June, 24 Oct 1867.

(ii) The articles in the *Bee-Hive* 1871–5 were almost entirely devoted to the legal and political aspects of the Labour Laws' agitation. There were thirty-two articles in all. Among them may be noted: 'The Trades Union Bill', 1 July 1871; a series on the Criminal Law Amendment Act: 31 May, 14 and 21 June 1872; a series on the Master and Servant Acts: 15 and 22 Feb, 1 Mar and 12 Apr 1873; three articles on independent labour politics: 8 Feb and 8 Mar 1873, 31

Jan 1874; and two articles on labour spies: 5 and 12 Dec 1874. The following writings of Harrison were published after his *Memoirs* appeared in 1911 and were not therefore included in the bibliography: 'Among my Books', *Engl. Rev. 10*, 10–23, 210–24, 425–441, 568–83, and *11*, 19–36, 177–88 (Dec 1911–May 1912); Preface to Lady Mary Agatha Russell, *Golden Grain* (1912); 'The Future of Woman' in H. R. Steeves, *Representative Essays in Modern Thought* (1913) 502–18; 'How to read', in *Essays for College Men*, compiler N. Foerster (1913) 362–90; Introduction to M. B. Edwards, *The Lord of the Harvest* [1913]; *The Positive Evolution of Religion; its moral and social reaction* (1913); *A Critical Year* [an address] [1913]; '1913', *Engl. Rev. 13* (Jan 1913) 183–99; 'Frederic Harrison's Warning, January 1913', ibid., *18* (Sep 1914) 196–203; *The Old Garden City. In Praise of Bath* [repr. from *Cornhill Mag. 36* (Apr 1914), [1914]]; *The Meaning of the War for Labour* (1914) 8 pp.; Introduction to A. Harrison, *The Kaiser's War* [1914]; 'Old Books in Wartime', *Engl. Rev. 19* (Mar 1915) 389–404; *20* (Apr 1915) 13–24; *The German Peril: forecasts 1864–1914, realities 1915, hopes 191–* [1915]; 'Do it now', *Engl. Rev. 24* (Feb 1917) 132–8; *Memoirs and Essays of Ethelbertha Harrison* (Bath, 1917) 40 pp.; *On Society* (1918); *On Jurisprudence and the Conflict of Laws*, with annotations by A. H. F. Lefroy [repr. from *Fortn. Rev.* and revised, 1919]; *Obiter Scripta, 1918* (1919), 'Of ninety years', *Nation 28*, 23 Oct 1920, 128–9; (edited with F. S. Marvin and S. H. Swinny) *The New Calendar of Great Men* (new ed. rev., 1920); *Novissima Verba: last words, 1920* (1921); 'Lamenting the Past', *Nation 30*, 1 Oct 1921, 13–14; *The City of Bath. An appreciation* [Bath, 1921]; 'Victorians on themselves', *Nation 31* 22 Apr 1922, 117–18; 'Future of Empire and of England', *Engl. Rev. 34* (June 1922) 577–82; 'England and France', ibid., *35* (Sep 1922) 249–51; *De Senectute – more last words* [1923]; 'Romance of the Peerage' in *Modern English Essays* (1923); *The Decay of Parliament* (n.d.); *Selected Essays, Literary and Historical*, ed. with Introduction and Notes by A. Jhā (1925).

Sources: (1) **MSS:** E. S. Beesly papers, University College, London; Richard Congreve papers, BM and Bodleian Library, Oxford; Frederic Harrison papers, LSE; George Howell Coll., Bishopsgate Institute, London; Positivist archives, Le Musée d'Auguste Comte, 10 rue de M. le Prince, Paris; Webb Coll., LSE; Working Men's College archives, London. (2) **Theses:** W. K. Lamb, 'British Labour and Parliament, 1865–1893' (London PhD, 1933); W. L. Presswood, 'The Influence of Auguste Comte and the Rise of Positivism in England up to the Formation of the English Positivist Society in 1867' (Sheffield PhD, 1935); H. W. McCready, 'Frederic Harrison and the British Working Class Movement, 1860–1875' (Harvard PhD, 1952); D. R. Moberg, 'George Odger and the English Working Class Movement, 1860–1877' (London PhD, 1954); R. J. Harrison, 'The Activity and Influence of the English Positivists upon Labour Movements, 1859–1885' (Oxford DPhil., 1955); S. Coltham, 'George Potter and the *Bee-Hive* Newspaper' (Oxford DPhil., 1955); R. A. Buchanan, 'Trade Unions and Public Opinion, 1850–75' (Cambridge PhD, 1957); S. Eisen, 'Frederic Harrison: the life and thoughts of an English Positivist' (John Hopkins PhD, 1957); A. D. Bell, 'The Reform League from its Origins to the Reform Act of 1867' (Oxford DPhil., 1961); P. Adelman, 'The Social and Political Ideas of Frederic Harrison in Relation to English Thought and Politics, 1855–86' (London PhD, 1968); C. A. Kent, 'Aspects of Academic Radicalism in mid-Victorian England: a study in the politics of thought and action with special reference to Frederic Harrison and John Morley' (Sussex DPhil., 1969). (3) **Secondary:** S. and B. Webb, *The History of Trade Unionism* (1894); *DNB* (1922–30); A. Harrison, *Frederic Harrison. Thoughts and Memories* (1926); B. Webb, *My Apprenticeship* (1926); F. E. Gillespie, *Labor and Politics in England, 1850–1867* (Duke Univ. Press, 1927); J. E. McGee, *A Crusade for Humanity* (1931); S. Maccoby, *English Radicalism, 1853–1886* (1938); E. C. Mack and W. H. G. Armytage, *Thomas Hughes* (1952); M. St John Packe, *Life of John Stuart Mill* (1954); H. W. McCready,

'British Labour and the Royal Commission on Trade Unions, 1867–69', *Univ. of Toronto Q. 24* (1955) 390–409; idem, 'The British Labour Lobby, 1867–75', *Canad. J. Econ. Pol. Sc. 22* (1956) 141–60; *The George Eliot Letters*, ed. G. S. Haight, vols *4* and *6* (Oxford Univ. Press and Yale Univ. Press, 1956); B. C. Roberts, *The Trades Union Congress, 1868–1921* (1958); R. Harrison, 'E. S. Beesly and Karl Marx', *Int. Rev. Social Hist. 4* (1959) 22–58; idem, 'Professor Beesly and the Working Class Movement', *Essays in Labour History*, ed. A. Briggs and J. Saville (1960) 205–41; R. V. Clements, 'British Trade Unions and Popular Political Economy, 1850–75', *Econ. Hist. Rev. 14* ser. 2 (1961) 93–104; A. M. McBriar, *Fabian Socialism and English Politics 1884–1918* (Cambridge, 1962); B. Semmel, *The Governor Eyre Controversy* (1962); W. M. Simon, *European Positivism in the Nineteenth Century* (Cornell, 1963); H. Collins and C. Abramsky, *Karl Marx and the British Labour Movement* (1965); R. Harrison, *Before the Socialists* (1965); W. S. Smith, *The London Heretics 1870–1914* (1967); S. Eisen, 'Frederic Harrison and Herbert Spencer: embattled unbelievers', *Victorian Studies, 12*, no. 1 (Sep 1968) 33–56; P. Adelman, 'Frederic Harrison and the "Positivist" Attack on Orthodox Political Economy', *Hist. Pol. Economy, 3*, no. 1 (Spring 1971) 170–89; R. Harrison, *The English Defence of the Commune* (1971); F. M. Leventhal, *Respectable Radical: George Howell and Victorian Working Class Politics* (1971). OBIT. *Manchester Guardian* and *Times*, 15 Jan 1923; *Positivist Rev.* 1 Feb 1923; *Sociological Rev.*, 15 Apr 1923, 158 [by E. J. Gould]; *Engl. Rev. 36* (May 1923) 410–13 [an address by Sir Frederick Pollock].

NOTE: This entry is the result of a collaboration of a number of scholars, to whom the editors are greatly indebted. A preliminary draft was prepared by Professor Royden Harrison, who commented also on subsequent drafts. Mr Alan Jones provided most of the material on the labour laws agitation; Mrs M. 'Espinasse wrote the text of the George Eliot matter and of the evaluation which follows; and Professor C. Kent (Univ. of Saskatchewan) and Dr P. Adelman both gave detailed comments.

JOHN SAVILLE

See also: Robert APPLEGARTH; *Edward Spencer BEESLY; Thomas Joseph DUNNING; George HOWELL; *Thomas HUGHES; *George POTTER.

HARRISON, James (1899–1959)
LABOUR MP

Born on 30 August 1899 at Sawley, Derbyshire, James Harrison was the son of two lacemakers, George Harrison and his wife Mary (née Beresford). After an elementary school education he began work with the London, Midland and Scottish Railway Co. and was soon active in trade union affairs, joining the NUR in 1916 and becoming, at the age of nineteen, chairman of the 1200-strong NUR branch at Toton, Notts. In 1920 he was awarded a scholarship by the NUR which enabled him to study economics and political science in London at the Central Labour College. Returning to railway work, he became an engine driver at the age of twenty-four and served for a number of years as chairman of the Nottingham no. 8 branch of the NUR. In 1942 he was appointed to the National Executive Committee of the NUR as a representative of the Midland District, and was re-elected in 1943 and 1944. During the war years he was also the deputy chief warden for Long Eaton.

Harrison had joined the Labour Party in 1916 and while studying in London had acted as the secretary of the South Kensington Labour Party; for many years he was president of the Party's South Derbyshire branch. He continued his association with the NCLC by part-time lecturing for a number of years in politics and economics. At the 1945 general election he entered the Commons as Member for East Nottingham, and when boundary changes led to the disappearance of this division, Harrison was elected for North Nottingham in 1950, 1951 and 1955. During the period of the Labour Government he was chairman of the Party's transport group, vice-chairman of the colonial group and a member of groups dealing with social insurance and industrial organisation. He was also a member of the Fabian Society. In 1947 he travelled to China with the Parliamentary Goodwill Mission.

In the Commons he was regarded as a conscientious back-bencher of pleasant disposition who belonged to the right wing of the Labour Party. He was a regular speaker on various subjects, but especially on matters affecting his constituents and issues such as pensions and the railways. Occasionally he was outspoken in his views, as when, after racial disturbances in Nottingham in August 1958, he advocated that restrictions should be placed on immigrants from the Commonwealth. In March 1958 he put down a Commons motion with E. G. Gooch (Norfolk N.) and Sidney Dye (Norfolk S.W.) protesting that U.S.A. rocket bases were being concentrated in the eastern areas of England instead of being sited more widely.

By religion a Wesleyan, Harrison was a teetotaller and temperance advocate. For a number of years his hobby was poultry-keeping and this led to his membership of the Poultry Association of Great Britain. On his election to Parliament he became a vice-president of the Lace Federation, but resigned from that body in 1953 after it had been suggested that he should consult with them before making public statements about the trade.

Harrison's death occurred on 2 May 1959 at the Royal Free Hospital, London, three days after he suffered a heart attack on the Nottingham–St Pancras train. He was cremated at Wilford Hill on 7 May after a service at the Derby Road Wesleyan Church, Long Eaton. He left effects to the value of £4123 in his will. In 1924 he had married Gladys Mary Anne Earnshaw who survived him. They had one child, a daughter, who taught in a school until her marriage to a farmer.

Sources: C. Bunker, *Who's Who in Parliament* [1946]; *Dod* (1958); Labour Party *Report* (1959); *WWW* (1951–60); P. S. Bagwell, *The Railwaymen: the history of the National Union of Railwaymen* (1963); W. W. Craik, *The Central Labour College*

1909–29 (1964); biographical information: NUR; personal information: Mrs G. M. A. Harrison, Nottingham, widow; Mrs Arthur Wilmot, East Leake, daughter. Obit. [Nottingham] *Guardian Journal*, 4 May 1959; *Times*, 4 May 1959; *Hucknall Dispatch*, 8 May 1959.

DAVID E. MARTIN

See also: †Sidney DYE.

HEADLAM, Stewart Duckworth
(1847–1924)
CLERGYMAN, EDUCATIONALIST, SOCIAL REFORMER

Headlam was born in Wavertree, Liverpool, on 12 January 1847, the son of Thomas Duckworth Headlam, an insurance underwriter; these comfortable circumstances obviated the need for him to have paid employment. The family were strong Evangelicals, though Headlam was early initiated into Anglican controversy since an uncle was a High Churchman. Moving to the south in the early 1850s, the family settled at Tunbridge Wells. Headlam was entered for Eton at the age of thirteen in 1860, and belonged to the house of J. L. Joynes, whose son was later a leading figure in the early years of the Social Democratic Federation. Headlam's first leanings towards political radicalism came during his five years at Eton.

He was a member of Trinity College, Cambridge, from 1865 to 1868. Here he was a student under the Christian Socialist Frederick Denison Maurice, whose influence on Headlam was to be equalled by only one other man (in a very different sphere), Henry George. Maurice, who was Professor of Moral Philosophy, was then less important to Headlam as a Christian Socialist than as a theologian. His Broad Church views made Christianity much more attractive and humane than the narrow Evangelicalism of the day. It was under Maurice's influence that Headlam decided to enter the priesthood.

His experience as a clergyman was confined to London, where his first curacy, late in 1870, was at St John's, Drury Lane, an area of mixed social class. Here he met the

Rev. Thomas Wodehouse, another Christian Socialist who influenced his thought. He also met many theatrical people, beginning an interest which became a passion. At St John's Headlam had his first of many brushes with ecclesiastical authority. His enthusiastic advocacy of Maurice's teaching, particularly with regard to the after life, did not endear him to orthodox clergy, and in 1873 he was asked to resign as curate. Not long before he had been ordained a priest.

Headlam's second curacy was at St Matthew's, Bethnal Green, where he lived in a newly-built working-class 'model' flat. He remained in Bethnal Green for five years, saying later that he had spent there 'some of the best years of my life'. (It was a district whose elected local representative he was to be for thirty-three years.) His rector was Septimus Hansard, a Broad Churchman well disposed towards social reform. He encouraged Headlam to seek out the working-class leaders of the district and to spread art and culture among his flock. Headlam gave active support to trade unionism, especially among women. He also continued the practice, begun at Drury Lane, of taking school-children swimming and sightseeing in the West End. At the same time, while he always remained personally loyal to Maurice, his religious view took another turn. Under the influence of H. D. Nihill of Shoreditch and the famous curate, Arthur Henry Stanton of St Alban's, Holborn, Headlam moved into the Anglo-Catholic camp.

His interest in the working classes and the theatre were responsible for his dismissal from Bethnal Green. Headlam and Father Stanton were among the Sunday evening lecturers at a Bethnal Green workingmen's club, the Commonwealth Club. On 7 October 1877 Headlam delivered a lecture entitled 'Theatres and Music Halls', which was subsequently published in the *Era* newspaper. The lecture supported these forms of entertainment and added: 'Above all, don't let us speak with scorn of the ladies who dance on the stage.' Septimus Hansard and the Bishop of London, John Jackson, were shocked by the lecture, and early in 1878 Headlam was asked to leave Bethnal Green. In the same month he was married to Beatrice Pennington. According to Bernard Shaw [Winsten (1951) 9] Headlam's wife was a homosexual; the couple separated after a period, and Headlam never subsequently referred to his marriage.

In his life in East London Headlam came into contact with the secularist movement and its leader, Charles Bradlaugh. He attended many secularist meetings, defended Christianity with vigour ('I ... fired away for my ten minutes', he characteristically wrote on one occasion), and created between the secularists and himself a considerable degree of friendship and respect. Indeed, Headlam regarded secularists as staunch allies against the narrower forms of orthodox Christianity, and on occasion went out of his way to help them, notably in the organisation of their science classes. His support for the disestablishment of the Church of England also made Headlam congenial to secularists.

This relationship brought out important aspects of his character; his absolute fearlessness, his flamboyance, his unconventionality. In 1877 he had agreed to give evidence for Bradlaugh and Annie Besant in the famous birth control trial, though in fact he was not called on to do so. In 1880 during Bradlaugh's campaign to gain admission to the House of Commons Headlam sent him a telegram: 'Accept my warmest sympathy. I wish you good luck in the name of Jesus Christ, the Emancipator, whom so many of your opponents blaspheme.' This resulted in a stern rebuke from the Bishop of London. It was the same qualities of fearlessness, flamboyance and unconventionality which induced Headlam to befriend Oscar Wilde during the latter's trial and imprisonment in 1895-7, an attitude which cost Headlam many friends and supporters. But unconventionality had to struggle on occasion with sacramentalism; though a lifelong campaigner against Puritanism, Headlam refused to marry Charles Stewart Parnell in 1891 to the divorced Kitty O'Shea.

Headlam moved from Bethnal Green to St Thomas's, Charterhouse, where he was curate to the Rev. John Rodgers, a well-known figure of the day and an early member of the London School Board. Here he stayed until 1881 when, after Rodgers' death, he moved on to St Michael's, Shoreditch, serving as curate under one of the clergymen whom he most admired, Father Nihill. But the two men did not work happily together, and in December 1882 Headlam wrote to a friend: 'Just got the sack for being political'. It was his last regular post in the Church. Further attempts to obtain a curacy failed, and Headlam was refused a licence to preach. When Frederick Temple succeeded Bishop Jackson in 1885 Headlam hoped for reinstatement, but his views on the relations between church and stage antagonised Temple, and the ban was not revoked until 1898.

His suspension as an Anglican clergyman enabled Headlam to follow many diverse but related activities during the 1880s. He continued his connections with the theatre, in particular the Church and Stage Guild which he had formed in 1879 and which recruited 470 members in its first year. He took up journalism and wrote extensively, and participated actively in radical-socialist politics and demonstrations. Most important, at the end of the decade he began the work in London education which henceforth dominated his life.

It was in 1877 that Headlam and some of his Bethnal Green congregation formed the Guild of St Matthew as a parish organisation. The Guild soon became a national body with Headlam as its permanent leader, and from 1884 much of its energy was spent on social as well as church reform. In that year it printed a list of twenty-four lecturers who were prepared to speak on one hundred and thirty subjects. Among its members were such well-known Christian Socialist priests as Thomas Hancock, C. W. Stubbs, Charles Marson and Conrad Noel. The secretary was the layman Frederick Verinder, Headlam's lifelong friend and supporter. Writing in 1968, the Rev. Kenneth Leech commented: 'The association of Maurician theology and Socialism with Anglo-Catholicism was one of the crucial features of Headlam's life, and his permanent legacy to English Christianity.' As Leech points out, to Headlam more than any other single person is due the left-wing tradition within Anglo-Catholi-cism, for in his early years in the Guild radicals among the clergy were not usually noted for High Church attitudes.

For Headlam Christianity and Socialism were opposite sides of the same coin. As he put it in 1892: 'If you want to be a good Christian, you must be something very much like a good Socialist.' The Guild supported a number of secular reforms, including shorter working hours, better elementary education and, more generally, 'a better distribution of the wealth created by labour', as it demanded in a resolution passed in 1884. A striking declaration sent as a memorial to the Pan-Anglican Conference of 1888 asserted:

The startling contrast between the hovels of the poor and the houses of the rich within the same city, between the pitiful wage of the labourer and the vast income of the idler, between the poverty of the tenant and the luxury of the landlord, especially in our large towns, has been put before English society with startling vividness. A wave of Socialist thought has swept over England.

The Guild's most important political demand was land reform. It was totally committed to the land taxation proposals of Henry George, that 'man sent from God', as Headlam once called him. As early as 1882 Headlam had declared that George's attack on Malthus had shown him the means of ending poverty (*Malthusian*, Nov 1882). In a lecture delivered to the Fabian Society in 1892 (which, printed as a Fabian Tract in the same year, sold extensively over a long period), Headlam declared that land reform was 'the main plank in the platform of the Christian Socialist, the chief political reform at which he aims'. 'Landlordism' was 'the root question, the bottom question', in the fight against poverty. Headlam's lieutenant Frederick Verinder was secretary of the English Land Restoration League and toured the country in its famous red vans.

The Guild of St Matthew, although it lasted for thirty-two years, never had a large membership. In 1877, its first year, there were forty members, and the peak seems to have been reached in 1895, when there were 364 members, ninety-nine of them clergymen. But as the most socialistic of Christian groups before the twentieth century and the rise of the Church Socialist League, the Guild's influence far exceeded its numbers. Despite a certain vagueness in its aims and programme (critics said that the Guild's solution to a social evil was to read a paper on it), its activities did much to turn the attention of Christians to social reform. As the pioneer Christian Socialist body (though not the first modern British socialist society, as is sometimes claimed), the Guild both forged links between Christianity and the labour movement, and led to the form- ation of other social reforming bodies of Christians. Thus its activities influenced the establishment in 1889 of the Christian Social Union, a larger, more influential and more moderate body than the Guild of St Matthew.

The Guild's organ was the *Church Re- former*, a monthly journal begun in January 1882 and taken over by Headlam as pro- prietor and editor from the end of 1883. Headlam continued the paper until the end of 1895, by which time the Guild had suffered a good deal of internal dissension and Headlam had lost £1200 in the *Re- former*'s support. It was full of information on both theological and secular subjects, which to Headlam as to Maurice were in- divisible and essentially religious in character [Jones (1968) 159]. The *Reformer* cam- paigned for democracy and equality within the Church of England, for the abolition of Church patronage and the end of social abuses. It hailed Headlam's hero Henry George and publicised his speaking tours. It supported the free speech demonstrations in London in the 1880s and the London dock- ers' strike in 1889. It was a weapon in the fight for an improved system of elementary education in London. In fact, the *Church Reformer* was one of the most important and respected of the radical journals of its day – as well as 'a mine of material for the social historian' [Jones (1968) 127, n. 2]. A hostile critic asserted, quite accurately, that its motto should have been 'The Mass and the Masses'.

Headlam called himself a Socialist, and the *Church Reformer* 'an organ of Christian Socialism'. He also called himself a Liberal. It is clear that he was both, Socialist in aim but unwilling to break his ties with his Liberal allies. (He was, by the 1890s, notably reluctant to support the Independent Labour Party and the demand for large numbers of working-class MPs.) Clear as to objects, he was muddled over methods, and eventually his political programme became fossilised around education and land reform. Headlam was for many years a leading mem- ber of the Fabian Society, and in particular a friend of Bernard Shaw, but in some respects he was never at home among the Fabians. This was in part because his intellectual analysis of social problems and his social programme were in many respects, though by no means all, less advanced than theirs. More importantly, it was because the Fabians had not Headlam's vision of a new and socially just society. As his biographer, F. G. Bettany, said: 'It was the sentimental, the emotional side of Socialism that struck a response from him.' Moreover, in the 1880s, easily his most radical decade, Headlam consistently and unhesitatingly supported socialist and radical causes. It is arguable that his broad vision and fearless propa- ganda were as effective in their own way as the Fabians' cautious, pragmatic and gradu- alist programme.

Headlam's philosophy was well brought out in his educational activity. He served on the London School Board from 1888 until its end in 1904, an event which he bitterly opposed, notably among his fellow Fabians. After a three-year gap caused by the hostility which surrounded the death of the Board, Headlam was elected to the London County Council, and served on the Council, its education committee and a number of sub- committees until his death in 1924.

Headlam stood for the London School Board in Hackney (including Bethnal Green) in 1888 as part of a Liberal-Socialist coali- tion, a common front of three candidates made possible by the multiple system of voting used in School Board elections. His address to the Hackney voters included the then novel demand for trade union wage rates to be paid for School Board works. Schools should be free and so too should school dinners. The money for these reforms, he added, should come from 'those huge land values which . . . industry creates and the landlords appropriate'. Above all, he wanted to make children

> discontented with the evil circumstances which surround them. There are those who say that we are educating your children above their station. That is true; and if you return me I shall do my utmost to get them such knowledge and such discipline as will make them thoroughly discontented, not indeed with that state of life into which it shall please God to call them, but with that evil state into which anarchy and monopoly has [sic] forced them, that so by their own organised and disciplined effort they may live fuller lives than you have been able to live, in a more beautiful world than you have had to toil in.

(Headlam repeatedly used modified forms of this passage, notably in his Fabian lecture delivered over three years later.) Such uncompromising language endeared him to the Marxists of the Social Democratic Federation, in whose paper *Justice* he wrote during the election campaign, calling on SDF members to 'sow the good seed of Socialism' among the clergy.

Headlam also pledged himself to work for the abolition of religious teaching in the Board schools. In opposing the non-secretarian 'School Board religion' of the day he as usual ranged himself with radicals and against the vast majority of his Church colleagues. This was indeed to stir up a hornet's nest, for not only was religion a permanent source of dissension on the School Boards, but the London clergy participated actively in elections: in 1888 Headlam was one of sixteen Anglican clergymen elected among the fifty-five members of the London School Board. His stand for secular education caused him to be regarded as anti-Christ in some orthodox circles, and met lively opposition even within the Guild of St Matthew. Headlam also wanted the Church of England to close its own schools, or at least wanted the state to end financial support for voluntary schools. His opposition to existing

religious instruction in the Board schools was based on the fact that it relied totally on the Bible. 'The children', he wrote, 'are practically taught to put it in the place of the eternal universal word of God.' It is not surprising that Headlam, a High Churchman, opposed the exclusive use of the Bible as tending towards Nonconformity. But his solution of a total separation between education and religion was followed by few of his fellow Anglicans.

Headlam's candidacy aroused controversy in Hackney, and at least one church hall was closed to him. Spending little on his campaign, he finished fourth among the five successful candidates. The radical *Star*, delighted by his victory, commented: 'Before many weeks are over we fully expect to see the new Board given its first lesson in the art of theatrical dancing.' Another of Headlam's activities in the autumn of 1888 was taking the chair at the lectures later published as *Fabian Essays in Socialism*. The socialist journal *To-day* reported that at one of them he was 'anxious as to the future of the Alhambra [Theatre] under Socialism'.

Headlam's long career in education began with a dazzling radical burst. Early in 1889 the London School Board became the first elected body to pass a resolution in favour of paying trade union wage rates. In 1890 a resolution was passed in support of free schools, an event which contributed to the decision to abolish most school fees by Act of Parliament the following year. Headlam played a leading role in these and other radical resolutions, and in 1890–1 was also prominent in a movement to supply pianos to schools with halls for use in drill and singing lessons. Opposition to pianos was intense, part of the never-ending effort to keep Board school education cheap and 'elementary' in the derogatory sense. One example of the adverse reaction was a postcard sent to Headlam by 'A Hater of All Faddists', calling him a 'cursed hound' and suggesting that he 'pay for the pianos out of your own pocket, you Robber, not out of the ratepayers'. Veterans of the election of 1891 remembered it as the 'piano election'. Headlam also worked for other progressive causes on the Board, including swimming baths, higher grade schools and smaller classes.

Thomas Gautrey, who was for a period a colleague of Headlam's, wrote in his history of the London School Board that Headlam 'held a unique place at the Board'. He was chairman of the Evening Continuation Schools Committee from 1897 (when the Liberals and Socialists of the Progressive Party gained control of the Board) until 1904, and presided over a remarkable growth. According to his biographer the eighty evening institutes with 9000 students of 1894 became by the new century 395 institutes with 147,000 students. Gautrey, who gives slightly lower figures of growth, comments that 'the splendid system ... was, in large measure, the creation of Mr Headlam'. Headlam also carried out vigorously the school visiting duties of School Board Members. He was immensely popular in Bethnal Green, and a colleague wrote of him in later life: 'To join him in a walk through its streets was to be in the company of a Pied Piper of Bethnal Green.' Headlam's seventeen years on the London County Council (where he represented S.W. Bethnal Green) were spent entirely in opposition, but his energies never flagged, and his record of attendance at Council and committee meetings as given by his biographer was nearly perfect.

Although Headlam remained active in political, religious and literary causes all his life, his great era was the 1880s and early 1890s. In 1895 he lost his journal, the *Church Reformer*, and in 1909 his organisation, the Guild of St Matthew. His liberal-socialist politics were overtaken from the left by working-class organisations and by the militants of the Church Socialist League. From 1904 he lost his position as a leading force in the determination of London education policy, and in any case many of the educational issues about which he felt most strongly were settled in his School Board period, or – as with free school meals – soon afterwards. When the First World War broke out in 1914 he was already nearly seventy and his support for a 'great and righteous War' further distanced him from contemporary left-wing opinion. Thus his last twenty years formed a long anti-climax to his earlier career.

Headlam died on 18 November 1924. The funeral service was held at All Souls', St Margaret's-on-Thames, and he was buried at East Sheen Cemetery. There were many obituaries, and a London County Council school was renamed the Stewart Headlam School. His gross estate was £5753.

Headlam was reputed, even by his friends, to be somewhat irascible and inflexible. (These qualities, among others, were brought out by Shaw in his portrayal of the Rev. James Mavor Morell in *Candida*, a portrayal generally supposed to be based in part on Headlam.) His character, together with his uncompromising faith in social justice, the theatrical world and secular education, rendered impossible a successful career in the Victorian Church of England. But in his day Headlam was the most important of Christian Socialists. He helped to form a bridge between Christianity and the labour movement, to improve the education of Londoners and to turn the attention of the middle classes to social reform.

Writings: *The Church Catechism and the Emancipation of Labour* [1875] 4 pp.; *The Doubts of the Faithful Sceptic the Confirmation of True Theology. A sermon* [on Ps. cxliii.12] etc. (1875) 14 pp.; *Priestcraft and Progress: being sermons and lectures* (1878); *The Service of Humanity, and Other Sermons* (1882); *The Sure Foundation. An Address given before the Guild of S. Matthew, at the Annual Meeting, 1883* [1883] 17 pp.; 'Plea for Peace among Socialists', *To-day*, 8, no. 46 (Sep 1887) 78–81; *Lessons from the Cross. Addresses given in Oxhey Parish Church on Good Friday, 1886* (1887) 46 pp.; *The Theory of Theatrical Dancing*, edited from C. Blases' Code of Terpsichore with original plates by S. D. Headlam (1888); *The Laws of Eternal Life: being studies in the Church Catechism* (1888, 2nd ed. 1897, 3rd ed. 1905) 56 pp.; *The Function of the Stage: a lecture* (1889) 37 pp.; *The London School Board in 1890: an address etc.,* (1890) 16 pp.; *The Guild of St Matthew, an Appeal to Churchmen: being a sermon* [on 2 Corinthians iv. 6] etc. (1890) 20 pp.; *The Duty of the Clergy towards Board Schools and Elementary Education* [1891?]; *Christian Socialism* (Fabian Tract no. 42, 1892) 15 pp.; *The Ballet* [a paper read to the Playgoers' Club] (1894) 16 pp.; *The Catholicity of the English Church* (1898); *Classical [English] Poetry: a lecture* (1898) 27 pp.; *Evening Continuation Schools in London* (repr. from *The School World* (Feb 1901) [1901] 8 pp.; *The Place of the Bible in Secular Education. An Open Letter to the Teachers under the London School Board* (1903) 38 pp.; *Disorders in the Church. An address etc.* [1904] 4 pp.; *Municipal Puritanism* [1905] 16 pp.; *The Meaning of the Mass: five lectures, with other sermons and addresses* (1905); *Secular Schools: the only just and permanent solution* (1906) 27 pp.; Preface to J. Clayton, *The Bishops as Legislators* (1906); *The Secular Work of Jesus Christ, his Apostles and the Church of England* [a lecture given before the East London branch of the National Secular Society in 1876] [1906] P; *Charles Bradlaugh: an appreciation* [with an introduction by George Standring] (1907) 15 pp.; *The Socialist's Church* (1907); (with Rev. J. Clifford, Rev. P. Dearmer and J. Woolman) *Socialism and Religion* (Fabian Socialist Series, no. 1, 1908); *Fabianism and Land Values* (1908) 16 pp.; *Maurice and Kingsley: theologians and socialists: a lecture* (1909) 14 pp.; *The Re-Organisation of the Evening Schools* (1912) 28 pp.; Preface to J. Reeves, *Recollections of a School Attendance Officer* [1913]; *Some Old Words about the War* [1915] 16 pp.; *The Clergy as Public Leaders* (n.d.).

Sources: (1) MSS: None known in this country, though an interesting Headlam letter (quoted by W. S. Smith (1967) 187) survives in the Pierpont Morgan Library, New York. F. G. Bettany's biography of Headlam refers (pp. v–vi) to a family memoir by Headlam's sister, Constance Coote, 'certain fragments of memoirs' and 'large stores of correspondence' which do not appear to have survived; (2) Secondary: The standard biography is F. G. Bettany, *Stewart Headlam: a biography* (1926). This contains correspondence, autobiographical writing and long reminiscences by contemporaries. See also: S. Webb, *Socialism in England* (1890); *Labour Annual* (1895) 175; A. V. Woodworth, *Christian Socialism in England* (1903); J. Adderley, *In Slums and Society* (1916); E. R. Pease, *The History of the Fabian Society* (1916); E. Bernstein, *My Years in Exile* (1921); *WWW* (1916–28); D. O. Wagner, *The Church of England and Social Reform since 1854* (New York, 1930); G. C. Binyon, *The Christian Socialist Movement in England* (1931); T. Gautrey, '*Lux Mihi Laus*': *school board memories* [1937]; M. B. Reckitt, *Maurice to Temple: a century of the social movement in the Church of England* (1947); S. Liberty, 'Stewart Duckworth Headlam', *Christendom 15* (Dec 1948) 268–73 and *16* (Mar 1949) 12–16; S. Winsten, *Salt and his Circle*, with a preface by Bernard Shaw (1951); A. H. Nethercot, *The First Five Lives of Annie Besant* (1961); A. M. McBriar, *Fabian Socialism and English Politics, 1884–1918* (Cambridge, 1962); K. S. Inglis, *Churches and the Working Classes in Victorian England* (1963); W. S. Smith, 'Stewart Headlam and the Christian Socialists', *Christian Century 80* (1963) 201–4; B. Simon, *Education and the Labour Movement, 1870–1920* (1965); S. Mayor, *The Churches and the Labour Movement* (1967); W. S. Smith, *The London Heretics, 1870–1914* (1967); P. Thompson, *Socialists, Liberals and Labour: the struggle for London, 1885–1914* (1967); P. d'A. Jones, *The Christian Socialist Revival, 1877–1914* (Princeton, New Jersey, 1968); K. Leech, 'Stewart Headlam 1847–1924 and the Guild of St Matthew', in *For Christ and the People* ed. M. B. Reckitt (1968); D. Rubinstein, *School Attendance in London, 1870–1904: a social history* (Hull, 1969); idem, 'Annie Besant and Stewart Headlam: the London School Board election of 1888', *East London Papers 13*, no. 1 (Summer 1970) 3–24; D. Tribe, *President Charles Bradlaugh, M.P.* (1971). OBIT. *Times*, 20, 25 and 29 Nov 1924; *Saturday Rev. 138*, 29 Nov 1924, 543–544.

DAVID RUBINSTEIN

See also: *Annie BESANT; *Charles BRADLAUGH; John Malcolm Forbes LUDLOW, for

Christian Socialism, 1848–54; Conrad NOEL; *Frederick VERINDER.

HINDEN, Rita (1909–71)
FABIAN ANTI-COLONIALIST AND SOCIALIST WRITER AND EDITOR

Although she refused ever to return there even for a short holiday, Rita Hinden's childhood and schooldays were happily spent in Cape Town, South Africa, in the security of a comfortably-off Jewish family. She was born there in her maternal grandparents' house, the second child of Jacob Gesundheit and Bella Harris, on 16 January 1909. Her father registered her as Rebecca, a name that she never used. At the time of her birth her parents were living in a village in the countryside where her father ran an ostrich farm. The failure of this venture resulted in the family moving into Cape Town when she was three years old. In December 1925 she matriculated at the Seminary of Good Hope and afterwards attended the local university for a year. In 1927 the whole family left for Palestine. Her father was a keen Zionist and an orthodox Jew who had long dreamt of going to live in the Holy Land as soon as he was rich enough to afford it. All his four children had been given an intensely Jewish education – at this time Rita could speak Hebrew fluently. They were the first family to emigrate from South Africa to Palestine, and the farewell they were given on the quayside left a deep imprint on her memory.

It was soon discovered that there was no opportunity for Rita to continue her education in Palestine. She was sent to England, to Liverpool for a year and then to the London School of Economics and Political Science. Here she gained second-class honours division I in the B.Sc. (Econ) in 1931. By this time she had met her future husband, Elchon Hinden, who had qualified in medicine at Cambridge. She returned to Palestine after graduation; he followed later and they were married on 14 February 1933; but after the honeymoon they came back to London to enable Elchon to pursue higher professional training for a couple of years. They were ardent Zionists, and they joined the Willesden branch of the Independent Labour Party, considering themselves well to the Left in Labour politics. Many of their friends had become members of the Communist Party and they were strongly pressed to follow their example, but its anti-democratic views and disregard for the truth repelled them. In 1935 they set off to settle in Palestine, believing they were leaving England for good.

What followed was a complex and disturbing experience for both of them, but especially for Elchon. Rita found it very much easier than her husband to get satisfactory work and gain acceptance in the new society. She was soon busily employed in journalism and research, and took up contacts with the Labour movement and the official Jewish Agency in Palestine. But both of them became increasingly estranged from the whole of their religious upbringing and ended as agnostics. They were also more and more disenchanted with the nationalist streak in Zionism which the rise of Hitler in Germany had accentuated among the Palestinian Jews. In the summer of 1938 they came on holiday to England, and after much heartsearching, decided to stay. This was to be their homeland and there could be no reversal of the decision.

By now they had two children, but Rita was not a housewife, and she was restless and unsettled. She lacked work that adequately stretched her abilities – or indeed any clear conception of what it was she wanted to do. Early in 1939 she joined the Labour Party and the Fabian Society. She had registered as a research student at LSE, working in an area largely based on economic studies begun with David Horowitz (later president of the Bank of Israel) in Palestine between 1933 and 1938; and in 1939 she obtained her doctorate for a thesis entitled 'Palestine – an experiment in colonisation'. It was during this period as a research student that she met R. R. Kuczynski, the eminent demographer, who was a Reader at LSE, and it was he who suggested that the colonial field might be the most suitable for her future work. She discussed the idea with various people, and in 1940 the Fabian Colonial Bureau was born with herself as its first secretary and Arthur Creech

Jones as chairman. This proved to be a most fruitful political partnership, dissolved only when Creech Jones became first Under-Secretary and then Secretary of State for the Colonies in the post-war Labour Government. Rita Hinden and Creech Jones had complementary qualities. He had a wise head, a wealth of experience at home and abroad and standing in the Labour movement. She had drive and imagination, was an able writer, and quickly showed that she was a gifted organiser too.

The venture was a great success and a new world of activity was opened up for Rita which she thoroughly enjoyed. As secretary of the Bureau she organised the production of a stream of pamphlets on colonial affairs which soon gave the Bureau an international reputation. Her own book *Plan for Africa* appeared in 1941. The time was ripe for action, the liquidation of the Empire had to come; but how? The Fabian Colonial Bureau developed a unique and crucial role that has been well described by Sir W. Arthur Lewis, who was closely involved in its early work:

> Rita gave substance to Labour's colonial policy. By keeping in touch day by day with what was going on in the colonies, especially in Africa and in the Caribbean, she was able to feed a constant stream of questions into Question Time in the House of Commons, as well as up-to-date and ordered material into MPs' speeches. Officials at the Colonial Office came to respect her knowledge, judgement and persistence, so she effected changes as much by influencing their actions as by her public protests. Suddenly, colonial leaders found they had a spokesman in London who reached right into the Commons and into the Colonial Office itself [*Socialist Commentary* (Jan 1972) 18].

One problem much discussed at the time was how the colonial countries could best develop democratic institutions which would prove viable after their independence. It was believed that the same institutions which had served the growth of the British Labour movement – local government, trade unions and co-operatives – would also pave the way for an enduring democracy in the colonies. Conferences were held on these subjects, and collective publications appeared advancing practical proposals in the Fabian tradition. Under its self-denying ordinance the Fabian Society had no agreed policy on anything, but at this time its Colonial Bureau displayed a far-reaching consensus on its political objectives; these were, in a phrase, to speed independence, but independence with democracy.

In 1950 Rita Hinden handed over the secretaryship of the Fabian Colonial Bureau to her deputy, Marjorie Nicholson. Her resignation was not due to any loss of interest in the subject or in the causes for which she had stood. She remained associated with the Bureau's work and continued her writing on colonial and commonwealth affairs. As an authority in this field she served on various advisory committees of the Labour Party, the Colonial Office and Chatham House. In the same year she was appointed a member of the Parliamentary Committee on British Guiana (now Guyana) to inquire into the riots that led to the suspension of the constitution there and to advise on a future constitution. Her reputation was at its peak. But the Fabian job had lost its earlier creative challenge, and she was looking for new worlds to conquer. She found what she was seeking in Socialist Union and *Socialist Commentary*, as secretary of the one and editor of the other. The present writer's own closer political co-operation with her began at this time, since he was chairman of both.

Socialist Union had a limited life throughout the fifties. It was formed to do a particular job, and when this was completed it disbanded. The conception that brought it into being was that the exhaustion and confusion in the Labour Party which followed the completion of its immediate post-war programme could only be overcome by a re-examination of the underlying principles of Socialism and their application to the conditions of the modern world. Its membership, recruited mainly from those who were already associated with the monthly *Socialist Commentary*, was never very large and it was possible to adopt the method of group discussion. Drafts were prepared by committees and then presented for criticism and agreement to the whole of the membership. The first document prepared in this way, *Socialism – A New Statement of Principles*, was published in 1952. Attlee welcomed it as expressing 'in far better language than I command the views which I hold and the faith which I believe'. Although its reception within the Labour Party was mixed, it immediately received world-wide publicity as a serious attempt at reformulating a modern Socialist philosophy. Discussions continued and principles were applied to practice. *Socialism and Foreign Policy* came out in 1953, and three years later *Twentieth Century Socialism*, dealing with economic policy and the nature of a Socialist economic system. The latter was published as a Penguin Special, translated into a dozen foreign languages and enjoyed the honour of a review by R. H. Tawney in *Socialist Commentary* (July 1956). Two other statements followed in 1958, the one on Education and the other on Social Services, and that completed the programme. Rita's part in all this was crucial. Drafts have in the last resort to be written by individuals, and most of the drafting fell upon her shoulders. At the same time the experience was very valuable to her in clarifying and deepening her own convictions as a Socialist, and it was firm fidelity to principle which characterised her editorship of *Socialist Commentary*.

She edited this monthly until her death, for the best part of twenty years, making it, by sheer perseverance as well as by her flair as an editor, an influential organ of opinion within the Labour movement. It was closely identified with Hugh Gaitskell, who had served as treasurer of the supporting organisation, Friends of Socialist Commentary, before he became Leader of the Labour Party. It parted company from him, however, on the question of Britain's entry into Europe, where it consistently took a strongly positive line. One of the many innovations for which she was responsible as editor, and which exemplify the unique character of her contribution, was the preparation of special supplements dealing in depth with some major issues of policy and, on one occasion, with Party organisation. Their production usually involved bringing together a group of highly argumentative experts who were not always equally expert in communicating their thoughts to others. The fact that it eventually proved possible to publish a coherent document, interestingly written, with a clear line of argument leading to practical recommendations, was largely Rita's doing. She gave these supplements their shape and style with a strong sense of what was effective political journalism.

But it would be a mistake to stress only her intellectual side. Her Socialism owed much to Tawney, and like him, she combined passion with learning. (Appropriately his literary executors asked her to edit a posthumous volume of his essays, which appeared under the title *The Radical Tradition*.) Socialism was for Rita Hinden first and foremost an ethical creed. It meant acceptance of a trinity of ideals, equality, freedom and fellowship, and the unremitting striving for their fuller realisation in society. They were not for her arid abstractions but values that she felt deeply about, as can be seen in all her writings, not least in the monthly editorials of *Socialist Commentary*. On these ideals, she argued, enduring Socialist structures could be founded, but dogmatism had to be avoided in the choice of Socialist means. Here revisionism was in place, because circumstances change, and lessons can be learnt from experience. This distinction between ends and means proved to be influential in Labour's doctrinal conflicts in the fifties.

In the whole of her political life Rita Hinden may be said to have sought influence rather than power. She had no illusions about the part played by power in politics, but she was temperamentally unsuited to participate in the rough and tumble of the struggles for power. She was too modest and too gentle a person, easily hurt even by hard words. Instead she made the politics of influence into an art, proving that in a democracy they could be a force even if they brought less personal glory and public recognition. In the exercise of political influence her personality found full expression and her latent gifts were strongly developed. She had, for example, an almost unlimited capacity for making and keeping friends, as well as creating beyond that circle relations of confidence and trust. And because she won people's hearts she gained their co-operation. She was effective, too, because of the intensity of her commitment to the causes that filled her life. Though she was in no sense a solemn person, her feelings about what she thought to be right were deep and were not swayed by loss of popularity. Against all the current trends and the weight of the experts' arguments she held to her conviction that the African people, given a fair chance, could make a democratic system work. It offended her sense of equality to agree that democracy was not for the blacks.

Family ties were very important to her and fortified her political life. She had a devoted and appreciative husband, to whom she turned daily for counsel and support. She always retained close and intimate relations with her two children, Jonathan and Judith, and lived to see their children. Her brother and sisters lived in Israel, but they saw each other quite frequently. Rita had, indeed, a continuing interest in Israel, and not only on account of her many relatives there. She was greatly concerned about the future of the country, and belonged to several Jewish organisations. After a period of ill-health she died in Whipps Cross Hospital on the evening of Thursday, 18 November 1971, and was cremated at the Golders Green Crematorium. She left an estate valued at £17,340. After her death a Rita Hinden Memorial Fund was established mainly for the purpose of arranging an annual lecture in her memory. The *Times* obituary (20 Nov 1971) was headed: 'A Dedicated Socialist'.

Writings: (with D. Horowitz), *Economic Survey of Palestine* (Jewish Agency for Palestine Economic Research Institute Tel Aviv, 1938); 'The Fertility and Mortality of the Population of Palestine' *Sociological Rev. 32* (1940) 29–49; *Plan for Africa* (1941); 'The Economic Issues' in *Freedom for Colonial Peoples* (National Peace Council [1940?]) 5–11; *The Colonies and Us* (Fabian Society Socialist Propaganda Committee, no. 4: 1943) 26 pp.; Editor of *Co-operation in the Colonies* (1945); 'The Challenge of African Poverty' and 'How a Political Society Functions' in H. N. Brailsford et al. with an introduction by A. Creech Jones *Fabian Colonial Essays*, ed. R. Hinden (1945) 56–66 and 249–61; *Socialists and the Empire* (Fabian Colonial Bureau, 1946) 27 pp.; 'The Labour Government and the Empire' in *Socialism the British Way*, ed. D. Munro (1948); *Empire and after* (1949); *Common Sense and Colonial Development* (Fabian Colonial Bureau, 1949) 47 pp.; Editor of *Local Government and the Colonies* (1950); *The Way Forward* (Controversy ser., no. 7, Fabian Colonial Bureau, 1950); *The United Nations and the Colonies* (Peacefinder ser., no. 9, UNA, 1950) 17 pp.; *A World of Peace and Plenty* (LP Discussion Pamphlet, 1951) 30 pp.; *Challenge to the British Caribbean* (Fabian Colonial Bureau with Gollancz, 1952) 37 pp.; (with A. Flanders), *Twentieth Century Socialism* (Penguin, 1956); *Problems of Self-Determination* (Peacefinder ser., no. 24, UNA, 1957) 12 pp.; *No Cheer for Central Africa* (Fabian Commonwealth Bureau, 1958) 38 pp.; 'Socialism and the Colonial World', in *New Fabian Colonial Essays* ed. A. Creech Jones (1959) 9–18; (with M. A. Abrams and R. Rose), *Must Labour Lose?* (Penguin, 1960); *Africa and Democracy* (Encounter Pamphlet no. 8, [1961?]); Editor's preface to R. H. Tawney, *The Radical Tradition* (1964) 8–10; numerous articles in *Fabian Q.*, *Guardian*, *New Statesman*, *Socialist Commentary* and *Venture*.

Sources: *Observer*, 8 July 1956; M. Cole, *The Story of Fabian Socialism* (1961); *Hugh Gaitskell*, ed. W. T. Rodgers (1964); *Evening Standard*, 8 June 1968; personal knowledge. OBIT. *Times*, 20 Nov 1971; *Guardian*, 30 Nov 1971; *Socialist Commentary*, Dec 1971 and Jan 1972; *Venture 24*, no. 1 (Jan 1972) 4.

ALLAN FLANDERS

See also: *Hugh Todd Naylor GAITSKELL; *Arthur Creech JONES; *Richard Henry TAWNEY.

HOLE, James (1820–95)
OWENITE SOCIALIST, CO-OPERATOR AND
ADULT EDUCATIONALIST

James Hole was born in London in 1820 (*Boase*, 5, 685 gives 1819) but apparently spent part of his youth in Manchester, where as a boy in the 1830s he was a member of the Mechanics' Institute and attended a mutual improvement class. He went to Leeds early in the 1840s as foreign correspondent and confidential clerk to Messrs Simon Bros, of Bedford Street, a firm of stuff merchants engaged in the export of worsted. There is no evidence that Hole was ever more than an employee of this firm, although J. M. F. Ludlow could describe him in 1851 as 'the managing man in one of the large firms of the town'. Hole's reputation was based on his work in Leeds, where he had a wide circle of friends and acquaintances among social reformers. He was a member of the literary group which centred on the *Truth Seeker*, a periodical edited in Leeds from 1846 to 1850 by F. R. Lees and George Searle Phillips ('January Searle'), and was an acquaintance of William Howitt's.

The first public mention of Hole was in 1845, as a foundation member of the Leeds Redemption Society, a communitarian venture in the Owenite tradition. Hole edited the society's paper, the *Herald of Redemption* (later, the *Herald of Co-operation and Organ of the Redemption Society*), 1847–8, and elaborated his communitarian philosophy in its pages. The society acquired an estate in South Wales, but the venture did not flourish, and in 1855 it was wound up. Simultaneously Hole was involved in the movement to establish consumers' co-operation. He was one of the pioneers of the Leeds District Flour Mill Society founded in 1847, from which came the Leeds and District Co-operative Flour and Provision Society in 1853. Through this work he came into contact with the Christian Socialists, and was a member of the Co-operative League which they formed in 1852. His social philosophy at this time was most fully expressed in a collection of essays published in 1851 under the title, *Lectures on*

Social Science and the Organization of Labor (these had appeared previously in the *Truth Seeker*, 1849–50). Hole's work was an important Socialist critique of capitalist society, derived from Owenite premises. But he repudiated Owenite solutions and advocated 'Association', including within his definition of Socialism almost any social or co-operative enterprise, from communities to civic wash-houses.

As an example of successful association Hole frequently cited mechanics' institutes. He was active in the Leeds Mechanics' Institute by 1845, and from 1847 to 1865 was a member of the general committee and various sub-committees. In 1858 and 1861 he was elected vice-president. It was, however, through the larger body of the Yorkshire Union of Mechanics' Institutes that Hole made his main contribution to adult education. From 1848 to 1867 he was honorary secretary of this flourishing adult education organisation. For twenty years he guided the general policy of the Union and saw to its day-to-day running. He lectured, gave addresses at soirées, and chaired meetings throughout the West Riding. Among his innovations was the Yorkshire Union Village Library, an itinerating library scheme that from 1852 supplied boxes of books on loan for six months to rural groups. His views on adult education were set out in his Society of Arts Prize Essay, published in 1853 as *An Essay on the History and Management of Literary, Scientific, and Mechanics' Institutions*, and also in the *Annual Reports* of the Yorkshire Union of Mechanics' Institutes. Hole showed a remarkable grasp of the needs and possibilities of workers' education at a time when all too many middle-class sympathisers were content to encourage entertainment rather than learning.

Hole deprecated reformers who were interested only in one aspect of social reform, and he engaged in numerous activities based on the 'associative principle'. Among these was national education. In his prize essay, *Light, more Light! – on the present state of education amongst the working classes of Leeds, and how it can best be improved* (1860), he demonstrated the inadequacy of educational facilities. The work was not primarily an interpretation of educational policy but rather a survey of existing agencies in Leeds. It covered day, Sunday, evening and secondary schools, mechanics' institutes, local educational institutes, the School of Art, the education of paupers and criminals, as well as 'social education' through such agencies as popular literature, savings banks and cheap concerts; and the result was to expose the failure of voluntaryism to provide a national system of education. In his practical work in education Hole was particularly concerned with technical instruction. He was chairman of the Leeds School of Art (formerly the School of Design); and when the West Riding Educational Board was formed in 1859 to supervise the local examinations for Oxford, Cambridge and Durham Universities, the Society of Arts, and the Science and Art Department, he was one of the representatives on it from the Yorkshire Union. When there was renewed interest in technical education in 1866-8, Hole actively supported the proposals for a Central College in the West Riding; and he was present at the special conference on technical education called by the Society of Arts in London in January 1868.

For a social reformer of Hole's stamp it was but a short step from education to working-class housing. Impressed by the success of the model village of Akroydon (Halifax), Hole and a group of co-operators and Redemptionists founded the Leeds Society for the Erection of Improved Dwellings, backed by the Leeds Permanent Building Society (of which Hole was a director). The Society purchased small plots of land, erected model houses on them at a cost of £150-200 per house, and sold them to working men at cost price. By 1866 some eighty-seven houses had been built. Hole's approach to the problem was expounded in another prize essay which he published in 1866, *The Homes of the Working Classes*. Like his survey of education, Hole's book contains a mass of detailed statistical information, but it also includes a good deal more of his social philosophy, and in this it is reminiscent of his *Lectures on Social Science*. His earlier belief in the power of the working classes to transform society by their own efforts (which was at the root of the idea of the Redemption of Labour) had, however, become considerably modified by 1865; for after considering the various agencies by which improved housing for the working classes might be obtained, he opted for state assistance as the only practical solution. He was a member of the committee of the Yorkshire Penny Bank from 1859, and approved of temperance [Winskill, 2 (1897-8) 48]; but he was convinced that self-help by working men could only be practical on any socially significant scale if it was backed up by government legislation. Yet, unlike many of his old friends, Hole's name does not appear as a supporter of the Leeds Working Men's Parliamentary Reform Association in 1861. Instead, he remained true to his earlier Owenite distrust of political action, especially 'this loud hullabaloo about Reform, that will lead to nothing'.

In 1867 Hole left Leeds for London, to become the agent (or organising secretary) of the Associated Chambers of Commerce, and he held this position until his death twenty-eight years later. In London he continued his work for social reform. His advice was sought by all kinds of reformers, and in later years, as an elder statesman of the cause of social reform, his name was frequently solicited for use on prospectuses. The *Times* obituary could consequently praise him as 'a practical philanthropist', while Engels saw him similarly, though without praise, as 'a bourgeois philanthropist'. Typical of his interests at this time was his membership of the council of the Trades Guild of Learning, established in 1873 by Henry Solly to secure trade union support for a programme of technical instruction and liberal studies. In the same year he also contributed a series of articles, 'On Association', to Solly's *Workman's Magazine*. He was a member of the committee of management of the Central Co-operative Agency Society from 1869 to 1874, and was later a supporter of the Guild of Co-operators. His work for improved housing was continued through the Adelphi

Permanent Benefit Land, Building and Investment Society, of which he was a director. He was on the council of the Society for Promoting Industrial Villages (1884), and in his last years he was secretary of the Commons Preservation Society.

His final effort was in yet another field: the nationalisation of the railways. His book, *National Railways: an argument for state purchase*, was published in 1893. Beginning with an examination of the anomaly that the railways are at once private property and public necessities, he ends with proposals for their ownership by the state, so that they may be controlled solely in the public interest. If his condemnation of *laissez faire* and the competitive system still echoes the *Lectures on Social Science*, with their Owenite ring of the 1840s, his detailed proposals for the taking over of the railways by the state are close to the collectivism of the Fabians.

In his writings Hole scrupulously avoided all sectarian religious matters, as causing irrelevant divisions among reformers. He was the [anonymous] translator of the first English edition (1864) of Ernest Renan's *The Life of Jesus*, and his preface indicates an admiration for the works of F. W. Newman, Bishop Colenso, and the authors of *Essays and Reviews*.

Virtually nothing is known of Hole's private life. Of his two sons, James died in 1913; and Edward J. Hole became clerk to E. O. Greening, the co-operator. Both were educated at the Leeds Mechanics' Institute day school and evening classes. Hole died on 24 February 1895 at his home in London; no will has been located.

Writings: *Lectures on Social Science and the Organization of Labor* (1851); *An Essay on the History and Management of Literary, Scientific, and Mechanics' Institutions* (1853); *Light, more Light! – on the present state of education amongst the working classes of Leeds* (1860); [anon.] trans., E. Renan, *The Life of Jesus* (1864); *The Homes of the Working Classes, with Suggestions for their Improvement* (1866); *National Railways: an argument for state purchase* (1893).

Sources: (1) MSS: Minute books, 1847–60, Leeds Co-operative Society; Ludlow papers, Cambridge University Library; Solly papers, LSE; (2) Other: *Herald of Redemption* (Isle of Man, 1847); *Herald of Co-operation* (Isle of Man, 1847–8); *Truth Seeker* (1846–50); *Christian Socialist* (1850–1851); *Annual Reports, Yorkshire Union of Mechanics' Institutes* (1847–68); *Annual Reports, Leeds Mechanics' Institute* (1847–1865); P. T. Winskill, *Temperance Standard Bearers of the Nineteenth Century*, 2 vols (Manchester, 1897–8); C. R. Raven, *Christian Socialism 1848–1954* (1920); G. D. H. Cole, *A Century of Co-operation* (Manchester [1945?]); J. F. C. Harrison, *Social Reform in Victorian Leeds: the work of James Hole, 1820–1895* (Leeds, Thoresby Society, 1954) [this is the main source for all statements and references in this entry]; J. F. C. Harrison, *Learning and Living* (1961); J. F. C. Harrison, *Robert Owen and the Owenites in Britain and America* (1969). OBIT. *Leeds Mercury* (Supplement), 23 Feb 1895; *Times*, 26 Feb 1895; *Leeds Co-operative Record* (Apr 1895).

J. F. C. HARRISON

See also: †Edward Thomas CRAIG; †Edward Owen GREENING; †Patrick Lloyd JONES; †John Minter MORGAN.

HOUSE, William (1854–1917)
MINERS' LEADER

Born on 18 January 1854 at Pittington, Durham, House was the son of a colliery engineman. The family moved to Bishop Auckland, and after a rudimentary education House began work at the age of ten in a local pit. In 1867 he went underground as a driver, and six years later, when he was nineteen, he began working at the coal face as a hewer. He became involved in trade union activities as a young man, and in 1880 was elected as a delegate to the council of the Durham miners. He had served for some years on the executive council of the DMA when in 1899 he was appointed agent to the Association, with sole charge of the Joint Committee that had just been established in consequence of the passing of the

Workmen's Compensation Act. In the following year, House succeeded J. Forman as president of the DMA and continued in this position until his death. He represented the DMA on the executive committee of the MFGB in 1908 and 1913 and was vice-president of the MFGB from 1914. Although somewhat brusque in manner he carried great weight among the miners, and his negotiating skill was widely remarked upon.

The years before 1914 witnessed a number of important changes within the DMA. The ILP began to make a special agitational effort in Durham, and the appointment of Matt Sim in 1905 as their organiser was followed by a notable increase in the Party's strength. The Durham miners voted to join the MFGB in 1907, and when the latter decided to join the Labour Party in 1908 Durham was part of the new affiliation, although because of a legal technicality a ballot was never held by the DMA [Gregory (1968) 73]. Considerable tensions – political, between the miners' traditional support for the Liberals and their new alliance with the Labour Party, and industrial, around the issue of the eight-hour day – continued, however, to exist within many mining constituencies, and House was the victim of these disagreements on the three occasions when he stood as parliamentary candidate. In his youth he had been a radically-minded Liberal, but he accepted the switch to the Labour Party. He was preparing himself as a candidate for South-East Durham when J. M. Paulton, the sitting Liberal member for Bishop Auckland, announced his coming retirement before the next election, and the DMA thereupon transferred House to this constituency. The Liberal Party was traditionally supported by many miners; moreover, the negotiation by the DMA of the three-shift system (in order to implement the Eight Hours Act) aroused intense hostility among the rank and file, so that it was clear to contemporary observers that House had no chance of success; and in a three-cornered contest in January 1910 he was bottom of the poll, with a landowning Liberal easily the victor. In the second general election of 1910 (December) House lost again to the Liberal

candidate, but he improved his voting figures by a few hundred, beating the Conservative into third place. House's third attempt to enter Parliament was even more humiliating than the earlier ones. The DMA put him up in a by-election for Houghton-le-Spring in 1913. Although John Wilson had won the seat in 1885 he had lost it in the following year and the constituency remained a safe Conservative one until after 1900, when the Liberal Party gained ascendancy. The DMA, as a result of the Osborne judgement, were short of election funds in 1913; but it was politics, not money, that defeated House. Gregory [(1968) 80] describes the contest:

> The local Liberals selected a commercial traveller named Tom Wing, and as the campaign developed it became apparent that thousands of miners preferred even this unlikely candidate to the president of their own union running on the Labour ticket. Nearly every lodge in the constituency was represented at Wing's adoption meeting, and, according to its chairman, the Houghton-le-Spring Liberal Association was made up almost entirely of miners. House, of course, was not without supporters, and very soon quite unprecedented and extraordinary situations arose. Every lodge and every village was split from top to bottom, and on a good many evenings half of the lodge's officials were to be found speaking from House's platform whilst the other half were helping Wing. And, now that the miners were divided and forced to take sides, the extent to which they had been previously identified with the Liberals came out even more clearly.

House came bottom of the poll, with the Unionist above him and the Liberal returned; and he never tried again. Houghton-le-Spring returned a miner to Parliament from 1918 on, but before that House was dead. Just before his death he paid a warm tribute to the work of the socialist president of the MFGB, Robert Smillie: interesting because of the political differences between them.

Like so many of his generation of miners'

leaders House pioneered working-class representation in local affairs. He was elected in 1893 to the Durham County Council, and later became chairman of the County Health Committee and an alderman. He also served on the Auckland RDC, was a member of the Auckland Board of Guardians and a governor of the local hospital. A staunch co-operator, he was for a number of years president of the Auckland Co-operative Society. He was made a J.P. in 1908. During the First World War, which he fully supported, he was a member of the County Appeals Tribunal.

He died on 7 May 1917, survived by a wife and large family, and left effects valued at £950. The funeral service was conducted at the local Primitive Methodist chapel, of which House had been an active member for many years. In a brief valedictory resolution of regret, Sam Roebuck of Yorkshire later said of him: 'He was blunt and rough in exterior, but fundamentally he was a fine fellow, and represented in a very real sense the aspirations of his organisation.'

Sources: *Durham Chronicle*, 19 Oct 1900; John Wilson, *The Story of the Durham Miners* (1907); S. Webb, *History of the Durham Miners* (1921); R. Page Arnot, *The Miners*, vols *1* and *2* (1949 and 1953); H. Pelling, *Social Geography of British Elections 1885–1910* (1967); R. Gregory, *The Miners and British Politics 1906–1914* (Oxford, 1968); biographical information: Mrs V. Mason. Obit. *Durham County Advertiser* and *Times*, 11 May 1917.

JOHN SAVILLE

See also: †Thomas ASHTON, for Mining Trades Unionism 1900–14; †Thomas Henry CANN; †John WILSON (1837–1915).

HOWELL, George (1833–1910)
TRADE UNION LEADER AND LIB-LAB MP

George Howell was born in Wrington, Somerset, on 5 October 1833, the eldest of eight children of Edwin John Howell and Mary Welsh. Edwin Howell was, like his father before him, a mason by trade, but after his marriage he became self-employed as a general builder, sub-contracting for railway bridges and other projects in Somerset and Monmouthshire. Uncertain prospects and financial reversals caused the family to move often during George's early years, and in 1843 Edwin Howell was ruined in a law suit when he failed to recover several thousand pounds from a defaulting contractor. Until the age of ten George Howell attended village schools and, in the early 1840s, a Church of England boys' school in Bristol. After his father's disaster, his education, interrupted for stints as a plough boy, became more sporadic, although he attended evening classes until the age of twelve and Sunday school for several more years. However rudimentary his formal schooling, he read voraciously, beginning with works like Foxe's *Book of Martyrs, Pilgrim's Progress* and Hannah More's *Bible Rhymes*. In 1845 Howell began to assist his father, working as a mortar boy and time-keeper. The arrangement was not a happy one, and two years later he was apprenticed to a Wrington shoemaker. The three-year agreement stipulated that Howell was to receive one shilling per week after the first six months and a regular weekly wage after the first year for a fourteen-hour day.

The workshop completed Howell's education, exposing him for the first time to political discussion and to Radical newspapers. His fellow workers introduced him to the *Northern Star*, the *Working Man's Friend*, and the *British Controversialist*, this last valuable as a guide to further reading. In 1848 he was inducted into a local Chartist group and, more significantly, underwent conversion from nominal Anglicanism to Wesleyan Methodism. He became a proselytising teetotaller and taught Methodist Sunday school classes. His reading during this period followed the typical pattern of a working-class autodidact. His Wesleyan class leader lent him Isaac Watts's *On the Improvement of the Mind*, and *Paradise Lost*, which instilled in him an enthusiasm for Milton shared by Samuel Bamford and Mark Rutherford's Zachariah Coleman. Although he enjoyed Plutarch and the poetry of Crabbe and Clare, he favoured religious tracts, notably the works of Baxter, Wesley, and John Gregory Pike.

When his apprenticeship ended in 1851, Howell moved to Weston-super-Mare and then to Bristol, where he worked at shoe-making and joined an improvement society affiliated with a Reformed Methodist chapel. He acquired experience in public speaking, addressing meetings on temperance and on the Master and Servant Acts, and organised an informal study group to read Coleridge, Whately, and Paley. In addition, he helped to found the St James's Square YMCA, which provided a reading room abundantly stocked with periodicals. Upon his parents' move to Bristol in 1853 Howell was prevailed upon to return to the building trade. Prevented from working as a mason by union regulations which prohibited more than one son from pursuing his father's craft except after serving a full apprenticeship, he turned to bricklaying. But his sights were already set on London, which had attracted him ever since his first visit at the time of the 1851 Exhibition. He had already begun to harbour ambitions unlikely to be attained were he to remain tied to family surroundings. With confidence in the efficacy of self-improvement, Howell formulated three goals for himself: to write a book, to speak in Exeter Hall, and to enter Parliament.

Arriving in London in July 1855, he found it impossible at first to secure employment as a journeyman bricklayer. He worked as an improver at wages of a guinea for the standard fifty-eight-and-a-half hour week. Within a few months, however, he was receiving the journeyman's wage of thirty-two shillings per week and by 1859 had risen to become a deputy foreman. His many jobs in this period included a residential crescent in the Caledonian Road, the City Road drainage scheme, and the new Foreign Office building. London brought him into contact with a number of former Chartists and foreign exiles, men like Robert Hartwell, J. B. Leno, Benjamin Lucraft, Mazzini, Kossuth, and Marx. Through his political and industrial activities he also came to know G. J. Holyoake, Charles Bradlaugh, John

Malcolm Ludlow, E. S. Beesly, and Frederic Harrison. More important for his development in these years were the numerous informal groups in which he participated – improvement societies, debating clubs, and temperance organisations – more cosmopolitan versions of associations he had encountered in Bristol. Through these Howell met other aspiring working-class politicians and began to establish a network of connections within which he was to construct a career. The movement in the building trades was to give this element cohesion and to serve as the catalyst in the revival of working-class Radicalism in the 1860s. His compulsive self-improvement persisted all through the early London years, although his preoccupation with religion was tempered by a growing political consciousness. Soon after his arrival he enrolled in classes on penmanship, commercial arithmetic, and book-keeping. He later studied geometry and architectural drawing at the Charterhouse School of Art, took lessons in Latin and Greek, and frequented T. H. Huxley's lectures to working-class audiences at the Museum of Practical Geology. Once he had acquired a reader's permit, he spent much of his spare time at the British Museum, immersed in Bacon, Hume, Gibbon, Macaulay, Carlyle, and Mill.

It was the nine hours dispute in the building trades from 1859 to 1862, a watershed in Victorian labour history, that prompted Howell to join the London Order of the Operative Bricklayers' Society and brought him into close association with the men who were to dominate the world of London unionism for the next generation: William Allan, Robert Applegarth, Edwin Coulson, and George Potter. As a newcomer to the union, Howell played little part in the initial stages of the strike and lockout, but by the end of 1860 his effectiveness as a debater and his organisational skills gained recognition, and he was appointed to represent the London Bricklayers at the January 1861 Derby conference, at which Potter established the United Kingdom Association for Shortening the Hours of Labour in the Building Trades. In March Howell was elected a member of the Bricklayers' strike committee, assuming major responsibility for negotiating with employers and communicating with provincial societies. He also piloted through a constitutional reorganisation of the London Order on 'New Model' principles and launched the *Operative Bricklayers' Society Trade Circular* in September 1861. His increasing prominence in union affairs posed a threat to Coulson's domination of the Bricklayers, and a bitter rivalry ensued. Howell repudiated Coulson's attempts to encroach on the territory of the Manchester Unity of Bricklayers, and his endorsement of greater union involvement in politics clashed with Coulson's preoccupation with trade questions. With his friend Charles Shearman and the former secretary, Henry Turff, Howell began a systematic campaign to undermine Coulson's authority, widening a breach which ultimately led him to resign from the London Order in 1871 and to join the Sheffield Lodge of the Manchester Unity the next year. Throughout the 1860s he polled well in elections to the union's executive council, but he consistently failed to displace Coulson as general secretary. Howell and Coulson were able, however, to ignore their mutual antipathy when required, in order to promote policies they both favoured. In the International, in the London Trades Council's struggles against Potter, and later in the work of the Conference of Amalagamated Trades, vital working-class interests pushed enmities into the background. Nonetheless, Coulson emerged indisputably as the victor in the contest within the Operative Bricklayers' Society. Howell's attempts to wrest the leadership from him were repeatedly foiled, and his failure reinforced his inclinations towards political, rather than industrial activity.

Howell encountered fewer obstacles to his progress on the London Trades Council and was elected to its executive in May 1861. Within three weeks of his election he was named as secretary, a position he held until July 1862, when ill-health and his deepening conflict with Coulson led to his resignation. Both as secretary and during his subsequent tenure on the Council from 1865

to 1867 he and George Odger, with the support of Applegarth, struggled to convert trade unionists to a belief in the efficacy of political action. It was Howell's task in December 1861 to respond to the fraternal greetings of the General Neapolitan Society of Working Men and to affirm the Council's solidarity with the cause of Italian freedom. In 1865 he re-emerged as a partisan in the Junta campaign against Potter's independent industrial policy. Howell's stint as secretary provided valuable organisational experience, and in the following years he was to ally himself more closely with the Junta, thus laying the foundation for his accession to the secretaryship of the Reform League.

While his political career prospered in the early 1860s, Howell's involvement in the Bricklayers' strike committee had resulted in his being blacklisted by London builders. Unable to find work, he moved to Surrey in 1862 and did not return to London until June 1864, when a former employer re-hired him as foreman, a position he was to retain until he gave up bricklaying to accept the secretaryship of the Reform League in April 1865. During his enforced absence from London he continued to participate in political activities and was one of the initiators of the Trade Unionists' Manhood Suffrage and Vote by Ballot Association in October 1862, along with Odger, Applegarth, and W. Randal Cremer. He spoke at the celebrated St James's Hall meeting on 26 March 1863, convened by Professor Beesly to express working-class sympathy for the North in the American Civil War. At a Working Men's Shakespeare Tercentenary celebration on Primrose Hill in 1864 it was Howell who proposed a national political organisation to widen the scope of reform agitation, a suggestion which bore fruit in the formation of the Reform League the next year. He was also a member of the National League for the Independence of Poland in 1863, the Garibaldi Reception Committee in 1864, the Marquis of Townshend's Universal League for the Material Elevation of the Industrious Classes in 1864–5, and of the General Council of the International Working Men's Association from 1864 to 1869, although he took little part in its affairs after 1866. These spheres of activity tended to overlap, fostering a political alliance of reformers that straddled class lines.

Established in February 1865 with Edmond Beales as president, the Reform League was the first national organisation to mobilise the urban artisans effectively for franchise agitation. Committed to a program of manhood suffrage and vote by ballot, the League operated through a network of local branches – over 400 by 1867 – and by means of public meetings, lectures, and the dissemination of propaganda, all co-ordinated through a central office in London. As secretary of the League from April 1865 until its dissolution in the spring of 1869 and its only full-time, paid functionary, Howell was responsible for implementing the instructions of the executive committee, for keeping the financial records, and, above all, for the vast correspondence through which the organisation kept in touch with branches, potential contributors, and sympathetic politicians. He took charge of fund-raising, of arranging meetings, deputations, and demonstrations, and of setting up branches throughout the country. Sensitive to criticism and continually embroiled in personal conflicts, he nevertheless proved to be an adept administrator. Realising that survival depended in large measure upon middle-class subsidies, Howell sought to contain working-class militancy, a policy which accorded with his own aspirations towards respectability. The League endorsed the Liberal Reform Bill of 1866 and was slow to sponsor outdoor demonstrations, such as that in Hyde Park in July. After the defeat of Gladstone's bill, the League, aided by contributions from Samuel Morley and other Radical donors, expanded its activities to include lecture tours and frequent demonstrations. With the enactment of franchise reform in 1867, Howell linked the League more closely with the Liberals as the best hope of securing those political and social reforms, such as the ballot and trade union rights, that still awaited parliamentary action. During the 1868 general election he administered a special fund, amassed by the

Liberal Whips, to mobilise working-class support for Liberal candidates in a number of marginal constituencies. His policies during and after the election evoked sharp criticism from certain of his contemporaries, and some later historians (of whom the most important is Royden Harrison, *Before the Socialists* (1965) ch. 4) have been notably unflattering in their assessment of his role at this time.

Howell's administrative experience in the Reform League and his close ties with Liberal politicians opened up new career opportunities. In 1869 he launched a private Liberal Registration and Election Agency, financed mainly by Morley and James Stansfeld, but the project proved abortive. At the same time he helped to establish the Labour Representation League, serving on its executive until 1876. Along with other moderates in the League, like Applegarth and Potter, he tried to devise an arrangement whereby the Liberal managers would promote working-class candidacies in a few select boroughs in return for League support of official nominees in the majority of contests; but the plan foundered on Liberal recalcitrance. From 1868 to 1874 Howell was employed as paid secretary of Walter Morrison's Representative Reform Association, an organisation advocating schemes of proportional representation, and in 1871–1872 he served as Chairman of the Working Men's Committee for Promoting the Separation of Church and State, an offshoot of the Liberation Society. He was a member of the executive committees of both the National Education League and the Liberation Society, undertaking occasional lecture tours in their behalf. In addition, he held the positions of paid secretary of the Plimsoll and Seamen's Fund Committee from 1873 to 1875 and of financial agent for John Stuart Mill's Land Tenure Reform Association. In 1871 he was also elected to the Vestry of St Mary's, Newington.

Throughout the late 1860s and early 1870s Howell tried to carve out a position of financial security based upon his experience in the labour movement. Although his earnings were considerably higher during this period than they would have been in bricklaying, most of the organisations from which he derived income tended to be of short duration, and he found it impossible to obtain both financial independence and security of tenure. In 1870–1 he started the Adelphi Permanent Building Society to lend money to working men for the purchase of their own homes, but he lacked the business acumen and the sources of capital needed to make it a profitable venture. He also served briefly as the secretary of the People's Garden Company, an investment society seeking to acquire land for recreational purposes, and was employed by Thomas Brassey to locate slum properties for rehabilitation.

Despite the abandonment of his trade, Howell retained close links with London union officials. In April 1867 he had appeared as a witness before the Royal Commission on Trade Unions and had testified to the success of unions, not merely in improving wages and hours, but also in creating an atmosphere of moral restraint which curbed drunkenness. While the Junta leaders, by now constituted as the Conference of Amalgamated Trades, remained aloof from the first meetings of the Trades Union Congress in 1868–9, Howell attended the Birmingham Congress in August 1869 as their unofficial representative. His active, self-assured participation in the proceedings enhanced his reputation among the delegates, and within the next two years he was to eclipse Potter, who had cultivated the provincial union leaders, as the dominant London figure in TUC affairs. By 1871 he not only secured election to the first parliamentary committee, but also emerged as secretary, a position he held until his voluntary retirement after the 1875 Congress. Under the leadership of Howell and Alexander Macdonald of the miners, the parliamentary committee strove to obtain the repeal of the Master and Servant Act and the Criminal Law Amendment Act of 1871, as well as other reforms beneficial to miners and industrial workers. Howell's technique of private lobbying of Liberal politicians aroused the disapproval of trade union allies, like Beesly and Harrison, and his policy of seeking partial concessions was criticised at the Leeds TUC in 1873. He

found himself with less room for personal manoeuvre after the Leeds Congress, but his personal ascendancy within the parliamentary committee was never again challenged. Prospects for success improved in 1873 with the increase in working-class agitation, stimulated by the London gas stokers' strike, and the conversion of more MPs to the cause of repeal. In 1873–4 A. J. Mundella agreed to sponsor bills for the repeal of the Criminal Law Amendment Act, but it was not until 1875 that the Conspiracy and Protection of Property Act removed the constraints on strike activity and granted trade unions a full charter of rights.

By 1876, when Henry Broadhurst replaced Howell as secretary of the parliamentary committee, the TUC had earned a recognised place among the voluntary institutions of the nation. For five years Howell had personified the committee and, in some ways, the Congress itself. It was Howell as secretary who shaped its policies and who embodied its virtues and failings. Although his administrative talents made him the ideal person to direct a large, but decentralised campaign for legislative reform, he was not always able to subordinate personal ambition to long-term objectives and was susceptible to the blandishments of Liberal politicians. Pragmatic, cautious, unresponsive to the more radical currents in the movement, he worked assiduously to promote the interests of trade unionism as he conceived them. He regarded compromise as the only way to win the benevolent indulgence of middle-class reformers. Remote from the rank-and-file union membership, Howell rejected militant tactics in favour of intricate negotiations. If his methods were too accommodating, they reflected his conviction that success depended upon an astute advocacy of labour's demands and the conversion of men of influence. However narrow his perspective, his tenure as secretary was a personal and public success, establishing him in the forefront of the labour movement.

Although Howell continued to try to make a career for himself in working-class politics after his resignation from the TUC, the most important phase of his career was over, and he was never again to achieve the prominence he had attained in these years. He remained a useful, if not essential man, active on innumerable committees and in arranging meetings, but he lacked the opportunities and the abilities to rise into the middle class. He had achieved the status of a labour statesman, whose advice and whose participation in movements were sought, but if he shared in the activities of middle-class reformers, he never became one of them, remaining in spite of himself firmly rooted in the world of labour. In 1876, 1879, and 1882 Howell served as the secretary of the London School Board election committees and held the office of parliamentary agent of the Women's Suffrage Committee in 1878–9. He failed to secure appointment, however, as an inspector of schools or as a factory inspector. Unable to find steady employment, he turned increasingly to writing as a source of income. He contributed regularly to the *Bee-Hive* in the 1870s, and in 1876 published *A Handy Book of the Labour Laws*, a popular guide to the recent legislation. The favourable reception accorded the work encouraged him to produce a full-scale study of trade unionism, *The Conflicts of Capital and Labour*, in 1878. The next year he returned to political organising and founded the National Liberal League, with himself as chairman, Broadhurst as secretary, and William Morris as treasurer. It was another attempt to enlist working-class voters in the Liberal camp, but it attracted even less support than the Labour Representation League, and disintegrated by 1882. In the meantime Howell had begun to work as London business agent for Ellis Lever, a Manchester coal merchant, a position he held until 1885. In 1881, with the Rev. Henry Solly, Howell edited the short-lived labour weekly, *Common Good*, and from 1881 to 1885 he took an active role in the management of the *Labour Standard*, a successor to the *Bee-Hive*.

Despite his loyalty to the Liberal party, Howell received scant encouragement in his efforts to win election to Parliament. In 1868 he stood as a Liberal candidate in Aylesbury, but hampered by lack of funds and of a local reputation, he finished third. In 1871 he was prevailed upon by Liberal officials to withdraw from a by-election contest in Norwich rather than risk splitting the Liberal vote. While party leaders professed their enthusiasm for working-class candidates, in practice they repeatedly barred them from available constituencies. Without a ready source of income, the Labour Representation League, which endorsed Howell's candidacy in Norwich and again in Aylesbury in 1874, simply could not afford to sponsor independent nominees, and the trade unions, some of which had the funds, were reluctant to intervene in electoral politics. Howell rejected invitations to seek the nomination in the Forest of Dean in 1873, in Greenwich in 1878, and in Kidderminster in 1880, but he decided to contest Stafford, where Macdonald's death had created a vacancy, in 1881. Supported by the Liberal organisation, he was attacked by local Irish interests who exploited resentment against the Coercion Act to ensure Howell's defeat.

In 1885 he was adopted by the local Liberal and Radical organisations for the newly-created constituency of North-East Bethnal Green. In contrast to his earlier ventures, Howell now had ample time in which to cultivate support and to obtain financial backing from Morley and Brassey. With Liberals dominant in London, he was elected with a comfortable majority, secured re-election in 1886 and 1892 (the latter with SDF opposition), but lost his seat in the 1895 Conservative landslide. Although his parliamentary tenure was productive, Howell refrained from assuming an independent role as a labour spokesman, content to follow the lead of the London Liberal contingent in the Commons. His bill to substitute manhood suffrage for the existing franchise and to reduce residential qualifications to three months, introduced annually from 1886 to 1895, failed to win support, but he was able to prod the Government into publishing a working man's edition of the Statutes, and was active in the deliberations over the Statute Law Revision Bill in 1891. Howell replaced Samuel Plimsoll as the principal advocate of legislation for the improvement of seamen's conditions, and was instrumental in carrying a Merchant Shipping Bill in 1889 which regulated the load-line on ships, and a measure to secure the inspection of provisions in 1892. He also sponsored a bill exempting trade union provident funds from the income tax.

During his years as an MP Howell relied mainly on journalism for his livelihood, but in 1886–8 he was engaged to edit the *Imperial White Books*, a compilation of official papers and parliamentary speeches, and in 1889–90 was employed by the National Home Reading Union. *Trade Unionism New and Old*, published in 1891, revealed his sharp divergence from the progressive forces in the labour movement. Defending the older craft unions for their success in overcoming public hostility, Howell denounced the New Unionists for espousing a reckless strike policy, for transforming unions into agencies for socialist propaganda, and for demanding a statutory eight-hour day. With his political ideas rooted in the mid-Victorian faith in self-help and bourgeois benevolence, he found the new militancy uncongenial. After 1895 Howell withdrew entirely from political life, devoting himself to articles and to his last book, *Labour Legislation, Labour Movements and Labour Leaders*, a major study of the progress of the working classes in the nineteenth century, which appeared in 1902. A commissioned biography of Ernest Jones was completed, only to be rejected by the publisher, and Howell was obliged to sell it for serialisation in the *Newcastle Weekly Chronicle*. Failing eyesight and deteriorating health made it difficult for him to work in his later years. After his appeal for a Civil List pension was rejected in 1897, his friend Applegarth raised a £1650 testimonial fund to buy him an annuity. In 1904 he was stricken with partial blindness, and Applegarth again assumed responsibility for raising money, this time to buy his library. This second subscription amassed £1000, part of it from Andrew Carnegie, and the books and papers were presented to the Bishopsgate Institute at the invitation of its librarian, C. W. F. Goss. In July 1906 the Liberal Government awarded Howell a Civil List pension of £50 per year.

It was as an organiser and administrator that Howell left his mark on the history of the Victorian labour movement. From the time he abandoned his trade at the age of thirty-two, he found an avenue for his talents in working-class politics. The extension of democracy and the growth of labour institutions afforded him the opportunity to build a career as a professional bureaucrat. His success as an administrator turned him into an organisational entrepreneur, discovering in the achievements of pressure-group politics the means to his own advancement. Once he had mastered the formula, he was continually trying to establish new organisations or to find a secure position in existing ones. To each he brought the same combination of self-interest and diligence, relishing the thousands of letters he had to write and the contacts with public figures. However deferential, Howell performed a crucial task in interpreting working-class opinion to men of influence. While he never fully appreciated the power that organised labour might exert, he was an articulate exponent of its interests, and was instrumental in persuading well-disposed politicians that concessions were necessary. He discovered in the principles of Gladstonian Liberalism the embodiment of his own personal values, never outgrowing the cautious Radicalism of his early years. The ideal of self-improvement, in his view, did not imply that the working class should seek to better its position unaided, but rather in partnership with the more enlightened leaders of the country.

Howell took pride in his contribution to the progress of English workers during his lifetime, but he regarded his own career as something of a failure. His expectations of wealth, honour, and position were never realised. In his last years he came to be discredited as an apologist for Liberalism, and his reputation never revived. In the more militant, class-conscious phase of the labour movement at the end of the century he seemed an anachronism, his ideas irrelevant to the aspirations of a younger generation.

In 1856 Howell married Dorcas Taviner the daughter of George Taviner, a Wiltshire farmer. She died in 1897. They had one son, George Washington Taviner (1859–80).

Howell died at his home in Shepherd's Bush on 16 September 1910. His funeral three days later at Nunhead Cemetery was attended by a number of prominent trade unionists and representatives of labour and co-operative organisations. His estate was valued at £210.

Writings: The most important of Howell's works are: Evidence before R.C. on Trade Unions, 1867 XXXII Qs 1629–748; *Books and Reading* (1875) P; *A Handy Book of the Labour Laws* (1876); 'Working Men and the Eastern Question', *Cont. Rev.* 28 (Oct 1876) 866–72; *Waste Land and Prison Labour* (1877) P; *The Conflicts of Capital and Labour Historically and Economically considered* (1878); 'The History of the International Association', *19th C. 4*, no. 17 (July 1878) 19–39; 'The Caucus System and the Liberal Party', *New Q. Mag. 10* (Oct 1878) 579–90; *Land Tenure Reform* (1879) P; 'Strikes: their cost and results', *Fraser's Mag.* 20 n.s. (Dec 1879) 767–83; *Conciliation and Arbitration in Trade Disputes* (1880) P; 'The Financial Condition of Trades Unions', *19th C. 12*, no. 68 (Oct 1882) 481–501; 'The Work of Trade Unions', *Cont. Rev.* 44 (Sep 1883) 331–49; 'Trades Union Congresses and Social Legislation', *Cont. Rev.* 56 (Sep 1889) 401–418; *Trade Unionism New and Old* (1891); 'Liberty for Labour' in T. MacKay, *A Plea for Liberty: an argument against socialism and socialistic legislation* (1891) 109–41; 'Working Class Movements of the Century', *Reynolds's Newspaper*, 23 Aug 1896 to 4 Jan 1897; 'Ernest Jones the Chartist', *Newcastle Weekly Chronicle*, Jan to Oct 1898; *Labour Legislation, Labour Movements and Labour Leaders* (1902; 2nd ed. 2 vols, 1905).

Sources: (1) MSS: Howell Coll., Bishopsgate Institute, London (diaries, letters, minute books); Gladstone papers, BM: Add. MSS 44347, 44439; Frederic Harrison Papers, LSE; Liberation Society papers, London County Record Office; Henry Solly papers, LSE; Webb Trade Union Coll. LSE. (2) Theses: W. K. Lamb, 'British Labour and Parliament, 1865–93' (London PhD, 1933); H. W. McCready, 'Frederic Harrison and the British Working Class Movement, 1860–75' (Harvard PhD, 1952); R. J. Harrison, 'The Activity and Influence of the English Positivists upon Labour Movements, 1859–85' (Oxford DPhil., 1955); S. W. Coltham, 'George Potter and the *Bee-Hive* Newspaper' (Oxford DPhil., 1956); R. A. Buchanan, 'Trade Unions and Public Opinion, 1850–75' (Cambridge PhD, 1957); A. D. Bell, 'The Reform League from its Origins to the Reform Act of 1867' (Oxford DPhil., 1961); F. M. Leventhal, 'George Howell, 1833–1910: a career in radical politics' (Harvard PhD, 1967); R. G. G. Wheeler, 'George Howell and Working-Class Politics, 1859–95' (London MA, 1969). (3) Secondary: The major source is F. M. Leventhal, *Respectable Radical: George Howell and Victorian Working Class Politics* (1971). The most useful additional sources are: *Operative Bricklayers' Society Trade Circular* (1861–71); *The Bee-Hive* (1862–78); *TUC Reports* (1869–75); *Reynolds's Newspaper*, 3 Feb 1895; A. Watson, 'George Howell', *Millgate Monthly*, 3, no. 35 (Aug 1908) 665–71; DNB; *Documents of the First International, 1864–68*, 2 vols (1961, 1963). See also: H. Evans, *Sir Randal Cremer* (1909); W. J. Davis, *The British Trades Union Congress* (1910); A. W. Humphrey, *A History of Labour Representation* (1912); H. Evans, *Radical Fights of Forty Years* (1913); A. W. Humphrey, *Robert Applegarth* (1913); R. W. Postgate, *The Builders' History* (1923); F. W. Soutter, *Recollections of a Labour Pioneer* (1923); F. E. Gillespie, *Labor and Politics in England, 1850–67* (Durham, North Carolina, 1927); S. Maccoby, *English Radicalism, 1853–86* (1938); G. D. H. Cole, *British Working Class Politics, 1832–1914* (1941); G. Tate, *London Trades Council, 1860–1950* (1950); W. H. G. Armytage, *A. J. Mundella* (1951); H. W. McCready, 'British Labour's Lobby, 1867–75', *Canad. J. Econ. Pol. Sc.* 22, (May 1956) 141–60; B. C. Roberts, *The Trades Union Congress, 1868–1921* (1958); H. J. Hanham, *Elections and Party Management* (1959); *Essays in Labour History*, ed. A. Briggs and J. Saville (1960); W. S. Hilton, *Foes to Tyranny* (1963); R. T. Shannon, *Gladstone and the Bulgarian Agitation, 1876*

(1963); S. W. Coltham, 'George Potter, the Junta, and the *Bee-Hive*', *Int. Rev. Social Hist.* 9 (1964) 391–432, 10 (1965) 1–85; A. D. Bell, 'Administration and Finance of the Reform League, 1865–67', *Int. Rev. Social Hist.* 10 (1965) 385–409; H. Collins and C. Abramsky, *Karl Marx and the British Labour Movement* (1965); R. Harrison, *Before the Socialists* (1965); F. M. Leventhal, 'The George Howell Collection', *Bull. Soc. Lab. Hist.* 10 (Spring 1965) 38–40; P. Thompson, *Socialists, Liberals and Labour* (1967). OBIT. *Times* and *Daily Chronicle* and *Daily News*, 19 Sep 1910.

F. M. LEVENTHAL

See also: †William ALLAN and for New Model Unionism; Robert APPLEGARTH; *Edward Spencer BEESLY; *Charles BRADLAUGH; Henry BROADHURST; *Edwin COULSON; *William Randal CREMER; Frederic HARRISON; *Robert HARTWELL; *Thomas HUGHES; *Ernest JONES; †Patrick Lloyd JONES; *John Bedford LENO; †Alexander MACDONALD; *George ODGER; *George POTTER; *George SHIPTON.

HUCKER, Henry (1871–1954)
TRADE UNIONIST

Henry Hucker was born on 11 January 1871 at Park Gate, Teddesley Hay, near Stafford, one of the large family of William and Louisa Hucker (née Bartlett). He attended the local village school until the age of twelve, when he left to work on a farm. His first duty was scaring the birds away from growing corn with clappers, for which he was paid 3s for a seven-day week. At the age of seventeen, when his earnings had risen to 10s a week, he gave up farm work to become a platelayer on the former London and North Western Railway, at a wage of 18s per week. After five years as a platelayer he became a signalman, working first in the signal box at Anglesey sidings, Brownhills and then in the No. 1 box at Bescot, Walsall. After working for ten years at Bescot, he was transferred in 1907 to the signal box at Pleck Junction, where he worked alternate eight-hour shifts with Joseph Thickett.

Hucker and Thickett were already close friends by virtue of their association in the Walsall No. 2 branch of the Amalgamated Society of Railway Servants and their involvement in the activities of Walsall Trades Council. The latter, which had been re-established in 1890 after a lapse of some years, was reconstituted as the Trades and Labour Representation Council in 1906. Later, they both took an active part in forming the Walsall Labour Association in 1912. This organisation was established specifically 'to get representation on the Town Council, Board of Guardians and Education Committee ... and to aspire to Parliamentary honours' and was the immediate precursor of the Walsall Labour Party, in which Hucker and Thickett became leading figures.

For more than thirty years the working lives, trade union activities and political careers of these two were inextricably intertwined. Their abilities and personalities complemented each other in a remarkable way, Thickett's flamboyance, wit and oratorical flair being balanced by Hucker's administrative ability and capacity for organisation. These qualities served Hucker well during his forty-five years as secretary of the Walsall No. 2 branch of the Amalgamated Society of Railway Servants (from 1913 the National Union of Railwaymen). They were reflected in the growth of the union's strength in the Walsall area. When Hucker was first elected to the position of secretary in 1902, membership of No. 2 branch of the Amalgamated Society of Railway Servants was just over 100. Just over a decade later, when the Railway Servants amalgamated with the General Railway Workers' Union and the United Pointsmen's and Signalmen's Society to form the NUR, membership had grown to 900, and thereafter the railwaymen provided a solid basis of trade union support for the developing Labour Party in Walsall.

In April 1914, after two unsuccessful attempts to win a seat on the Walsall Town Council, Hucker was returned unopposed to fill a casual vacancy in Caldmore ward, so joining Joseph Thickett, who had been elected to the Council in the previous year.

He continued to represent Caldmore until 1928, Birchills ward in 1929 and 1930, and Pleck ward in 1931. Then from 1932 until the time of his death he represented Palfrey ward, thus completing forty years' unbroken membership of the Council. During the First World War, which he supported, he worked hard in connection with the domestic food-growing campaign. He was chairman of the Small Holdings and Allotments Committee and had overall responsibility for the 5000 allotments within the borough of Walsall; and his energy and organising ability were main factors in the success of the campaign in the town. After the war he maintained his interest in this sphere with work for the Ryecroft Cottage Holdings scheme for ex-Servicemen.

With the resumption of normal political activity after the end of the war Hucker came to be an outstanding figure in the civic life of Walsall. He was appointed a magistrate in 1921, and five years later became a member of the magistrates' Licensing Committee. He served on this committee until his retirement from the bench, being chairman for several years. In 1946 he became chairman of the Walsall bench, and held this position until May 1950, when he was forced to relinquish it under the provision of the Justices of the Peace Act 1949 which required magistrates to retire on reaching the age of seventy-five. On his retirement his fellow magistrates presented him with a radio set and a cheque for £10. He then served on the magistrates' supplementary list until his death. In 1924 he had succeeded Joseph Thickett as Mayor of Walsall, an event which was marked by the directors of what had now become the London, Midland and Scottish Railway with the installation of a plaque in Pleck Junction signal box, bearing the inscription: 'This tablet commemorates the fact that Signalman J. Thickett and Signalman H. Hucker filled the office of Mayor of the Borough of Walsall during the years 1923–24–25 respectively while being employed as signalmen in this box.'

Hucker was created an alderman in 1928 and retained this office until his death. The fact that the Labour Party remained a minority group on Walsall Council until 1945, by which time he was seventy-four years old, precluded him from chairing any of the council's major policy-making committees, but he had been chairman of the Watch Committee for many years, and also of the Health Committee for a shorter time.

Hucker retired from his work as a signalman in 1936 after forty-eight years on the railway, but he continued as secretary of the Walsall No. 2 branch of the NUR for a further eleven years, only retiring from this position on 30 June 1947. The coincidence of his retirement with the nationalisation of the railway was particularly fitting, as Hucker had been a lifelong advocate of state ownership. In other ways too, Hucker's political attitudes reflected his trade union background. He supported the 'sane patriots' during the First World War and stood loyally by the Labour Party at the time of the MacDonald defection in 1931. To him, as to many other trade unionists of his generation, the Attlee Governments of 1945 to 1951 were the culmination of a lifetime's hope and aspiration, and the Bevanite resignations were a matter for sorrow as much as anger.

Hucker was twice married. His first wife predeceased him in 1942. In 1949 he married his second wife, the former Miss Blanche Wright of Walsall, who survived him. His death occurred at the home of his daughter, Mrs H. M. Butler, 158 Wednesbury Road, Walsall, on 11 July 1954. After a service in Walsall Parish Church, Hucker was buried in Ryecroft Cemetery on 15 July. Another two daughters of Hucker's first marriage also survived him, together with four granddaughters and one grandson. He left an estate valued at £3021, probate of which was granted to Fred Thickett, the son of his old friend Joseph Thickett.

Sources: Reports of Walsall Town Council meetings, Trades Council, ASRS and NUR activities in *Walsall Advertiser* 1900–14, *Walsall Free Press* 1900–1903, *Walsall Observer* 1900–54, *Walsall Times* 1925–54; P. S. Gupta, 'History of the Amalgamated Society of Railway Servants 1871–1913' (Oxford DPhil., 1960); P. S. Bagwell, *The*

Railwaymen (1963); K. J. Dean, 'Parliamentary Elections and Party Organisations in Walsall 1906–45' (Birmingham MA, 1969); idem, *Town and Westminster: a political history of Walsall from 1906–1945* (Walsall, 1972); personal information: F. Thickett, B.E.M., JP, Walsall, May 1972. OBIT. *Wolverhampton Express and Star*, 12 July 1954; *Walsall Observer*, 16 July 1954. [Photographs with obituaries, also in *Walsall Red Book*, 1924 (in Mayor's robes); 1929.]

ERIC TAYLOR

See also: *Joseph Thomas DEAKIN; †Benjamin DEAN; †William MILLERCHIP; Joseph THICKETT.

HUDSON, Walter (1852–1935)
TRADE UNION LEADER AND LABOUR MP

Walter Hudson was born at Richmond Station, Yorkshire, on 5 February 1852, the second son and the youngest of three children of Henry Courtley Hudson, a gas stoker who later became a North Eastern railwayman, and a Miss Young. Both his parents died young, his mother at the early age of thirty. The orphaned Walter Hudson was at first cared for by his father's relatives, but when hard times came he was sent to the workhouse, being later rescued by members and friends of his mother's family. He attended Richmond National School until he was nine years of age. Thereafter he picked up what knowledge he could in Sunday schools, evening classes and debating societies.

Hudson began work on a farm near Malton at the age of nine and stayed in this kind of employment until he was twenty. He then entered the service of the North Eastern Railway, first as one of a navvy gang laying down new lines, then successively as a shunter (at Croft Junction, Darlington), under-guard, mineral-line guard and main-line guard. In October 1882 Hudson joined the Darlington No. 1 branch of the ASRS. Three years later he was elected its secretary and held the office until he became a full-time official in 1898. In 1888 he took a leading part in what became

known as the Darlington Programme, which included demands for a maximum fifty-four hour week for shunters, overtime rates at one and a quarter times, and Sunday duty at one and a half times the normal rates. At the Hull Congress of the ASRS in 1889 these demands formed the core of the union's first national programme.

In 1890, after his election to the executive committee of the ASRS, Hudson quickly made his mark. When the president of the Society, the newspaper proprietor P. S. MacLiver, died in 1891, a number of delegates at the annual conference wished to continue the practice of appointing another 'outsider' to the office. The favourite candidate was F. A. Channing, Liberal MP for East Northamptonshire; but an amendment in favour of the election of a bona-fide working president of the union was carried by thirty-four votes to twenty. Hudson was subsequently elected to the presidential office, and he continued to be re-elected annually until 1898. In that year he resigned both from service with the railways and from presidential office, to take up the difficult assignment of full-time ASRS secretary in Ireland. By this time he was widely known in his own union, and in the second ballot for the election of a general secretary in June 1898 to the ASRS he secured 14,518 votes against Richard Bell's 22,671.

As a result of the bitter experiences of his working life as a railwayman Hudson had become a passionate advocate of improved safety precautions on the railways. By 1893 he was head train foreman at Darlington, one of the largest shunting stations in England, and he always regarded himself as fortunate in having sustained no worse injury than a crushed thumb, although on three occasions he had found himself under moving trains. He wrote in 1906, just after his election as an MP: 'of from twenty to thirty young fellows who entered the Company's service at the same time as I did and at about the same age, I could count on the fingers of one hand those who remained in the same grade of service when I left, the others having been cut down by fatal or permanent injuries' [*Pearson's*

Weekly, 5 Apr 1906]. Hudson was a persistent and persuasive campaigner for safer methods of railway working, and in 1899 he was appointed a member of the Royal Commission on Accidents to Railway Servants. Parts of the report of the Commission were implemented in the following year when the Railway Employment (Prevention of Accidents) Act [63 and 64 Vict. c. 27] was put on to the Statute book, incorporating a number of the reforms Hudson had been advocating for many years.

Hudson was an early supporter of the cause of independent labour representation in Parliament. At the annual conference of the ASRS in Newport (Mon.) in October 1894, he advocated 'one common standard for the cause of labour, alone, clear and distinct from either of the two political parties'. In 1903 he was adopted as LRC candidate for Newcastle upon Tyne, and in the following year became a member of the executive committee of the Labour Representation Committee. In the general election of January 1906 he stood as LRC candidate in Newcastle's double-member constituency and came top of the poll with 18,869 votes; the other successful candidate, Thomas Cairns, a Liberal, polling 18,423. During his election campaign he adopted an intransigent attitude towards the Liberal Party, emphasising the importance of a Labour group in Parliament that was free from any commitments or agreements. The absence of a second Liberal candidate in the Newcastle election was in fact the result of the MacDonald–Gladstone secret entente of 1903 [Pelling (1967) 325], but whether Hudson was aware of the arrangement or not, it made no difference to his attitude. He came top of the poll, just ahead of the Liberal, and his supporters in fact divided their votes mainly between himself and the Liberal candidate. The *Manchester Guardian* wrote after the result that Hudson

had pursued his campaign with impeccable rectitude on independent lines, refusing to endorse the Liberal; but of his almost 19,000 votes only 1000 were 'plumpers', and less than 500 split with either of the Conservative candidates: the remainder were all split with the Liberal [17 Jan 1906].

Hudson's election programme was typical of LRC candidates at this time. He stood for Free Trade ('But they could not afford at this juncture to allow that question to obscure every other question of importance that affected the well-being of the workers'); one man, one vote; female suffrage; the feeding of schoolchildren; the extension of the Unemployment Act to provide more work for the unemployed; and the Chinese labour question. On this last issue, which figured so prominently in the election campaign as a whole, Hudson made some typical comments – flavoured with a not uncommon pinch of anti-semitism:

Proceeding to refer to the present state of South Africa and Chinese labour, Mr Hudson said the South African millionaires – he ought to say the alien millionaires (Hear, hear) – the Wall Street and the Park Lane gentlemen who almost had to have an interpreter even when they sang the National Anthem (laughter) had had the late Conservative Government tightly within their grip, and, as a result, they had not got the white man's country that was promised; but, on the Government's own returns, they had no fewer than 48,000 Chinese coolies in South Africa. That ought to be thought about. They were told it was not slavery; but under the ordinance sanctioned by the late Conservative Government the subject imported could not serve any other master unless he was transferred by a deed, which was practically selling human flesh (Hear, hear). It was slavery in every sense of the word . . . [*Newcastle Daily Chronicle*, 20 Dec 1905].

During the election campaign the Rev. W. E. Moll was one of his most active supporters, and among those who spoke on his behalf was Michael Davitt, who during this election made a tour of the Labour constituencies whose candidates the United Irish League had endorsed [Moody (1953) 74]. Soon after Hudson's election to the

House of Commons he replied to W. T. Stead's request for the books which had most influenced him, in the following terms:

The books most useful to me in my early days were the Bible, Bunyan's *Pilgrim's Progress*, J. Stuart Mill's *Principles of Political Economy*, Dickens, Scott's Waverley novels, one or two works on Theology, Field's *Hand Book*, a few snatches of the classics (very limited, of course). Many of Burns' and Hood's poems have been favourites. Ruskin's works (pocket edition) are invaluable.

The Wesleyan East Road, Darlington, Mutual Improvement Society, my starting point, to think and work seriously [*Review of Reviews* (1906)].

Inside the House of Commons Hudson maintained the independent line he had so long advocated, and he disapproved strongly of his colleague Richard Bell for voting too frequently with the Liberal majority in Parliament. At the end of March 1906 Hudson moved the second reading of the Trade Unions and Trade Disputes Bill which became law later that year as the Trades Disputes Act. In his speech he emphasised the desire of the trade unions to free themselves completely from judge-made law. From 1908 he made repeated efforts to carry an Eight Hour Bill for railwaymen. Although he was never successful in securing its enactment, the publicity given by the reports of the parliamentary debates paved the way for the introduction of this reform after the end of the War (1919). In evidence given to the R.C. on the Railway Conciliation Scheme in 1911 he favoured the election of composite rather than sectional (i.e. grade) boards, basing his opinion on his experience as secretary of the composite conciliation board of the North Eastern Railway since 1906.

When the National Union of Railwaymen was created in 1913 through the amalgamation of the ASRS, the General Railway Workers' Union, and the United Pointsmen's and Signalmen's Society, Walter Hudson was appointed one of the four assistant secretaries of the new union, the others

being J. H. Thomas, S. Chorlton and T. Lowth. He had been president of the Irish TUC at Newry in 1903, and he presided over the Labour Party's annual conference at Hull in 1908. Hudson took a great interest in the NUR's newspaper, the *Railway Review*, and for many years served as one of the directors of the Kings Cross Publishing Company, a subsidiary concern formed in 1900, with capital provided by the ASRS to manage the paper.

He had been returned to Parliament in the two general elections of 1910, but in the 'coupon election' of December 1918 he lost his seat, being defeated in the Newcastle East constituency. He had loyally followed the decision of the special Labour Party Conference, held the previous month, that no further support should be given to the War Cabinet; but he did accept from Lloyd George the OBE for services to Labour during the war.

When he retired on the Union's pension at the end of December 1919 he continued to live in the London borough of Lambeth to which he had removed on his first election to Parliament. He served there as a JP in the Juvenile Court and in Petty Sessions He died at his home in Atherford Road, Stockwell on 18 March 1935 at the age of eighty-three. The funeral service was conducted in the High Street Methodist Church, Clapham, where he had been a member for many years, and he was buried in Lambeth Cemetery. He was survived by his wife, sons and daughters and left effects valued at £169.

Sources: (1) MSS: Labour Party archives: LRC; (2) Other primary sources: ASRS, *Executive Committee Minutes* (1889–1912) and AGM *Reports*; 'How I got on', *Pearsons Weekly*, 5 Apr 1906; *Review of Reviews 33* (Jan–June 1906) 574–5; (3) Secondary: *Railway Rev.*, 5 Oct 1894; *Newcastle Daily Chronicle*, 20 Dec 1905, 3, 4, 9 and 11 Jan 1906; *Times*, 16 Dec 1905, 17 Jan and 31 Mar 1906; Evidence before R.C. on the Working of the Railway Conciliation and Arbitration Scheme 1912–13 XLV Qs 5962–6379; G. D. H. Cole and R. Page Arnot, *Trade Unionism on the Railways*

(1917); *WW* (1918); G. Alcock, *Fifty Years of Railway Trade Unionism* (1922); T. W. Moody, 'Michael Davitt and the British Labour Movement', *Trans Roy. Hist. Soc.* 5th ser. 3 (1953) 53–76; F. Bealey and H. Pelling, *Labour and Politics 1900–1906* (1958); P. S. Bagwell, *The Railwaymen* (1963); H. Pelling, *Social Geography of British Elections 1885–1910* (1967). OBIT. *Times*, 20 Mar 1935; *Brixton Free Press*, 22 Mar 1935; *Railway Rev.*, 22 and 29 Mar 1935.

PHILIP BAGWELL

See also: Richard BELL; George LANSBURY, for British Labour Party, 1900–13; *William Edmund MOLL; George James WARDLE.

HUGHES, Edward (1856–1925)
MINERS' LEADER

Born on 22 March 1856 at Berthengam, Flintshire, Hughes was the son of an agricultural labourer, Hugh Hughes of Fford, Faen, Trelogan, and his wife Maria, and was educated at a village school run by the Calvinistic Methodists at Trelogan. When he was seven he began working in the washings at the local mine, gathering lead and baled. For this he received 3*d* a day for a ten-hour day in the summer and a nine-hour day in the winter. At twelve years of age he went to work with his brother at the Mostyn Quay Colliery, where he carted coal for 2*s* a day, and he later obtained work at Hanmer Colliery, Mostyn. In 1875 he walked to Liverpool to get the train for the Durham coalfield, where he obtained employment at South Hetton Colliery, Easington, and was prominent in at least one major dispute.

In October 1887 Hughes returned to Trelogan, worked at the coal face at Point of Ayr Colliery until the following year when, having led a successful three weeks' strike, he was appointed the colliery's first checkweighman. It was not until the early 1890s that a successful attempt was made to organise the miners in North Wales, when the Denbighshire and Flintshire Miners' Association was formed. Hughes was appointed financial secretary in 1891, general

secretary in 1897, and permanent agent in the following year. The union was renamed the North Wales Miners' Association in 1903, and Hughes held office as secretary and agent until his death in 1925. For seven years between 1899 and 1919 he represented the North Wales Miners on the executive of the MFGB; he was a member of the Federation's Board of Conciliation in 1903; and he took some part in the closing stages of the South Wales Cambrian Combine strike in 1911. In 1914 at the inquiry into the Senghenydd Colliery disaster, he gave evidence on behalf of the MFGB, and the S. Wales Colliery Enginemen, Stokers and Surface Craftsmen's Association.

Hughes was a persuasive negotiator and a good organiser, and during his long service as secretary and agent membership rose from 2732 to 15,229. Like many miners' leaders he was also active in local affairs, as a member of the Denbighshire County Council from 1901 and from 1907 as a county alderman, serving until 1918; in 1908 he was made a county JP. In 1877 he married at Easington, Elizabeth, daughter of William and Sarah Hughes of Lloc, Whitford, Flintshire, and there were two daughters and a son. The latter, Hugh, succeeded his father as agent to the North Wales Miners' Association in 1925. Edward Hughes died on 10 March 1925 at his Wrexham home survived by his wife and family, and was buried at Wrexham Borough Cemetery on 13 March. He left effects valued at £457.

Sources: G. G. Lerry, *The Collieries of Denbighshire Past and Present* (Wrexham, 1946); *Dictionary of Welsh Biography* (1959); personal information: J. C. H. Jones, nephew of E. N. Hughes (grandson of Edward Hughes) and E. R. Luke, County Librarian, Denbigh, OBIT. *Wrexham Leader*, 13 March 1925.

JOYCE BELLAMY
JOHN SAVILLE

See also: †Thomas ASHTON, for Mining Trade Unionism, 1900–14; *Arthur James COOK, for Mining Trade Unionism, 1915–1926; †Hugh HUGHES.

HUTCHINGS, Harry (1864–1930)
MINER

Born on 25 June 1864 at Harrowbarrow, Cornwall, Harry Hutchings was the son of Thomas Hutchings and his wife Marina (née Trewarthar). The family moved to Northumberland in 1873 and Harry continued his education at the Presbyterian school, Seaton Delaval. He began work at the age of twelve as a trapper in the Ann Pit, Cramlington (one of seven pits owned by the Cramlington Coal Co. Ltd.) and three years later had an accident to his left foot, as a result of which he spent six months in Newcastle Old Infirmary and the foot was eventually amputated. Hutchings found the loss of one foot less crippling than he had expected, and he returned to the mines in the Cramlington area. His involvement in trade unionism was not immediate, but by 1900 he was branch secretary and delegate for Betsy Pit and served for a time on the executive committee of the Northumberland Miners' Association (the practice being for each branch to send a member in turn). When the Betsy Pit closed he went back to work at Ann Pit, and became a prominent local leader. He was made chairman and checkweighman of Ann Pit, positions he retained until his death; he was local compensation secretary for many years; secretary of the joint accident fund of the Cramlington collieries' workmen; chairman of the group committee for the Cramlington Pits; secretary and treasurer of a funeral hearse fund. When the Northumberland Aged Mineworkers' Homes Association built cottages in Cramlington, Hutchings was appointed deputy-landlord.

In his middle years he had been a member of the Cramlington Liberal and Radical Association but he accepted the movement among the miners towards the Labour Party after 1906. He represented Cramlington on the County Council for the last eleven years of his life, and he was also a member of the Cramlington Urban District Council, and a member of the Earsdon Joint Hospital Board. Of notably intemperate habits when a young man, he underwent a 'conversion' to Primitive Methodism about 1895, and became a Sunday school teacher and a trustee of his chapel (and no doubt took the 'pledge'). He married Ellen Stansbury, whose parents came from Tavistock, in September 1897 at Blyth Primitive Methodist Chapel. He died at his home on 24 January 1930; after a service in the Wesleyan Church he was buried in Cramlington Churchyard.

Sources: R. Page Arnot, *The Miners*, vols 1 and 2 (1949 and 1953); R. F. Wearmouth, *Social and Political Influence of Methodism in the Twentieth Century* (1957). Obit. *Newcastle J.*, 27 Jan 1930; NMA, *Monthly Circular* (1930).

VALERIE MASON

See also: †Thomas ASHTON, for Mining Trade Unionism, 1900–1914; †Thomas BURT; *Arthur James COOK, for Mining Trade Unionism, 1915–26; William STRAKER.

IRONSIDE, Isaac (1808–70)
CHARTIST, OWENITE AND ANARCHIST

Isaac Ironside was born in 1808 at Masbrough, near Rotherham, a major centre of the Industrial Revolution and an important centre of Dissent in that both the celebrated Walker ironworks and a Congregationalist College had been established there in the eighteenth century. The township also had associations with Tom Paine, who had lived there while negotiating with the Walkers to build an iron bridge of revolutionary design and who, in local tradition, wrote at least part of his *Age of Reason* here. That the bridge project was frustrated, and that the tradition is suspect, are alike unimportant. The political tradition lived on, in the minds of such men as Ebenezer Elliott (an early political associate of Isaac Ironside and a man who, celebrated as the Corn Law Rhymer, was to become a champion of popular education) whose father was supposed to have been horse-whipped by an officer of Pitt's hated dragoons.

Although shortly after Isaac's birth the Ironside family moved the few miles to Sheffield, where Samuel, the father, secured a position as a clerk in an ironworks, they remained characteristic products of their native Masbrough. Obviously a family which was later to boast of its descent from a 'notorious English Jacobin' was unlikely to mellow in Sheffield, itself the home of Radical and Dissenting traditions. It was here that Isaac Ironside's father became a lay preacher and class leader at Queen Street Congregational Chapel, an institution that had long had close links with Masbrough, and here, too, that the Ironside family as a whole became known for their forthright Radical views.

Isaac Ironside's ultra-Radical leanings were thus rooted in a pre-Chartist, pre-Owenite age. It is also, perhaps, peculiarly appropriate that one of the most vigorous and imaginative contributors to the movement for popular education in the nineteenth century should himself have been an outstanding product of an initial stage of that movement.

His early educational experiences were at Queen Street Sunday School, already well known as a powerhouse of educational effort in South Yorkshire – even in the 1850s adult education in Sheffield was said to be dominated by 'The Saints of Queen Street' – and at the Sheffield Lancasterian School for Boys founded in 1809. These experiences were, in fact, unusually rewarding; and, although he left the Sheffield Lancasterian School at the age of twelve to become apprenticed in the heavy trade of stove-grate fitter, he continued his studies at the night school run by the redoubtable John Eadon, an institution from which Ironside ultimately emerged as the winner of mathematical prizes offered by the Edinburgh Review. Like many another earnest young man, indeed, he found ecstatic escape from the demands of a harsh industrial age in the books which, thanks to the creation of the Sheffield Mechanics' and Apprentices' Library in 1823, were now readily available to the products of the Lancasterian School. It was, we may assume, the combination of heavy manual labour and midnight study that produced in 1833 the breakdown in health which led to Isaac's becoming a partner in the accountancy and estate agency business begun by his father the year before. In the

eighteen-forties Isaac took over complete control of the business, the flourishing nature of which allowed him to devote an increasing amount of time, and money, to ultra-Radical causes.

Meanwhile he played a lively part in the educational and political life of the town. In December 1830, ably supported by other young ultra-Radicals, he moved an amendment at a meeting called by the local Whigs in Paradise Square to consider a cautiously-phrased petition for 'an extension of the suffrage, the shortening of Parliaments and an alteration in the mode of taking votes at elections'. Characteristically, Ironside, 'having read and studied the plan propounded by the immortal Jeremy Bentham', moved for universal suffrage, the ballot and annual parliaments.

The extremist stand of Isaac Ironside and his colleagues, illustrating as it did the inclinations and latent power of the emergent working classes at that period, undoubtedly influenced the thoughts and actions of middle-class leaders in the region. The immediate reaction of the Sheffield moderates was to bring Ironside within the framework of the Sheffield Political Union, established on the Birmingham model in January 1831, and subsequently he became campaign secretary for T. A. Ward, the 'popular' but unsuccessful candidate in Sheffield's first election in December 1832.

A temporary alliance with the Liberals in the political field – in later years Ironside explained this aberration by drawing attention to the fact that T. A. Ward had long campaigned for a national system of education – was matched by a period of co-operation in the educational field. The golden age of liberal politics in Sheffield coincided with the period of Ironside's most wholehearted involvement in the affairs of the Sheffield Mechanics' Institute, an establishment that was, in a real sense, an offshoot of the Political Union in the town. The first major meeting of the Mechanics' Institute, held in October 1832, heard a short speech from the young Radical and made him a member of the organising committee. A scrutiny of the minute book of that committee provides evidence of his energy; indeed his incisive-ness there was later satirised by John Holland in a local publication. Convinced of the need to strike while the iron was hot, he almost immediately urged the committee to act 'with all possible dispatch' in securing premises for the Institute. A latent propagandist instinct and a natural intolerance of long-windedness led him to support motions for the distribution of pamphlets outlining the aims of the Mechanics' Institute and for restricting the length of committee meetings. By 21 November 1832, when the first general meeting of the institution was held, with Dr Holland in the chair, the committee had prepared not only plans for general management, but also a comprehensive scheme of education embracing public lectures and classes.

For a period after 1832 Ironside concentrated his public energies in the Sheffield Mechanics' Institute and in the local Mechanics' Library, of which he became honorary secretary. But the policies of the Whigs after 1832 ultimately alienated him. The last straw, as for so many ultra-Radicals, was Lord John Russell's famous declaration on the 'finality' of the Great Reform Bill. In September 1838, at a crowded Chartist meeting in Paradise Square, he appeared as a convinced supporter of the Chartist cause.

Nor was his disillusionment confined to the political sphere. Initially Ironside had simply believed that the work of Mechanics' Institutes, apart from its intrinsic importance in the educational sphere, would 'do something towards breaking in pieces the remaining fetters by which the lower classes were enslaved'. But by 1839 it was becoming increasingly clear that the more obvious and direct linking of educational effort and working-class political aspiration which Ironside was eager to bring about could hardly take place with such orthodox institutions as the Mechanics' Library and the Mechanics' Institute. Indeed, in December 1839 a special meeting of the members of the latter accepted the formal adoption of the rule, hitherto an unwritten one, that the discussion of 'controversial' subjects should be excluded. Meanwhile, Ironside had been dismissed from his post as honorary secre-

tary of the Mechanics' Library, principally on the ground that he had infringed the regulation which excluded books 'subversive to the Christian religion' by admitting a number of books including some of Abram Combe's Owenite writings and John Minter Morgan's *Hampden in the Nineteenth Century* (1834).

It is, in fact, at this point that Ironside appeared as Owen's leading supporter in South Yorkshire. As early as September 1838, in a speech to a Chartist meeting, he had called for the establishment of agrarian communities, and on 17 March 1839, Robert Owen and Ironside opened in Buckingham St, Sheffield, the first building specifically designed as an Owenite Hall of Science. Subsequently, as the person 'more publicly connected with the Sheffield Institutions than any other member', he was able to put a highly individual stamp on an institution whose major festivals celebrated the birthdays of Christ, Robert Owen and Tom Paine, and whose leading supporters were in many cases drawn from the ranks of local Chartists. Ironside himself, however, materially withdrew from Chartism in the early eighteen-forties. Like Ebenezer Elliott he deprecated the violence reflected in Holberry's alleged plot to burn down Sheffield, although he was willing to provide a surety for Richard Otley, who, along with G. J. Harney, was arrested after a Chartist meeting in Lancashire.

The Sheffield Hall of Science reflected the independent working-class spirit that was the essence of both Chartism and Owenism. The opening announcement in the Sheffield newspapers stated that the 'new and handsome building in Rockingham Street was to be used by the Socialists "for the exposition of their views"', and many of the early lectures were devoted to 'developing the principle on which to establish home colonies, which are the only remedies for the numerous evils that are now affecting all classes of the community'. The connection between propaganda and education, was nowhere more clearly mirrored than in the activities of the Sheffield Hall of Science. A spirit of fearless inquiry was deliberately cultivated, and the supporters of the Hall of

Science constantly encouraged individuals and organisations publicly to challenge Owenite principles. In 1840 a local clergyman, the Rev. R. S. Bayley, was induced to debate 'Marriage and Divorce' with a Socialist champion called Mrs Martin, and later in the same year James Campbell clashed with the Rev. John Brindley, the most scurrilous and abusive of all the anti-Owenite clerics. In 1842 the local Free Trade Society was invited to send 'a champion or champions' to a Socialist function, and in 1843 Ironside himself publicly challenged the editor of the *Sheffield Mercury* to an open discussion. The activities of the Hall of Science were conceived in the broadest terms. It had a religious and social, as well as an educational character. Hymns were sung at certain of its functions, and it was registered as a place of worship and licensed to solemnise weddings. To the Owenites the social activities of their institution were no less 'holy' than their earnest educational discussions. They organised festivals, balls, parties, soirées and masquerades, and in thus bringing ordinary people together to enjoy themselves in a relaxed and friendly atmosphere, the Owenites, as Socialists, considered themselves to be fulfilling a genuinely religious duty.

Although the creation of a Workers' Educational Institute at the Hall of Science was announced in November 1847, it is clear that the Hall itself was ceasing to be the focal point of Isaac Ironside's activities by that date. A number of reasons for this state of affairs might be suggested. Ironside, although to the end of his life remaining to some extent a disciple of Owen, had been involved in the agonising end of Owen's Queenwood community experiment. It was, in fact, Isaac Ironside who had brought a number of issues out into the open by the blunt statement of his belief that 'Mr Owen had no idea of money'; although he had subsequently tried to keep some sort of community experiment going by taking over the lease of some of the Queenwood property.

It was also at this point that Ironside emerged as undisputed leader of the Sheffield Chartists, a group whose activities he managed to keep within the bounds of moral force ideas, and whose *Address to the French Provisional Government* he personally took to Paris in 1848. He now began to build an ultra-Radical party (subsequently known as the Democrats) within the Sheffield Town Council. Certainly, if his aim was to create interest in local affairs (where he was helped by the fact that a local household suffrage existed), there is much evidence that he achieved a high degree of success. By their enthusiasm, honesty, and the unusually excellent organisation of ward committees and a central organising body, his allies came well to the fore in local elections. In November 1849, the total number of Chartist-sponsored candidates in the Sheffield Town Council was twenty-two; and Ironside had already forced debates in the council chamber on the People's Charter and on the need to establish a national system of education. On a more obviously practical level, his vigorous campaigning led to the setting up of a model workhouse farm and the establishment of a Health Committee of the Town Council which in 1847 commissioned an important sanitary report. The creation of a workhouse farm at Hollow Meadows was of particular interest. In February 1848 Ironside, in the Town Council, attacked the system that was 'grinding paupers into a most woeful state'. As alternative employment, work began on a moorland site in May 1848 and by 1854 some twenty-two acres had been reclaimed and planted. It was claimed that the project proved 'beyond dispute that pauper labour can be productive', but Ironside was more concerned with the new dignity that this hard but productive labour gave to the heads of destitute families.

As the writer of his obituary was later to remark, at this point it seemed as if Sheffield, in defiance of national trends, might ultimately have a Chartist mayor. It speaks much for Ironside's personal hold over his followers, however, and also for the complex nature of his motivation, that at this critical point in his career he was able to enlist the support of the 'Ironside Party' for a series of experiments, based on anarchist theory, in the field of political education.

Ironside's spiritual guide in this period of his career was Joshua Toulmin Smith, an English antiquary and anarchist whose most exhaustive work was *Local Self Government and Centralization* (1851), and whose writings were later to be drawn on by Prince Kropotkin in his classic *Mutual Aid* (1902). In the eighteen-fifties Smith was the leading exponent of 'the science of direct legislation'.

From 1850 to 1870 Ironside's activities come clearly under the heading of a version of Anarchism. His aim was to create circumstances in which ordinary people could take an interest in and exert influence on public affairs. As an Owenite, and as a Moral Force Chartist, he had long believed that real human progress was based on moral advance. Education was the key, but increasingly he came to believe that, in his own words, 'the only hope of properly educating the masses was to interest them in something that touched their pockets'.

The tangible product of Ironside's involvement with Smith was the 'wardmote', the 'little local parliament' attended by all interested citizens. Stimulated by Ironside's enormous energy, an Ecclesall wardmote began to meet in November 1851, and by the end of the year there were similar bodies in the St Philip's and Ecclesall wards of Sheffield.

The pretensions of the wardmotes ultimately led to disaster: they claimed the right to elect aldermen in open meeting, thus challenging the authority of the Town Council, and their existence led Ironside to make a wholly disastrous attempt to promote without Act of Parliament a second gas company for Sheffield between 1851 and 1854. But they served to illustrate the striking way in which the social philosophies of the first half of the nineteenth century underpinned an evolving ultra-Radical educational philosophy. As with the Hall of Science, the very breadth of the activities of various local groups emphasised rather than detracted from their essentially educational nature. In December 1851, for instance, a 'band of jolly fellows' met at the Queen's Arms, Portmahon, to discuss the state of the local watercourses; to consider the victimisation of Sheffield trade unionists; to weigh the implications of the Kaffir War; and to express concern at Palmerston's recognition of the new regime in France. Here, indeed, was an approach to the 'science of direct legislation', and underlying the whole was the urge to raise the moral worth of those who could be induced to take part. Ironside, who continued to sit in the Town Council for virtually the rest of his life, constantly stressed the importance of 'that practical education which the revivification of our institutions would certainly create'. Nor were the practical achievements of this period to be ignored: as chairman of the Sheffield Highway Board Ironside effectively used the 'permission' of the wardmotes to spend money on the building of deep sewers – something that was strictly illegal under the orthodox powers conferred by the Act.

Personal relations between Toulmin Smith and Ironside were ruptured, however, when the latter (who had played a leading part in securing the election of J. A. Roebuck for Sheffield, as *The Times* had noted) failed to get Smith – who refused to contribute to his own election expenses – sent to Westminster. By the mid-eighteen-fifties Ironside had become a leading supporter of David Urquhart – and a valuable ally at that, for by this time the Sheffield agitator had secured financial control of the *Sheffield Free Press*, a newspaper to which a penniless Karl Marx was persuaded to contribute. For some months in 1854 Ironside played a leading part in the Sheffield area in the agitation which led to J. A. Roebuck's celebrated attack on Lord Aberdeen and the collapse of the Aberdeen Ministry. Subsequently he joined in the attack on Palmerston, who was accused by Urquhart of being a Russian agent, and tool of the Antichrist Tsar. The work of denunciation on platforms and in the *Free Press* (subsequently the *Diplomatic Review*) was supported by the Sheffield Foreign Affairs Committee which was formed in June 1855. Ironside was an energetic member of this committee and continued to play an active part until his death in 1870: spurred on by his enthusiasm (he was a man who found Blue Books 'as thrilling as the most romantic novels'), the members of the Foreign Affairs Committee studied diplomatic documents and often produced radical judgements. Once again, as with the wardmotes, Ironside was seeking to vest power in small local units and to raise the moral worth and self-confidence of their members.

Isaac Ironside illustrated the impact of Robert Owen on contemporary educational thought. By equating knowledge with reason, and reason with morality and social improvement, Owen gave the stimulus of an essentially practical goal, infusing the work of his disciples with an intense, religious, but far from sanctimonious spirit. By emphasising the power of the environment to mould character, Owen taught his followers to look beyond the textbook and the classroom and to carry his ideas into the whole field of social reform. It was these principles which underlay Ironside's career long after the collapse of Queenwood. He was one of the most controversial figures in a town remarkable for the virulence of its personal conflicts. Yet it is equally true that he was consistently admired for his honesty as a political campaigner, his kindness as an employer, his sagacity as a business man, and his qualities as a husband and father. Nor was his career without personal triumphs of a lasting nature, more particularly in the sphere of education and public health. The continuing existence of the Sheffield Mechanics' Institute owed much to his energy and support. The threat of Ironside's Hall of Science to orthodox educational thinking stimulated the appearance of the Sheffield People's College, an institution which influenced the wider work of F. D. Maurice. The effective draining of the centre of the town was peculiarly Ironside's triumph, although perhaps an even greater achievement was to make Sheffield 'health conscious'. Above everything else, however, Ironside stood for a belief in the power of the intellect to analyse and solve the problems of industrial man. Curiously, a man who was associated with more aspects of ultra-Radicalism than almost any other contemporary figure worked within the framework of a single belief, succinctly stated by Ebenezer Elliott:

> Our *minds* have holy light within,
> And every form of grief and sin,
> Shall see and feel its fire.

Isaac Ironside died at his home, Alma Grange, Fir View, Sheffield, on 20 August 1870 and was buried in Sheffield General Cemetery. His wife died in 1867; he had four daughters. No will has been located.

Writings: Ironside was a compulsive writer to newspapers, but his publication in other forms was limited, apparently to four pamphlets: *Brindley and his Lying Braggadocio* (Sheffield, 1840); *The Question is Mr Urquhart a Tory or a Radical?* (Sheffield, 1856); *The Part of France and Russia in the Surrender by England of the right of Search: correspondence between the Sheffield Foreign Affairs Committee (I. Ironside, chairman) and the Lord Advocate* (1866); *Trades' Unions: an address* (Sheffield, 1867).

Sources: There is no collection of material on Ironside but see (1) MSS: Leader Coll., Sheffield PL; Owen Coll., Co-operative Union, Manchester and Gladstone papers, BM. (2) Newspapers and journals: *New Moral World*; *Northern Star* and the following Sheffield papers: *The Iris, The Independent, Sheffield Times, Sheffield Free Press, The Free Press* and *The Diplomatic Rev.* (3) Other: W. Shepherd, *Starting a Daily in the Provinces* (1876); G. J. Holyoake, *Sixty Years of an Agitator's Life*, 2 vols (1892); *DNB 18* [s.v. Joshua Toulmin Smith] and *20* [s.v. David Urquhart]; R. G. Gammage, *History of the Chartist Movement* (1894; repr. with an Introduction by John Saville, New York, 1969); F. Podmore, *Robert Owen: a biography* 2 vols (1906, repr. in one vol., New York, 1968); G. Robinson, *Some Account of David Urquhart* (1921); J. H. Gleason, *The Genesis of Russophobia in Great Britain: a study of the interaction of policy and opinion* (Harvard Univ. Press: Cambridge,

1950); W. H. G. Armytage, 'Sheffield and the Crimean War', *History Today 5*, no. 7 (July 1955) 473–82; Asa Briggs, 'David Urquhart and the West Riding Foreign Affairs Committee', *Bradford Antiquary 8* n.s. pt 39 (Apr 1958) 197–207; A. R. Schoyen, *The Chartist Challenge* (1958); J. Salt, 'Isaac Ironside and the Hollow Meadows Farm Experiment', *Yorks. Bull. Econ. and Social Research 12*, no. 1 (Mar 1960) 45–51; idem, 'The Sheffield Hall of Science', *Vocational Aspect 12*, no. 25 (Sep 1960) 133–8; J. F. C. Harrison, *Learning and Living 1790–1960: a study in the history of the English Adult Education Movement* (1961); H. Collins and C. Abramsky, *Karl Marx and the British Labour Movement: years of the First International* (1965); J. Salt, 'Local Manifestations of the Urquhartite Movement', *Int. Rev. Social Hist. 13*, pt 3 (1968) 350–65; J. F. C. Harrison, *Robert Owen and the Owenites in Britain and America* (1969); J. Salt, 'Isaac Ironside, 1808–1870, the Motivation of a Radical Educationalist', *Brit. J. Educ. Studies, 19*, no. 2 (June 1971) 183–201; E. Yeo, 'Robert Owen and Radical Culture', in *Robert Owen Prophet of the Poor*, ed. S. Pollard and J. Salt (1971); R. G. Garnett, *Co-operation and the Owenite Socialist Communities in Britain, 1825–45* (Manchester Univ. Press, 1972). OBIT. *Sheffield Daily Telegraph*, 22 Aug 1870; *Sheffield and Rotherham Independent*, 22 Aug 1870; *Sheffield Times*, 27 Aug 1870.

JOHN SALT

See also: *Samuel HOLBERRY; *Robert OWEN

JOHNS, John Ernest (1855/6–1928)
CO-OPERATOR

Johns was born in the mid-1850s in Bavaria, but no details of the date or locality or of his parents are known. His grandfather, a Welshman, had apparently emigrated to that country, but when Johns's own father died, he came to England in the early 1860s unable, at that time, to speak English. He soon began to learn the language, and after about a year started work at Merthyr Tydfil. He later moved to Reading, where he attended an evening college in West Street and obtained employment at a large Reading tin works, subsequently becoming a foreman there. In 1885, when he was twenty-nine, he was successful in an application for British citizenship, and he continued to reside in the Reading area, where he was active in the co-operative and friendly society movements and was also a pioneer in the adult education field. But it was his co-operative work especially which brought him national recognition.

He had joined the Reading Co-operative Society in 1878, served on its management committee from 1887 to 1907, was president in 1894, and contributed largely to the expansion of the organisation. He left the Society in 1907, on his election to the board of the CWS of which he remained a member until he retired in 1926 under the age rule. He served on the board's grocery committee, and visited co-operative tea estates in India and Ceylon. His knowledge of German enabled him to address co-operative conferences in Austria and Germany in their own language. In 1916 he was elected to assist the Food Controller (Lord Devonport) in the wartime supervision of the tea trade, and continued to serve on the tea advisory committee under three successive food controllers. Early in 1917 Johns, acting for the CWS, had joined with M. J. Flavin, an Irish MP, and Will Thorne in pressing the Government to introduce an order which should make illegal the practice of including the weight of paper when weighing packets of tea [Lockwood (1949) 40–1]. In the early years of the First World War, a parliamentary committee had inquired into the selling of tea by gross weight, and as a result of its recommendations that tea should be sold by net weight, the Tea (Net Weight) Order 1916 was passed and became effective from 1 May 1917. In June 1917 Johns was one of four members appointed to represent the English CWS on a joint committee of the English and Scottish Wholesale Societies which was concerned with wartime food control. From 1922 to 1924 Johns served as chairman of the CWS board's wages committee.

His work for the friendly societies movement was also considerable. He joined the Reading Excelsior Lodge of the Manchester Unity Order of Oddfellows on 12 October 1874, was chairman of the Lodge in 1885 and 1886, served as lodge auditor and delegate to the district meeting on a number of occasions, and was trustee of the lodge. In addition he was on the committee of the Juvenile branch of the Oddfellows and was treasurer of this for a time. He also served the district as auditor and lodge book examiner, and in December 1891 was elected deputy grand master, becoming grand master in the followng year; from 1900 to 1908 he was provincial corresponding secretary of the Reading District. He was also a Freemason, having been initiated to the Morland Lodge in 1905, and for some years was superintendent of Christ Church Sunday School.

Johns was also interested in adult education. He was present at the inaugural meeting of the 'Association to Promote the Higher Education of Working Men' held at Oxford in 1903 under the chairmanship of Dr Percival, Bishop of Hereford. The founding conference of the Reading branch of the organisation was held on 1 October 1904 at the Palmer Hall, Reading. This was promoted by the Reading Industrial Co-operative Society under the auspices of the 'Association for the Advancement of the Higher Education of the Working Classes' – a title which was changed in 1905 to Workers' Educational Association. Johns, who was president of the Reading Co-operative Society at the time, was present at the 1904 meeting. Three weeks later an organising committee was formed, of which Johns became chairman. At a meeting on 15 November 1904 the Reading WEA branch was formed – the first of many to be established throughout the country. At the meeting Johns was elected president, an office he held for two years; he then became treasurer for a year; but he does not appear to have taken an active part in WEA work after 1907. Together with W. M. Childs, the Principal of the University College of Reading, he had, however, assisted in drafting the federal constitution of the Reading branch, which became a model for later WEA branches.

Johns died at his Reading home on 20 July 1928 at the age of seventy-two or seventy-three. After a service in All Saints' Church on 23 July he was buried in Reading Cemetery. He was survived by two sons, J. E. and P. R. Johns. No will has been located.

Sources: A. Mansbridge, *An Adventure in Working Class Education: being the story of the Workers' Educational Association 1903–1915* (1920); T. W. Price, *The Story of the W.E.A.* (1924); P. Redfern, *The New History of the C.W.S.* (Manchester, 1938); A. Lockwood, *Co-operation in the Thames Valley* (Reading, 1949); W. J. Souch, *The History of the Reading Branch of the Workers' Educational Association* (Reading, 1954); biographical information: D. S. Roberts, assistant secretary, Independent Order of Odd Fellows Manchester Unity and Mrs D. R. North, Reading District secretary of the Order; F. C. Padley, Reading; Home Office, London. Obit. *Reading Standard*, 28 July 1928 [photograph].

NOTE: Readers will notice discrepancies in the spelling of the word 'Oddfellows' and 'Odd Fellows' in several biographies in this volume. So far as the Independent Order of Odd Fellows is concerned its name was originally spelt as two words but these were contracted to one about the time of the foundation of the Manchester Unity of the Independent Order in 1810. About 1925 a deliberate reversion to the two separate words was made and this form is used at the present time. For a discussion of the meaning of the word 'Oddfellow' see R. M. Moffrey, *A Century of Oddfellowship* (1910) ch. 1. Further details of the Oddfellows' Societies are also given in P. H. J. H. Gosden, *The Friendly Societies in England 1815–1875* (Manchester Univ. Press, 1961).

JOYCE BELLAMY
H. F. BING

See also: Robert HALSTEAD; †Percy REDFERN, for Co-operative Wholesaling.

JOHNSON, Henry (1869–1939)
LABOUR COUNCILLOR

Henry Johnson was born on 16 January 1869 at 17 Darwin Street, Aston, Birmingham, the son of William Johnson, a tortoiseshell worker, and his wife Jane. He was educated at Bristol Street Wesleyan Elementary School until the age of twelve, when he started work as a repairer of wire mattresses. In 1886 he entered the Royal Navy, where he remained for eight years. On the outbreak of the First World War, he re-enlisted and served for the duration.

On being demobilised he set up as a wire mattress repairer in April 1919, and subsequently became managing director of the Ideal Wire Mattress Co. Ltd. He continued, however, to champion the Labour cause. He had joined the ILP in 1906, and on one occasion explained the basis of his political position:

I have been through the usual troubles that befall the workers, unemployment (eight months at one time and several shorter periods), low wages, overwork and short time. Just as I felt the injustice of my experiences, so I feel even more those suffered by the workers to-day, and, believing that they need not exist, I am anxious to do all in my power to change the system that is the cause [*Birmingham Gazette*, 12 May 1939].

In 1928 he entered the City Council as a Labour representative for the Small Heath ward, and served until 1931 when he failed to secure re-election. In 1934 he again became a member of the Council and sat for a further three years until ill-health brought his retirement.

With the threat of war, Johnson, despite his poor health, formed the first body of ARP workers in the district of Small Heath where he lived. He was the area's chief air raid precautions officer for a period of about eighteen months, and it was following a meeting of the ARP that he collapsed and died on 10 May 1939. He had married a daughter of S. H. Bailey in 1897; his wife, three sons and a daughter survived him. Johnson, who was popular with both political friends and opponents, had for some forty years been a member of the Adult School movement. He left effects to the value of £1075.

Sources: *Cornish's Birmingham Year Book* (1937–8). Obit. *Birmingham Mail* and *Evening Despatch*, 11 May 1939; *Birmingham Gazette*, 12 May 1939.

DAVID E. MARTIN

See also: Percy Lionel Edward SHURMER; *Joseph Edward SOUTHALL.

JOHNSON, William (1849–1919)
MINERS' LEADER, LIB-LAB AND THEN LABOUR MP

Born on 31 March 1849 at Chilvers Coton, Warwickshire, William Johnson was the youngest of the eleven children of John Johnson and his wife Susan (née Wood). His father and grandfather were colliers. When he was three years old his parents moved to Collycroft, near Bedworth, and after attending the local school he began work in a nearby factory at the age of twelve, and later was employed in a silk-weaving factory at Ryton-on-Dunsmore. Although the male members of his family and relatives were mostly all miners he himself worked only occasionally in the pits, and he remained in factory work until he was appointed a full-time trade union organiser. It was, in fact, his economic independence from the mining industry that allowed him to begin acting, first as an unpaid organiser to the Warwickshire miners from the later 1870s and then, in 1885, when the county union was on a reasonably stable basis, as part-time general secretary and agent to the Warwickshire Miners' Association. Three years later, in 1888, the position of agent was made permanent and Johnson now began his career as a full-time, paid official. He remained in a full-time capacity until 1916, when he resigned the secretaryship but remained as agent until his death. He represented the Warwickshire miners at the famous Newport Conference in November 1889 which inaugurated the MFGB; stood, unsuccessfully, for the provisional executive committee and again at the first annual conference of January 1890; and was first elected in 1892. Between that date and 1916 he served nine terms on the MFGB executive. For many years he was also treasurer of the Midland Miners' Federation.

Johnson was a moderate in industrial and political matters, and his influence in the Warwickshire coalfield was strongly reflected in the absence of major disputes during his many years of office. In religion he was a practising member of the Church of England and in politics he was a Liberal. He stood unsuccessfully for the Tamworth constituency in 1892, having failed to win the Liberal nomination for Nuneaton. In 1900 he stood as a Lib-Lab candidate for Nuneaton but was again defeated. In the general election of 1906 he stood again for Nuneaton as a Lib-Lab under the auspices of the MFGB (following the acceptance by the MFGB in 1901 of the 'Pickard' scheme), and on this occasion he was successful. By the time the next general election took place the miners were affiliated to the Labour Party. Johnson retained the seat in January 1910 and again in the second election of 1910. He retired from Parliament at the time of the general election of 1918.

Shortly before the First World War owing to dissatisfaction with his administration of the union, a breakaway organisation was established called the North Warwickshire Miners' Association. This was formed by G. H. Jones. Soon after the war the breach was healed, G. H. Jones becoming agent to the Warwickshire Miners' Association while William Johnson the younger was secretary. G. H. Jones was also appointed to the secretaryship of the Midland Miners' Federation.

Although his formal education had been limited Johnson widened his intellectual range by attending evening classes at Coventry, obtaining seven first class certificates in the examination of the Science and Art Department, South Kensington. In 1887 he won the first prize of three guineas for an essay on 'Working men as co-operators' in a competition organised by the working men's clubs movement; and in 1888 he won the second prize in the Cobden Club competition with an essay on 'Co-operation in its relation to labour and capital'. In the same year he contributed a series of articles on 'Machinery v. human labour' to the *Nuneaton Observer* and these articles were later published in book form, although no copy has so far been found. Johnson is also said to have published an essay on 'Mazzini's Duties of Man', but again no copy has yet been discovered.

Like many miners' leaders, he was active in local affairs, including the co-operative movement. In 1889 he was among the first members of the County Council for Warwickshire when he was elected to represent Bedworth, and he served continuously on the Council until his death, being made a county alderman in 1915. In 1894 he became chairman of Bedworth parish council, and from 1892 to 1910 he was on the Foleshill Board of Guardians. In 1907 he was appointed a JP for Warwickshire, and among his other local interests was that of governor of Nicholas Chamberlain's Charity. In 1918 he was awarded the MBE.

He was twice married: first to the daughter of a butty collier and then, after her death, to Mrs Annie Copson, of Leicester. There were four sons and three daughters of the two marriages. He died on 20 July 1919 at his Bedworth home, and was survived by his wife and some members of the family. One of his sons – William Johnson – was at the time of his father's death still an official of the Warwickshire Miners' Association.

Sources: W. Hallam, *Miners' Leaders* (1894: photograph); 'How I got on', *Pearson's Weekly*, 1 Mar 1906; *Dod* (1918); *WWW* (1916–28); R. Page Arnot, *The Miners: 1889–1910* (1949); H. Pelling, *Social Geography of British Elections* (1967); biographical information: Warwick Public Library, Nuneaton Public Library. OBIT. *Nuneaton Chronicle*, 25 July and 1 Aug 1919; *Nuneaton Observer*, 25 July 1919.

JOYCE BELLAMY
JOHN SAVILLE

See also: †Thomas Ashton, for Mining Trade Unionism, 1900–14; †Benjamin Pickard, for Mining Trade Unionism, 1880–99.

KELLEY, George Davy (1848–1911)
TRADE UNION LEADER AND LABOUR MP

The son of Thomas Kelley, a cooper, and his wife, Sarah Frances (née White), Kelley was born on 4 March 1848 at Ruskington, Lincs. He was educated at the village school and for two and a half years served as a pupil-teacher. His parents' wish that he should enter the Anglican Church failed to be realised, and he was instead apprenticed to a lithographic printer. He followed this trade first at York, and later, after his apprenticeship had expired, in London, Birmingham, Leeds and Bradford.

In Bradford he managed a small printing establishment for some five or six years, during which time he rose to prominence in the trade union world. In 1873 he became the president of the newly-established Bradford Society of Lithographic Printers. He led a campaign for the amalgamation of the various societies within the trade, becoming in 1876 a member of the amalgamation committee established for that purpose. At a conference held at Liverpool in 1879 he was elected as the first general secretary of the new Amalgamated Society of Lithographic Printers, a post he retained until his death. As the headquarters of the ASLP were established in Manchester, Kelley took up residence in that city and also acted as secretary to the union's Manchester branch.

Under his direction the ASLP became one of the most powerful trade societies in Britain; its membership was not large, but it was well-organised. By the mid-1890s the union was operating a closed shop by refusing to allow its members to work with non-union labour. As well as organising claims for higher wages and shorter working hours, Kelley was also a key figure in the establishment of the Printing and Kindred Trades' Federation. In March 1890 he wrote on behalf of his executive to various kindred societies 'proposing a conference of printers and allied trades, with a view to forming a federation' [Musson (1954) 249]. A meeting was held at Manchester on 8 September 1890, at which ten organisations were represented, and in 1892 the PKTF was established with Kelley as its first secretary, a position he held until 1911. In 1896 he became president of the International Congress of Lithographic Artists and Printers. He was a member of the parliamentary committee of the TUC in 1871, 1883, 1887 and again in 1890–1.

In addition to these trade union activities, Kelley was involved in several other causes. Early in the 1880s he was appointed secretary of the Manchester and Salford Trades and Labour Council, and this post in turn brought him into contact with a variety of movements. Among these was the Bimetallic League, of which he was a vice-president. In May 1889 he gave a short address as a member of a League deputation that waited on the Prime Minister and the Chancellor of the Exchequer. It appears that Kelley's enthusiasm was the main cause of the Trades Council's support for bimetallism, although a minority of its members believed the League to be part of the 'fair trade' movement, to which they were opposed. Kelley continued to be interested in questions of this sort for some years: in 1899 he was vice-president of the Trade Union Monetary Reform Association, of which Thomas Greenall, agent of the Lancashire Miners' Federation, was treasurer and James Mawdsley, the cotton spinners' leader, J. R. Clynes and Ben Turner members of the executive. For many years Kelley was secretary of the Lancashire Federation of Trade Councils, and held the same post after an amalgamation with the Councils of Cheshire in 1902. The Lancashire and Cheshire Federation of Trade Councils was the largest body of that type in the country.

In the 1890s Kelley was noted for his opposition to the ILP and SDF. Early in 1893 he refused the assistance of the Manchester and Salford Trades Council in a demonstration that was being organised by the ILP to celebrate May Day. He attacked the ILP for spoiling the chances of Liberal candidates at elections, and thus allowing the Tory to slip in. This brought a fierce response from Leonard Hall, who accused the Trades Council of being undemocratic and often contemptible and the richer and more skilled unions of 'unspeakable respectabilities' [*Clarion*, 1 Apr 1893].

Though more sympathetic to Liberalism than Socialism, Kelley for several years attempted to maintain a balance within the Trades Council so that it became neither too closely identified with, nor directly opposed to, the Liberal Party. While most members of the Council were Liberals, they did not wish to see their organisation become a creature of the Liberal Party and so they maintained a politically independent line. Many of them believed there was a need for more labour representatives on public bodies and in 1890 the Council became affiliated to the TUC-sponsored Labour Electoral Association, with Kelley acting as a delegate to the Association's congress. The Association was devoted to obtaining the election of working men to municipal councils, school boards and similar bodies as well as keeping alive the question of working-class parliamentary representation. Kelley was one of its most active supporters. In 1888, 1889 and 1890 he was its vice-president. At the 1889 Congress, held in Sheffield, he seconded a motion calling for land nationalisation, while in April 1890, when the LEA met at Hanley he gave the chairman's address. He took the chair again at the 1891 Congress, held at Westminster Town Hall, when he accused the landowners and the capitalist class of protecting their own interests to the injury of the public. On this occasion he renewed his demand for land nationalisation, and in the following year when he was president at the Leicester Congress, he called for 'a solid body of labour members who will form the foundation of the Parliamentary labour party, and who from the House of Commons shall proclaim a labour programme around which all the workers of the country can gather' [Labour Electoral Association, *Report* (1892) 9].

For many years Kelley hoped that the Liberal Party would espouse labour representation. In 1890 there was a move to promote him as a candidate for St George's ward, Manchester, in the municipal elections, but he was unwilling to oppose the retiring Liberal councillor and received some criticism as a result. In the 1891 School Board elections he stood, with the Trade Council's support, as a Labour candidate, but was unsuccessful. A few months earlier, in February, he had filled unopposed a vacant seat that had arisen in St Clement's ward, thus becoming the first representative of the labour interest to sit on Manchester City Council; but he lost the seat in 1895 to a Conservative opponent. In the following year he again stood for the City Council but failed to secure election. During his spell as a councillor, Kelley paid particular attention to the contracts negotiated by the City Council to ensure that standard wages were being paid, an issue with which the Trades Council was much concerned.

Despite his criticisms of the propertied classes' control of Parliament, Kelley accepted the view that the fundamental interests of employers and workers were the same. He wished to minimise the conflict between capital and labour, and was for a time a member of the National Industrial Association which had been formed in 1900. Other trade unionists belonging to this body were Richard Bell and Alexander Wilkie, while several employers also gave their support.

In February 1900, as the delegate of the Manchester Trades Council, Kelley attended the Memorial Hall conference that led to the foundation of the Labour Representation Committee. In the following June, John Hodge addressed the Trades Council, asking for its affiliation to the LRC; the Council agreed, and was one of the first in the country to take such a step. Kelley's break with the Liberals was now in sight. In February 1900 the LRC held its conference in Manchester and he attended as delegate. When the Manchester and Salford LRC was formed he was adopted as a parliamentary candidate for South-West Manchester and at a meeting held early in 1904 he publicly announced that he was no longer associated with the Liberal Party, which had given the working men 'many advantages and benefits' in the past but was no longer 'doing all that the people had a right to expect from them' [*Manchester Guardian*, 4 Feb 1904].

At the general election of 1906 the operation of the MacDonald–Gladstone agreement gave Kelley a straight fight with the sitting member, W. J. Galloway (Unionist), and he secured a comfortable majority. Although he had shown a brief interest in Chamberlain's tariff reform campaign, he had abandoned such views by the time of the election and he received Liberal and free trade support as well as that of the Irish (Michael Davitt spoke at his meetings). His platform emphasised trade union and unemployment measures, Home Rule and free trade. On entering Parliament he resigned from the Trades Council, being succeeded in the secretaryship by Tom Fox.

Kelley was a member of the Commons for just four years; in June 1908 he announced that, acting on medical advice, he would not contest another election. As a trade union negotiator, Kelley had been noted for the conciliatory tone he adopted with employers; 'I can always get more over the tables with a chat,' he claimed, 'than by an appeal to force.' In Parliament, too, he was noted for his moderate views, and although sitting on the Opposition benches he did not hesitate to express his support for the Liberal Government's social legislation. His gifts were less those of the politician than of the organiser; it was in the painstaking day-to-day duties of the trade union official that he excelled.

Many aspects of social reform interested him, and he was a keen advocate of technical education. He served as a member of the council of the Manchester Technical School and as a governor of the Whitworth Institute. In 1902 he travelled to the United States as a member of the Mosely Industrial Commission, and visited the USA and Canada in 1900 and 1906 to observe the state of the lithographic trade. Nor did these comprise the full range of his activities: for more than thirty years he was a member of the Manchester and Salford Co-

operative Society, and in 1896 he was elected to the board of the Co-operative Printing Society. He was also a JP, joining the magistrates' bench in 1892 and serving until his death.

In many respects Kelley was representative of the type of man who led skilled trade unionists in the late nineteenth century. He was fully committed to the principle of trade unionism and its entitlement to take part in public life, but his political opinions were no more advanced than those of the Gladstonian Liberal. He regarded socialist doctrines with suspicion and only gradually accepted the idea of independent labour representation. He had, too, some of the labour aristocrat's coolness towards the unskilled worker who could not hope to organise on a craft basis. Kelley was remembered by one colleague as being a somewhat austere character; it was by steady application that he built up the ASLP, and he demonstrated the same characteristic in his work with innumerable reforming organisations.

Kelley died suddenly at his home, 70 Cecil Street, Manchester, on 11 December 1911, shortly after he had returned from a visit to Scotland. When he was buried at Ardwick Cemetery on 21 December his funeral was attended by representatives from many trade union and co-operative societies. In his will he left effects to the value of £3388. His wife, Mary, survived him.

Writings: Labour Electoral Congress, 'Chairman's Address' *Report* (1890) 6–8; *Report* (1891) 7–10; *Report* (1892) 7–9; *Mosely Industrial Commission to the United States of America, Oct–Dec 1902* (1903) 233–41.

Sources: Labour Electoral Congress, *Reports* (1888–92); Manchester and Salford Trades Council, *Annual Reports* (1892–1912); *Dod* (1906–10); T. Sproat, *The History and Progress of the ASLP and Auxiliaries of G.B. and Ireland, 1880–1930* (Manchester, 1930); T. W. Moody, 'Michael Davitt and the British Labour Movement' *Trans of the Roy. Hist. Society* 5th ser. 3

(1953) 53–76; A. E. Musson, *The Typographical Association: origins and history up to 1949* (1954); L. Bather, 'A History of Manchester and Salford Trades Council' (Manchester PhD, 1956); F. Bealey and H. Pelling, *Labour and Politics 1900–1906* (1958); H. A. Clegg et al., *A History of British Trade Unions since 1889* vol. 1: *1889–1910* (Oxford, 1964); P. F. Clarke, *Lancashire and the New Liberalism* (Cambridge, 1971); biographical information: Bradford City Library; Dr R. H. C. Hayburn; Manchester Graphical Society. OBIT. *Manchester Evening Chronicle, Manchester Evening News* and *Manchester Guardian,* 18 Dec 1911; *Manchester Courier* and *Times,* 19 Dec 1911; *Manchester City News,* 23 Dec 1911; Manchester and Salford Trades Council, *Annual Report* (1911); *TUC Report* (1912).

DAVID E. MARTIN

See also: Tom Fox; *William Leonard HALL; George LANSBURY, for British Labour Party, 1900–13.

LANSBURY, George (1859–1940)
SOCIALIST, PACIFIST AND LABOUR LEADER

George Lansbury was born on 22 February 1859, according to Somerset House records, although his autobiography and other sources give 21 February. He was one of the older of the nine children of George Lansbury and his Welsh wife Mary Anne Ferries. The elder George was a railway timekeeper for Thomas Brassey and Co., the railway contractors who were engaged to construct the British railway system in Victorian days; which accounts for the fact that young George entered life in a toll-house in East Anglia midway between Lowestoft and Halesworth in Suffolk. George's childhood was thus passed in a thoroughly working-class atmosphere among people who lived a rough and ready semi-nomadic life moving from one encampment of wooden huts to another; and this was deeply impressed on him. Even when he had become comparatively well-off and owned his own business, he always thought of himself as working class,

and his children were brought up in that conviction. His father, like many of the navvies with whom he worked, drank heavily, and his mother also gave way to drink, with the result that their son became a strict teetotaller and temperance advocate, though he never cut himself off from comrades whose practice was different.

In 1866 his father gave up the roving life, the railway boom being over, and went to London with his family, first to Sydenham, where little George attended a dame school of traditional type – and threaded his teacher's needle for her when he had been a good boy – then to Greenwich and Bethnal Green, settling finally in Whitechapel, where in 1875 he died; his widow soon afterwards married again. Young George had a little more schooling before he was fourteen, at Anglican elementary schools, where he learned his three R's and also, from an intelligent and enthusiastic master at St Mary's School in Whitechapel, a good deal of geography and English history; but his main education was conducted out of school, in a brief period of paid work when he was eleven, in what his mother told him about her great Liberal heroes like Gladstone, Bright, and Cobden, and also in conversation with John Hales, one-time secretary of the International Working Men's Association. From Hales he heard tales of the Commune of Paris and of the bloody vengeance exacted by Thiers on its participants.

On the death of his father he had to go to work to help in the keep of the younger children, and with his elder brother Jim took a job as coal-heaver, where his big frame and strong muscles served him well and developed further – though not without strains at times, and a partial breakdown which put him into a rural hospital or convalescent home for some weeks in the spring of 1879. In 1875 he had begun 'walking out' with a pretty girl of fourteen named Elizabeth Brine, who had attended St Mary's School while he was there. Her parents, who were in a slightly more solid economic position than the Lansburys', decided that she would be 'lowering herself';

and what with that and his own financial insecurity – he had got into debt during his illness – it was not until 1880 that they were joined together, in a marriage of great affection on both sides, which endured at full strength until Bessie died in 1933. She bore him twelve children, of whom two died very young: his second son Edgar, who later was manager of his business and like his father Mayor of Poplar, married as his second wife the actress Moyna McGill and was the father of Angela Lansbury, the stage and screen star; his third daughter Dorothy was also active in public life, a member of the London County Council and married to Ernest Thurtle, MP; and his fourth daughter Daisy became his personal secretary for all the years of his active life, and was also the wife and collaborator of the journalist, author, and Labour historian Raymond Postgate.

During the formative years before his marriage the strongest influence in Lansbury's life was that of the Reverend J. Fenwick Kitto, Vicar of Whitechapel, whose saintly character and beautiful services attracted many worshippers to his church. Lansbury had been put off Christianity by the illiberal social practices of many members and dignitaries of the Anglican Church – indeed, on one occasion he and a friend helped to rescue Charles Bradlaugh from an angry mob in Hyde Park. But he was really *anima naturaliter Christiana*, and Kitto and his Whitechapel Young Men's Association with its emphasis on social service and straightforward piety soon brought him to a simple Christian faith. During the last decade of the century, it is true, under the influence of his friends in the Socialist societies, he for a while abjured Christianity, joined the Ethical movement, sent his children to an Ethical Sunday School and refused to have those who were born at that time baptised – an omission repaired, when he returned to the fold, by a mass christening which greatly annoyed at least one of those who endured it. Once reconciled to the Church, he remained a believing Christian, even though towards the end of his life he joined the theosophists – without however

taking any active part in their church. This inclination may have been in part due to admiration of Annie Besant, the former Fabian and Freethinker, who was converted to theosophy and subsequently became one of the great early leaders of Indian nationalism. He was never anything of a bigot: as First Commissioner of Works in the Second Labour Government he kept restrictions in the royal parks to the minimum, and did what he could to soften the austerities of the English Sunday.

For some years after his marriage Lansbury was in fairly low financial water. Trade was not good, and after trying various experiments he succumbed to propaganda from the Colony of Queensland, and in May 1884, with his wife, their three small children, and a younger brother, set sail on an emigrant ship. They had a miserable journey out, and when they arrived in Brisbane they found that like many another emigrant they had been duped. They were not wanted: Lansbury could not get work except under conditions which he found unendurable, and after two years they returned to England on money provided by Bessie's father, who also gave his son-in-law work in the timber business which he owned. Lansbury, with six children, was still poor; but he managed after hours to run a partially successful protest against deceitful propaganda on emigration, and to act as unpaid ward secretary for the local Liberal Party. During the 1886 election he was given leave to be agent to Samuel Montagu (afterwards Lord Swaythling), got him returned with an enhanced majority, and was made general secretary (still unpaid) to the Liberal Party in Bow. He was, however, beginning to move away from Liberalism; and two events in 1889 helped to make up his mind. The first was a visit he made to Ireland as a member of a twelve-man delegation from the radical clubs of the East End 'to see what crimes are being committed in our name' [Postgate (1951) 34]. The second, soon after he returned from Ireland, was his attendance at a national Liberal Conference in Manchester where he attempted to move, on behalf of all London Liberals, a motion urging the eight-hour day; but there was a great deal of noisy opposition from old-style Liberals, and he was not allowed to complete his speech. This treatment re-inforced the arguments which he had heard from the Socialists, above all from H. M. Hyndman of the Social Democratic Federation, that neither Tories nor Liberals offered any real hope to the working man. So, though the London Liberals deserved the name better than some of the national figures, and Montagu had offered to back him for a 'safe' parliamentary con-stituency, he changed his allegiance, stayed with the local Liberals long enough to bring his candidate home in the 1892 election (with the help of Keir Hardie), and there-after spoke and wrote as a confirmed Socialist, a member first of the Social Democratic Federation, later of the Inde-pendent Labour Party and of the Labour Party after its formation. He was political secretary of the SDF in 1897, but he was also for some years a member of the Fabian Society; within the movement his sympathies were catholic. From 1892 then, and particularly after his father-in-law's death in 1895 had left him the owner, until the outbreak of the First World War, of the timber firm, socialist propaganda and active efforts towards reform played an in-creasing part in his life. In 1889, the year of the London dock strike, he had joined Will Thorne's Gasworkers' Union.

He stood, as a Socialist, for the Wal-worth division of Newington (London) at a by-election in May 1895 and again at the general election in July of that year but on both occasions received few votes (347 and 203). In 1900, at the 'khaki' election, he contested the Bow and Bromley division of Tower Hamlets, scoring the respectable vote of 2258; but his major concern, during the first years of his political life, was with local government and the Poor Law.

He was elected to the Board of Guard-ians in 1892, and in subsequent years, with the help of Will Crooks and some other vigorous campaigners, brought the handful of East End Socialists to a position of con-siderable influence on both the Board and the Poplar Borough Council, which had

come into being in 1900; he early set the example of visiting in person the work-houses and other institutions for which 'elected persons' were nominally respon-sible, and in a famous incident (described in his autobiography) he forced an improve-ment in the inmates' diet by challenging the chief officer to eat just one mouthful of the dirty porridge served up to the 'paupers'; in 1894 his persistence in ferret-ing out cases of peculation and other ir-regularities resulted in an inquiry by the Local Government Board and the eventual dismissal of the offending officials. His activities so impressed the authorities that he was called upon in 1894 to give evidence in the House of Lords, to the Royal Com-mission on the Aged Poor, of which the Prince of Wales (Edward VII) was a mem-ber; and he used reports of his conversa-tions with the Prince on matters such as the food of paupers to shame the loyal Guardians into being more generous. In many other ways he endeavoured to humanise conditions for the indigent, and even to provide work for them instead of miserable idleness; the Laindon Farm Colony and the Hollesley Bay estates, both started with financial help from the Ameri-can soap king Joseph Fels of 'Fels-Naphta', were tangible instances of his efforts, as was for several generations the Poplar Training School. On 6 November 1905 he led a large deputation of women to the House of Commons to explain to Balfour the misery inflicted by the Poor Law; this, and the influence which his constant speechifying in different parts of the country was beginning to produce, may have been part of the reason which promp-ted Mr J. S. (later Sir James) Davy, In-spector under the Poor Law in 1905, to urge upon his political masters the appoint-ment of a Commission to investigate the Poor Law with a view to ensuring that the 'principle of the 1834 Poor Law' be not whittled away, and in the following year himself to preside over an official inquiry into the administrative behaviour of the Poplar Board of Guardians.

This inquiry, as a whole, misfired, not-withstanding a barrage of evidence from persons heavily biased against the humaner practices of the Poplar Board; though some irregularities were brought to light, Lansbury and Crooks, who were Davy's chief targets, came out of the ordeal unscathed, and no one was punished. The Royal Commission was even less satisfactory to Davy, who unfortunately for him had prematurely disclosed to Beatrice Webb his plans for inducing the Commission to reaffirm the 1834 'principle of less eligibility' [B. Webb, *Our Partnership* (1948) p. 322] viz. that the lot of the person receiving poor relief should be in all respects less agreeable than that of the poorest independent labourer. Mrs Webb showed herself more adept than Mr Davy at bulldozing a committee; and Lansbury, though he had no hand in the actual writing of the famous Minority Report, one of the great State papers of this century, both signed it and played a considerable part in the Commission's deliberations and in the following nationwide campaign to have the Poor Law completely abolished. But even while that campaign was being defeated by Lloyd George's Insurance Acts of 1911–12, Lansbury was showing himself more and more of a crusader.

He was not elected to Parliament in 1906, having unwisely left the East End in order to fight Havelock Wilson, the sailors' leader, who had thrown in his lot with the Liberals in Middlesbrough; returning in 1910 to the East End, he was unsuccessful in the first election of that year, but at the second defeated L. S. Amery for the Bow and Bromley division; in the same year he became one of the LCC members for Woolwich. From outside Parliament he had written and spoken for Victor Grayson in the latter's brief and furious campaign as Member for Colne Valley against the ILP leaders; after he had been re-elected he spoke fiercely against Party policy over the Insurance Bills and the alliance with the Liberals; and in the summer of 1912 worked himself into such a heat of passion over the government's treatment of the militant suffragettes that he insulted Asquith to his face and was expelled from the House. In 1913 he was himself arrested and imprisoned under the once famous Cat and Mouse Act; he embarked at once on a hunger and thirst strike, was soon released, and thereafter let alone. When he failed to persuade the Labour Party to vote against *all* Government measures (including the Home Rule Bill) until they brought in a Bill to enfranchise women, he allowed the Pankhursts to persuade him to resign his seat; in the subsequent by-election he lost it, and was out of Parliament until 1922. He recognised his tactical mistake, and thereafter said his motto was 'Never Resign'. The loss of his parliamentary income, such as it was, was however soon made up; in 1913 he became editor of the *Daily Herald*.

The *Daily Herald* was born, first, in January 1911, as a printers' strike sheet. As such it lasted for three months only; but a year later, in April 1912, it was restarted, optimistically, by a committee of trade unionists, who had collected a ridiculously small sum to found 'a permanent daily for trade unionists'. It was from the beginning an explosive journal of the left, reflecting the excitement and the 'labour unrest' of the immediately pre-war years. Its position was made more precarious by the efforts being made by Clifford Allen of the ILP (later Lord Allen of Hurtwood) to collect funds for an official Labour newspaper – which in October 1912 came out as the *Daily Citizen*; on more than one occasion the very appearance of the next day's issue was in doubt until the last moment. The *Herald* had a succession of editors until at the end of 1913 Lansbury, then chairman of the board of directors, finally succeeded Charles Lapworth; but it had a team of brilliant contributors: Hilaire Belloc, G. K. Chesterton, Will Dyson the Australian cartoonist, Rebecca West, Ben Tillett of the dockers, the Oxford Socialists William Mellor and G. D. H. Cole; its politics were anti-capitalist and pro-strike, syndicalist or Guild Socialist, pro-suffrage, pro-Irish Nationalist and supportive of James Larkin's locked-out Dublin workers, pro-India, and anti-war. To help its circulation Lansbury founded the Herald League of supporters in various towns up and down the country, a move which at one and the same time helped to build up a circulation and made 'G.L.' into more of a national father-figure. When he became editor in full charge he endeavoured, without breaking his promise of 'no censorship', to modify some of his colleagues' savage attacks on those Labour men they disagreed with.

When war came the *Herald*'s circulation dropped rapidly, and in September 1914 it became a weekly (the *Daily Citizen* faded out altogether by May 1916). As a weekly, after a short interval during which it shared the almost universal sentiment of bewildered patriotism, it soon became, of all anti-government publications, the most influential among the working classes and leftish intellectuals. It attacked the 'profiteering' which began almost as soon as the war; it supported all efforts by trade unions and others to maintain the standard of living against heavy rises in prices; it attacked and exposed scandals wherever it could find them; when conscription and the wartime 'dilution' of skilled labour came in it supported the conscientious objectors and the shop stewards who led unofficial strikes in centres of war production like the Clyde; before the war was a year old it had begun gathering proposals for a just post-war settlement. Gradually, under the guidance of Lansbury, who was deeply pacifist by nature, it took up a strong anti-war position, which was intensified by the revolution in Russia – when the Tsar abdicated the Herald League helped to organise an immense joyful meeting in the Albert Hall – and by Lloyd George's successful sabotage of the projected Stockholm conference of the Socialists of the warring nations. In May of 1918 the *Herald*, along with the *Manchester Guardian*, published the text, found by the Bolsheviks in the Russian state archives, of the 'secret treaties' in which the Allied governments had recorded their agreement to divide the spoils after the war. This created widespread anger; though it did not have much effect either in the snap general election of 1918 or on the provisions of the peace treaties.

After the war was over and disillusionment began to set in, the mood of the working classes was sufficiently inflamed for the *Herald* to be re-started in March 1919 as a daily, with Lansbury again in command. He had raised the bulk of the capital (though not nearly the amount initially budgeted for). Some of the pre-war contributors, such as Chesterton and Dyson, who disagreed with the anti-war policy, had been lost; but they were replaced by others quite as effective. W.N. Ewer, E. M. Forster, Bertrand Russell, Osbert Sitwell, Havelock Ellis, Aldous Huxley, Herbert Farjeon, Rose Macaulay – these are only a handful of the best-known names in a team of widely differing personalities who were all happy to work under Lansbury. The new daily continued to press the policies and practice of its predecessor in home, imperial and foreign affairs; it vigorously supported the national railway strike (and other strikes) of 1919, and deplored the 'betrayal' of Black Friday, 1921; it backed the nationalist movements in Ireland, India and Egypt, and played a considerable part in bringing to an end the British support of White Russian counter-revolutionaries and of Poland in the Russo-Polish war; it was a well-recognised thorn in the side of the Government. Two of Lansbury's infrequent books, *Your Part in Poverty* and *What I saw in Russia*, give a good idea of what it meant to him.

But its days of glory did not last. The *Herald* had strong enemies, many among advertisers, whose contribution was not nearly enough to offset the lack of initial capital, and after the post-war bubble of prosperity burst, circulation began to fall away. Lansbury, though elected to Parliament in 1922, had exhausted his fundraising capacities; later in that year he handed over the paper to the Trades Union Congress and a new editor, Hamilton Fyfe To smooth over the transition he agreed to remain as general manager; but he was unhappy over the changes that were made, and in February 1925 he resigned – not, however, to leave the world of journalism. For in the same month appeared the first numbers of *Lansbury's Labour Weekly*, with many of the former *Herald* contributors and some new names, such as those of Ellen

Wilkinson, the future Minister of Education, and the cartographer and cartoonist J. F. Horrabin; it had a good deal of support, some of it financial, from trade union men such as A. J. Cook of the Miners and George Hicks of the Bricklayers, who were indignant with the poor performance of the first Labour Government. The *Weekly* began life with a good circulation, but it survived only until the middle of 1927. This failure was due in the first instance to the Communist Party, which started almost immediately the competitive *Sunday Worker*, thereby repaying very ill the staunch support which Lansbury had always given against the efforts of official Labour to destroy the Party. Lansbury was not, and could never have been, a Communist Party member; his pacifist principles and his hatred of authoritarianism had prevented it. But he believed that the Communists, though he disagreed with them and often thought their tactics unbelievably silly, were essentially on the side of the working class and should not be hounded; this naturally, if ironically, earned him plenty of suspicion in orthodox Labour circles. To this setback was added the disaster of the 1926 General Strike, which the *Weekly* had of course backed to the hilt. It was losing money rapidly, and in July of 1927 amalgamated with the ILP's *New Leader*. Lansbury never again had a paper of his own.

This did not mean, however, that his influence had waned; in fact, it was growing by other means, though paradoxically the scene of growth was local, not national. In 1919, the unexpectedly radical results of the local council elections had put Labour in control of Poplar Borough and made Lansbury its Mayor until 1922 – he was still on the Board of Guardians. But before that date he had collided violently with the central authorities. After the post-war boom had ended, unemployment grew rapidly. By the middle of 1921 the numbers out of work had grown to over a million, of whom many had exhausted their claim to insurance benefit and so had to appeal to the Guardians for relief – which relief had to be paid for out of the borough rates. This meant that boroughs like Poplar, which had a very low rateable

value, would quickly become bankrupt if they tried to maintain even moderately decent scales of relief. There were other very poor boroughs in the provinces, such as Merthyr Tydfil, which had once had Keir Hardie as its MP; but the plight of the East London boroughs was made more glaring by contrast with the riches of West London boroughs like Westminster and Kensington. Lansbury and a group of his colleagues on the Poplar Council decided that they would neither starve out the victims of the depression nor raise the rates to a height which the residents of the borough could not possibly pay. Instead, they announced that Poplar would refuse to pay the 'precepts' which the London County Council and the Metropolitan Asylums Board were legally able to levy on the borough councils for various centralised services – Poplar's bill from the LCC in 1921 amounting to £270,000. When the councillors were summoned in July to the High Court they marched in procession from Bow, with the mace-bearer at the head and a banner carried in front saying *Poplar Borough Council marching to the High Court and possibly to* PRISON. They were, of course, ordered to levy the precept, refused, and in September were jailed *en masse* for contempt of court, the women going to Holloway, the men to Brixton, where they were the despair of the warders. They refused to work; they demanded newspapers and footballs, and every day Lansbury spoke to crowds through the bars of his cell. (The women in Holloway had less fun, and Edgar Lansbury's wife Minnie suffered privations which may have contributed to her death a few months later.) The news spread: the Borough Council of Bethnal Green followed the Poplar example, and other boroughs were contemplating similar action.

Despite the anger of Herbert Morrison and other 'moderate' Labour mayors, the Government gave way. The High Court released the recalcitrants to enable them to attend a conference as a result of which a Bill was introduced for the partial equalisation of rates over the whole of the LCC area, and Poplar's rates fell immediately by 6s 6d in the £. In the following year, however, the Ministry of Health, having learned nothing, it would seem, from the earlier governmental experiences with the Poplar Guardians, sent down a Mr Cooper, clerk to the Guardians of Bolton, to investigate their methods. His report suggested that £100,000 a year could be saved if Poplar put into effect the principles of 1834. After some argument with Edgar Lansbury, who was then chairman of the Board, the Minister fixed what he considered correct rates for payment of relief and also for the wages to be paid to officers of the Board; and the district auditor then surcharged the Guardians individually for all monies paid out in excess of the Minister's ruling. The Guardians took no notice, and when shortly afterwards the Lloyd George coalition fell, the Conservative Government which succeeded it decided that it had had enough tangling with 'Poplarism', now a word of national significance, and let the whole business lapse. 'Poplarism' may, however, have played some part in the omission of Lansbury from the Labour Cabinet of 1924, though Lansbury himself always believed that it was the King who had objected to have kissing his hand a man who, he thought, wished to cut off his head. Be that as it may, in 1929 MacDonald invited Lansbury, who had been chairman of the national Labour Party the year before, to join his cabinet as First Commissioner of Works – a post, as Philip Snowden dryly noted, in which he could do very little harm – and Buckingham Palace acquiesced. (In fact, when the First Commissioner met his sovereign in face-to-face discussion they got on very well.)

Lansbury took his official job, which included the care of the royal parks and historical monuments as well as the buildings belonging to other departments, very seriously, and collected by his actions a good deal of personal popularity. Most notable was his institution of public bathing and sun-bathing (Lansbury's Lido) in Hyde Park; but he also endeared himself to antiquaries by his willingness to listen to their troubles and visit their sites, and to a large part of the public by his readiness to abandon obsolete restrictions on behaviour – though he was attacked furiously by a body calling itself the London Public Morality Council, and a *Times* leader described him as 'the Caliban of the Parks'. But any pleasure he may have found in these exercises was vitiated by his experiences when appointed, with J. H. Thomas, Tom Johnston and Oswald Mosley, to draw up plans for relieving unemployment. This combination would have been unlikely to produce anything useful at the best of times; when the great depression began, only months after the Government had taken office, the position became rapidly impossible. Lansbury almost at once began to work out proposals for relief, all of which were turned down for one reason or another, either by Thomas or by Snowden as Chancellor of the Exchequer. In the spring of 1930 he collaborated with Johnston and Mosley in combining their various suggestions into a document to be drafted by Mosley, which he, as Thomas refused, brought before the Cabinet. This was the famous 'Mosley Memorandum', which was rejected on a very narrow vote by the Party Conference in October, 1930; this led to Mosley's resignation and the formation of his 'New Party'.

Lansbury did not resign; in the autumn of 1930 he was still loyally supporting MacDonald's Government, if only for its foreign policy and its attitude generally to problems such as were presented by India, for example. But as the situation worsened he grew more and more unhappy, and began to wonder whether he was right to continue to stifle his doubts. The situation was resolved for him, painfully, by the formation of the National Government in the summer of 1931. He had of course no doubt as to where his sympathies lay; and he, no more than anyone else in the Labour movement, anticipated the crushing result of the general election. As he and he alone of the Labour Cabinet survived it – for Bow and Bromley as before – he inevitably became leader of the handful – forty-six – of Labour members in the new House of Commons; Clement Attlee, the future Prime Minister, who had been Postmaster-General, was his deputy, and Sir Stafford Cripps, ex-Solicitor-General, who after some hesitation had declined to follow the Lord Chancellor

(Sankey) into MacDonald's National team, became his other chief aide. Both were devoted to Lansbury and served him well; he was probably the best leader the attenuated and desperate Party could have had, not only because of his long experience of parliamentary procedure, but also because of his strong faith, his ability to work with the most difficult personalities among 'comrades', and his invincible – and sometimes irrational – optimism. In his room at the House, as at 39 Bow Road, he was always ready to advise, and to comfort.

He worked hard and deployed his small and not very able battalion effectively: though there was no chance of defeating the Government in a vote, as time passed and the panic of 1931 subsided it was possible, by the use of question time, by speeches in the Commons and extra-parliamentary agitation, to bring about modifications in government policy. His personal life was not happy; he was short of money (there was no salary, in those days, for the Leader of the Opposition), and in order to meet his many commitments and generosities (and to pay his postage bill!) he had to supplement his £600 from Parliament and the proceeds of his autobiography, *My Life* (1928), by undertaking a good deal of journalism. In March 1933 his wife died, and he lost the support which had been his for more than half a century. (Edgar, the son on whom he most relied, died in 1935.) It was not very surprising that in December of the same year he broke his thigh stepping out in the dark after a big Labour meeting, and was seven months in hospital; what did surprise him was the flood of anxious and loving correspondence which reached him on his sickbed and served to dispel for the time being the doubts he had felt about his fitness to be leader.

The doubts returned, however, in full force over the question of rearmament. The conviction that the ambitions of Hitler and the Nazis could not be stopped except by force of arms was slowly growing; in 1934 the Peace Ballot showed a substantial majority in the country favouring the use of force by the League of Nations if need be. This necessitated, eventually, rearmament in Britain, which Lansbury's pacifist convictions forbade him to accept. This brought him into disagreement with some of the leading trade unionists, notably Ernest Bevin of the Transport Workers and Walter Citrine, secretary of the TUC. Lansbury offered to resign the leadership, but was not allowed to; and at the Party Conference of 1935 the situation was abruptly resolved. The executive committee proposed a resolution calling on the Government to use 'all necessary measures' through the League to stop the imminent invasion of Ethiopia by the Italians. Lansbury made a moving appeal against calling men to take up arms, but the conference was not with him. Bevin attacked him in a speech of calculated ferocity, and when he tried to reply, the microphone was turned off. The motion was carried by an immense majority, and Lansbury then resigned. Thereafter, though he was Mayor of Poplar again in 1936, he gave his main attention to a desperate individual effort to prevent the coming war, visiting personally, during the years 1936 and 1937, the heads of state in all the principal foreign countries, including Hitler whom, he believed, he had turned from his purposes; and under the banner of the Peace Pledge Union, of which he was president, addressing anti-war meetings up and down his own country. When at last it became clear to him that all his efforts had failed, he began to lose heart, and his health to fail. He died, of cancer, on 7 May 1940, only a few months before the Luftwaffe destroyed his home in Bow Road. His funeral service was held at Bow Parish Church, followed by cremation. He left an estate valued at £1695 gross (£916 net), and directed that his ashes should be thrown into the sea somewhere off Land's End: 'I desire that', he had declared, 'because although I love England very dearly and consider this lovely island the best spot in the world, I am a convinced internationalist.' In 1951, as part of the South Bank Exhibition prepared by the third Labour Government before its fall, a part of war-damaged Poplar was entirely rebuilt as a model urban community, and named Lansbury after him.

MARGARET COLE

Writings: Lansbury wrote his autobiography, *My Life* (1928) which had an Introduction by Harold Laski and in 1935 published a volume of reminiscences entitled *Looking Backwards and Forwards*; his political and social views were expressed in *Your Part in Poverty* ([1916], fourth impression, 1918); *These Things shall be* [1919]; *My England* [1934]; *Labour's Way with the Commonwealth* (1935) and *Why Pacifists should be Socialists* (*Fact*, no. 7, 1937); and he described some particular events in his life in *What I saw in Russia* (1920); *The Miracle of Fleet Street: the story of the 'Daily Herald'* [1925] and *My Quest for Peace* (1938). Apart from these works he was a prolific writer of pamphlets and articles and the files of the *Daily* and *Weekly Herald*, of *Lansbury's Labour Weekly* and *Reynolds News* contain much of his literary output although he also contributed to other, non-Socialist journals such as *John Bull*. Most of his published works, apart from those listed above, are quoted below and have been divided into pamphlet and periodical literature. Many of his publications were prepared with the help of his son-in-law, Raymond Postgate. Lansbury's contributions to parliamentary debates in *Hansard* are an indispensable source.

Pamphlets: *The Principles of the English Poor Law* (1897) 14 pp.; *The Development of the Humane Administration of the Poor Law under the Poplar Board* [1907] 15 pp.; *London for Labour* [1909] 11 pp.; *Unemployment: the next step* [1909] 16 pp.; *Socialism for the Poor: the end of pauperism* (Pass on Pamphlet no. 12 [1909] 20 pp.; *Smash up the Workhouse* [1910] 13 pp.; *The Chief Need of the Labour Movement* [1911?] 8 pp.; (with W. C. Anderson et al.), *War against Poverty* [1912] 19 pp.; *In France* [1915] 15 pp.; (with others), *Russia free: report of speeches made on 31 March at the Royal Albert Hall* (1917) 23 pp.; compiler of *The First Socialist Republic: being the full text of the Russian Constitution* [1918] 24 pp.; *My Impressions of Soviet Russia* (repr. from *Politiken*, Sweden by People's Russian Information Bureau, Apr 1920) 6 pp.; *Socialism versus Protection: the battle*

cry of the election (1923) 6 pp.; *Jesus and Labour* [1924?] 7 pp.; *If we could live on Rice and do without Sleep altogether* (LPD, 1925) 4 pp.; *The I.C.W.P.A. at work* [a speech delivered in Moscow, British Section of the International Class War Prisoners' Aid, Nov 1926) 26 pp.; *This way to Peace* [1940].

Articles: 'Report of the Vagrancy Committee', *Econ. J. 16* (June 1906) 303–7; 'Unemployment', *Econ. Rev. 17* (July 1907) 299–308; 'Hollesley Bay' [LCC and Labour colonies] *Soc. Rev. 1* (May 1908) 220–33; 'A Year of the Poor Law', *Soc. Rev. 4* (Nov 1909) 189–202; 'The Power that re-makes men' in *Labour and Religion*, ed. W. A. Hammond (1910); 'Poplar and the Labour Party: a defence of Poplarism', *Lab. Mon. 2* (June 1922) 383–91; 'Tom Mann', *Plebs 15* (Dec 1923) 534–6; 'Socialist', *English Rev. 38* (Feb 1924) 158–66; 'All aboard for Birmingham', *Labour Mag. 7* (Oct 1928) 245–9; 'The Message of May Day', *Labour Mag. 12* (June 1933) 59–62; 'These Great Men came to Power – but what have they done?' *Labour 1* (Sept 1933) 6–7; 'My Comrade, Will Thorne', *Labour 1* (July 1934) 250; 'Anti-Semitism in the East End', *Spec. 157*, 24 July 1936, 133–4.

Sources: (1) MSS: Lansbury papers, LSE; Webb Coll., LSE. (2) Lansbury's own biographical reminiscences (for which see above) must be supplemented by Raymond Postgate's authorised and full biography, *The Life of George Lansbury* (1951). Family recollections are to be found in Edgar Lansbury's *My Father* (1933) and in two articles by Daisy Postgate 'A Child in George Lansbury's House', *Fortnightly 164* (Nov 1948) 315–22 and (Dec 1948) 390–4. There is an appraisal in Margaret Cole, *Makers of the Labour Movement* (1948) 268–87. (3) *See also:* Evidence before R.C. on the Aged Poor Vol. III 1895 XV Qs 13697–14053; *Labour Annual* (1896; 1897; 1898); R.C. on Poor Law 1909 XXXVII; A.F.B. [A. Fenner Brockway] 'Life Story of Mr George Lansbury', *Christian Commonwealth*, 12 Jan 1910; *East London Observer*, 24 Sep 1910; *Dod* (1912); 'Mr Smillie and Mr

Lansbury: will they clear their characters?' *Spec. 125*, 4 Sep 1920, 292-3; M. Fels, *Joseph Fels His Life-Work* (1920); *Who's Who in the New Parliament*, ed. T. W. Walding (1922); S. V. Bracher, *The Herald Book of Labour Members* (1923); *Dod* (1923); C. J. Sheridan, 'Creatures of Circumstance no. 2, Mr George Lansbury', *Outlook*, 21 June 1924; C. Langdon Everard, 'Mr George Lansbury, MP. The John Bull of Poplar', in *The Book of the Labour Party, 3* ed. H. Tracey [1925] 309-317; *Labour Who's Who* (1927); *An Admirer of Lenin: Mr George Lansbury. . . . Chairman of the Labour Party in 1928* [1929] 51 pp.; E. Wertheimer, *Portrait of the Labour Party* (1929); *WWW* (1929-50); 'Uncle George', *Sat. Rev. 149*, 1 Mar 1930, 253-4; *DNB* (1931-40) [by M. A. Hamilton]; E. S. Pankhurst, *The Suffragette Movement* (1931); 'George Lansbury', *Sat. Rev. 155*, 21 Jan 1933, 67; P. Snowden, *An Autobiography*, 2 vols (1934); *Labour Party Annual Report* (1935); 'Occasional biographies: Mr Lansbury', *Spec. 155*, 4 Oct 1935, 499; G. D. H. Cole and R. W. Postgate, *The Common People 1746-1938* (1938; rev. ed. 1946: 4th ed. 1949); M. A. Hamilton, *Arthur Henderson* (1938); Watchman, *Right Honourable Gentlemen* (1939); F. Brockway, *Socialism over Sixty Years: the life of Jowett of Bradford (1864-1944)* (1946); G. D. H. Cole, *History of the Labour Party from 1914* (1948); idem, *Short History of the British Working Class Movement* (1948); *The British Labour Party: its history, growth, policy and leaders*, 3 vols, ed. H. Tracey (1948); B. Webb, *Our Partnership* ed. B. Drake and M. I. Cole (1948); M. I. Cole, *Growing up into Revolution* (1949); E. Estorick, *Stafford Cripps* (1949); *Beatrice Webb's Diaries 1912-1924*, ed. M. I. Cole (1952); G. G. Eastwood, *George Isaacs* (1952); T. Johnston, *Memories* (1952); H. Nicolson, *King George the Fifth: his life and reign* (1952); C. R. Attlee, *As it happened* (1954); H. A. Clegg, *General Union: a study of the National Union of General and Municipal Workers* (Oxford, 1954); J. McNair, *James Maxton: the beloved rebel* (1955); *Beatrice Webb's Diaries 1924-1932*, ed. M. Cole (1956); G. D. H. Cole, *Socialist Thought: The Second International 1889-1914*, 2 vols (1956, repr. 1967); S. R. Graubard, *British Labour and the Russian Revolution 1917-1924* (1956); H. Dalton, *The Fateful Years: memoirs 1931-1945* (1957); F. Bealey and H. Pelling, *Labour and Politics 1900-1906* (1958); G. D. H. Cole, *Socialist Thought: Communism and Social Democracy 1914-31* 2 vols (1958-60, repr. 1969); A. Bullock, *The Life and Times of Ernest Bevin, 1: 1881-1940* (1960); H. Morrison, *An Autobiography* (1960); R. J. Minney, *The Private Papers of Hore-Belisha* (1960); D. Sommer, *Haldane of Cloan: his life and times 1856-1928* (1960); C. Tsuzuki, *H. M. Hyndman and British Socialism* (Oxford, 1961); M. Foot, *Aneurin Bevan: a biography* (1962); A. M. McBriar, *Fabian Socialism and English Politics 1884-1918* (1962, repr. 1966); G. Blaxland, *J. H. Thomas: a life for unity* (1964); Lord Citrine, *Men and Work: an autobiography* (1964); R. E. Dowse, *Left in the Centre: the Independent Labour Party 1893-1940* (1966); T. Jones, *Whitehall Diary*, 2 vols (1969); K. Middlemas and J. Barnes, *Baldwin: a biography* (1969); K. D. Brown, *Labour and Unemployment* (Newton Abbot, 1971); M. Cole, *The Life of G. D. H. Cole* (1971); M. Cowling, *The Impact of Labour 1920-1924: the beginning of modern British politics* (Cambridge, 1971); P. Rowland, *The Last Liberal Governments: unfinished business* (1971). OBIT. *Times*, 8 May 1940; J. J. Mallon, 'Man of the People', *Spec. 164*, 10 May 1940, 656; *New Statesman and Nation 19*, 11 May 1940, 614; *East London Observer*, 11 and 18 May 1940; *Reynolds News*, 12 May 1940; *Labour Party Report* (1940).

See also: Reginald Clifford ALLEN; *Clement Richard ATTLEE, for British Labour Party, 1931-51; *Richard Stafford CRIPPS; William CROOKS; †Arthur HENDERSON, for British Labour Party, 1914-31; *Herbert MORRISON; Daisy POSTGATE; Raymond William POSTGATE; and below: British Labour Party, 1900-13.

British Labour Party, 1900-13:

(1) MSS: Cole Coll., and Fabian Society archives, Nuffield College, Oxford; Herbert

Gladstone papers, BM; J. Keir Hardie correspondence and other papers formerly in the custody of Mr Francis Johnson, ILP, now being catalogued by Mr R. Bruce Aubry at Bristol but not yet available (1973) for research; Henderson and LRC papers, Labour Party archives; Lansbury papers, LSE; J. Ramsay MacDonald papers, LSE and in the possession of the family; Webb Coll., LSE; and see also lists in H. Pelling, *The Origins of the Labour Party 1880–1900* (1954, 2nd ed. 1965), F. Bealey and H. Pelling, *Labour and Politics 1900–1906* (1958) and A. M. McBriar, *Fabian Socialism and English Politics, 1884–1918* (1962).

(2) **Theses:** D. Good, 'Economic and Political Origins of the Labour Party from 1884–1906' (London PhD, 1937); W. L. Guttsman, 'A Study of the Social Origins and Character of British Political Leaders, 1886–1936' (London MSc, 1950); E. J. Hobsbawm, 'Fabianism and the Fabians 1884–1914' (Cambridge PhD, 1950); D. W. Crowley, 'The Origins of the Revolt of the British Labour Movement from Liberalism, 1875–1906' (London PhD, 1952); J. Bonner, 'The British Labour Party' (Liverpool MA, 1954); D. Cox, 'The Rise of the Labour Party in Leicester' (Leicester MA, 1959); P. R. Thompson, 'London Working-Class Politics and the Formation of the London Labour Party 1885–1914' (Oxford, DPhil., 1964); D. M. Chewter, 'The History of the Socialist Labour Party of Great Britain from 1902 until 1921 with Special Reference to the Development of its Ideas' (Oxford BLitt., 1966); K. O. Fox, 'The Emergence of the Political Labour Movement in the Eastern Sector of the South Wales Coalfield, 1894–1910' (Wales, Aberystwyth, MA, 1966); G. B. Woolven, 'Publications of the Independent Labour Party 1893–1932' (Bibliography for London Univ. Diploma in Librarianship, 1966 [copy in Brynmor Jones Library, Hull Univ.]); M. Warner, 'The Webbs: a study of the influence of intellectuals in politics (largely between 1889 and 1918)' (Cambridge PhD, 1967); R. S. Barker, 'The Educational Policies of the Labour Party, 1900–1961' (London PhD, 1968); B. J. Atkinson, 'The Bristol Labour Movement, 1868–1906' (Oxford DPhil, 1969); K. J.

Dean, 'Parliamentary Elections and Party Organisations in Walsall 1906–45' (Birmingham MA, 1969); R. I. McKibbin, 'Evolution of a National Party: Labour's political organisation, 1910–24' (Oxford DPhil., 1970); J. M. Winter, 'The Development of British Socialist Thought 1912–18' (Cambridge PhD, 1970); R. K. Alderman, 'Discipline in the Parliamentary Labour Party from the formation of the Labour Representation Committee in 1900 to 1964' (London PhD, 1971); R. Davidson, 'Sir Hubert Llewellyn Smith and Labour Policy 1886–1916' (Cambridge PhD, 1971); L. B. Simpson-Holley, 'The Attitude of British Labour Members of Parliament towards the Empire, 1895–1914.' (Southampton PhD, 1971).

(3) **Reference Works:** *McCalmont's Parliamentary Poll Book: British Election Results 1832–1918* (1879; eighth ed. with Introduction and additional material, ed. J. Vincent and M. Stenton, Brighton, 1971); *Labour Annual*, 1895–1900 subsequently *Reformers' Year Book*, 1901–9 (Repr. Brighton, 1971); *Dod* (1900–13); LRC, *The Labour Party Foundation Conference and Annual Conference Reports 1900–1905* (Repr. 1967); LRC and Labour Party, *Annual Reports*, 1906–13; The Times, *House of Commons 1910: with brief biographies of members and full details of the polls* (1910); Pall Mall Gazette Extra, *The New House of Commons 1911: 'mems' about members, 600 portraits and caricatures* (Jan 1911); J. Stammhammer, *Bibliographie der Social-Politik*, Band II *1895–1911* (Jena, 1912); S. V. Bracher, *The Herald Book of Labour Members* (1923); C. A. Gulick, R. A. Ockert and R. J. Wallace, *History and Theories of Working-Class Movements: a bibliography* [1955]; U. Fedeli, *Storia del Movimento Operaio: bibliografia* (Centro di Sociologia della Cooperazione, Milano, 1958); J. Brophy, 'Bibliography of British Labour and Radical Journals, 1880–1914', *Labor History 3* (1962) 103–26; D. W. Butler and J. Freeman, *British Political Facts 1900–1960* (1963, 3rd ed. (to 1968), 1969); *Labour Party Bibliography* (1967); World Microfilms Publications, *Check List of British Labour History Ephemera 1900–1926* [1971].

(4) **The most important secondary works**

(excluding most biographical works) are: A. W. Humphrey, *A History of Labour Representation* (1912); G. D. H. Cole, *The World of Labour* (1913, 4th ed. 1928); M. Beer, *A History of British Socialism* (1920); *The Book of the Labour Party: its history, growth, policy, and leaders*, 3 vols ed. H. Tracey [1925]; E. Halévy, *A History of the English People, 5: Imperialism and the rise of Labour 1895–1905* (1926, 2nd ed. 1952) and *6: The Rule of Democracy* (1905–1914) (1932: paperback 1961); G. D. H. Cole, *British Working Class Politics, 1832–1914* (1941); *The British Labour Party*, 3 vols ed. H. Tracey (1948); H. Pelling, *The Origins of the Labour Party 1880–1900* (1954, 2nd ed. 1965) [with an excellent bibliography]; R. T. McKenzie, *British Political Parties* (1955, 2nd ed. 1963) [with bibliography]; J. H. S. Reid, *The Origins of the British Labour Party* (Univ. of Minnesota Press, 1955); F. Bealey and H. Pelling, *Labour and Politics 1900–1906: a history of the Labour Representation Committee* (1958); G. D. H. Cole, *A History of Socialist Thought 3*, pt 1: *The Second International 1889–1914* (1958, 3rd repr. 1969); P. P. Poirier, *The Advent of the Labour Party* (1958); R. Miliband, *Parliamentary Socialism: a study in the politics of labour* (1961; new ed. 1973); A. M. McBriar, *Fabian Socialism and English Politics, 1884–1918* (1962); H. Pelling, *Social Geography of British Elections 1885–1910* (1967); P. Thompson, *Socialists, Liberals and Labour: the struggle for London 1885–1914* (Studies in Political History, 1967); R. Gregory, *The Miners and British Politics 1906–1914* (Oxford, 1968); *The Social and Political Thought of the British Labour Party*, ed. F. Bealey (1970).

(5) **See also**: W. Sanders, *The Political Reorganisation of the People* (1902); J. Burns, *Labour and Free Trade* (1903) 19 pp.; *Modern Socialism*, edited with an Introduction by R. C. K. Ensor (1903, 3rd ed. 1910); J. B. Glasier, *Labour: its politics and ideals* [1903] 15 pp.; Anon., 'Labour Members and Liberals', *Sat. Rev. 96*, 1 Aug 1903, 133–4; J. K. Hardie, 'Federated Labor as a New Factor in British Politics', *N. Amer. Rev. 177* (Aug 1903) 233–41; idem (with

others), *Labour Politics: a symposium* (1903) 16 pp.; H. M. Hyndman et al., *Liberalism and Labour* [1903?] 19 pp.; Anon., 'Labour and its Leaders', *Sat. Rev. 98*, 10 Sep 1904, 321–2; P. Snowden, 'The Labour Party and the General Election', *Ind. Rev. 6* (Aug 1905) 132–46; W. Crooks, 'The Prospects and Programme of the Labour Party', *Nat. Rev. 46* (Dec 1905) 621–32; J. Burgess et al., *What Labour wants* [1905] 16 pp.; W. Diack, 'The British Labor Party; its aims and aspirations', *Arena 35* (1905) 476–80; G. W. Kitchin, *A Letter to the Labour Party: thoughts on the future of labour* (1905) 38 pp.; J. R. MacDonald, *The Labour Party* [1905] 16 pp.; J. C. Wedgwood and T. B. Greig, *Should the Labour Party unite with the Liberals?: a debate* (repr. from *Staffordshire Sentinel*, [1905?]); Anon., 'Liberals and the Labour Party', *Sat. Rev. 101*, 20 Jan 1906, 69–70; J. K. Hardie, 'Labour at the Forthcoming Election', *19th C. 59* (Jan 1906) 12–24; H. Vivian, 'Pretended Labour Parties', *Fortn. Rev. 85* (Jan 1906) 151–62; J. K. Hardie, 'The Labour Party: its aims and policy', *Nat. Rev. 46* (Feb 1906) 999–1008; J. R. MacDonald, 'The Labour Party and its Policy', *Ind. Rev. 8* (Mar 1906) 261–9; H. Seton-Karr, 'The Labour Party – A Unionist View', *19th C. 59* (Mar 1906) 471–82; P. Snowden 'The New Power in Politics', *20th C. Q. 1*, no. 1 (Apr 1906) 46–55; C. Roberts, 'The Labor Party in England', *World's Work 12* (June 1906) 7668–72; W. H. Mallock, 'The Political Powers of Labour: their extent and their limitations', *19th C. 60* (Aug 1906) 202–14; idem, 'The Intellectual Conditions of the Labor Party', *Mon. Rev. 25* (Oct–Dec 1906) 9–24, 25–34, 1–19; P. Snowden, 'Socialism in the House of Commons', *Edin. Rev. 204* (Oct 1906) 273–305; L. A. Atherley-Jones, 'The Story of the Labour Party', *19th C. 60* (1906) 576–86; J. K. Hardie, 'The Labour Movement', ibid., 875–82; C. Noel, *The Labour Party: what it is and what it wants* (1906); H. Morgan-Browne, 'Problems of Labour: the Labour Party', *Fortn. Rev. 86* o.s. (1906) 916–24; J. K. Hardie, *The Labour Party* (Madras, 1907) 18 pp.; R. Hunter, 'The Congress of the British Labor Party',

Int. Soc. Rev. 7 (Mar 1907) 513–27; A. Wollerton, *The Labour Movement in Manchester and Salford* (Manchester ILP Branch Pamphlets, no. 1: Manchester, 1907); J. R. MacDonald, 'Socialism and the Labour Party', *Soc. Rev. 1* (Mar 1908) 13–23; W. Temple, 'The Church and the Labour Party: their ideals', *Econ. Rev. 18* (Apr 1908) 190–202; S. G. Hobson, 'The Socialist Policy', *New Age, 3* n.s. 4 and 11 July 1908, 188–9 and 209–10; E. Porritt, 'The British Socialist Labour Party', *Pol. Sc. Q. 23* (Sep 1908) 468–97; G. R. S. Taylor, 'The New Labour Party', *New Age 3* n.s. 3 Oct 1908, 444; V. Grayson, 'Socialism and Labor in Great Britain', *Int. Soc. Rev. 9* (Mar 1909) 660–8; R. Hunter, 'The British Labor Party – A Reply', [reply to V. Grayson] ibid., (Apr 1909) 753–64; J. K. Hardie, 'The British Labor Party', ibid., *10* (May 1909) 985–8; M. Beer, 'The Labour Party and the Portsmouth Conference', *Soc. Rev. 3* (Apr 1909) 148–57; H. M. Hyndman, 'Socialism and Labourism in England', *Int. Soc. Rev. 10* (Oct 1909) 351–3; W. Thompson, 'The Position of the British Labor Party', ibid., (Nov 1909) 418–21; F. H. Rose, *The Coming Force: the Labour Movement* (ILP Salford, 1909); K. Kautsky, 'The British Labour Party', *Soc. Rev. 5* (May 1910) 223–40; R. Robinson, 'The Labour Party and Class Politics', ibid., (June 1910) 313–16; H. Quelch, 'B.L.P.', *Int. Soc. Rev. 11* (July 1910) 17–19; J. Koettgen, 'Let us reform the Labour Party', *Soc. Rev. 6* (Dec 1910) 289–301 and J. R. MacDonald, 'A Rejoinder', ibid., 301–5; J. R. Clynes, *Laws to smash the Labour Party* (Manchester, [1910?]) 15 pp.; L. Hall et al., *Let us reform the Labour Party: a protest and appeal* (Manchester, 1910) 16 pp.; E. Porritt, 'The British Labor Party in 1910', *Pol. Sc. Q. 25*, no. 2 (June 1910) 297–316; W. Thompson, *A. Victor Grayson, M.P.: an appreciation and a criticism* (Huddersfield, 1910); H. Cox, 'The Despotism of the Labour Party', *19th C. 70* (July 1911) 187–200; idem, 'The Danger ahead', ibid., (Sep 1911) 414–27; *Official Report of the Socialist Unity Conference held at Caxton Hall, Chapel St, Salford on Saturday, September 30th and Sunday, October 1st 1911* [1911] 32 pp.; D.

L. George, *The People's Insurance* (1911) P; J. R. MacDonald, *The Socialist Movement* (1911); S. Skelhorn, *Socialist Fables: a reply to the case for the Labour Party* (1911) 11 pp.; F. W. Jowett, 'Discussion: Socialism and the Cabinet System', *Soc. Rev. 9* (Apr 1912) 153–60; T. Rothstein, 'What of the British Labor Party', *Int. Soc. Rev. 13* (Dec 1912) 488–94; H. M. Hyndman, *Further Reminiscences* (1912); G. S. Penfold, *The Labour Party under a Searchlight* (1912) 32 pp.; Bishop Welldon, 'The Church and the Labour Party', *19th C. 73* (May 1913) 943–59; E. R. Pease, *History of the Fabian Society* (1916, 2nd ed. 1925); T. Mann, *Tom Mann's Memoirs* (1923); F. W. Soutter, *Recollections of a Labour Pioneer* (1923); T. F. Tsiang, *Labor and Empire: a study of the reaction of British Labor, mainly as represented in Parliament, to British Imperialism since 1880* (New York, 1923); J. K. Hardie, *Speeches and writings, from 1888–1915* [1925?]; A. Shadwell, *The Socialist Movement, 1824–1924, pt 1 : The First and Second Phases 1824–1914* (1925); W. Thorne, *My Life's Battles* [1925]; J. Clayton, *The Rise and Decline of Socialism in Great Britain, 1884–1924* (1926); W. S. Sanders, *Early Socialist Days* (1927); S. Bryher, *An Account of the Labour and Socialist Movement in Bristol* (repr. and published by *Bristol Labour Weekly*, 1929–1931); A. Plummer, *Labour's Path to Power* [1930]; P. Snowden, *An Autobiography*, 2 vols (1934); C. R. Attlee, *The Labour Party in Perspective* (1937); J. R. Clynes, *Memoirs, 1869–1924*, 2 vols (1937); J. H. Thomas, *My Story* (1937); C. F. Brand, *British Labour's Rise to Power* (California, 1941); R. C. K. Ensor, *England, 1870–1914* (Oxford, 1941); R. Redmayne, *Men, Mines and Memories* (1942); F. Brockway, *Socialism over Sixty Years: the life of Jowett of Bradford* (1946); G. D. H. Cole, *Short History of the Working-Class Movement* (1948); M. I. Cole, *Makers of the Labour Movement* (1948); B. Webb, *Our Partnership*, ed. B. Drake and M. I. Cole (1948); F. Williams, *Fifty Years' March: the rise of the Labour Party* (1949); Labour Party, *Marching on, 1900–1950: the golden jubilee of the Labour Party* (1950) 16 pp.; J. A. Yates, *Pioneers to*

Power: in celebration of the fiftieth anniversary of the Labour Representation Committee, Feb 1900 (1950); G. R. Shepherd, *Labour's Early Days* (Tillicoultry, 1950) 48 pp.; F. Williams, 'The Program of the British Labour Party: an historical survey', *J. of Politics 12* (May 1950) 189–210; G. D. H. Cole, *British Labour Movement – retrospect and prospect: Ralph Fox memorial lecture, April 1951* (1951) 20 pp.; *Beatrice Webb's Diaries 1912–1924*, ed. M. I. Cole (1952); H. Dalton, *Call back Yesterday: memoirs 1887–1931* (1953); S. Maccoby, *English Radicalism 1886–1914* (1953); *The Challenge of Socialism*, ed. H. Pelling (1954); F. Bealey, 'The Electoral Agreement between the Labour Representation Committee and the Liberal Party', *J. of Modern Hist. 28* (1956) 353–73; Labour Party, *Voice of the People: commemorating the jubilee of the Parliamentary Labour Party, 1906–1956* (1956) 21 pp.; A. L. Morton and G. Tate, *The British Labour Movement, 1770–1920: a history* (1956); H. Pelling, *America and the British Left: from Bright to Bevan* (1956); F. Bealey, 'Keir Hardie and the Labour Group', *Parliamentary Affairs 10* (1956–7) 81–93, 220–33; M. Cole, *The Story of Fabian Socialism* (1961); H. Pelling, *A Short History of the Labour Party* (1961); C. Tsuzuki, *H. M. Hyndman and British Socialism*, (Oxford, 1961); W. L. Guttsman, *The British Political Elite* (1963); E. Shinwell, *The Labour Story* (1963); K. O. Fox, 'Labour and Merthyr's Khaki Election of 1900', *Welsh Hist. Rev. 2* (1964–5) 351–66; C. F. Brand, *The British Labour Party: a short history* (Oxford, 1965); I. Bulmer-Thomas, *The Growth of the British Party System 1: 1640–1923* (1965); K. O. Fox, 'The Merthyr Election of 1906', *National Library of Wales J. 14* (1965–6) 237–41; B. B. Gilbert, *The Evolution of National Insurance in Great Britain: the origins of the Welfare State* (1966); W. T. Rodgers and B. Donoughue, *The People into Parliament: an illustrated history of the Labour Party* (1966); A. Marwick, 'The Labour Party and the Welfare State in Britain, 1900–1948', *Amer. Hist. Rev. 73* (1967) 380–403; C. Rover, 'The Labour Party' in *Women's Suffrage and Party Politics in Britain* (1967) 146–69; E. P. Wilmot, *The Labour Party: a short history* (1968); R. Barker, 'The Labour Party and Education for Socialism', *Int. Rev. Social Hist. 14* (1969) 22–53; G. R. Smith, *The Rise of the Labour Party in Great Britain* (1969); R. I. McKibbin, 'James Ramsay MacDonald and the Problem of the Independence of the Labour Party', *J. of Modern Hist. 42* (1970) 216–35; C. Parry, *The Radical Tradition in Welsh Politics: a study of liberal and labour politics in Gwynedd, 1900–1920* (University of Hull, 1970); H. S. Weinroth, 'The British Radicals and the Balance of Power 1902–14', *Hist. J. 13* (1970) 653–82; J. A. Garrard, *The English and Immigration, 1880–1910* (Oxford Univ. Press, 1971); R. Barker, *Education and Politics, 1900–1951: a study of the Labour Party* (Oxford, 1972).

LAWSON, John James
(Lord Lawson of Beamish) (1881–1965)
MINERS' LEADER AND LABOUR MINISTER

'Jack' Lawson as he preferred to be called, was born at Whitehaven on 16 October 1881, and christened John James after his father. His mother, Elizabeth (née Savage), was a very dominant woman whom Lawson remembered as stern and quick-tempered, and strong enough to wrestle with poverty in order to feed and clothe her ten children. The father was a mariner in the merchant service and came of a seafaring family, but he also worked for periods as a coalminer, and was known as a good pitman. At the early age of three Lawson began his education, in the local National school. The family moved to the village of Flimby, between Maryport and Workington, and after a year, when Lawson was nine, they moved to Boldon in Durham. Leaving school when he became twelve years old, he began work as a trapper at Boldon Colliery which was some four miles north-west of Sunderland and was then owned by the Harton Coal Company. There he worked a ten-hour day, for which he received tenpence. After a few months he was promoted to driver with charge of a pony, and by the time he had been working in the mine for eleven years, he had passed through every class of work from the shaft to the coal face.

During these early years Lawson extended his elementary education by voracious reading; before he was twenty-one he had carefully read Gibbon's *Decline and Fall*, and this love of books was to continue for the rest of his life. Though he remembered the 'Three Months' Strike' of 1892 in Durham, it was some years before Lawson became interested in politics; but at about the age of twenty he seriously adopted Wesleyan Methodism and soon became locally known as a preacher. At about the same time he began to read the *Labour Leader*, the *Clarion* and other socialist literature, and to speak regularly at meetings of his trade union branch. In 1904 he joined the ILP, and by regular purchases at a Newcastle bookshop extended his knowledge of industrial and social problems. He had begun working as a hewer in the same year, was soon elected as the hewers' assistant checkweighman, and became a member of the Miners' Lodge Committee. By the age of twenty-three Lawson considered himself a Socialist. He had achieved one ambition, to work on the coal face, and had gone a good way to realising another – that of becoming an educated man. Towards this latter end he started attending evening classes and, with others, organised an adult school. In 1906 he took a further step by going to Ruskin College, Oxford. He had married Isabella Scott in that year, and with her encouragement, and financial assistance from his parents and a local clergyman, together with the proceeds of selling their newly-acquired possessions, he was able to go to Ruskin. His wife worked as a domestic servant in Oxford during his two years at the College. In spite of a number of offers to enable him to stay longer and graduate, his intention was not to educate himself out of the ranks of the manual workers, and he preferred to return to mining.

Back in Durham, Lawson occupied himself with union affairs and was active as a speaker for the ILP. He was Pete Curran's agent at the January 1910 general election when Curran unsuccessfully defended the Jarrow parliamentary constituency which

he had won at a by-election in 1907. In 1911 Lawson was appointed checkweighman at a coalmine in West Pelton. In 1913 he was elected to the Durham County Council, on which he served for ten years, the last four as an alderman. During the First World War Lawson served as a driver in the Royal Artillery, and soon after he was demobilised he was adopted as a candidate for Parliament. Though unsuccessful in contesting the Seaham Division in the general election of 1918, at a by-election in the following year he was elected MP for Chester-le-Street, and continued to represent the constituency until he retired in 1949. Lawson was a member of the Labour Party's commission to Ireland in 1920, and was one of the delegates who visited Egypt in 1921 in connection with that country's independence negotiations. In the Commons he was much occupied with the pension problems of ex-Servicemen. When MacDonald was elected leader of the Parliamentary Labour Party in 1922, he appointed Lawson as one of his parliamentary private secretaries. The other was Attlee, and this was the beginning of a close and enduring friendship between the two men. There was a certain likeness in temperament between them and on many public issues their opinions were similar. In the Labour Government of 1924 Lawson served as financial secretary to the War Office.

Immediately after the 1926 General Strike, Lawson urged the Government to adopt a more conciliatory attitude towards the miners' leaders and he was very critical of government policy on the coal industry. He pressed the Government to utilise their powers to compel the owners to settle with the men, and demanded a reorganisation of the mining industry to achieve greater efficiency. He also condemned the action of the Minister of Health, Neville Chamberlain, in suspending the Chester-le-Street Guardians who refused to abide by the official regulations which precluded the giving of relief to single men. Although this Board of Guardians was not the most liberal in the country, it had, from the beginning of the dispute, insisted on making payments to unmarried miners who had no other source of income and the case received much publicity at the time [Mason (1967) 378–85].

In the second Labour Government, Lawson was parliamentary secretary to the Minister of Labour, Margaret Bondfield. At the general election of 1931, when a large number of Labour MPs were defeated, he kept his seat with a comfortable, though reduced, majority. In Parliament he spoke most frequently on questions concerning unemployment, particularly as they affected his mining constituency, which was part of a depressed area. The occasions when he spoke on foreign affairs were often connected with the interests of soldiers in the British Army. His political position was towards the centre of the Labour Party; he was a good example of the reformist and constitutionally-minded working man without militant attitudes, whose approach to social questions could indeed be justly said to owe more to Methodism than to Marxism.

In the 1930s Lawson did a certain amount of writing: his vivid autobiography, *A Man's Life*, appeared in 1932, and he also wrote biographies of Peter Lee and Herbert Smith. He visited Spain in 1938 along with Bevan, Shinwell and Tom Williams. From 1939 until 1944 he was the Deputy Regional Commissioner for Civil Defence, Northern Region, and during the war he travelled to Greece and China with parliamentary delegations. When he joined Attlee's Labour Cabinet in 1945 as Secretary of State for War, his object was to complete demobilisation as quickly and fairly as possible, and he believed it should be done on the 'first in – first out' principle. In September and October 1945, he explained the Government's policy to troops in Egypt, India, Singapore, and other countries, and when it was suggested that doctors should be released out of turn, Lawson threatened to resign. As a major re-organisation of defence was in hand, however, he stayed on at the War Office until it had been completed, and then offered his resignation, at the beginning of October 1946.

In 1949 he was the first working man to be made Lord Lieutenant for Durham, an office he held until 1958. He was a DCL of Durham University and a member of the Court of the University. In 1950 he was created a peer as Baron Lawson of Beamish. During his public career Lawson was also a member of the Imperial War Graves Commission, 1930–47; vice-chairman of the National Parks Commission, 1949–57; and was made a Privy Councillor in 1945. He held the decorations of Knight of the Order of St John of Jerusalem and the Order of the Brilliant Star with Grand Cordon (China).

In retirement, Lawson continued to live in the miners' cottage at Beamish, Co. Durham, where he had spent much of his adult life. He had maintained his early interest in Methodism and was a Wesleyan lay preacher for sixty years. There were three daughters of his marriage; an adopted son was killed in the Second World War. He died at Chester-le-Street General Hospital on 3 August 1965, and his funeral service took place at West Pelton Wesleyan Chapel. The obituary notice in the *Times* remarked that Lawson 'brought to high office in the service of state and country those qualities of sturdy self-respect, natural dignity, and robust vigour which flourish in the hardy mining communities of Durham'. A memorial service was held at Durham Cathedral on 13 September, when Lord Attlee was among those present. In his will Lawson left £3461 gross. Lady Lawson, herself active in social and political work, died in 1968, and was buried with her husband at the village churchyard in West Pelton.

Writings: *A Minimum Wage for Miners: answer to critics in the Durham Coalfields* (ILP Publications Department, n.d. [1912?]) 14 pp.; speech on the church and the labour movement printed in *Labour's Dynamic* (Labour Publishing Co., 1922) 34–8; 'Ebby Edwards', *Labour Mag.* 10 (Apr 1932) 530–533; *A Man's Life* (1932, new ed. 1944, ed. and abridged 1951) [an autobiography]; *Under the Wheels* (1934) [a novel]; *Peter Lee* (1936, revised ed. 1949 with foreword by C. R. Attlee); *Labour Fights for Workmen's Compensation* (The Labour Party, 1939) 8 pp.; *The Man in the Cap: the life of Herbert Smith* (1941); *Who Goes Home?* (1945) [broadcasts and sketches]; 'The

Discovery of Sidney Webb' in *The Webbs and Their Work* ed. M. Cole (1949) 187–98.

Sources: (1) MSS: papers in possession of the Hon. Mrs I. Lawson, Chester-le-Street; (2) Other: Labour Party, *Report of the Labour Commission to Ireland* (1921); S. V. Bracher, *The Herald Book of Labour Members* (1923); J. Lawson, *A Man's Life* (1932); R. Jenkins, *Mr Attlee: an interim biography* (1948); *Dod* (1949); R. Page Arnot, *The Miners in Crisis and War* (1961); Rev. Spencer Wade, 'The Pitman who became Lord Lieutenant of Durham', *Newcastle Evening Chronicle*, 27 Nov 1964; *WWW* (1965); A. Mason, 'The Miners' Unions of Northumberland and Durham, 1918–1931, with special reference to the General Strike of 1926' (Hull PhD, 1967); W. R. Garside, *The Durham Miners 1919–1960* (1971); personal information: the Hon. Mrs I. Lawson, daughter. OBIT. *Newcastle J.*, 4 Aug 1965; *Times*, 4 and 7 Aug 1965; *Newcastle Evening Chronicle*, 6 Aug 1965; *Labour Party Report* (1965).

JOYCE BELLAMY
DAVID E. MARTIN

See also: *Clement Richard ATTLEE, for British Labour Party, 1931–51; *Arthur James COOK, for Mining Trade Unionism, 1915–26; Peter LEE, for Mining Trade Unionism, 1927–34.

LEE, Peter (1864–1935)
MINERS' LEADER

Born on 20 July 1864 at Duff Heap Row, Fivehouses, Trimdon Grange, County Durham, Peter Lee was one of eight children of Thomas Lee, a miner whose father had also been a miner. Thomas Lee's grandfather had been a gipsy before settling down in Lancashire, and Thomas had been living in the same county before moving to Durham in the early 1860s. Peter's mother Hannah (née Simpson) was Thomas's second wife; she was an educated woman whose own father was a mill foreman, and she did much to broaden the minds of her family; in Peter's early years his father moved regularly between pits in Durham and Lancashire. Peter started work in a cotton mill near Oldham soon after his ninth year, in a part-time job, which also required his attendance at school for part of the week; but he disliked school, lost the job and went to work full time in a brickyard. His family returned to Durham when he was ten and he then started as a pony driver at the Littletown Colliery, Sherburn Hill. He was hewing coal when he was sixteen and a half, and between 1879 and 1886 his early nomadic existence continued, for he worked at fifteen different collieries in Cumberland, Durham and Lancashire. He was of strong physique and J. J. Lawson, in his biography of Lee, gave this vivid word picture: 'six-foot-one and a half, body steeled by hard labour, great straight-looking grey eyes set in a fine face, thick black hair curled round his cap' [Lawson (1949) 33].

In 1886 he left for America where he worked in mines in Ohio, Pennsylvania and Kentucky, but returned in the following year, disillusioned by working conditions and homesick. His experiences there, however, had widened his general outlook, and he began to attend miners' lodge meetings. He had already shown some organising ability and in 1887 was elected as a delegate of the Wingate Lodge to the Durham Miners' Association. He also attended evening classes, and on his marriage in 1888 was converted to Primitive Methodism. Before this event he had been a drinker but thereafter he became a teetotaller and non-smoker.

During the next few years he moved around various pits in Durham, and experienced some victimisation as a result of his union activities. In 1892 he was elected a checkweighman, but after four years, he left his wife and four children to seek his fortune in the gold mines of South Africa. As before when he had visited America, his stay abroad was short, and in 1897 he returned to Durham and began work at Thornley Pit. He settled down at last, took an increased interest in union meetings and continued to extend his early, somewhat meagre, education. His conversion to Primitive Methodism was now complete, and he became a popular local preacher.

In 1902 Lee was again appointed a check-weighman, and in the next two decades his rise to prominence in local and union affairs was rapid. The administrative ability and reforming zeal which became evident in his local government work undoubtedly shaped his subsequent career in mining trade unionism. He was a member of the Wingate School Board and in 1903 was elected to Wingate parish council; in 1907 he was elected to the Easington Urban District Council, and in 1909 became a Labour member of the Durham County Council. During the First World War he was District Food Controller in the Easington area and in 1919 was elected the first Labour chairman of Durham CC. He held this office until May 1921 and served again as chairman from May 1929 to May 1932: he continued as a member of the Council until March 1934. During his twenty-five years' service he played an important role in improving the living standards in Durham County, especially in the fields of education, housing, sanitation and water supplies. He was, for example, largely responsible for the formation of the Durham County Water Board.

It was shortly after the end of the First World War that Lee was appointed to an official position in the Durham Miners' Association. In 1915 he had been one of five candidates chosen for a ballot to elect a successor to John Wilson as agent of the DMA, but he was not successful on that occasion; in December 1919, however, he secured a majority of 31,938 votes over J. Gilliland, his nearest rival, and was appointed financial secretary of the DMA [Garside (1971) 73–4]. In the following year the Government failed to honour its pledges in the Sankey Commission Report concerning nationalisation, and the miners became dissatisfied with the Government proposal for wage increases based on higher output. Lee pressed for strike action; and when the Datum Line strike of October 1920 began, Durham miners were unanimous in their decision to cease work [Garside (1971) 126 ff.]. Lee represented the Durham miners on the MFGB executive on seven occasions between 1921 and 1934. In 1930, after the

death of W. P. Richardson, he became general secretary of the DMA and in 1931 served as vice-president of the MFGB. In the following year Lee reached the peak of his mining career: he was elected president of the MFGB and was at the same time chairman of the Miners' International Conference. In 1934 Peter Lee and J. A. Hall were chosen by the MFGB as their representatives at the Inquiry into the Gresford Colliery Disaster when 265 men and boys lost their lives.

By the standards of the inter-war years Lee was a moderate in Labour politics, although on occasion he could be severe in criticism. He commented in 1931 on the results of the scaremongering general election:

We are experiencing today what misrepresentation can do amongst people who have no convictions . . . The working people by this election, will recognize that the Liberals and Conservatives are dead against them and that they form one solid mass against Labour being in power in this country [Garside (1971) 342].

And in 1934, at the International Congress of Miners at Lille, Lee made a harsh attack upon Ramsay MacDonald, whose apostasy the Labour movement in the 1930s bitterly resented. After referring to the menace of Fascism in Europe, destroying 'the liberty of the common people' Peter Lee went on:

In my own nation we have a Prime Minister who once stood firm for justice and right, a man of the people. He now associates with those who wear fine raiment, live in castles and have always been the enemies of the people; and as we look round the nations of Europe we find others with similar or worse experience of trust and eventual betrayal [Arnot (1961) 196–97].

In the previous year, speaking as president of the MFGB, Lee had warned the Government of the danger of a national strike when it had refused to meet miners' representatives for discussions on a national wage for the industry. He was a strong opponent of district agreements: as he said at a meeting of miners at Ferryhill in November 1933:

War as a rule is a hard and cruel way of

settling disputes but there are times when injustice, poverty and hardship are worse to bear than to fight in endeavouring to remove those evils. We shall never again rest content under district agreements; if trouble comes I hope and trust that the miners of this country will join their strength in resisting the evil forces which are directed against them [Garside (1971) 252].

Apart from his local government and trade union activities, Lee continued his interest in the Primitive Methodist Church and for many years held a class for young men. He was also, for a time, president of Wheatley Hill Co-operative Society. When he had married Alice Thompson, a miner's daughter and childhood friend, to whom he owed much, he had been a rough man of little education, but he was an idealist with great physical and moral courage and with foresight – characteristics which brought him to the forefront of mining leadership in Durham. Although he was president of the MFGB in the last years of his life he was not, perhaps, of national stature. Evidence for this kind of statement is, as in this case, often impalpable, but some at least of his contemporaries seem to have had doubts when comparing him with other trade union leaders of his day. He was still DMA secretary at the time of his death, and to the end retained a very fine presence and an impressive manner of speech. He died on 16 June 1935 and, in accordance with his wish, was buried in Wheatley Hill Cemetery. No will has been located. As a tribute to his work for the people of Durham, his name is perpetuated in the new town of Peterlee.

Writings: 'The Mining Situation', *Labour Mag. 12* (May 1933) 11–14.

Sources: J. Lawson, *Peter Lee* (1936; rev. ed. 1949 with a Foreword by C. R. Attlee); R. Page Arnot, *The Miners in Crisis and War* (1961); W. R. Garside, *The Durham Miners 1919–1960* (1971); biographical information: Durham County Library; Clerk's Department, Durham CC; personal information: Dr R. Page Arnot. OBIT. *Times*, 17 June 1935; *Durham County Advertiser*, 21

June 1935 [photograph]; *Labour Party Report* (1935); NMA, *Monthly Circular* (1935).

JOYCE BELLAMY
VALERIE MASON

See also: *Arthur James Cook, for Mining Trade Unionism, 1915–26; and below: Mining Trade Unionism, 1927–44.

Mining Trade Unionism, 1927–44:

(1) **For MSS**, see individual biographical entries.

(2) **Theses:** W. J. Anthony-Jones, 'Labour Relations in the South Wales Coal Mining Industry, 1926–1939' (Wales PhD, 1959); J. E. Williams, 'The Political, Social and Economic Factors influencing the Growth of Trade Union Organisation amongst the Derbyshire Coal Miners 1880–1944' (Sheffield PhD, 1959); A. R. Griffin, 'The Development of Industrial Relations in the Nottinghamshire Coalfield 1550–1930' (Nottingham PhD, 1963); A. Mason, 'The Miners' Unions of Northumberland and Durham, 1918–31, with special reference to the General Strike of 1926' (Hull PhD, 1967); W. R. Garside, 'The Durham Miners' Association, 1919–1947' (Leeds PhD, 1969); M. W. Kirby, 'Aspects of the Coal-mining Industry in Great Britain in the inter-war period (1919–1939)' (Sheffield PhD, 1971).

(3) **Parliamentary Reports:** Board of Trade, *Report on the Working of the Mining Industry Act 1926*: 1928–9 VIII; 1929–30 XVI; 1930–1 XV; 1931–2 XXII; 1933–4 XIV; 1934–5 X; 1935–6 XIV; 1936–7 XIII; 1937–8 XIII; 1938–9 XIII; Coal Commission, *Report*: 1939–40 V; 1945–6 XIII; Departmental Committee on Miners' Welfare Fund, *Report*: 1932–3 XV; Coal Mines Reorganisation Commission, *Report*: 1933–1934 XIV; *Report of Special Enquiry into the Working of Overtime in Coal Mines in Lancashire*: 1933–4 XIV, *in Scotland*: 1934–1935 X; R. C. on Safety in Coal Mines, *Report*: 1938–9 XIII; *Coal Mines (War Levy) Scheme*: 1940–1 VIII; *Coal Mines Guaranteed Wage Levy*: 1940–1 VIII; 1941–1942 IX; *White Paper on Coal* (June 1942) Cmd 6364.

(4) **Secondary:** R. Page Arnot, 'The Miners'

Struggle and International Unity', *Lab.Mon.* 9 (Jan 1927) 36–45; A. Hutt, 'The Tactics of the Miners' Struggle', *Plebs 19* (Jan 1927) 11–15; C. F. G. Masterman, 'The Coal Conflict and after', *Cont. Rev. 130* (Jan 1927) 7–17; A. J. Cook, 'The Conflict of Ideas in British Trade Unionism', *Lab. Mon.* 9 (Feb 1927) 96–9; J. Hamilton, 'A Chapter in the Miners' Struggle', *Plebs 19* (Feb 1927) 53–5; A. Horner, 'The Need for One Mineworkers' Union', *Lab. Mon.* 9 (Mar 1927) 146–54; W. Lawther, 'One Miners' Union-now', *Plebs 19* (Apr 1927) 124–7; W. H. Wynne, 'The British Coal Strike and after', *J.P.E. 35* (June 1927) 364–389; J. A. Bowie, 'A New Method of Wage Adjustment in the Light of Recent History of Wage Methods in the British Coal Industry', *Econ. J. 37* (Sep 1927) 384–94; E. T. Good, 'Mines Nationalization', *Engl. Rev. 45* (Oct 1927) 408–11; W. Lee, *Commonsense about Coal* (Economic League, 1927) 8 pp.; Liberal Publication Department, *The Miners' Charter as adopted by the Grand Conference of Welsh Miners held at Cardiff on 17 December 1927 and based on the Coal and Power Policy of the Liberal Party* (1927) 4 pp.; G. Spencer, *The Trade Unions Bill vindicated by a Labour MP* (Anti-Socialist and Anti-Communist Union, 1927) P; TUC et al., *The Mining Situation, an Immediate Programme* [1927?] 18 pp.; A. Horner, 'The Significance of the Miners' March', *Lab. Mon.* 10 (Jan 1928) 23–30; W. Fox, 'Spencerism in Notts – A Non-Union Coal Field', *Soc. Rev. 27* (Mar 1928) 40–4; G. A. Hutt, '"Democracy" in the Scottish Miners' Union', *Lab. Mon. 10* (June 1928) 348–56; W. Gallacher, 'The Position in the Scottish Coalfield', ibid., (Nov 1928) 675–80; H. P. Carter, *The Problem of the Unemployed Miner and its Solution* (1928) 16 pp.; A. J. Cook, *The Efficiency of a Longer Working Day in British Coal Mines* (1928) 8 pp.; W. Hannington, *The March of the Miners: how we smashed the opposition* (National Unemployed Workers' Movement, 1928) 34 pp.; A. Horner and G. A. Hutt, *Communism and Coal*, pt 1: The Economic Situation of Coal Capitalism, pt 2: The Miners and their Struggle (1928); ILO, *Wages and Hours of Work in the Coal Mining Industry* (Studies

and Reports, ser. D, no. 18; Geneva, 1928); J. R. Raynes, *Coal and its Conflicts: a brief record of the disputes between Capital and Labour in the Coal Mining Industry of Great Britain* (1928); G. A. Hutt, 'Coal, Charity and the Class Struggle', *Lab. Mon. 11* (Mar 1929) 143–50; W. Allan, 'The Position of the Scottish Miners', ibid., (May 1929) 278–84; J. H. Jones, 'Organised Marketing in the Coal Industry', *Econ. J. 39* (June 1929) 157–71; J. Ancrum, 'The WIR [Workers' International Relief] in the Dawdon Lockout', *Lab. Mon. 11* (Sep 1929) 555–8; G. Williams, 'The Mining Situation', ibid., (Nov 1929) 686–93; I. Lubin and H. Everett, *The British Coal Dilemma* (New York, 1929); D. H. Macgregor, 'The Coal Bill and the Cartel', *Econ. J. 40* (1930) 35–44; D. F. Parsons, 'Finance Capital and the Coal Bill', *Lab. Mon. 12* (June 1930) 339–347; A. J. Cook, 'The Real Coal Problem', *Labour Mag. 10* (July 1931) 104–5; E. Shinwell, 'The Mines for the Nation', ibid. (Oct 1931), 260–1; E. Loughlin, 'The Miners' Fight for Seven Hours', *Lab. Mon. 14* (June 1932) 369–76; H. H. Merrett, *I fight for Coal* (1932); P. Lee, 'The Mining Situation', *Labour Mag. 12* (May 1933) 11–14; MFGB, *The Position of the Coal-Miner: the facts!* (1933) 36 pp.; J. H. Richardson, *Industrial Relations in Great Britain* (ILO, Geneva, 1933); A. M. Neuman, *Economic Organization of the British Coal Industry* (1934); H. M. Watkins, *Coal and Men: an economic and social study of the British and American Coalfields* (1934); Economic League, *The Miners' Campaign* (1935) 4 pp.; USA Bureau of Labor Statistics, 'Miners' Welfare Activities in Great Britain', *Mon. Labor Rev. 40* (May 1935) 1208–19; W. D. Stewart, *Mines, Machines and Men* [On the Condition of the Coal Industry] (1935); J. P. Dickie, *The Coal Problem: a survey: 1910–1936* (1936); W. L. Ellis, 'The Miners' Struggle in Notts', *Lab. Mon. 18* (Jan 1936) 34–9; W. Hannington, *Unemployed Struggles 1919–1936* (1936); J. J. Lawson, *Peter Lee* (1936); PEP, *Report on the British Coal Industry* (1936); M. Slater, *Stay Down Miner* [An Account of a Strike at Nine Mile Point Colliery] (1936); *The Miner's Two Bob*, ed. W. H. Williams (Labour Research

Dept, 1936); W. Prest, 'The Problem of the Lancashire Coal Industry', *Econ. J.* 47 (June 1937) 287–96; CPGB, *Free the Harworth Prisoners* (1937) 15 pp.; CPGB, *Notts united* (1937) 15 pp.; G. A. Hutt, *The Post-war History of the British Working Class* (1937); R. Kidd, *The Harworth Colliery Strike: a report to the executive committee of the National Council for Civil Liberties* (1937) 15 pp.; P. H. Massey, *Portrait of a Mining Town* (Fact no. 8, 1937); G. Orwell, *The Road to Wigan Pier* (1937); F. J. C. Hearnshaw, 'Moscow and the Miners', *Nat. Rev.* 110 (Feb 1938) 183–9; J. Jones, *Unfinished Journey* (1938); I. Thomas, 'Coal in the Commons', *Pol. Q.* 9 (Apr 1938) 226–37; B. L. Coombes, *These Poor Hands: the autobiography of a miner working in South Wales* (1939); idem, *I am a Miner* (Fact no. 28, 1939); idem, 'Twenty Tons of Coal', *New Writing*, 2nd ser., no. 3 (1939) 159–74; J. H. Jones et al., *The Coal Mining Industry: an international study in planning* (1939); W. Hannington, *Ten Lean Years* (1940); J. J. Lawson, *The Man in the Cap: the life of Herbert Smith* (1941); Board of Investigation into Coal Mining Industry, *The Immediate Wages Issue* (1942); A. L. Horner, 'Coal and the Nation's War Effort', *Lab. Mon.* 24 (June 1942) 180–4; T. Stephenson and H. Brannan, *The Miners' Case* (ILP, 1942) 18 pp.; Anon., 'Conciliation in the Mining Industry', *Labour* 5 n.s. (May 1943) 267–71; Anon., 'Coal Fields Conciliation', ibid. (July 1943), 335; Anon., 'Miners' Wages', *Lab. Mon.* 26 (Apr 1944) 114–19 and (May 1944) 146–50; D. R. Llewellyn, 'Why Miners Strike', *Left*, no. 90 (Apr 1944) 90–3; Anon., 'Miners move for a National Union', *Labour* 7 n.s. (Sep 1944) 14–16, 21; B. L. Coombes, *Those Clouded Hills* (1944); M. Heinemann, *Britain's Coal: a study of the mining crisis* (1944); A. Beacham, 'Efficiency and Organisation of the British Coal Industry', *Econ. J.* 55 (June-Sep 1945) 206–16; B. L. Coombes, *Miners Day* (1945); W. H. B. Court, 'Problems of the British Coal Industry between the Wars', *Econ. Hist. Rev.* 15, no. 1–2 (1945) 1–24; J. Jones, *Me and Mine: further chapters in the autobiography of Jack Jones* (1946); W. Gallacher, *The Rolling of the Thunder* (1947); G. D. H. Cole, *A History of the Labour Party from 1914* (1948); W. H. B. Court, *Coal* [History of the Second World War, U.K. Civil Ser.] (1951); W. Gallacher, *Rise like Lions* (1951); R. Page Arnot, vol. 2 *The Miners: years of struggle* (1953); H. A. Clegg, 'Some Consequences of the General Strike', *Trans of the Manchester Statistical Soc.* (Jan 1954) 1–29; W. A. Lee, *Thirty Years in Coal 1917–1947: a review of the coal mining industry under private enterprise* (1954); R. Page Arnot, *A History of the Scottish Miners* (1955); C. L. Mowat, *Britain between the Wars* (1955); E. D. Lewis, *The Rhondda Valleys* (1959); A. Bullock, *The Life and Times of Ernest Bevin*, vol. 1: 1881–1940 (1960); A. Horner, *Incorrigible Rebel* (1960); R. Page Arnot, vol. 3 *The Miners in Crisis and War* (1961); M. Foot, *Aneurin Bevan: a biography*, vol. 1: 1897–1945 (1962); A. R. Griffin, *The Miners of Nottinghamshire, 1914–1944: a history of the Nottinghamshire Miners' Unions* (1962); S. Pollard, *The Development of the British Economy 1914–1950* (1962); J. E. Williams, 'Labour in the Coalfields: a critical bibliography', *Bull. Soc. Lab. Hist.* no. 4 (Spring 1962) 24–32; idem, *The Derbyshire Miners* (1962); W. H. Chaloner, 'The British Miners and the Coal Industry between the Wars', *History Today* 14 (1964) 418–26; A. Moffat, *My Life with the Miners* (1965); A. J. P. Taylor, *English History 1914–1945* (Oxford, 1965); R. Skidelsky, *Politicians and the Slump* (1967); J. Griffiths, *Pages from Memory* (1969); A. Mason, *The General Strike in the North-East* (Univ. of Hull Occasional Papers in Economic and Social History, no. 3: 1970); W. R. Garside, *The Durham Miners 1919–1960* (1971); A. R. Griffin, *Mining in the East Midlands 1550–1947* (1971); W. Paynter, *My Generation* (1972).

LINDGREN, George Samuel
(Lord Lindgren of Welwyn Garden City)
(1900–71)
TRADE UNIONIST,
LABOUR COUNCILLOR AND MP

The son of George William Lindgren, a carpenter in the piano-making trade, and his wife, Emily Maud (née Hyam), George Samuel Lindgren was born on 11 November 1900 in Islington, London. His grandfather was a Swede who had settled in England in about 1870. George had an elementary education at the Hungerford Road Primary School, Holloway, and although he was an avid reader, at the age of thirteen he had to leave school and take a job. He obtained employment as a clerk in the civil engineer's office of the LNER at St Pancras, and continued to work as a railway clerk until 1945.

Becoming interested in political questions while a young man, Lindgren joined the Labour Party at the age of nineteen and served as secretary to the St Pancras branch of the ILP from 1923 to 1926. After his marriage to Elsie Olive Reed in July 1926 he set up home in Welwyn Garden City, and there soon became secretary of the Labour Party, holding the post until 1930 when he became, for three years, the honorary secretary of the St Albans divisional Labour Party. His membership of the Labour Party led to an active interest in local government. He was elected to Welwyn Garden City Urban District Council in 1927 and served until 1946; he led the Labour group on the Council and was its chairman in 1933–4. In 1931 he was the first Labour member to be elected to the Hertfordshire County Council and in 1939 was raised to the aldermanic bench. As the Council was Conservative-controlled, Lindgren did not hold any major posts, although he was for a short time in 1949 the chairman of its Civil Defence Committee. In that year he was not re-elected as an alderman, but in 1958 he again became a county councillor and in 1960 was once more created alderman, and remained so for the rest of his life. He became a JP for Hertfordshire in 1935 and later served as chairman of the Welwyn bench until his death. From 1942 until the end of the war he was Deputy Regional Commissioner for Civil Defence in the Midlands.

In parallel with this work in local politics, Lindgren was active in trade union affairs. He joined the Railway Clerks Association in 1918, served for many years as a branch officer, and sat on its national executive committee from 1933 to 1939 and 1942 to

1946. He was chairman of the London Trades Council from 1938 to 1942.

At the general election of 1935 he unsuccessfully contested Hitchin, a safe Conservative seat. Ten years later he entered the Commons as MP for Wellingborough at the general election, and was immediately appointed to office. From August 1945 to October 1946 Lindgren was Parliamentary Secretary to the Ministry of National Insurance. He was appointed in the same capacity to the Ministry of Civil Aviation where he continued until March 1950 when he became attached to the Ministry of Town and Country Planning, again as Parliamentary Secretary. In January 1951 this latter department was reorganised as the Ministry of Local Government and Planning, with Lindgren continuing to act as Parliamentary Secretary until the defeat of the Labour Government in October. The Minister, Hugh Dalton, found him 'very easy to work with, industrious, cheerful, sensible and loyal' [Dalton (1962) 351].

Lindgren's parliamentary interests included national insurance, local government and transport, and he was especially concerned with these during the years his party spent in opposition. But although these domestic matters were a chief area of activity, he travelled abroad on several occasions, visiting Russia, Poland and China in 1954 and undertaking a number of lecture tours in South America. His majority in the 1951 general election was reduced to 2201 and four years later he retained Wellingborough by only 926 votes; in 1959 he was narrowly defeated in a straight fight with the Conservative candidate.

In 1956 he had become treasurer of the Transport Salaried Staffs' Association and on losing his seat in Parliament he returned to work as a £800-a-year clerk with British Railways. In January 1961 he was created a life peer and resigned from his post with the TSSA. Following the election of a Labour Government in October 1964, Lindgren was appointed Parliamentary Secretary to the Ministry of Transport. He held this post until January 1966 when he moved, again as Parliamentary Secretary, to the Ministry of Power where he remained for only a few weeks until the general election. The Right Hon. Tom Fraser, Minister of Transport, provided the remarks which follow on Lindgren's political activities and attitudes:

I would say that George Lindgren's first love in his public life was his Trade Union, the Railway Clerks Association (RCA) which later became the Transport Salaried Staffs Association (TSSA) and was for many years its Treasurer.

When George Lindgren came to Parliament in 1945 it was quickly evident that he adopted in politics the careful middle of the road position which had been for long the attitude of the RCA. He never changed.

During the 1950s he never showed any sympathy towards the Bevanite faction in the Parliamentary Labour Party and indeed he could never quite understand why this group should so deliberately 'rock the boat'. He believed it to be of the utmost importance for the Labour Party to make the widest possible appeal to the community as a whole and the policies exemplified by leaders such as Attlee and Morrison seemed to George Lindgren to be essential to the success of the party. He never at any time supported any group within the Labour Party who could see advantage in pursuing policies which were claimed to be more socialistic than those acceptable to the majority if this meant being out of office. He always seemed to regard the objective in politics as that of winning power and being the Government of the day. He might even have carried this attitude a little too far in his own mind to the length that even his friends would have regarded George as being over-willing to trim Labour's policies when in Government in order to avert defeat at the polls in a subsequent election.

It follows from all this that he was a supporter of Hugh Gaitskell for whom he had a very high regard and, like so many others, he saw Hugh Gaitskell's death as a great tragedy for the Labour Party. At this point it is worth recording, however, that when Harold Wilson was elected to lead the Party George Lindgren very quickly adjusted himself to acceptance of the new leadership and I believe that he was just as loyal to Harold Wilson as to any former leader. Indeed it could be said of George Lindgren that loyalty to his Union, to the Labour Party and to the Leader for the time being was a condition of mind never to be questioned. It again follows from all this he never at any time went in for unilateralism [letter of 3 Oct 1972].

Lindgren's activities at both local and national level involved him in a variety of interests. These included his governorship of several local schools, while, from 1966 until his death, he was a deputy lieutenant for Hertfordshire. From the age of eighteen he had belonged to the St John's Ambulance Brigade and for several years he was a member of the national executive of the WEA. He was passionately fond of bowls and represented Hertfordshire and England. His other main recreation was swimming, and in all seasons he began each day with an early-morning bathe.

In the last years of his life, Lindgren was involved in difficulties connected with his work as a magistrate. Complaints by a defence solicitor against Lindgren were upheld by the High Court, and there was a good deal of adverse publicity (*Times*, 11 and 12 July, 24 and 25 Oct, 1 Nov, 5, 12 and 30 Dec 1969). Lindgren complained bitterly at the time that he was never allowed to represent his own case. On his death, however, a number of warm tributes were paid to him for his service on the Welwyn bench.

While on holiday in Majorca, he developed peritonitis and died on 8 September 1971 in hospital at Palma, where the funeral also took place. Lindgren, who belonged to no religious denomination, was survived by his wife and the only child of the marriage, Graham, who became an engineer. He left an estate valued at £5087.

Sources: C. Bunker, *Who's Who in Parliament* [1946]; *Dod* (1946–58); H. Dalton, *High Tide and After: memoirs 1945–1960* (1962); *WW* (1971); biographical information: Clerk to Hertfordshire CC; personal information: Mrs Mary G. Lindgren, Welwyn Garden City, daughter-in-law; the Rt Hon. Tom Fraser, Lanark. Obit. *Times, Welwyn Times* and *Hatfield Herald*, 10 Sep 1971; *Transport Salaried Staffs Journal* (Oct 1971).

DAVID E. MARTIN

See also: *Clement Richard ATTLEE, for British Labour Party, 1931–51.

LOCKWOOD, Arthur (1883–1966)
CO-OPERATOR, LABOUR AGENT,
EDUCATIONALIST

Lockwood was a Yorkshireman, born in Darnall, Sheffield, on 23 October 1883. He was the third son in a family of twelve. His father, William Lockwood, was born at Thurgoland near Penistone, and was the son of a Mr Coldwell and a Miss Lockwood who had married some time after William's birth. William attended the Penistone Grammar School until he was seventeen (most probably in the name of Coldwell), and was then apprenticed to wire-drawing, at a wire-mill owned by his uncle on the Lockwood side. For some unknown reason he left the mill and migrated to Sheffield, taking a job at Pickard's stone quarry, Handsworth. In due course he became a stone-dresser, and remained at the quarry until he was sixty. In Sheffield he lodged with a Mrs Rands (who had come to Sheffield from Spalding in Lincolnshire), and he married her daughter, at Darnall Church. It was probably at this time that he resumed the name of Lockwood.

Arthur Lockwood's early education was at an ordinary elementary school of the period, and he left school at fourteen to start his working life at Fisher Son and Sibray, nurserymen and seedsmen of Handsworth. (The firm existed until a few years ago.) After this he seems to have tried many different kinds of work. It was when he was employed at Hadfields Steel Foundry Co. Ltd as a pattern-maker that his spirit of unrest began to manifest itself and his fight for better conditions for his fellow-men started. He would hold meetings at the works gates, which did not please his employers and resulted in his dismissal from the firm. To earn a living he became an insurance agent for the Royal Liver Friendly Society.

In his early teens he joined the Darnall Congregational Church. Attached to this church was a branch of the Rechabites Temperance Friendly Society, in which he became an active member: he passed through all the various offices connected with it. To further his education he joined the Workers' Educational Association (the first WEA branch was formed at Reading in 1904) and about this time became active in local politics. In due course he joined the Independent Labour Party and then the Attercliffe Labour Party. For recreation, he was a member of a male-voice choir. He also wrote short plays, and any songs in them were written so that they could be set to the tune of 'The Red Flag'.

About this time he met his future wife, Ellen Keziah Drinkall of Goxhill, near Barton upon Humber. She was on a visit to an aunt who lived next door to the Lockwoods. An invitation to supper, followed next day by a visit to a Derbyshire beauty spot, resulted in their going next day to see his mother in order to introduce her as his future wife. Miss Drinkall, one of a family of fourteen, was the daughter of a police sergeant, whose family was Church of England and Conservative in politics; Lockwood by this time was an agnostic and a Socialist. But difficulties were overcome, they married, and remained a happy pair for the remainder of their lives.

The Attercliffe Labour Party had purchased two or three small shops, converting them into a small hall, with living accommodation. This work was largely carried out by volunteers, who included Lockwood, and it was here that he started his married life.

On 1 November 1912 Lockwood stood as a Socialist candidate for the Darnall ward of Sheffield, but was soundly beaten by the Liberal, C. H. Wilson, who afterwards joined the Labour ranks. In the general election of December 1918 he stood for Parliament for the Hillsborough constituency. He was defeated, the result being as follows:

A. Neal, Coalition Liberal   11,171
A. Lockwood, Co-operative Party   4,050

But by his work in this constituency he paved the way for A. V. Alexander (afterwards Lord Alexander of Hillsborough) to become the Labour member in 1922. Not long after the election Lockwood left Sheffield and came south to London to act as agent for Alfred Barnes, MP for East Ham South. This post was soon followed by his appointment as political organiser with the London Co-operative Society, in order to build up a strong Co-operative Party.

In 1922 the Reading Labour Party decided to appoint a full-time agent and Lockwood was the successful candidate. As was usual with this type of appointment, the agent had to help to provide his own salary. He was so successful in building up the Reading Party that in 1924 Reading elected its first Labour Member of Parliament in the person of Dr Somerville Hastings. In the same year Lockwood started the *Reading Citizen*, being both editor and circulation manager in its initial stages. This has been Reading's only Labour paper, and it ran for twenty-four years.

He soon became active in the local co-operative movement and was elected to the Reading Co-operative Society's Management Committee in 1937, remaining until 1959. On the resignation of the president, Councillor Harry ('Peggy') Wooldridge in 1947, Lockwood was elected to the presidency, a position he held until 1959. As the Labour agent he naturally wanted to be involved in local politics, and he attempted to get on the Town Council as early as 1923, but failed to do so.

When *Reynolds News* was purchased from Lord Dalziel by the co-operative movement in 1929 its circulation was very small for a national newspaper, and in 1930 Lockwood resigned his agent's post in Reading to take a position with the co-operative movement which culminated in his being made circulation manager for *Reynolds*. He remained in this post until he retired from full-time work in 1947.

The daily journey to London did not alter his wish to serve on Reading Town Council, and in 1932 he succeeded in winning Katesgrove ward (then a compact working-class ward) which he held till 1939. But the war period was a trying time and although he still remained president of the Co-operative Society as well as taking classes for the Workers' Educational Association, he dropped his Council work. He was co-opted on to the Town Council in 1944 but ill-health caused him to retire in 1945. On his retirement from *Reynolds* in 1947 he was appointed a member of the Southern Electricity Board, and served from 1948 until 1953. During the same period he was chairman of the Southern Electricity Consultative Council.

By 1954 he felt well enough to undertake Council work once again, and he was elected to the Council for Battle ward, representing it for four years. In 1956 he became Mayor of the Borough. He and Mrs Lockwood had a busy year of office, the great social event of the year being the visit of H.M. Queen Elizabeth II. After a civic reception the Queen went to open the first building to be built on the Whiteknights Park site for the University of Reading. Another busy year followed for the Lockwoods as Deputy Mayor and Mayoress. In 1958 he was elected to the alderman's bench, and the town gave him its highest award in making him a Freeman of the Borough. At a ceremony on 29 July 1958 an engrossed parchment in a wooden casket was presented to him – a well-deserved mark of the high esteem in which he was held by the people of Reading. At seventy-five he was entitled to rest on his laurels, and gradually dropped out of civic life.

In spite of the heavy duties entailed by his numerous posts in the 1940s – as circulation manager of *Reynolds News*, editor of the *Reading Citizen*, president of the Reading Co-operative Society, tutor for WEA classes, member of the Southern Electricity Board and president of the Southern Electricity Consultative Committee, he nevertheless found time and energy to write a book, published in 1949, on the history of co-operation in the Thames Valley. His recreations were gardening – the garden of his house at 308 Tilehurst Road, Reading, was beautifully kept – and walking, especially if it could be on the Berkshire Downs. In stature he was short and somewhat stocky in later years, with a rather high-pitched voice, which, however, carried well even in the open air in the days before the use of microphones.

Mr and Mrs Lockwood had one son John (Jack) now a civil servant, and one daughter, Margaret, who with her schoolmaster husband has returned to live in Yorkshire, in Huddersfield. The last few months of the Lockwood's life was spent together in an old people's home, situated across the park which his own house looked out on. He was somewhat saddened by the fact that many of the acquaintances he had made over his forty years in Reading seemed to have forgotten him, at a time when he would have welcomed their friendship. Mrs Lockwood died on Christmas Day 1965, aged seventy-eight, and Arthur Lockwood on 19 February 1966, in his eighty-third year. After a service at St Michael's Church, Tilehurst, he was cremated. No will has been located.

Writings: *Co-operation in the Thames Valley*, with a Preface by A. E. Hannay, secretary of the Reading Co-operative Society (Reading, 1949); many articles in the *Clarion* and the *Reading Citizen*, some under the pseudonym of Frank Coldwell.

Sources: A. Mansbridge, *An Adventure in Working-Class Education: being the story of the Workers' Educational Association 1903–1915* (1920); *Reading Standard*, 9 Dec 1960; biographical information: Reading Library; personal information: Miss Jane Lockwood, Sheffield, sister; J. A. Lockwood, Reading, son; Mrs D. Preston, Reading; and personal knowledge. Obit. *Reading Chronicle*, 25 Feb 1966.

FREDERICK C. PADLEY

See also: †Albert Victor ALEXANDER, for Co-operative Party; John (Jack) BAILEY; †William Henry BROWN; for Retail Co-operation, 1900–45; John Ernest JOHNS.

LONGDEN, Fred (1886–1952)
LABOUR AND CO-OPERATIVE MP

Born in humble surroundings at Ashton-under-Lyne on 23 February 1886, Fred Longden was the second eldest of seven sons of an iron-moulder, Harry Longden, and his wife, Elizabeth Ann (née Royle). They were clearly an able family: five of the sons became engineers, and the eldest, John, was also a sculptor of some competence. Because his father's search for work took him and his family to many towns, Fred attended a number of elementary schools until at the age of thirteen he took a job as a railway 'nipper' – apparently an errand and messenger boy. After a few months he became apprenticed to his father's craft, at which he remained for several years. In later life, Longden recalled that his father taught him 'the old Tory maxim of "Hard work and none of that reading for a good workman"', but that his mother, who had been a silk-weaver, encouraged him to take an interest in politics. At sixteen he entered the labour movement by helping to form the Irlam and Cadishead branch of the ILP, and later he played a prominent part in establish-a local trades council and debating society. He became a member of the co-operative movement at the age of twenty, and this began an active association which lasted for the rest of his life. He also took part in the work of the Friendly Society of Iron-founders; he joined the society in 1907, and though his membership lapsed in 1917, he re-entered at Birmingham in 1944, by which time it was the National Union of Foundry Workers.

During his youth, Longden was resolved to improve the meagre education he had received, and towards this end he attended WEA classes. This led, in 1912, to a recommendation from Manchester University and the WEA that he should receive a preparatory tutorship, and after attending Ruskin College, Oxford, in 1914 he was awarded the University's diploma, with distinction, in economic and political science. In 1913 Longden had won the Hodgson Pratt travelling scholarship, instituted a few years earlier as a memorial to Pratt's work for co-operation; the scholarship allowed him to travel to Belgium where he studied apprenticeship conditions in foundries. He published an account of his findings in 1915. In the course of supplementing his formal education, Longden also obtained the Manchester University certificate for tutorship and a first-class certificate for sociological studies under the Co-operative Union.

After the outbreak of war in 1914 Longden joined the Union of Democratic Control, which he helped to organise in the Birmingham area. A speech in which he appealed for immediate peace negotiations led to his arrest, and though offered exemption on the grounds of his trade and his health, he chose to refuse military service as a conscientious objector, for which he spent over two years in prison. After the war Longden resumed agitation for co-operative and socialist causes, which included speaking as a Clarion Vanner for several years. During the 1920s and 1930s he was a full-time lecturer and tutor in the WEA and did a considerable amount of speaking on behalf of the co-operative movement. He was an able public speaker and wrote a book on the art, to which Sir Cedric Hardwicke contributed an introduction. On the Left of the ILP, Longden co-operated with CPGB members in launching the *Sunday Worker*, which appeared for the first time in March 1925. The group to which Longden belonged was probably a minority within the ILP at that time, but it was sufficiently important to weigh as a factor with Clifford Allen when he resigned from the ILP in October 1925. Allen wrote to Maxton explaining that his position had been made 'exceedingly unpleasant' by the activities of Ayles, Sandham, Longden, and others, while Maxton's 'political irresponsibility' made it hopeless [Marwick (1964) 101]. In the General Strike, Longden, as a member of the National Council of the ILP, declared in the 4 July issue of the *Sunday Worker* that the Left should be united in making effective the policy of embargo on the handling of blackleg coal.

In 1922, 1923 and 1924 he unsuccessfully fought the Deritend division of Birmingham, was elected for the constituency in 1929,

only to be defeated again in 1931. In his maiden speech on 4 July 1929 he attacked the 'parasites' who exploited the workers, and later he was a severe critic of proposals to reduce unemployment benefits, stating on 28 September 1931 that the Government was 'expecting a man, woman and child to live a whole week in all their being upon as large a sum as Hon. Gentlemen opposite spent at a dinner or upon their pet dogs during the week'.

At the general election of 1935 Longden again unsuccessfully challenged the sitting member for Deritend, J. Smedley Crooke. In the Second World War he did some lecturing to members of the armed forces in his locality but the authorities ended this venture, Longden believed on account of his views on the war. At the Co-operative Party Conference in March 1940 he had moved an amendment (which was defeated) to the executive's 'pro-war' motion. He declared that he was unconditionally opposed to the war, describing it as 'a clash of rival imperialism' that could only bring misery to Europe. In 1945 the voters of Deritend returned Longden to Parliament with a substantial majority, and when the constituency was reorganised to become Small Heath, he continued to sit as a Labour and Co-operative MP. (He had first been sponsored as a Co-operative candidate in the 1924 election.) In the general elections of 1950 and 1951 he enjoyed the largest majority of all the Birmingham MPs. In the Commons, Longden continued to represent the ILP tradition and belonged to the Left of the Labour Party, being regarded by some critics as a 'fellow traveller'. In 1949 he was among the sixty-four Labour Members to receive a letter from Maurice Webb, the chairman of the PLP, and William Whiteley, the Government Chief Whip, warning them about their conduct towards the Party. This followed the expulsion of two MPs from the Party, and the dismissal of four parliamentary private secretaries for voting against the Government on the Ireland Bill. Longden was resolutely opposed to the partition of Ireland, and regarded Ulster as part of an oppressive British Empire. In 1950 he was vice-president of the League for Democracy in Greece, and he always took an active interest in the politics of that country. One well-known case that he campaigned for was on behalf of Mrs Betty Ambatielos, whose communist husband was imprisoned in Greece. He also remained anti-militarist, declaring in 1947 that the outstanding menace to world peace was neither Stalin nor Truman, but Churchill, and in March 1952 he was one of the fifty-seven Labour MPs who defied their leaders by forcing a division at the end of the defence debate.

The outspoken and uncompromising way in which Longden expressed his views meant that he was often a source of embarrassment to the leaders of his party. In the last few months of the Labour Government he answered an American critic in the pages of the *Daily Worker*, sending his letter to that paper when the *Daily Herald* refused to publish it: 'I do object', he wrote, 'to my country being used as a stationary air-deck for your bombers. Were war to come, which heaven forbid, it is my people, not yours, that would suffer the hellish effects.' As a rebel, he never had the opportunity of ministerial office but made his views known from the back benches inside the Commons and by writing and lecturing outside. The British co-operative movement has not been noted for producing militants but Longden was an exception, and his markedly left-wing opinions also embraced a commitment to the principles of co-operation. However, his efforts to shift the co-operative movement into a more socialistic position were for the most part met with indifference; his writings were regarded as obscure and his views as extreme.

Although as a young man he had for several years attended the Cadishead Protestant Church, and had been a member of the choir, in later life Longden regarded himself as a humanist. He once claimed to believe, like the philosopher T. H. Green, in the 'disinterested performance of self-imposed duties' and, while expressing admiration for Christ the man, he could be a hostile critic of organised religion.

During the 1951 Parliament Longden was able to take his seat in the House on only a few occasions, as his health was deterior-ating. For the last few weeks of his life he was confined to his home in Erdington, Birmingham, where from his bedroom he attempted to continue working; he died there on 5 October 1952.

Julius Silverman, who also became a Birmingham MP in 1945, has written of him: 'Fred Longden was a somewhat retiring man, and completely lacked the extrovert qualities which are usually characteristic of a member of Parliament. Fortunately his wife Alice provided these in a very marked degree for the purpose of contact with the constituents, electioneering, and social occasions' [letter of 30 Mar 1972]. He had married Alice, daughter of Robert Sherlock of Cadishead, in 1914. His wife was a JP and active in labour and co-operative politics in the City of Birmingham: she sat on the City Council for forty-two years, at first as a councillor for the St Bartholomew's ward of the Deritend division, and later as an alderman; she died on 22 July 1970. There was one child of the marriage, now Mrs Freda Longden-Parker, who worked as a hospital radiographer and has been a Labour councillor in Birmingham since 1958. Longden's funeral took place at Yardley Crematorium on 9 October. In his will he left effects to the value of £1420.

Writings: several books, pamphlets and articles on political and social issues, including: *Apprenticeship in Ironmoulding: a comparison of apprenticeship conditions in English and Belgian foundries* (Hodgson Pratt Memorial, [1915]) 57 pp.; 'The ILP "Programme of Work"', *Lab. Mon.* 7 (Jan 1925) 44–51; *Shekels and Talents: an open letter to Mr Joseph Bibby* [1925] 8 pp.; *A Simple Appeal to Remember!* . . . (n.d.) 10 pp.; *Why this Unemployment? a socialist view to the origin and solution* (ILP, n.d.) 11 pp.; *Why a Feud between Co-operation and Labour?* . . . (Burton-on-Trent, 1935) 23 pp.; *Essentials of Public Speaking*, with an Introduction by Sir C. Hardwick (Birmingham [1937]); *A Case and a Plea for Peace at Once* (n.d. [1940?]) 15 pp.; *Co-operative Politics inside Capitalist Society: a reply to 'Consumers' Co-operatives in Great Britain'* . . . (Birmingham, 1941);

'Municipal Election Prospects – in Birmingham', *Lab. Mon.* 27 (Sep 1945) 270–1; *Can Consumers' Co-operation survive without a Socialist Philosophy?* (Nottingham, 1945) 8 pp.; *The Proletarian Heritage* (Glasgow, 1951).

Sources: C. Bunker, *Who's Who in Parliament* [1946]; *Dod* (1952); *Birmingham Post Year Book* (1952–3); *WWW* (1951–60); R. P. Hastings, 'The Labour Movement in Birmingham 1927–1945' (Birmingham MA, 1959); H. J. Fyrth and H. Collins, *The Foundry Workers: a trade union history* (Manchester, 1959); E. J. Meehan, *The British Left Wing and Foreign Policy: a study of the influence of ideology* (New Brunswick, New Jersey, 1960); A. Marwick, *Clifford Allen: the open conspirator* (1964); T. F. Carbery, *Consumers in Politics: a history and general review of the Co-operative Party* (Manchester, 1969); J. Klugmann, *History of the Communist Party of Great Britain*, vol. 2: *1925–7* (1969); biographical information: His Excellency Mr T. A. K. Elliott, Helsinki; personal information: Edward Longden, Manchester, brother; Mrs F. M. Longden-Parker, Birmingham, daughter. OBIT. *Birmingham Gazette, Birmingham Mail, Birmingham Post, Daily Worker,* and *Times,* 6 Oct 1952; *Co-op. News,* 11 Oct 1952; *Amalgamated Union of Foundry Workers' Journal and Report,* Nov 1952; *Labour Party Report* (1953).

DAVID E. MARTIN

See also: †Albert Victor ALEXANDER, for Co-operative Party; *Clement Richard ATTLEE, for Labour Party, 1931–1951.

LOVETT, Levi (1854–1929)
MINERS' LEADER

Lovett was born on 2 February 1854, at Hugglescote, Leicestershire, the son of Robert Lovett and his wife, Sarah. When he was about a year old his parents, who were publicans, transferred to Swannington, where they kept the Robin Hood Inn, and Lovett continued to live in this village for the remainder of his life. He was educated at Coalville British School until he was twelve years old when he commenced work in the mines at Swannington No. 3 Pit. He extended his early education by private study, passed through all grades of mining work, and took a keen interest in trade unionism and other working-class movements. He was early invited to be a checkweighman at Swannington Colliery and also at Ellistown Top Seam Colliery, but he continued to work as a miner until he was thirty-two when, in September 1885, he accepted an invitation to be checkweighman at Snibston No. 2 Pit. In the same year he chaired many district meetings held in secret to organise the miners of Leicestershire, and was largely responsible for the formation of the Coalville and District Miners' Association, of which he was made president in 1887 with Thomas Chambers as general secretary. The Association was later renamed the Leicestershire Miners' Association and Lovett continued as president until 1900. He then acted as the Association's secretary for a short time, and in September 1902 was appointed miners' agent for the LMA, whose membership had risen from 2241 when Thomas Chambers represented it at the Liverpool TUC in 1890 to 5491 in 1910, with eighteen branches. For a number of years from 1902, Lovett served on the English and North Wales Conciliation Board, and represented the Leicestershire miners on the executive of the MFGB in 1905, 1911, 1916 and 1920. At an MFGB conference in 1920 he supported Herbert Smith's appeal to Robert Smillie to withdraw his threatened resignation as president of the Federation at the time of the Datum Line discussions.

On account of ill-health Lovett retired as agent at the end of 1923, after thirty-six years' work for the Leicestershire miners. He was especially noted for his extensive knowledge of the old indemnity case law, on which workers depended for claims against employers before the passing of the Workmen's Compensation Acts. The first of these latter became law in 1897, and its scope included the mining community. Lovett also became a specialist in compensation legislation.

Apart from his union interests, he was for a time an overseer of Swannington parish and a member of the parish council, of which he was chairman at the time of his election as miners' agent in 1902: he then resigned to concentrate on his work for the miners. He was president of the village horticultural society, was energetic in securing ground for allotments, and watched carefully to see that public footpaths were kept open. He was also active in the friendly society movement, holding several offices in the Order of Oddfellows in Leicestershire: at twenty-four he was a lodge secretary and was later deputy grand master to the Order. He was a governor of Leicester Infirmary and was made a JP for the County in 1916. Ill-health forced him to decline an invitation in 1917 to be a prospective Labour candidate for the Bosworth Division.

In 1876 he had married Bessy Hickling and had two sons and two daughters. One son died in infancy and the other in a swimming accident when he was sixteen. One of the daughters married a mining engineer, who pioneered the development of the Kent coalfield and whose father was general manager of a group of collieries at Eckington and Staveley. Their daughter married Charles W. Percival, who worked as a mining engineer for over forty years, first as under-manager at Bagworth Colliery, Leicestershire and then as manager of Oxcroft Colliery, Derbyshire. For twenty-six years he was a district inspector of mines in Nottinghamshire. Their two sons are respectively a senior management consultant and a company representative. Lovett's second daughter married an engineer and they also had two children, a son who became a senior official of the Royal Insurance Co. and a daughter who is a dental nurse.

Levi Lovett died at his Swannington home on 7 April 1929, and his funeral service was at St George's Church, Swannington, on 10 May 1929. His wife had predeceased him by six years, but a daughter, three grandchildren and two great-grandchildren survived him. He left an estate valued at £5927.

Sources: W. Hallam, *Miners' Leaders* (1894) [photograph]; Evidence before R.C. on Mines vol. III 1908 Qs 36917–37183; F. R. Batt, *The Law of Master and Servant* (1929); R. Page Arnot, *The Miners* 2 vols (1949) and (1953); personal information: Miss E. I. Clay, Birstall and Mrs F. E. Percival, Coalville, grand-daughters; the late J. A. McHugh, Ellistown near Coalville; copy of scrapbook of news cuttings and family papers: Brynmor Jones Library, Hull University. OBIT. *Leicester Mercury*, 9 Apr 1929; *Coalville Times*, 12 Apr 1929.

JOYCE BELLAMY

See also: †Thomas ASHTON, for Mining Trade Unionism, 1900–14; *Arthur James COOK, for Mining Trade Unionism, 1915–1926; †Benjamin PICKARD, for Mining Trade Unionism, 1880–99.

LUDLOW, John Malcolm Forbes (1821–1911)
CHRISTIAN SOCIALIST

John Ludlow was born on 8 March 1821 at Nimach in India, the son of Colonel John Ludlow CB who came from the same family as Edward Ludlow (1617–98), the Cromwellian general and regicide. His father died soon after his birth. His mother, Maria Brown, was the daughter of the runaway son of a Scottish presbyterian minister, Murdoch Brown, who became a merchant prince of India and bitterly opposed Company rule. Both sides of his family supported the Whigs. His widowed mother, with her son and three daughters, decided to live in Paris, where they attended the ministrations of a Liberal protestant divine, Athanèse Coquerel. The sight of the royalist army during the 1830 revolution fleeing from the populace, and of a polytechnician being able to calm the latter by moral force caused the precocious nine-year-old Ludlow to abandon thoughts of a military career.

Educated at the *Collège Bourbon*, now the *Lycée Condorcet*, he was brilliant at school, acquiring the *Bachelier-ès-lettres* in 1837. Ambitious of making a career for himself in France, Ludlow was shattered by his mother's gentle insistence that his dead father would have wanted him to be an Englishman. 'With a heavy heart' he came with his mother to London in 1838, and in 1839 they rented a house in Cadogan Square off Sloane Street, beyond which stretched fields of oats and rye. Ludlow was consequently nicknamed 'Johnny Townsend' by his fellow Christian Socialists, and often used the name or the initials J.T. as a *nom de plume*. He read for the Bar, to which he was called in 1843, under a distinguished aristocratic Whig lawyer, Bellenden Ker. However, he made no English friends until 1848, spent many holidays in France, and kept a diary in French. An alien in English society, which he found uncultured and snobbish, he thought of committing suicide. He brooded on political reforms. '*Quels immenses changements*', he wrote in his diary, 28 September 1839, '*n'y a-t-il pas encore à introduire à nos moeurs avant que nous n'ayons acquis cet esprit d'égalité, la seule base solide de tout édifice politique de nos jours*'. During the same year he underwent a conversion of an evangelical type which caused him to make contact with French pastors of *Le Réveil* in Paris, but secular ambitions remained mixed with his unworldly pietism. He envisaged, as he wrote in his unpublished autobiography, a future for himself as Prime Minister of England, who would pass certain necessary reforms and would then become a clergyman in the East End of London. Meanwhile he read some of the works of the French Socialist writers, notably those of Charles Fourier, and in 1841 wrote a *Confessio Fidei* which embodied the idea that Christianity was the fulfilment of whatever was good in Socialism. One of his school friends, Charles de Riancy, a Legitimist, who died young, had introduced him to liberal Catholic circles in Paris. Ludlow read some of the works of Lamennais, whom he described in his diary, 5 June 1839, as '*grand, terrible, sublime, déplorable, tout à la fois*'. Yet he always denied that his Christian Socialism owed anything to Roman Catholic sources. He was much influenced by Dean Stanley's *Life of Dr Thomas Arnold* (1844), in particular by Arnold's headmasterly notion of a sixth-form élite dedicated to bringing about national unity and justice.

Meanwhile he was acquiring a good deal of legal knowledge which he would later use on behalf of the developing working-class associations. Bellenden Ker was an expert on the laws of partnership, and promoters of joint stock companies came to him to obtain the charter of incorporation which had been required since the Bubble Act of 1720. Ludlow, who was his favourite pupil, 'devilled' for Ker on these charters, and in 1844 assisted him in drawing up the Joint Stock Regulation Act and an act to regulate Joint Stock Banks. In 1848–9 he himself arranged for the passage through Parliament of two minor amendments which he drew up, concerning the winding-up of joint stock companies, thus learning how through wire-pulling and technical expertise such changes could be brought about. Earlier some of his Whig relatives had brought him into contact with the British India Society, the Anti-Slavery Association and the Anti-Corn Law League. His interest in the latter had caused him to visit Birmingham and Manchester in 1841, where the industrial revolution, and an educated working class, participating in politics, greatly impressed him. Ludlow came to appreciate the role which voluntary organised associations with branches, acting as pressure groups, could play in promoting particular measures.

His religious conversion caused him to be interested in those who were outside the sphere of political activity. In 1846 he came into contact with a French Lutheran pastor, Louis Meyer, who worked in Paris with the Calvinist pastors of *Le Réveil*. Ludlow became interested in Meyer's *Société des Amis des Pauvres*, a body of celibate young men dedicated to visiting the poor. He decided that with some other law students he would form a religious fellowship and visit in 'the foully vicious neighbourhood of the Inns of Court'. In 1847 he called on F. D. Maurice, the chaplain of Lincoln's Inn. 'I felt his kindness, but hoped for direction and found none', Ludlow wrote subsequently; and at the time he described Maurice to his mother as 'a good man but very impractical'.

His relationship with Maurice, however, was transformed by the 1848 revolution. Ludlow immediately travelled to Paris to look after his sisters, and was delighted to see 'the whole town transformed into an Athenian *agora*'. He noted that the speakers were now talking not of political but of social questions, and that the crowds were not, as in 1830, hostile to religion. Ludlow concluded that this Socialism of Paris would spread throughout the world, but that only if it was 'christianised' would it be a blessing and not a curse, and that only 'a social christianity' could achieve this. He decided to throw up his legal career in London and start in Paris a journal, *La Fraternité Chrétienne*, to proclaim this message. However, he wrote to F. D. Maurice, on whom the 1848 revolution likewise had a catalytic effect, enhanced by Ludlow's letter. They now corresponded and met frequently. Maurice seemed to provide a theological basis for Ludlow's capacity for executive action. 'The veil was lifted and I felt this new friend was the greatest man I had ever met', he wrote later in life. Regarding himself as an *homme du peuple* Ludlow refused to join the forces of law and order as a special constable when on 10 April the Chartist demonstration took place at Kennington Common. Remaining in his chambers, he was visited by Charles Kingsley, up from the country to see what he could do to avert a clash between the Chartists and the forces of law and order, and Kingsley and he went to view the Chartist demonstration, only to find it was dispersing. The two men decided that a journal 'of a broad outspoken christianity ready to meet all social and political questions' must be started in England. With Ludlow assisting, Kingsley plastered the streets of London with posters addressed 'To the workmen of England'.

Subsequently Maurice and Ludlow became joint editors of the short-lived weekly journal *Politics for the People* (6 May–27 Aug 1848). Ludlow was the most prolific and constructive contributor. He criticised the charter, but demanded the extension of the franchise to 'those who paid taxes and had some kind of education', as a preliminary to universal suffrage; he attacked the New Poor Law, insisted on the 'right to work', which was to be organised through a revitalised parish, and drew the lesson from 'the June Days' in Paris that 'the machinery' as well as the spirit of society must be altered to remove class conflict. The journal, whose circulation never reached much more than 2000, helped him to gather round Maurice a group of what he called 'tried moral men', 'a band of brothers like Nelson's captains before Trafalgar', whom he organised through Maurice's Bible class, 'the very core of the movement while it lasted'. Among those thus collected were Charles Mansfield, a brilliant young scientist who was Ludlow's closest friend till he was fatally injured in one of his own experiments in 1855; Thomas Hughes, with whose family Ludlow and his mother shared from 1852 to 1859 a specially-built house at Wimbledon, 'a communist experiment'; F. J. Furnivall, a loyal supporter of Ludlow in spite of differences of belief; Lord Goderich, later Marquis of Ripon, with whom, as a wealthy aristocrat, Ludlow was unable to fraternise. Through a scripture reader named Self, the *Politics for the People* was read by a few Chartists, and Ludlow was then able to arrange that Maurice and some of 'the band of brothers' should hold a series of meetings with Chartists now disillusioned with politics and returning to social Owenite objectives. These meetings began on 29 April 1849 at the Cranbourne coffee house. Walter Cooper, tailor and Straussian lecturer, and Lloyd Jones, a life-long friend of Ludlow, were the chief working-class leaders to throw in their lot with 'the band of brothers' as the result of these meetings.

During a second visit to Paris in the summer of 1849, Ludlow was impressed by a number of co-operative experiments. 'Never before or since,' he wrote later in life, 'have I ever seen anything to equal the truly brotherly spirit which pervaded these workshops.' He determined to set up something similar in England. Early in 1850, in spite of Maurice's resistance, he inspired his friends to form a Society for Promoting Working Men's Associations which began by setting up a tailors' association off Oxford Street, with Cooper as manager, to be followed by two more tailors', three shoemakers', two builders', one piano-makers', one painters', and one smiths'. Links were also established with co-operative workshops elsewhere in the country. Meanwhile Maurice changed his mind, decided to join the new venture and, to Ludlow's surprise, suggested a series of *Tracts on Christian Socialism*; Ludlow contributed nos 4, 5 and 6 of these, and later, *Tracts by Christian Socialists* nos 3 and 4, a discussion of Mayhew's *London Labour and the London Poor*. Furthermore, on 2 November 1850 Ludlow founded a new journal, *The Christian Socialist*, of which he was the sole editor. Working men, notably Gerald Massey, wrote for this. Among Ludlow's own contributions was an account of 'a co-operative tour' taken with Tom Hughes in the North of England during the autumn of 1851. The new journal which, with the workshops, was widely discussed by the working class, was used by Ludlow as a means of arousing interest in and collecting evidence for a change in the law affecting co-operative organisations. Ludlow was the first witness before an 1850 parliamentary committee which discussed the problems involved; and there was a second committee in 1851. In the following year there was passed the Industrial and Provident Societies Act, drawn up by Ludlow, and sometimes called 'the Magna Carta of Co-operation'. Ludlow drafted the Act, which gave producer and consumer co-operatives special terms by which they could register with the Registrar of Friendly Societies (a state-paid barrister, appointed in 1829, had been given this title in 1846), and thus have legal protection for their funds. Ludlow had also tried to obtain limited liability for co-operatives as small businesses in which the workers were often shareholders and participated in the profits, but he argued that this should not be granted to larger businesses without safeguards against profiteering. Limited liability, though discussed for this measure, was rejected, but was granted to joint stock companies in 1856 and to co-operatives in 1862. Those who advocate the reform of company law in the interests of workers' control and profit-sharing have seen Ludlow as the pioneer of their ideas.

Ludlow helped to organise a co-operative conference, on 26 and 27 July 1852, at the Hall of Association, constructed by the builders' co-operative in Red Lion Square. By now, however, he was at odds with some of his colleagues, particularly with Vansittart Neale, a late arrival, who financed not only co-operative workshops, but also a consumers' store and a Central Co-operative Agency independently of the SPWMA. Ludlow, who believed the co-operative producers, of whom he was a lifelong champion, should control the consumers, and who also noticed that Neale did not attend the Bible class, proposed on 6 November 1851 the expulsion of Neale and others who worked with him from the SPWMA. When this was heavily defeated he himself resigned from the Society on 13 November and also from the editorship of the *Christian Socialist* on 27 December. Maurice insisted that the latter should change its name to *Journal of Association* and only supply non-controversial information. Under the editorship of Tom Hughes, circulation fell, until Ludlow took it on again in April 1852, to complete the six months volume at the end of June, when the paper ceased publication. During the final stage it recovered its former militant Christian Socialist character.

In September 1852 Ludlow issued his *Thoughts*, suggesting that 'the band of brothers' with Maurice at its head must give allegiance to the Christian faith, and under a mixed constitution have more authority over the workshops; it would thus form an élite, 'a true and holy Jesuitry', which 'could bid defiance to all parties and classes and effect a change in social conditions in England more mighty and blessed than has been effected since the gospel turned Saxon robbers into cultivators and then into citizens'. Ludlow's *Thoughts*, however, were rejected by the few members of the SPWMA to whom they were shown (though Hughes admitted that a similar conception, less clearly stated, had occurred to him). Moreover, Ludlow had disagreed with the suppression by Maurice of a pamphlet by Lord Goderich defending Christian democracy. In an exchange of letters, Maurice (8 Sep 1852) insisted that he was only 'a digger' of foundations, and Ludlow replied that if that was the case, Maurice was 'a philosopher and not a Christian', while he himself was 'a builder . . . building being the whole work of Christianity'. In spite of these differences Ludlow agreed to rejoin the SPWMA, renamed after the passing of the Industrial and Provident Societies Act of 1852, The Industrial and Provident Societies Union. The rules of the IPSU were revised on principles which were the complete reverse of Ludlow's own. Only as a result of Ludlow's intransigence, principally against Neale, was any allusion to Christianity preserved in the rules at all, while the Union claimed to offer only inspiration, advice and assistance and neither a prescribed creed nor any form of control over the workshops – control being no longer necessary, it was argued, since they could obtain safeguards under the 1852 Act. Finally, at a meeting in 1854 at Leeds, which Ludlow refused to attend, with representatives from co-operators of the North, it was decided that the committee then formed should take over the work of the IPSU. Ludlow now realised that Maurice was 'throwing over Christian Socialism' to concentrate on the Working Men's College, at first regarded as only one manifestation of the movement. He considered suggestions by a minority that he should take over the leadership, but – although never sure in his subsequent life that he had made the correct decision – he decided not to do so, as he felt inadequate for the task. As a result he came to consider that he was unfit to lead in any, even an inferior, cause, and described himself henceforth as '*vox et praeterea nihil*'.

However, this was to be an underestimation of his subsequent activities. He continued to assist co-operators, especially after 1867 when E. O. Greening drew the co-operators of London back into association with those of the North. Ludlow gave legal advice to the Rochdale Pioneers and the Wholesale Society, among others, at the nominal fee of two guineas a time. He drew up the Industrial and Provident Societies Act, 1871 (34 & 35 Vic. c. 80) which gave co-operators the power to hold and deal with land. He was active at co-operative congresses between 1869 and 1873,

editing the proceedings of the first one, advocating a Co-operative Central Board and Co-operative Bank, and suggesting that trade unions should provide funds for setting up co-operative workshops.

Ludlow also played an important role as a defender of the 'New Model' trade unions. The case of the then newly-formed Amalgamated Society of Engineers, whom he had helped to set up workshops during the 1852 strike or lockout, was put by him very ably in the *Journal of Association* (Jan 1852); and he claimed to have demolished the wages fund theory, which was used by opponents of trades unions. In a series of lectures delivered in February and published as *The Master Engineers and their Workmen* (1852), he gave a clear account of the structure of the 'New Model' union and a defence, with quotations from political economists, of its right to exist. Here, too, he was the first to suggest that to protect their funds trade unions should register at the Friendly Society Office. Registration was granted in 1855, but declared invalid after the case of *Hornby* v. *Close* in January 1867. Ludlow had a long connection with the ASE and later claimed that he became 'virtual standing counsel for the ASE, had their cases referred to me, settled a complete amendment of their rules'. From 1858, with other Christian Socialists, he co-operated in defending trade unions with a group of Positivists, notably Frederic Harrison and the Lushington twins who, like Ludlow, taught at the Working Men's College. Like them he was a member from 1858 to 1860 of the committee of the National Association for the Promotion of Social Science; each of the committee members undertook to examine a strike; Ludlow examined the North Yorkshire Colliery Strike of 1858, and contributed papers to the NAPSS on this strike and on strikes in general. It was in his rooms in 1859 that the NAPSS committee met the trade union leaders during the builders' strike of 1859 to 1861, and Ludlow revised two letters to *The Times* (Feb 1861) written by Frederic Harrison and signed by the group of Christian Socialists and Positivists, putting the builders' case. He also drew up the minority report of the NAPSS which advocated full legal recognition for trade unions, giving his views in two notable articles for *Macmillan's Magazine* (Feb and Mar 1861), 'Trade Societies and the Social Science Association'. He was disappointed that he was not invited to serve on the Royal Commission on Trade Unions of 1867–9, as some working men wished, though this may have been in effect a blessing, as Ludlow was not prepared to grant them the special status suggested by Frederic Harrison, whereby they received legal protection for their funds as corporate bodies, but could not be sued as such. Ludlow was also a pioneer advocate of arbitration tribunals in trade disputes (see especially his two articles in *Commonwealth*, 17 and 24 Mar 1866).

In 1867, with Lloyd Jones, he produced a small book, *The Progress of the Working Class*, which described the enabling and paternalistic legislation to assist workmen passed since 1832, and justified an extension of the suffrage on the ground of the workers' increased education and higher morality. The book was translated into German, and it inspired the director of the Prussian Statistical Bureau, Ernst Engel, and the social historian and economist, Lujo Brentano, to visit England in 1867 to study co-operative partnerships. Ludlow told Brentano that the British workers were then more interested in trade unions than in co-operation, and gave him letters of introduction to Frederic Harrison, Lloyd Jones, William Allan and William Newton of the ASE, and others. Brentano, who much later, described Ludlow in *Mein Leben* (Jena [1931]) as 'an economic genius', borrowed much from his writings. Brentano's first essay, published in 1870, was dedicated to Ludlow and the famous two-volume *Die Arbeitergilden der Gegenwart*, which had such an influence in Europe, owed much to the intellectual friendship with Ludlow. Brentano described to Ludlow the activities of Ferdinand Lassalle, about whom Ludlow wrote an article in the *Fortnightly Rev.* (Apr 1869) in which he indicated that Lassalle had derived his doctrines from Karl Marx. This led to an exchange of letters between Marx and Ludlow. Since Ludlow

read German, Marx decided to send him his last copy of Volume I of *Das Kapital*, which he hoped Ludlow would review. Ludlow failed to do this, but did review, not unfavourably, Marx's *Eighteenth Brumaire of Louis Bonaparte* [*Spec.* (1869) 1017–8]. Chiefly through Brentano, Ludlow came to influence both a number of the German *Katheder Socialisten*, (Socialists of the Chair), whom he assisted with their researches in England, and also the Austrian statesman, J. M. Baernreither, whom he helped with his *English Associations of Working Men* (1889) writing a preface for it. His friendly relationship with Brentano and other Germans was marred by Ludlow's strong reaction against the annexation of Alsace-Lorraine. A letter, signed first by Ludlow, then by some Positivists and working men, advocating British intervention, military, if necessary, to prevent this, appeared in the *Bee-Hive* (7 June 1871).

For the rest of his life Ludlow wrote repeatedly of the menace of the German Empire to European peace. He wrote in a somewhat divided spirit on the Paris Commune in a much later article (*Commonwealth* 1 (1896) 145–6).

Earlier Ludlow had been struck by other events overseas. In a series of lectures in the Working Men's College, published in two volumes in 1858 as *British India, its Races and its History*, Ludlow violently denounced Company rule and the annexationalist policy of Lord Dalhousie. He advocated a government by a multi-national Christian élite for what was then British India. According to J. S. Mill's *Autobiography* Ludlow and Hughes were the first Englishmen to come out in favour of the North after the outbreak of the American Civil War. Ludlow, who, throughout his life, was a passionate opponent of any form of racial discrimination, saw slavery as the key issue from the first, though he also felt strongly about the Union. He wrote a number of books and articles on American history, especially on President Lincoln whom he passionately admired. He was on the Jamaica Committee (1865) which attempted to force a prosecution of Governor Eyre. His championship of this cause, with which John Stuart Mill was passionately involved, caused a breach with Charles Kingsley.

A change in Ludlow's life took place when in 1869 he married his cousin, Maria Forbes, with whom he had been in love since 1843. Partly as a means of acquiring a more settled income, he became secretary of the Northcote Commission on Friendly Societies from 1870 to 1874 and from 1875 to 1891 the first Chief Registrar. The report of the Commission, which Ludlow wrote, contains a full history of all the working-class self-help organisations of the time. The Friendly Society Act (1875), which he drew up, by its definition of a Friendly Society with branches, strengthened the great Orders such as the Foresters or the Oddfellows. He also drew up similar acts in 1876 for co-operatives and trade unions which wished to register. As Chief Registrar he described himself as a 'minister of thrift', and in his annual reports mercilessly exposed fraud and incompetence, particularly if found in high places, and encouraged and aided the inexperienced. Representing Friendly Society opinion, he opposed Canon Blackley's state insurance scheme before a parliamentary committee in 1884–5; yet from his correspondence with a new Danish friend, Harold Westergaard, the economist and statistician, whom Ludlow had first met in 1878, and who subsequently started a Christian Socialist movement in Denmark, it is evident that Ludlow came to accept the necessity for state-sponsored old age pensions and sickness insurance. But in his final report (1891) he insisted that the latter could only be introduced in Britain when the country was 'more democratic and decentralised'. He did persistently, but without result, advocate the provision by the state of a funeral benefit, as here there could be no 'malingering'; and he strongly criticised the door-to-door collecting burial societies. During the period 1888–9 he also welcomed the registration of many of 'the new unions' though he was dubious about their survival without the Friendly Society benefits of the craft unions. He arranged with Vansittart Neale, with whom he was now on terms of complete amity, that a list should be made of the co-operative workshops registered in his

office; and in 1884 he helped to found the Labour Association, of which he was president in 1897. The Association was later, much to his annoyance, renamed the Labour Co-partnership Association. From 1884 he was a member of the Imperial Federation League, whose ideals of Empire he shared. From 1892 to 1903 he served on the committee of the London branch of the Christian Social Union. Almost up to his death at the age of ninety-one he continued to occupy himself with speeches, articles and good works of various kinds. Notable among these was the collecting, in 1899, along with a German refugee, Eugene Oswald, of 605 signatures, many of them working men's, to thank 'the representatives of the true France' for the stand they had made in defence of Dreyfus.

In 1910 Ludlow's wife died at the age of ninety, and he survived her for less than a year. On 17 October 1911 he died at his Kensington home, 35 Upper Addison Gardens. His funeral took place at Wimbledon, and he left an estate valued at £5379 net. He had no children, and he made a number of charitable bequests, including legacies to the Working Men's College, the Society for the Promotion of Christian Knowledge and other religious charities. He donated books to the British Museum, the Labour Association and the Working Men's College.

Ludlow had a French consistency of mind and sense of commitment which were not found among his fellow Christian Socialists. He was a small, shy man who avoided the limelight and whose influence was largely exercised through others. Nevertheless, more than anyone else he was responsible both for founding and giving concrete substance to the Christian Socialism of England, and in his later life he may be regarded as a constructive forerunner to those who have created the modern welfare state.

Writings: (1) Evidence before: S.C. on Investments for the Savings of the Middle and Working Classes XIX 1850 Qs 1–144; S.C. on Best System of National Provident Insurance against Pauperism X 1885 Qs 1409–570; and R.C. on Labour XXXIX pt 1 1893–4 Qs 1740–1936; (2) Other: *Letters on the Criminal Code* (1847); articles in: *Politics for the People* (weekly nos 1–17, 6 May 1848–July 1848), and *Christian Socialist. A Journal of Association, conducted by several of the Promoters of the London Working Men's Associations* (weekly, 3 Jan 1852–28 June 1852) [Authorship of articles identified for *Politics for the People* (complete) and the *Christian Socialist, 1*, in C. E. Raven, *Christian Socialism 1848–1854* (1920) App. A]; 'Froude's Nemesis of Faith', *Fraser's Mag. 39* (May 1849) 545–560; *The Joint Stock Companies Winding-up Acts* 2 vols (1849–50); *The Working Associations of Paris* (Tracts on Christian Socialism, no. 4 [1850?]) 22 pp.; Preface to *The Society for Promoting Working Men's Associations* (Tracts on Christian Socialism, no. 5 [1850?]) 23 pp.; *Prevailing Idolatries or Hints for Political Economists* (Tracts on Christian Socialism, no. 6 [1850?]) 11 pp.; 'Labour and the Poor', *Fraser's Mag. 41* (Jan 1850) 1–18 (repr. with revisions as Tracts by Christian Socialists, no. 3, pt 1 [1851?]) 12 pp.; *Labour and the Poor*, pt 2 (Tracts by Christian Socialists, no. 4 [1851?]) 23 pp.; *Christian Socialism and its Opponents, a Lecture* (1851); *The Master Engineers and their Workmen. Three lectures on the Relations of Capital and Labour* (1852); [A Barrister of Lincoln's Inn], *King's College and Mr Maurice: No. 1, The Facts* (1854) 53 pp.; *The War in Oude* (1858) 58 pp.; *British India, its Races and its History, considered with reference to the Mutinies of 1857* 2 vols (1858); *Thoughts on the Policy of the Crown towards India* (1859); 'Trade Societies and the Social Science Association', *Macmill. Mag. 3* (Feb 1861) 313–25 and (Mar 1861) 362–72; (with others), *Tracts for Priests and People* (1861); 'On the Investigation of Trade Differences and the Relative Credit due to the Testimony of the Employer and the Employed', *Trans NAPSS* (1862) 693–710; *A Sketch of the History of the United States from Independence to Secession* (1862); *Popular Epics of the Middle Ages of the Norse-German and Carlovingian Cycles*, 2 vols (1865); 'Some Thoughts on Strikes and Lock-outs', *Good Words 6* (May 1865) 372–9; *Women's Work in the Church*

(1865); *President Lincoln Self-Portrayed* (1866); *A Quarter Century of Jamaican Legislation* (1866); *Trade Societies and Co-operative Production* (Manchester, 1867) 10 pp.; 'On some New Forms of Industrial Co-operation', *Good Words 8* (Apr 1867) 240–248; (with Lloyd Jones), *The Progress of the Working Class 1832–67* (1867); (with Lloyd Jones), 'The Progress of the Working Classes', Essay 10 in *Questions for a Reformed Parliament* (1867) 277–328; 'The Social Legislation of 1867 and the New Year Gifts for 1868', *Cont. Rev. 7* (Jan–Apr 1868) 86–97; 'Mr Hare's Scheme of Parliamentary Representation', *Cont. Rev. 9* (Sep–Dec 1868) 80–97; 'Ferdinand Lassalle, the German Social Democrat', *Fortn. Rev. 11* (Apr 1869) 419–53; 'Old Guilds and New Friendly and Trade Societies', ibid., *12* (Oct 1869) 390–406; Edited *Proc. of the Co-operative Congress* (1869); *Co-operative Banking* (paper read at Bury Co-op. Conference, 1870); 'Gilds and Friendly Societies', *Cont. Rev. 21* (Mar 1873) 553–72 and (Apr 1873) 737–62; (with Lloyd Jones), *The War of American Independence* (Epochs of Modern History ser., ed. E. E. Morris, 1876); Preface to C. B. and R. B. Mansfield, *Aerial Navigation* (1877); Preface to J. M. Baernreither, *English Associations of Working Men* (1889, 2nd ed. 1893); 'A Dialogue on Co-operation', *Econ. Rev. 2* (Apr 1892) 214–30; 'Building Societies', ibid., *3*, no. 1 (Jan 1893) 64–86; 'The Bill to amend the Building Societies Act', ibid., *3* no. 2 (Apr 1893) 242–4; 'The Industrial and Provident Societies Bill', ibid., *3*, no. 3 (July 1893) 411–413; 'The Report of the Select Committee of the House of Commons on the Building Societies, no. 2 Bill', ibid., *3*, no. 4 (Oct 1893) 565–9; 'The Christian Socialists of 1848 . . . I', ibid., *3*, no. 4 (1893) 486–500 and 'Some of the Christian Socialists of 1848 and the Following Years II', ibid., *4*, no. 1 (Jan 1894) 24–42; 'Mr Benjamin Jones and the Early Christian Socialists', *Labour Co-partnership 1* (1894) 36; 'Building Societies and Properties in Possession', *Econ. Rev. 4*, no. 3 (July 1894) 396–7; 'Building Society Bills', ibid., *4*, no. 3 (July 1894) 393–6; 'Two Dialogues on Socialism', ibid., *4*, no. 3 (July 1894) 328–44; 'Report of the Chief Registrar of Friendly Societies for 1893', ibid., *4*, no. 4 (Oct 1894) 541–3; 'The National Free Labour Association', ibid., *5*, no. 1 (Jan 1895) 110–18; 'The Labour Association', ibid., *5*, no. 1 (Jan 1895) 131–2; 'Co-operative Production in the British Isles', *Atlantic Mon. 75* (Jan 1895) 96–102; 'The Building Society Returns', *Econ. Rev. 5*, no. 2 (Apr 1895) 256–7; 'Two Books on Socialism by "Nunquam" and "Nemo"', ibid., *5*, no. 4 (Oct 1895) 538–43; 'The Industrial Union of Employers and Employed', ibid., *5*, no. 4 (Oct 1895) 549–56; 'Some Words on the Ethics of Co-operative Production', *Atlantic Mon. 75* (1895) 383–8; 'Two New Social Departures', ibid., *77* (1896) 360–7; 'The Paris Commune of 1871', *Commonwealth 1* (1896) 145–6; The Tenth Report of the Labour Association', *Econ. Rev. 6*, no. 1 (Jan 1896) 85–88; 'The Christian Socialist Movement of the Middle of the Century', *Atlantic Mon. 77* (Jan 1896) 109–118; 'Trade Unions and the Post Office Savings Bank', *Econ. Rev. 6*, no. 2 (Apr 1896) 247–9; 'Thomas Hughes and Septimus Hansard', ibid., *6*, no. 3 (July 1896) 297–316; 'Cardinal Manning and the Christian Socialist Movement', ibid., *6*, no. 3 (July 1896) 402; 'Friendly Societies and their Congeners', ibid., *6* (Oct 1896) 481–502; 'Is Co-operation a failure?', ibid., *7*, no. 4 (Oct 1897) 450–9; 'The Local Co-operative Press', ibid., *8* (Apr 1898) 240–6; 'Co-operation in Russia', ibid., *9* 'Centenarian Friendly Societies', *Cont. Rev. 82* (Oct 1902) 546–54; 'The Origin of the College' in *The Working Men's College 1854–1904*, ed. J. Llewelyn Davies (1904) 13–21; 'Trade Unionism and Individualistic Radicals', *Econ. J. 14* (Dec 1904) 649–50.

NOTE: This is not a complete list of Ludlow's writings and for further material in the *Cont. Rev., Fortn. Rev., Fraser's Mag., Macmill. Mag.* and *N. Brit. Rev.* see the *Wellesley Index to Victorian Periodicals, 1824–1900*, ed. W. E. Houghton, *1* (Univ. of Toronto Press, 1966) and *2* (Univ. of Toronto Press, 1972).

Sources: (1) MSS: University Library, Cambridge; George Howell Coll., Bishopgate Institute, London; Goldsmith's Library, London University; London Working Men's College; Bunderarchiv, Coblenz. (2) Secondary: The only full scale biography is N. C. Masterman, *John Malcolm Ludlow: the builder of Christian Socialism* (Cambridge, 1963) although there is an unpublished thesis by P. N. Backstrom (Boston, U.S.A. PhD, 1960) for details of which see *Christian Socialism, 1848–54* below. The standard work on mid-Victorian Christian Socialism is C. E. Raven, *Christian Socialism, 1848–54* (1920), supplemented by T. Christensen, *Origins and History of Christian Socialism, 1848–54* (Aarhus, 1962). See also: *DNB 11* (1901–11); Sir H. Cotton, *Indian and Home Memories* (1911); J. J. Dent, *John Malcolm Forbes Ludlow CB, Christian Socialist and Co-operator, 1821–1911* (Manchester, 1921) 16 pp.; C. E. Raven, 'J. M. Ludlow', in *Christian Social Reformers of the Nineteenth Century*, ed. H. Martin (1927) 143–162; L. Brentano, *Mein Leben* (Jena, 1931); G. D. H. Cole, *A Century of Co-operation* (Manchester, [1945?]); E. C. Mack and W. H. G. Armytage, *Thomas Hughes* (1952); B. Semmel, *The Governor Eyre Controversy* (1962); P. d'A. Jones, *The Christian Socialist Revival, 1877–1914* (Princeton, 1968). OBIT. *Times*, 19 Oct 1911; *Co-op. News*, 21 and 28 Oct 1911; *Scottish Co-operator*, Oct 1911; *Commonwealth*, Nov 1911; *Co-partnership*, Nov 1911; E. J. Greening, 'J. M. F. Ludlow', *Working Men's College J. 12* (1911–12).

NEVILLE MASTERMAN

See also: †William ALLAN; Robert APPLEGARTH; †William COOPER; *Frederick James FURNIVALL; *Thomas HUGHES; *Ernest Charles JONES; †Patrick Lloyd JONES; *Charles KINGSLEY; *Frederick Denison MAURICE; †John Thomas Whitehead MITCHELL; †Edward Vansittart NEALE; William NEWTON; and below, Christian Socialism, 1848–54.

Christian Socialism, 1848–54:
(1) **MSS:** see individual biographical entries. (2) **Theses:** H. W. West, 'The Social and Religious Thought of Charles Kingsley, and his Place in the Christian Socialist School of 1848–1854' (Edinburgh PhD, 1947);

D. C. Morris, 'The History of the Labour Movement in England, 1825–1852: the problem of leadership and the articulation of demands' (London PhD, 1952); P. N. Backstrom, 'John Malcolm Forbes Ludlow, a little known Contributor to the Cause of the British Working Man in the Nineteenth Century', (Boston, U.S.A. PhD, 1960); J. Parkyn, 'The Political Thought of some of the Founders of Christian Socialism' (London MA, 1962).

(3) **Other:** [J. W. Croker], 'Revolutionary Literature', *Q. Rev. 89* (Sep 1851) 491–543; Society for Promoting Working Men's Associations, *First Report* (1852); V. A. Huber, *Ueber die cooperativen Arbeiterassociationen in England* (Berlin, 1852) 35 pp.; W. R. Greg, *Essays in Political and Social Science*, 2 vols (1853); *Report of the Co-operative Conference at Manchester, August 1853* (1853); R. G. Gammage, *History of the Chartist Movement* (1852; 2nd ed. 1894 and repr. with an Introduction by John Saville, New York, 1969); A. J. L. St André, *Five Years in the Land of Refuge* (1854); V. A. Huber, *Reisebriefe aus Belgien, Frankreich und England in Sommer 1854*, 2 vols (Hamburg, 1855); J. S. Mill, *Autobiography* (1873); M. Nadaud, *Histoire des Classes Ouvrières en Angleterre* (Paris, 1872); idem, *Les Sociétés Ouvrières* (Paris, 1873); G. J. Holyoake, *The History of Co-operation in England, 1: The pioneer period 1812–1844* (1875), *2: The constructive period 1845–1878* (1879); Charles Kingsley, *His Letters and Memories of his Life*, ed. by his wife, 2 vols (1877); C. Kingsley, *Alton Locke, Tailor and Poet: an autobiography* with a Prefatory Memoir by Thomas Hughes Esq. QC (1881); L. Brentano, *Die Christlich-soziale Bewegung in England* (Leipzig, 1883); *The Life of Frederick Denison Maurice, chiefly told in his own Letters*, 2 vols ed. F. Maurice (1884); J. Llewelyn Davies, *Social Questions from the Point of View of Christian Theology* (1885); E. R. A. Seligman, 'Owen and the Christian Socialists', *Pol. Sc. Q. 1* (1886) 206–49 (repr. in his *Essays in Economics*, New York, 1925, 20–63); J. Tulloch, *Movements of Religious Thought in Britain during the Nineteenth Century* (1885; repr. with an Introduction by

A. C. Cheyne, Leicester Univ. Press, 1971); M. Kaufmann, *Christian Socialism* (1888); B. Potter, *The Co-operative Movement in Great Britain* (1891); T. Hughes, 'Edward Vansittart Neale as a Christian Socialist', *Econ. Rev. 3* (1893) 38–49, 174–89; B. Jones, *Co-operative Production*, 2 vols (Oxford, 1894; repr. in one vol. New York, 1968); S. and B. Webb, *History of Trade Unionism* (1894); J. M. Ludlow, 'The Christian Socialist Movement of the Middle of the Century', *Atlantic Mon. 77* (Jan 1896) 109–118; *Life and Letters of Fenton J. A. Hort*, 2 vols ed. J. A. Hort (1896); L. Camazian, *Kingsley et Thomas Cooper. Étude sur une Source d'Alton Locke* (Paris, 1903); C. L. Graves, *The Life and Letters of Sir George Grove CB* (1903); A. V. Woodworth, *Christian Socialism in England* (1903); C. Webb, *Industrial Co-operation* (1904; 4th ed. rev. 1910); G. J. Holyoake, *Bygones worth remembering*, 2 vols (1905); J. McCabe, *Life and Letters of George Jacob Holyoake* (1908); 'Charles Kingsley and the Christian Socialist Movement, 1819–1875', in R. Balmforth, *Some Social and Political Pioneers of the Nineteenth Century* (1900) 133–43; *Life of Octavia Hill as told in her Letters*, ed. C. E. Maurice (1914); H. U. Faulkner, *Chartism and the Churches* (Columbia Univ., 1916); P. W. Slosson, *The Decline of the Chartist Movement* (Columbia Univ., 1916); M. Beer, *A History of British Socialism*, 2 (1920); C. E. Raven, *Christian Socialism 1848–1854* (1920); L. Wolf, *Life of the First Marquess of Ripon*, 2 vols (1921); *Christian Social Reformers of the Nineteenth Century*, ed. H. Martin (1927); F. E. Gillespie, *Labor and Politics in England, 1850–1867* (Duke Univ. Press, 1927); D. O. Wagner, *The Church of England and Social Reform since 1850* (New York 1930); G. C. Binyon, *The Christian Socialist Movement in England* (1931); S. C. Carpenter, *Church and People, 1789–1889: a history of the Church of England from William Wilberforce to 'Lux Mundi'* (1933); C. E. Elliott-Binns, *Religion in the Victorian Era* (1936); G. D. H. Cole, *A Century of Co-operation* (Manchester, [1945?]); J. B. Jefferys, *The Story of the Engineers* [1945]; M. B. Reckitt, *Maurice* to Temple (1947); U. Pope-Hennessy, *Canon Charles Kingsley* (1948); E. C. Mack and W. H. G. Armytage, *Thomas Hughes* (1952); J. F. C. Harrison, *A History of the Working Men's College* (1954); J. Saville, 'The Christian Socialists of 1848', in *Democracy and the Labour Movement*, ed. J. Saville (1954) 135–59; idem, 'Sleeping Partnerships and Limited Liability, 1850–6', *Econ. Hist. Rev. 8* (1955) 418–33; A. R. Schoyen, *The Chartist Challenge* (1958); R. B. Martin, *The Dust of Combat. A Life of Charles Kingsley* (1959); T. Christensen, *Origin and History of Christian Socialism, 1848–54* (Aarhus, 1962); P. N. Backstrom, 'The Practical Side of Christian Socialism in Victorian England', *Victorian Studies 6*, no. 4 (June 1963) 305–24; K. S. Inglis, *Churches and the Working Classes in Victorian England* (1963); N. C. Masterman, *John Malcolm Ludlow: the builder of Christian Socialism* (Cambridge, 1963); P. R. Allen, 'F. D. Maurice and J. M. Ludlow: a reassessment of the leaders of Christian Socialism', *Victorian Studies 11*, no. 4 (June 1968) 461–82; P. d'A. Jones, *The Christian Socialist Revival, 1877–1914* (Princeton Univ. Press, 1968).

LUNN, William (Willie) (1872–1942)
MINERS' LEADER AND LABOUR MP

Born on 1 November 1872 at Rothwell, an Urban District in the West Riding of Yorkshire four miles south-east of Leeds, Lunn was the eldest of eight children of Thomas Lunn, a miner and active trade unionist and his wife, Mary. After attending Rothwell Board School, he started work with his father at the local colliery (Rothwell Haigh) when he was twelve. Willie Lunn, the name by which he was always known, never forgot the problems of his early working-class life, and like his father soon became involved in trade union affairs. When only sixteen he was victimised for leading a pony drivers' strike, and this strengthened his determination to continue to struggle for improved working conditions. In November 1889 he obtained employment at Middleton Colliery in Leeds County Borough, which involved a long walk each day, but he continued his

trade union activities, and succeeded his father as chairman of the Rothwell miners' branch of the Yorkshire Miners' Association when he was only nineteen. In 1900, at the early age of twenty-seven, he was elected checkweighman at Middleton Colliery and served in that position until December 1918. He was regularly elected by the local miners to represent them at meetings of the YMA, and he attended many international conferences.

In his early youth he became deeply interested in politics, and during the 1893 coal strike helped to form the Rothwell branch of the Independent Labour Party of which he was a branch officer from the outset and for many years. He was one of Pete Curran's most ardent supporters at the notorious Barnsley by-election of 1897, when Curran stood as an ILP candidate and adopted the programme of the MFGB which included the provision of an eight-hour day. At that time Yorkshire miners' leaders were vigorously opposed to Curran, as they favoured the continued election of Liberal candidates sympathetic with the Labour cause; but there was growing support among some of the rank-and-file miners for independent Labour representation in Parliament and a break from Liberalism. During the 1890s Lunn also began a lifelong interest in local government affairs: he was a member of the Rothwell School Board from 1895, of the Rothwell School Management Committee in 1898, and from 1903 to 1918 a member of the Rothwell Urban District Council, of which he was chairman from 1915 to 1917. He joined the Fabian Society (probably in the early 1890s), and later became secretary of the Normanton Labour Party.

A man of fine physique with a strong somewhat bluff personality, he was also a forceful speaker; these attributes, combined with his reforming zeal and wide experience in trade union and local government affairs, led to his selection in 1909 as one of five Yorkshire miners' leaders to contest parliamentary constituencies. His first opportunity to fight a seat came in 1912, when, owing to a by-election in the Holmfirth constituency caused by the retirement of the Liberal member, he was unanimously chosen as prospective Labour candidate. Although a nominee of the Yorkshire Miners' Association, he did not receive wholehearted support from miners in the constituency, but his short campaign – of less than a fortnight – witnessed a remarkable exhibition of extensive canvassing and public speaking by prominent Labour MPs, trade unionists and members of the ILP. Among those who supported his campaign were W. C. Anderson, G. N. Barnes, Fred Hall (the miners' leader), Keir Hardie, Arthur Henderson, John Hodge, George Lansbury, Ramsay MacDonald, Ben Riley, Robert Smillie and Ben Turner. For the first time, some of the women's suffrage organisations took part, notably the National Union of Women's Suffrage Societies and the Women's Freedom League. Altogether 170 well-attended meetings were held during the short campaign. Lunn's election manifesto advocated the establishment of a living wage, an eight-hour day, nationalisation of the mines and railways, and votes for women. On this last issue he pledged, if elected, to vote against the third reading of the Franchise and Registration Bill, then being discussed in Parliament, unless women were to be enfranchised. Although he was unsuccessful in this particular election, he doubled the previous Labour vote, and his campaign was regarded as a decisive factor in the final severance of the long-standing connection between the Yorkshire miners and the Liberal Party [Gregory (1968) 116–17]. He was invited to become a candidate again at the next general election, but the outbreak of the First World War intervened.

At the first election after the war, Lunn entered Parliament as Labour MP for Rothwell, and retained this seat until his death, contesting in all seven parliamentary elections between 1918 and 1935. In the House his forthright manner of speech made a considerable impression. He spoke on international issues (self-determination for Egypt, for example) as well as on obvious domestic topics such as the nationalisation of the mines. He was notably active in matters of local interest: in 1920, for instance, he upheld the cause of the smaller urban councils by opposing the inclusion of Rothwell within the Leeds boundary.

In October 1920 Arthur Henderson initiated a debate in the House of Commons on Ireland, and demanded an independent investigation into the 'causes, nature and extent of reprisals on the part of those whose duty is the maintenance of law and order'. When he failed to obtain this Henderson persuaded the Labour Party executive to set up its own commission of inquiry, of which he was appointed chairman and of which Lunn was a member. The commission spent a fortnight in Ireland, and published its report in January 1921. This was followed by meetings throughout the country which undoubtedly helped to alter public opinion and led to the Irish Treaty of 1921. In September of that year Lunn, with other MPs visited Egypt to make inquiries relating to its independence, which was granted by the British Government in February 1922. In the same year (1922) he was appointed a Labour Whip and in the Labour Government of 1924 served as parliamentary secretary to the Overseas Trade Department of the Board of Trade, with Sidney Webb as his President. At this time Lunn became interested in the emigration of children to Canada and his Department sent Margaret Bondfield and others to Canada to investigate the conditions experienced by these immigrants.

In the second Labour Government of 1929 to 1931 Lunn was Under-Secretary of State for the Colonies and for the Dominions Office successively, again serving under Webb [*Beatrice Webb's Diaries 1924–1932* (1952) 198]. He maintained his interest in emigration as chairman of the Overseas Settlement Committee and was also vice-chairman of the Empire Marketing Board. He travelled widely as a member of the Empire Parliamentary Association; attended a number of international labour conferences and studied mining conditions in Austria, Belgium, France and Germany. A member of the Parliamentary Labour Party executive for a number of years, he also served on various Select Committees and was a personal friend of many of the Labour leaders, including Clement Attlee.

Apart from his long service at Middleton Colliery and his almost equally lengthy local government and parliamentary career, Lunn served from 1911 on the Hunslet Board of Guardians for many years, was an active member of the Marsh Street Primitive Methodist Church, Rothwell, and a co-operator, a lifelong member of the Rothwell Temperance Society, Band of Hope and Independent Order of Rechabites. For fifteen years he played in the Rothwell Temperance Prize Band. In 1929 he became a JP for the West Riding of Yorkshire.

He had married in 1902 Louisa Harrison (née Hall), who was a widow with two daughters and who bore him three sons. One of his sons became an insurance inspector and Labour councillor in Leeds, another entered the police force and the third, whose health was affected through war service, settled in the Isle of Wight where he participated in local politics and ran a post office. Lunn was assisted in his constituency work by his two stepdaughters. His wife, who shared his interest in community work was made a JP of the West Riding in 1922, and was the first woman to sit on the West Riding Bench at Leeds. Lunn died on 16 May 1942 in Leeds General Infirmary and was buried in Rothwell Cemetery. His wife and family survived him and he left an estate valued at £2756.

Writings: 'Yorkshire Miners and Politics', *Northern Democrat* (Oct 1909) 6.

Sources: *Labour Leader*, 12 Apr, 13, 20 and 27 June 1912; *Aldersgate Mag.* (June 1920) 425–6; *Hansard*, 20 Oct 1920; Labour Party, *Report of the Labour Commission to Ireland* (1921); *Times*, 20 Sep 1921; S. V. Bracher, *The Herald Book of Labour Members* (1923); E. S. Pankhurst, *The Suffragette Movement* (1931); M. A. Hamilton, *Arthur Henderson* (1938); *Kelly* (1938); *Dod* (1941); J. Lawson, *The Man in the Cap* (1941); *WWW* (1941–50); F. Brockway, *Socialism over Sixty Years: the life of Jowett of Bradford (1864–1944)* (1946); G. D. H. Cole, *A History of the Labour Party from 1914* (1948); *Beatrice Webb's Diaries 1912–1924*, ed. M. I. Cole (1952); C. L. Mowat, *Britain*

between the Wars 1918–1940 (1955); R. Gregory, *The Miners and British Politics 1906–14* (1968); biographical information: Rothwell Public Library; personal information: Mrs Lilian Briggs, Rothwell, stepdaughter; F. Lunn, Wroxall, Isle of Wight, son. OBIT. *Times*, 18 May 1942; *Rothwell Advertiser* and *Wakefield Express*, 23 May 1942 [photographs]; *Labour Party Report* (1942); *TUC Report* (1942).

JOYCE BELLAMY

See also: †Thomas ASHTON, for Mining Trade Unionism, 1900–14; *Pete CURRAN; †Arthur HENDERSON, for British Labour Party, 1914–31; †Benjamin PICKARD, for Mining Trade Unionism, 1880–99.

MACARTHUR, Mary (1880–1921)
TRADE UNION ORGANISER

Mary Reid Macarthur was born in Glasgow on 13 August 1880, the eldest daughter of John Duncan Macarthur and his wife Anne Elizabeth (née Martin). Her family was well-to-do, as her father, who was a Conservative in politics, owned a drapery business with several branches. During the first few years of her life Mary lived in Glasgow and Kilmacolm and at the age of twelve went to the Glasgow Girls' High School. In 1895 the family moved to Ayr and in the following year Mary continued her education by spending a year in Germany. On returning to Ayr she worked for a time as a book-keeper in her father's business, and, accepting her family's political opinions, was an active member of the Primrose League.

Early in 1901 she attended a meeting organised by the Shop Assistants' Union which was addressed by John Turner, who spoke in favour of establishing a branch of the Union in Ayr. Miss Macarthur recalled this meeting as the occasion of her conversion to trade unionism, for, although she had attended as a sceptic, the eloquence of Turner's appeal led to a change of mind. Her employment with her father meant that she was eligible for membership of the Union, which she joined shortly after, and within a few months she became the first chairman of the Union's Ayr branch.

Approaching her new-found work with characteristic energy and enthusiasm, she made such a notable impact that in 1902 she was elected president of the Scottish National District Council of the Shop Assistants' Union. In this capacity she headed the Scottish delegation to the Shop Assistants' annual conference held during Easter 1902 at Newcastle, where she met Margaret Bondfield, then the Union's assistant secretary. At the 1903 conference she was elected to the National Executive of the Union. Having become fully committed to trade unionism, Mary Macarthur was also moving towards Socialism. In the North-East Lanark by-election of September 1901 she assisted Robert Smillie in his campaign. Smillie, who, according to C. F. G. Masterman, represented her ideal type of labour leader, had tried to dissuade her from taking an active part in canvassing, knowing that it would lead to a breach with her parents. Although this did happen, they later came to respect their daughter's new-found beliefs and her friendship with Socialists such as W. C. Anderson and J. J. Mallon.

In June 1903 Miss Macarthur moved to London, where with the help of Margaret Bondfield she obtained the post of secretary to the Women's Trade Union League. Established in 1874 by Emma Paterson and others, the WTUL, despite the efforts of Lady Dilke and Gertrude Tuckwell, its honorary secretary, was at a low ebb. Under the direction of Mary Macarthur the League was revitalised. She encouraged those trade unions that admitted women to their membership to affiliate to the League, and addressed many meetings of women workers in those trades in which organisation hardly existed. In two years some 14,000 new members joined the League, bringing its total strength up to about 70,000; but it was part of Mary Macarthur's confident and optimistic attitude that she thought of herself as the spokesman for all women, not just those belonging to the WTUL. As a platform speaker she was outstanding, with a simple eloquence that could charm an indifferent or hostile audience, while the enthusiasm and fixity of purpose with which she pursued her campaigns impressed the officials of

both government departments and the male-dominated world of trade unionism. This ability to command the attention of those who heard her speak is illustrated by an incident that J. A. Salter recalled:

She went one morning to an employer in North London who paid the girls working for him less than a living wage. She had no success. 'If they can't sell their labour for as much as they want', he replied brutally, 'let them sell themselves.' She left his office in a fury just as the girls were coming out, across a big yard, for their midday meal. She jumped on a tub and poured out her anger. Just at that moment the employer himself came out. 'I suddenly realized' she told me, 'that if I didn't at once stop them they would tear him limb from limb. I found then that I had something in me that might be valuable – but might also be dangerous' [Salter (1967) 56].

Mary Macarthur travelled to Berlin in 1904 as one of the British delegates to the International Congress of Women, and in a similar capacity, visited the United States in 1908, giving several lectures and attending the Chicago Industrial Exhibition. She was for a time the only woman delegate to the London Trades Council and also served as a member of its executive.

In order to extend the organisation of women workers, in 1906 Miss Macarthur founded the National Federation of Women Workers which operated on the model of a general labour union. She acted first as president of this new organisation (while remaining secretary of the WTUL, and serving both bodies until her death), and then in 1908 became its general secretary in place of Gertrude Tuckwell, who took over the post of president. Also in 1906 she joined the executive of the Anti-Sweating League, the outcome of the Exhibition of Sweated Industries which she had helped in encouraging the *Daily News* to sponsor. In the autumn of 1907 Mary Macarthur further publicised her cause by launching the *Woman Worker*, a penny newspaper at first appearing monthly and then weekly and with a peak circulation of some 20,000 copies. Describing itself as 'the only woman's paper which assumes that its readers are not dolls or drudges, but WOMEN', it was edited by her until the end of 1908, when she returned to devoting her full efforts to organising women workers in sweated industries. In 1908 she gave evidence before a Select Committee on Home Work and agitated for effective control by trade boards, the first of which were established, in 1910, for four industries (chain-making, machine lace-making, paper-box making, and the wholesale and bespoke tailoring trades). Working with C. H. Sitch and Julia Varley she organised a strike among the chainmakers of the Cradley Heath district in the first months of the new board, in order to establish the minimum wages laid down, and in Nottingham helped in setting up the lace-making trade board. In the summer of 1911, together with Alfred Salter and Marion Phillips, she worked to organise a number of strikes that had broken out among women workers in Bermondsey. Miss Macarthur and her helpers were involved in some twenty strikes and negotiated pay rises of between one and four shillings a week. In the years before the First World War she continued to work for the establishment of minimum standards for female labour, and tried where possible to put pressure on the Liberal Government.

Some of her contemporaries were supporters of the 'Votes for Women' agitation, but Mary Macarthur did not become associated with this movement as she regarded herself not as a feminist, but as an egalitarian, who fought for the underprivileged, whatever their sex. With Margaret Llewelyn Davies, she was honorary secretary of the People's Suffrage Federation, a body which campaigned for adult suffrage, employing the traditional and constitutional methods of the pressure group.

From 1909 to 1912 Mary Macarthur was a member of the National Council of the ILP, but at the outbreak of war in 1914 she did not, unlike many ILP members, actively oppose the war. Rather than join with the struggling anti-war minority, she directed her efforts towards salvaging what could be saved. She became a member of the War Emergency Workers' National Committee as the WTUL representative, and tried to ensure that the large number of women newly brought into the labour market were treated fairly. At first the problem had been one of unemployment, but this stage did not last long and by the end of the war something like a million and a half extra women were working for wages. Throughout the war she insisted that trade union standards should be maintained for women workers, and even when serving on official committees such as the Central Committee on Women's Training and Employment (of which she was honorary secretary) and the National Insurance Advisory Committee, she did not allow her principles to be compromised. In these years she continued to work at full capacity and to show her characteristic impatience with authority if it appeared to be using bureaucratic processes to block her way. A sense of frustration often reduced her to tears which sometimes melted opposition, although those who knew her well suspected that on occasion the tears were less genuine than the motives behind them. Lloyd George, who could be equally eloquent and shrewd, regarded Miss Macarthur as a thorn in his flesh and relations between them were always strained. On the other hand, she established a close working friendship with Queen Mary, the consort of George V. This began in August 1914, when both were concerned with the Central Committee for Women's Training and Employment which had grown out of the Queen's Work for Women Fund, and so well did they get on together that it was humorously spoken of as 'the strange case of Mary M. and Mary R.' [Pope-Hennessy (1959) 494]. By learning more of Socialism from Mary Macarthur, the Queen came to modify her views about the labour movement and probably played a part in persuading King George that it provided no real threat to the stability of society. Mary Macarthur refused offers of government posts and may have rejected the honour of Dame of the British Empire, although there is some evidence that Lloyd George vetoed this award [Markham (1956) 97n]. She was on the left of the Labour Party and sympathetic to the Russian

Revolution – one of those, Beatrice Webb noted, who were 'playing with Bolshevik ideas' [*Beatrice Webb's Diaries* (1952) 107].

The war years were a great strain on Miss Macarthur's physical resources. Overworked and affected by what appeared to be the madness of the European nations, she also suffered the loss of both parents. Early in 1919, another death, that of her husband, dealt a blow from which she never recovered. In 1911 she had married W. C. Anderson, who became MP for the Attercliffe division of Sheffield in 1914. When he contested the division at the general election of 1918, she helped in his campaign, but he was defeated, as she, too, was at Stourbridge, where she was runner-up to the 'coupon' candidate. In April 1919, after her husband's death, her friends persuaded her to go to America, which she had first visited in 1907. She again crossed the Atlantic in October 1919, as adviser to the British workers' delegation at the first conference of the International Labour Organisation. After attending the Labour Party conference at Scarborough in June of the following year, she travelled to Geneva with Susan Lawrence and Madeleine Symons to take part in the conference of the Second International.

These activities, however, brought little solace, and her own health had become impaired, although she carried on with her work. In 1919 she was elected to the national executive of the Labour Party and in the following year became a JP in Hendon. Though she sat as a magistrate for only a few months, observers noticed the sensitive manner with which she heard cases. In September 1920 she attended the Portsmouth conference of the TUC to press for greater recognition of women trade unionists on the TUC executive. But her health was waning. Earlier in 1920 she had undergone an operation for cancer; it was not successful, and despite a second operation in October she died at her home in Woodstock Road, Golders Green, on 1 January 1921 – the day upon which the NFWW merged with the Women Worker's Section of the National Union of General Workers. The

funeral took place on 4 January at the crematorium, Golders Green. A large number of mourners attended the ceremony including representatives of many organisations. At the close of the service William Morris's 'The March of the Workers' was sung. In her will she left effects valued at £7264.

She was survived by a daughter, Nancy (Anne Elizabeth), who had been born in July 1915. Another child, a son, had died at birth in 1913. Nancy Anderson was brought up by an aunt until the age of twelve when she went to Bedales School, as her mother had stipulated (following the advice of Ramsay MacDonald who had a high opinion of J. H. Badley, the School's founder). From the age of eighteen she lived in London with Susan Lawrence and spent some time with her guardian, Madeleine Symons. Before her marriage in 1939 to I. H. Bargrave-Deane, a naval officer, she was active in labour politics and helped Miss Lawrence in the Stockton-on-Tees campaign against Harold Macmillan in 1935.

Mary Macarthur's death was mourned far beyond the labour movement, not only because she had died shortly after Will Anderson and at the height of her powers, but because of her exceptionally vivid and sympathetic personality. She was admired by almost all who met her; in Masterman's opinion, 'most men fell a bit in love with her', and Sir William Ashley smiled as he recalled 'that she was a very attractive young woman' [Hamilton (1944) 114]. The warmth of her appeal undoubtedly contributed to her success, while a secure middle-class background gave her the education and self-confidence to pursue her aims whatever the circumstances. She did not have an intellectual approach to problems; rather she wrote and spoke in a simple and direct way, appealing to the common sense of her audience.

Although Mary Macarthur's upbringing had been Presbyterian, she, like her husband, was atheist in her adult years, and her daughter was never christened because of this. But it was not an atheism that denied the supernatural; Masterman described her faith as having something of Tolstoi in it and something of the early Quaker element. After her husband's death she developed a somewhat mystical attitude and at times disturbed her friends by reporting conversations she had had with his spirit.

Within the labour movement she was held in an unusually wide and deep regard and many warm tributes were recorded after her death. In one of these, Beatrice Webb related her personality to her political work:

What was the secret of Mary Macarthur's compelling charm and power of guiding the thoughts and actions of her fellow citizens? She was neither pre-eminently beautiful or pre-eminently intellectual; and yet in any committee, in any group or organisation in which she worked, she was always the centre of attraction, the axle round which the machine moved. I think that the origin of this outstanding personal significance was the combination in her nature of an exuberant and contagious joy of life with a consistently held social purpose to which when necessary, she sacrificed physical comfort and worldly success. It was by the charm of her comradeship that she led men and women along the path she desired them to take. I well remember occasions when I had, wittingly or unwittingly, followed her to her desired end, how she would turn round, and in the warmest tones and with a most delightful smile, congratulate me on having discovered such an excellent way to the right conclusion. To have lost this beneficent influence exactly when it was most precious in a Labour and Socialist movement, growing with distracting speed, is the biggest calamity since the death of W. C. Anderson. It is grievous to think how these two together might, through their combined charm, sanity, and power of work, have defined and ennobled the methods and aims of the British people [Labour Woman (Feb 1921) 23].

Her work is commemorated in the Mary Macarthur Homes for Working Women, the first of which was opened by Queen Mary in 1924, and the Mary Macarthur Educational Trust. This latter body provides scholarships for working women, and an appeal was launched by Dame Anne Godwin at the beginning of 1971 with a view to increasing the capital resources of the Trust in order to make twelve such scholarships available each year.

Writings: numerous articles in *Christian Commonwealth, Daily News, Labour Leader, Woman Worker, Women's Trade Union Review* etc.; 'Trade Unions' in G. M. Tuckwell et al., *Woman in Industry from Seven Points of View* (1908) 61–83; 'Women and State Insurance', *Women's Trade Union Rev.* (July 1911) 7–14; 'The Working of the Trade Boards Act', *Englishwoman 19* (Sep 1913) 270–6; (with Mary Crosbie) 'Making Women like the Factory' *System 30* (Oct 1916) 249–256; appendix on C. Dilke and labour questions in S. Gwynn and G. M. Tuckwell, *The life of the Rt Hon. Sir Charles W. Dilke*, vol. 1 (1917) 365–7; (with A. Susan Lawrence) memorandum in *Women in the Engineering Trades*, ed. B. Drake (1917) 111–12; 'The Future of Women in Industry' in *Problems of Reconstruction*, ed. Marquess of Crewe (1918) 151–62; 'The Women Trade Unionists' Point of View' in *Women and the Labour Party*, ed. M. Phillips (1918) 18–28; Evidence before S.C. on Home Work 1907 VI Qs 2690–853; 1908 VIII Qs 1770–1787, 2222–70; Departmental Committee on Sickness Benefit Claims under the National Insurance Act 1914–16 XXX Qs 11325–592, 14091–667 [examined jointly with Honora Enfield].

Sources: *Reformer's Year Book* (1906) and (1909); L. W. Papworth and D. M. Zimmern, *Women in Industry: a bibliography* (Women's Industrial Council, 1915); B. Drake, *Women in Trade Unions* [1920]; *DNB* (1912–22) [by J. J. Mallon]; *WWW* (1916–1928); R. Smillie, *My Life for Labour* (1924); G. H. Stuart-Bunning, 'Mary Macarthur', *The Civilian*, 17 May 1924, 158–9; J. J. Mallon, 'Memoirs of an Agitator', *Railway Service Journal* (May 1925) 139–40, (July 1925) 213–14; M. A. Hamilton, *Mary Macarthur: a biographical sketch* (1925); idem,

'Mary Macarthur' in *Great Democrats* ed. M. Barratt Brown (1934); idem, *Remembering My Good Friends* (1944); M. Bondfield, *A Life's Work* [1949]; *Beatrice Webb's Diaries 1912–1924* ed. M. Cole (1952) V. Markham, *Friendship's Harvest* (1956); J. Pope-Hennessy, *Queen Mary 1867–1953* (1959); A. Salter, *Slave of the Lamp: a public servants' notebook* (1967); personal information: Mrs Nancy Bargrave-Deane, Petersfield, daughter. OBIT. *Times*, 3 and 5 Jan 1921; *Hendon and Finchley Times*, 7 Jan 1921; *South London Press*, 7 Jan 1921; *Nation*, 8 Jan 1921 by C.F.G.M. [Masterman]; *Shop Assistant*, 22 Jan 1921 by J. Turner; *Labour Woman* (Feb 1921) by G. M. Tuckwell, A. Henderson, R. Smillie, B. Webb, V. Markham, J. R. Clynes; *Woman Worker* (Feb 1921) by M.G.B. [Bondfield]; *Cont. Rev.* (Mar 1921) by Margaret Crewe; *Labour Party Report* (1921).

DAVID E. MARTIN

See also: William Crawford ANDERSON; Margaret BONDFEILD; *Susan LAWRENCE; *Marion PHILLIPS; Charles Henry SITCH; *Gertrude TUCKWELL; *Madeleine SYMONS.

MESSER, Sir Frederick (Fred)
(1886–1971)
TRADE UNIONIST, PACIFIST AND LABOUR MP

Fred Messer was born on 12 May 1886 at Islington, London, the seventh of ten children of Robert Rouse Messer, a Poor Law officer and workhouse master, and his wife Louisa Tubb (née Dean) who died when Fred was twelve. Fred had a spinal disability – probably caused by tuberculosis – which developed in early boyhood and which became much worse in later years. This did not prevent him from attending the Thornhill Board School, Islington, but ill-health somewhat retarded his education. Soon after his mother died Fred left school and started work in a factory, where he trained as a French polisher. Reading gave him much pleasure. Apart from the Bible and the works of Dickens, Kingsley and Scott, other books which interested him included Haeckel's *Riddle of the Universe*, Edward

Bellamy's *Looking Backward*, and Henry Fielding's *Tom Jones* – which his father forbade him to read!

By the time that Fred had reached his early youth his elder brother and sisters were married, and when he was only sixteen he was looking after his two younger sisters, both of whom died of tuberculosis. Fred's father was an educated man, but a heavy drinker; by contrast his son was teetotal from his teens, and became a Sunday School teacher at the Ragged Robins Mission, West Green, Tottenham. The young Fred also interested himself in trade union affairs, and in 1909 joined the French Polishers' Union. He was elected chairman of the labour side of the French Polishers' Joint Committee which regulated wages and hours in the industry, and was chosen to represent the men in any dispute with the firm. He led several strikes during the First World War, one of which lasted for thirteen weeks. He served on the union's executive for six years and from 1917 to 1921 was the union's general treasurer.

After the war the Manor House Hospital at Golders Green, which had been used for the care of wounded soldiers during hostilities, was taken over by the Industrial Orthopaedic Society. Fred Messer's employer was chairman of the Society; Fred became vice-chairman, and from 1922 to 1924 acting general secretary. His association with the work of the Society was the beginning of a lifelong interest in hospitals, and in 1925 he left his employment with a piano company to become southern area organiser for this Manor House Hospital, also known as the Labour Hospital, which was maintained by a membership subscription of 1*d* per week. Messer held this position until his election to Parliament in 1929.

Fred Messer had been actively interested in Labour politics since 1906; he took part in general election campaigns, spoke at outdoor meetings of the ILP, and knew Keir Hardie. In 1920 he was elected chairman of the South Tottenham Labour Party, a position he held until he entered Parliament. As chairman of his local Labour Party, Messer was closely associated with Professor Tawney, who contested the South Tottenham constituency at the 1922 general election, and he was much influenced by Tawney's speeches and writings. This interest led to an involvement in local government activities, and in 1925 Messer was elected to the Middlesex County Council for the Town Hall ward of Tottenham; he was made a JP in 1928 and a county alderman in 1938, a position he retained until his retirement from local government in 1952. From 1925 to 1940 he chaired the Council's Labour Group and served on many of the Council's committees, including the one responsible for health matters; he was vice-chairman of the Middlesex CC in 1946, and chairman in the following year.

In his early twenties Messer attended the West Green Baptist Mission, where he met his wife, but subsequently he worshipped at the Etherley Road Mission, Tottenham, where he often preached. In his forties he frequently spoke at the Brotherhood Pleasant Sunday Afternoon meetings which were held mainly in London and the Home Counties. On one occasion when his theme was practical Christianity, he roused the wrath of a local clergyman when he said:

What is the good of speaking to a man about mansions in the sky when what he wants is a three-roomed house down here? What is the good of telling him he wants a change of heart when what he needs is a change of shirt or the change of a ten bob note?

A staunch pacifist, Messer did not register for war service in the First World War and possibly on account of changes in address, he was not located by the recruiting authorities until 1918, just as the war ended. In the post-war years he continued his interest in pacifism and became an ardent supporter of the No More War Movement which was founded on 24 February 1921 in London. He gave lectures for the organisation, was particularly active in its North London branch, and when he contested South Tottenham at the 1929 general election his views on peace and disarmament were included in his election address: 'As one who believes the most important ques-

tion of modern life is this question of peace, I appeal to you to give me an opportunity to carry those principles of peace and humanity for which I stand into the law-making assembly of this country.' He was elected, but lost the seat in 1931.

After his defeat, Messer became a Labour Party propagandist and toured the country speaking to constituency parties. They provided hospitality, and his other expenses were met by the Party, which at the same time published a news sheet, the *Victory for Socialism Campaigner*, with which Messer was involved. He was re-elected Labour MP for South Tottenham in 1935, and at the 1945 general election held the seat with a majority of 13,853. By 1950 he had joined the Co-operative Group in the House of Commons, and at the general election in that year contested and won the newly created constituency of Tottenham in the Co-operative and Labour interest; he held the seat until his retirement from Parliament in 1959. He had been associated with the co-operative movement for many years. After his election to Parliament in 1929 he edited one of the local *Citizen* papers published by the Co-operative Press. During the 1935 election their total circulation reached two and a half million copies. Messer continued to edit the *South Tottenham Citizen* during some of the period when he was not in Parliament. He was a conscientious constituency MP and continued to hold his Friday evening 'surgeries' even in the years when he was out of Parliament. He was also a well-known speaker at open meetings on Thursday evenings at Salisbury Corner, Haringey, and on Sunday evenings at West Green, Tottenham.

Towards the end of the Second World War, Fred Messer's son Eric was a member of the Committee against Race Hatred, whose chairman was Will Cove, Labour MP for Aberavon and the author of a pamphlet, *Against Race Hatred and for a Socialist Peace*. The aim of the Committee was to oppose the ideas of Lord Vansittart on the war guilt of the whole German people. Fred Messer supported the Committee and spoke at some of its regional conferences. When his son and others decided to broaden the scope of their work – from the issue of peace terms to general left-wing policies – he assisted in the drafting of manifestos for their campaign, which was inaugurated in 1943 as the Victory for Socialism Group. At that time H. G. McGhee, MP for Penistone, was chairman of the Group and Eric Messer the secretary. In a publicity leaflet for the organisation, Fred Messer questioned whether the Labour Party had enough socialist drive to effect the transition from capitalism to Socialism and appealed to 'convinced Socialists who are prepared to live and work for Socialism' to join the group. Several national conferences were organised by the Victory for Socialism campaigners but were condemned by the Labour Party on the grounds that the authority of its national executive was being usurped and an unofficial group within the Party created. At a conference arranged by this 'ginger group' in September 1944 at Birmingham, to which constituency parties were invited, the agenda included the following items: (i) The Truce and the Coalition; (ii) A Socialist Programme for the next General Election; (iii) Post-war Europe, with special reference to Governments in 'liberated' territories and to the treatment of enemy peoples; and (iv) Democratic Reform of the Labour Party.

In the following year the Group received the support of 100 Labour MPs in an attempt to secure re-affiliation of the ILP with the Labour Party; but discussions between the ILP Council and the LP executive failed to achieve this result. A conference arranged by the Group in 1955 was cancelled after intervention by the LP executive, but in the mid-1950s the Group was reorganised when the *Tribune* MPs joined, and Fred Messer was elected president. In 1956, when another conference was being convened, Fred Messer wrote in reply to a complaint from Morgan Phillips (then secretary of the LP), that the conference was not on a national scale and could not 'be said to usurp the functions of any national authority'. He challenged the criticism that the object of the organisation was to 'create the structure of an unofficial group', and said that he would 'strongly oppose anything

that was against the "Spirit and Purpose of the Party" or which was in conflict with the Party constitution' [private letter, 12 Mar 1956: For the later history of VFS, see entry for Stephen Swingler in *DLB III*].

Messer's early involvement in hospital administration continued with his appointment as chairman of the North Middlesex Hospitals Committee in 1935, and throughout his parliamentary career he took a keen interest in matters relating to health and welfare. Although his own physical disability – curvature of the spine – did not prevent him from leading a very active life (till he was forty he was a keen cyclist who toured East Anglia and the South Coast with his son), he was especially sympathetic towards organisations whose aims were the amelioration and prevention of suffering. In December 1937 he made a forthright attack in the House of Commons on Sir Francis Fremantle, a doctor and MP for St Albans who was a member of an official committee inquiring into nurses' working conditions. Sir Francis spoke against a private member's Bill to provide a forty-eight-hour week in municipal hospitals. This was the Local Authorities (Hours of Employment in Connection with Hospitals and Institutions) Bill, which Sir Francis opposed on the ground that this would 'sacrifice the spirit of service that comes down from the days of the religious houses and from more recent times up to the present of the great voluntary hospitals'. He was sternly rebuked by Messer who was able to quote the excellent results obtained at the Middlesex hospitals where a forty-eight-hour week was worked. Messer also took a close interest in the passage through the Commons in 1938 of the Blind Persons Bill, some parts of which he strongly criticised.

He took a major interest in the debates in 1939 on the Military Training Bill and he was largely responsible for the inclusion of an amendment which enabled conscientious objectors to have a more adequate review procedure. From 1944 to 1945 he was parliamentary private secretary to the Minister of Labour, Ernest Bevin. In the years of the post-war Labour Governments he is especially remembered for his interventions in the debates on the National Health Service Bill in 1946. He spoke on a number of occasions, and during the second reading criticised the insufficient regard for illness prevention and after-care service. He was also against the method of appointment to regional hospital boards, preferring the elective principle rather than the submission of names to the Minister of Health. He was himself the first chairman of the North-West Metropolitan Regional Board, a position he held until 1953, when the pressure of parliamentary duties forced him to resign. In recognition of his knowledge of hospital service, he was appointed in 1948 chairman of the Central Health Services Council, an organisation created by the Labour Government to advise it on health matters. He was also active in related fields: as chairman from 1944 to 1956 of the Ministry of Education's Advisory Committee on Handicapped Children, chairman of the Old People's Welfare Council, a member of the National Association for Prevention of Tuberculosis, the Nuffield Trust for the Care of Aged People, and the Tottenham advisory committee dealing with the Disabled Persons Act. He was also an officer brother of the Order of St John, and held office in the British Council for the Welfare of Spastics, the Cripple Reform League, and the Tottenham Branch of the League of the Blind. He served on the governing boards of several London schools – Hornsey County, Mill Hill and Tottenham Grammar – and was also a governor of St Ignatius College and the Stationers' Company School.

Official recognition of his long record of public service came with the award of a CBE in 1949 and a knighthood in 1953, and in 1955 he received the Freedom of the Borough of Tottenham. On the latter occasion, Ald. A. Reed paid tribute to Sir Frederick as being a man who 'had devoted the whole of his life to the great cause of humanity and the minimisation of suffering'. In 1958, just before his retirement from Parliament, Messer moved from Southgate to Croydon, where his public service continued. From 1961 to 1964 he chaired the Croydon Hospital Management Committee, and he was elected president of the Broad Green Old Age Pensioners' Club, West Croydon. He continued to take a lively interest in health matters, and in the year before his death wrote a letter to *The Times* (2 Apr 1970) supporting the proposals for reorganising the National Health Service which were then under discussion in the House of Lords.

He had married on 1 August 1908 Miss Edith Beatrice Chapman, and there were two sons and a daughter of the marriage. The younger son was killed in an accident in 1913 when he was only two-and-a-half years old, and their daughter died of tuberculosis in 1952 when she was twenty-seven. The elder son, Frederick Alfred (Eric), a co-operative insurance agent from 1935 to 1971, had in 1929 founded the League of Youth in Tottenham and was its first chairman. He was elected to the Croydon County Borough Council in 1949, and on two occasions contested parliamentary elections in the Labour interest: Esher in 1955 and Croydon South in 1959.

Fred Messer died on 8 May 1971 at St Johns Nursing Home, South Croydon, and was cremated after a service at the Croydon Crematorium conducted by a personal friend, the Rev. W. C. Elliott. He was survived by his son Eric, with whom he had lived from 1964, Mrs Messer having predeceased her husband in 1960. He left an estate valued at £7180.

Many tributes were paid to Fred Messer's life and work. He had a quick wit which was not always appreciated by those who were its object, but he was, in the words of a friend of forty years and one-time colleague, Douglas Clark:

quite the most warm-hearted man – many thought him a secular saint – one could know . . . he amazed me and indeed all who knew him. Born a hunchback, crippled all his life and scarcely ever free from pain he never complained nor allowed his condition to handicap him. This was all the more remarkable because he never earned more than a pittance by today's standards. He was poor, crippled and working class. He had to walk. Yet to see him was to see a giant – a gentle, involved and caring giant whose heart was bigger than his body.

In public life health was his consuming passion. No matter what the set subject of any meeting might be all knew that within five minutes of Fred starting to speak he would be on about hospitals and research and home help, etc. And everything he said was listened to with rapt attention be the audience the Royal College of Surgeons or a local society, political, religious or social.

When the story of the ending of the scourge of TB is written there will be his lasting memorial. His layman's contribution over thirty years and more in this one field earns him his immortality . . . He was free from all cant, ever cheerful and encouraging, recognized no barriers of class or politics or religion (*Times*, 14 May 1971).

Writings: 'The Work of a Health Committee' *Labour Councillor*, 2 no. 5 (May 1950) 33–34; *The National Health Service: a miracle of social welfare. Can it be saved?* with a preface by L. Pavitt MP [London Co-operative Society Political Committee] (1971).

Sources: J. W. Graham, *Conscription and Conscience* (1922); *Report of Central Board of Co-operative Union* (1935–6) and (1936–1937); A. M. Carr-Saunders et al., *Consumers' Co-operation in Great Britain* (1938); *Dod* (1946) and (1958); *Co-op. News*, 4 Feb 1950; *Co-op. News*, 14 Mar 1953; *Tottenham Calling: monthly news-sheet of the Corporation of Tottenham*, 7, no. 3 (Mar 1955); personal information: Mrs M. L. Eyles Monk, Barnet; Eric Messer, Old Coulsdon, son. OBIT. *Guardian* and *Times*, 11 May 1971; *Tottenham and Edmonton Weekly Herald*, 14 May 1971; H. Williams, *Health* (Summer 1971); *Labour Party Report* (1971).

JOYCE BELLAMY

See also: *Clement Richard ATTLEE, for British Labour Party, 1931–51; †Arthur HENDERSON, for British Labour Party, 1914–1931; *Stephen SWINGLER.

MIDDLETON, George Edward (1866–1931)
MINERS' LEADER

George Middleton was born on 3 August 1866 at Mickley Square, Mickley, near Prudhoe on the River Tyne in Northumberland, the son of Thomas Middleton, a coalminer. He had a longer education than most children at that time, having stayed at school until he was fifteen, when he began working in the mines. While still in his teens he helped to form the Mickley branch of the Northumberland Miners' Association, became its president when still a young man and held this position until 1918. By this date Middleton was well known throughout his county. He had been a delegate to the council of the NMA for many years and was also a member of its executive committee. He was also a member of the first committee of the Northumberland Aged Mineworkers' Homes Association when this was formed in 1900 and, on the death in 1918 of John Wilson, the Association's first secretary, Middleton was appointed to replace him in this full-time salaried post which, like Wilson, he held until his death. He was, according to a jubilee souvenir of the Association published in 1950, a 'gently philosophic and persuasive' man who with the other founders of the organisation, among whom were Hugh Boyle, John Cairns, Billy Golightly, Willie Hogg, George Shield and William Straker, guided it, 'worked for it and inspired others to work for it, from the day it was founded until either they were physically incapable of doing more, or until they died' [*Souvenir* (1950)].

Middleton's local activities, apart from his work for the miners, were numerous, especially in local government. He was elected to the Mickley Parish Council on its formation; was a member of the Hexham RDC and was chairman, for three years, of the Prudhoe Urban District Council, when, largely on his initiative, this was created. He also served for four years on the Northumberland County Council and for many years was on the Hexham Board of Guardians. An ardent co-operator, he was a director of the Prudhoe District Co-operative Society for a number of years. He was also widely known for the part he played in the Working Men's Club and Institute Union movement. He served on the organisation's national committee and was for many years a leading figure of the Union in Northumberland. Middleton was a popular sportsman, helped to form the Mickley Football Club, was a playing member for fifteen years and then took an active part in the management of the Club up to the time of his death. He became a member of the Council of the Northumberland Football Association in 1902, and served as vice-president for several years before being elected president in 1917.

Middleton had literary ability and was a regular contributor to the *Hexham Courant*, writing notes on association football and other sports. He originated the 'Prudhoe Jottings' column and in a tribute following his death the *Courant* obituary referred to 'his wide knowledge of the district, his crisp judgment in local matters, his clarity of view and, above all, his abounding sense of humour'. He had married Margaret Jane Paisley, daughter of a Mickley miner, in 1901. His wife was an active worker in the Labour women's movement, and her sudden death, in August 1925, was a severe shock to George Middleton from which he never recovered. His remaining years, after his wife's death, were marred by increasing mental depression and he took his own life – by gassing himself in the kitchen of his hime – on 30 October 1931. At his funeral service, conducted by the vicar of Mickley, there was a large gathering of mourners from all parts of Northumberland and Durham; and William Straker paid tribute to his work as secretary of the Aged Miners' Homes Association. He left effects valued at £662.

Sources: B. T. Hall, *Our Fifty Years: the story of the Working Men's Club and Institute Union* (1912); *Jubilee Souvenir of the Northumberland Aged Mineworkers' Homes Association from 1900–1950* [1950] [40] pp. OBIT. *Newcastle J.*, 2 Nov 1931; *Hexham Weekly News*, 6 and 7 Nov 1931; *Hexham Courant*, 7 Nov 1931; NMA, *Monthly Circular* (1931).

ANTHONY MASON
JOHN SAVILLE

See also: †Thomas ASHTON, for Mining Trade Unionism, 1900–14; †Thomas BURT; *Arthur James COOK, for Mining Trade Unionism, 1915–26; William STRAKER; John WILSON (1856–1918).

MILLINGTON, Joseph (1866–1952)
CO-OPERATOR AND TRADE UNIONIST

Joseph Millington was born on 9 April 1866 at Holbrook Moor, near Belper, Derbyshire, the son of Jacob Millington, a general labourer, and his wife, Emma (née Sherlock). At the age of nine he started work in a local cotton mill as a half-timer, and while still young also worked as a hotel page, office boy and pony driver in a coalmine, before becoming a railway employee in Derby, where he worked up to the age of twenty-five.

From 1891 to 1906 he was a first-class signalman on the Midland Railway at Saltley, Birmingham. This occupation took Millington into trade union officialdom; he was chairman of the local branch of the Amalgamated Society of Railway Servants for a time and secretary of a joint committee of eight branches in Birmingham with a combined membership of 3000. He was also a delegate to the annual congress of the ASRS and represented the Birmingham branch at the 1900 Trades Union Congress.

Millington was a prominent member of the Birmingham Trades Council, serving as its president from 1899 to 1902. During his term of office he worked with Arthur Eades, the Council's secretary, in organising an Industrial Polytechnic Exhibition with the object of raising funds to provide scholarships to Birmingham University for working-class students. In 1897 he stood as a Trades Council candidate in the School Board election, but was defeated. A supporter of the principle of labour representation, he joined the Labour Representation Committee at its inception, and was chairman of the local branch.

In 1898 he was elected as a Poor Law

Guardian, and in 1906 he left the service of the Midland Railway to become relieving officer of the Aston Board of Guardians, a post he held until his retirement in 1931. He was appointed a city magistrate in 1926.

But it is for his valuable and almost lifelong service to the co-operative movement that Millington was best known. He joined the Birmingham Co-operative Society when he moved to the city in 1889, and in 1895 he became a member of its management committee, upon which he served continuously until 1936, when he reached retiring age. For the last fourteen of these years he was president of the Society, and in 1933 when the Co-operative Congress met in Birmingham, he was president of the Congress. In his inaugural address he reviewed the history of the co-operative movement, especially in the Birmingham area, and spoke of the future progress of co-operation. In January 1918 he became a member of the Birmingham and District Co-operative Representation Council. This organisation was formed as a result of the decision of the 1917 Co-operative Congress that co-operators should seek representation on national and local administrative bodies, and it subsequently adopted two candidates for the general election of December 1918. They were Tom Hackett (King's Norton) and F. Spires (Sparkbrook); neither was successful.

From 1912 until 1939 Millington sat on the Midland section of the central board of the Co-operative Union, for several years as chairman. He served as a member of the Midland Sectional Co-operative Hours and Wages Council and sat on the executive committee of the Midland Co-operative Convalescent Fund. He was also for a time chairman of the Co-operative Coal Trade Association. These offices led to appointments on several other bodies, notably ones concerned with the coal industry, including, in 1936, membership of the government committee of investigation under the 1930 Coal Mines Act.

Millington's later years were spent in retirement. He died at his home in Moseley Road, Birmingham, on 7 April 1952, aged eighty-five, and he was interred at Brandwood End Cemetery on 10 April. He had married in 1886 and had three sons and a daughter. In his will he left an estate valued at £14,533.

Sources: Anon., *History of the Birmingham Co-operative Society Limited 1881–1931* (Birmingham, 1931); *Co-op. Congress Report* (1933); J. Corbett, *The Birmingham Trades Council 1866–1966* (1966); S. Pollard, 'The Foundation of the Co-operative Party' in A. Briggs and J. Saville, *Essays in Labour History*, vol. 2: *1866–1923* (1971) 185–210. OBIT. *Birmingham Mail* and *Evening Despatch*, 7 Apr 1952; *Birmingham Gazette*, 8 Apr 1952; *Co-op. News*, 12 Apr 1952; *Birmingham Post Year Book* (1952–3).

DAVID E. MARTIN

See also: †Fred HAYWARD, for Co-operative Union; Arthur EADES; Thomas HACKETT; John Valentine STEVENS.

MITCHISON, Gilbert Richard (Baron Mitchison of Carradale) (1890–1970)
BARRISTER AND LABOUR POLITICIAN

Gilbert Richard, Baron Mitchison of Carradale, was a good example of a man of the upper income bracket who became, rather late in life, a Socialist and solid supporter of the Labour Party in Parliament. He was born on 23 March 1890, the son of Arthur Maw Mitchison and Mary Emmeline Russell. His family were well-to-do, and he was educated at Eton, as an oppidan, and then at New College, Oxford, where he obtained a first in Literae Humaniores ('Greats'). He had hoped to be elected to a fellowship at All Souls, but failed; he then turned to the law, and was called to the Bar at the Inner Temple in 1917, the reason for the delay being, of course, the First World War. At its outbreak he joined the Queen's Bays Regiment, where he rose to the rank of major; he served in France, and was seriously wounded in the head, but recovered sufficiently to become GSO2. in the British Mission to the French Forces in Italy, and to win the Croix de Guerre.

Earlier, in 1916, he had married Naomi Haldane, the young sister of the distinguished geneticist J. B. S. Haldane, who had been his contemporary at Eton, and after the war they settled in London, eventually in a large house on Hammersmith Mall, where they raised a family and entertained freely a wide circle of friends and notabilities of the left in art, literature and politics. Mitchison was making his way rather slowly – in part because of the effect of his war wound – as a barrister, and his wife in 1923 published her historical novel, *The Conquered*, which had a considerable success and started her on a long and prolific literary career.

Mitchison, meanwhile, was rather marking time; though a painstaking worker, he was not deeply interested in his largely commercial law practice, and was not very well satisfied with the role of genial host to his wife's artistic and literary friends; his own political inclinations, though generally radical, were ill-defined, and he was generally regarded as something of a light-weight. A marked change came, however, when under the influence of G. D. H. Cole and his wife he joined the left-wing Socialist movement of the early thirties which in 1931 produced the New Fabian Research Bureau, and which, at the end of the decade, was to transform the moribund Fabian Society into a live political force and to nourish so many future Labour Ministers.

In the following year, with his fellow-barrister Sir Stafford Cripps, he took part in the Socialist League; and as in the 1931 election he had succeeded G. D. H. Cole as candidate for the former constituency of King's Norton, and fought it again, without success, in 1935, he became fully committed to Labour politics. As one of the richest members of this grouping he naturally became treasurer of the NFRB and held that post until it amalgamated with the Fabian Society in the summer of 1939: he further signalised his conversion by publishing in 1934 a quasi-Utopian description of *The First Workers' Government*, which assumed the disappearance, *inter alia*, of the House of Lords and the City. This book combined with his close association with Cripps and

Aneurin Bevan to render him a recruit slightly suspected by the official leaders of the Labour Party other than Lansbury, but the differences were not pressed.

A year or two before the Second World War broke out he had bought a fair-sized property at Carradale in Argyll, to which he soon in effect transferred his family, lodging with the Coles for his London work. During the war Mrs Mitchison turned Carradale House into a home of refuge for those needing to escape from bombs in the cities or from Nazi invasion of their own countries; and it became gradually, and after the war increasingly, a centre of much discussion, as well as rest and recreation, for left-wingers of all types, artistic and political – many friendships were forged within its walls or in shooting or fishing in its policies. Mitchison himself spent much of the war in social research, in 1940 for the manpower survey which Sir William Beveridge undertook for Ernest Bevin's Ministry of Labour and from 1941 to 1943 as lieutenant in the London area for G. D. H. Cole's large-scale Nuffield Social Reconstruction Survey. This survey was abruptly terminated when government support was withdrawn, but the contacts it brought him with leading administrators on both sides of industry and with prominent figures in local government and the civil service widened and deepened his experience, so that when he decided to seek a more promising constituency he found no difficulty in being adopted for Kettering in Northamptonshire, a district which included a strong co-operative movement as well as a block of workers from Clydeside imported for employment by Stewarts and Lloyds in the developing area of Corby.

He was elected to Parliament, with a comfortable majority, in 1945, and retained the seat through all elections until his elevation to a life peerage in 1964. From first entry it became clear that all suspicions had melted away. He took to the new environment like a duck to water, made friends on all sides, and as a colleague showed himself willing to put his legal knowledge – he took silk in 1946 – freely at the disposal of any Labour member anxious to draft a question, move an amendment, make out a case in debate, or present a private Bill. Any aspirations he may have had for office were well concealed, and he was pleasurably surprised when at his first attempt, in 1955, he was elected to the Committee of the Parliamentary Party, i.e. to the Front Bench of the Opposition. His first speech as front-bencher was a fierce attack on the Rating and Valuation Bill, a subject peculiarly suited to his talents; and thereafter he led for the Party in a good many debates on housing, local government and cognate subjects. He held strong views on the issue of the atomic bomb, and was a fierce opponent of the death penalty. In 1961 he was made front-bench spokesman on science and technology, a task which he greatly enjoyed, until he was made to relinquish it to R. H. S. Crossman; instead, he led on pensions, which he liked much less. In the summer of 1964 he was asked by his party leader to stand down from the Kettering seat, and to accept a life peerage. Sir Geoffrey de Freitas became the candidate in his place. When Mitchison was offered congratulations on his peerage, he was quoted as saying: 'I am not so sure that I want congratulations. I dislike leaving Kettering very much. But you can't help getting older. Mr Wilson is, after all, the judge of what are the needs and interests of the Labour Party, and in these circumstances if you are asked to do this kind of thing you have to give some reason for not doing so.'

When Labour came to power after the general election of October 1964, he was considered too old to undertake a major ministry, but he was appointed parliamentary secretary to the newly created Ministry of Land and Natural Resources. As the Labour team in the Lords was still scanty in numbers, he was frequently called upon to answer there for Ministries other than his own, which he did to good effect. He was a highly respected member of his Government when in 1968 he had a serious illness. He made a partial recovery; but relapsed and died on 14 February 1970, leaving a widow, two daughters and three sons of distinction in science: his estate in England and Scotland was valued at £75,399.

MARGARET COLE

Writings: *Industrial Compensation* [1932] 20 pp.; *Banking: being a chapter from the history of the 1935 Socialist Government, written in 1970* [1932?] 29 pp.; 'The Russian Worker' in *Twelve Studies in Soviet Russia*, ed. M. I. Cole (1933) 75–103; (with G. D. H. Cole) *The Need for a Socialist Programme* [1933?] 17 pp.; *The First Workers' Government; or, New Times for Henry Dubb*, with an introduction by Sir S. Cripps (1934); 'Unity Manifesto', *New Statesman and Nation 13*, 23 Jan 1937, 115–16; 'Wages and the Cost of Living', in *Democratic Sweden*, ed. M. Cole and C. Smith (1938) 182–207; 'Retail Trade and the Co-operative Movement', ibid., 208–25; Edited with R. I. Simey, *Arnould on the Law of Marine Insurance and Average* (12th ed. 1939); 'Economic Importance of French Colonies', *New Statesman and Nation 19*, 29 June 1940, 800.

Sources: M. Ashley and G. T. Saunders, *Red Oxford* (Oxford University Labour Club, 1931); *Dod* (1945); E. Estorick, *Stafford Cripps* (1949); M. Cole, *The Story of Fabian Socialism* (1961); idem, *The Life of G. D. H. Cole* (1971). OBIT. *Northamptonshire Evening Telegraph* and *Times*, 16 Feb 1970; *Times*, 19 and 20 Feb 1970; *Kettering Leader*, 20 Feb 1970.

See also: *George Douglas Howard COLE.

MURNIN, Hugh (1865–1932)
MINERS' LEADER AND LABOUR MP

Hugh Murnin was born on 12 July 1865 at Durhamtown, Bathgate, Linlithgowshire, the son of Michael and Elizabeth Murnin. The family was of Irish descent, part of that very large migration into the Scottish coalfields in the middle of the nineteenth century which brought into existence an extensive Irish Catholic community in the midst of Presbyterian Scotland. On leaving elementary school at the age of nine, Hugh Murnin entered the mines, and in his early youth worked in almost every Scottish coalmining district. After twenty-one years as a miner, he was elected checkweighman at Bannockburn Colliery, Cowie, Stirlingshire, and six years later he became agent to the Stirlingshire Miners' Association. He was one of the first agents of the Association and retained the position until his death, although in his later years in an honorary capacity.

During his younger days he was active in the United Irish League, and throughout his life his prominence within both the trade union movement and the Labour Party was regarded by his fellow Catholics as one of the safeguards of their rights. During the First World War, which he supported, Murnin sat on recruiting tribunals and was a member of the Profiteering Appeal Court for the counties of Stirling, Dumbarton and Clackmannan.

Murnin became president of the National Union of Scottish Mineworkers in 1920, being replaced by Robert Smillie in 1922, with Murnin stepping down to vice-president. He served on the MFGB executive in 1912 and 1924. It was during his period of office as vice-president of the NUSMW that Murnin was involved in the serious internal factional fights of the late 1920s that led, *inter alia*, to the establishment of the United Mineworkers of Scotland. Murnin, who himself had been defeated in the ballots during all these bitter struggles, took the side of the existing officials of both Fife and the Scottish federation (and in particular William Adamson) and campaigned against the younger, more militant, and often Communist elements in the Scottish coalfields. Ballot votes in 1927 had resulted in a defeat of all the old officials who had thereupon (it seems quite unlawfully) refused to accept the results on the ground mainly that the total number participating had been fewer than normal [Arnot (1955) Ch. 8].

In the early 1920s Murnin turned his attention to parliamentary affairs and was elected Labour MP for Stirling and Falkirk at the 1922 general election (the first Labour candidate to be successful in the constituency); was defeated in 1923 and re-elected in 1924 and 1929. At the general election of 1931 he was again defeated. Except for his maiden speech during a debate on mining he almost never spoke in the House of Commons; although his considerable and expert knowledge on workmen's compensa-

tion, unemployment payment and pension rights was always at the service of his constituents. It was at the local and regional level that he was most active, and it was his moderate social Catholicism that provided much of the driving force of his personality. He was always prominent in the affairs of his local church, and his only son became a Catholic priest.

Hugh Murnin was also a leading figure in the local co-operative movement, being a director of a number of societies, chairman for three years of the Stirling Society, and one of the promoters of the Education Guild. He was a vigorous advocate of co-operative principles within the Labour Party.

Murnin was made a JP for both the burgh and county of Stirling in the early 1920s, and he later became a member of the advisory council for the appointment of JPs. He had married in his early manhood the daughter of James and Margaret McBryde of Denny and there were a son and three daughters of the marriage. His wife predeceased him and he himself died on 11 March 1932 at the home of his married daughter in Glasgow. After the celebration of Requiem Mass at St Mary's Church, Stirling, conducted by his son, he was buried at Bannockburn Cemetery. He left £379 personal estate.

He was succeeded as Labour candidate for Stirling by Joseph Westwood (who defeated James Barbour for the position) and Westwood regained the seat for the Labour Party at the 1935 general election.

Sources: S. V. Bracher, *The Herald Book of Labour Members* (1923) [with photograph]; *Dod* (1923) and (1929); *Labour Who's Who* (1927); *WW* (1931) [Mr Murnin's name appeared in *WW* annually up to 1959]; R. Page Arnot, *A History of the Scottish Miners* (1955); personal information: Miss E. A. Liversidge, Stirling. Obit. *Stirling J.*, 17 Mar 1932; *TUC Report* (1932).

JOYCE BELLAMY

See also: *Robert SMILLIE, for Scottish Mining Trade Unionism; Joseph SULLIVAN.

NEWTON, William (1822–76)
TRADE UNIONIST AND RADICAL

Born in Congleton, Cheshire in 1822, William Newton was the son of a journeyman mechanic. He became an apprentice at Kirk's Foundry, Etruria, Staffordshire, and joined the Hanley branch of the Journeymen Steam Engine and Machine Makers' Friendly Society (the 'Old Mechanics') in 1840. Soon after he moved to London and immediately became active in engineering union circles. He was elected to the 1843 Delegate Meeting, continued to represent London at the meetings of 1845, 1847 and 1848 and played a leading part in all the discussions of the later 1840s that led ultimately to amalgamation between existing unions. By 1848 he had risen to the position of foreman in an engineering firm named Robinsons, in the East End of London, and in this year he was dismissed for his trade union activity. He then took over the Phoenix Tavern, Ratcliffe Cross, already the meeting place of the East London branch of the 'Old Mechanics', and from this base greatly extended the influence of the union in local engineering shops and factories. William Allan had become general secretary of the 'Old Mechanics' in 1848, and the friendship and collaboration between Newton and Allan was to be an important factor in the eventual fusion of some of the existing societies into the Amalgamated Society of Engineers (ASE) on 6 January 1851. The membership of the ASE at the time of its formation was only 5000 – smaller than that of the 'Old Mechanics' in 1850, but its growth was rapid and by June 1851 there were over 9000 members organised in 100 branches.

William Newton played a leading part in all the detailed discussions both in London and nationally which preceded amalgamation; and on 4 January 1851 he began publishing and editing the *Operative*, a weekly paper which while not the official organ of the ASE yet devoted most of its space, in its early numbers in particular, to the problems of engineering trade unionism, arguing in a reasoned way the advantages of amalgamation.

Within the new amalgamated union it was Newton who moved the momentous resolution on the executive council: 'That all engineers, machinists, millwrights, smiths and pattern-makers cease to work systematic overtime and piece-work after 31 December 1851'; the resolution which precipitated the famous lock-out of the early months of 1852. The lock-out began on 10 January 1852 when the Lancashire and London employers closed their works. Newton was indefatigable during this critical period, addressing meetings all over the country, including one in the Manchester Free Trade Hall (described as 'the greatest indoor meeting ever held by the working class of England' *Operative*, 28 Feb 1852). The employers' representative, Sidney Smith, attributed the entire lock-out to 'a Mr Newton who went among them [the engineers] and propagated certain doctrines'. Although the engineers who were locked out remained solid to the end, the engineering employers won the day. Later, in the *Operative* (8 May 1852) Newton emphasised the hostility and misrepresentation of the press – 'of *The Times* particularly' – as a major factor in their defeat, although it was freely admitted that there were other reasons, not least the unpreparedness of the union as a whole for a prolonged strike.

At the executive council of the ASE which brought the lock-out to an end Newton moved a resolution which was unanimously agreed:

> That in the opinion of this meeting, the resistance of Labour against Capital is not calculated to enhance the condition of the labourers. We therefore advise that all our future operations should be directed to promoting the system of self-employment in associative workshops as the best means of effectually regulating the conditions of labour.

Thus began the short-lived association of the ASE with the Christian Socialists, chronicled by C. E. Raven among others [*Christian Socialism 1848–1854* (1920) pp. 231 ff.]. Newton himself, as his sponsorship of the resolution made clear, was wholeheartedly in support of the attempts 'to destroy the redundancy in the labour market' by co-operative workshops. He was not, however, opposed to independent political action by the working class – as were many who supported the idea of associative workshops at this time – and at the general election of July 1852 he stood as an independent working-class candidate for the Tower Hamlets seat against both Liberal and Tory. He received overwhelming support at the hustings and obtained the quite creditable vote of 1095 at the bottom of the poll. The fourteen points of his election address (*Operative*, 12 Apr 1852) included, besides the Chartist demands of universal suffrage and parliamentary reform, proposals for universal education, legislative protection for co-operators, state insurance for the unemployed and a revision of the Patent Laws 'so as to enable the poor inventor to secure for himself at small expense, the reward of his own ingenuity'. In his candidature he was strongly supported by the *Star of Freedom* (formerly the *Northern Star*) at this time edited by George Julian Harney. In the next few months, after the general election, there took shape a most interesting development, a coming together of trade unionists, co-operators and veteran Chartists such as Harney within a loose organisation that might have provided the basis for an independent working-class party. Newton led the movement in London together with the working-class Christian Socialists Richard Isham and Walter Cooper, and A. E. Delaforce of the Metropolitan Trades Delegates; and in September Newton published a long letter in the *Star of Freedom* (11 Sep 1852) setting forth the aims and policies of a 'National Party'. He argued for a limitation of their demands to the one aim of manhood suffrage – on the ground that all the other points of the Charter would follow once the suffrage was obtained – and he called for a public meeting to launch the new organisation. It was a call which, in the period of political disarray following the decline of Chartism after the events of 1848, had much to commend it to contemporary radicals; but it immediately encountered formidable obstacles. For one thing Harney himself was sceptical about

limiting the 'National Party's' demands to the single issue of manhood suffrage, and he was resolutely opposed to the implications of working with certain middle-class radicals. Even more important was the implacable hostility of Ernest Jones towards any alliance with the middle class or to a watering-down of the Chartist programme, and Jones commanded the respect and loyalty of the greater part of the working men who still adhered to the Charter. Newton himself was apparently quickly discouraged by the lack of response to his ideas, and Harney also began to consider the idea of a new movement premature. By the end of October 1852 the 'National Party' was stillborn and the *Star of Freedom* itself ceased publication in November.

Newton had already given clear evidence in the columns of the *Operative* – which had ceased publication in the spring of 1852 – of his political radicalism and of the Chartist context in which his ideas still moved. Editorials in the *Operative*, which although unsigned could only have been written by Newton, spoke in Chartist terms about the need for working-class representation in the House of Commons. They urged unions such as the ASE to take up social questions, such as the revision of the Master and Servant laws; they insisted that only an alteration in the political structure would open the way for social reform; and they emphasised in general the need for a unity of working people against the capitalist class. There was, moreover, a vision of a different order of society:

And behind these reforms, greater ones, affecting society as well as politics, rise up from the darkness of the future – that future which may be the beginning of a bright and glorious end, when those who make the wealth of the world shall be treated as justly as the ox which was not muzzled when treading out the corn [*Operative*, 9 Aug 1851].

The radical tone and temper of these writings and speeches was soon to be lost. His publishing and editing of *The Englishman* still, however, reflected the influence of Chartism. He wrote of the franchise, for example, that it would never be granted to working men 'unless the masses by organisation make power for themselves' (11 Feb 1854); but his ideas were already beginning to change by the middle of the decade and in the later years of the 1850s he was becoming an example of the labourist radical of the second half of the nineteenth century – one who was aware of and who retained memories of the Chartist years, but who now turned to engage in the practical problems of the day and in so doing became increasingly identified with the Liberal Party. In 1857 Newton founded, and edited, the *East London Observer*, and it is because of his editorial writing and the extensive reporting of his speeches that we have an unusually full account of the ways in which his political ideas altered. His political and social career in the last twenty-five years of his life may be taken as a paradigm of the labourist philosophy and practice which were to come to full development from the 1870s on.

Although Newton was never fully involved in an organisational way with the ASE after the early 1850s, he remained a close friend and associate of William Allan and he was often called upon to speak publicly in the name of the engineers. He still described himself as an engineer in his evidence before the 1856 S.C. on Masters and Servants (Equitable Councils Etc.) and on industrial issues he was consistent throughout his life. By the mid-1850s he was firmly against the unions becoming involved in political matters as such [S.C. of 1856, Qs 1574–6]; he defended on many occasions both the principles and the trade practices of the skilled unions; and he consistently advocated compulsory boards of conciliation as the way to regulate the industrial relations between employers and their workmen. As he said in a major speech at the time of the general election of 1868:

He knew there were difficulties existing between the working classes and their employers, and he also knew that the working classes, when addressed in bodies, would ask for nothing beyond fair justice. Now, there were employers who asserted they had the greatest difficulty in dealing with their workmen, stating that they would not listen to fair justice. This antagonistic state of things all arose from a want of proper communication between the two bodies. If there was a good feeling on the part of the labourer toward the employer on the one hand, and a proper consideration of the labourer by the employer on the other, there would not be the slightest difficulty in arriving at proper conclusions. He believed if there were opportunities afforded the working men of submitting their differences to arbitration at proper times and places, strikes and lock-outs, and all their evil effects, would be avoided . . . he was in favour of a court of arbitration being constituted under a legal statute, and that both parties should be compelled to submit to the decision of the arbitrators [*East London Observer*, 8 Aug 1868].

In October 1859 Adam Black, MP for Edinburgh and a member of the well-known publishing house, delivered an anti-union lecture on 'Wages, Trade Unions and Strikes' which obtained national publicity. The Edinburgh trades called a special meeting to answer Mr Black's attacks and Newton was sent by the council of the ASE to represent their case since the rules and practices of the ASE had been a main target of criticism. Newton's speech was later republished as a pamphlet. He began by a vigorous polemic against 'mere popinjays of men, who had entitled themselves not to stand upon any very high pedestal, and to lecture at working men upon duties which they knew fully better than they could be told by such gentlemen'. He then continued to defend at great length the regulations and union rules of the ASE, and attacked vigorously Black's proposition that labour was as much an article of commerce as corn or sugar. 'The great mistake of political economists', Newton went on, 'lay in first telling us that labour was a simple commodity, and then talking about the duties of servants.' And he ended on a very typical note, common to so much of the discussion from the side of the working men in the middle decades of the century:

After quoting from J. S. Mill, Adam Smith, and other political economists in favour of his views, Mr Newton maintained that working men were only attempting, by their trades' unions, to protect their own interests, and if Mr Black was so anxious that they should not do so, why did he not throw his own trade open, and abolish the copyright law? Why did he not let others sell the books which he claimed a right to sell? The only reason he knew was because it would not be profitable to do so, and he stated the same reason on behalf of trades' unions [Daily Scotsman, 12 Nov 1859].

A further example of the close association that Newton maintained with his trade union colleagues and friends came in the closing years of the 1860s. The Sheffield outrages and the Hornby v. Close decision put the unions under great pressure from an increasingly hostile public opinion, and Newton was as prominent as ever in stating their position. When the ASE convened a meeting at Exeter Hall on 21 February 1867 to consider the approach that should be adopted towards the newly established Royal Commission on Trade Unions, it was Newton who was called to the chair by the 3800 working men who were present. In his opening address he agreed that an inquiry into the outrages at Sheffield might not be unreasonable, but he protested vigorously at the extension of such an inquiry to cover the organisation and the working of Trade Societies like their own. The meeting agreed with him, and unanimously adopted resolutions condemning the Hornby v. Close decision, and expressing their serious dissatisfaction with the social composition of the Royal Commission [Full and Authentic Report ... (1867)].

With the foundation of his own East End newspaper in 1857 Newton became increasingly involved in local, and general London, politics. In 1855 Sir Benjamin Hall's Act had established the Metropolitan Board of Works which brought together

for certain administrative purposes the vestries of twenty-two of the larger parishes, fifteen district boards of works covering the other fifty-six parishes, and the local board of health for Woolwich. As its name suggested, the Metropolitan Board of Works was concerned with matters of sanitation, water supply and like problems. Newton was first elected to the Board as representative for the Mile End Vestry, and later he became for a period chairman of the Board and chairman of its parliamentary committee. His own career for the next twenty years until his death in the mid-seventies was closely bound up with the history of the Board's activities, and as a result of his prominence he was involved in a number of legal actions, one or two of which achieved more than local publicity. He took a major part in the developing controversy over the future structure of London's government, and a speech of his in 1870, in which he urged the establishment of 'one great central authority' (along the lines of the London County Council established in 1889), was reprinted and widely circulated. The East London Observer gave much prominence to the social conditions of the people of the East End, and in particular to the problems of pauperism and poor law policy [G. Stedman Jones, Outcast London (1971) Ch. 13 esp. 243 ff.]. Newton continuously advocated the equalisation of the poor rates between the various districts – 'the battle of the East End against the West End', as one of his supporters put it in the election campaign of 1868 – and the debates and discussions of these years on this particular question would have been warmly applauded by George Lansbury.

But despite his very close involvement with East End affairs, Newton did not remove himself entirely from the national politics of his period. He remained a consistent supporter of the secret ballot and of manhood suffrage, and he seems to have been especially active in the late 1850s and early 1860s on the franchise question. He attended, for example, the conference organised by Ernest Jones in 1858, as did his friend William Allan [Saville, Ernest Jones (1951) 68]; and he constantly stressed the need for working-class representatives in Parliament. During the early years of the American Civil War he developed an interesting variation on the minority radical opposition to political support for the Federal Cause. At an East End meeting called in December 1862 to discuss financial support for the relief of destitute Lancashire operatives, Newton said that:

His own feeling was that there was little to choose between north and south. He could not go so far as the gentleman who spoke last, for he could see little difference between candidly avowing a liking for slavery, and refusing, as was generally the case throughout the north, to sit in the same railway carriage, the same pew, or worship at the same altar as a negro [*East London Observer*, 13 Dec 1862]

Whether Newton changed his mind and became more favourable to the Northern cause after Lincoln's Emancipation statement – as a number of radicals did – is not known; but his attitude illustrates the complexities and differences of opinion within the working-class movement [Harrison (1965) Ch. 2]. The central theme of his political activity was, however, the demand for the working-class franchise which the Chartist movement had bequeathed to its successors; and linked with this demand was the problem of the relationships between working-class radicals and their allies – potential, actual or illusory – among the middle classes. Here Newton exhibited the common tendencies of these middle decades; and by the late 1860s he had thoroughly identified himself with the Liberal Party and its leader, W. E. Gladstone. His eulogies of the latter are quite remarkable in their fulsomeness, considering that at the same time he was capable of stringent criticism of the Whig element in the party. In the year before his death Newton presided over a meeting of the Labour Representation League, of which he was president, called, among other purposes, to regret the retirement of Gladstone from the leadership of the Liberal Party. For the achievements of the 1868–74 Gladstone government, Newton said:

... they were indebted to his intense love of justice and to his great ability, his unceasing application, and his commanding eloquence ... as long as Mr Gladstone required rest, and it might suit him to remain in quiet, he would carry with him to his retreat the thanks of the working men of the United Kingdom for the benefits he had conferred on the entire nation [*East London Observer*, 6 Feb 1875].

Newton again stood as parliamentary candidate for Tower Hamlets in the general election of 1868. It was a complicated local situation, with four Liberal candidates and one Tory. The two 'official' Liberal candidates were A. S. Ayrton, who had represented the East End for a good many years, and J. d'A. Samuda, a Whig. Edmond Beales of the Reform League was the other radical candidate besides Newton himself. Newton was supported by local businessmen and vestrymen as well as by some of the leading personalities of the metropolitan trades, including the secretaries of the ASE, Carpenters, Shipwrights and Ironfounders. Tom Hughes sent an open letter:

... I believe you would be of more use in the House than any of us, from the fact that you speak with the supreme authority of actual experience on questions in which we are only amateurs [*East London Observer*, 3 Oct 1868].

Newton claimed to have over 6000 local signatures in support of his candidature. The main point of his election programme called for the improvement of the 1867 Reform Act, the disestablishment of the Irish Church, a national and unsectarian system of education, the equalisation of poor rates ('pauperism, being a national calamity, should be supported by a national rate'), and compulsory industrial arbitration. At one public meeting during the election campaign Newton explained at length his support for Gladstone's proposals to disestablish the Irish Church. He emphasised his abhorrence of 'Fenianism and violence', but argued that the basic principle of disestablishment must not be obscured:

He hoped, however, that the greatest amount of respect would be paid to the properties attached to the Church: he would not advocate taking a tittle of that which was private property, but he would appropriate that which had come to the Church by confiscation to other purposes tending to the education of the people [*East London Observer*, 8 Aug 1868].

Newton was strongly opposed in the election by the *Bee-Hive* which was backing A. S. Ayrton and Beales; and George Potter was especially active on Ayrton's behalf. The latter was a subscriber to a confidential appeal by the *Bee-Hive* for financial help, to further its circulation among working-class voters, and 'to guide them at this important crisis in sustaining the LIBERAL PARTY . . .'. The story of intrigue and financial corruption surrounding the 1868 Election in the matter of working-class candidates and the Reform League has been told in detail in Harrison, *Before the Socialists* (1965) Ch. 4; and it provides a necessary part of the background to Newton's own intervention. His candidature was, it is clear, largely rooted in his local influence. It was resented by George Potter and George Howell, for their own special reasons and from evidence of Newton's public meetings it was vigorously opposed by many of the rank and file of the Reform League in the East End. In the event Newton came bottom of the poll, the results being:

A. S. Ayrton	9839
J. d'A. Samuda	7849
O. E. Coope	7416
E. Beales	7160
W. Newton	2890

In the year before his death, Newton stood as parliamentary candidate again, in a by-election at Ipswich. One of the sitting members – a Conservative – had died and under the accepted custom the Liberal Party decided not to contest the seat. An Ipswich branch of the Labour Representation League had been formed in 1875, the prime mover of which was George Hines, and it was Hines who was largely responsible for the invitation to Newton. The local unions and other working-class organisations warmly supported his candidature and the contest aroused more than local interest. Newton made an important speech on 18 December 1875 which was later reprinted as a pamphlet, and which once again is a useful source for the labourist ideology of these years. 'I am here, then', he insisted 'not to divide, but rather to consolidate and sustain the Liberal interest; to support all sections of Liberal reformers, and to endeavour, if possible, to unite them in one body against the common opponent.' The policy he put forward was couched in general and moderate terms; apart from calling for the total revision of the Land Laws and of the Game Laws, and the assimilation of the franchise in the county districts with the urban boroughs, there was hardly a specific reform mentioned in his speech. His only criticism of the Liberal Party – to which he paid enthusiastic tribute for its past history – was the failure to consult with their working-class supporters on the choice of candidates: a theme which was to be much more strongly emphasised by Lib-Labs in the following decade. The election took place on 1 January 1876 and Newton polled 1607 votes against the Conservative's 2213.

Newton died a few months after the Ipswich by-election. He had been ill for little over a month, suffering, among other things, from a mild form of Bright's disease and he died at his home at Stepney Green on Thursday 9 March 1876. Of his family life little is known: he was married and had at least one daughter, who married into a local business family. Newton left effects valued at under £6000. He had been given several public testimonials in his day. In 1860 the ASE had presented him with a silver goblet and a purse of £300, 'in recognition of his devoted services'; and in 1873 at the Albion Tavern friends presented him with a purse of 1000 guineas and a service of plate to the value of £250.

Writings: In *The Operative*, 1851–2, *The Englishman*, 1853–4 and the *East London Observer*, 1858–76, all of which Newton edited; Evidence before the S.C. on Masters and Operatives (Equitable Councils, &c.) 1856 XIII Qs 1514–676; 'The Origin, Progress and Recent Position of the Amalgamated Society of Engineers', *Trans NAPSS* (1861) [paper read but not printed]; *Speech at Mile End Vestry on 29 April 1868 on the Metropolitan Board of Works and the Taxation of the Metropolis* (n.d.) 11 pp.; *Statement . . . at the Mile End Vestry in relation to the charges in Mr Beal's pamphlet against the Metropolitan Board of Works* [1870] 16 pp.; *The Government of London: speech on 22 April 1870 at Metropolitan Board of Works* [1870] 16 pp. *Speech at the Metropolitan Board of Works on 6 December 1872 on the Subject of Freeing the Metropolitan Toll Bridges and the Coal and Wine Duties* (1872) 16 pp. [repr. from *The Metropolitan*, 7 Dec 1872]; *Speech on Municipality of London Bill at meeting of Metropolitan Board of Works 19 March 1875* (1875) 15 pp.; *A Speech delivered at Ipswich by Mr William Newton, President of the Labour Representation League, 18 December 1875* (n.d.) 15 pp.

Sources: *Operative*, 8 Mar, 9 Aug and 6 Sep 1851; 28 Feb, 10 and 12 Apr and 8 May 1852; *Star of Freedom*, 11 and 25 Sep, 9 Oct 1852; *East London Observer*, 1858–76 *passim* and especially 13 Dec 1862; 8 Aug and 3 Oct 1868; 6 Feb 1875; *Daily Scotsman*, 12 Nov 1859; *J. of the Typographic Arts*, 2 Aug 1860; NAPSS Committee, *Trades' Societies and Strikes* (1860, repr. New York, 1868); *Nat. Reformer*, 18 Mar 1861; Discussion following papers on the employer and the employed by J. M. F. Ludlow and Frederic Harrison, *Trans NAPSS* (1862) 798; *Bee-Hive*, 31 Oct, 7, 14, 21 Nov 1868; [L. Brentano], 'The Growth of a Trades-Union', *N. Brit. Rev. 53* (Oct 1870) 59–114; S. & B. Webb, *The History of Trade Unionism* (1894); G. Howell, *Labour Legislation, Labour Movements and Labour Leaders* (1902); A. W. Humphrey, *A History of Labour Representation* (1912); C. E. Raven, *Christian Socialism 1848–1854* (1920); F. E. Gillespie, *Labor and Politics in England, 1850–1867* (Duke Univ. Press, 1927); R. Ratcliffe, History of the Working Class Movement in Ipswich, 1 [typescript, 1935; Ipswich Borough Library and microfilm Hull University Library]; G. D. H. Cole, *British Working Class Politics 1832–1914* (1941, 4th impression, 1965); J. B. Jefferys, *The Story of the Engineers* [1945]; AEU, *William Newton 1822–1876* (1951) 9 pp. [Tower Hamlets Central Library]; J. Saville, *Ernest Jones: Chartist* (1952); B. C. Roberts, *The Trades Union Congress 1868–1921* (1958); A. R. Schoyen, *The Chartist Challenge: a portrait of George Julian Harney* (1958); R. Harrison, *Before the Socialists* (1965); G. S. Jones, *Outcast London* (1971); F. M. Leventhal, *Respectable Radical: George Howell and Victorian Working Class Politics* (1971). OBIT. *Minutes of Metropolitan Board of Works*, 10 and 24 Mar 1867; *East London Observer* and *Suffolk Chronicle*, 11 Mar 1876; ASE, *Monthly Report* (Mar 1876) [by John Burnett].

The assistance of Mrs Marion Miliband in collecting material for this entry is gratefully acknowledged.

JOHN SAVILLE

See also: †William ALLAN, and for New Model Unionism; *George Julian HARNEY; †George Lelly HINES; George HOWELL; *Ernest Charles JONES; John Malcolm Forbes LUDLOW, and for Christian Socialism, 1848–54.

NOEL, Conrad le Despenser Roden (1869–1942)
CHRISTIAN SOCIALIST

Conrad le Despenser Roden Noel, priest of the Church of England, was born on 12 July 1869, in one of the Royal cottages at Kew, lent for the occasion by an aunt who was Lady-in-Waiting to the Queen. His grandfather was the Earl of Gainsborough, his father (reluctantly) a Groom of the Privy Chamber; the powerful, freebooting Norman Despensers were among his ancestors, and the influential Buxtons among his relatives; so Noel seemed from the start destined for the high places of church or state. This expectation was doubtless heightened by his conventional course through the brutalities of prep. and two public schools – Winchester and Cheltenham – and by his subsequent behaviour at Cambridge where he cut loose in the raffish, riotous style customary among the sons of the gentry. In addition to a riotous and mocking defiance of authority, Noel flaunted 'shocking opinions' which included, according to Buxton cousins, the advocacy of anarchism, the ridiculing of 'Arthurian Ideals', 'save your soul' religion, and marriage; and a deriding of such Buxton family heroes as Lord Shaftesbury, Wilberforce and Elizabeth Fry. A sobering duly came: rustication for a year; shame at heavy debts piled up for his father to pay; falling in love with Miriam Greenwood; conversion to Socialism through hearing Annie Besant lecture and reading *The Socialist Catechism* by J. L. Joynes – some or all of these things steadied him. He did not return to Cambridge, but was privately tutored for entry to a theological college by Herman Joynes, brother of J. L. In the interim came doubts about the validity of Christianity and about his vocation. But by reading widely in other world religions, he satisfied himself that none was so near the truth for humanity as Christianity. He then studied nonconformity and romanism, and emerged convinced that in England the national church had more of true Christianity in its best thought and tradition than the other churches had. At Chichester Theological College, which he entered in 1893, he discovered that the fathers of the early church held revolutionary views on usury, private property and the oppression of poor men by rich men; he was thus strengthened in his belief that Christianity was relevant to contemporary social and economic problems, and that in politics a Christian could be no other than a Socialist.

On leaving college, Noel volunteered to help Father Robert Dolling who, after years of devoted mission work in the slums of Portsmouth, was in trouble with the Bishop of Winchester, and was soon afterwards to be dismissed. But before this happened, Noel, seeking ordination, had gone to join Father Charles Chase at All Saints, Plymouth. Like Dolling, Chase was an extreme

ritualist, using a debased continental ceremonial, knowing no other; but unlike Dolling, Chase was deeply committed to the dogmas and authoritarianism of the Roman Church, and in due time made his capitulation to it. Uneasy at some of Chase's beliefs, Noel nevertheless respected him because of his work among the poor and destitute. But association with Chase increased official suspicion of Noel. When the time came he was refused ordination by the Bishop of Exeter on grounds – mutually contradictory, according to Noel – of 'pantheism and romanism'.

Perhaps it was these encounters with the miseries of the very poor in Portsmouth and Plymouth that led Noel to seek closer acquaintance with the destitute by masquerading as a tramp and living in London doss-houses. Moved and concerned as he was with the plight of the outcasts, he came away from the adventure certain that it was not possible to 'build a new society out of the material of slum dwellers and waifs and strays'; and his education in these matters was enlarged when he spent some time with Percy Dearmer, curate of St Anne's, Lambeth, a Fabian Socialist. Both Dearmer and his vicar, W. A. Morris, were members of the Guild of St Matthew, the Church Socialist Group founded in 1877 by Stewart Headlam; and in 1895, immediately after their marriage, both Noel and his wife Miriam Greenwood joined the Guild also. Morris was revered by the working people in the parish for the simplicity of his life among them, and for his ardent championship of the gas workers in their battle for union rights and better conditions.

Fuller enlightenment came when Noel, still seeking ordination, moved north to Floweryfield, Cheshire – where the vicar, T. M. Tozer, exhausted by a long and apparently hopeless struggle to train his congregation in correct responses, stances and gestures in church, gladly allowed his energetic assistant to liven up services and ceremonial and to begin a series of Sunday afternoon lectures on Socialism and Catholicism. Crowds came, but few of them were regular churchgoers. There were protests from the more influential pew-renters. Bishop Jayne of Chester sent for Noel and ordered him to cease work among agnostics, atheists and dissenters, and devote himself to churchgoers only. Noel would not, was refused ordination and dismissed from his post. He was to be unemployed for two years.

Among secular socialist societies, Noel chose to join the doggedly Marxist Social Democratic Federation, 'dogmatic socialism being the obvious expression in the political sphere of dogmatic social democratic catholicism in the theological . . .'. He was aware, however, of the faults of the SDF — its rigid determinism, its ill-digested and narrow atheism, which resulted, he declared, in 'a hard and unlively and unattractive presentation which has small powers of conversion'.

The Noels remained in the north, Noel earning a precarious livelihood by book-reviewing and other writing, and occasionally by paid lecturing. He gave most of his time to the Socialist movement, and became popular among those artisans, operatives and miners who, with their Socialist and co-operative societies, study classes, drama and literary groups, Clarion cycling clubs, choirs, orchestras and brass and silver bands, were creating in their midst a piece of that new society for which they were striving. In them Noel saw the people capable of overturning the old order and making a new life. In his view, these were the kind of people who had gathered round Jesus, and founded the early Christian communities.

Bishop Charles Gore rescued Noel from unemployment by finding him a place at St Philip's, Salford, under the tolerant Canon Hicks, who made no objection to Noel's extra-parochial activities among the Socialists, nor to the prominent part he took in the 'free speech' tussle at Boggart Hole Clough, for which he was three times arrested. Ordained priest in 1898, Noel became assistant at St Philip's, Elswick, Newcastle, to the Vicar, W. E. Moll, a veteran; the other assistant priest was Percy Widdrington, a younger member of the GSM. After two stirring years of campaigning

for social-democratic catholicism Noel moved on to St Mary's, Paddington Green, London, where the vicar, A. L. Lilley, an Anglo-Catholic with Socialist sympathies, was in close touch with advocates of 'modernism' and reform among French Roman Catholics.

Noel's main activity at St Mary's was mission work in the Paddington slums. In spite of much effort, he found the hard-pressed slum dwellers indifferent to the social gospel, and indeed, to any gospel. He had some success, however, with the children, using imaginative, liberating methods of teaching which were rare at the time. Being in London, Noel was able to take a more active part in the affairs of the GSM, and served as honorary secretary in 1903 and 1904. Towards the end of 1904, Noel was invited by Percy Dearmer to become assistant priest at St Mary's, Primrose Hill. Here Dearmer was replacing the fussy, frilly Roman ceremonial, slavishly imitated by most Anglo-Catholics, by the magnificent usages of the pre-Reformation English Church. The social gospel, the colour and significance of the ceremonial, and the music were drawing crowds to the church. Noel went there gladly and learnt much that was to be of use to him in later years.

Leaving Paddington meant moving home. Noel's cousin, Noel Buxton, was seeking a suitable tenant for the old house he had bought at Coggeshall, Essex, called Paycock's. It had been shamefully neglected and needed considerable repair. The Noels wanted a home, Dearmer was generous, and Noel's parish duties were considerably concentrated from Friday nights to Monday mornings; so the Noels, with their year old daughter Barbara, moved in to Paycock's. For nearly five years the Noels lived there, enduring much discomfort, but encouraging, guiding and helping a local carpenter Ernest Beckwith in a superb restoration of the lovely old house.

In spite of his duties at St Mary's, Noel continued to be busy in the GSM, to write for Socialist papers, to review books occasionally for the *Daily News*, and to speak at Socialist meetings all over Britain. In July 1906, stimulated by the massive victory of the Liberal Party in the election of that year, and presumably even more by the return of twenty-nine supposedly independent Labour members, Noel, Widdrington, Moll, Arnold Pinchard and some others formed the Church Socialist League, a body more avowedly Socialist and more directly active in the labour movement than the old GSM. The CSL defined its Socialism as 'the political, economic and social emancipation of the whole people, men and women, by the establishment of a democratic commonwealth in which the community shall own the land and capital, and use them co-operatively for the good of all'. It was and was meant to be the 'economic socialism' of the secular societies. In the 'immediate work' the Church Socialists had 'as their comrades Messrs Hyndman, Hardie, Blatchford and Shaw, but their standpoint and their power is the philosophy of the Gospels, the tradition of the Church, and the driving force of the Holy Spirit'.

In 1907, Noel gave up his work with Dearmer to be, until 1910, the League's organising secretary. During those years, Noel was telling Socialist men and women up and down the country that the Church was founded to be 'the social-democratic organ of the Kingdom', 'the sacraments were social pledges of the Kingdom', 'the creeds had a social-democratic significance', the Liturgy of the Church of England was 'soaked in Socialism'; and that 'the Church of England, in taking its stand at the Reformation on not the Bible only but the Bible as interpreted by early Christian writers, is possibly committed to communist principles which go beyond our modest Socialist proposal'. Churchgoers 'must at least be Socialists and work with their fellow Socialists, Christian and non-Christian alike, for the establishment of God's international commonwealth', for in economic Socialism was to be found 'the practical and scientific form for our day and in one important sphere for the realisation of those very objects which the Church has always had at heart'.

In its first three years, the CSL grew, and though never a large body, had considerable influence. But, in spite of Liberal promises and social legislation, the rich were growing richer, the poor poorer. The workers turned their backs on Labour and most of the ILP leaders as being little more than hirelings of Liberal Capitalism, and began a series of strikes; other rebels, such as suffragettes and Irish, added to a mounting hostility to Government and social system. Younger men left the Socialist societies in order to preach syndicalism and industrial action, and these societies began to droop and decline.

Forced to look again at Socialism and the Socialist societies, Noel, like many, clung to old formulas while proclaiming the need for new ones. The Victor Grayson election of 1907 and the protest of 1908 brought a campaign for a united and militant Socialist party, in which the CSL, and Noel as its leading and most flamboyant personality, were prominent. The British Socialist Party (a union of the SDF with a number of ILP branches) was eventually established, but the growing tide of rebellion rolled past it, leaving it in the shallows.

Besides organising, speaking for the CSL, and other Socialist groups, and campaigning for a united revolutionary Socialist party, Noel was doing Sunday duties for Canon Steele at Saffron Walden, and writing *Socialism in Church History* and *By-Ways of Belief*. In all this immense activity he had little fresh to say on the problems of the movement. He suggested that the CSL would go on growing and become more influential in the Church and labour movement, though in fact, like all the Socialist societies, it was losing ground. The Church, he wrote, needed a 'reinterpretation of the creeds and their application to the practical life of men, the democratisation of the Church, an effective desire to meet both Nonconformists, Atheists and Agnostics, listen to their criticisms, and, with their help, rebuild the national religion without sacrificing a single essential principle'.

In December 1909 he was speaking for Victor Grayson in the Colne Valley during the election, and in January 1910 was inspiring an unlikely audience of parsons and county people at Warwick Castle. Soon afterwards, Lady Warwick offered him the living of Thaxted, one of the five churches in the valley of the Essex Chelmer of which she owned the patronage as lady of the manor at Easton. For centuries a thriving market town, by 1910 Thaxted had shrunk to a small place of under two thousand souls, dependent for a living mainly upon farming and a modest sweet-making factory. Visiting the place for the first time, Noel was depressed by what he saw of church and town, and had almost decided to turn the living down, when some inner prompting caused him to change his mind and accept it.

News of his appointment brought angry protests from residents and outsiders. The protests continued during the summer; and at Noel's induction on 21 September 1910, crowds gathered in the churchyard and in the streets outside, some of them hostile. The presence of Lady Warwick, several Buxtons, and many parsons, among them CSL members, probably stifled any intended protest; the ceremony was undisturbed. Noel made his changes slowly, but met opposition at once. His Socialism had already alienated the gentry and some farmers and businessmen; his Catholicism, promptly dubbed 'popery' by the less scrupulous of his opponents, antagonised some working people and traders who might otherwise have accepted his Socialism. Some churchgoers resented changes in familiar ways of worship, and identified that resentment as opposition to Socialism and Catholicism. The changes were sweeping: Noel moved the heavy choir stalls from the chancel to the west end of the church, lengthened the altar, moved the altar rails farther down into the body of the church, cleared the beautiful nave pillars and wide spaces of the building from the clutter of chairs clogging them, and replaced the tawdry ornaments, gloomy furnishings and sombre hangings with simple handwoven tapestries, banners, a few pictures and several small shrines and altars, the arrangement of which was largely the work of Miriam Noel; he introduced unaccompanied singing and plainsong, sat the choir of men and boys with the congregation, and made a sung Communion and not Matins the main Sunday service, explaining that 'the Lord's service' commemorated the sacrifice of Jesus and of countless saints and rebels for the cause of God's kingdom on earth; and that with its sharing of the good things of life, symbolised in the nourishing bread and the merry wine of fellowship, it was a foretaste of life in that kingdom.

Indignation among the more conventional parishioners swelled. The surpliced choir and the lady organist departed. So did the chief churchwarden and several other regular churchgoers when Noel abolished reserved seats in the church. A number of Noel's opponents stayed, to resist the innovating vicar. Others hesitated, confused by the topsy-turvy situation created by Noel's actions. The social and political proprieties, in which landowner, parson, farmer and businessman were Tories, went to church and ruled the countryside to uphold the *status quo*, while shopkeeper, workman and farmhand were Liberals, went to chapel, and constituted the reforming opposition, were in disarray. The big landowner and the parson, both of unquestionable aristocratic lineage, were championing the cause of the working people and being opposed by Tories and Liberals, in a town where Liberals were strong enough to win the County Council seat and where the only factory was owned by a Liberal. Real and imaginary lines of division were fast disappearing. Yet neutrals, and some avowed enemies of Noel's Socialism, found themselves involved in activities sprouting from the church. Thus crowds of children and young people, some of whose parents were hostile or indifferent to the social gospel, went along joyfully enough to the stimulating Sunday schools and catechism classes run by Noel and his helpers. The common people of Thaxted, unknown to their governors, had cherished in their cottages and taverns fragmentary survivals of the long-submerged culture of the English people; and becoming aware of this, and prompted by Miriam Noel, Noel was moved to arrange classes in country dances, and to revive the not long disbanded Morris team. The response astonished everyone. Children, young people, and adults came in crowds and took naturally to the music and dancing. Many commoners and young people likewise took to the ceremonial and the rest of it. As Noel, in those early years, groped towards a full expression of his social-democratic Catholicism, and, by instinct rather than design, towards the renewal of an indigenous culture, he shaped the rites, the music, the dancing, the common life, the drama of the Mass and of the Christian-Pagan festivals of the year not only into a summons to social salvation and a premonition of Christ's kingdom on earth, but also, at its fullest, into an imaginative exploration and statement of man's place in the natural order and in divine creation. To this people responded emotionally, and imaginatively.

Thaxted undoubtedly had a considerable effect on Noel; and the presentation of his social-democratic Catholicism liberated him partially from obligations to institutions and the political contentions of the hour. But only partially. In mundane matters contention continued; and Noel remained involved with the institutions and doctrines, though endeavouring to sharpen and modernise the formulations.

In January 1911 Noel began the publication of *Country Town* – a vigorous, well-produced monthly journal. He organised a series of evening lectures in the church, and initiated debates with local nonconformist ministers. When, with misgivings, he agreed that the assistant priest George Chambers – also a Socialist – should take over the almost moribund boy scout organisation, there was again an unusually enthusiastic response from the young, and approval from their parents.

During 1911 and 1912, Noel was as active as ever in the CSL and Socialist societies, and prominent in the campaign for and the foundation of the British Socialist Party, serving for a period on its executive committee. All was not well, however, with the Socialist societies; amid the tumult of rebellion all over Britain, the societies were losing members and direction. Uneasily aware of this, and contrasting the condition of the groups with what was going on at Thaxted, Noel argued that the whole

Catholic religion was essential to social revolution and social salvation, and that the CSL could activate itself and the secular rebel movements only along such lines. The League, he pointed out, was open to anyone belonging to the Church of England who also accepted economic Socialism. But doctrines held by some members were the theological equivalents of belief in capitalist individualism. The League should base itself on a restated, renovated Catholic theology.

Discussions on the theology of social-democracy Catholicism took place in the CSL, and at private gatherings at Thaxted. Most League members, however, remained obdurate in their conviction that Protestants could be Socialists (if members of the Church of England); and, though the Thaxted talks were more useful, no agreed body of doctrine emerged from them. Discussions, renewed intermittently, faded with the outbreak of war in August 1914; the League's membership and activities diminished; its future seemed uncertain. It was divided over the war. So, too, was the British Socialist Party, which in 1916 split on the issue, the pro-war minority walking out after defeat at conference. Noel supported the war against 'Prussianism' from the start, but with important reservations, chiefly a strong and, as the war went on, a growing belief that there must be energetic war also on 'Prussianism at home'; an early supporter of Guild Socialism, he was at the 1915 London conference where the National Guilds League was formed, and was elected to the executive.

Noel was stirred to renewed assault on the quiescent CSL members by the Irish Rebellion of Easter 1916, with its passionate affirmation that without the shedding of blood there could be no social or national redemption. In the autumn of that year, at a long-overdue League conference, Noel presented the document *Some Articles of the Faith* to the executive, asking that it should be placed before conference as the proposed basis for future League membership and work. This the executive refused to do – though the document was read to the Conference – whereupon Noel resigned, intending, according to the report in the *Church Socialist*, to start 'A Company of the Redemption, to embody his reading of the great truths and implications embodied in our Catholic faith'.

It was to be another nineteen months before the new group was founded, months that brought two revolutions in Russia and the final agonies of the war. On 10 April 1918 a handful of people met at Thaxted vicarage and resolved to set up 'the Catholic Crusade of the Servants of the Precious Blood to transform the Kingdoms of the world into the Commonwealth of God' – a title shortened before long to the Catholic Crusade. By the time of the Armistice, the Crusade's first handwritten statement had given way to a printed one, and, by the end of that year, Noel and others had composed a manifesto, *The Catholic Crusade*, which was to remain the definitive statement of the group.

It was Noel's most powerful and persuasive statement of social-democratic Catholicism. All of a piece, matter and manner fused with remarkable success, the manifesto caught up in style and argument not only the revolutionary excitements of the hour but also a centuries-old rebel and Socialist tradition. With its publication the Crusade began enrolling members in Thaxted from the young men returning from the war, and the young women coming home from the munition factories in the north; and outside, from members of the CSL and the National Guilds League.

In 1919 and 1920, Noel was contributing to George Lansbury's *Daily Herald*, speaking and writing for the CSL, the NGL, the Catholic Crusade; taking part in a series of lectures organised by the Catholic Crusade in London in support of the Russian Revolution and the Irish struggle for national independence, and for an English revolution; in touch with Sylvia Pankhurst and her East End Workers' Federation; and, through her and her paper, the *Workers' Dreadnought*, following the negotiations between the newly-founded Communist International and various British groups for the formation of a British Communist Party. Busy also with the Free Catholic

Movement, which aimed at uniting dissenters and the Church of England round a catholic belief and order, Noel hoped to win the growing Anglo-Catholic movement to his social gospel. But his passionate belief that 'worship divorced from social righteousness is an abomination in the sight of God' was too much for most Anglo-Catholics, who were concerned, said Noel, only with 'what went on in church'. And Church authorities in many dioceses, armed with new powers by Parliament, were persecuting the more fervent Catholic priests. Noel spoke at various protest meetings, condemning the persecution but urging Catholic churchmen to root their ceremonial and parish life in the social gospel. In 1919, Thaxted Church took a prominent place in this struggle when Noel defied the Bishop of Chelmsford's ban and went ahead with Thaxted's annual Midsummer Festival procession on Saturday 28 June, in which the Host was ceremonially elevated. He described the event as 'the uplifting of the Son of Man as the God of Justice in our midst'. The Catholic Crusade advertised in the *Church Socialist* and the *Church Times*, inviting 'all who wish to join in the Procession of the Divine Outlaw' to attend. Militant anti-papist protestant organisations summoned supporters to Thaxted, declaring their intention of breaking up the procession by force, and on the day crowds poured into the village. The storm raged in the streets as the procession made its way from the church down the main street and back again. The crowds billowed out into the road as attempts were made to attack the procession, the police watching but obviously instructed not to interfere. Amid mounting turmoil, which reached a crescendo as the Host was elevated on the steps of the Moot Hall, the assaults were constantly checked by lines of soldiers, supporters, and, significantly, by Thaxted residents, who, but for a diminishing though virulent minority, had come to respect Noel if not always to agree with his views. A reporter watching noted that the hostile elements were from the outside: 'Thaxted people showed an extraordinary devotion and loyalty to their vicar.'

Bishop Watts Ditchfield put Thaxted church under interdict, dismissed the Brentwood curate, Stanley Joad, who had elevated the Host, and threatened proceedings for Noel's removal unless he conformed. Noel replied by accusing the bishop of heresy, and refusing to obey him. A sort of truce was reached between the two men during 1920, when Noel's health worsened – he had been diagnosed as diabetic in 1913 – and he was compelled to absent himself from Thaxted for periods, leaving Jack Bucknall, assistant priest since 1919, in charge.

By 1921, the post-war revolutionary tide was ebbing – wartime promises and 'reconstruction' schemes were, as Noel had foreseen, being discarded. Unemployment was rising, wage reductions were threatened, and the first to be attacked were the miners. On 12 April 1921, Noel was among the speakers at a Kingway Hall meeting in support of the miners called by the University Socialist Federation and attended by over 2000 people, one of numerous expressions of support for solidarity against employers and government. Three days later the miners' partners in the Triple Alliance withdrew their strike notices, the miners were left to fight alone, and labour's rout had begun.

The opposition to Noel at Thaxted grew bolder, and sought, with help from Conservative newspapers, to force Noel to abandon the social gospel and its ceremonial and symbols, or resign as vicar. Hostile newspaper comments on the flags in Thaxted Church became more frequent – three flags were all that remained of a display put around a shrine at the onset of war in 1914; it had included the old flag of Ireland and the English flag. In 1915 or early 1916 Noel had added the Red Flag, and, after the 1916 Easter uprising in Dublin, substituted the tricolour of Sinn Fein for the old Irish flag. Little notice was taken of this for several years, but now, with Irish nationalists at war with British Government forces, and the Red Flag of world labour being erroneously and maliciously identified with the flag of 'Bolshevik' Russia, Thaxted's flags became the focus of

considerable argument and agitation. Noel, without doubt, revelled in the controversy; it was a good example of his way of teaching essential and living themes by the use of symbols. The flags of England and Ireland symbolised love of country and the right of national self-determination. The Red Flag gave balance to the love of national freedom by representing the aspirations of labour for equality of men within the nation, and for a federation of nations within a world commonwealth.

On Sunday 24 April 1921, a reporter from the *Daily Chronicle* visited Thaxted church. He noted placards outside denouncing rich men and their Government as warring against the workers and the Irish, equating them with those who had crucified Jesus; and he saw that 'on either side of the noble chancel hung the red flag of the revolution and the flag of the Irish Sinn Fein Republic'.

The three flags were carried in church procession on Sunday 1 May. A day or so later the Red Flag was stolen. Another was put in its place. That one was taken by a raiding party of Cambridge undergraduates, and this raid received much publicity. Angry editorials in national newspapers, and questions in Parliament, demanded action by Church and Government against Noel.

On Empire Day, 24 May 1921, the town was invaded by over a thousand undergraduates, Conservatives and other assorted rowdies and the wild scenes in the streets were widely reported. On 26 June night raiders broke into the church, pulled the flags down, burnt them in the church stove and hoisted Union Jacks across the chancel. In the morning churchgoers hauled down the Union Jacks and replaced the missing flags. On Saturday 9 July came the most formidable raid of all, when Army officer cadets and others advanced on the town in three motorised columns, and, while the police stood and watched, after a scuffle in the church with Noel, Bucknall and some women, pulled down the flags and carried them out into the street. There the Red Flag was set on fire, but, because of the truce suddenly agreed on in the Irish War, the tricolour was handed over to the police. Two new flags were again placed in the church.

On 22 January 1922 six Thaxted residents petitioned the Consistory Court of the Diocese for a faculty for the removal of the flags. These petitioners, and the hostile newspapers, had long insisted that Noel spoke for only a minority of Thaxted's churchgoers. The opposition prepared, therefore, for elections on 12 April to the newly-established Parish Church Councils. To their surprise and chagrin, Noel's supporters won all the seats easily, polling five-sixths of the total votes cast, a result unreported in the newspapers that said Noel spoke for a minority. On Empire Day, the town was again invaded, and for hours noisy crowds paraded the streets. The petition was heard at Chelmsford on 8 July 1922, and the Chancellor of the Diocese, in a strongly partial, unjudicial decision, ordered the flags to be removed. 'An insult to the people of the Irish Free State, and to the workers of this country', said Noel.

The Catholic Crusade, equipped with Manifesto, several tracts and a little book of devotions which included 'The Red Mass', was growing in a few other areas, though its membership was never high. It recruited selectively; a period of probation was enforced on applicants; and only after scrutiny and debate at the Crusade's annual chapter was full membership granted. But the main reason why the Crusade grew so slowly was that it could create groups and a common life only around a parish church, conducted by a Crusade priest; it made its point not only, or even mainly, in words, but in the life of the church and the parish; in ceremony as well as Socialism, in sacrament as well as sermon, in plainsong as well as politics.

Livings for Crusade priests were hard to come by. Bishops were hostile to Socialism or Catholicism, or both. Even tolerant vicars recoiled from the furore created by a Crusade curate; and as the church filled with young people, with 'dissenters and riff-raff', regular churchgoers protested, wealthy patrons departed, collections fell. Only exceptional circumstances made a prolonged stay possible for the Crusade priests in the 1920s – as at St Michael's, Poplar; at St John's, Delabole, and at Sneyd Church, Burslem, which became a centre of social-democratic Catholicism throughout the 1920s and into the 1930s. Here, and at a handful of other churches in the 1930s, in spite of much harassment by the authorities, Noel's points were made fluently and powerfully: that the Church of the Establishment, of the powers that be, could become again the church of the true English nation, and that the common people would respond eagerly to the social gospel in industrial as well as in rural areas.

Thaxted remained the heart of the movement, and here, as the young people Noel had won at the beginning became men and women, his position became assured. The town and much of its life was being shaped to the Church and what went on in it and around it. The orchestral music and choral singing, developed by Gustav Holst in the war years; the founding of the Morris Ring and its Whitsun gathering at Thaxted; the beauties of the Church, its furnishings and ceremonial, the crowds at the year's high festivals – it all expressed the revolutionary social gospel.

The world collapse of the capitalist economy, and the ignominious fall of the Labour Government in 1931, brought Noel and his Catholic Crusade comrades more attention from ecclesiastics, startled into examining society's problems in search of remedy for economic ills. Noel and some of his comrades were invited to write for Church journals, to address weekend schools and conferences. But few cared to join a group so small, so absolute, so extreme in its demands. Soviet Communism became fashionable among intellectuals and church dignitaries; Noel, though on the executive committee of the Communist-controlled League Against Imperialism for some years, was never a supporter of Communist doctrine, even in the years when he had strongly defended the Russian Revolution.

Much of his activity was necessarily curtailed by a worsening of his diabetic condition in the early 1930s. By 1935, his twenty-fifth year as vicar of Thaxted, he had became wholly blind. Nevertheless he remained active in the causes of the period – the protest against unemployment, the colonial struggles for independence, the campaign against German and Italian Fascism, the support for the Spanish Republican Government, and always, the saving power and grace for mankind of the social gospel.

Stalinism was infecting all left-wing groups at the time, including the Catholic Crusaders. Factional disputes drove out John and Mary Groser and the group at Christ Church, Stepney, in 1932; and four years later, agreement became impossible; the Crusade was wound up at its Chapter at Burslem, Noel joining with several others to found the Order of the Church Militant. Despite his growing disabilities, Noel continued to take services, to preach, to write. He completed the final chapters of his impressive *Life of Jesus*, published in 1937; he discussed with interest some aspects of the recently-established 'Oxford Group'; and he began writing an autobiography, which remained unfinished.

He recovered his sight partially, but knew he was suffering from an incurable cancer. In 1941–2 he was able to observe, with wry amusement, Thaxted Communists and Conservatives uniting under the imperialist Union Jack and Russian Flag, that 'red flag of Bolshevism' he had falsely been accused of displaying in the Church.

He died of cancer on 22 July 1942 at the age of seventy-three. He had been vicar of Thaxted for thirty-two years and three months.

His funeral was the occasion of a remarkable demonstration of the love, affection and respect which he had built around him during his life. Friends and parishioners kept vigil during one night over the coffin and on the next day a Requiem Mass was sung by Jack Putterill, assisted by George Chambers and Jim Wilson. The Thaxted singers sang Bach's introit, 'The Lord is ever at my side', and after the epistle, singers and congregation sang to the tune of Beethoven's Ninth Symphony some verses of William Morris's poem 'All for the Cause'. The Bishop of Chelmsford, Dr Henry Wilson, gave an address, in which

he said, 'I believe it to be literally true that Conrad Noel was the greatest personality among the clergy of this diocese, as a student, as a writer, as a religious and political leader, as a man of artistic and musical sense, and most of all as a saint of God'. Among the many clergy present was Lewis Donaldson, now very old, a Canon of Westminster Abbey, who had led the march of the unemployed from Leicester to London in 1905.

Noel's wife Miriam, and their daughter, survived him. He left effects valued at £942 to his widow. His daughter, Barbara, had married Jack Putterill in September 1921, and Putterill, who had been assistant to Noel for several years, and who had always been one of his most active and fervent supporters, took over the parish on Noel's death.

Writings: *The Day of the Sun* (1901); *The Labour Party: what it is and what it wants* (1906); *Objections to Socialism* (Thaxted, n.d.); *Socialism in Church History* (1910); *Socialism and Church Tradition* (n.d.); *By-Ways of Belief* (1912); 'The Church in the Great State', in *Socialism and the Great State*, ed. G. R. S. Taylor, Lady Warwick and H. G. Wells (1912); *The Catholic Crusade* (Elland, 1918); *Uplifting the Son of Man as the God of Justice in our Midst* (Thaxted, 1919); *Creative Democracy* (Thaxted, 1920); *The Battle of the Flags* (1922); *The Kernel of Christ's Teaching* (Burslem, 1930); *The Meaning of Imperialism* (n.d.); *The Law and the Prophets* (Burslem, n.d.); *The Sacraments* (Burslem, n.d.); *Render Unto Cæsar* (Burslem, 1933); 'Jesus', in *Christianity and the Social Revolution*, ed. J. Lewis, K. Polanyi, D. K. Kitchen (1935); *The Life of Jesus* (1937); *Jesus the Heretic* (1939); *Autobiography*, ed. Sidney Dark (1945); *see also* journals listed under Sources.

Sources: (1) MSS: Noel papers: Brynmor Jones Library, Hull University; (2) Other: *The Commonwealth* (monthly) 1896–1929; *The Optimist* (Quarterly) 1906–1908, which became *The Church Socialist Quarterly* 1909–11, and then *The Optimist* 1912–16;

Justice, 1909–14; *The Church Socialist*, monthly 1912–1917, bi-monthly 1918–21; *Country Town* (Thaxted) 1911–12; *The New World*, 1928–30; *The Catholic Crusader*, Dec 1930–Dec 1934; *The Challenge* 1935–1936; *The Church Militant*, 1936–42; F. G. Bettany, *Stewart Headlam* (1926); G. C. Binyon, *The Christian Socialist Movement in England* (1931); N. Dearmer, *The Life of Percy Dearmer* (1940); R. Woodifield, *Catholicism, Humanist and Democratic* (1954); M. Reckitt, *P. E. T. Widdrington* (1961); R. Shaw, *The Flag* (1965); R. Groves, *Conrad Noel and the Thaxted Movement* (1967); P. d'A. Jones, *The Christian Socialist Revival in England 1874–1914* (1968); R. Woodifield, 'Conrad Noel, 1869–1942, Catholic Crusader', in *For Christ and the People*, ed. M. B. Reckitt (1968) 135–79; R. Groves, *The Catholic Crusade 1918–1936* (1970). OBIT. *Manchester Guardian* and *Times*, 24 July 1942.

REG GROVES

See also: Stewart Duckworth HEADLAM; Malcolm SPARKES, for Guild Socialism.

O'GRADY, Sir James (1866–1934)
TRADE UNION LEADER AND MP

The son of Irish parents, John and Margaret O'Grady, James was born on 6 May 1866 at Bristol. He received a few years' education at St Mary's Roman Catholic School before starting his first job at the age of ten. This was in a mineral water factory, and he had several other jobs before he was fifteen, when he found an employer willing to apprentice him as a cabinet-maker. As a youth he joined the Army, but after having second thoughts he was bought out by his employer. At the age of twenty-one, having completed his apprenticeship, he married Louisa James; and being unable to find suitable employment in Bristol, he went on the tramp. A ready workman and skilled at his trade, he supported himself by working in various parts of the country for some three years, after which he returned to Bristol. In the course of his travels, he had come into contact with the socialist ideas that were being discussed in the industrial centres, and he

began to take an interest in trade unionism and local politics.

He made his first public speech in 1892 in support of the Bristol dockers who were on strike. At this time he was an emotional though fluent speaker, with a noticeable Irish brogue. His evident sincerity commanded the respect of his audiences, and he became a popular figure in the local labour movement. O'Grady was a founder member of the local Clarion Cyclists, who operated as both a social and a propaganda organisation, and he served as president of the Bristol Trades Council. In 1896 he contested the District Ward for a seat on the city council, and though defeated on this occasion, was successful in the following year when he became the Labour representative of the newly-constituted Easton Ward. He was one of four Labour councillors, and he and his colleagues stimulated further interest in Labour questions by holding frequent public meetings to discuss their work on the council. O'Grady sat on the council for two years, during which time he helped to lead a successful campaign to create scholarships for promising schoolchildren.

In 1898, at the age of thirty-two, he was president of the Trades Union Congress which met at Bristol. His lengthy presidential address covered a wide range of issues from a distinctly Socialist standpoint. He proposed that a scheme be formulated for the political organisation of the trade union world, and ended by quoting the closing lines of Morris's 'The Day is coming':

. . . Come cast off all fooling, for this at least we know, That the Dawn and the Day is coming, and forth the Banners go.

The speech was widely commented upon as being the first occasion that a president of the TUC had advocated Socialism as an objective of the trade union movement, while it also foreshadowed the decision of the 1899 TUC to establish what was to be known as the Labour Representation Committee. Shortly after, O'Grady moved to London on becoming a national organiser for his union, the National Amalgamated Furnishing Trades' Association.

During his time as a journeyman he had

visited Leeds, and in April 1904, sponsored by his union, he was chosen by the local Branch of the LRC as their prospective candidate for East Leeds. The constituency had a large Irish population and was subject to the MacDonald–Gladstone agreement which precluded a Liberal challenger. At the general election of 1906 O'Grady was elected to Parliament in a straight fight against the sitting Unionist. He remained there until 1924; in the general elections of 1910 he held the seat with comfortable majorities on both occasions, and in 1918, when the constituency became part of South East Leeds, he was returned unopposed. In 1922 and 1923 he had substantial majorities over Liberal opponents.

On entering the House of Commons, O'Grady was one of the more able of the members of the Parliamentary Labour Party. He claimed to have read extensively in economics and sociology: he mentioned Marx and Engels, and George's *Progress and Poverty* had, he told W. T. Stead, made a deep impression; but his 'solace and inspiration' was Carlyle [*Review of Reviews* (1906) 578]. Some fellow MPs regarded him as too impetuous and too fearless in taking a minority view. For example, he belonged to both the SDF and the Fabian Society, and, himself an ardent volunteer, he campaigned for the 'Citizen Army', a project dear to the SDF, but generally looked upon with disfavour by the rest of the labour movement – particularly the ILP. In 1911 he again disagreed with a majority of his colleagues on the financing of the proposed system of national insurance. On this occasion he took the view of a section of the ILP in opposing the contributory principle, and acted with Lansbury as a teller for the Noes in the third reading of the Bill. Hardie abstained, but the majority of the Labour Party followed MacDonald in support of the Bill, though Jowett, Snowden and Thorne also voted against.

During the war years O'Grady adopted a firmly patriotic stance, describing himself as a 'Labour Imperialist'. In August 1915 he visited the front, and on his return called for greater efforts in shell production. He joined the British Workers' League as a vice-president in 1916 but left it in 1918. He was given the rank of captain in 1918 for a recruiting campaign that he undertook in Ireland, where conscription had not been introduced. In April 1917 he had been entrusted with a more important task, that of travelling to Russia to impress on the Kerensky Government the vital importance of continuing the war against Germany. He was accompanied by Will Thorne and W. S. Sanders, who acted as the delegation's secretary. The British Ambassador in Petrograd, Sir George Buchanan, considered O'Grady and Thorne to be 'splendid types of the British working man', but they made little headway in their mission. While they were in Russia the ILP issued a statement repudiating the delegation as representatives of the British Government and not of the labour movement. H. M. Hyndman and others sent a telegram to Kerensky denouncing the ILP statement, and these counter-charges were widely used by the delegation. They noted in their Report to the War Cabinet that the telegram 'proved most useful'. On the whole they seem to have been received sympathetically, except by the extreme left, but on returning to England at the end of May they reported in gloomy terms to the Cabinet, although they ventured to suggest that things would have been much worse had the old regime still existed. On their journey home they stayed in Stockholm, where they held discussions with Branting, Huysmans and others on the proposed separate conferences between the various socialist majorities and minorities. It was feared that unless England and France were represented 'the German influence would be very strong with the highly susceptible Russian Socialists' [Report to War Cabinet (June 1917) 6].

In November 1919 O'Grady, still an Army Captain, was appointed to negotiate with Litvinov on the exchange of British prisoners of war and civilians in Russia. The two met in Copenhagen, and although Litvinov was the more skilful in the arts of negotiation, O'Grady brought his characteristic good humour to the proceedings, and ultimately an agreement was reached between the British and Russian Governments.

When the threat of war with the young Soviet republic developed in August 1920, O'Grady was one of those who signed the manifesto against war, and he represented the Labour Party on the Council of Action [Graubard (1956) 104–5]. In the early 1920s O'Grady again visited Russia as an administrator of famine relief on behalf of trade unions in many countries. On one occasion, in March 1922, he passed a piece of famine 'bread' around the chamber of the House of Commons to show that it was largely composed of clay. After a journey in Russia at the end of 1922 he contracted smallpox.

In addition to his other activities, which included appointment in 1916 as a magistrate for London, O'Grady continued to work as a trade union official. During his years as a Member of Parliament, he was, at various times, an official of the Furnishing Trades Association; a member of the executive of the Engineering and Shipbuilding Trades' Federation; a member of the GFTU (from 1912 to 1918 he was president of its board of management); and secretary of the short-lived National Federation of General Workers. Established in 1917, the NFGW was responsible for national negotiations in several industries, including chemicals, quarrying and flour-milling. Although some members of the GFTU had envisaged such an organisation, it owed its origin mainly to the system of national bargaining created by wartime conditions. In the 1920s it rapidly lost ground to the general unions and disappeared.

Untypically for a trade union leader, O'Grady paid much attention to foreign questions. On first entering Parliament he had specialised in Indian affairs and was a hostile critic of Morley's policies; his trade union work had taken him abroad on several occasions, and during the war he travelled extensively and gained a reputation for patience and tact. With the formation of the first Labour Government in 1924, it was strongly rumoured that if Soviet Russia was diplomatically recognised, he would be appointed as British Ambassador to Moscow. This did not come about, but in October 1924 he was made Governor of Tasmania and created a KCMG. Although O'Grady

had mellowed politically, the appointment of a Socialist to such a position was a subject of criticism. Those who predicted his failure were confounded: during the six years he spent in Tasmania, O'Grady was recognised by all sections as an able and popular official. Lady O'Grady had to be left behind when he sailed for Tasmania, since she was suffering from a painful and serious complaint. She died in 1929. O'Grady returned to England in April 1931, and after a month received another colonial post, that of Governor and Commander-in-Chief of the Falkland Islands. Among his luggage was a crate of boxing gloves, which he took in the hope of interesting the islanders in his favourite sport, but he was unable to complete his tour of duty in the south Atlantic because of illness. His health had for some time been indifferent, and when, in the middle of 1933, he contracted blood-poisoning he had to return to England for specialist treatment. He remained on sick leave until his death, in a London nursing home, on 10 December 1934. He was a practising Catholic all his life. He was survived by two sons and seven daughters and in his will he left effects to the value of £9228.

Sources: (1) MSS: Labour Party archives: LRC; (2) Other: W. T. Stead, 'The Labour Party and the Books that Helped to Make It', *Review of Reviews 33* (June 1906) 568–582; *Dod* (1907, 1923); W. J. Davis, *The British Trades Union Congress: history and recollections* vol. 2 (1916); *Report of the Visit of the Labour Delegation to Russia, April–May 1917* [printed for the War Cabinet June 1917: PRO Cab. 24/3] 7 pp.; S. V. Bracher, *The Herald Book of Labour Members* (1923); G. Buchanan, *My Mission to Russia and other Diplomatic Memories*, 2 vols (1923); S. Bryher, *Labour and Socialist Movement in Bristol* (Bristol, 1929); *WWW* (1929–40) *Kelly* (1932); H. W. Lee and E. Archbold, *Social-Democracy in Britain* (1935); W. P. and Z. K. Coates, *A History of Anglo-Soviet Relations* (1945); S. R. Graubard, *British Labour and the Russian Revolution 1917–1924* (Cambridge, Mass., 1956); F. Bealey and H. Pelling, *Labour and Politics 1900–1906* (1958); B. C.

Roberts, *The Trades Union Congress 1868–1921* (1958); A. M. McBriar, *Fabian Socialism and English Politics 1884–1918* (Cambridge, 1962); H. A. Clegg et al., *A History of British Trade Unions since 1889*, vol. 1: *1889–1910* (Oxford, 1964); B. J. Atkinson, 'The Bristol Labour Movement 1868 to 1906' (Oxford DPhil., 1969); K. D. Brown, 'The Labour Party and the Unemployment Question 1906–10', *Hist. J.* (1971) 599–616; idem, *Labour and Unemployment* (Newton Abbot, 1971); R. Douglas, 'The National Democratic Party and the British Workers' League', *Hist. J. 15*, no. 3 (1972) 533–52; J. O. Stubbs, 'Lord Milner and Patriotic Labour, 1914–1918', *English Hist. Rev. 87*, no. 345 (Oct 1972) 717–54. Obit. *Daily Herald, Leeds Mercury* and *Yorkshire Post*, 11 Dec 1934; *Times*, 11 and 13 Dec 1934; *Labour Party Report* (1935); *TUC Report* (1935).

DAVID E. MARTIN

See also: †Arthur HENDERSON, for British Labour Party, 1914–31; George LANSBURY, for British Labour Party, 1900–13; †William James THORNE.

PARKER, James (1863–1948)
LABOUR MP

Parker was born on 9 December 1863 at South Thoresby, Authorpe, near Louth in Lincolnshire, the son of George Parker, a farm labourer. His mother died while he was still a small boy and this led to his being brought up by a relative at Carlton, near Leeds. He attended a Wesleyan school at Louth and then the Bramhope School near Leeds, until at the age of twelve he started work as an assistant to a milk roundsman. During his teens he worked successively as a greengrocer's assistant, doctor's groom, milkman and barman, until at the age of nineteen he moved to Halifax where he became employed first as a labourer with the Corporation and later as a packer and warehouseman.

In his youth Parker had attended the Guiseley and Yeadon Mechanics' Institute, and in Halifax he joined the Brunswick Church Mutual Improvement Society, where he took part in debates. He was an early member of the local branch of the ILP, and became its full-time secretary. As such he assisted in a number of elections, including those of John Lister at Halifax (1893 and 1895), Hardie at East Bradford (1896), Pete Curran at Barnsley (1897), Tom Mann at Halifax (1897), Robert Smillie at North-East Lanark (1901) and Snowden at Wakefield in 1902. He served for a number of years on the ILP National Administrative Council, and was a member of the Labour Representation Committee, being a delegate at the Memorial Hall Conference of February 1900.

Parker's activities at local level also included membership of the Halifax Trades Council, of which he was for a time president, and the Chamber of Commerce, of which he was a member from 1895 to 1906. His first attempt to join the Halifax Borough Council in 1893 was unsuccessful, as was his candidature for the Board of Guardians in 1896. In 1897, however, he was elected to the town council as a Labour member for North Ward, sitting until 1906, and serving for four years as chairman of the Waterworks Committee.

At the 1900 general election when Parker contested Halifax he was returned at the bottom of the poll. But in 1906 the working of the agreement reached between Herbert Gladstone and Ramsay MacDonald meant that Parker had only one Liberal opponent for the two-member constituency of Halifax, and he was elected. He had made more sure of winning the seat by advising his supporters to vote for J. H. Whitley, the Liberal, as well as himself, in the calculation that Liberal voters would in turn give him their support, a strategy that angered other ILP leaders. Whitley and Parker served together until 1918, and as a result of the collaboration between the local parties became known as 'Our Harry and your Jim'.

On moving to London, Parker shared rooms for a time with Fred Jowett and Thomas Summerbell in a small hotel near Westminster. His years of service with the ILP gave him some standing, but he was possibly its least able member in the 1906 Parliament. Nevertheless he was secretary of the Labour Party in the Commons from 1909 to 1912, and its vice-chairman from 1912 to 1913. In this latter post he was, in the absence of MacDonald, the Chairman, responsible for replying to the address on the opening of Parliament in March 1913. Glasier recalled the time when Parker was a 'plodding' party secretary at Halifax and noted that the House of Commons job was too big for him. Beatrice Webb took a more scathing view, referring to Parker as a 'feeble creature' for his lack of enthusiasm for the 'War against Poverty' campaign of 1912 [*Beatrice Webb's Diaries* (1952) 10]. About a year later, Glasier, always a critic of those who had done well out of their political convictions, recorded that Jowett had been told by Parker that he had only £40 in the bank on entering Parliament, but had since increased his savings to £900 [Thompson (1971) 162]. Parker was a Labour representative on the select committee that inquired into the Marconi scandal of 1912, and signed the majority report of 1913 exculpating Lloyd George, Rufus Isaacs and others from financial impropriety.

With the outbreak of war in 1914 Parker was one of the minority within the ILP that took a pro-war line. He became a member of a government joint committee to stimulate recruiting, and in January 1917 was appointed to a minor office, that of a Junior Lord of the Treasury, in the Coalition Government. He spoke often at meetings on the War Savings Certificate Scheme, which he claimed to have originated. At the 1916 ILP conference, when an attempt was made to withdraw support from Parker along with Clynes, MacDonald spoke against the move, but Parker was disowned when he accepted a government post. By this time, however, Parker had largely abandoned his ILP stance, although he still found favour with a majority of his party and was the chief Labour Whip in the Commons from 1916 to 1918. He held his Treasury post until October 1922, and acted as a Whip for the Coalition Government from 1918 to 1922. For services to the savings and recruiting campaigns he was made a Companion of Honour in 1918 and in the same year installed as a freeman of Halifax. At the general election of December 1918 he stood for Cannock, Staffordshire, as a Coalition Labour candidate and was returned in a straight fight against an Asquithian Liberal; he then chose to leave the Labour Party rather than give up office. In November 1922 he contested the same seat as an Independent with National Liberal support, but was defeated by the Labour candidate. His last few years in Parliament were lucrative, as he showed a readiness to pick up investment tips dropped to him by the wealthy [Cowling (1971) 23].

Parker retired from politics after 1922, and spent the remainder of his life in Halifax. He had contributed articles to local newspapers for many years, and he continued to write a weekly column of philosophical reflections in the *Halifax Courier and Guardian*. He was also fond of reading. In 1906, in response to W. T. Stead's inquiry about the books that had influenced him, he wrote:

I have been a desultory reader, and have devoured almost everything that has come my way, from the Bible to Balzac, and from Darwin's *Origin of Species* to Mark Twain's *Innocents Abroad*. Many books have helped me in my work. Perhaps I owe more to Thomas Carlyle than to any other writer. The philosophy of the 'Sage of Chelsea' always appealed to me from the time I first opened *Heroes and Hero Worship*. *Sartor Resartus* is, I think, the book I would save from my library if my house was on fire and I could only escape with one book. Emerson, Mazzini, Huxley, Frederic Harrison and Ruskin have all helped to mould my opinion. Among the novelists, I am familiar with the writings of Charles Dickens, Thomas Hardy, George Meredith, George Moore, Victor Hugo, Zola, Balzac, George Eliot and many others.

The *History of the English People* by John Richard Green, Thorold Rogers' *Six Centuries of Work and Wages*, Ashley's *Economic History*, Marshall's *Economics of Industry*, and a multitude of books dealing with social and political topics have helped to form my political and economic faith.

Whitman, Shelley, and Edward Carpenter are also favourites, though I am familiar with most of the major and some of the minor poets. I could never settle down to any system of reading and possibly am the worse for it.

This same article described him as a Nonconformist in religion [*Review of Reviews* (1906) 578].

He died at his home in Chester Road on 11 February 1948, aged eighty-four, and was buried at All Souls Cemetery, Halifax. In 1887 he had married Clara Oram, who died in 1933; he was survived by a son. Parker left effects to the value of £9652 in his will, which included a bequest of £500 to a local holiday home for children.

Writings: newspaper articles for local and labour journals.

Sources: (1) MSS: Labour Party archives: LRC; (2) Other: W. T. Stead, 'The Labour Party and the Books that helped to make it', *Review of Reviews* 33 (June 1906) 568–82; *Dod* (1909–21); *WWW* (1941–50); F. Brockway, *Socialism over Sixty Years; the life of Jowett of Bradford* (1946); B .Webb, *Diaries 1912–1924* ed. M. I. Cole (1952); F. Bealey and H. Pelling, *Labour and Politics 1900–1906* (1958); P. P. Poirier, *The Advent of the Labour Party* (1958); K. D. Brown, *Labour and Unemployment 1900–1914* (Newton Abbot, 1971); M. Cowling, *The Impact of Labour 1920–1924: the beginning of modern British Politics* (Cambridge, 1971); L. Thompson, *The Enthusiasts: a biography of John and Katharine Bruce Glasier* (1971). OBIT. *Times*, 12 Feb 1948; *Halifax Courier and Guardian*, 14 Feb 1948 [photograph]; *Labour Party Report* (1948).

DAVID E. MARTIN

See also: †Arthur HENDERSON, for British Labour Party, 1914–31; George LANSBURY, for British Labour Party, 1900–13.

PARKINSON, John Allen (1870–1941)
MINERS' LEADER AND LABOUR MP

Born on 15 October 1870 at the hamlet of Hindley Green, a few miles south-east of Wigan in Lancashire, John Parkinson was the son of a colliery manager. After attending the United Methodist Free Church School at Hindley Green he began working as a half-timer at the age of ten, changing to full-time two years later. From the age of seventeen he became a committed and active trade unionist, and after working underground for twenty-three years was elected checkweighman at the Mains Colliery, Bamfurlong, near Wigan, succeeding Henry (Harry) Twist who had just been appointed Miners' Agent for Wigan. In 1917 he himself was appointed a full-time agent for the St Helen's district of the Lancashire and Cheshire Miners' Federation, and he represented his area on the executive committee of the MFGB in 1913 and again in 1925.

Like many miners' leaders Parkinson was active in local politics. The Lancashire miners were in advance of many mining areas in their support for a working-class party [Gregory (1968) 82 ff.], and in 1906 he became president of the Ince parliamentary division of the Labour Party, a position he continued to hold for many years. He was elected a member of the Abram Urban District Council in 1908 and retired only in 1917, when he became agent. He also served on the Lancashire County Council from 1915 to 1919. In the 'coupon' general election of December 1918 he defeated the sitting Conservative MP for Wigan – Mr (later Sir) Reginald J. N. Neville, K.C. – and retained the seat at all subsequent elections until his death. At the last election, in 1935, he had a majority of 10,304 over his Conservative opponent. In the first Labour Government of 1924 Parkinson was appointed Comptroller of the King's Household and also a Labour Whip; and in the second Labour Government he was a Lord Commissioner of the Treasury from June 1929 to 13 March 1931 and then, in the closing months of the Government, became parliamentary secretary to the Minister of Transport, Herbert Morrison. Throughout the 1920s Parkinson played a fairly prominent role within the Parliamentary Labour Party. He spoke frequently for the PLP on mining and transport matters in particular; and in 1930 he was a member of the Joint

Select Committee on East Africa investigating the possibilities of closer union among the countries in that area. He maintained his interest in African affairs for the remainder of his parliamentary career: in 1932 he urged the Government to raise the standard of living of the native populations by a comprehensive reorganisation of their colonial policy and in subsequent years pressed for the extension of the Native Co-operative Union scheme of Kilimanjaro to other colonial areas and for the setting up of a Labour Department for Northern Rhodesia. He also took an interest in labour conditions in other British colonies. He was equally concerned about the depressed areas of Britain, especially Lancashire, and Wigan in particular; was critical of government policy on coal and favoured nationalisation of the mines. In 1932 he suggested the setting up of a national disaster fund for the coal industry. He also maintained his earlier interest in transport matters, especially in the programmes for trunk roads.

He was made a JP in 1908; was a member of the Mine Managers' Examination Board from 1928 to 1929; and was awarded the CBE in 1931. He was a keen gardener, especially interested in roses, and was an enthusiastic pigeon-fancier up to his middle years, being for a time secretary of the local federation of Homing Societies. In religion he was associated with the Hindley Green United Methodist Church in early life, and later with the Hope Congregational Church, Wigan. He married twice: first, Alice, daughter of J. Pilkington, who died in 1904 and by whom he had a son, Thomas, who became a joiner; and then in 1905 Mrs Ida Alice Elliott, daughter of W. Atkinson, by whom he had a daughter, Margaret Ida, who became a nurse and married a doctor. His second wife, who had two sons by a previous marriage, William Elliott, who became a joiner, and John Holland Elliott, an electrician, also took part in public work and was a magistrate for the county.

He himself died, after some years of failing health, on 7 December 1941. After a service at the Hope Congregational Church, Wigan, he was buried at Hindley Cemetery on 11 December. He left a widow

and grown-up family and his effects were valued at £3123.

Sources: S. V. Bracher, *The Herald Book of Labour Members* (1923); *Dod* (1940); *WWW* (1941–50); R. Page Arnot, *The Miners: years of struggle* (1953); R. Gregory, *The Miners and British Politics, 1906–1914* (Oxford, 1968); personal information: Mrs J. Dunlop, Wigan, step-grand-daughter. OBIT. *Times,* 8 Dec 1941; *Wigan Observer and District Advertiser,* 9 Dec 1941.

JOHN SAVILLE

See also: †Thomas ASHTON, for Mining Trade Unionism, 1900–14; *Arthur James COOK, for Mining Trade Unionism, 1915–26; †Arthur HENDERSON, for British Labour Party, 1914–31; Henry (Harry) TWIST.

PARROTT, William (1843–1905)
MINERS' LEADER AND LIB-LAB MP

Born on 18 December 1843 at Row Green, near Wellington, Somerset, William Parrott was the son of James Parrott, a miner, and his wife Susannah (née Martin). When he was very young his parents moved to Yorkshire, and William began work in a brickyard at eight years of age, entered a factory when he was nine, and went into the mines at West Normanton, Yorkshire, just before his tenth birthday. After working nearly twenty years as a miner, he was appointed their first checkweighman by the miners of Good Hope Pit, Normanton Common in 1872. In 1876 he was elected assistant secretary of the West Yorkshire Miners' Association when Benjamin Pickard was promoted to the secretaryship after the death of John Dixon; Parrott held this office until 1881 when, on the fusion of the South and West Yorkshire Miners' Associations to form the Yorkshire Miners' Association, he was appointed agent. Throughout the 1880s he worked alongside Pickard and Cowey. In 1890 he attended the first international conference of miners at Jolimont, was one of the miners' representatives at the Rosebery Conference of 1893, a member of the Conciliation Board which followed it, and served on the MFGB executive from 1892 to 1903.

The miners' leaders in Yorkshire before 1900 were all Liberals. Bealey and Pelling write that 'Pickard had bound the union to the Liberal Party by an electoral alliance' [(1958) 223]; and the ILP made little headway in the Yorkshire coalfield during the 1890s, as was demonstrated by the famous Barnsley by-election of 1897 when Pete Curran polled less than ten per cent of the total vote. Only at Hemsworth, in the Barnsley division, did the ILP have a branch of any size, and it was from the Hemsworth lodge that a resolution went forward in 1902 asking for two more parliamentary candidates to be sponsored by the Yorkshire miners. Parrott was selected, later in the same year, as Lib-Lab candidate for East Leeds. When, however, Ben Pickard died early in February 1904, Parrott became the candidate for Pickard's constituency of Normanton and was successful at the by-election.

At this time the Yorkshire miners were involved in the aftermath of the Denaby Main strike and subsequent legal action which spread over the years from 1902 to 1906. Industrial relations had worsened steadily, and the union was in a state of great uncertainty and strain [Bealey and Pelling (1958) 223 ff]. Ned Cowey died in December 1903; Ben Pickard and John Frith in February 1904; and Parrott himself in November 1905. As the *Times* obituary recorded, he was the last of the band of four 'who more than any others were responsible for the creation of the Yorkshire Miners' Association as it exists today'.

In addition to his work for the miners' union, Parrott served on the Barnsley School Board from 1889 to 1892 and was vice-chairman when he retired. Elected to the Barnsley Town Council in 1893, he was defeated at the end of his term of office, but subsequently re-elected in 1899 and returned unopposed in 1901. In November 1904 he was made a JP for Barnsley. He died at his Barnsley home on 9 November 1905, and was survived by his wife, the former Eliza Thompson of Methley, whom he had married in 1868, and by a son and three daughters. He left effects valued at £944.

Sources: W. Hallam, *Miners' Leaders* (1894) [photograph]; *Dod* (1905); *WWW* (1897–1915); F. Bealey and H. Pelling, *Labour and Politics 1900–1906* (1958); F. Machin, *The Yorkshire Miners* (Barnsley, 1958); H. Pelling, *The Origins of the Labour Party, 1880–1900* (2nd ed. rev., Oxford, 1965). OBIT. *Times*, 10 Nov 1905; *Barnsley Independent*, 11 Nov 1905.

JOYCE BELLAMY
JOHN SAVILLE

See also: †Alexander MACDONALD, for Mining Trade Unionism, 1850–79; †Benjamin PICKARD, for Mining Trade Unionism, 1880–99.

PASSFIELD, 1st Baron Passfield of Passfield Corner, see **WEBB, Beatrice and Sidney James**

PEASE, Edward Reynolds (1857–1955)
SOCIALIST AND SECRETARY OF THE FABIAN SOCIETY

Edward Pease, historian and founder-member of the Fabian Society, and for many years its secretary, was born at Henbury Hill House, Henbury, near Bristol, on 23 December 1857, the eldest son of Thomas Pease, a retired woolcomber, by his third wife, Susanna Ann Fry. Both his parents were Quakers, and he was a cousin of the well-known family of coalowners, the Peases of Darlington. He was never sent to school but was taught by a resident tutor; and in 1872 he was made to take employment in the City of London, becoming a clerk in the office of Sir Thomas Hanbury, where he remained until in 1878 he went into partnership with a stockbroker. But it was not a happy period in his life; for at some time – it is not known exactly when – he made acquaintance with the writings and speeches of the early Socialists, particularly William Morris, and fairly soon came to the conclusion that stockbroking was an immoral occupation, and that he ought to keep himself by the work of his hands. He was not capable of doing so immediately; but when in 1884 his father died leaving him £3000, he promptly left the City for ever, and apprenticed himself for three years to a cabinet-maker in Newcastle upon Tyne. Before then, however, he had come, almost accidentally, upon what was to be the major interest of his life.

A cousin of his, named Emily Ford, who was a keen spiritualist, had introduced him to another spiritualist, Frank Podmore, the biographer of Robert Owen – who also ended his days as a believer in spiritualism. Pease, though he himself had gifts as a water-diviner, had little use for the occult in any form; but he made friends with the other young man, and was persuaded by him to go and watch for a ghost in an empty house in Hampstead. No ghost appeared, but Pease and Podmore spent the night in happily discussing the problems of the world, as a result of which Pease, at Podmore's invitation, attended, towards the end of 1883, a meeting of a small society calling itself the Fellowship of the New Life, which had been founded by the eccentric 'wandering philosopher' Thomas Davidson for the purpose of improving the world at large; one of its objects was 'the 'attainment of a perfect character by all and each'. This particular object struck some of those attending the meetings of the Fellowship as somewhat utopian and verging upon the unattainable; and when, in order to help carry this out, some of the Fellowship proposed, according to Bernard Shaw, to 'found a colony in Brazil and live on one another's pass-books', Hubert Bland, the future treasurer of the Fabian Society, and a handful of others revolted; and in the following January nine or ten of them met together in Pease's rooms in Osnaburgh Street, St Marylebone, and then and there decided to form a society with the rather less ambitious object of helping to establish a Socialist economy. This they called the Fabian Society, deriving its name from a motto (provided by Podmore) which ran:

For the right moment you must wait, as Fabius did most patiently, when warring against Hannibal . . . but when the time comes you must strike hard, as Fabius did, or your waiting will be vain and fruitless.

Thus was born the Fabian Society, longest-lived of all Socialist societies. Bernard Shaw joined it at its third meeting, Sidney Webb shortly afterwards: Pease, a year or two older than either of them, took on the job of voluntary secretary, and kept the minute-book until he went to Newcastle, when he was succeeded for a while by Sydney Olivier, the third of the 'Big Four' of Fabianism, who later became governor of Jamaica and was made a peer by Ramsay MacDonald in the first Labour Government.

When Pease returned from the North he found the tiny Fabian Society just entering upon its first period of growth. The series of lectures given by seven leading Fabians in the autumn of 1888, when published in the new year under the title *Fabian Essays in Socialism*, had enjoyed a startling success. The membership of the Society and of local Fabian Societies rose so rapidly that in the following year the Society felt itself rich enough to risk £1 a week on the part-time employment of a paid secretary. Pease was an obvious candidate, though Hubert Bland's wife (E. Nesbit of *The Treasure-Seekers* and other children's books) and a few of her friends made a fuss, to which H. G. Wells later attached erroneous importance, over any member of the Society receiving any money from its funds. Pease was, however, appointed, Webb ensuring his acceptance by appointing him as his own personal secretary for another weekly pound. 'I did not feel then', wrote Pease in a chapter of reminiscence published after Webb's death, 'and I do not think now, that the work I did had any value to him or to anybody else' [*The Webbs and their Work*, ed. M. Cole (1949) 19]. The gesture, he was certain, was a characteristic Webbian way of resolving an awkward situation without catastrophe – and a year later the Society assumed responsibility for the whole forty shillings.

Pease, who in 1889 had married a fellow-Fabian, Mary Gammell Davidson, was very grateful to Webb. They had been friends for some time previously: in his Morris phase Pease had constructed for Webb a 'geological cabinet' (which after Webb's interest in geological specimens had faded, found a home in the Fabian offices) and in 1888 had gone with him on a three-months visit to Canada and the United States during which 'he [Webb] made all the plans and I kept the accounts'; but after this act of calculated generosity he regarded Webb with an admiration only this side of idolatry. 'In the first thirty years of the Fabian Society', he wrote in the chapter already quoted, 'Webb dominated the Executive Committee, not because he was in the least dictatorial but because he was always wise and right. All the initiative came from him.' And again: 'I cannot think of any moral faults or weaknesses which can be attributed to him. I knew him for sixty years, and for much of that period had constant dealings with him, and if anyone says that I seem to regard him as a perfect character, I shall not gainsay it' – as an encomium this could scarcely be surpassed. For Beatrice, though he could hardly fail to be impressed by her qualities, he had nothing like the same feeling; and she for her part, found him a good deal of a bore. 'Worthy' was the damning epithet she applied to him in her *Diary*.

Webb and the Fabian executive had thus acquired an absolutely faithful henchman, who could be relied upon to promote the pure milk of the collectivist world without unnecessarily antagonising (as Shaw so often did) those persons whom it was desirable to influence. He was hard-working and capable, and did effective organisational work in forcing the Liberal Party in 1891 to adopt the semi-socialist Newcastle Programme, and in the following year for the Progressive victory in the LCC elections – this was the first time Webb was elected for Deptford. Three years later, in 1894, he found himself a trustee under the will of Henry Hutchinson, out of whose estate the London School of Economics was founded (*see* Beatrice and Sidney Webb) and acted as secretary and as Webb's reliable lieutenant in the work of administering the Trust. When in 1900 the Fabian Society, along with the other Socialist societies, received the summons to the Memorial Hall conference which founded the Labour Representation Committee, Pease duly attended on its behalf, selected himself to represent

it on the executive committee of the new organisation, and reported to his own executive that the conference had behaved in an adequately Fabian manner. 'It was', he wrote of the Labour Party at a later date, 'from the first purely Fabian in its policy, both in the measures which it advocated and in its tolerance of Liberalism'; and the party of that date appeared to acquiesce in this opinion, for Pease was frequently called upon to draft resolutions and reports for conferences. He remained on the Labour executive for fourteen years doing this kind of useful but unspectacular work: as the Fabian leaders paid little attention to the Labour Party until after the failure of the Poor Law campaign of 1909 to 1911, he was left pretty much to his own discretion.

Within the Fabian Society itself, however, his patience was much tried by the newcomers who flocked in after the radical victory of 1906 and seemed to want to make radical changes in Webb's own society. Everything which ran counter to established Fabian tradition, or embodied the faintest criticism of Sidney Webb, was anathema to him; he scrutinised severely the credentials of applicants for membership, coming once within an ace of rejecting the future Prime Minister, Clement Attlee, and he rejoiced wholeheartedly in the defeat of H. G. Wells. 'So the Old Gang triumphed' runs as a *leit-motif* through the relevant chapters of his *History of the Fabian Society*. Wells himself, in this case more generous than his opponent, remarked that in Pease the Fabian executive had an employee who did the work of a cabinet minister for the salary of a clerk.

In 1913 Joseph Storrs Fry, an uncle of his, died and left him a legacy sufficient to provide him with a living; and to the considerable relief of Mrs Webb, who found him too unwilling to try any sort of experiment, he resigned his paid post in favour of Stephen Sanders, himself remaining as honorary secretary. It was thus as an outraged member of the Fabian Old Guard and not as a paid officer that he joined in the battle with the Guild Socialist rebels just before the war. Sanders took his place on the Labour Party executive.

It had been his intention to retire, except in so far as attendance on the Fabian executive was concerned, to Limpsfield in Surrey, where he had been living since 1893, and there to engage in local politics – Limpsfield being well known in the early twentieth century as a haven for many persons of 'advanced' views – while writing the official history of the Fabian Society. The book was duly completed and came out in 1916; but the rest of the programme had to wait. For in the autumn of 1915 Sanders was called up for army service. Pease persuaded Webb to accept appointment to the Labour Party executive – 'the second best day's work I ever did' – and he himself had perforce to return and hold the fort for the Fabian Society in its recently-acquired premises in Tothill Street, Westminster. There he found that the Guild Socialists, under the leadership of G. D. H. Cole and, until the Military Service Acts carried them off to gaol, of William Mellor and Page Arnot, had captured the Fabian Research Department which the Webbs had so hopefully founded, and were running it as a highly effective combination of a research and inquiry bureau for trade unions, trades and labour councils and shop stewards, with a general forum for left-wing discussion and propaganda.

These Guild Socialists, young, ebullient and much lacking in respect for Webb and the other Fabian collectivists, occupied a couple of rooms on the middle floors of 25 Tothill Street, overflowed into the Fabian bookshop, the Fabian Hall, and the Fabian commonroom, and generally treated the elderly secretary to something between a revolution and a romp [M. Cole, *Growing Up Into Revolution* (1949) Ch. 6]. Pease bore the invasion on the whole very well, merely making gruff complaint from time to time of the noisy and casual habits of the Guild Socialist volunteers; but he cannot but have been relieved when at the end of the war the Fabian – by now the Labour – Research Department removed itself, volunteers and all, to a lodging in the Labour Party's new headquarters. Sanders returned as general secretary until he got into Parliament, when F. W. Galton was appointed in

his place. Pease remained as honorary secretary until 1938, when he finally retired, to live at Limpsfield until his death. For some years before that he had been completely deaf, but that did not hinder him from taking a keen interest in what was going on in the world. He welcomed, in fact, the take-over in 1939 of an almost moribund Fabian Society by the younger Socialists of the New Fabian Research Bureau, many of whom had been Guildsmen in their youth, and was delighted to welcome a visit from some of them, thereby proving that the gruff intransigence which he seemed to some of them to have displayed in past days was due partly to shyness and partly to the determined loyalty to Sidney Webb already described, and not to any innate obscurantism. Like his hero, he was a modest man and sought no glory for himself; but the Fabian Society could scarcely have had a more efficient or more devoted secretary.

He died at his home on 5 January 1955, aged ninety-seven, and was cremated. He left an estate valued at £37,593 net. His wife had predeceased him in 1950 but their two sons, Michael, born 1890, and Nicolas, born 1894, survived their father. Both were ardent Fabians almost from the cradle: the elder son died in 1966; the younger remains a staunch Fabian still.

MARGARET COLE

Writings: 'Towards Democracy: a note on Edward Carpenter', *To-Day* 6 (Aug 1886) 37–46; 'Labour Federation', ibid., 7 (June 1887) 171–7; *Parish Council Cottages and how to get them* (Fabian Tract no. 63: 1895, 3rd ed. rev., 1900) 4 pp.; *A Program for Workers* (Fabian Tract no. 66: 1895) 2 pp.; *Liquor Licensing at Home and Abroad* (Fabian Tract no. 85: 1898, 3rd ed. 1906) 15 pp.; *Municipal Drink Traffic, with a Criticism of Local Veto and Other Reform Projects* (Fabian Tract no. 86: 1898, 6th ed. 1909) 19 pp.; 'The National Housing Committee', *Econ. Rev. 10*, no. 2 (Apr 1900) 246–8; *How Trade Unions benefit Workmen* (Fabian Tract no. 104: 1900) 4 pp.; *The Case for Municipal Drink Trade* (1904, 2nd ed. 1908); *The Abolition of Poor Law Guardians* (Fabian Tract no. 126: 1906) 23 pp.; *More Books to read on Social and Economic Subjects: a supplement to 'what to read'*, containing publications from October 1901 to October 1906 (Fabian Tract no. 129:1906) 19 pp.; 'The Extravagance of the Poor Law', *Cont. Rev. 89* (June 1906) 856–866; *Capital and Compensation* (Fabian Tract no. 147:1909) 15 pp.; *Railway Nationalisation and the Railway Workers* (1910) 8 pp.; *Gold and State Banking: a study in the economics of monopoly* (Fabian Tract no. 164:1912) 19 pp.; *Profit-sharing and Co-partnership: a fraud & a failure?* (Fabian Tract no. 170; 1913 repr. 1926) 16 pp.; *The History of the Fabian Society* (1916, rev. ed. 1925, repr. 1963 with a new Introduction by M. Cole); T. Kirkup, *A History of Socialism*, rev. and partly rewritten by E. R. Pease (1920); idem, *A Primer of Socialism*, rev. and partly rewritten by E. R. Pease (1920); 'Webb and the Fabian Society', in *The Webbs and their Work*, ed. M. Cole (1949) ch. 2, 17–26.

Sources: The literature on the Fabian Society is considerable. Margaret Cole's *The Story of Fabian Socialism* (1961) is an important contribution in addition to Edward Pease's own *History*; and there is a comprehensive bibliography in A. M. McBriar, *Fabian Socialism and English Politics 1884–1918* (Cambridge, 1962). *See also:* (1) MSS: Cole Coll. and Fabian Society archives, Nuffield College, Oxford; Webb Coll., LSE; 'Recollections for my Sons', autobiographical notes and reminiscences by E. R. Pease [including 'Some reminiscences of E.R.P.' by Marian F. Pease] (unpublished typescript, 1953), N. A. Pease, Limpsfield, son (copies also in BM and Brynmor Jones Library, Hull University). (2) Other: Fabian Society, *Annual Reports* 1890 to date; S. G. Hobson, *Pilgrim to the Left* (1938); R. D. Howland, 'Fabian Thought and Social Change in England from 1884–1914', (London PhD., 1942); B. Webb, *Our Partnership* (1948); M. Cole, *Growing up into Revolution* (1949); *The Webbs and their Work*, ed. M. Cole (1949); E. J. Hobsbawm, 'Fabianism and the Fabians 1884–1914' (Cambridge PhD., 1950); *Beatrice Webb's Diaries 1912–1924*, ed. M. Cole

(1952); G. D. H. Cole, *A History of Socialist Thought 2: Marxism and Anarchism* (1954, 4th repr. 1969); H. Pelling, *The Origins of the Labour Party, 1880–1900* (1954, 2nd ed. Oxford, 1965); G. D. H. Cole, *A History of Socialist Thought 3: The Second International 1889–1914* (1956, repr. 1963); *Beatrice Webb's Diaries 1924–1932*, ed. and with an Introduction by M. Cole (1956); G. D. H. Cole, *A History of Socialist Thought 4: Communism and Social Democracy 1914–1931* (1958, 3rd repr. 1969); S. Caine, *The History of the Foundation of the London School of Economics and Political Science* (1963); B. Simon, *Education and the Labour Movement, 1870–1920* (1965). OBIT. *Times*, 7 Jan 1955; 'Edward R. Pease 1857–1955: a tribute' [G. D. H. Cole and S. K. Ratcliffe], *Fabian J.* no. 15 (Mar 1955) 6–8.

See also: Beatrice and Sidney WEBB.

PEASE, Mary Gammell (Marjory) (1861–1950)
FABIAN SOCIALIST AND LABOUR COUNCILLOR

Mary Gammell Davidson, who became Mrs Edward Pease, called herself Marjory after her marriage, for what reason nobody now remembers. She was born on 11 December 1861 at the Manse, Kinfauns, near Perth, where her father, the Rev. George S. Davidson, was Presbyterian minister. She was his only daughter, and was educated first in Edinburgh and then at Cheltenham College, where she took a teacher-training course which enabled her to come to London and teach in several schools under the London School Board which educated the elementary schoolchildren of London until that task was transferred to the LCC. She became a Socialist in her early days and in 1886 joined the Fabian Society, which was then a little-known society with only a handful of members. There she met Edward Pease, married him in September 1889 soon after he returned from Newcastle, and helped him in his work as Fabian secretary. During her early married life, in London and at Limpsfield in Surrey, Mrs Pease's time was much occupied with household affairs and with bringing up two sons, Michael and Nicolas, but as soon as she felt free enough she engaged in political and social problems in Surrey. Early in the new century, while there was still no possibility of a Labour Party in Surrey, she formed and was honorary secretary of a women's Liberal association in Oxted and Limpsfield; and in the election of 1906 she was largely instrumental in bringing the Liberal candidate safely home by a small majority.

She took a strong interest in the living conditions of farm-workers, which in those days were poor; and in 1907 she helped to form a Land Club League for Kent and Surrey, which agitated for small holdings, provision of housing in rural areas, and wages boards for agricultural workers – this was the first occasion on which wages boards for agriculture were proposed. A little later the Land Club League joined with other societies to form on a national scale the all-party Land and Home League with the same objects. Mrs Pease was for six years its honorary secretary, but little progress was registered in the matter of farm-workers' wages until the war was nearly over. In housing, however, she had rather more success: in 1911 she fought an election and won a seat on the Rural District Council on a policy of building cottages, and forced the Council to build, at a time when scarcely any rural district council in the kingdom was using its powers under the Housing Acts. She was also one of the first women to be made a JP, and sat on a number of school, hospital, welfare and war pensions committees. She transferred her allegiance from Liberal to Labour as soon as the 1918 reorganisation of the Labour Party made Labour a possible if not a very hopeful cause in Surrey; and in the 1922 election stood unsuccessfully for the East Surrey constituency. She did not again try her hand at national politics; but in her later years her experience and knowledge of local government made her a formidable force whether in Fabian debate or in the counsels of her very Conservative county. She retained firm Socialist views until her death on 23 February 1950 at the Oxted and Limpsfield Hospital, Surrey. She left an estate valued at £4394, probate being granted to her son Nicolas, then a retired civil servant.

Sources: personal information: Nicolas Pease, son; personal knowledge.

MARGARET COLE

See also: Edward Reynolds PEASE.

PIGGOTT, Thomas (1836–87)
IRONWORKERS' LEADER

Piggott was born on 18 July 1836 in the Lyng, West Bromwich, the son of a miner, and began work at the age of eight at the Bromford Works of Dawes and Sons, Oldbury, where he eventually became a forehand puddler. At this time the Black Country iron industry was organised on a sub-contracting system. The ironmaster himself was not directly concerned with the process of production. He furnished the plant and raw materials, but production was carried on by sub-contractors or forehands who were usually supervised by a works manager, though in some small firms this might be done by the master himself. Each overhand was responsible for a specific process, employing such labour as he thought necessary. The men and youths so employed were the underhands and were controlled absolutely by the sub-contractor. The ironmaster dealt only with his sub-contractors and it was they whom he thought of as his workmen. The sub-contractor was paid by the ironmaster on a piece-rate basis, but paid his underhands day wages. Maximising his own income therefore involved the sub-contractor in maintaining or increasing the output of his team and keeping their wages under control. Under this system there was obviously considerable scope for abuse and exploitation by the forehand, but the custom of the trade was usually strong enough to prevent this. By this custom underhands' day wages moved up and down with variations in sub-contractors' piece rates, so that when sub-contractors obtained an increase of 1s per ton they usually raised underhands' wages by 2d per day and the reverse applied when tonnage rates fell. The skilled sub-contractors were thus the key figures in the trade and the support or otherwise of the underhands was quite irrelevant in any contest with the ironmasters. Organisation, where it developed, was confined almost exclusively to the sub-contractors until as late as the early 1870s.

For various reasons the puddlers were the most militant of the skilled sub-contractors: they were the worst paid, and as the puddling process was fairly uniform across the Black Country they were able to feel a sense of common interest to a greater degree than the rollers and millmen who exercised a wider range and variety of functions than did the puddlers. Through the first half of the nineteenth century puddlers' unions rose and declined according to the state of trade and the strength of the masters' association, but in 1863 a lasting basis of organisation was established when a strike over puddling rates at Brierley Hill gave rise to the Associated Ironworkers of Great Britain. Piggott played a major part in establishing the union by bringing out the Bromford men in support of the Brierley Hill strikers, and over the next four years, along with William Aucott and James Capper, he was one of the main props of the struggling union. Then, in 1867, a year of depression for the Black Country iron trade, Piggott left South Staffordshire for Cumberland, where he worked as a puddler at the Workington Iron Company and became president of the local union lodge. After two years he returned to West Bromwich, working for a short time at the Roway Ironworks before returning to the Bromford Works, where he spent the rest of his working life.

When the Associated Ironworkers' union was wound up in 1868, the Black Country ironworks were organised by the Amalgamated Malleable Ironworkers of Great Britain, and on his return to South Staffordshire Piggott took an active part in organising support for John Kane's union. He was also one of the leaders of the movement, which developed with the spread of the Amalgamated Ironworkers into the Black Country, to establish a board of conciliation for the South Staffordshire trade similar to that already operating in the North of England. Agitation, partial strikes, and confusion over price- and wage-fixing led to conferences between representatives of the masters' association and a deputation of the puddlers and millmen, one in 1871 (September) and then three in 1872 (January, February and June). From these resulted the South Staffordshire Iron Trade Board, and a sliding scale (see William Aucott). In 1875 an agreed reduction of five per cent in wages, to operate until the end of the year, was implemented in the North of England, but in South Staffordshire a partial strike ensued and the board broke up.

In spite of the board's failure the ironworkers' leaders remained convinced that a system of conciliation based on strong organisation was possible and indeed essential, and Piggott worked closely with William Aucott and James Capper to organise a series of meetings across the Black Country with the object of reconstructing the board. The response was sufficiently encouraging for the men's leaders to begin negotiations with the owners for the re-establishment of the board, and in March 1876 it was reconstituted as the South Staffordshire Mill and Forge Wages Board. This consisted of twelve employers and twelve workmen, of whom Piggott was one, these latter being chosen on a works basis and not necessarily union members. The chairman was the current chairman of the Ironmasters' Association, and as leader of the operatives William Aucott became vice-chairman. There was a paid secretary for each side, James Capper for the men and Daniel Jones for the employers. In addition there was an independent president, chosen from outside the trade, to whom any difference which the board could not resolve was to be referred. He was in fact an arbitrator and his award in cases of dispute was final. The first president was Joseph Chamberlain, then Mayor of Birmingham.

The new board ran into difficulties almost immediately, when no agreement could be reached on the basis for a new sliding scale. The owners' proposals involved a reduction in existing wages, which the ironworkers refused to accept, on the grounds that wages were already at subsistence level and the reductions of the previous two years had brought no improvement in trade. Chamberlain's arbitration involved reductions both for puddlers and millmen in 1876 and again in 1878. He awarded an increase towards the end of 1879, at the same time strongly recommending the establishment of a sliding scale.

By this time there was considerable dissatisfaction on both sides of the board with the existing method of referring disputes to arbitration, and with the upturn of trade the employers felt able to take up Chamberlain's suggestion regarding the sliding scale. Early discussions foundered on the question of a premium above level shillings for pounds, which the Black Country men claimed 'in lieu of northern extras', and this was finally fixed at 6d per ton by Richard Chamberlain, who had succeeded his brother as president when Joseph became President of the Board of Trade in 1880.

In the same year Piggott became vice-chairman of the board, William Aucott having left the industry. In this position he worked closely with James Capper to maintain the board's authority and prevent the decline of union influence from impairing its successful operation. Piggott also took a leading part in the parallel attempt to restore the fortunes of the ailing Malleable Ironworkers' Association, and was among the West Bromwich delegation to the Manchester Conference in April 1887 which took the decision to reorganise the union as the Associated Iron and Steel Workers of Great Britain. This move coincided with the reorganisation of the South Staffordshire Mill and Forge Wages Board as the Midland Iron and Steel Wages Board, and together these two developments placed industrial relations in the Black Country iron and steel industry on a much firmer basis; ironically, Piggott, whose qualities of industry and integrity had done so much to bring this about, did not live to see it come to fruition.

Piggott's dedication to the welfare of his fellow working men was also shown in his notable contribution to the friendly society movement in the Black Country. He was for many years secretary of the Court Brave Old Oak of the Ancient Order of Foresters, and at the time of his death was secretary of the Pride of England Lodge of the Order of United Free Gardeners, having been a founder member of this body. He frequently represented both societies at national conferences.

Piggott died suddenly at his home in Littleton Street, West Bromwich, on 24 August 1887, in the midst of the union and wages board reorganisation. For about fourteen weeks before his death he had been out of work because of the closure of the Bromford Works. Added to his existing heavy commitments, his exertions on behalf of the welfare of the other six hundred Bromford men thrown out of work by the closure had seriously impaired his health and was undoubtedly a factor in his premature death. He was buried in West Bromwich Cemetery. His wife and seven children, four of them still at home, survived him. No evidence of a will has been located.

Sources: Accounts of proceedings of South Staffordshire Mill and Forge Wages Board and union activities in *Dudley Herald, Ironworkers' J., West Bromwich Chronicle, West Bromwich Free Press*, and *Wolverhampton Chronicle*, 1876–87; *Labour Tribune*, 1886–1887; G. C. Allen, *The Economic Development of Birmingham and the Black Country 1860–1927* (1929, repr. 1966); A. Fox, 'Industrial Relations in Birmingham and the Black Country 1860–1914' (Oxford BLitt., 1952); J. C. Carr and W. Taplin, *History of the British Steel Industry* (Oxford, 1962); J. H. Porter, 'Management, Competition and Industrial Relations: the Midland manufactured iron trade 1873–1914', *Business History, 11*, no. 1 (Jan 1969) 37–47. OBIT. *Labour Tribune, West Bromwich Free Press* and *West Bromwich Weekly News*, 27 Aug 1887; *Ironworkers' J.* (Sep 1887).

ERIC TAYLOR

See also: William AUCOTT; James CAPPER; *John KANE.

POINTER, Joseph (1875–1914)
TRADE UNIONIST AND LABOUR MP

Joseph Pointer was born on 12 June 1875 at 4 Bressingham Road, Sheffield, the son of John Pointer and his wife, Elizabeth (née Herbert). His father, who worked as an engine tenter, was a native of Norfolk. Pointer received a better education than most working-class children: he attended the Attercliffe Board School, and went on to the Central Secondary School. Later, at the age of about twenty-four, he went to Ruskin College for six months to study history and sociology.

In 1889 Pointer was apprenticed as an engineers' pattern-maker, and at the age of twenty he joined the United Pattern Makers' Association, in which he was to hold a number of unpaid offices. He worked in this trade for various firms until 1907. In that year a sixteen-week local strike of pattern-makers in Sheffield was defeated. Pointer had been in a small minority opposing the strike before it began, but he fully accepted the majority decision and played a leading part in picketing and other strike activities, for which he was victimised once the dispute was over. Unable to obtain employment in his own trade, he took a series of temporary jobs; at the time of his election to Parliament in May 1909 he was working in a laundry.

Pointer became active in the Attercliffe branch of the ILP probably in the early 1900s, and served in time as secretary and president. The division between those sections of the working class which continued to support the Lib-Lab position and those which campaigned for an independent stance was more sharply defined in Sheffield than in almost any other major urban centre. It was a division which was geographical as well as industrial. The central area of Sheffield contained the traditional 'light trades' – makers of cutlery, saws, edge-tools, files, etc., whose political attitudes had been Lib-Lab for several decades; but from around the middle of the 1890s the growth of steelworks and the heavy engineering trades began to shift the centre of gravity of working-class politics to the Brightside and Attercliffe areas, in the eastern parts of the city. The attachment to the Liberal Party in this relatively new, modern proletariat was much weaker than in the older trades, and Socialist ideas spread fairly rapidly after the establishment of the national ILP at Bradford in 1893.

By the time Joe Pointer became active in politics, the bitterness between the Lib-Labs and those who campaigned for an Independent Labour position had reached a high pitch of intensity. The Sheffield Federated Trades Council (SFTC), which had long been the main organisation expressing working-class political objectives, was dominated by Lib-Labs, and although the Sheffield Labour Representation Committee affiliated to the SFTC in 1903, the majority on the latter remained vigorously opposed to any break with the Liberal Party. From 1905, when the first Independent Labour candidate stood for Attercliffe, Lib-Lab and Independent Labour fought each other at local government elections. In June 1908 the Labour Representation Committee (by now no longer connected with the SFTC) established a separate Trades and Labour Council; and thus between 1908 and 1920 Sheffield had two rival trades councils. The SFTC contained delegates from most of the old staple trades, together with the labourers' unions, while the new Trades and Labour Council took in the remainder, particularly the steelworkers and the numerous unions in the metal trades [Pollard (1959) 197 ff.; Mendelson [1958?] 46–8; 58].

In 1906 and 1907 Pointer stood in the local elections for Darnall Ward, being defeated on both occasions; but in 1908 he was successful for Brightside. He sat on the City Council for three years only, not seeking re-election in 1911. By this time he was already in the House of Commons. In January 1908 he had been accepted by the local Labour Party in South Leeds as their candidate in the next parliamentary election; but he was opposed by London, and in the end the Pattern Makers also withdrew their support. The death, however, of the sitting Liberal MP for Attercliffe in 1909 soon reopened the way to Westminster. Attercliffe was the only one of the five Sheffield constituencies to return a Liberal at every election since 1885 (the Conservatives did not contest the seat in 1900; had they done so they would probably have won). Now that Pointer was standing as an Independent Labour candidate against the official Liberal, it was likely that the Conservative and Unionist Party would succeed in this by-election. The Conservative candidate was, however, a stranger to the city, and Councillor A. Muir Wilson, a well-known Sheffield man, was determined to contest as an Independent Conservative. The result of an exciting five-cornered contest long remembered in the city, was that Pointer won with a majority of less than 200 over the official Conservative candidate; and the cause of Independent Labour received tremendous encouragement throughout the city. At the time he was president of the local branch of the ILP.

Pointer had to fight two more elections within twenty months, both in 1910. On both occasions he was opposed only by a Conservative candidate, and won fairly comfortably, an understanding having been reached with the Liberals, who in return were given a clear run in the Brightside division. Pointer's election address, dated November 1910, called for vigorous measures to reduce unemployment, including a Right to Work Bill and the legislative establishment of an Eight Hour Day; the lowering of the age limit for Old Age Pensions; the nationalisation of the land, railways, shipping and coal; the continuation of Free Trade; adult suffrage for women as well as men; free and unfettered education for all, including the extension of school feeding, medical inspection and school clinics; the abolition of the Poor Law on the lines suggested by the Minority Report; Home Rule for Ireland; complete reversal of the Osborne judgement; and support for the Liberal Government in their attack upon the House of Lords. He ended his election address: 'Workers! Arouse yourselves! The WORKERS must triumph. The noble idlers must be beaten.'

The agreement with the Liberal Party led to a good deal of friction, with a section of the local Liberals declaring themselves dissatisfied with Pointer's conduct on certain issues of the day, while from the Social-Democratic Party in particular came criticisms that Pointer's Socialism had become enfeebled. He was attacked, for instance, for his lukewarm attitude towards women's suffrage: while he favoured enfranchisement,

he did not consider the issue sufficiently important to risk bringing down the Liberal Government. The Socialist Left were also constantly criticising his rapid shift to a moderate Labour position, and Alfred Barton (the husband of Eleanor Barton), a prominent figure in the left-wing movement in Sheffield, was several times suggested as an alternative candidate for the parliamentary seat. A much publicised occasion in 1912 especially aroused the anger of the Sheffield Left. Tom Mann had recently been sentenced to a term of imprisonment, along with Fred Crowsley, Guy Bowman, and the printers, for circulating a 'Don't Shoot' leaflet; and Pointer failed to support a proposal for the adjournment of the House of Commons to allow a discussion of the case. He further infuriated his former colleagues in Sheffield by suggesting in the *Sheffield Guardian* (the weekly journal of the ILP, established 13 January 1906) than Mann deserved his sentence. Most members of the Parliamentary Labour Party were, however, hostile to the syndicalists, and the fact that Pointer was made a junior Whip in 1912 suggests that he had the confidence of most Labour MPs. But he did not always follow the majority. In 1911 he had agreed with Fred Jowett's criticism of Ramsay MacDonald on the issue of the National Insurance Bill, and he defied the party Whips in a number of divisions, although on the crucial third reading he voted with the majority of the Labour Party. His political independence was illustrated by another episode. The strike which began at Ruskin College on Monday 29 March 1909 was over the enforced resignation of Dennis Hird, the Principal. Pointer, together with J. T. Macpherson, was among the most active Labour MPs supporting Hird, and Pointer became a member of the Provisional Committee set up to establish the breakaway Central Labour College. In supporting the Ruskin strikers in these ways Pointer must certainly have been among a small minority of his parliamentary colleagues [Craik (1964) Chs. 5 and 6].

The Osborne judgement of 1909 created immediate problems for those like Pointer who were supported by their unions. A member of the Pattern Makers' Society took out an injunction to prohibit any expenditure in the future on Pointer's candidature at elections; and after appealing for voluntary contributions, the Pattern Makers ultimately decided to discontinue their support of all parliamentary candidates [Mosses (1922) 212 ff].

Pointer joined the Fabian Society in 1910. Two years later he visited the West Indies on a fact-finding tour; but his career was soon to be abruptly ended. On the oubreak of war he was appointed as one of the Labour members of the National Recruiting Committee, but he insisted that his name should be taken off the list of the Committee, on the grounds that, being himself a pacifist, he could not ask others to fight. He had fallen ill in the middle of 1914, and on 19 November he died of leukaemia at his home in Sheffield, aged thirty-nine. He was cremated on 22 November, and Fred Jowett was among the mourners. In 1902 he had married Jane Annie Tweddle, the daughter of a Middlesbrough sub-postmaster; his wife, two daughters and a son survived him, and a second son was born three months after his death. He left effects valued at £405. In order to finance her family his wife ran a post office which was subsequently taken over by her younger daughter, Dora. The elder daughter, Ruth, went into hairdressing and still has (1973) a salon in Sheffield. The elder son, Harold, went to New Zealand where he worked as a bus traffic manager; and the second son, Joe, became a plumber. Pointer had been a Wesleyan Methodist lay preacher but his beliefs later changed, and in 1910 he defined his religion as coinciding with the New Theology of the Rev. R. J. Campbell. He was a total abstainer. W. C. Anderson, another ILP member succeeded him in the Attercliffe division in December 1914.

Writings: Parliamentary column in the *Sheffield Guardian*, 1909–1914.

Sources: (1) MSS: Labour Party archives: LRC; Sheffield City Library. (2) Other: *WWW* (1897–1916); *Dod* (1910–14); W. Mosses, *The History of the United Pattern Maker's Association 1872–1922* (1922); J.

Mendelson et al., *The Sheffield Trades and Labour Council 1858 to 1958* (Sheffield, [1958?]); S. Pollard, *A History of Labour in Sheffield* (Liverpool, 1959); A. M. McBriar, *Fabian Socialism and English Politics 1884–1918* (Cambridge, 1962); W. W. Craik, *The Central Labour College 1909–29* (1964); H. Pelling, *Social Geography of British Elections, 1885–1910* (1967); personal information: Mrs Ruth Dalrymple, Sheffield, daughter. OBIT. *Sheffield Daily Independent, Sheffield Daily Telegraph* and *Times*, 20 Nov 1914; *Sheffield Guardian*, 27 Nov 1914.

DAVID E. MARTIN
JOHN SAVILLE

See also: †Mrs Eleanor BARTON; *Frederick William JOWETT, for Independent Labour Party, 1893–1914; George LANSBURY, for British Labour Party, 1900–13.

POSTGATE, Daisy (1892–1971)
SOCIALIST

Daisy Lansbury, wife for fifty-two years of the author and gastronome Raymond Postgate, was born at Bow in the East End of London on 9 December 1892. She was the sixth of the ten surviving children of the Labour leader George Lansbury and his wife Elizabeth Jane (née Brine). One of her younger sisters, following the frequent Victorian pattern, died in infancy. At the time of her birth her father was a journeyman veneer dryer and the family was in straitened circumstances; and though three years later their prospects began to improve when Lansbury, on the death of his father-in-law, became owner of a small timber and veneering business, the size of the family, combined with the amount of time spent by the father on unpaid political work, meant that their standard of living, and mode of life, was very much the same as that of their more strictly working-class neighbours in Bow. Daisy wrote very little; but she has left on record, in a chapter contributed to Margaret Cole's *Roads to Success*, and in two articles on 'A Child in George Lansbury's House', some amusing detail about her upbringing. She tells of being dressed as a child in a woollen knitted vest, a red 'staybelt' and a series of red and pink flannelette petticoats topped on Sundays by a white cambric one with embroidery; of being bathed on Saturday nights in the big kitchen copper; and of the children watching from upper windows the red flag which Lansbury waved from the train when setting out for one of his many meetings.

Until she was fourteen she attended the local elementary school; then, as she was unlikely to pass the examination which led elementary school girls to careers as 'pupil-teachers' or in the lowest-paid ranks of the civil service, she helped her mother in the home for three years; at the end of which, younger siblings being available to take her place there, she took a course in shorthand and typing, and about 1910 went as typist and book-keeper to her brother Edgar in the timber business. After two years of this she had shown herself so competent that her father invited her to became his personal secretary, a post which she kept through all vicissitudes until his death in 1940. At the time of her appointment Lansbury, though he had lost his parliamentary seat a year or two previously, had recently been elected to the London County Council as one of the councillors for Woolwich, and was an active member of both the Poplar Borough Council and the Poplar Board of Guardians, as well as manager – shortly to become editor – of the young, struggling and vociferous Daily Herald; so the job of being his personal secretary was both strenuous and educative. Daisy found herself involved with very many of the 'comrades' who sought help from Lansbury, in Bow and in Fleet Street, during the years of turmoil which preceeded the First World War; on one occasion, when warning had been received that the police were waiting to arrest the Socialist suffragette Sylvia Pankhurst, she disguised Sylvia in her own coat and hat, and was herself duly arrested by disappointed constables. When war broke out she and other East End friends became part of the 'Bow Brigade' of volunteers who worked in left-wing organisations such as the Independent Labour Party, the Labour Research Department, and the National Guilds League; and through these organisations she met and married Raymond Postgate in 1918 just before the Armistice. Thereafter, in addition to bearing two sons (John Raymond, afterwards professor of microbiology at the University of Sussex, and Richard Oliver, independent scriptwriter and cartoonist in children's television) she became as much her husband's secretary as her father's; she typed his books and articles, and gave him the help and encouragement he needed in all his avocations. This job became more and more important in later years: when Raymond began work on the Good Food Guide, and the editorial side of it, for a dozen years, was done in their house at Hendon; she was responsible for the organising (and finding!) of the many collaborators, and was indispensable to the production. In the late sixties, her health began to fail, and she only survived Raymond's death by a few weeks. She died on 20 April 1971 after a short illness in hospital at Canterbury and left an estate valued at £16,199. Her two sons survived her.

MARGARET COLE

Writings: 'The Private Secretary' in The Road to Success: twenty essays on the choice of a career for women, ed. M. I. Cole (1936); 'A Child in George Lansbury's House', Fortnightly 164 (Nov 1948) 315–321 and (Dec 1948) 390–4.

Sources: G. Lansbury, My Life (1928); E. S. Pankhurst, The Suffragette Movement (1931); M. Cole, Growing up into Revolution (1949); R. W. Postgate, The Life of George Lansbury (1951); personal knowledge: Dame Margaret Cole. OBIT. Times, 22 and 30 Apr 1971.

See also: George LANSBURY; Raymond William POSTGATE.

POSTGATE, Raymond William (1896–1971)
JOURNALIST, AUTHOR AND GASTRONOMIC EXPERT

Raymond Postgate was born in Cambridge on 6 November 1896, the second child and eldest of the four sons of John Percival Postgate, classical scholar and Fellow of Trinity College, who later became Professor of Latin at the University of Liverpool. Raymond's grandfather was Dr John Postgate of Birmingham, a reformer who, having started work in mid-Victorian times as a grocer's boy, became so sickened by the shady practices of his masters that he transferred himself to a job with an apothecary and used the knowledge he obtained there and the amount he could save from his wages to get himself a medical degree; armed with that, he set himself the task of securing legislation to check the scandal, and after long-continued efforts, in which he received remarkably little outside assistance, succeeded in achieving the passage of the Adulteration Acts [see *DNB* 16]. Raymond's radical tendencies may have been partly attributable to inheritance from his grandfather – who was dead long before Raymond was born; but the penurious existence which Dr John's unpaid public activities imposed upon his family made a deep impression on John Percival, the eldest of a family of seven, causing him to have a lifelong fear of indigence and an emotionally violent antipathy to any person or groups (such as the Labour Party when it came into being) whom he suspected of intending to deprive him of his own earnings and savings. John Percival himself was a Latin scholar of considerable distinction, editor of the *Corpus Poetarum Latinorum* and of some of the classical Latin poets, compiler of a Latin Grammar, for a great many years a teacher and lecturer in the cloistered atmosphere of Cambridge University, and a pioneer, with W. D. Rouse of the Perse School, of the modern pronunciation of Latin and the 'direct method' of teaching it to children – not least his own. It was while lecturing to students of Girton College that he met Raymond's mother, Edith Allen, a woman of vivid personality who had come from Miss Buss's North London Collegiate School for Girls to be one of the early female aspirants to honours in the Classical Tripos; he married her in 1891, not long after members of college common rooms had been permitted to marry, and

they lived in Cambridge until his Trinity appointment terminated in 1909 and he was elected to the Chair at Liverpool.

Raymond attended a small private school until he was nine, when he was sent to the Perse under Rouse, and after the move, to Liverpool College. But from a very early age he received a severe indoctrination in the language of Caesar and Cicero; along with his elder sister Margaret (later the wife of G. D. H. Cole) and the second son he was made to converse and answer questions in Latin and was taught the elements of scansion in Latin verse; though he and they resented his father's discipline and his irritable impatience with the errors of small children, he nevertheless absorbed sufficient of the essence of the classics to enable him in after years to keep up a scholarly interest and even to produce, and publish, his own translation of the *Pervigilium Veneris* and the *Agamemnon* of Aeschylus.

Early in the First World War he won a classical scholarship to St John's College, Oxford; but he had already moved far away from his father's outlook. During his time at Liverpool College he had discovered the 'Labour movement' of the pre-war years whose effect was so marked in Liverpool, where an extremely hot week in August 1911 saw the strikes of dockers, seamen, railwaymen, tramway workers and the city scavengers combining to produce something like a general strike in miniature – to be followed by the long-drawn-out miners' strike, the sinking of the *Titanic* with its scandals about the rescue of first-class passengers, and the internecine warfare of James Larkin's Irish Transport Workers' Union with Dublin employers, a struggle with particular significance for Liverpool with its large Irish population. The Liverpool schoolboys formed a political discussion group which turned several of them into ardent Socialists – and Socialists, moreover, of the extreme left. A contemporary named J. A. Kaufmann – who later, as Alan Kaye, became assistant secretary to that breakaway movement in the Fabian Society known as the Fabian Research Department – introduced Raymond to the first book of the young G. D. H. Cole, *The World of Labour* which, as he said, 'opened a completely new world to me. The education which I and every other middle-class boy had received, had not referred to one single thing mentioned in the book.' He went up to Oxford, therefore, in the autumn of 1915, a committed Guild Socialist, a regular reader of the explosive weekly *Herald* edited by George Lansbury, and a Marxist believer in the class war as the only war in which a Socialist could be concerned.

Under these circumstances it was not surprising that when the Military Service Acts imposed conscription on the young men Raymond Postgate was one of the earliest conscientious objectors. In 1916 a military tribunal rejected his appeal, notwithstanding support by Professor Gilbert Murray and some Oxford Quakers: he was called up to Cowley Barracks, and when he refused to obey an order was sent to gaol by the magistrates. He did not, however, remain there long, for he fell ill. At this early stage the government was unsure of its procedure towards young men who came from the cultured classes, and an adverse medical report resulted in temporary release. Later, however, he was again called up, and this time, like many of his generation, became a C.O. 'on the run'. His father, meantime, had repudiated him and forbidden him to visit his home or see his mother. During this period he had managed to exist by doing some odd jobs of writing, sometimes for the *Herald*, and had lived with the growing number of anti-war groups of various kinds and their friends of non-British nationality; and just before the Armistice had fallen in love with, and married, Daisy Lansbury, one of the editor's large family.

Towards his father-in-law, whose biographer he eventually became, he felt lifelong love and admiration. In 1919, when the *Herald* again became a daily, Lansbury offered him a job as foreign sub-editor, and he became for some years a full-time working journalist, as well as sharing in the exciting coups (such as the publication of the text of the 'secret treaties' for dividing up among the allied powers the territories of their enemies which the Russian Bolsheviks had found in the Tsarist archives after the revolution) with which in the immediate post-war years the *Daily Herald* delighted its supporters. It was during those years that he published his first books, *The International during the War* (1918) and *The Bolshevik Theory* (1920); it was then also that he became a regular supporter of the Plebs League, the left-wing Labour educational body, and a tutor for the National Council of Labour Colleges.

Postgate was a founder-member, in 1920, of the Communist Party of Great Britain, and thereafter first served for a short time as assistant editor of its weekly journal, *The Communist*, and then, in July 1921, took over the editorship from Francis Meynell; but as the principle of 'democratic centralism' was imposed firmly by Moscow on the British party he rather noisily severed connections in May 1922 and went back to work on the *Daily Herald*. That paper, however, was steadily losing money, and after the Trades Union Congress assumed responsibility for it in 1922 there were many changes made. Lansbury retired from the editorial chair in 1925, and his son-in-law lost his job. Soon after, they were back in Fleet Street, Lansbury as editor of *Lansbury's Labour Weekly* and Postgate as his assistant. In this capacity he covered the General Strike of 1926, and did a good deal of building-up of his collection of historic Labour documents (some of which were later deposited in the library of the Institute of Social History, Amsterdam); but after the collapse of the strike the journal slumped rapidly, and in 1927 it ceased publication. Thereafter Postgate and his family were in low financial circumstances for a while until he was unexpectedly summoned by J. L. Garvin of the *Observer*, who was English editor of the post-war (14th) edition of the *Encyclopaedia Britannica*, and was possibly influenced by Postgate's patronymic to put him in charge of the section dealing with ancient history and the classics. (This involved him in visits to New York, where he made acquaintance with a publisher of left-wing leanings, Alfred Knopf, for whom he became European representative from 1930 to 1940.) In the twenties and thirties he was steadily gaining reputation as a serious writer on Labour and radical history: in 1920 he brought out a large documented study on *Revolution* from 1789 to 1906; two years later he accepted an invitation from the National Federation of Building Trades Operatives (then still committed to Guild Socialist ideas) to write for them the official *Builders' History*. Later he wrote informed popular biographies – of John Wilkes [*That Devil Wilkes* (1930)] and *Robert Emmett* (1931) – and in 1951 the official life of George Lansbury. In 1938 appeared the most solid and long-lasting of his historical works, *The Common People*, written in collaboration with his brother-in-law G. D. H. Cole. As the years went on he widened the scope of his literary efforts: in 1932 he produced a somewhat immature semi-autobiographical novel, *No Epitaph*, and 1940 saw the appearance of the (very successful) first of three detective novels, *Verdict of Twelve*. His only 'straight' novel, *Every Man is God*, was not published until 1959.

Throughout the inter-war years, whether or not he held a full-time post in journalism, he remained a committed supporter of left-wing Labour; he was an early member in 1930 of the Society for Socialist Inquiry and Propaganda which, founded originally with the object of gingering up the second Labour Government and inducing it to adopt a more Socialist programme and policy, led eventually to the revival of the Fabian Society as an important political influence; and he was concerned with more than one of the groupings which during the thirties endeavoured with little success to break the grip of the National Government which followed the crisis of 1931. In 1932 he was a member of the team which the New Fabian Research Bureau sent to report upon the institutions of Soviet Russia; and in 1937 joined a similar expedition which investigated 'Democratic Sweden'. He wrote chapters in both reports; but in general he was handicapped by having no directly political or parliamentary ambition – he was at that time an indifferent speaker – and by his commitment to left-wing views, while at the same time his quarrel with the tactics

of British Communism meant that paid work for Communist journals was closed to him. He remained at heart a journalist of the *Daily Herald* in its great and irreverent days; and after the job on the *Encyclopaedia* had come to an end life was difficult for him until in 1937 a young admirer of Lansbury named Rudolph Messel put up the money for Postgate to edit a monthly called *Fact*. This consisted of a small book, in appearance like a Penguin; each issue contained, besides reviews and editorials, a long study by a single contributor of one of the important issues of the day, which had already been criticised, sometimes shatteringly, by the 'contributing editors', who included H. G. Wells, Stephen Spender the poet, the novelist Storm Jameson, and Joseph Needham the expert on China. *Fact* lasted rather over a couple of years, after which, in 1940, George Strauss and Aneurin Bevan decided to rescue the weekly *Tribune* from the control of its communist-sympathising staff who were making it, in Strauss's words, 'an organ of the Nazi-Soviet pact', and invited Postgate to take over the editorship and run it as a journal of Socialist resistance to Hitler. This he did very willingly, for he felt very differently towards the Second World War. He had no urge towards conscientious objection; though too old for combatant service, he joined the Home Guard soon after its foundation and served in it with enthusiasm, and in 1942 he became a temporary civil servant in the Board of Trade, where his principal task was to persuade small manufacturers in, for example, the fur and furniture trades, to 'concentrate' their businesses. He remained in the Board of Trade until 1950, writing books the while. But before he left it he had already embarked upon the enterprise which in his sixties was to bring him, quite unexpectedly, the nation-wide reputation which had eluded him so long – the Good Food Club.

Postgate had for many years been appreciative of good food and drink; and even in his most impecunious days had made himself, so far as funds permitted, a connoisseur of wine and cookery. Now, in the unpropitious circumstances of 1948–9 he conceived the idea of coming to the rescue of Britain's appalling reputation for public eating by pioneering an amateur guide of the nature of the French *Club des Sans-Club*. His idea was that a team of volunteer enthusiasts, working without fear or favour, would visit, sample, and report upon the food and drink provided in British hotels and restaurants, and would endeavour to shame their keepers into raising their standards to something reasonably comparable to establishments on the continent of Europe. Initially, Edward Hulton, proprietor of the famous weekly *Picture Post*, had half-promised to run the reports in one of his papers; but he changed his mind, and Postgate with a band of volunteer helpers, who included some names well known in the gastronomic world, decided to start on his own. The first *Good Food Guide*, edited by the 'President of the Good Food Club' (Raymond Postgate), appeared in 1951, with a trenchant preface by the editor, explaining in vigorous detail what were the main sins of British caterers and what reforms were immediately necessary. The editorial was followed by a series of reports on individual establishments, drawn up and signed by initials or names of 'reporters', members of the Club; these reports were all supervised and vetted by the editor, and bore the plain stamp of his personal style. The *Guide* carried no advertisements; its reporters were forbidden to accept hospitality of any kind from the establishments which they visited: very small honoraria were paid to those who converted the rapidly-growing number of reports spontaneously sent in into printable entries and when some paid staff became essential their numbers were kept to a bare minimum.

This policy – which was a matter of principle – naturally precluded the making of any considerable profit. Nevertheless, the reputation of the *Guide* grew steadily; and of its editor also, in places which had never before heard of him. Postgate's first *public* recognition of this kind came, appropriately, in France, where in the mid-fifties the organised vintners of St Emilion in the Bordeaux country showed their appreciation of his labours and his published work on wine

(see Bibliography) by conferring upon him the status of Honorary Bourgeois, rising to that of Grand Chancelier d'Ambassade pour la Grande Bretagne. In his own country he broadcast, and his mellowing features appeared on TV screens demonstrating how spaghetti ought to be eaten. He was engaged for fat fees to write in an expensive magazine first-hand penetrating reports on the gastronomic provision in various holiday resorts; one of these landed him in a libel action brought by a large firm which asserted that one of their widely-advertised products had been adversely and incorrectly described. It was an anxious moment, for the firm had plenty of financial resources and Postgate practically none; but with cheers from his fellows he stuck to his guns, and in the courts he beat the money-bags.

By 1962 the circulation of the *Guide* and the work connected with it and the Club had increased beyond the capacity of Postgate's own home; and it was handed over, lock, stock and barrel, to the Consumers' Association, to be edited by him from the Association's central London office. He continued as editor, running it on the same lines as before, until the autumn of 1968, when serious illness forced him to retire to the country. For another year he stayed on as 'adviser', but retired finally at the end of it. After a very short illness he died on 29 March 1971 at the Kent and Canterbury Hospital and left an estate valued at £24,980. His wife died three weeks later on 20 April, but both sons survived their parents.

During the last dozen years of his life Postgate was most widely known as a connoisseur of and writer upon food and drink; the prefaces he wrote to successive editions of the *Guide* have become almost collectors' pieces, and though the venture did not quite realise his hopes of revolutionising British catering as a whole, it certainly did a great deal towards raising British standards, and the expectations of the British public, from the miserable levels of 1948. But he never thought of this as the whole or even the most important part of his work in the world. He continued to be a Socialist, a social historian, and a writer at large. In

1957 he published a translation of Colette's *Mitsou*; in 1955 a volume of 'instant history' called *The Story of a Year: 1848*, which was succeeded in 1969 by a companion volume on 1798; he took part in no less than four revisions of H. G. Wells's great *Outline of History*; and in 1969 brought out the *de luxe* edition of the *Agamemnon*, with his own notes and translation. The award of the OBE, which he received in 1966 during the time of the Wilson Government, was earned, so he believed, by his services to history and literature rather than the more-publicised contributions; and so he would have maintained in any autobiography, for which, though often urged to write it, he never produced more than a few articles of reminiscence.

As an amateur of many interests, who never held any official position, it is not easy to make definite assessment of his influence; but he was a 'character' in the best sense of the term, a lively companion and colleague, in whom a mellowing by experience gradually replaced, without cramping his style, an early truculent combativeness, and a welcome adviser to younger men in his fields.

MARGARET COLE

Writings: As journalist and author, Postgate produced a large number of books and articles. His major political writings are listed separately below as are his works on food and wine and other subjects. His writings in the *Daily Herald, Guild Socialist, Lansbury's Labour Weekly, Tribune, Holiday* and other papers and periodicals are omitted.

Political:
The International (Socialist Bureau) during the War (1918); *Doubts concerning a League of Nations* [1919] 23 pp.; *Revolution from 1789 to 1906: documents selected and edited with notes and introduction* by R. W. Postgate (1920; repr. of 1962 ed. Gloucester, Mass., 1969); *The Workers' International* (1920); *The Bolshevik Theory* (1920); (with T. A. Jackson) 'Four Years: the story of the Russian Revolution', *Communist 1* no. 1, 5 Aug 1920; 'Friedrich En-

gels', *Plebs 12* (Dec 1920) 224–6; 'Louis Blanc and Louis Pujol', *Plebs 13* (Feb 1921) 35–8; 'A Leader of the Commune: Th. Ferre', *Plebs 13* (Mar 1921) 68–71; 'Mr Smith' [Rev. J. H. Smith – working-class sympathiser] *Plebs 13* (May 1921) 135–7 and (June 1921) 169–72; 'Admiral Parker', *Plebs 13* (Oct 1921) 302–4 and (Nov 1921) 336–9 [Nore Mutiny, 1797]; Historical introduction to K. Marx, *The Civil War in France* (1921) 49 pp.; 'The Webbs' Young Man' [Laski], *Plebs 14* (Mar 1922) 69–72; 'Too Clever by Half' [An attack on the WEA], *Communist*, 8 Apr 1922; 'A Year of Ourselves', ibid., 20 May 1922; Literature and Communism', ibid., 27 May 1922; 'Horatio Bottomley', ibid., 10 June 1922; 'The Chartist Rising, 1839', ibid., 24 June 1922; 'The Fall of the Commune of Paris', *Communist Rev. 3* (June 1922) 77–89; *Out of the Past: some revolutionary sketches* [1922]; *Chartism and the "trades union"* (1922); 'The German Revolution', *Plebs 15* (June 1923) 287–8; 'William Cobbett', *Plebs 15* (July 1923) 333–6; 'How Labour goes wrong', *Plebs 15* (Sep 1923) 396–8; *Periods of Working Class History* (Labour Research Department Syllabus Series no. 7 [1923–]); *The Builder's History* [1923]; (with R. P. Arnot, M. P. Price, M. Starr and E. Wilkinson), 'A Century of Labour 1825–1925', *Plebs 17* (Jan 1925) 5–29; 'Mussolini plays all his cards', *Plebs 17* (Feb 1925) 65–72; 'Labour's Press: daily', *Plebs 17* (Oct 1925); *Papers of the First International. Communication about the George Howell Collection preserved at the Bishopsgate Library, London* [1926]; *A Short History of the British Workers etc.* (1926); 'The Dons are coming' [comment on controversy about condition of British workers in late eighteenth and early nineteenth centuries], *Plebs 19* (May 1927) 160–164; 'Who won Waterloo?', *Nation 41*, 24 Sep 1927, 802–3; 'Francis Place: enemy of the people', *Plebs 19* (Dec 1927) 384–7; (with J. F. Horrabin and E. Wilkinson) *A Workers' History of the Great Strike* (1927); *That Devil Wilkes* (1930); 'Reverend Nicholas Sheehy', *New Statesman and Nation 2*, 1 Aug 1931, 139–40; *Robert Emmet* (1931); 'Unfortunate Mr Harvey', *New*

Statesman and Nation 4, 1 Oct 1932, 372–3; 'A Letter to a Friend upon War and Sadism', *Soc. Rev.* (July 1933) 177–82; 'Iron Tonic for Labour', *New Statesman and Nation 6*, 7 Oct 1933, 410–11; 'Review of *Lenin*, by R. Fox', *Soc. Rev.*, (Nov 1933) 492–3; *Karl Marx* (1933); *How to make a Revolution* (1934); 'Communist Comedy', *Soc. Rev.*, (Apr 1934) 1–6; (with A. Vallance) *Those Foreigners. The English People's Opinion on Foreign Affairs as reflected in their newspapers since Waterloo* (1937); *A Pocket History of the British Workers to 1919* (Fact, no. 5: 1937); (with G. D. H. Cole) *The Common People 1746–1938* (1938; 2nd ed. revised and partly re-written with title changed to *1746–1946*, 1946; 4th ed. 1949; The first American edition was called *The British Common People* which was changed to *The British People* in a later edition); *Let's talk it over. An argument about Socialism for the unconverted* (Fabian Society: Socialist Propaganda Committee pamphlet no. 2, 1942) 32 pp.; *Pocket History of the British Working Class* (N.C.L.C. Tillicoultry, 1942, 3rd ed. 1964); *The Life of George Lansbury* (1951); Revised edition of H. G. Wells, *The Outline of History* (1920) brought up to the end of the Second World War by R. W. Postgate (1951; rev. ed. 1956); *Story of a Year: 1848* (1955); *Story of a Year: 1798* (1969); 'A Socialist remembers', *New Statesman 81*, 9, 16 and 23 Apr 1971, 495–6, 526–7, 558–559; (with G. P. Wells) revised edition of H. G. Wells, *A Short History of the World* (1922) brought up to date (1971).

Food and Wine:
The Plain Man's Guide to Wine (1951, rev. ed. 1970); *The Good Food Guide* (1951–2 and later editions); 'On buying Claret', *New Statesman and Nation 48*, 20 Nov 1954, 651–2; 'Wines from the Commonwealth', *New Statesman and Nation 50*, 12 Nov 1955, 622; 'Plaques for Britain', *Spec. 195*, 18 Nov 1955, 657–8; *An Alphabet of choosing and serving Wine* (1955); 'How to invest in Wine', *Spec. 199*, 22 Nov 1957, 691; Wine revisions in P. Reboux, *Food for the Rich* (1958); 'Eating in the City', *Spec. 203*, 27 Nov 1959, 798; 'Thought for Food',

Spec. 203, 11 Dec 1959, 888; *The Home Wine Cellar* (1960); 'Hambrosia', *Spec. 204*, 8 Apr 1960, 493; 'Report from Yugoslavia', *Spec. 207*, 24 Nov 1961, 754; 'Which Wine', *New Statesman 68*, 20 Nov 1964, 784–6; *The Good Food Guide to London* [1968]; *Portuguese Wine* (1969).

Other Writings:
Edited and translated with a Commentary, *Pervigilium Veneris* (1924); *Murder, Piracy and Treason. A Selection of Notable English Trials* (1925); *The Conversations of Dr Johnson*. Extracted from the Life by James Boswell and edited with an introduction by R. W. Postgate (1930, repr. London, 1969; New York, 1970); 'Allo! Allo!' [on broadcasting], *New Statesman and Nation 2*, 4 July 1931, 7–9; *No Epitaph: a novel* [1932; published in U.S.A. as *Felix and Anne: a novel* (New York, 1933)]; 'The B.B.C.', *Soc. Rev. 15* (May 1933) 87–90; 'Radio, Press and Publishing' [in Soviet Russia] in M. I. Cole, *Twelve Studies in Soviet Russia etc.* (1933) 225–47; *What to do with the B.B.C.* (1935); 'Journey to Sweden', *New Statesman and Nation 15*, 9 Apr 1938, 610; 'Publishing, Press and Radio' in *Democratic Sweden: a volume of studies prepared by members of the New Fabian Research Bureau*, ed. M. Cole and C. Smith (1938); *Verdict of Twelve* [a novel] (1940; repr. in several languages 1947–69); *Detective Stories of Today chosen by R. W. Postgate* (1940); *Somebody at the Door* (1943); 'Problem of International Language', *Pol. Q. 14* (Jan 1943) 46–59; Editor of M. Maclaren, '*By me*' . . . *A report upon the apparent discovery of some working notes of William Shakespeare in a sixteenth century book* (1949); *The Ledger is kept* [a novel] (1953; repr. 1958); Translated *Mitsou; or the Education of Young Women* (no. 10 in *Uniform Edition of Works by Colette*, 1957); *An Introduction to R. S. Magowan, Oxford and Cambridge* (1964); Edited with an Introduction, a Commentary and a Translation into Modern English Prose, *The Agamemnon of Aeschylus* (Cambridge, 1969).

Sources: *DNB 16* [entry on John Postgate];

T. Bell, *The British Communist Party: a short history* (1937); M. Cole, *Growing up into Revolution* (1949); M. Foot, *Aneurin Bevan: a biography*, vol. *1: 1897–1945* (1962); Lord Citrine, *Men and Work* (1964); D. N. Pritt, *Autobiography 1: From Right to Left* (1965); L. J. Macfarlane, *The British Communist Party: its origin and development until 1929* (1966); J. Klugmann, *History of the Communist Party of Great Britain* vol. *1: 1919–24* (1968); *Co-op News*, 2 May 1970 [a profile]; M. Cole, *The Life of G. D. H. Cole* (1971); F. Meynell, *My Lives* (1971); R. W. Postgate, 'A Socialist remembers', *New Statesman 81*, 9, 16 and 23 Apr 1971, 495–6, 526–7, 558–9; personal knowledge. OBIT. *Guardian* and *Times*, 30 Mar 1971.

See also: *Aneurin BEVAN; *George Douglas Howard COLE; Daisy POSTGATE; George LANSBURY and for British Labour Party, 1900–13; *Kingsley MARTIN; *William MELLOR; *Francis MEYNELL.

POTTS, John Samuel (1861–1938)
MINERS' LEADER AND LABOUR MP

John Potts was born on 12 August 1861 at 20 Salt Houses in the Derby Ward of Bolton, the son of a coalminer, Robert Potts, and his wife Mary Elizabeth (née Kirkman). The family moved to Durham where at the age of eleven John started as a surface worker at the Sacriston Colliery, and a year later went underground. He stayed at this colliery for eight years, then worked for a year at the Stargate Colliery, near Newcastle, having by this time passed through all grades of underground work. He then moved to Yorkshire about the year 1879 and found employment as a coal-hewer at Hemsworth Colliery, where he began to take an active part in trade union and local government affairs. He became a checkweighman at the early age of twenty-eight, and remained in this position for twenty-five years. He represented his colliery for many years at meetings of the Yorkshire Miners' Association. It was only after forty-three years of manual work in the pits that he was elected in 1915 to an official position

as miners' agent and treasurer. He held office until 1922 when he became Labour MP for Barnsley. Sir Joseph Walton, Liberal, who was unopposed in 1918, had been kept in this seat by the Yorkshire miners' officials since 1897 because he was in favour of the Eight Hour Act; Potts was one of the miners who signed Walton's nomination papers in 1897. This was a famous election, in which Pete Curran was the ILP candidate [Arnot (1949) 302]. From 1895 to 1922 Potts had also been an elected member of the Joint Board of Owners and Workmen and was particularly knowledgeable on matters relating to mining wage scales. His expertise was utilised by the MFGB in 1919, when on 15 March he gave evidence on hours and output before the Sankey Coal Commission and in particular emphasised the advantage of reduced hours in lessening the liability to accidents for miners. From 1920 to 1922 he represented the Yorkshire miners on the MFGB executive.

He held his parliamentary seat from 1922 until he was defeated in the general election of 1931. He then worked in the miners' offices at Barnsley until 1935, when he was re-elected for Barnsley. Although an authority on financial matters and noted for quoting statistics in his political speeches, he spoke little in parliamentary debates; but he was a regular attender and introduced an Employers Liability Bill (which was rejected by the House). He was also active in local politics and when Hemsworth became a Rural District Council in 1894 he became leader of the Labour group. He served on the County Council, the Board of Guardians, and the School Board, and continued a family connection with the co-operative movement by joining the Barnsley Co-operative Society on his marriage. He was a JP for Barnsley from 1929, a strong temperance advocate, and at one time a Wesleyan Methodist local preacher.

His health was affected by the shock of a colliery disaster at Wharncliffe Woodmoor in 1936, and he died on 28 April 1938 at his Carlton home, near Barnsley, after a long illness. His wife had predeceased him, but he was survived by two sons. He left effects valued at £1454.

Sources: Evidence before the Coal Industry Commission 1919 XI Qs 9044–9147; R. Page Arnot (compiler), *Facts from the Coal Commission* (1919); S. V. Bracher, *The Herald Book of Labour Members* (1923); *Labour Who's Who* (1927); *WWW* (1929–1940); *Dod* (1937). OBIT. *Times*, 29 Apr 1938; *Barnsley Chronicle*, 30 Apr 1938; *Labour Party Report* (1937–39).

JOYCE BELLAMY

See also: *Arthur James Cook, for Mining Trade Unionism, 1915–26; †Arthur Henderson, for British Labour Party, 1914–31; Peter Lee, for Mining Trade Unionism, 1927–44.

PRINGLE, William Joseph Sommerville
(1916–62)
TRADE UNIONIST AND LABOUR COUNCILLOR

William Pringle was born on 10 November 1916 at Putney, London, one of four children of William Mather Rutherford Pringle and his wife, Lilas Patrick (née Sommerville). W. M. R. Pringle was a barrister and was Liberal MP for North-West Lanarkshire from 1910 to 1918 and for the Penistone division of Yorkshire from 1922 to 1924; a Scot and a Presbyterian, he believed in a high-principled liberalism and was a firm opponent of Lloyd George in the 1920s. His son went to Bembridge School, Isle of Wight, and to study science and technology at the Chelsea Polytechnic; he also studied economics in his spare time and took an external BSc (Econ.) degree of London University. From 1937 to 1950 Pringle was employed as an analytical and research chemist at the Cereals Research Station, St Albans, and from 1950 until his death he worked at the Edgbaston Coal Survey Laboratory of the National Coal Board. He published papers dealing with the composition of cereals and coal; most of these were of course technical papers for specialists, but one which he and two colleagues published in 1944 was of general interest as well, an 'Analysis of Barley from King Tutankhamen's Tomb' [*Nature 153* (1944) 288].

Although his father had died in April 1928, when William was only eleven, he was a very formative influence, and his extensive library came into the son's possession. Pringle remained 'liberal' in his outlook, but he joined the Labour Party, which he regarded as the only practical alternative to Conservatism, and he was a member of the Fabian Society from 1944. From 1945 to 1947 he was a Labour member of the St Albans City Council and he served in a similar capacity on the Hertfordshire County Council from 1946 to 1949. On moving to Birmingham in October 1950 he continued his association with the labour movement and fought the Edgbaston division in the 1951 general election, but was defeated by the Conservative candidate. In the general election of 1955 he was again unsuccessful when he contested another safe Conservative seat, the Hall Green division of Birmingham. On this occasion he referred in his election address to the three objectives that governed his political actions; to fight economic injustice; to establish equality of opportunity; and to work for the reward of ability. He also unsuccessfully fought a number of elections at City Council level, in difficult wards where Labour supporters were in a minority.

Hospitals and education were among his other local interests; while working in St Albans he had for two years been a member of the Mid-Hertfordshire Hospital Management Committee, and after he moved to Birmingham he served on the management committee of Highcroft Hospital, Erdington. He was a co-opted member of the Birmingham Education Committee. His leisure-time interests included opera, ballet, stamp collecting, tennis and walking.

Pringle was an active trade unionist for most of his adult life. For many years he represented the West Midlands area on the executive committee of the Association of Scientific Workers and he was active in the World Federation of Scientific Workers for about eight years, during which time he travelled widely on behalf of the Federation. His special responsibility on the executive council of the Federation was the organisation of the joint activities of the West European groups. Shortly before his death he attended an international conference of scientific workers in Moscow. Professor C. F. Powell, the Nobel prize winner and president of the World Federation wrote an appreciation after Pringle's death:

He was a good and devoted man of the highest principles. I knew him most intimately because of his work in the World Federation, and his critical and constructive approach to all that he did for that organisation was of the very greatest value to it. His clean and honest pronouncements in great issues were in the best tradition of English science and of the English Trade Union movement, and we shall miss him for a long time.

Pringle died of a heart attack on 21 October 1962, aged forty-five. In 1946 he had married Dr Mia Lilly Kellmer, the psychologist and authority on child welfare, who survives him. There were no children of the marriage. He was a humanist, like his wife, and the cremation ceremony took the form of five valedictory addresses by friends and colleagues. These were from A. J. Hughes, Coal Survey Officer, NCB West Midlands Division; Alderman Mrs F. E. Hammond, Chairman of the Birmingham Labour Party; J. K. Dutton, general secretary of the Association of Scientific Workers; Miss Janet M. Calder, a family friend; and Dr W. A. Wooster, hon. treasurer of the World Federation of Scientific Workers. His widow published the addresses in a memorial brochure with a frontispiece full-page photograph and a list of Pringle's published papers. In his will he left effects to the value of £6172.

Writings: numerous scientific papers in technical journals.

Sources: *Birmingham Post Year Book* (1960–1961); personal information: Dr M. L. Kellmer Pringle, London, widow. Obit. *Birmingham Post*, 23 Oct 1962; *William Joseph Sommerville Pringle 1916–1962* [privately printed memorial (Nov 1962) 10 pp.]

DAVID E. MARTIN

See also: *Cecil Frank POWELL.

PRYDE, David Johnstone (1890–1959)
MINERS' LEADER AND LABOUR MP

Born on 3 March 1890 at Roslin, Midlothian, the younger son of Matthew James John Maitland Pryde of Gorebridge, Midlothian, a miner, David Pryde was educated at Lasswade Public School and later extended his education through private study and the Scottish Labour College (at a time when John Maclean was a tutor). After working for two years as a colliery clerk, he entered the mines and was soon involved with trade union and political affairs. As a young man he was a member of the ILP and also of the Fabian Society. He worked for the Mid and East Lothian miners from 1921 and was victimised for his activities during the General Strike of 1926. From 1927 to 1929 he was organiser for the Lothian miners and from 1927 to 1932 president of the Lothian Miners' Association. He served on the national executive of the Scottish Mineworkers' Union from 1923 to 1933.

A fluent speaker, he twice acted as election agent for Joseph Westwood, and in 1935 contested the South Midlothian and Peebles constituency but was unsuccessful; in 1945, however, he won the seat for Labour. The constituency was readjusted in 1950 when it became Midlothian and Peebles, and Pryde held the seat in a three-cornered fight. The Conservative candidate was Miss (later Dame) Florence Horsbrugh. He won the election of 1951 in a straight contest and when the constituency was once again altered in 1955, Pryde won the new division of Midlothian. Before entering Parliament he was also active in local government affairs: a JP for Midlothian from 1933, a member of the Bonnyrigg and Lasswade Town Council in 1939, and in 1941 and 1944 senior Bailie of the Council from which he resigned when he was elected an MP. For his services to the Council he was made the first freeman of the burgh in 1958.

He had married, in 1916, Marion, daughter of Henry Rue Grandison of Edinburgh and had a son and a daughter. He died at his Bonnyrigg home on 2 August 1959 and was buried at Lasswade cemetery. His wife had died in the previous year but he was survived by his children. He left an estate valued at £1508. He was followed in his parliamentary seat by James Hill, a miner and checkweighman who was elected MP for Midlothian at a by-election later in 1959.

Sources: *Dod* (1953); *WWW* (1951–60); *Kelly* (1955); R. Page Arnot, *A History of the Scottish Miners* (1955); biographical information: His Excellency Mr T. A. K. Elliott, Helsinki. OBIT. *Times, Scotsman* and *Edinburgh Evening News*, 3 Aug 1959; *Labour Party Report* (1960).

JOYCE BELLAMY

See also: *Robert SMILLIE, for Scottish Mining Trade Unionism; Joseph WESTWOOD.

RAE, William Robert (1858–1936)
CO-OPERATOR AND EDUCATIONALIST

Born at Stromness in the Orkneys on 17 August 1858, William Rae was the son of John Rae, a bookseller and his wife Janet (née Clouston). He was educated at Edinburgh University and a teachers' training college before taking an appointment in Newcastle where he was in charge of one of Dr Rutherford's Bath Lane schools. It was in Newcastle that he met his wife, a Miss Herdman, whose father was a well-known public figure and a founder of the Town Moor temperance festival. They were married in 1882 and three years later Rae transferred to Sunderland as headmaster of Hendon School, from which position he retired in 1921.

Rae devoted much of his time to the co-operative movement and from 1898 to 1936 was associated with the central board of the Co-operative Union, being its chairman for a number of years and only retiring from the board shortly before his death. He was president of the Co-operative Congress in 1909 and for some years was a director of the Co-operative Press. His special interest lay in the educational side of the movement and he was chairman of the Co-operative Union's education committee from 1901 to 1936. Much of the success achieved in the educational field was due to his enthusiasm. He helped to keep the idea of a Co-operative College before the members of congress and, with Fred Hall, contributed largely to the establishment of the College in 1919.

Rae was associated with the foundation of the Workers' Educational Association in 1903, was a member of its first executive committee and was frequently consulted by the Board of Education. He served on a number of national committees as an educationalist and co-operator. During the First World War he sat on a number of trade advisory boards.

He had been invited at different times to stand for Parliament in both the Liberal and Labour interests but preferred to remain outside party politics. In his Newcastle days he had ardently supported Joseph Cowen and in his later years his sympathies lay with moderate labourist ideas. By religion a Congregationalist, he first attended the Union Congregational Church in Sunderland and then tranferred to the Grange Church. His intense interest in youth was reflected in his work for a local mission where Sunday night services for boys were held, and in his acting as chairman of the juvenile advisory committee of the Sunderland Employment Exchange from its inception. He was also associated with the temperance movement and was a JP for Sunderland.

He died at his Sunderland home on 6 February 1936 and was survived by two sons and two daughters, all married. His wife had predeceased him by two years. His services to the co-operative movement were commemorated by the establishment, after his death, of a scholarship in his name tenable at the Co-operative College.

Writings: *Co-op. Congress Handbook*, edited by W. R. Rae (1894); *Work of an Education Committee* (Manchester, 1901) 16 p.; *How best can Co-operative Societies utilise their Educational Funds in view of the Educational Facilities now provided by Municipal and Local Authorities* (Manchester, 1904) 12 p.; *The Training of Co-operative Managers* (Manchester, 1904) n.p.; *The Co-operative Union and the Unification of its Forces* (Manchester, 1916) 8 p.; *Co-operative Education and the Programme of the Central Education Committee* (Manchester, 1916)

8 p.; *Rule by Committee* (Manchester, 1920) 8 p.; *Employment of Women and Girls* (Minimum Wage Series: n.d.) 4 p.

Sources: *Co-op. Congress Handbook* (1909); A. Bonner, *British Co-operation* (1961). OBIT. *Sunderland Echo*, 6 Feb 1936; *Co-op. Congress Report* (1936).

JOYCE BELLAMY

See also: †Fred HALL, for Co-operative Education; †Fred HAYWARD, for Co-operative Union.

REEVES, William Pember (1857–1932)

NEW ZEALAND POLITICIAN, HISTORIAN AND LIBERAL COLLECTIVIST

Born at Lyttelton, Canterbury, on 10 February 1857, three weeks after his parents arrived in New Zealand from London, William Reeves was educated mainly at Christ's College Grammar School, Christchurch. Here he received a sound classical education on English public school lines, won a Senior Somes scholarship in 1873, and a university entrance scholarship a year later. His father, a Gladstonian Liberal, first entered the House of Representatives in 1868 and became a minister in the Fox administration in 1871; and the family background of liberal politics became a formative influence on young Reeves. In 1874 it was decided he should go to Oxford to read law, but he experienced a severe breakdown in health, and after just over a year he returned home, to spend the following year on a large sheep and cattle farm in order to recuperate. The next few years were spent mostly in sporting activities – he became an excellent cricketer – but he was finally admitted as a barrister and solicitor in 1880. He disliked the law, however, began writing for his father's paper, the *Lyttelton Times*, and in 1885 he became editor of the *Canterbury Times*, a weekly also under the control of his father.

During these years he was becoming increasingly absorbed in politics. In 1887 he founded the Canterbury Electors' Association and in July stood as a candidate supporting the Stout-Vogel Government. He proved himself an excellent organiser and an increasingly fluent speaker. His election campaign was aimed especially at the working-class voter. It was one of the first elections in Christchurch to be fought on class lines and although Reeves won the seat, the group he was associated with lost control of the Government. By the end of his second session in the House, he was being reckoned as one of its best speakers, and by the time John Ballance was elected leader of the opposition, just before the 1889 session, an organised party was beginning to emerge in which Reeves himself was to play a prominent part. In the same year (1889) he became editor of the *Lyttelton Times* and in collaboration with G. P. Williams published his first volume of verse; but of greater significance for his later career was the shift in his ideas towards a moderate socialist position. In April 1890 he began publishing, under the pseudonym 'Pharos', a series of articles in the *Lyttelton Times* on Socialism and Communism; and these later appeared in sixpenny booklet form under the title *Some Historical Articles on Communism and Socialism: their dreams, their experiments, their aims, their influence.* He still used the name 'Pharos', although his authorship was by now becoming well known. These articles revealed wide reading on Reeves's part in European and American socialist and radical literature, and he was particularly influenced by the German Socialist, Lassalle, and the English Fabians, whose seminal *Fabian Essays in Socialism* had been published the previous year. Like the Fabians, Reeves understood the progress of Socialism as inherent in the evolution of modern societies and as involving the increasing use of state power to remedy inequalities and injustices, as well as the nationalisation of monopolies, including land.

This booklet by Reeves was the first socialist publication in New Zealand; and from this time he was increasingly identified with the cause of labour. The *Lyttelton Times* gave considerable prominence to the London dock strike of August–September 1889 and, what was more important, to the growing strength of the New Zealand trade union movement, in particular, to the activities of the Maritime Council which had been formed in Dunedin in 1889, representing the seamen, wharf labourers and some miners' and labourers' unions. A number of strikes in 1890 were supported by Reeves in public statements and through reports in his own press, and in the general election at the end of 1890 he was able to count upon the solid support of the unions and the working-class vote as a whole. He himself topped the poll in his Christchurch constituency, and the Liberal Party, under Ballance, won an overall victory. In the new ministry Reeves became Minister of Education and Justice.

This was the beginning of five years of intensive radical politics. In 1891 and 1892 the Legislative Council threw out or mutilated most of the labour legislation that Reeves introduced on behalf of his government (he became Minister of Labour in 1892), and the internal struggles within the Liberal Party – notably between Reeves and Richard John Seddon – did almost as much damage to the reforming cause. When Ballance died in 1893 Reeves fought unsuccessfully against the succession of Seddon to the premiership. The Conservatives were overwhelmingly defeated in the general election of November 1893, with Reeves once more heading the poll in his own constituency. He was again Minister for Labour and Education in the new Seddon government and he was to put through the statute book the most comprehensive and advanced system of labour legislation that had so far been developed in any part of the British Empire. Like many radicals and liberals in Australia and New Zealand – and Britain – Reeves was hostile to Asian immigration. His Undesirable Immigrants Bill of 1894 sought almost to prohibit Chinese immigration and intended to exclude paupers and cripples as well. These latter provisions, rather than the restrictions on Chinese, led to much public criticism. His Shop Acts, regulating shopping hours and thus interfering with public social habits, were even more controversial. His best known measure was the Industrial Conciliation and Arbitration Act of 1894. Its aim was twofold: first 'to

facilitate the settlement of industrial disputes'; and second, to encourage the establishment of trade unions and protect them in what Reeves believed to be a permanently unfavourable labour market situation. It was a measure, as he saw it, to obviate strikes – which he thought the unions were likely to lose – and thereby to strengthen labour.

The Arbitration Act of 1894 was a major piece of legislation that had considerable influence outside New Zealand. It directly influenced Australian legislation, and was widely discussed in radical and liberal-collectivist circles in Britain. There is no doubt that without Reeves the Seddon administration would have been much less radical in its general legislation, and there is equally no doubt that Reeves's social reforming measures have provided the framework within which New Zealand's social legislation has further developed throughout the twentieth century. The opposition he aroused in his own country was both vigorous and inevitable, and the remaining years of his political life in New Zealand were shot through with conflict and dissension. As one of his biographers suggests, 'Perhaps he was too sensitive and of too fine a temper for the rough-and-tumble of practical politics'; and in the event he accepted, by December 1895, the position of New Zealand Agent-General in London. His wife had enormously enjoyed a visit to England that she had made in 1894, and this must have been another influence making for his decision.

Reeves arrived in England in March 1896, his family following him in May. He began to be well known in London circles almost as soon as he arrived, and for the first few years of his appointment his prominence in political affairs was such that the New Zealand papers were full of news of him. He was an excellent public speaker and was inundated with requests from a wide range of organisations. 'His wit, clarity, brevity and apparently inexhaustible fund of amusing stories, always appropriate (which he sometimes summarised in his journals for future use) made him an admirable after-dinner speaker. In 1898 an English periodical [*Echo*, 3 Jan 1898] described him as one of the best in London' [Sinclair (1965) 248–9].

The Fabians, as well as other British socialist groups, had already become interested in the labour reforms with which Reeves had been associated in New Zealand, and Reeves quickly made the acquaintance of the Webbs, Bernard Shaw (of whom he became a close friend) and other Fabian intellectuals. In June 1896, after he had been in England only a few months, he lectured under Fabian auspices on industrial arbitration; and among his audience of 500 were Bernard Shaw and Graham Wallas. In December 1896 he wrote *The State and its Functions in New Zealand* (Fabian Tract no. 74), and although he never formally joined the Fabian Society, believing that his official position made it improper to belong to any political organisation, he remained close to the leading Fabians for many years. His wife, however, did later join the Society and for some years after 1900 was to play quite an active part in its internal affairs.

Reeves was a collectivist Liberal, although in his early years in London he was probably more sympathetic to the Fabian group around the Webbs than to any other; but his range of political and social acquaintances was extremely wide. In his work as New Zealand Agent-General he was in daily contact with commercial and financial circles in the City of London, and he proved remarkably successful in his official duties. Joseph Chamberlain was Colonial Secretary, and Reeves, as an ardent imperialist, was in sympathy with many of Chamberlain's ideas, although he was to adhere to a free-trade position when Chamberlain later embraced imperial preference.

Reeves touched British politics at many points. He became a member of the Rainbow Circle, formed in 1894 by J. A. Hobson, Herbert Samuel, William Clarke, Ramsay MacDonald and Richard Stapley, and he became a close friend of Herbert Samuel. At the Webbs' house in Grosvenor Road, Westminster, he met many who were later to become front-rank politicians, among them Lloyd George and Balfour. Following discussions and debates on the Boer War, the

Webbs invited a small group to join a dining club which became known as the 'Co-efficients'; Reeves was among the first dozen at the original meeting on 8 December 1902. As a social reformer and an imperialist he admirably fitted the purposes that the Webbs had in mind [Semmel (1960) Ch. 3 especially 72 ff.].

His fellow countrymen in New Zealand, however, much misunderstood his attitude towards the Boer War. As a liberal imperialist he accepted both the superiority of British civilisation and its extension over more backward peoples; but he disliked the bullying aspects of British policy and detested the jingoistic enthusiasm that engulfed so many of the British people. By chance his somewhat divided views became known in New Zealand and he was denounced as a pro-Boer, while in London he was still regarded as a Government supporter. Broadly, he shared the views of the Webbs and Shaw expressed in the well-known pamphlet *Fabianism and the Empire* (drafted by Shaw).

Like many other colonial statesmen, Reeves had ambitions to enter more effectively into British political life. His main aim when he had first landed in Britain had been to return to New Zealand politics at the earliest possible opportunity, but as has already been noted he was increasingly involved in British problems, and his experience of various kinds of state control of social and industrial affairs was much drawn on by men of all parties. His friends pressed him hard to stand for a parliamentary constituency on the Liberal ticket in the general election of 1900, but in the end he decided against it, largely on the ground of finance; and he never again came as close to acceptance, although for the next few years the idea of a parliamentary seat continued to interest him. Moreover, he was never able to overcome completely the conflict between his involvement in British politics and his political roots in his home country. He himself described his position in 1905:

. . . I have for the past ten years lived in London with my eyes turned half the time towards the Antipodes. Thus all my life I have been, as it were, looking across the sea [he is referring to his childhood reading about England]. Without ceasing to be a New Zealander I have also become an Englishman. Yet in talking over affairs with English friends our point of view seems almost always not quite the same. On the other hand I do not look at things quite as I should if I had never left New Zealand. It is a detached kind of position [quoted Sinclair (1965) 278].

Throughout his life in England Reeves retained his keen interest in literature. Before he left New Zealand he had already published some poetry – rather light satire for the most part; and in 1898 he published in London *New Zealand and Other Poems*, a volume which contained some of his best poetical writing. He was, however, a much more effective prose writer than poet. His commissioned *The Story of New Zealand* appeared in April 1898, and the much more ambitious, and highly successful, *The Long White Cloud*, later in the same year. This is the best known of all his books, and some indeed rank it as one of the best short histories in the English language. A second edition was published in 1899 and a third in 1924. Two further editions appeared after his death. In 1902 he produced a scholarly and well-documented two-volume work, *State Experiments in Australia and New Zealand* (reprinted by photographic process in 1923 and reissued in 1968) and in 1908 a general, rather chatty survey of New Zealand's customs, social life and topography.

By the early 1900s Reeves had become an established figure in London political and social circles. His appointment as Agent-General had been successively renewed until 1904 when he became the first New Zealand High Commissioner. At this time he was closely involved with attempts to enlarge the decision-making processes in the Anglo-Saxon colonies of the British Empire and he was moving towards the concept of what was much later to become the British Commonwealth. He was still only in his early fifties, yet there was now a degree of stodginess about him that was in sharp contrast to the liveliness of the Agent-General

of 1896. Beatrice Webb noted in her diary in early May 1904 that he was 'the same in opinion – but he has grown stale in English politics and is settling down to a certain plaintive dullness of spirit and aim'. When John Seddon died in June 1906 Reeves made the final decision not to return to New Zealand politics. Two years later he resigned from the position of High Commissioner, having already accepted appointments as Director of the London School of Economics and as a director of the National Bank of New Zealand; although he continued for just over a year to act as financial adviser to his home government.

Both Reeves's predecessors at the London School of Economics – W. A. S. Hewins and H. J. MacKinder – were fellow 'Coefficients'. Reeves was not Sidney Webb's first choice, and he was not by any means a success in the position, although his careful financial husbandry greatly helped the School through the early years of the First World War. His health deteriorated badly by 1915, and in the years immediately before his resignation as Director in 1919 he had virtually lost both interest and control in the affairs of the School. In October 1917 he had been elected chairman of the National Bank, and financial affairs proved more congenial to him than academic matters. But what really excited him and occasioned a renewed upsurge of intellectual interest and political activity was a passionate involvement with Greek affairs. For most of his life Reeves had been an ardent Philhellene. He visited Greece and Crete in the early 1900s, became a vigorous supporter of Greece during the Balkan wars, and in 1913 helped to found the Anglo-Hellenic League. He was the League's first chairman, and he became indefatigable in publicising the Greek cause during the years of the First World War. He was a close friend and devoted admirer of Eleutherios Venizelos; the University of Athens awarded him an honorary doctorate of philosophy; and he accepted the honour of High Commander of the Order of the Saviour and later that of Grand Commander of the Order of George I. When the war ended Greece remained for several years the dominant interest in his life, and it was only in 1925, after serving for twelve years, that he resigned the chairmanship of the Anglo-Hellenic League.

In the same year, in November 1925, he made what became a triumphal tour of his home country; but despite his enthusiasm for what he saw, and his approval of the changes that had come about, he was never tempted to remain. Returning to England, he lived in partial retirement near Wisborough in Sussex, although he retained his chairmanship of the Bank until December 1931. He died from cancer of the prostate, on 15 May 1932, and was cremated at Golders Green Cemetery. His estate at death was valued at £12,547.

Pember Reeves entered British political life at the time when collectivist ideas were gaining ground. The social and industrial legislation with which he had been associated in New Zealand in the early 1890s had a considerable influence upon liberal and labourist opinion both in England and in America (where Henry Demarest Lloyd became a close friend), and Reeves was an important channel of information and source of ideas. He was able to affect in some ways the trends in liberal thinking and, through his association with the Webbs and the Fabians, even more perhaps the shaping of labourist policies. He lacked, however, the emotional and physical toughness of the first-rate political leader, and one senses that his very considerable potential was never fully realised, although he remains one of New Zealand's notable personalities.

He married Magdalen Stuart Robinson in 1885. Maud, as she was always called, was a remarkable women in her own right, who became best known for her excellent survey of working-class women, *Round about a Pound a Week*, published in 1913. There were three children of the marriage: Amber (who became Amber Blanco White, well known in English literary circles), Beryl, and Fabian. The last-named was killed in the First World War, a tragedy which had a profound effect on both his parents. Maud died on 13 September 1953 and was cremated at Golders Green Crematorium on 16 September.

Writings: *Canterbury Rhymes*, 2nd ed. (Christchurch, 1883) [ed. W. P. Reeves]; (with G. P. Williams), *Colonial Couplets: being poems in partnership* (Christchurch, 1889); 'Pharos' [W. P. Reeves], *Some Historical Articles on Communism and Socialism: their dreams, their experiments, their aims, their influence* (Christchurch, 1890); with G. P. Williams, *In Double Harness: poems in partnership* (Christchurch, 1891); *The State and its Functions in New Zealand* (Fabian Tract no. 74: 1896) 16 pp. [written anonymously but attributed to Reeves]; *The Fortunate Isles* [1896] 23 pp.; (with others), *Reform and Experiment in New Zealand* [1896] 44 pp.; (with J. A. Cockburn), *The Working of the Women's Suffrage in N. Zealand and S. Australia* [1897] 16 pp.; 'The Eight Hours' Fight in New Zealand—The State and Labour Conciliation' [an interview with the Hon. W. P. Reeves], in *Notes on the Engineering Trade Lockout 1897-8* [n.d.] 47-9: Ludlow Coll. Goldsmiths Library, London; *New Zealand* [1898]; *The Long White Cloud: Ao Tea Roa* [History of New Zealand] (1898, 4th ed. with an additional chapter by A. J. Harrop and an Introduction by Sir J. Hight, 1950; 5th impression, 1956); 'Protective Tariffs in Australia and New Zealand', *Econ. J.* 9 (Mar 1899) 36-44; Introduction to H. D. Lloyd, *A Country without Strikes* (1900); 'The Minimum Wage Law in Victoria and South Australia', *Econ. J.* 11 (Sep 1901) 334-44; 'Mr Wise's Industrial Arbitration Act', *Econ. J.* 12 (Sep 1902) 320-6; *State Experiments in Australia and New Zealand* (1902, reissued with an Introduction by J. Child, 1968); 'Colonial Ideals', *Ind. Rev.* 1, no. 3 (Dec 1903) 365-79; 'The Labour Ministry in Australia', ibid., 3, no. 9 (June 1904) 108-123; 'New Zealand Today', in C. S. Goldman, *The Empire and the Century: a series of essays* (1905) 462-77; *New Zealand*. Painted by F. & W. Wright; described by W. P. Reeves (1908); Introduction to G. H. Scholefield, *New Zealand in Evolution* (1909); *Studies in Economics and Political Science, Bibliographies* [ed. W. P. Reeves] (1909) and *Geographical Studies* [ed. W. P. Reeves] (1910); *New Zealand* (1911, 2nd ed. 1927); 'Land Taxes in

Australasia', *Econ. J. 21* (Dec 1911) 513–26; 'Greek Fire; a Byzantine ballad', *Spectator, 107*, 16 Sep 1911, 417; *Albania and Epirus* (1913) 8 pp.; *A Plea for a Civilised Epirus* [1913] 11 pp.; *Memorandum by the Director of the London School of Economics on the development of higher commercial education after the war and the position of the London School of Economics* [c. 1916] 12 pp.; *An Appeal for the Liberation and Union of the Hellenic Race* (1918) 23 pp.; *The Great Powers and the Eastern Christians. Christiani ad leones! A Protest* (1922) 16 pp.; *The Passing of the Forest and Other Verse* (1925). Reeves also contributed biographies to the *DNB* 22 of Sir Harry Atkinson, John Ballance, James Edward Fitzgerald, Sir William Fox, Sir Julius Vogel, all of whom were prime ministers of New Zealand and of Sir George Grey, governor of South Australia and New Zealand. He contributed articles on New Zealand and on New Zealand statesmen to 10th, 11th and 14th editions of the *Encyclopaedia Britannica*.

Sources: (1) MSS: LSE archives and Passfield papers, LSE; H. D. Lloyd Coll., Wisconsin State Historical Society; W. P. Reeves papers, Alexander Turnbull Library, Wellington and for additional MS sources in New Zealand see K. Sinclair, *William Pember Reeves: New Zealand Fabian* (Oxford, 1965). (2) Other: *Fabian Essays in Socialism*, ed. G. B. Shaw (1889; sixth ed. with an Introduction by Asa Briggs, 1962); *Echo*, 3 Jan 1898; A. Métin, *Le Socialisme sans Doctrines: la question agraire et la question ouvrière en Australie et Nouvelle-Zélande* . . . (Paris, 1901; 2nd ed. 1910); A. Siegfried, *La Démocratie en Nouvelle-Zélande* (Paris, 1904) [trans. E. V. Burns, *Democracy in New Zealand*, with an Introduction by W. D. Stewart (1914)]; E. R. Pease, *History of the Fabian Society* (1916, 2nd ed. 1925); B. Webb, *My Apprenticeship* (1926, repr. 1971); *Bookman*, 77 no. 401 (Feb 1930) 273–4 [Portrait and reference to Reeves's poetry]; *WWW* (1929–40); H. G. Wells, *Experiment in Autobiography* (1934); *Dict. of NZ Biography*, 2 (1940); Viscount Samuel, *Memoirs* (1945); F. A. Hayek, *The*

London School of Economics 1895–1945 [1945?] 16 pp. [repr. from *The Economist*]; W. H. Beveridge, 'The London School of Economics and the University of London' in *The Webbs and Their Work* ed. M. Cole (1949) 39–53; *Beatrice Webb's Diaries 1912–1924* ed. M. I. Cole (1952); B. Russell, *Portraits from Memory and Other Essays* (1956); K. Sinclair, *A History of New Zealand* (1959, repr. 1960); Lord Beveridge, *The London School of Economics and its Problems 1919–1937* (1960); J. Beveridge, *An Epic of Clare Market* (1960); B. Semmel, *Imperialism and Social Reform: English Social-Imperial Thought* (1960); M. I. Cole, *The Story of Fabian Socialism* (1961); A. M. MacBriar, *Fabian Socialism and English Politics 1884–1918* (Cambridge, 1962); Sir S. Caine, *The History of the Foundation of the London School of Economics and Political Science* [1963]; *Bernard Shaw: collected letters*, 2 vols, ed. Dan H. Laurence (1965) and (1972); J. Amery, *Joseph Chamberlain and the Tariff Reform Campaign: 1901–1903* and *1903–1968* (1969); personal information: T. A. Blanco White, QC, London, grandson; Director, Golders Green Crematorium. OBIT. *Manchester Guardian*, 18 May 1932; *Times*, 19 and 25 May 1932; *London Mercury*, 26, no. 152 (June 1932) 99; *Econ. J. 42* (Dec 1932) 666–9 [by J. B. Condliffe].

NOTE: This entry is largely based upon the definitive biography of Pember Reeves by Professor K. Sinclair (Oxford, 1965). The editors are further indebted to Professor Sinclair for an early draft of a biographical entry for the *DLB*.

JOHN SAVILLE

See also: William CLARKE; †John Atkinson HOBSON; †James Ramsay MACDONALD; Beatrice and Sidney WEBB.

RICHARDSON, Robert (1862–1943)
MINERS' LEADER AND LABOUR MP

Born on 1 February 1862 at West Auckland, County Durham, the eldest of eight children. His parents moved to Ryhope, near Sunderland, when he was two years old and he was educated at Ryhope National School. When he was nine he began work at Ryhope Colliery, first as a surface worker and then underground successively as trapper, putter and hewer. He continued his earlier education by receiving special lessons from his former headmaster in his spare time. In his early youth he became interested in trade union affairs and in 1879 was elected to the Ryhope miners' lodge committee as a putters' representative. In 1885 he was made assistant lodge secretary and two years later became secretary, a position he held until 1919. From 1900 to 1918 he was employed as a checkweighman at Ryhope Colliery, and he was a member of the Durham Miners' Association executive from 1897 to 1919.

The Liberal tradition, although not unchallenged, had remained vigorous within the Durham coalfield down to the years of the First World War. Houghton-le-Spring, for example, which Richardson was to represent for over a decade, had returned T. Wing, a Liberal, in a by-election in 1913 thereby defeating William House, the Labour candidate sponsored by the DMA. When the war ended the miners' leaders in Durham made determined efforts both to establish Labour Party organisations throughout the country and to return miners as Labour candidates in all constituencies. Richardson had a three-cornered fight at Houghton-le-Spring, and he won the seat in 1918 with 7315 votes against 6626 for the sitting Liberal member and 6185 for J. Lindsley, the British Workers' League candidate. Richardson retained his seat with increased majorities at all the four subsequent elections during the 1920s and played a fairly active role on the Labour backbench, taking a special interest in matters affecting the coal industry, health, pensions and the poor law. In the Labour Governments of 1924 and 1929–31 he served as a Parliamentary Charity Commissioner. In the crisis election of 1931 he lost his seat to R. Chapman, a Conservative member of South Shields Town Council and a Deputy-Lieutenant of Durham County. In April 1932 he was defeated at a selection conference by six votes, the successful candidate being W. J. Stewart. Stewart, a former employee of Boldon Colliery was unemployed at the time, but he was well known in the division and the county, having served on the executive committee of the DMA, the Durham County Council (since 1922) and having been vice-president of the Houghton-le-Spring Labour Party since 1926. He won the seat in the general election of 1935.

This rejection by his former constituents ended Richardson's part in national politics; but he had always been deeply involved in the affairs of his own region. He was a member of the Ryhope Parish Council from its inception in 1893 until 1922; and he was re-elected in 1937 and served until his death. From 1904 to 1922 he was a member of the Ryhope Board of Guardians. In 1901 he was elected to the Durham County Council, became an alderman in 1917 and retired in 1925. During these years as a county councillor he was a member of a number of the council's committees, including agriculture, finance, health and maternity and child welfare; but he was especially interested in educational matters and was vice-chairman of the education committee in 1915–16 and served as chairman 1920–1. He took a personal interest in the Ryhope Secondary School which he opened in 1911, serving initially as chairman of the governors from 1911 to 1920 and as a member of the governing body until his death. In 1936 the school was renamed the Robert Richardson Grammar School in his honour. He also served from 1904 to 1922 on the Sunderland RDC and was chairman of the council from 1910 to 1913.

In 1902 he had been a founder-member of Ryhope Working Men's Club and he remained vice-president until his death. In 1905 he became vice-president of the Durham County Working Men's Club Union and president in the following year. He was later elected to the national committee of the Working Men's Club Union and served as president from 1922 to 1938.

Richardson took a lively interest in the Durham Aged Miners' Homes and founded the Durham Aged Miners' Cup Competition to raise money to support the Homes. He was a local magistrate for many years and, rather unusually for a Durham miners' leader, he was a member of the Anglican Church.

He had married Elizabeth Fletcher in 1886 by whom he had a son and three daughters, and he died at Ryhope on 28 December 1943. His effects were valued at £795.

Sources: (1) Minutes of the Durham County Council; Hansard; files of the *Durham Chronicle* and *Sunderland Echo*; (2) S. Webb, *The Story of the Durham Miners (1662–1921)* (1921); *Labour Who's Who* (1927); Anon., *A Short History of the Working Men's Club and Institute Union 1862–1926* (1927); *Dod* (1929); *WWW* (1941–50); E. Shinwell, *The Labour Story* (1963); W. R. Garside, *The Durham Miners, 1919–1960* (1971).

ARCHIE POTTS
JOHN SAVILLE

See also: †Thomas ASHTON, for Mining Trade Unionism, 1900–14; Peter LEE; †Benjamin PICKARD, for Mining Trade Unionism, 1880–99; *William Pallister RICHARDSON; *William WHITELEY; †John WILSON (1837–1915).

RITSON, Joshua (Josh) (1874–1955)
MINERS' LEADER AND LABOUR MP

Born on 16 June 1874 at Farlam, Cumberland, he was one of the nine children of a farm labourer well known locally for his radical views. Although Josh's father is known to have been a farm labourer for a good deal of his life, Somerset House records indicate that he was working as a coalminer when Josh's birth was registered. Josh himself began working underground at Midgeholme Colliery in Cumberland at the age of twelve, and then worked for the next ten years at a number of collieries in Northumberland and Durham. In his early twenties he moved to Sunderland where he joined the borough police force, serving as a constable for eight years and then resigning after leading an unsuccessful movement to improve conditions of service in the Sunderland force. He next worked for a time as

a labourer at the North Eastern Marine Engineering Works, and then went back to the mines, taking a job as a hewer at Wearmouth Colliery. He soon won a place on the lodge committee and then on the Durham Miners' executive committee, and became a checkweighman in 1912. He was also active in the co-operative movement, and from 1914 to 1921 and again from 1933 to 1935 he served on the committee of the Ryhope and Silksworth Co-operative Society.

In 1918 he was sponsored by the Durham Miners' Association and stood as Labour candidate for the Durham Division in a straight fight against a Coalition Unionist, but was beaten by 218 votes. He stood against J. W. Hills, the sitting member, in 1922 and was elected. He won the following three elections but lost his seat in 1931 to a National Liberal candidate by 270 votes, regaining it in 1935 and remaining at Westminster until 1945 when he retired at the age of seventy. He was succeeded as MP for Durham by C. F. Grey, a coal hewer from Elemore. During his time in the House of Commons Ritson confined himself almost entirely to the problems of the coal industry and the working conditions of miners; although in 1937 he supported Hugh Dalton's attempts to dissuade the Parliamentary Labour Party from voting against the Defence Estimates.

He was active in local government and was elected to the Sunderland Town Council in 1912; in 1928 he was made an alderman and a JP. He resigned from the council in 1938, was re-elected in 1945, served as mayor 1945–6, and returned to the aldermanic bench in 1947. He served on many council committees but always took a special interest in the work of the health and hospital committees, and was a governor of the Sherburn Hospital for many years. He served as a River Wear Commissioner from 1948 to 1955. In 1948 he was awarded a CBE in recognition of his public work, and in 1951 was made an honorary freeman of the borough of Sunderland. Throughout his life he was a member of the Wesleyan Church.

He married, in 1900, Elizabeth, daughter

of Irvin Dinning, of Cambois, Northumberland, and there were two sons and four daughters of the marriage. Ritson died at Sunderland on 5 February 1955, his wife having predeceased him by four years. He left effects worth £1235.

Sources: (1) Primary: Records of the Ryhope and Silksworth Industrial and Provident Society; files of the *Sunderland Echo*; *Sunderland Year Books*; (2) Secondary: S. V. Bracher, *The Herald Book of Labour Members* (1923); Dod (1923) and (1944); W. Barkley, *A Reporter's Notebook* (1948); H. Dalton, *The Fateful Years: memoirs 1931–1945* (1957); J. E. McCutcheon, *A Wearside Mining Story* (1960); WWW (1951–60); W. R. Garside, *The Durham Miners, 1919–1960* (1971). Obit. *Sunderland Echo* and *Times*, 7 Feb 1955; *Durham County Advertiser*, 11 Feb 1955.

ARCHIE POTTS

See also: *Clement Richard ATTLEE, for British Labour Party, 1931–51; †Thomas Henry CANN; *Arthur James COOK, for Mining Trade Unionism, 1915–26; †Arthur HENDERSON, for British Labour Party, 1914–1931.

ROBSON, James (1860–1934)
MINERS' LEADER

Born on 1 April 1860 at West Auckland, Durham, James Robson attended the local village school and at the age of ten entered the local coal mine. He worked long hours, leaving home at 5 am and not returning until 7 pm, for which he was paid 10d per shift. In 1871 the family moved to Langley Moor where Robson worked at Littleburn Colliery and joined the local miners' lodge. He extended his earlier education through private study and in 1890 was appointed checkweighman at Broompark Colliery; in 1897 he was chosen to represent the Broompark lodge on the executive committee of the Durham Miners' Association. In 1900 he became checkweighman at Bearpark and served continuously on the DMA committee until 1911, when he succeeded John Johnson as agent.

In 1915 he represented Durham on the executive committee of the MFGB and when William House died in 1917, Robson succeeded him as president of the Durham Miners' Association, and he continued in the office until his death. From 1918 to 1921 he was treasurer of the MFGB, being succeeded by another Durham leader, W. P. Richardson.

Robson was awarded the OBE for his war service, presumably mainly in connection with recruiting, although he was a member of the National Coal Advisory Board in 1917. In the immediate post-war years he took a prominent part at the national level in the complicated negotiations between Government, owners and miners. At the time of the Sankey Commission he was chairman of an MFGB sub-committee which decided, on 7 March 1919, to appoint four witnesses to present the Federation's case on different aspects of their claims. W. Straker (Northumberland) dealt with the issue of nationalisation; J. Potts (Yorkshire) with wages; J. Robertson (Scotland) with the miners' living standards; and Vernon Hartshorn (South Wales) with hours of work. The Government's handling of the Sankey Commission's recommendations received very sharp criticism from most of the Durham officials, including Robson who commented that 'the Prime Minister has been the object of strong solicitations by the coal owners and financiers of the country' (*Durham Chronicle*, 22 Aug 1919); but there were some compromising opinions, especially among the older officials. T. H. Cann, for example, representing the Lib-Lab tradition in the coalfield, was willing to excuse the Government on the grounds that the country was in a difficult and weak financial position. Cann also made a sharp criticism of Robson's part in the negotiations which preceeded the 'Datum Line' strike of October 1920. Robson, who favoured the strike was, however, backed by a large majority on a ballot vote of the Durham miners. Robson, it should be added, voted in favour of the return to work at the end of the month [Garside (1971) 118 ff].

Robson was a senior official of the DMA

during the most difficult and trying period of its history. Most of his time was inevitably given to his official duties, but like most miners' leaders he played an important part in the general life of his community. In 1894 he had been elected to the RDC for Broompark and from 1901 until 1911 he was a county councillor. He served for a term on the Durham Board of Guardians and was made a JP for the city in 1917. He decided to offer himself for Seaham Harbour as a miners' sponsored candidate in the Labour interest in 1919 but withdrew early in 1920; and in his place Sidney Webb was finally chosen [Garside (1971) 328]. He was always especially concerned with welfare work, was an enthusiastic supporter of the Durham Aged Mineworkers' Homes Association, and took an active part in the purchase of Conishead Priory as the first miners' convalescent home to be opened in the county. The home, which provided accommodation for 170 people, was jointly opened on 23 August 1930 by Robson and the president of the Durham Coal Owners' Association. In 1929 when the Carnegie United Kingdom Trustees provided money for a Distressed Coalfields Committee, Robson became a member of the local committee for Northumberland and Durham; and was especially interested in its general educational activities.

As far as can be discovered Robson was moderate Labour in his politics; but like many he was outraged at the action of Ramsay MacDonald in 1931. In the general election of October 1931 MacDonald stood for Seaham Harbour against the official Labour candidate, W. Coxon, and G. Lumley, a Communist who was a checkweighman at Ryhope Colliery and a member of the executive committee of the DMA. The DMA executive supported Coxon, and although Robson was unable to take an active part in the election campaign because of ill-health he published a vigorous letter of support for Coxon (who was defeated by MacDonald), in which he said:

The Durham miner and his wife never had a greater responsibility cast upon them than in giving their vote on this occasion. The question is as to whether we should give a political home to men who, to say the least, have turned traitors to the Labour movement [*Durham Chronicle*, 23 Oct 1931].

Robson was a member of the Methodist New Connexion. He married Jane Arnold of Langley Moor by whom he had two sons, one of whom died of malaria in Malta during the First World War. The surviving son was a member of the DMA staff. Robson himself, after a long illness, died at his Durham home on 7 September 1934. Following a funeral service at the Bethel Methodist Church he was buried at St Margaret's Cemetery: his wife and son survived him. He left an estate valued at £2495.

Sources: *Durham Chronicle*, 7 Dec 1917; *Report on the Activities of the Northern Committee of the Distressed Coalfields Committee under the National Council of Social Service* (1929–33); J. Lawson, *Peter Lee* (1949); R. Page Arnot, *The Miners: years of struggle* (1953); A. Mason, *The General Strike in the North-East* (Univ. of Hull, 1970); W. R. Garside, *The Durham Miners, 1919–1960* (1971); biographical information: NUM (Durham); Mrs Valerie Mason, Kenilworth. OBIT. *Times*, 8 Sep 1934; *Durham County Advertiser*, 14 Sep 1934; *NMA, Monthly Circular* (1934).

JOHN SAVILLE

See also: †Thomas Henry CANN; *Arthur James COOK, for Mining Trade Unionism, 1915–26; Peter LEE, for Mining Trade Unionism, 1927–44; John ROBSON.

ROBSON, John (1862–1929)
MINER

Born on 21 June 1862 at West Auckland, Durham, John Robson came of a long line of Durham miners. When John was nine years old his father moved to Littleburn Colliery; and although the parents wished to give their children a good schooling, John at least proved recalcitrant, and after playing truant for extended periods, he started work in the pit. He was converted to religion in his late teens and joined the United Methodist Connexion, but in later years ceased being a practising member. When still quite a young man he became active in trade unionism. The manager of the pit he was working in refused to accept trade unionists, and on three occasions elected delegates to the county committee meetings were dismissed. Robson, a single man, was finally elected and when the manager gave him the usual notice to quit, Robson brought the whole colliery out on strike. After a fortnight 'Robson's Strike', as it was later called, was ended by the reinstatement of Robson himself. He became president of the Littleburn Lodge and in 1898 was elected on to the executive committee of the DMA. He served ten years and was also a member of the Durham County Wages Board. In 1907 he was appointed agent to the Northumberland and Durham Permanent Relief Fund and on the death of George Robson in 1921 he succeeded to the secretaryship; and he remained in this position until his own death.

Robson played some part also in local affairs outside the pits. He was for a few years a member of Brandon Urban District Council and for five years was a committee member of Brandon Co-operative Society. He became increasingly incapacitated in the last years of his life with creeping paralysis, and he died on 5 October 1929 at his home in Newcastle; no will has been located. He was a younger brother of James Robson, born in 1860, who served as an agent of the DMA from 1911 until his death in 1934 and as president of the DMA from 1918 to 1934.

Sources: J. Wilson, *History of the Durham Miners' Association* (Durham, 1907); R. Page Arnot, *The Miners*, vol. *1* (1949); biographical information: Dr A. Mason, Univ. of Warwick. OBIT. *Durham County Advertiser*, 10 Oct 1929; NMA, *Monthly Circular* (1929).

JOHN SAVILLE

See also: †Thomas ASHTON, for Mining Trade Unionism, 1900–14; †Thomas Henry CANN; †William CRAWFORD; †Benjamin PICKARD, for Mining Trade Unionism, 1880–99; James ROBSON.

ROWSON, Guy (1883–1937)
MINERS' LEADER AND LABOUR MP

Born on 30 May 1883 at Ellenbrook, Worsley, near Manchester, Guy was the son of Joseph Rowson, a miner and his wife Mary (née Clare). He began working in coal-mining at the age of twelve and passed through all the various grades of work in the pit. He became active in trade union affairs and was for ten years a delegate from the Tyldesley miners' branch to the Lancashire and Cheshire Miners' Federation. In 1923 he was appointed miners' agent for the Federation, the first to be elected by a membership ballot and not at a delegate conference, and he was responsible for organising the miners in the Wigan district. He represented the Lancashire miners on the MFGB executive in 1932, in which year also he was appointed a JP for Lancashire County.

In 1907 Rowson joined the SDF and in 1910 contested a seat for the Tyldesley Urban District Council as a Socialist candidate, but was defeated. He succeeded, however, in 1919, in which year also he was returned unopposed to the Lancashire County Council and served as a representative of the Tyldesley district until 1925. In the following year he was chosen by the LCMF as a prospective parliamentary candidate to succeed Tom Greenall, the Labour MP for Farnworth and president of the Federation. Greenall had announced his intention to retire and Rowson was elected at the 1929 general election in a three-cornered contest but lost the seat in 1931. Re-elected for the same constituency in 1935, he was shortly afterwards appointed parliamentary private secretary to C. R. Attlee, then Leader of the Opposition, but his early death, two years later, cut short what Attlee himself described as a promising career in politics. He had taken a special interest in Parliament in workmen's compensation and was as popular and helpful towards his parliamentary colleagues as he was with the miners and the public generally in his native county. He promoted a Holidays with Pay Bill as a private members' measure in 1936 but died before this finally received the Royal Assent in 1938.

He married a Miss Gregory of Tyldesley by whom he had two sons and a daughter. He died in a Wigan nursing home on 16 November 1937, following an operation, and was buried in Tyldesley Cemetery. His wife and family survived him and he left effects valued at £1288.

Sources: *Labour Who's Who* (1927); *WWW* (1929–40); *Times, House of Commons*, (1929) (1931) and (1935); *Dod* (1936); C. R. Attlee, *As it happened* (1954). OBIT. *Bolton Evening News* and *Times* 17 Nov 1937; *Labour Party Report* (1937–9).

JOYCE BELLAMY

See also: *Arthur James COOK, for Mining Trade Unionism, 1915–26; †Arthur HENDERSON, for British Labour Party, 1914–1931.

RUST, Henry (1831–1902)
MINERS' LEADER

Born on 5 May 1831 at Stroud, Gloucestershire, Henry Rust was the son of Samuel Rust, an agricultural labourer, and his wife Hannah. By the age of nine, after a rudimentary schooling, he was working on canal boats operating between the West Country and South Staffordshire. He followed this occupation for about four years before settling in Oldbury, an 'island' of Worcestershire within Staffordshire, and entering the mines. As a young man he was converted to Primitive Methodism, and for nearly fifty years served the Church as lay preacher, Sunday School class leader and superintendent. Also as a young man, Rust began what was to prove a lifelong association with the Liberal Party. In later life he was for many years an active member of the North Worcestershire Liberal Council, and his influence in a predominantly working-class constituency was an important factor in the electoral successes of Benjamin Hingley, the Liberal MP for the North Worcestershire division from 1885 to 1895, whose admiration for Gladstone and belief in the cause of Home Rule, Rust shared.

Rust's radicalism led naturally to an in-volvement in trade unionism, and he took part in a number of abortive attempts to establish lasting organisation among his fellow Black Country miners until, in 1863, this was finally achieved with the establishment of lodges at Bilston and Willenhall. By the following year the West Bromwich Miners' Association had been established, and as one of its leaders Rust played a prominent part in the four month strike of that same year. He was consequently victimised by the coal owners, and his further involvement in the strike of 1874 intensified their hostility until he was forced to leave the mines altogether. He then took a small shop in Oldbury, combining this with work as an agent for the Wesleyan and General Assurance Society. He retained an active interest in the affairs of the West Bromwich Association as a trustee, however, and in the middle eighties he played a major part in reviving the fortunes of the Association, which resulted in his being appointed its paid agent in 1890. The Association had been declining since the dismissal in 1880 of Thomas Griffiths – the Association's first agent and its main inspiration and driving force – and the publicity which attended the court action which Griffiths brought for wrongful dismissal. The reasons for Griffiths's dismissal from his union position remain obscure, but it may have been occasioned by his candidacy for a seat on the West Bromwich School Board in 1877, in opposition to the official Liberal candidates. He was not successful, but his intervention had provoked widespread criticism within the union, and from other Black Country working-class leaders. Moreover, the Association was already losing membership with the decline of the Black Country coal industry. Rust was well suited to restore its failing fortunes, since he was an eloquent and compelling speaker and an able organiser; and he held the position of paid agent from 1890 until his death.

The nineties were difficult years for trade unionism among the Black Country miners. From the formation of the first Midland Federation in 1881, representing the South Staffordshire (Darlaston) Association, West Bromwich, Old Hill, Cannock Chase, Shropshire and North Staffordshire, there had been a divergence of view between the Black Country associations on the question of sliding scales. The West Bromwich representatives on the Federation Management Committee, of whom Rust was one, and the Darlaston representatives were strongly in favour of sliding scales, while the Old Hill representative was equally strongly opposed to them, and by the end of the decade these conflicting views had widened into an open breach. When the first South Staffordshire and East Worcestershire Wages Board was formed in 1883, committed to sliding scales and arbitration, the Old Hill Association remained outside, supporting instead the growing national movement towards policies of restricting output and limiting hours. The Wages Board was destroyed by the strike of 1884, but the establishment of the second Midland Federation two years later brought the conflict between the Old Hill miners and the other Black Country associations into the open once more. The second Federation's opposition to sliding scales meant that, except for Old Hill, the Black Country unions played only a token part in its activities, and when the Midland Federation affiliated to the MFGB in 1889 the great body of Black Country miners withdrew from it, leaving their wages to be governed by the sliding scales of the second South Staffordshire and East Worcestershire Wages Board established the previous year.

As vice-chairman of the Wages Board from 1889 Rust became the leading Black Country advocate of sliding scales. The unsuccessful strikes of 1864, 1874 and 1884 had all been strikes 'against the market' – strikes for restriction of output, undertaken in a vain attempt to stiffen prices and therefore wages at times when these were declining. Their failure persuaded Rust of the futility of trying to resist wage reductions in falling markets, and through the operation of sliding scales he and his followers sought to secure the same strict correspondence between wages and prices in rising as in falling markets. This philosophy brought Rust into bitter dispute with Ben Winwood, agent of the Old Hill miners since 1883, who had

been vice-chairman of the Wages Board for the first year of its operation, before resigning to lead the Old Hill Association into the MFGB, along with the other constituent unions of the Midland Federation.

The breach between Rust and Winwood and their rival associations took a decade to heal. By the early nineties the West Bromwich Association had absorbed the Darlaston Association and a number of other unions, and now controlled organisation and policy over the whole Black Country district except for the Old Hill, Blackheath and Halesowen area, which was organised by Winwood's Association. Though it became increasingly apparent through the nineties that Black Country wages rates were effectively governed by those in the Federation districts, the sliding scale remained in existence, and only in 1899 did the West Bromwich Association finally respond to the influence of Tom Mansell, who had been steering it in this direction since becoming secretary in 1894, by rejoining the Midland Federation and hence affiliating to the MFGB. The Wages Board then became a Board of Conciliation, with Rust continuing as vice-chairman until his death.

Rust died on 29 May 1902 at his home in Green Street, Oldbury, after a long illness. He left a grown-up family. He was buried in Oldbury Cemetery on 2 June.

Sources: Reports of activities of West Bromwich Miners' Association, Midland Miners' Federation and South Staffordshire and East Worcestershire Coal Wages Board in *Dudley Herald, West Bromwich Chronicle* and *West Bromwich Free Press*, 1880–1902; *Labour Tribune*, 1886–94; T. E. Lones, *History of Mining in the Black Country* (Dudley, 1898); G. C. Allen, *The Industrial Development of Birmingham and the Black Country 1860–1927* (1929, repr. 1966) pt 2 ch. 6 and pt 4 ch. 2; A. Fox, 'Industrial Relations in Birmingham and the Black Country 1860–1914' (Oxford BLitt., 1952). OBIT. *Midland Advertiser, Smethwick Weekly News* and *West Bromwich Weekly News*, 31 May 1902; *Wolverhampton Chronicle*, 4 June 1902.

ERIC TAYLOR

See also: *Samuel EDWARDS; *Thomas MANSELL; Benjamin WINWOOD.

SAMUELSON, James (1829–1918)
LIBERAL AND WORKING-CLASS
SYMPATHISER

James Samuelson was born in Hull in April 1829, the son of Samuel Henry Samuelson, a forwarding agent. The family moved to Liverpool when James was a child. At the age of seven or eight he entered his first school, 'a classical, mathematical and commercial academy', run by the Rev. George Stokes in Norton Street, Liverpool. Samuelson's major recollection of the academy was the flogging ability of Stokes. However, he later entered the school of the Rev. John Brunner in Everton, where he received enlightened instruction involving the Pestalozzi method, which was then new. He found 'education there . . . a pleasure and not a task'. The curriculum included not only classical and mathematical studies but also French, German, Chemistry and Physics.

On leaving school he was apprenticed to a large mercantile firm, but after its bankruptcy he went back to Hull in 1847, when he was eighteen, and worked as a representative in his father's business. In October 1853 he was married at Gainsborough to Miss Fanny Worsley, the eldest daughter of the Rev. William Worsley of Gainsborough. In 1857 he returned to Merseyside and established the firm of James Samuelson and Sons, seed crushers and oil cake manufacturers. The works were situated at the West Float, Birkenhead, with an office in Castle Street, Liverpool. He ran the firm for the next fifty years.

From his early youth Samuelson had shown an interest in a wide variety of activities, and he gradually became a well-known and respected figure in the area, making his mark in business, science, education, literature, politics and industrial relations. He was also a considerable traveller and visited many European countries, the U.S.A. and India. Such overseas tours were not only for pleasure but also gave him an opportunity to gather knowledge of the industrial, commercial and cultural affairs of the countries he visited.

His earliest trip took place in 1846 when he was sent to Germany by his father to visit some of the firm's correspondents. In the winter of 1849–50 he was in Russia for the same purpose. In 1856 he travelled to Königsberg in Prussia as agent for a large salt works in Winsford as well as for his father's firm. It was there that he began to study natural history, taking lessons at the university. He pursued the study of science on his return to England, and in 1861 passed examinations at South Kensington to secure a first class lecturer's certificate in geology and animal physiology. While he was studying these subjects he was also a law student at the Middle Temple, on the invitation of Sir William Fairbairn; and in 1860 he was called to the Bar. He rarely appeared in court, but his legal training was to prove useful in industrial affairs at a later date. At this time, however, he was more interested in science education and scientific journalism: in the early 1860s, with the aid of Sir William Brown, he founded the Liverpool School of Science, thus starting the first technical classes in Liverpool. His desire to popularise science led him to collaborate with Robert Hardwick in 1861 in founding *The Popular Science Review*, which he edited for a couple of years. He then started in 1864 the *Quarterly Journal of Science*, which he edited for seven years. On his resignation he was presented with a complimentary address, the signatories including Charles Darwin and Sir John Herschel.

By 1870 Samuelson was emerging as something more than a figure of minor local importance. He had published two works on natural history (1858 and 1860) and his first book of more general interest *The German Working Man* (1869). He was now poised to develop his growing ambitions in politics and local industrial affairs. In the ensuing fifteen years he achieved considerable local prominence and admiration.

In politics Samuelson came from a family with strong Liberal traditions. Five of his brothers were Liberals, including Sir Bernhard Samuelson who was Liberal MP for Banbury for many years. His elder brother

Edward was, in contrast, a Conservative, who became a leading figure in the Liverpool Council. James's somewhat radical views and championship of the working classes prevented him from being accepted with any great enthusiasm by the local Liberal Party caucus. On the two occasions that he sought to become a local MP his election campaigns were marred by recrimination between party factions. Indeed, in the 1874 election the Birkenhead Liberals were both unprepared and divided, and no official party candidate was sponsored. A group of radical Liberals, however, together with a number of working men, were determined to put up a candidate, and Samuelson was invited to stand against the Conservative candidate, John Laird, three days before polling took place. Not surprisingly he lost, Laird securing a majority of over 2000. Samuelson's election address exhibited his 'advanced' views; he advocated compulsory state education, the extension of household suffrage to agricultural labourers, workmen's compensation for injury at work, support for Plimsoll in his campaign to protect seamen, and self-government for Ireland.

In the general election of 1885 he was adopted as the Liberal candidate for Kirkdale, Liverpool – after a good deal of controversy. Kirkdale was a working-class constituency, and well before the election Samuelson had accepted an invitation from the Liverpool Trades Council and a number of trade unions to stand as a candidate representing the working man's interests. He did not regard this as signifying any breach with the Liberal Party, and as the election drew nearer he sought adoption by the Kirkdale Liberal Association as the official Liberal candidate. The Association was deeply divided. Samuelson was not only an outsider in that he lived in Birkenhead, but he was also a radical, and under suspicion as a nominee of working men. The Association took the unusual step of submitting the case, with Samuelson's approval, to arbitration. John Morley, the prominent Liberal MP, adjudicated in favour of Samuelson as the most likely person to defeat the Conservative candidate. But the controversy over his candidature

scarcely helped his campaign, and he was defeated in a three-cornered fight, the result being:

G. S. Baden-Powell (Conservative)   3391
J. Samuelson (Liberal)   1981
J. E. Redmond (Irish Nationalist)   765

This election marked the climax of Samuelson's efforts to enter Parliament. Although he contested East Renfrewshire as a Liberal in 1886, where he polled 2438 votes against the Conservative candidates 3806, his ambition had always been to represent a Merseyside constituency, and by the 1890s he had virtually given up active politics.

It is clear that the Liverpool Liberals never wholly accepted Samuelson. His radical views, his persistent support for the lower paid, the poor and the weak of Merseyside, and his advocacy of trade unionism created suspicion among the traditionally minded local party officials. Considerate treatment for his own employees, who enjoyed a co-operative scheme, was his own private affair, but his agitation on behalf of the working classes from the early 1870s soon disenchanted local Liberal opinion, although Samuelson remained a loyal party member and sought, wherever possible, to further the Liberal cause.

Samuelson had sprung into prominence during the considerable local labour agitation of 1872. The trade boom of the early 1870s, together with the spread of the agitation for a nine hour day encouraged Merseyside workers to press for shorter hours and/or increased wages. Although William Simpson emerged as the protagonist on behalf of Liverpool's unskilled workers, Samuelson played a considerable if less dramatic role. In October and November 1871 he chaired meetings of railwaymen in their agitation to secure a nine-hour day. By the end of the year they had secured a fifty-seven hour week. Throughout 1872 Samuelson chaired meetings of the Shop Assistants' Association and gave it every encouragement in its efforts to secure shorter working hours by early closing. Marginal gains were achieved, although Samuelson felt that success depended ultimately on earlier closing of public houses, and an employers' union to compel the public to shop earlier. The operative bakers and the carters were other work groups that sought Samuelson's advice during this turbulent year. By mid-1873 the agitation had run its course and the ensuing years of depression witnessed a collapse of militancy.

The great waterfront dispute of 1879 provided a more dramatic setting for Samuelson's intervention. For five weeks the Liverpool and Birkenhead docks were paralysed by a strike of seamen for a wage increase and of dock labourers in protest against a wage cut. Although William Simpson played the major role, Samuelson attended many meetings of the dock labourers (he played no part in the seamen's dispute), supported Simpson in his efforts to resolve the strike, recommended compromises and, finally, arbitration. Although his recommendations were rejected and ultimately he withdrew, the climax of his career as mediator came after the strike had collapsed. During the conflict he pressed the men to form a union; in March 1879 he chaired a meeting that created the Birkenhead Amalgamated Dock Labourers' Union and Benefit Society. In the same year a similar union was formed in Liverpool. There is no doubt that the creation of these two unions derived from Samuelson's persistent advocacy of organisation among the dock labourers. By early 1880 the dock labourers were agitating once again to restore their pre-1879 wage rate. The unions, under Samuelson's influence, sought to prevent another major strike, and the employers were prepared to accept arbitration. Lord Derby agreed to make the final decision, and Samuelson was nominated as the dockers' representative. Ultimately Lord Derby recommended the restoration of wages to the men, and Samuelson was hailed as architect of the dockers' victory. It was in the wake of this success that local trade unions invited him to become a candidate for the Kirkdale parliamentary constituency.

Samuelson's ideas were certainly radical for the time. He held progressive views on compensation for industrial injuries and on profit sharing. He was among the handful of enlightened middle-class reformers who genuinely and unswervingly supported the spread of trade unionism to all sectors of the working classes in the interests of industrial harmony. His fundamental belief was in the virtue of conciliation and, if all else failed, arbitration. The best means to achieve conciliation was the meeting of representatives of employers and employees to resolve industrial differences. Hence the need for strong trade unions to provide intelligent and peaceable representatives. In this way strikes would be avoided, to the benefit of all. Moreover, trade unions could provide some measure of protection against the problems of sickness, unemployment, etc. through friendly society benefits. Samuelson failed to appreciate that what was appropriate to skilled men in craft societies was not appropriate to men in unskilled and casual employment, where abundance of labour kept wage rates low, and where the regular occurrence of bouts of unemployment destroyed the viability of friendly society schemes.

It is not surprising that after 1885 Samuelson's influence declined sharply. Samuelson liked to be consulted and offer his advice: there was a strong element of paternalism in his attitude to trade union and working-class desires for economic and social justice. The development of Socialism was far removed from his radical Liberalism, and the emergence of militant trades unions along the Liverpool waterfront was alien to his concept of the function of unions. Nevertheless in the Liverpool dock strike of 1890 he sought, briefly, to bring both sides together to resolve the dispute, with arbitration to settle outstanding points. It was, however, the employers who brushed aside his suggestion of conciliation.

In the 1890s as unemployment returned various local schemes were devised to alleviate distress. To these Samuelson gave money and support. He played some part in the formation of a Board of Conciliation and Arbitration that was designed to deal with local labour disputes, but in 1893 he felt that 'the feud between employer and employed [was] likely for some time to come to be bitter'.

By then he was in his sixties and had withdrawn from active politics. He had, over the years, published a considerable number of books on a wide variety of subjects. His philanthropic interests spread to relieving the sufferings of slum children, and in the early years of the twentieth century he founded the Liverpool Summer Camp for Girls which provided a seaside holiday for the needy. His firm remained in existence until 1905 when – presumably – he retired. He had lived for a time in Birkenhead, but moved to Hoylake, Cheshire, where as an octogenarian he led an active life. By 1913 he had left Merseyside and moved to Bath House, Sidmouth. Mrs Samuelson died on 5 March 1916. They had two sons, one of whom lived in Hoylake, the other in the south of England. As late as April 1917, when he was eighty-eight years old, he published an article in the *Cotton Factory Times* on the Russian textile industry. Samuelson died on 14 April 1918, a few days before his eighty-ninth birthday. He had been in failing health for some time, hastened by the death in the war of his only grandson. He left an estate valued at £6644.

Although by 1918 he was largely forgotten on Merseyside, during the last third of the nineteenth century he had played a considerable role as a radical Liberal seeking to raise the dignity of the working man through the encouragement of trade union organisation.

Writings: (assisted by J. B. Hicks) *Humble Creatures. The Earth Worm and the Common House Fly* (1858, 2nd ed. 1860); (assisted by J. B. Hicks) *Humble Creatures (Pt 2): the honey bee, its natural history, etc.* (1860); *The German Working Man* (1869); *Continuity in Civilisation* [an essay read before the Liverpool Literary and Philosophical Society] (1869); *Trade Unions and Public Houses. A letter to the Rt Hon. H. A. Bruce* (1871) P; *Views of the Deity, Traditional and Scientific: a contribution to the study of theological science* (1871); *Work, Wages, and the Profits of Capital: an essay on the Labour Question* (1872); *The Natural Foundations of Religion* (1876); *The History of Drink. A Review, Social, Scientific and Political* (1878, 2nd ed. 1880); *Useful Information for Intending Emigrants to the Western Prairies of the United States* (1879); *National Reform Union. W. E. Gladstone, Scholar, Statesman, Orator and Financial Reformer. An address . . . to the Liberals of Preston* (1880), 14 pp.; *Roumania, Past and Present* (1882); *A Digest of the Corrupt Practices Act (46 and 47 Vic. c. 51), Its Aims and Chief Provisions* [1883] 8 pp.; *Shall Russian Treachery win the Day? An appeal to Englishmen* (1886) 14 pp.; *Bulgaria Past and Present* (1888); *India, Past and Present* (1890); *Boards of Conciliation and Arbitration for the Settlement of Labour Disputes* (1891) 32 pp.; *Boards of Conciliation in Labour Disputes . . . A Short Address to the Artizans and Labourers of Liverpool* (1892) P; *Labour-saving Machinery. An essay on the effect of mechanical appliances in the displacement of manual labour in various industries* (1893); *Greece: her present condition and recent progress* (1894); Editor of *The Civilisation of our Day* (1896); *Footsteps in Human Progress, Secular and Religious. A Short Series of Letters to a Friend* (1898); *Drink and Compensation. An Essay on Licensing Reform* (1903) 48 pp.; *James Samuelson's Recollections* [1907]; *The Lament of the Sweated* (1908); *The Human Race: its past, present and probable future. An Essay* (1910); *The Children of our Slums* (Liverpool, [1911]); *Drink, Past, Present and Probable Future, with some of its Bearings on the War: an essay* (Liverpool and Sidmouth, [1916]) 43 pp.; 'Russian Textile Industry: its rise and development', *Cotton Factory Times*, 20 Apr 1917.

Sources: *Birkenhead News; Liverpool Daily Courier, Liverpool Daily Post, Liverpool Mercury* and their weekly editions; *Liverpool Review; Porcupine*, 35 (Apr 1893); Lord Russell of Liverpool, *Personal Books 2* (n.d.); E. L. Taplin, *Liverpool Dockers and Seamen 1870–1890* (University of Hull, 1974). Obit. *Liverpool Echo*, 15 Apr 1918; *Liverpool Daily Post and Mercury* and *Liverpool Daily Courier*, 16 Apr 1918; *Birkenhead News*, 17 Apr 1918.

ERIC TAPLIN

See also: William SIMPSON.

SCHOFIELD, Thomas (1825–79)
CO-OPERATOR

Thomas Schofield was born on 21 October 1825 in Oldham, his father dying when he was still a child. After a limited education at Old Jacob's School, he started work at the age of seven as a piecer at Rowland's Mill. Later he acquired some additional education at the Church Sunday School, and spent some hours every evening reading and teaching himself mathematics. A founder of the Oldham Industrial Co-operative Society (1850) and elected one of its first two auditors, he became on 20 October 1858 the first permanent manager of the Society and did much to carry it through its early difficult years and establish it on a sound basis.

Schofield was one of the first subscribers to the Oldham Building and Manufacturing Co. Ltd (later the Sun Mill Co. Ltd) and in February 1863 was elected a director. In April 1868 he resigned this post and that of manager of the Oldham Industrial Co-operative Society to become the Company's salesman and market man. Within a few months of his appointment he had rescued the Company from severe difficulties by clearing away large stocks of faulty yarn that had accumulated, and by acquiring enough customers to make production pay. In 1869 he and the Company's treasurer, J. J. Midgley, resigned to found a yarn agency. David Wilkinson, secretary of the Sun Mill, wrote: 'I always found Mr Thomas Schofield one of the best business men I ever came across. He seemed to weigh everything in a balance, was never in a temper, always kind and cautious, and ever ready to reason with anybody, however humble.' His resignation was a great loss to the Company and to the Oldham Co-operative movement.

He was a member of Oldham Parish Church and a churchwarden until his death at 3 Queen's Road, Oldham, on 6 December 1879. His wife Mary, to whom he left his estate, valued at under £200, survived him.

Sources: *Textile Manufacturer* (1885) 195; *Oldham Co-operative Record*, 3, no. 7 (Nov 1896); J. T. Taylor, *Jubilee History of the Oldham Industrial Co-operative Society Ltd 1850–1900* (Manchester, 1900); R. E. Tyson, 'The Sun Mill Company Limited – A Study in Democratic Investment, 1858–1959' (Manchester MA, 1962); biographical information: Education Secretary, Oldham Industrial Co-operative Society Ltd.

H. F. BING
R. E. TYSON

See also: †James LEES; †William MARCROFT.

SEDDON, James Andrew (1868–1939)
TRADE UNION LEADER AND LABOUR MP

James Seddon was born on 7 May 1868 at Prescot in south-west Lancashire, the eldest son of Thomas Seddon and his wife, Marion Heggie. At the time of his birth his father was a nail maker, but a few years later he became an employee of the local Board of Guardians, which he served for over thirty years. James was educated in Huyton and Prescot at National and Board schools. At the age of twelve he became a grocer's assistant, and this was to be his occupation for sixteen years, until he obtained a post as a commercial traveller, in which he remained for a further ten years. As a young man he was associated with local Congregational and Independent Methodist bodies, and served in the Sunday School and Pleasant Sunday Afternoon movement. He was also a member of the Rechabites and a teetotaller.

He entered the trade union world as an organiser of shop assistants in the St Helens area. In 1898 he became a member of the executive committee of the National Amalgamated Union of Shop Assistants, and in 1902 held the office of president. At this time he belonged to the ILP, and worked on behalf of the St Helens Labour Council, which he also served as president.

In a letter written to W. T. Stead in 1906 Seddon gave some account of the influences that had shaped his early development:

> My boyhood was spent in a strong Radical and Noncomformist home. The books, chiefly the Bible, Carlyle, and Chartist

literature. In early manhood I began to speak and study social questions, which brought me into contact with the Labour movement. I read anything and everything that came my way. Through a book club I secured a fair library, which contains Carlyle's works and most of the textbooks, or well-known authorities on social and Labour questions, and last but not least most of the poets.

I think the first step to my present political views was prompted by Kidd's *Social Evolution.* I cannot, however, give any special course adopted. I read a deal, did what I could for my class, and by accident got into Parliament [*Review of Reviews* (1906) 579].

In the general election of 1906 he was the LRC candidate for the Newton division of Lancashire, a constituency a few miles from St Helens which had a large number of miners among its electors. Earlier, Sam Woods of the Lancashire and Cheshire Miners' Federation had intended to contest the seat, but he withdrew because of ill-health, and an attempt to switch Tom Greenall from Accrington to Newton failed. Thus the way became clear for Seddon and in June 1904 he was unanimously elected as candidate for Newton by the local branch of the LRC. At that time he was registration agent for the Eccles LRC. The Newton division had been represented by a Conservative since 1885, and the sitting member was Col. R. Pilkington, whose family had extensive business interests in the area, but Seddon defeated him by 541 votes in a straight fight. He was described at the time of his election as 'an uncompromising Socialist, and much in request as a speaker' [*Reformers' Year Book* (1907) 32]. Seddon's victory was part of a notable swing in Lancashire against the Tories [Bealey and Pelling (1958) 265 ff.]. His election speeches were typical of the general run of LRC candidates at this time:

The Labour Party came forward, not in the interests of a class, but in the interests of the nation. John Morley said 'the workers are the nation', and the 90 Labour candidates before the country

were determined that the financiers who had made the House of Commons the annex to the Stock Exchange, the hutch for the guinea pigs, and the land flowing with milk and honey for German Jews, should in future be the workshop for social and industrial reform for the people of those isles [*Earlestown Guardian* 12 Jan 1906];

and in the same speech he had an interesting comment on the Chinese labour question in South Africa, an issue which played a prominent part in the election as a whole. The mineowners on the Rand, Seddon emphasised, wanted 'cheap, forced labour'. The local white miners naturally opposed the Chinese immigrants, but their meetings of protest were broken up by hired thugs and, as Seddon reported: 'The result of the Chinese importation was that they were a terror to every white woman, and their homes had to be protected by night against the yellow peril. What must be their idea of British liberty?'

At the general election of January 1910 Seddon retained the seat with a majority of 752 over Viscount Wolmer (Conservative), but in December the position was reversed when Seddon polled 144 votes fewer than Wolmer. Now out of Parliament for the next few years, Seddon concentrated on the trade union side of his career. In 1908 he had become a member of the TUC's parliamentary committee. He held this position until 1915, and in September of that year he gave the presidential address at the Bristol Trades Union Congress. Like the great majority of the labour movement, Seddon supported the declaration of war against Germany in August 1914; and as a 'super-patriot' he used all his influence to encourage pro-war attitudes. He travelled to the United States as a representative of the TUC to argue the British case for waging war. His services were recognised in 1918 when he was created a Companion of Honour. He was one of the signatories to the British Workers' National League manifesto, which called for an all-out effort to achieve victory. The League was inaugurated in 1916, and Seddon was then described as the chairman of its organisation committee. At the first annual conference of the League in March 1917, the main resolutions called for all-out support for the war effort; the co-operation of all classes for a higher standard of living for the workers; the development of national agriculture; the promotion of Empire development; and a restriction on the import of cheap manufactured goods. Seddon, as chairman of the organisation committee, presented the draft constitution to the conference.

In a speech in June 1917 as prospective National candidate for Hanley, Seddon explained the origins and aims of the British Workers' League:

The British Workers' League had come into being, not to make a new political party but to emphasise the lessons of the War. Soon after the statesmen of this country ceased to be politicians, and decided to present a united front to the enemy, it was discovered that there were agencies working subterraneously whose work was not in the interests of unity in the nation. The Labour Party were loyal to the truce in the House of Commons, but a certain section were disloyal – men like Mr MacDonald, men like Mr Snowden, men who ceased to be democrats and became enemies of their country and the friends of Germany ... As a League they stood first and foremost for the victory of our arms. Any negotiations until Germany had been crushed would be taken as a victory for Germany, and the German people, the docile victims of the Kaiser, would take it that Germany had not been beaten, but was waiting for a more favourable opportunity of working her vengeance on this country. The BWL stood also for the reconstruction of social life after the war. They laid down this fundamental principle – that in the future the first charge upon industry should be the workman, and not the investment ... [British Citizen, 16 June 1917].

His work in the BWL led Seddon outside the Labour Party. He joined the National Democratic Party, which was formed in 1918 and supported the Lloyd George Coalition; an offshoot of the British Workers' League, it received financial support from Conservatives and Coalition Liberals. At the general election in December he contested the Hanley division of Stoke-on-Trent as an NDP candidate endorsed by the Coalition, and he received £500 from the British Commonwealth Union [Stubbs (1972) 752]. He had three opponents standing against him – Harper Parker (Labour), R. L. Outhwaite (Independent Liberal) and L. L. Grimwade (Liberal) – and was elected with a majority of 336. Four years later, when he fought the constituency as an Independent with National Liberal support, he was runner-up to Parker in a three-cornered contest. In 1923 he again stood for the division, on this occasion as a Conservative, but was again unsuccessful.

The last years of his life were spent in political obscurity. He continued to lecture, and in 1929 he was appointed secretary of the Church Association. In 1936 he became secretary of the St Pancras Chamber of Commerce. Seddon collapsed and died at his home, 17 Western Parade, New Barnet, on 31 May 1939. In 1891 he had married Ellen Brown of Prescot; his wife and two daughters survived him. No record of his will has been traced.

Writings: *Why British Government supports the War* [1917] 12 pp. (French translation, 1918).

Sources: (1) MSS: Labour Party archives: LRC; (2) Other: W. T. Stead, 'The Labour Party and the Books that helped to make it' *Review of Reviews* 33 (June 1906) 568–582; *Reformers' Year Book* (1907); *Dod* (1909, 1921); *British Citizen*, 16 June 1917; *WWW* (1929–40); *Kelly* (1938); F. Bealey and H. Pelling, *Labour and Politics 1900–1906* (1958); R. Douglas, 'The National Democratic Party and the British Workers' League', *Hist. J. 15*, no. 3 (1972) 533–52; J. O. Stubbs, 'Milner and Patriotic Labour, 1914–18', *Engl. Hist. Rev.* (Oct 1972) 717–754. OBIT. *Times*, 1 June 1939; *St Pancras Chronicle*, 2 June 1939.

DAVID E. MARTIN

See also: †Arthur HENDERSON, for British Labour Party, 1914–31; George LANSBURY, for British Labour Party, 1900–13; *Robert Leslie (Leonard) OUTHWAITE.

SHACKLETON, Sir David James
(1863–1938)
TRADE UNIONIST AND LABOUR MP

David Shackleton was born on 21 November 1863 at Alma Cottages, Cloughfold, near Haslingden, in the Rossendale Valley, north-east Lancashire. He was the only son of William Shackleton, a power loom weaver employed at James Ashworth and Company's Hall Carr mill, Cloughfold, and his wife Margaret (née Gregory). At the age of five he attended a dame school and a year later continued his education at the Longholme Wesleyan Day School. He began work at the age of nine as a half-timer in the Hall Carr cotton mill, but after a short time his parents moved to Haslingden, where he again obtained a job in the weaving shed. Although still attending elementary school, he worked some thirty-six hours a week for a wage of two shillings, while in such spare time as he had he helped his father who had set up as a watchmaker. At thirteen he left school and became a full-timer. In 1878 he moved with his family to Accrington where in 1883 at the age of twenty, he married Sarah Broadbent at Antley Wesleyan Chapel. On one occasion, in 1906, when W. T. Stead asked him to say what books had influenced him, Shackleton looked back on these early years and replied:

> I cannot say that any particular book influenced me in my youth or early manhood. *The Manchester Guardian* was my chief instructor in political and social questions, and the practical experience gained since I was twenty of official trade union work has been my chief guide [*Review of Reviews 33* (1906) 579–80].

Shackleton's early interest in labour questions may have originated as part of a desire for self-improvement. As a young man he became a member of the Accrington Weavers' Association and was elected to its committee within fifteen months of joining, only to be dismissed by his employer, who disapproved of trade unionism. For the seventeen weeks of unemployment which followed this incident Shackleton had to live on the earnings of his wife, who was also a mill-worker. The experience failed to deter him from trade union work, and in 1889 he was elected president of the Accrington Association. While still working in the mill he was appointed a magistrate at the very early age of twenty-nine, the first working man to hold such a position in Accrington; ironically, as he recalled later in a short account of his early life, among his fellow magistrates was the employer who had discharged him [*Pearson's Weekly*, 15 Mar 1906]. In 1908 he was appointed a Lancashire county magistrate and in 1910 sat on the Darwen Borough bench.

In 1893 he became full-time secretary of the Ramsbottom Weavers' Association, and in the following year succeeded Joseph Cross in the post of secretary of the more important Darwen Weavers' Association, a position he held until 1907. He was elected to the Central Committee of the Weavers' Amalgamation, and was a member of the Lancashire delegation which went with cotton employers to America in 1902 in order to study employment conditions there and to inquire into the working of the Northrop loom.

Shortly after his return from the United States, in August 1902, Shackleton was elected unopposed as the MP for Clitheroe, succeeding Sir Ughtred Kay-Shuttleworth, a Liberal, who had been raised to the peerage. The return of a Labour candidate unopposed was unprecedented and came about through a combination of unusual circumstances [for which see the detailed account in Bealey and Pelling (1958) ch. 5]. Not the least important of these was Shackleton's political position. At one point the LRC had proposed Philip Snowden, but as the Clitheroe Liberals would almost certainly have contested the seat against a Socialist, the leaders of the ILP decided to support Shackleton. Only two years previously, Shackleton had declined a Liberal invitation to fight the Darwen constituency (though he had been returned in 1894 to

Darwen Town Council as a Liberal), and this background, together with his association with nonconformity and local trade unionism, worked in favour of his candidature. All the Lancashire Liberal MPs took the view that he should not be opposed and the most likely Liberal candidate, Philip Stanhope made it clear that he would not accept the local party's nomination. For the purpose of the election Shackleton described himself as 'a Labour man purely and simply', and if Socialists were disappointed that his platform was that of an advanced Liberal, they had the compensation that his union, the United Textile Factory Workers' Association, became affiliated to the LRC.

In Parliament Shackleton occupied an uncertain position, often being close to the Lib-Labs rather than to the tiny Labour group. On his introduction to the Commons he was to have been sponsored by John Burns and Richard Bell, but Keir Hardie replaced the latter after the intervention of the ILP. Shackleton's lack of commitment to the idea of an independent labour party was illustrated by his approval of Liberal candidates: in 1904 he spoke in support of Philip Stanhope who was contesting a by-election at Market Harborough, and he recommended J. W. Benn to the electors of Devonport. He was elected to the Labour Party executive in 1903, and in the following year became a member of the parliamentary committee of the TUC, a position he held until 1910. Shackleton was responsible for introducing into the Commons the Trade Disputes Bill, which sought to amend the legal situation created by the Taff Vale decision, but the Bill was defeated on the second reading in May 1903.

After the election of Arthur Henderson for Barnard Castle Shackleton and he became close friends; they were of the same age and had similar backgrounds, and both were Wesleyans, teetotallers and non-smokers. They shared lodgings in Kennington Road, Lambeth, while politically they shared cautious and reformist attitudes.

In the 1906 general election Shackleton was again returned to the Commons as member for Clitheroe, with a large majority over B. J. Belton, a brewer from Weybridge, Surrey, who appeared late on the scene as an independent Liberal-Unionist. The Labour Party now had twenty-nine members in the Commons. Shackleton stood against Hardie for the post of chairman of the newly-created Parliamentary Labour Party, failing by a single vote to secure election; instead he became vice-chairman, and acted as such until 1908. Though the ballot for chairman was secret (after a show of hands had produced a tie), it appears that MacDonald, who had earlier abstained, voted in favour of Shackleton [Elton (1939) 132]. A conscientious and capable parliamentarian, showing reliability and a capacity for hard work rather than more spectacular gifts, Shackleton took a prominent part in the passing of the Trade Disputes Act of 1906. He spoke against the half-time system, which was especially common in the textile industry, although having to admit that a majority of cotton workers favoured the system and that his own robust appearance and large frame – he was over six feet tall – provided no evidence for the views that its operation damaged the health of boys who were employed in factories. On most questions he was content to work with the Liberal Government; with his opposition to tariff reform and support for such issues as workmen's compensation, old age pensions and Irish home rule, his views were similar to many on the radical wing of the Liberal Party. When at the beginning of 1907, Victor Grayson announced his candidature for the Colne Valley by-election, the Labour Party executive set up a sub-committee to consider the matter. Shackleton, its chairman, successfully moved that it recommend not only a refusal to endorse Grayson, but also that no Labour officials should take part in his campaign. He was consistently opposed to the Socialist wing of the labour movement. In February 1910, for example, he commented on the Labour Party annual conference (held at Monmouth earlier in the same month) that 'We have had the usual attempts to alter the constitution in the direction of including the word "Socialism" in the title of our candidates, but I am pleased to say this has been overwhelmingly defeated, and the candidates will still be known under the simple title of Labour candidates' [*Cotton Factory Times,* 18 Feb 1910].

In addition to his parliamentary duties, Shackleton continued to be active as a trade union leader. On the death of David Holmes in 1906, Shackleton succeeded him in the post of president of the Weavers' Amalgamation. He was a TUC delegate to the American Federation of Labor in 1907, and was president of the Trades Union Congress in consecutive years (1908–9). At the general election of January 1910, after a straight fight with T. Smith (Unionist), Shackleton was re-elected for Clitheroe with a substantial majority. His election address called for the abolition of an hereditary House of Lords; adult suffrage for women as well as men; the abolition of plural voting; complete secular education in all state-aided schools; a total adherence to Free Trade principles; the public ownership of all monopolies including railways, canals, mines 'and, most important of all, Land'; and support for the recommendations of the Minority Report of the R.C. on the Poor Law. During this short Parliament, he continued to favour the policy of a majority of the Labour Party, that of giving qualified support to the Liberal Government. The situation arising from the Osborne judgement was a principal concern, and he was among those who led the demand for the payment of MPs.

Towards the end of 1910 Shackleton decided to give up his trade union work and to leave Parliament, having accepted the post of senior labour adviser offered by the Home Secretary, Winston Churchill. In the following year he was a special commissioner on the dock strike in Liverpool, and was later appointed a national health insurance commissioner, a post he filled until 1916. He had served on the Royal Commission on the Land Transfer Acts (1908–10).

During the War, as a commissioner on munitions factories he travelled to France in 1915, and later he negotiated on the question of labour dilution in Newcastle upon Tyne. When the Ministry of Labour

was created in 1916, John Hodge, who became the first Minister, selected Shackleton – to the chagrin of W. H. Beveridge – as permanent secretary, a post he occupied until 1921. A rearrangement of the Ministry in 1921 made him, until his retirement in 1925, chief labour adviser to the Ministry of Labour. He did not give up public work altogether, serving on the Industrial Transference Committee in 1928 and the South Wales Coal Mines Arbitration Tribunal in 1934. His work as a civil servant was recognised by the honour of Companion of the Bath in 1916 and that of Knight Commander of the Bath in 1917. Some account of this part of his career has been given by a fellow civil servant, Horace Wilson, who contributed a biography of Shackleton to the *DNB*. He noted that Shackleton's appointment to the Ministry of Labour in 1916 was unorthodox, 'for he had no administrative experience and no experience of the management of a large organization', but his familiarity with the leaders of the trade union movement and an 'ability to gain the loyal and warm-hearted support of his civil service colleagues' made the appointment a good one, and a succession of ministers of differing political views 'relied on his advice wth well-merited confidence'.

It is probable that if Shackleton had not left the labour movement in 1910 he would have continued to occupy a prominent position in it for many more years. His early career as a trade union official, when he represented a membership with a varied political complexion, taught him to walk warily and act with discretion. He saw this day-to-day experience of facing practical problems as the foundation of his approach to national politics. As a platform speaker and in the Commons, Shackleton did not rely on any of the devices of rhetoric; he addressed his audiences in a plain, commonsense manner which gave the impression of a calm, imperturbable, and even somewhat stolid, nature. Though there had been rumours of a government appointment, his departure from the Commons came as a surprise (unlike that of his colleague Richard Bell who also gave up politics to enter the civil service in 1910), and he continued to be respected by those leaders of the trade union movement with whom he came into contact. To the end of his life he retained an interest in the activities of the labour movement, and only a few months before his death attended the annual conference of the cotton unions at Blackpool.

The last few years of Shackleton's life were spent in retirement at Lytham St Annes, where he was honorary treasurer of the local branch of the League of Nations Union. He supported the local cricket club and, as befitted a Chief Ruler of the Order of Rechabites, continued to champion teetotalism. He died at his Beach Road home on 1 August 1938. His wife, a son, who was connected with the work of the League of Nations Union in London, and a daughter survived him. Shackleton left effects to the value of £7288 in his will. After a service at the Church Road Methodist Church, St Annes, he was buried at Darwen Cemetery on 5 August.

Tom Shaw, the textile workers' leader who became Minister of Labour in 1924, wrote of him in an appreciation:

Of all the men I have ever met Shackleton gave the highest 'percentage of efficiency'. No one could accuse him of being very widely read, indeed, outside his own immediate subject of weaving he did not seem to have any special knowledge. He never hurried, was never flurried, and apparently never tired. He worked slowly, but once a task finished, a revision was unnecessary. He was extraordinarily modest in his tastes, and if held up in any town during his journeys for a short time in bad weather, would just go to the railway station and pass the time in the waiting-room reading a book or a paper.

He was intensely Lancashire in his prewar outlook; looked upon Government action as interference and as reprehensible and left that view so deeply impressed in the Ministry of Labour that it still influences policy in a world that has changed almost completely. Outside his own immediate work he did not seem to have any hobbies, if one excepts his

religious interests and connection with the 'Rakkabites' (Rechabites) – he was a lifelong teetotaller, – and the six feet odd of him made a brave show dressed in the gallantry of sash and medal that went with his office in the order [*Manchester Guardian*, 2 Aug 1938].

Writings: (with J. K. Hardie and P. Snowden), *Labour Politics: a symposium* (ILP Tracts for the Times, no. 2, 1903) 15 pp.; 'How I got on', *Pearson's Weekly*, 15 Mar 1906; preface to G. M. Tuckwell et al., *Woman in Industry from seven points of view* (1908); *Labour and Protection* (Manchester 1910) 4 pp.; (with G. Bellhouse and W. W. Fletcher) *Report upon an Inquiry into the Alleged Dangers of the Transmission of Certain Diseases from Person to Person in Weaving Sheds by means of 'Shuttle-kissing'*, Cd. 6184 (1912) 24 pp.

Sources: (1) Labour Party archives: LRC; (2) Other: W. T. Stead, 'The Labour Party and the Books that helped to make it', *Review of Reviews 33* (June 1906) 579–80; *Dod* (1903–10); *Cotton Factory Times* (1906–10); *WWW* (1929–40); *DNB* (1931–1940) [by Horace Wilson]; J. Hodge, *Workman's Cottage to Windsor Castle* [1931]; M. A. Hamilton, *Arthur Henderson* (1938); Lord Elton, *The Life of James Ramsay MacDonald (1866–1919)* (1939); Lord Beveridge, *Power and Influence* (1953); F. Bealey, 'Keir Hardie and the Labour Groups' *Parliamentary Affairs 10* (1956–7) 81–93, 220–33; idem, 'The Northern Weavers, Independent Labour Representation and Clitheroe, 1902' *Manchester School 25* (1957) 26–60; F. Bealey and H. Pelling, *Labour and Politics 1900–1906* (1958); P. P. Poirier, *The Advent of the Labour Party* (1958); H. R. Hikins, 'The Liverpool General Transport Strike, 1911' *Trans of the Historic Society of Lancashire and Cheshire 113* (1961) 169–95; H. A. Clegg et al., *A History of British Trade Unions since 1889 vol. 1: 1889–1910* (Oxford, 1964); B. B. Gilbert, *The Evolution of National Insurance in Great Britain: the origins of the welfare state* (1966); E. Hopwood, *A History of the Lancashire Cotton Industry and the*

Amalgamated Weavers' Association (Manchester, 1969); P. F. Clarke, *Lancashire and the New Liberalism* (Cambridge, 1971); K. D. Brown, *Labour and Unemployment 1900–1914* (Newton Abbot, 1971). OBIT. *Daily Herald, Manchester Guardian* and *Times*, 2 Aug 1938; *Clitheroe Advertiser and Times, Colne Times, Lytham St Annes Express* and *Lytham Times*, 5 Aug 1938; *Labour Party Report* (1939).

DAVID E. MARTIN

See also: George LANSBURY, for British Labour Party, 1900–13.

SHANN, George (1876–1919)
SOCIAL REFORMER, LECTURER AND LABOUR COUNCILLOR

George Shann was born on 28 October 1876 in Chapel Street, Knaresborough, the son of George Shann, a labourer in a coal yard, and his wife, Annie (née Bramley). At the age of six he moved with his family to Bradford, where he received an elementary education at a Board School. He entered a spinning factory as a half-timer on reaching the age of ten, and later worked there full time. From fifteen to twenty he was employed at a woolcombing factory. Although he could apply himself to study only after a day's labour in the factory, such were his ability and energy that he was awarded a scholarship to the Bradford Technical College – where he took the first prize in French. On another occasion he went straight from work to the Scottish Preliminary examination in mathematics and applied mechanics at Glasgow University, and passed with the highest grade. At the age of twenty he went to Aberdeen University for two years to study Latin, Greek and English, in which subjects he completed his Scottish Preliminary.

By means of further scholarships and by teaching during vacations, he proceeded at the age of twenty-two to Glasgow University, where he proved to be an outstanding scholar: he obtained a high position in English and philosophy, and graduated with first class honours in economics. He was also Gladstone Prizeman in economics

and Edward Caird Prizeman and honours medalist in philosophy. While in Glasgow he was for four years warden of the students' settlement, which brought him into contact with the city's slum life. This increased his resolve to work for improved social conditions, which he decided could best be accomplished through political action. He became a member of the Glasgow Fabian Society and took part in the work of the local labour movement.

In 1904 he moved to Birmingham, where he lectured in economics and industrial subjects at the University. He also taught at the Woodbrooke Settlement, an educational institution belonging to the Society of Friends. Shann was especially active in the campaign to abolish sweating. He helped organise the *Daily News* anti-sweating exhibition held in London during May 1906, and contributed to the *Handbook* the sections on the Birmingham button and hook-and-eye carders, and the chainmakers of Cradley Heath. Shann was the first secretary of the National Anti-Sweating League, and he collaborated with Edward Cadbury in writing two books on the sweating system. In March 1908 he gave evidence before the Select Committee on Home Work.

His work among the unorganised led him naturally to the trade union movement. He joined the Workers' Union and took a full part in factory gate and strike meetings, becoming widely known in the Birmingham area for his vigorous condemnation of low wages and his insistence upon the role of trade unions in improving the workers' standard of life. He was also an active member of the ILP, of the Fabian Society and of the Birmingham Socialist Centre, and was a frequent lecturer to all these groups, as well as to the Adult School movement and the Labour Churches. He quickly involved himself in local government work. From 1904 to 1911 he served on the King's Norton Urban District Council, and, on the re-drawing of the local boundaries, was elected to the Birmingham City Council as a councillor for the Selly Oak Ward. He sat from 1911 to 1915, becoming the recognised head of the Labour group. As a member of the Council he interested himself especially in education. He was also, for a time, chairman of the local WEA.

After the outbreak of war in 1914, Shann became a member of a local emergency committee formed by the labour movement to deal with problems arising from the dislocation of trade and employment. At about the same time he resigned from the ILP. He regarded Britain's entry into the war as unavoidable, and believed that the nation would emerge uplifted and strengthened by the great changes that would take place. His statement on his position offers a useful insight into the political motives and ideals of those Labour members who ardently suported the war:

The I.L.P. has its head in the clouds. To the member of the I.L.P. living in his dream-world there are no such things as foreigners. Yet the war itself is proof of the terrific reality and potency of national aspirations and ambitions. The I.L.P. have beautiful dreams of a brotherhood of all nations. But they forget the practical fact that the British Empire covers at least one-fifth of the population of the world, and although we do not always keep the highest point of view, yet our national and Imperial policy is based on the principle of respecting the rights of small nations, and we seek to develop the liberty and freedom of the peoples over whom we rule.

It is the freedom of our Empire that holds it together. The magnificent rally of our brothers from the over-sea Dominions is the justification of our policy. The possibilities for Democracy in the British Empire are immeasurable. The Empire is the greatest experiment in political freedom the world has ever seen. A German victory would tell disastrously against freedom and liberty, and would plunge the world into war after war until Germany or some new Power gained the position that the British Empire now holds.

England does not want war. It has been forced upon her, and it is the duty of every Englishman to stand by his country in the hour of need. Our first business

is to beat the Germans. Then we will settle any little domestic differences we may have at home. Our soldiers are fighting for our homes, our wives, and children, and our freedom. The attitude of the I.L.P. is illogical, unpatriotic, and immoral. There is no other course for me than to resign my membership of that body.

Shann, as would be expected from one who held these views, was active in recruiting meetings, and in June 1916 he joined the mechanical transport section in the Army. While on active service the War Office allowed him to act as secretary to the government commission of inquiry into industrial fatigue as far as it affected the Midland counties. Though elected an alderman in 1916, he was prevented by war service from taking his seat until late 1918.

Shann fought the Yardley division of Birmingham as a Labour candidate in the general election of December 1918, being runner-up to the Coalition Conservative in a three-cornered contest. A day or two after the campaign he was taken ill, and on 2 January 1919 he died at his home in Linden Road, Bournville. He was survived by his wife, Mary Alice, and four children. In his will he left £657.

Writings: 'Birmingham Hook and Eye Carders'; 'Button Carders of Birmingham'; 'Chain Making', in *Sweated Industries, Being a Handbook of the 'Daily News' Exhibition*, compiled by R. Mudie-Smith (May 1906); (with Edward Cadbury and M. C. Matheson) *Women's Work and Wages: a phase in the life of an industrial city* (1906, 2nd ed. [Birmingham, 1909]); (with Edward Cadbury) *Sweating* (1907); 'Travail et Salaries des Femmes en Angleterre', *Revue Économique Internationale* (Paris) 7 (July 1908) 15–20; Evidence before S.C. on Home Work 1908 VIII Qs 551–693; *Trade Unionism and Speeding Up* (1914); articles in *Workers' Union Record*.

Sources: *Workers' Union (Midland District) Record* (Jan 1914) 5; 'Councillor George Shann, M.A.,' *Edgbastonia 35* (June 1915)

459–64 [photograph]; *Workers' Union Record* (Mar 1918); R. Hyman, *The Workers' Union* (Oxford, 1971). OBIT. *Birmingham Mail*, 2 Jan 1919; *Times*, 3 Jan 1919.

DAVID E. MARTIN

See also: John Arthur FALLOWS; Eldred HALLAS; Mary MACARTHUR; Charles Henry SITCH; John Valentine STEVENS.

SHURMER, Percy Lionel Edward
(1888–1959)
LABOUR COUNCILLOR AND LABOUR MP

The son of Edward Shurmer, a journeyman tailor, and his wife, Elizabeth Holtham, Shurmer was born on 21 October 1888 at Cheltenham and educated at the British and St Paul's schools, Worcester, before being apprenticed to the Merchant Service in 1902. After some time at sea, he had a variety of jobs ashore; he worked for a time in hotels as a boot-boy, kitchen porter and barman, and he was later employed as ostler, baker's vanman, miner, pit-head haulier, blast-furnaceman and accounts collector, before joining the engineering department of the Birmingham Post Office Telephone Service in 1912. During the First World War he served with the 48th Division of the Birmingham Territorial Army in Belgium and France until 1917, when he was demobilised after being wounded and gassed.

From the first he had taken an active part in Birmingham's labour and cooperative politics and in 1921 he was elected to the City Council for St Martin's ward. He and Jim Simmons, another newcomer to the council, were noted for their outspokenness, and they were dubbed 'the terrible twins'. In 1926, in consequence of speeches made by him in the Bull Ring and Calthorpe Park during the General Strike, Shurmer was charged with 'causing disaffection among the civilian population' and fined £10 with the option of fifty-one days' imprisonment. Because of this conviction he was dismissed from his employment with the Post Office. He then began work as a member of the clerical staff of the Birmingham Co-operative Society, and remained in this job until he entered Parliament in 1945. He was

elected alderman of the Birmingham City Council in 1934, serving until 1949, and became a JP in 1943. As a member of the Civil Defence organisation he received the King's commendation for rescue work during the air-raids of 1941.

At the 1945 general election he was returned as MP for Sparkbrook with a majority of 5634, and continued to represent the constituency until his death. The defeated Conservative candidate was L. S. Amery, then Secretary of State for India, who had held the division for the previous thirty-four years. The third candidate, R. Palme Dutt of the Communist Party, fought the election on Amery's colonial record. But Shurmer took little interest in colonial or foreign affairs. In Parliament he was first and foremost a 'constituency MP'; in the heat of oratory he once declared 'I am Birmingham'; he was proud of the fact that he continued to live in, and devote his energies to, Sparkbrook, 'and don't forget Sparkhill either', he would add in reference to the other part of his constituency. In many respects his House of Commons activities grew out of his long career in city politics, and his national activities were conditioned by his local experience. It was in committees and groups dealing with such questions as housing, pensions, local government and the problems of national servicemen that he was most active. Though short in stature he made sure he was heard, and he was well liked by his fellow MPs for his ebullient and sincere personality. In April 1951 he protested against the introduction of charges for dentures and spectacles, and at question time ministers often found him a lively opponent. He was a member of the Parliamentary Christian Socialist Group and was also a supporter of the Salvation Army.

Widely known in Birmingham as 'our Percy', he maintained a close contact with his constituents. He described social work as his recreation, and was active especially on behalf of children. Each year from 1920 he organised a children's Christmas party in Birmingham town hall, and his young guests came to be known as the 'Shurmer Sparrows'. He also arranged for groups of tubercular children to recuperate in Switzerland.

His interest in children was commemorated a few years after his death in the name of the Percy Shurmer Infant and Junior School, which was opened by a fellow MP, Denis Howell. Among his other local interests was the Birmingham branch of the Royal Shipwrecked Mariners' Association, which he helped to found. He was also a president of the Midland and Southern Markets Association and a member of the British Markets Association.

He died in Selly Oak hospital, where he was under treatment for heart trouble, on 29 May 1959. The funeral took place at Lodge Hill Crematorium on 4 June after a service at the Salvation Army Citadel in Birmingham. In 1908 Shurmer had married Maude, the daughter of Albert Taylor of Newport, Mon., and he was survived by his wife (who died in 1968) and a daughter, Mrs Zena Hazell, who was an officer in the Salvation Army; a second daughter died young. In his will he left effects to the value of £1362.

Sources: C. Bunker, *Who's Who in Parliament* [1946]; *Dod* (1959); *WWW* (1951–60); *Birmingham Post Year Book* (1958–9); R. P. Hastings, 'The Labour Movement in Birmingham 1927–1945' (Birmingham MA, 1959); personal information: Mrs M. Z. Hazell, Birmingham, daughter; C. J. Simmons, Birmingham. OBIT. *Birmingham Mail*, *Birmingham Post* and *Evening Despatch*, 30 May 1959; *Times*, 1 June 1959.

DAVID E. MARTIN

See also: *Clement Richard ATTLEE, for British Labour Party, 1931–51; *Joseph Edward SOUTHALL.

SIMPSON, William Shaw (1829–83)
RADICAL

William Simpson was born on 18 June 1829 at Lancaster, the son of a joiner. The family moved to Liverpool about 1839. His father died when Simpson was in his youth and his mother, a highly intelligent woman, was responsible for his education. Simpson's lifelong adherence to and advocacy of temperance derived from his mother's influence and involvement in the Liverpool teetotal revival of 1840; as a boy he was a noted vocalist and reciter at temperance meetings. He was not apprenticed to a trade or profession. At about the age of twenty-four he was working for Messrs Sewell, chronometer makers, South Castle Street, Liverpool, but a few years later he became manager of the Liverpool Zoological Gardens, near West Derby Road; and subsequently entered the shipping trade, becoming manager of the Rhyl Steam Packet Company and then of the New Steamship Company. On 1 September 1858 he started his own business as confectioner and caterer on the Prince's landing stage, one of the landing stages for the ferry across the River Mersey, under the newly created Mersey Docks and Harbour Board. In 1874 the landing stage and his restaurant were destroyed by fire, but a wooden refreshment room was built for Simpson as part of the reconstruction. This catering business remained his occupation until his death.

It was during the 1860s that Simpson gradually became a figure of local importance which derived from his well-publicised philanthropy and advocacy of temperance; and by the early 1870s he achieved considerable prominence through his political activities and championship of the labouring poor. His ambition was to become a public figure at both local and national level, but his disregard of political and social conventions alienated middle-class support. His flamboyant dress and manner, fearless attack upon political corruption and social abuse, support for those in distress, and supreme self-confidence in his own abilities resulted in a notoriety which earned him much enmity as well as the adulation of those he helped.

They were numerous. There was almost always someone seeking assistance at his home on the landing stage. His efforts to assist those in distress were genuine and sustained, though on occasion somewhat eccentric. He placed a bowl outside his catering establishment on the landing stage for the contributions of passers-by to worthy causes. 'Simpson's Bowl' became something of a Liverpool institution, with frequent press references to the amounts collected and the charity to be supported. The 'Bowl' contributed to relief over a wide range, from the Indian famine of 1866 to 1867 to colliery disasters and distress in Ireland. Some £3720 was collected for six charities and divided as follows: £1080 for distress in South Wales; £815 for distress in Birkenhead and Seacombe; £574 for Haydock Colliery disaster; £526 for Abercarne Colliery explosion; £522 for distress in the West of Ireland (Simpson went personally to Connemara to distribute the money to the Irish peasants) and £203 for the Indian Famine Fund. He originated the British Workman's Public House Company whereby one-penny tokens were sold in public houses to be distributed to street arabs and beggars for the purchase of food. In 1876, during a period of growing unemployment, he persuaded the Mayor to open a subscription list for the distribution of Lancashire hot-pot and bread to the destitute at Christmas time. This became an annual event and was still taking place as late as 1889. A more bizarre, though apparently successful, scheme was his idea of the hospital Saturday cages, an annual event in which parrot cages were suspended from lamp posts to encourage passers-by to contribute to local hospitals.

His political ambitions were largely unsuccessful. He began as a Conservative, but his trenchant criticism of the local party caucus led him to call himself an Independent Conservative, and by the early 1870s he was an Independent Radical seeking the support of the working classes. He was an Independent candidate in the general election of 1874, but came bottom of the poll. In the municipal election of November 1879 he contested the West Derby Ward as an Independent, though with Liberal support, and won by 232 votes over the Conservative candidate. His victory was short-lived. He was disqualified in 1880 on the grounds that as his residence on the landing stage was not rateable he was not entitled to be on the electoral register. In February 1882 a by-election took place in Preston. Simpson became an Independent Lib-Lab candidate three days before polling and without any

organisation was defeated by only 1833 votes. In November 1882, Simpson once again contested the West Derby Ward in the Municipal elections, this time as the official Liberal candidate. He was defeated by the Conservative opponent by 759 votes. This was his last attempt to seek election. His failures derived partly from the hostility of the established party caucuses; partly from the controversial nature of his political beliefs and ambitions, and partly from the principles of purity whereby he refused to canvass or use cabs for voters or indulge in what he generally termed 'corrupt methods'.

His greatest successes came from his active support for the unskilled workers of Liverpool and Birkenhead during the 1870s. The year 1872 was one of the most turbulent in Liverpool's industrial history. It was the time of the trade boom and the spread of the agitation for a nine-hour working day. Early in 1872 groups of unskilled workers in Liverpool were already trying to secure higher pay and/or shorter hours, often by means of brief strikes. William Simpson, and to a lesser extent James Samuelson, a radical businessman, became deeply involved. Between April and October 1872 Simpson took up the cases of no less than twelve groups of unskilled workers including the carters, cotton porters, omnibus employees and needlewomen. In setting himself up as the spokesman of the under-privileged Merseyside worker he was motivated by a strong desire to obtain justice for those who he believed were being treated badly and lacked adequate leadership to present their case. His strategy was simple enough: he would accept an invitation to chair a meeting and listen to the men's grievances; if he believed them to be just, he would lead a deputation to the employers, put the men's case, and seek an acceptable compromise; if this failed, he recommended arbitration. In the economic conditions of 1872 his persistent advocacy led to notable success in most cases. There is no doubt that Simpson enjoyed the publicity, and also the near adulation of the Liverpool unskilled, although he made many enemies among the employing classes.

The climax to his career as mediator for

the labouring poor came in the great waterfront dispute of 1879, when the Liverpool docks were paralysed for five weeks by a strike of seamen for a wage increase and of dock labourers in protest against a wage cut. The seamen formed a short-lived union, and Simpson attended all their meetings, met the employers, and waged a public campaign against the advance note and allotment note system which may have played a part in the passing of the Merchant Seamen (Payment of Wages, etc) Act of 1880. The mass meetings of dock labourers were always chaired by Simpson. His powerful speeches and genuine sympathy for the men had a profound effect upon the peaceable nature of the dispute. Simpson led a number of deputations to the employers, but met with a negligible response. When his ultimate recommendation to the strikers to accept arbitration was rejected, he withdrew from the dispute.

Simpson never expressed any support for trade unionism or working-class organisation. He deprecated strikes, believing that moral force was enough to secure a just resolution of grievances. If a liberal compromise proved to be impossible, he favoured arbitration. While his impressive oratory, fearless support for the oppressed, and talents as a mediator were undoubted assets, his failings were considerable: there was a good measure of opportunism in his activities, and he quickly lost interest in a cause when a new and more exciting challenge emerged. His egotism and love of publicity made him somewhat autocratic in his dealings with those he represented. He had, therefore, no interest in developing a working-class movement; support for the unskilled was an extension of his philanthropy, conceived in terms of personal crusade.

Simpson collapsed suddenly on 15 June 1883 and died at 3 a.m. on 16 June 1883, two days before his fifty-fourth birthday. His wife and six children (one son and five daughters) survived him. He had worshipped at Great George Street Congregational Chapel, although one account states he was a Quaker. At his funeral hundreds of working people lined the streets to mourn a man who had sought fearlessly for some twenty years to bring relief to the under-privileged. He was buried at Smithdown Lane Cemetery. Shortly after his death a committee was formed to provide a memorial, and on 11 July 1884 a memorial drinking-fountain at the corner of Chapel Street in front of St Nicholas' Churchyard, opposite the landing stage, was presented to the Corporation. This still exists (1972) but cannot be used and is in a condition of neglect.

Sources: *Liverpool Daily Courier; Liverpool Daily Post; Liverpool Liberal Review; Liverpool Mercury*; E. L. Taplin, *Liverpool Dockers and Seamen, 1870–1890* (University of Hull, 1974). OBIT. *Liverpool Daily Courier, Liverpool Daily Post* and *Liverpool Mercury*, 18 June 1883; *Liverpool Liberal Review*, 23 June 1883.

ERIC TAPLIN

See also: James SAMUELSON.

SITCH, Charles Henry (1887–1960)
TRADE UNIONIST AND LABOUR MP

Charles Sitch was born on 4 May 1887 at Saltney, Chester, the third son of Thomas Sitch, a chainmaker and trade unionist, and his wife Elizabeth (née Young). Two years after Charles's birth his father established the Chainmakers and Strikers' Association of Saltney, Pontypridd and Staffordshire. In 1894, when membership of the association had grown from its initial fifteen to 360, Thomas became its full-time secretary and returned with his family to his native Cradley Heath, the established centre of the chain trade. Charles then grew up in the Cradley Heath area. He left school at thirteen and for the next five years worked as an assistant in a grocer's shop. At the age of eighteen he went to Ruskin College, Oxford, where for two years he studied economics, industrial organisation and economic history. During this time he was supported by a grant from the funds of the Chainmakers' Association. The experience of Ruskin College, and his family background led naturally to an active interest in trade unionism, and from the age of twenty Sitch was intensely involved in trade union organisation in Cradley Heath and the surrounding districts of the Black Country.

For a short time he was associated with the Midland Counties Trades Federation, but this organisation was by now in decline as changes in the industrial structure of the Black Country rendered its type of unionism – pacific in outlook and limited to craftsmen – increasingly irrelevant. Accordingly Sitch turned his attention to the growing development of trade union organisation among women which stemmed from the establishment in 1906 of the National Federation of Women Workers. The Black Country had long been notorious for the conditions under which women were employed. The high proportion of women outworkers in many of its industries prevented effective control of wages, hours and conditions, whether by trade unions or government agencies, and led to all the abuses of the sweating system. While sharing many of the characteristics of other Black Country industries, chainmaking differed in two vital respects. It was still, up to 1914, an expanding industry – the number of workers employed more than doubled, to 6550, in the fifty years to 1911 – and it was effectively divided into two watertight sections. Large chain and very best quality small chain were made only in the factories, being quite beyond the scope of the outworkers who made all the other innumerable varieties of small chain. This division of the industry prevented the undermining of the factory workers' wages by the largely unregulated labour in the outwork section of the trade, and thus enabled the Chainmakers' and Strikers' Association to control the factory branch very tightly. In turn the relatively high wages of the factory workers provided the outworkers with an 'anchor' which was absent in other trades, and together with the expansion of the industry this prevented conditions deteriorating to the point reached in many other trades. It was therefore possible to put a statutory floor under wages in the hammered and dollied branches of the chain trade with the establishment of the Chain Trade Board under the Trade Boards Act of 1909. As secretary of the Hand-hammered Chain

Branch of the National Federation of Women Workers, Sitch played a leading part in the agitation preceding the Act, and was among the first members of the Board, which within four years, in addition to establishing a minimum wage, had raised piece rates by betwen 19 per cent and 67 per cent. It had also fostered the growth of voluntary organisation among the outworkers, so that by 1914 the local branch of the Women Workers' Federation included about 60 per cent of eligible workers, while a union of men employed in outshops had been established and covered about 70 per cent of workers eligible.

The success of the Chain Trade Board led to the organisation of other Black Country sweated industries on similar lines. Sitch worked closely with Mary Macarthur in bringing about this wave of organisation, becoming vice-chairman of the Stourbridge and District Firebrick Wages and Conciliation Board, and the representative of the women workers on the Hollow-ware Trade Board. He also became secretary of the Anchorsmiths, Shackle and Shipping Tacklemakers Association, and secretary of the Rowley Regis Trades and Labour Council; from 1914 to 1918 he was president of the South Staffordshire and Worcestershire Federation of Trades Councils. He was exempted from military service on medical grounds, being classified C3. In 1913 he became assistant secretary of the Chainmakers' and Strikers' Association of which his father was secretary. This was also the year of his marriage to Miss Mabel Jackson of Goole. She shared her husband's keen interest in amateur opera and played many leading parts in the productions of the Cradley Heath, Old Hill and District Amateur Operatic Society of which Sitch was secretary for many years, as well as being a leading performer himself. On his father's death in 1923 Charles succeeded him as union secretary.

Sitch's success as a trade union organiser provided the basis on which his political career was founded. He first entered politics in 1913 when he was elected as a Liberal for the Cradley Heath ward of the Rowley Regis Urban District Council. He left the

Liberal Party when it split at the formation of the Lloyd George Coalition Government in 1916, and at the general election of 1918 he was adopted as Labour candidate for the Kingswinford division, in preference to Samuel Edwards, the Old Hill Miners' agent (this seems to have been the immediate cause of his father's following him in change of allegiance). Despite very limited funds and an almost non-existent organisation – in a constituency about eight miles wide the party did not have a single vehicle at its disposal and Sitch frequently had to walk to and from meetings – an overwhelming personal vote in the chainmaking districts of Old Hill and Cradley Heath saw him elected by a majority of 2888, and maintained him in office until the landslide of 1931. During his thirteen years as an MP Sitch did not make much impact as a parliamentarian, although in his first three years as a member he put down oral and written questions on a large number of topics. From 1923 his interests were concentrated on the operation of the Trade Boards Act and the conduct and efficiency of the employment exchanges. Throughout his parliamentary life he did much excellent work as a constituency MP, and came to be held in high regard by local people of all political persuasions. By the time of his defeat he had succeeded his father as secretary of the Chainmakers' and Strikers' Association and had been made a magistrate.

Sitch's public career ended abruptly and tragically in 1933, when he was found guilty on charges of fraudulently converting the funds of the Chainmakers' and Strikers' Association and sent to prison for nine months. On his appointment as secretary of the Association in 1923 his salary had been an apparently substantial £12 10s per week. It was, however, a condition – an extraordinary condition – of his appointment that from this salary he must pay £4 10s per week to support his mother, and a further £2 per week for clerical assistance. He then accepted two salary reductions of £2 per week, and with the cessation of his parliamentary salary his personal income was reduced to a mere £2 per week. In face of the heavy demands made on a man of Sitch's

standing by local organisations of all kinds this income was quite inadequate, and the accessibility of the Chainmakers' Association funds provided the unfortunate solution. On his release from prison Sitch moved away from Cradley Heath and took no further part in public life. After living for a short time in Jersey, he moved to Leeds, where from 1937 he was employed by *Reynolds News* (later the *Sunday Citizen*).

The *Sunday Citizen/Reynolds News* during most of its period of co-operative ownership was largely maintained by contributions from the retail co-operative movement in a form known as the Collective Advertising Scheme. Under this scheme societies paid a fluctuating contribution per £ of their sales, to help maintain a national newspaper for the co-operative movement. Each of many hundreds of retail co-ops made its own decision on whether or not to support the scheme, sometimes by decision of its board, sometimes by vote of its members' meetings. A small staff of organisers was employed to service this scheme and maintain the contacts necessary to keep contributions going. Sitch was among the first of these organisers, dealing mainly with societies in Yorkshire and the North East. He continued to live in Leeds after his retirement in 1952 and he died at his home, 116 Harrogate Road, Chapeltown, Leeds, on 13 June 1960, survived by his wife and one son, Cedric. As a young man Cedric joined the Brigade of Guards as a private and served with them through the Second World War. Later he was employed by Hepworths, the tailors of Leeds, in an administrative capacity. No will for Charles Sitch has been located.

Sources: Reports of trade union and political activities in *County Advertiser* [for Staffordshire and Worcestershire]; *County Herald* [for Staffordshire and Worcestershire]; *Dudley Herald, Stourbridge County Express, Wolverhampton Express and Star* 1907–33; issue of warrant, committal proceedings, and trial *County Advertiser and Herald* [for Staffordshire and Worcestershire], *Dudley Herald* and *Stourbridge County Express*, 4 and 25 Mar, 1 July 1933; R. H. Tawney, *The Establishment of Minimum Rates in* the Chain-Making Industry (1914); G. C. Allen, *The Industrial Development of Birmingham and the Black Country 1860–1927* (1929; repr. 1966); personal information: Ewart Sitch of Warley, brother [by interview, March and April 1971].

ERIC TAYLOR

See also: *Samuel EDWARDS; Mary MACARTHUR; †Thomas SITCH.

SLOAN, Alexander (Sandy)
(1879–1945)
MINERS' LEADER AND LABOUR MP

Sloan was born on 2 November 1879 in the village of Rankinston, Ayrshire, eight miles south-west of Old Cumnock, the second son of John Sloan, an ironstone miner and his wife Esther (née McLoy). The family was a large one, of nine sons and two daughters, and was for many years in very poor circumstances. Sandy Sloan began work in an ironstone mine at the age of twelve, and the poverty of his early years made a lasting impression upon his personality. In later years he was to become known as the 'stormy petrel' of Ayrshire. After many years as a working miner, his first official trade union position was as a checkweighman at Littlemill, a small colliery owned by the Coylton Coal Co. which in 1925 had some two hundred employees. Following a dispute there he had to leave, but was able to change places with one of his brothers, a miners' agent at Burnfoothill. He subsequently became secretary of the Ayrshire Miners' Union, and in February 1936 came to the forefront of Scottish union affairs when he was appointed secretary of the National Union of Scottish Mineworkers. He resigned from this position in 1940, but continued to serve on the Union's executive committee. In 1938 he represented the Scottish miners on the MFGB executive, and also served on the Ayrshire Electricity Board and the Scottish Coal Board. At the MFGB conferences Sloan took a more and more leftward position: and in July 1942 at the Blackpool three-day annual conference he fought for and secured the inclusion of an emergency resolution for the liberation of India. This he moved in a speech extremely critical of the Coalition (Churchill) Government, whom he suspected of being ready to suppress Gandhi and Nehru by imprisonment – a suspicion which within a month was proved to be correct.

From early manhood he was active in local government work. In 1900 he was the first Labour member on the Coylton School Board, and he continued to serve until the Board's work was superseded by the 1929 Local Government Act which brought education under the County Council's jurisdiction. Elected to the Ayrshire County Council in 1919, he was convener of the Ayr District housing committee and after 1929 of the water and drainage committee. He made two unsuccessful attempts to enter Parliament, in 1929 and 1931, when he contested North Ayrshire and Bute respectively, but in April 1939 his years of local service were rewarded when he was elected MP for South Ayrshire in succession to James Brown.

In Parliament Sloan was critical of the Government's muddling of the fuel problem and was not afraid to suggest that the idolised parliamentary leaders Ernest Bevin and Winston Churchill were idols with feet of clay. He repeatedly voiced the mistrust of the miners towards Churchill which had begun when the latter was Home Secretary from 1910 and lasted for a third of a century afterwards. Although re-elected in 1945, Sloan was a sick man and died soon afterwards. His impaired health received a final blow when as one of the parliamentary delegation invited by General Eisenhower to inspect the Nazi concentration camps he witnessed the unspeakable horrors of Belsen.

Sloan was always well known for his independence of thought and the vigour of his political expression. His outlook in general broadened during the six years he was at Westminster and he came to be regarded as one of the most militant of the spokesmen for the Scottish miners. Throughout his life he was opposed to war and the military Establishment – he had been a conscientious objector during the First World War. His death occurred on 16 November 1945 in the Royal Infirmary, Glasgow, and he was buried at Coylton Cemetery, where tributes were paid to him by Abe Moffat, president of the Scottish miners, and William Gallacher, MP, with whom Sloan had worked more and more closely in the House of Commons. His wife had predeceased him by twenty years, but he was survived by a daughter and two sons, one of whom, Robert, was an insurance agent. He left an estate valued at £2714.

Sources: *WWW* (1941–50); biographical information: His Excellency Mr T. A. K. Elliott, Helsinki; Scottish Record Office, Edinburgh. OBIT. *Times*, 17 Nov 1945; *Ayr Advertiser*, 22 Nov 1945; *Ayrshire Post*, 23 Nov 1945; *Labour Party Report* (1946).

R. PAGE ARNOT
JOHN SAVILLE

See also: †James BROWN; *Robert SMILLIE, for Scottish Mining Trade Unionism.

SMITH, Herbert (1862–1938)
MINERS' LEADER

Herbert Smith was born on 17 July 1862 in the parish of Preston near Kippax, West Yorkshire. His father, a miner, had been killed in an accident a few days earlier and his mother died shortly afterwards. His early years were spent at the workhouse but he was then adopted by a childless couple, Samuel and Charlotte Smith and took their surname. It was a happy and, for those days, a comfortable working-class home. His early education was shared between a dame school at Glass Houghton, near Castleford, and the British School at Pontefract, and at the age of ten he entered the mines at Glass Houghton. He grew to manhood noted for his self-reliance and fearlessness, the epitome of Yorkshire bluntness and toughness. He was a good workman and a good trade unionist but until he was nearly thirty there was little sign of the future miners' leader. His experiences in coal-mining shaped and moulded the man who was to become one of the best-loved leaders in the history of the British miners.

As far back as 1879 Smith was a member of the Glass Houghton miners' union branch committee and in 1894 was appointed a checkweighman by the Glass Houghton miners; in the same year he became a delegate to the Yorkshire Miners' Association. He was being slowly attracted to Socialism. The great strike and lock-out of 1893 was an important influence on him, but more important was the famous intervention by Pete Curran in the Barnsley by-election of 1897 on behalf of the Independent Labour Party. Curran was backed by Robert Smillie, Keir Hardie and Tom Mann, while the Liberal Party candidate, a coalowner who was in favour of the eight hours movement, was warmly supported by Ben Pickard and the other Yorkshire miners' leaders. Henceforth Herbert Smith was an active Socialist and he stood upon a militant left-wing position.

In 1904 Smith was elected vice-president of the YMA and two years later became its president. From that time he was directly associated with the Miners' Federation of Great Britain until the year before his death. From 1908 to 1937 he represented the Yorkshire miners almost continuously on the executive committee of the MFGB, either as delegate or holding an official position in the Federation. He was vice-president of the latter from 1917 to 1921 and president from 1922 to 1929; he was also president of the International Miners' Federation from 1921 to 1929, was a member of the TUC general council, 1922 to 1924 and in 1931, and was a TUC delegate to Russia in 1924–5. From 1913 to 1916 he was a member of the parliamentary committee of the TUC.

He came to national prominence in the years after 1906, initially for the fearlessness he showed in rescue operations following colliery explosions; and he was a member of the Cttee on Spontaneous Combustion in Mines in 1914. According to his obituary in the *Barnsley Chronicle* 18 June 1938 he declined the award of an OBE during the First World War. After the war he was a Miners' Federation nominee on the Sankey Coal Commission of 1919 (his fellow trade unionists being Robert Smillie and Frank Hodges) and to the (Buckmaster) Court of Inquiry in April–May 1924. Smith, together with Tom Richards and A. J. Cook, presented the miners' case. He refused with the others to attend the (Macmillan) Court of Inquiry of early July 1925. In the discussions which followed on July 30 (before the Cabinet had accepted defeat and instituted a nine-month subsidy to the mineowners) it was Smith who, in response to the Prime Minister's request to the miners for a concession, uttered the phrase: 'Nowt, we have nowt to give.' On the composition of the Samuel Commission, from which workers' representation was excluded, Smith on September 23 was authorised 'to make a protest to the Prime Minister about the constitution of the Commission' and it was not until after a fortnight that representatives were authorised 'to take part in the proceedings'. During the General Strike of 1926 and the coalowners' lock-out, Smith was regarded as the most obdurate of the miners' leaders, although he was in fact prepared to compromise on one or two occasions.

In the three months' lock-out of 1921, Smith, as acting president, had carried out the national policy, to which both he and the Yorkshire Miners' Association were opposed; but in 1929, he resigned from the presidency of the MFGB over the question of hours of work, a matter on which his own Yorkshire Association was again at loggerheads with the majority in the Federation: the Yorkshire miners wanted a seven-hour day but the Labour Government and Federation compromised on a seven-and-a-half-hour day. Smith was subsequently nominated for president in 1931 and 1932 but was not elected. His work for the miners was, however, officially recognised in 1931 when a nation-wide tribute was paid to Herbert Smith and his wife. The 'Herbert Smith Testimonial' comprised the unveiling of a bust to Mr Smith which was placed in the Miners' Hall at Barnsley, personal gifts and the surplus for the erection of homes for aged miners in his name. Smith continued to be active in trade union work until his death in 1938 and took part in rescue operations until the last years of his life. He frequently told audiences at trade union meetings: 'I was brought up in the Union [referring to his early days in the

workhouse] and from that time onwards have never been out of a Union.'

Herbert Smith was the embodiment of the miners' cause in many ways. He carried the burden of leadership in an age in which the contraction of the mining industry was an historical necessity and he confronted the powerful and equally tough-minded mineowners at a time when conditions were heavily weighted against the miners. A prominent coalowner once described him as the 'Bismarck of the miners' movement'. His Socialism became much less militant in the years after the First World War and after 1926 he was vigorously opposed to the Communist Party and the National Minority Movement which the Communists inspired. At the Llandudno Miners' Conference in 1928 he tried even to use physical violence against Arthur Horner; and his hostility to A. J. Cook was compounded of anti-Welshness and anti-Communism – Cook being widely regarded in the mid-twenties as being in the control of the Communist Party [H. W. Booth: letter 17 May 1971: a statement which, however, requires important qualifications]. Smith travelled widely on behalf of the miners and had visited most European countries and the U.S.A.

In his early years, Smith had been very active in local affairs before the responsibilities of his work for the miners dominated his life. His first entry into community work was his election in 1890 to the School Board for Glass Houghton; he became a parish councillor in 1894 and was elected to the Pontefract RDC and the local Board of Guardians in the following year. In 1896 he was elected president of the Castleford Trades Council and served until 1904. In the previous year he was elected to the West Riding County Council and sat on various committees of the Council, only resigning these when he went to live in Barnsley in 1916. He had been elected to Castleford Urban District Council in 1903 and acted as chairman for two years. His only attempt to enter Parliament was at the January 1910 general election for the Morley constituency when he was defeated. From 1915 he was a JP for Barnsley and the County. He also served on the Barnsley Borough Council for a number of years; was Mayor in 1932–3 and towards the end of his life was chairman of the Water and Public Assistance Committees. Conscious all his life of his own meagre formal education, he was a fervent advocate of the expansion of educational facilities for the young trade unionist; and he never tired of explaining to his own people the benefits to be derived from attendance at the Barnsley Mining and Technical College. For fifty-five years he was a member of the 'Oak' Lodge of Free Gardeners, Glass Houghton. He was a keen sportsman, regularly attending matches of the Barnsley football and cricket clubs, and he was an assiduous supporter of local charities, and particularly of the Beckett Hospital, which he served for many years as vice-president.

He had married in 1885 Sarah Ann Ripley and had a long and happy married life with a family of four sons and five daughters. His death occurred on 16 June 1938 at the Barnsley office of the Yorkshire Miners' Association shortly after he had returned from voting at a by-election. The funeral service was at the Pitt Street Methodist Church, Barnsley on 20 June 1938, the day of the Yorkshire miners' annual demonstration and his body was carried along the twenty-mile route from Barnsley to Castleford Cemetery with crowds lining the streets on either side. He was survived by his widow, four daughters and three sons, two of whom, Arthur and Harold, were members of the Barnsley Borough Council at the same time as their father. Herbert Smith's effects were valued after his death at just over £12,000.

Sources: Evidence to R.C. on Mines vol. III 1908 XX Qs 31991–32327; Cttee on Spontaneous Combustion in Mines 1914 XLII; 1921 XV; W. H. Crook, *The General Strike* (Chapel Hill, 1931); *DNB* (1931–40) [by J. S. Middleton]; J. Lawson, *The Man in the Cap* (1941); R. Page Arnot, *The Miners: years of struggle* (1953); C. L. Mowat, *Britain between the Wars 1918–1940* (1955); R. Page Arnot, *The Miners in Crisis and War* (1961); J. E. Williams, *The Derbyshire Miners* (1962); A. J. P. Taylor, *English History 1914–1945* (1965); A. R. Griffin,

Mining in the East Midlands 1550–1947 (1971); personal information: Miss G. Smith, Gawber, near Barnsley; Mr H. W. Booth, Hove; biographical information: NUM (Yorkshire). OBIT. *Times*, 17 June 1938; *Barnsley Chronicle*, 18 June 1938; *TUC Report* (1938).

JOHN SAVILLE

See also: †Thomas ASHTON, for Mining Trade Unionism, 1900–14; *Arthur James COOK, for Mining Trade Unionism, 1915–1926; Peter LEE, for Mining Trade Unionism, 1927–44; †Benjamin PICKARD; *Robert SMILLIE.

SPARKES, Malcolm (1881–1933)
FOUNDER OF LONDON BUILDING GUILD AND PACIFIST

Malcolm Sparkes, Quaker and pacifist, was born in Rochdale on 4 October 1881. His father, Joseph John Sparkes, was a yarn salesman. Both his parents belonged to old Quaker families; his mother, Mary Sophia Pollard, was the daughter of William Pollard, part author of a book on the Quaker religion, *A Reasonable Faith* (1884). Malcolm attended schools at Ackworth (near Pontefract, Yorkshire) and Bootham, York, run, as they still are, by the Society of Friends. He had strong practical interests and after leaving school was apprenticed, by his own choice, to the London firm of architectural woodworkers, H. C. Cleaver Ltd. He remained with the firm until 1916, becoming a junior partner soon after the completion of his apprenticeship. In 1906 he began a correspondence with Elizabeth ('Leila') Jackson, whom he had first met while they were both at Ackworth, and who was then a student at Somerville College, Oxford. In 1910 they married and settled at Gerrard's Cross, Buckinghamshire.

In 1906, Sparkes initiated a Premium Bonus scheme at the Park Royal Works of H. C. Cleaver. The direction of his thought at this time was paternalistic, but he had an inquiring and open temperament and was constantly concerned with the problems of industrial relations and welfare, concerns which were reflected in the 'industrial' topics discussed at the reading circle in Gerrard's Cross which he had helped to form. As a Quaker, he was a pacifist, and the problems of pacifism and of industrial relations continued in an interrelated pattern throughout his life.

Sparkes maintained the role of 'model employer' until the London Building Trades dispute in 1914 forced him to consider his position more critically. He refused to issue the London Master Builders' Association's 'Document' in January 1914, and so isolated himself in the dispute, remaining firmly attached to the principle of collective bargaining. Since he had not issued the ultimatum, he retained staff until Easter 1914, when the building unions demanded that all employers still staffed should surrender their membership of Employers' Associations or themselves face a strike. This appeared inequitable to Sparkes, and he refused on the grounds that demands were being made on him which were the absolute reverse of those which he had made of his employees. After a complex period of demands and negotiations, a misunderstanding caused unjust accusations of spying and blacklegging to be made against one of his workmen. At this point Sparkes believed that the bitterness of the class war had unbalanced all normal human relations and that this dispute was only a microcosm of the larger industrial situation. It was this incident which influenced the subsequent direction of his political and industrial activities. He sought a solution to what he regarded as the inadequacy of the existing machinery for industrial co-operation and consultation. It came to him as a scheme for an Industrial Parliament, which he evolved in part under the influence of Guild Socialist ideas (he had read the *New Age* since 1907). His first suggestion for the scheme was made privately to the reading circle at Gerrard's Cross. This envisaged a Federal Parliament of Industry to be elected by National Parliaments of Industry drawn from all trades. The internationalism involved here reflects both the influence of Norman Angell – whose *Great Illusion* the group had studied – and of a certain trend of thought in the Society of Friends. Sparkes wrote:

. . . it would obviously be essential as a first stage to abolish unemployment completely throughout the civilised world, and this would lead up to the establishment of a full international code of minimum conditions, the standard minimum wage for all adult labour, the seven-hour day, standard minima of housing, child nurture, education and so forth (MS biography).

He continued to develop his ideas privately until 1916, when the February edition of *The Builder* issued notice to the building trades unions of a termination of working agreements. Sparkes saw this as threatening a repetition of the situation in 1914. Dubious of success and attempting to avoid suspicion of his position as an employer, he submitted his elaborated scheme to the Amalgamated Society of Carpenters and Joiners, through Stan Stennet of its London District Management. The ASCJ accepted it. It was then forwarded to the Building Trades Council, which put it before the National Federation of Building Trades Employers. This in turn accepted the scheme, which it was generally believed prompted the development of Whitley Councils. For J. H. Whitley, chairman of the Committee on Industrial Reconstruction, saw an article by Sparkes on his Industrial Parliaments published in the *Venturer* for December 1916, and asked him for more details. The request came through Arthur Greenwood, who wrote to Sparkes, then threatened with imprisonment as a conscientious objector; living under that threat, he prepared a memorandum for Whitley. He had resigned from H. C. Cleaver in June 1916 when the firm became 'controlled', and was then employed by the Garton Foundation through an association with its secretary, John Hilton. Attempts which were made to have the development of his scheme defined as work of national importance failed, and Sparkes was in prison when the outline of his scheme was incorporated into the *Whitley Report on Joint Standing Industrial Councils* issued on 9 March 1917. He had passed the final proofs of his own scheme on 28 January 1917, was arrested on 29 January and sentenced by court martial on 12 February 1917 to two years' hard labour, most of which was spent in Wandsworth prison. Despite representations by many officials and government servants, he was not released until the end of the war. Lord Parmoor's speech of 30 April 1918 in the House of Lords made clear the fact that Sparkes was acknowledged as a major influence on Whitley and 'really the author of the much praised Whitley Report'.

In prison, Sparkes's religious faith brought him a tolerance which overcame resentment, and enabled him to continue elaborating his ideas beyond the stage of Industrial Parliaments, which he saw as only a 'staging post' on the way to a Building Guild. This would be the real solution to the industrial impasse. In 1917 he wrote to his wife:

I am a keen National Guildsman. I am not, emphatically NOT a state socialist or collectivist. I believe that the Industrial Parliament is going to be a short cut to the National Guild and that in the principle of Constructive Goodwill and voluntaryism we are going to discover the true road of Industrial Advance (MS biography).

His ideas on Guild development brought him into contact with G. D. H. Cole, who visited him in prison in mid-1918 to discuss the formation of a Building Guild. Cole was not optimistic, but Sparkes continued to plan the Guild with the help of building trade operatives also imprisoned in Wandsworth as C.O.s. He may thus be accounted the originator of the practical Guild movement, although he was to share the praise for this with S. G. Hobson, whose publicity much outshone Sparkes's and who was the moving force of the development towards the National Guild which Sparkes considered always to be premature.

Sparkes was released from prison on 11 February 1919, having refused any remission on the ground of ill-health. He accepted a post with the publishers Headley Bros for the next six months, but constantly worked on his plans for a Building Guild. While so occupied he wrote, anonymously, the pamphlet entitled The Industrial Council

for the Building Industry, which was published by Harrison & Sons for the Garton Foundation. In the autumn of 1919, Sparkes's scheme was laid before the London District Council of the NFBTO, and it was while it was still under consideration that the Manchester Guild was launched on 20 January 1920 under the inspiration of S. G. Hobson, aided by Richard Coppock.

While both schemes were under discussion, the Walthamstow and Greenwich branches of the NFBTO had organised their own Guild Committees, and had begun negotiations with their local councils. The first Guild attempt – which was successful – was thus a rank and file demonstration of the possibilities of workers' control, although the larger organisation was to come through the London and Manchester groups. The initiative of the Walthamstow and Greenwich branches resulted in the offer of work if the Guild could become a legal entity. This prompted them, with other branches, to put resolutions before the London District Council of the NFBTO calling for the foundation of a Guild in London. The resolutions were accepted, and the meeting called for 28 April 1920 gave a unanimous vote for the foundation of the London Guild of Builders under the management of Malcolm Sparkes. Sparkes immediately set about the writing of a Prospectus, which was issued in May, and negotiations continued with the Ministry of Health until July, when an agreement on legal entity was made for both the Manchester and the London Guilds. A model contract was drawn up on 6 August 1920. The detailed history of the guilds has been told elsewhere [Matthews (1971)]. Sparkes's part in that history remained active and interested. Probably because of his more extensive business experience, he distrusted the moves towards amalgamation which were inaugurated by the Manchester Guild and supported by the NFBTO; but he could not defeat them, and the two major Guilds were united, if not legally, at least in fact, from 23 July 1921. By this time the Guilds were already working under the pressures of a deteriorating economic climate and of opposition from building trade employers and from the Government. Sparkes distrusted the financial operations of the Manchester Group, and on 26 May 1922, as the result of long-term disquiet, he and Harry Barham (secretary of the London Guild) issued a circular, *The Scheme for the Reorganisation of the National Building Guild Ltd*. The covering letter to this clearly indicated their alarm at the haphazard nature of the financial dealings of the National Guild. As a precaution they suggested the reorganisation of the Guilds as a grouping of autonomous units with a National Board over all. Hobson countered with a scheme which broke down the London Guild into ten areas, and offered Sparkes and Barham a place in the movement only if they accepted a fifty per cent reduction in salary. Refusing to accept this, they were dismissed on 13 July 1922. The fact that the London Group went on to re-constitute itself as a separate entity suggests that it did at least see the logic of Sparkes's argument while taking the opportunity to be rid of his person.

The history of the Guild movement from this point is one of decline. Sparkes, distrusted though vindicated by a conference of the NFBTO held in November 1922 to inquire into the whole working of the National Building Guild Ltd, retired to pursue his ideals in the formation of a new Guild. This, Guild Housing Ltd, was set up by Sparkes and Barham in August 1922. It suffered from managerial tensions, and in an attempt to underwrite his own security Sparkes established the separate firm of Drytone Ltd, to produce high-quality architectural woodwork in a range of finishes which he had developed. It was intended, also, to act as a feeder to Guild Housing Ltd. However, the attempt split his energies and may help to account for his resignation as manager of Guild Housing Ltd in June 1924 when, in any case, relations between Sparkes and the rest of the Board had become strained. Under new management the Guild was eventually forced to submit to a public inquiry into its affairs. The report, by W. H. Close, only partially vindicated Sparkes, and implied that there had certainly been an imbalance between office staff and those employed on site. This report was issued on 24 November 1924, and

the Guild subsequently went into liquidation. Sparkes continued to run Drytone Ltd until his death.

His basic failure was a vision which constantly caused him to overreach himself. His adoption as almost a motto of Maude Royden's declaration – ' . . . nothing will persuade me that the world is not ready for an ideal for which I am ready' – reveals a great deal about his approach to the problem of industrial melioration. Sparkes found it difficult to believe that goodwill was insufficient to solve the world's problems. His resultant idealism, while psychologically justifiable, gave rise to many practical problems, and it is clear that he was frequently exploited. It should not be forgotten, however, that he was the principal inspiration for the scheme of Industrial Parliaments which may have been – at least in the London area – an influence in converting building trades workers towards practical guild experiments. Without him the London Guild might never have assumed the organisation and philosophy which it eventually did. It would be fair to remember, also, that he believed – and the remaining evidence indicates the truth in the assumption – that without the amalgamation he might have been able to create in London a guild which could at least have co-existed as a viable and exciting alternative to the capitalist organisation of the building industry.

Sparkes continued to suggest methods of reconstruction within industrial society until the end of his life. These were mostly influenced by Guild Socialist ideas (e.g. his *Modern Industry: the Christian line of development* (1927)) and towards the end of his life, distressed by the economic depression, he was concerned in producing a scheme which he entitled 'The British Development Service' [The MS. was dated 19 Dec 1932]. This was intended to deal with the problem of industrial waste in the sense both of pollution and of unemployment. It suggested a nationally-administered scheme in which the unemployed could have specific training for the various areas of service envisaged. At the time of his death Sparkes was actively concerned in propagating this scheme, initially through the Society of

Friends. He died of angina pectoris on 6 April 1933; his wife, Elizabeth Sparkes, survived him for thirty-seven years, dying in 1970. There were two sons and two daughters of the marriage. He left an estate valued at £250. Sparkes had been Clerk to the Jordans Meeting up to the time of his death, and the funeral took place at Jordans Meeting. Among those who spoke at the service were Maurice Rowntree and Ernest Warner.

Writings: 'National Industrial Parliaments: an attempt to suggest the first steps towards a new Industrial Order founded upon the principle of the Kingdom of God', *Venturer* (Dec 1916) 5–18; *A Memorandum on Industrial Self-Government* (1917); 'Towards a National Building Guild', *Guildsman* (Apr 1919) 3; *The Industrial Council for the Building Industry* (Garton Foundation, 1919); *Prospectus of the London Guild of Builders* (1920) P; 'The Team Spirit in Industry' [The work of the Building Trades Parliament of Great Britain], *Engl. Rev. 30* (Feb 1920) 153–8; 'The Coming of the Guild of Builders', *Guildsman* (June 1920) 3; 'Industry organised for Service', *Justice*, 17 Feb 1921; 'A Guildsman's Reply', *Lab. Mon. 1*, no. 6 (Dec 1921) 520–6; 'Organising Industry for Service', *Engl. Rev. 36* (Feb 1923) 190–4; *How Socialists would run Industry* (ILP programme pamphlet no. 5 [1923/4?]) 16 pp.; *Letter to Subscribers to Guild Housing Ltd* (Jan 1924); *Modern Industry: the Christian line of development* (1927).

Sources: (1) MSS: biography by Mrs E. Sparkes entitled 'Malcolm Sparkes: constructive pacifist' in the Library, Friends' House, London which includes some of Sparkes's correspondence; microfilm copy of the ms. biography: Brymor Jones Library, Hull University. (2) Other: G. D. H. Cole, *Self-Government in Industry* (1917); C. Bechhofer and M. B. Reckitt, *The Meaning of National Guilds* (1920); N. Carpenter, *Guild Socialism* (New York, 1922); R. Postgate, *The Builders' History* [1923]; S. G. Hobson, *Pilgrim to the Left: memoirs of a modern revolutionist* (1938); M. Cole, *The Story of Fabian Socialism* (1961); F. D. Matthews, 'The Building Guilds', in *Essays in Labour History 2: 1886–1923*, ed. A. Briggs and J. Saville (1971) 284–331; personal information: W. H. Close, Hampstead; Dame Margaret Cole; the late Sir Richard Coppock, Cranleigh, Surrey; Mrs V. Penty, Isleworth, Middlesex; Mrs D. Thurtle, London; Mrs. E. Sparkes, Beaconsfield, widow. Obit. *Bucks Advertiser and Gazette*, 14 Apr 1933; *Friend*, 21 Apr 1933.

FRANK MATTHEWS

See also: *Sir Richard Coppock; *Samuel George Hobson; *Alfred Richard Orage and below: Guild Socialism.

Guild Socialism: (1) MSS: G. D. H. Cole papers, Nuffield College, Oxford; papers of F. W. Dalley, A. J. Penty and M. B. Reckett, on microfilm Brynmor Jones Library, Hull University; Webb Coll., LSE.
(2) **Theses:** B. Pribićević, 'The Demand for Workers' Control in the Railway, Coalmining and Engineering Industries, 1910–1922' (Oxford, DPhil., 1957); S. T. Glass, 'The Political Theory of the British Guild Socialists' (Oxford, BLitt., 1963); P. d'A. Jones, 'Christian Socialism in England, 1880–1914' (London PhD, 1963). Mr Frank Matthews, Dept of History, Univ. of Stirling, is currently (1973) completing a thesis on the history of Guild Socialism.
(3) **Reference works and periodicals:** Annual Reports of National Guilds League, 1915–21; *Labour Year Book* (1916), (1919); *New Age* ed. A. R. Orage, 1907–19; *Church Socialist*, 1912–1921; *The Guildsman*, 1916–1921, continued as *The Guild Socialist*, 1921–3 and then as *New Standards* to 1924; LRD *Monthly Circular*, Nov 1917–.
(4) **Secondary:** A. J. Penty, *The Restoration of the Gild System* (1906); G. D. H. Cole, *The World of Labour* (1913, 4th ed. 1928); S. G. Hobson, *National Guilds: an inquiry into the wage system and the way out*, ed. A. R. Orage [1914] (3rd ed. 1919); W. Mellor, 'The National Guilds League', *Plebs 7*, no. 7 (Aug 1915) 159–60 [a letter]; J. F. and Winifred Horrabin, 'Guild Socialism and Women in Industry', ibid., 7, no. 9

(Oct 1915) 200–5; National Guilds League, *A Catechism of National Guilds* (Leaflet no. 1, 1915) 8 pp.; idem, *Guild Socialism: the Storrington document revised* [1915] 12 pp.; idem, *National Guilds: an appeal to trade unionists* (pamphlet no. 1, [1915]) 20 pp;. Bernard Shaw, 'Guild Socialism' appendix to E. R. Pease, *History of the Fabian Society* (1916); National Guilds League, *The Guild Idea: an appeal to the public* (pamphlet no. 2, [1916] 2nd ed. [1918]) 19 pp.; idem, *Towards a Miners' Guild* [1917] 15 pp.; G. D. H. Cole, *Self Government in Industry* (1917); S. G. Hobson, *Guild Principles in War and Peace*, with introductory essay by A. R. Orage (1917); National Guilds League, *A Short Statement of the Principles and Objects of the N.G.L.* [1917?] 8 pp.; idem, *Towards a National Railway Guild* (1917) P; A. R. Orage, *An Alphabet of Economics* (1917); A. J. Penty, *Old Worlds for New: a study of the post industrial state* (1917); G. D. H. Cole, *An Introduction to Trade Unionism* (Fabian Research Dept Trade Union Ser., no. 4, 1918); idem, *The Payment of Wages: a study in payment by results under the wage system* (Fabian Research Dept Trade Union Ser., no. 5, [1918]); idem, *Labour in the Commonwealth* (1918); idem (with W. Mellor), *The Meaning of Industrial Freedom* (1918) 44 pp.; F. Goldwell, *Guild Socialism: a criticism of the national theory* (1918) 48 pp.; National Guilds League, *National Guilds or Whitley Councils* [1918] 20 pp.; M. B. Reckitt (with C. E. Bechhofer), *The Meaning of National Guilds* (1918, 2nd ed. rev. 1920); B. Russell, *Roads to Freedom: socialism, anarchism and syndicalism* (1918); G. D. H. Cole, *National Guilds and the Coal Commission* [1919?] 16 pp.; idem, 'National Guilds and the State', *Soc. Rev. 16* (Jan–Mar 1919) 22–30; P. Snowden, 'State Socialism and National Guilds', ibid., (Apr–June 1919) 116–23; F. Stewart, 'Industrial Democracy and the Shop Stewards' Movement' ibid., (July–Sep 1919) 277–82; G. D. H. Cole, *Guild Socialism: a lecture* (Nov 1919) (Fabian Tract no. 192, 1920 repr. 1922); J. W. Harper, 'Industrial Unrest: a plea for national guilds', *Hibbert J. 18* (Oct 1919) 113–124; A. J. Penty, *Guilds and the Social Crisis* (1919); G. R. S. Taylor, *The Guild State: its principles and possibilities* (1919); M. Beer, *A History of British Socialism*, vol. 2 (1920); Building Guild, *The Building Guild* (Manchester [1920]) 24 pp.; P. B. Bull, *Guild Socialism* [1920?] 8 pp.; N. Carpenter, 'The Literature of Guild Socialism', *Q. J. Econ. 34* (1920) 763–76; G. D. H. Cole, *Social Theory* (1920 rev. ed. 1921); idem, *Chaos and Order in Industry* (1920); idem, *Guild Socialism Restated* (1920); G. C. Field, *Guild Socialism: a critical examination* (1920); S. G. Hobson, *National Guilds and the State* (1920); idem, *Guilds of House Builders* [1920?] 4 pp.; London Guild of Builders, *Prospectus of the Guild of Builders [London] Ltd* (2nd ed. 1920) 6 pp.; W. Mellor, *Direct Action* (1920); A. J. Penty, *A Guildsman's Interpretation of History* (1920); H. Reynard, 'Guild Socialists', *Econ. J. 30* (Sep 1920) 321–30; S. and B. Webb, *A Constitution for the Socialist Commonwealth of Great Britain* (1920); G. D. H. Cole (with W. Mellor), *Gildensozialismus* (Cologne, 1921) 53 pp.; C. H. Douglas, *Credit Power and Democracy*, with a commentary on the scheme by A. R. Orage (2nd ed. 1921, 4th ed. 1934); J. H. Lloyd, *Guilds and the Salary Earner* (1921) 14 pp.; W. Mellor, 'A Critique of Guild Socialism', *Lab. Mon. 1* (July–Dec 1921) 397–404; W. Milne-Bailey, *Towards a Postal Guild* (1921) 12 pp.; National Guilds League, *Education and the Guild Idea* (1921) 18 pp.; idem, *The Policy of Guild Socialism* (1921) 23 pp.; idem, *Guild Socialism: a syllabus for class and study circles* (1921, 2nd ed. 1923) 20 pp.; W. A. Orton, *Labour in Transition* (1921); A. J. Penty, *Guilds, Trade and Agriculture* (1921) M. Sparkes, 'A Guildsman's Reply', *Lab. Mon. 1*, no. 6 (Dec 1921) 520–6; R. H. Tawney, *The Acquisitive Society* (1921); G. R. S. Taylor, *Guild Politics: a practical programme for the Labour Party and the Co-operators* [1921]; N. Carpenter, *Guild Socialism: an historical and critical analysis* (1922); A. Hewes, 'Guild Socialism: a two years' test', *Am. Econ. Rev. 12* (1922) 209–37; A. J. Penty, *Post-industrialism* (1922); R. G. Tugwell, 'Guild Socialism and the Industrial Future', *Int. J. of Ethics 32* (Apr 1922) 282–8; W. Leach,

'Guild v. Municipal Socialism', *Soc. Rev.* *21* (Mar 1923) 106–13; C. R. Attlee, 'Guild v. Municipal Socialism: a reply', ibid., (May 1923) 213–18; W. Leach, 'Guild v. Municipal Socialism: a rejoinder', ibid., *22* (July 1923) 35–40; E. D. Ellis,' Guild Socialism and Pluralism', *Am. Pol. Sc. Rev. 17* (1923) 584–96; A. J. Penty, *Towards a Christian Sociology* (1923); R. Postgate, *The Builders' History* [1923]; P. H. Douglas, 'Guild Socialism', in *A History of Political Theory: recent times:* ed. C. E. Merriam and H. E. Barnes (New York, 1924) 227–34; A. Shadwell, *The Socialist Movement 1824–1924,* vol. *2: The New Phase 1914–24* (1925); R. Page Arnot, *History of the Labour Research Department* (1926); S. G. Hobson, *The House of Industry: a new estate of the realm* (1931); M. B. Reckitt, *Faith and Society: a study of the structure, outlook and opportunity of the Christian Social Movement in Great Britain and the U.S.A.* (1932); B. Hastings, *The Old 'New Age': Orage and others* (Blue Moon Booklets, no. 16: [1936]); S. G. Hobson, *Functional Socialism* (1936); P. A. Mairet, *A. R. Orage: a memoir,* with an Introduction by G. K. Chesterton (1936); S. G. Hobson, *Pilgrim to the Left: memoirs of a modern revolutionist* (1938); M. B. Reckitt, *As it happened: an autobiography* (1941); G. D. H. Cole, *A Century of Co-operation* (Manchester, [1945?]); M. Cole, *Beatrice Webb* (1945); H. W. Laidler, *Social Economic Movements* (1948) Ch. 23; M. Cole, *Growing up into Revolution* (1949); C. D. King, *The Oragean Version* (New York, 1951); *Beatrice Webb's Diaries 1912–24,* ed. M. Cole (1952); G. D. H. Cole, *A History of Socialist Thought* vol. *3: The Second International* pt 1 *1889–1914* (1956 repr. 1963); *Beatrice Webb's Diaries 1924–32,* ed. and with an Introduction by M. Cole (1956); B. Pribićević, *The Shop Stewards' Movement and Workers' Control 1910–1922* (Oxford, 1959); M. Cole, *The Story of Fabian Socialism* (1961); S. T. Glass, *The Responsible Society: the ideas of the English Guild Socialists* (1966); W. Martin, *The 'New Age' under Orage: chapters in English cultural history* (Manchester, 1967); *Industrial Democracy in Great Britain: a book of readings*

and witnesses for workers' control, ed. K. Coates and A. Topham (1968); P. d'A. Jones, *The Christian Socialist Revival 1877–1914* (Princeton, New Jersey, 1968); M. Cole, *The Life of G. D. H. Cole* (1971); idem, 'Guild Socialism and the Labour Research Department', *Essays in Labour History* vol. *2: 1886–1923,* ed. A. Briggs and J. Saville (1971) 260–83; F. Matthews, 'The Building Guilds' ibid., 284–331; 'Guild Socialism: the Storrington document', ibid., 332–49.

STEVENS, John Valentine (1852–1925)
TRADE UNION LEADER AND LABOUR ALDERMAN

Stevens was born in Bristol on 13 March 1852. He was the youngest son of a large family and his father, a building worker, was killed in an accident when John was four. He therefore had to begin work at the early age of eight, although he was able to avoid joining the army of unskilled labourers, and in his teens he served an apprenticeship to the tin-plate working trade.

As a young man he went to Birmingham in search of work; he found a job on his first day, and lived in the city for the remainder of his life. At the age of twenty-two he joined the Tinplate Workers' Society, established in 1859, which set him on the road to trade union leadership. After six years as a member he became president of the society in 1880. One of the most important functions of the craft unions at that time was the provision they made for benefits, and Stevens was typical in regarding this aspect as being of first importance. In 1882 he initiated a scheme for a superannuation fund which paid out allowances to retired and disabled members of his society. Five years later he was appointed secretary of the Amalgamated Tinplate Workers' Association, and held the position until 1906. In 1909, however, the Birmingham society left the Amalgamation over the question of increased contributions, and when, during 1916 to 1919, negotiations took place for a more permanent amalgamation of tinplate workers on a national scale, it was Stevens who explained that Birmingham did not wish to turn its substantial superannuation fund over to a national body [Kidd (1949) ch. 11].

Towards the end of 1886 Stevens read a paper – probably later published, but no copy has been found – to the Tin Plate Workers' Society, recommending the adoption of the principle of co-operative production in the tinplate industry. The Society took up the suggestion with energy and enthusiasm; and towards the middle of 1887 the new organisation was registered as the Midland Productive Co-operative Tin Plate Workers' Society, 25 Masshouse Lane, Birmingham. The story of the early history of the Society is told in Ben Jones (1894) 486–7; and Stevens continued to be active in its affairs for many years. He was also closely involved with the friendly society movement. At the age of twenty-four – two years after he had first joined his trade union – Stevens was initiated into Court FRIAR TUCK, No. 1601 branch of the Ancient Order of Foresters (Birmingham Midland District) on the 25 May 1876. Men could join the 'Court' of their choice, and the initiation ceremony was highly elaborate. After initiation, various lectures were delivered to the member, and the following is an extract:

The Court, as the basis of the rest of the superstructure, first claims and deserves attention. Here are taught the first principles of duty and obedience; for here the practice of self-government is in full and constant operation. In the Court, and before the law, no one is greater than another. All meet there on terms of perfect equality. The Officers appointed to preside and to conduct the business of the Court are elevated to their positions of distinction and honour by the free and unbiassed votes of their compeers. The path of distinction and honour is open to all. As in the world of letters there is no Royal Road to learning, so in the Courts of our Order there is no privileged path to Power. No office is too high for the poorest to aspire to; no duty too humble

for the richest to stoop to. Intelligence to govern, ability to exercise authority with becoming humility, yet with the requisite firmness, and personal demeanour to ensure respect, are all the qualifications for office required; and these are in the power of every member to acquire. The Court, therefore, forms one of the best of schools in which the responsibilities of citizenship are taught.

In 1889 Stevens became the District Chief Ranger (the presiding officer) of the Midland District of the Foresters, and in both his trade union work and friendly society activity he exhibited the social and political attitudes typical of the skilled workers of his day. In March 1894 he gave evidence before the R.C. on the Aged Poor. Speaking for both his trade and friendly societies, Stevens emphasised the opposition to any contributory scheme for old age pensions that might compete with the existing benefits offered by trade and friendly societies. On the general issue of poor law policy Stevens drew the familiar Victorian distinction between the 'deserving poor' and the rest. In vew of these attitudes, it is surprising that within a few years he was actively associated with the campaign for old age pensions. In this he was not, of course, unusual; for by the closing years of the nineties many skilled workers had come to accept the demand for a state pension for the aged. In March 1899 Stevens, on behalf of the Birmingham Trades Council, joined with Arthur Eades in convening a meeting of over seven hundred people to hear Charles Booth state the case for non-contributory old age pensions. Two months later he became the first chairman of the National Committee of Organised Labour on Old Age Pensions, although most of its organisational work was undertaken by the paid secretary, Frederick Rogers.

For several years Stevens was the tinplate workers' representative on the Birmingham Trades Council, and during his association with the council served on several of its committees in addition to acting as its treasurer, and from 1887 to 1889 as its president. In 1897 the TUC met in Birmingham and

Stevens was chosen president; he conducted the business with admirable competence. His trade union activities led him into wider radical politics. In 1887 he was elected to the Birmingham School Board, upon which he remained for four years. As well as pressing for improved educational standards and secularism he sought to better the conditions of labour by demanding a fair wages clause in the contracts given out by the board.

At this time, like most leaders of 'craft' unions, he was a 'Lib-Lab' in politics, and with Liberal backing he contested St Thomas's ward for a seat on the City Council in 1889. At the time of the election, one newspaper characterised him in these terms: 'Like most self-educated men he is dogmatic to a degree and an energetic and vigorous speaker, with the faintest soupçon of a Gloucestershire accent, and just enough mis-aspirated h's to be frequently amusing. He has a vandalistic pleasure in smashing up an opponent. He hits hard, and does not foam if he's hit back' [*Birmingham Daily Times*, 29 Oct 1889]. Though his opponent was Austen Chamberlain, Stevens was elected in a hard-fought campaign by a majority of eleven votes. He remained on the council until 1907, and among the issues he raised was the acceptance by the council of the fair wages clause and the fifty-three hour week for labourers in municipal employment. He was a member of the Technical School Committee, and in 1900 was appointed a governor of King Edward's Grammar School for a term of six years, being the first working man to occupy such a position.

In July 1896 he was involved in an incident which led to his arrest by the Aston police. During the course of an open-air meeting in support of S. G. Middleton, a candidate for the Aston School Board, Stevens was taken into custody on a charge of shouting in the street. The meeting had been orderly and properly-conducted, and the action of the police aroused much indignation as it appeared to be an attempt to suppress free speech. On his appearance in court the local magistrates dismissed the charge. Stevens then brought an action against the police for illegal arrest, in which he was awarded £40 damages and costs.

During the early years of the century Stevens continued to work with the local Liberal Party, and contested three parliamentary elections under Liberal auspices. In 1900 he stood for East Birmingham against Sir J. Benjamin Stone (Conservative). During the course of the campaign, Joseph Chamberlain in a meeting he addressed on Stone's behalf suggested to his audience that Stevens ought not to be elected to Parliament as this would end the valuable work he was doing locally. Whether this ironic advice carried any weight is problematical, but Stevens, who had based his campaign on the demand for old age pensions, was defeated by 2154 votes. In the general election of 1906 he stood in South Birmingham against Lord Morpeth (Liberal Unionist) who was elected with a majority of 2900. His final attempt to enter Parliament was in December 1910 when he opposed D. Steel-Maitland, again in the East Birmingham division; on this occasion Stevens obtained 3449 votes fewer than his Conservative opponent.

In 1911, Stevens, who three years earlier had been appointed a JP, returned to the City Council as a Liberal, representing St Bartholomew's ward. He held this seat until 1920 when he was raised to the aldermanic bench. By this time he had joined the Labour Party; the precise timing of his conversion has not been discovered, but he quickly established himself and was chairman of the Labour group on the City Council from 1919 to 1923.

Stevens's death occurred on 14 August 1925 in an Edgbaston nursing home, and he was cremated at Perry Barr on 19 August, when a memorial service was conducted by the Rector of Birmingham. He was married with one son and one daughter. In his will he left effects of £3572.

Writings: Evidence before R.C. on Aged Poor 1895 XV Qs 17219–459; *The Housing of the Labouring Classes* [Public debate in the Central Hall, Birmingham, between J.V. Stevens and J. Moore Bayley] (Birmingham, [1901]) 24 pp.

Sources: *Birmingham Daily Times*, 29 Oct 1889; B. Jones, *Co-operative Production*, 2 vols (1894; reprinted in one vol., New York, 1968); 'Edgbastonians Past and Present: Councillor J. V. Stevens', *Edgbastonia 23* (July 1903) 145–51 [photograph]; F. H. Stead, *How Old Age Pensions began to be* [1909]; W. J. Davis, *The British Trades Union Congress: history and recollections* vol. 2 (1916); A. T. Kidd, *History of the Tin-Plate Workers and Sheet Metal Workers and Braziers Societies* (1949); A. Briggs, *History of Birmingham* vol. 2: *1865–1938* (1952); Birmingham and Midland Sheet Metal Workers' Society, *Centenary Souvenir* (1959); J. Corbett, *The Birmingham Trades Council 1866–1966* (1966); biographical information: C. A. Barnwell, Midland Society, Ancient Order of Foresters; A. E. Cooper, Birmingham and Midland Sheet Metal Workers' Society. OBIT. *Birmingham Post*, 17 Aug 1925; *Birmingham Despatch*, 18 Aug 1925.

DAVID E. MARTIN
JOHN SAVILLE

See also: Arthur EADES; †Frederick ROGERS.

STRAKER, William (1855–1941)
MINERS' LEADER

Born 13 July 1855 at Snitter, two-and-a-half miles west of Rothbury in Northumberland, William Straker was the son of an agricultural labourer. In 1861 the family moved to the village of Widdrington, seven miles north-east of Morpeth, and after schooling in various elementary institutions, William Straker began work as a farm boy, earning sixpence a day. In the beginning, for four or five years, he worked in the summer and went to school in the winter, although most of his education was self-instruction in later years. In 1872 he entered the mines as a putter boy at a time when there were few ponies, and boys had to push loaded tubs by hand. He often worked as many as fourteen hours a day, and during the winter months only saw daylight at weekends.

Straker was early involved in trade unionism, and in 1879 was elected delegate for the Widdrington lodge. Three years later he was elected to the executive committee of the Northumberland Miners' Mutual Confident Association; and between 1888 and 1905 he was a member of the joint committee of the miners' union, which had six representatives to meet six chosen by the employers, with an independent chairman annually elected by the two Associations. Straker continued to work in the mine until in 1905, at the age of fifty, he was chosen corresponding secretary of the union, which in that year had some seventy branches with 24,368 members, and by five years later in 1910 had 37,361 members in seventy-nine branches. But though membership increased thus rapidly, the union's funds, which were very nearly £70,000 at the beginning of 1901, and had risen to £156,084 at the beginning of 1910, suffered a catastrophic fall almost to £82,000 at the end of the year: the great strike on the North East Coast from January to April in connection with the implementation of the Eight Hours Act had cost nearly £84,000 in dispute pay. The Rt Hon. Thomas Burt MP did not retire from the general secretaryship until 1913, when Straker was appointed to that office, which in reality he had already filled, and which he held until his retirement in 1935. In 1929 the NMA made him a presentation to mark his fifty years' service to the union. He represented the NMA on the executive committee of the MFGB between 1908 and 1925 and attended innumerable conferences, at home and abroad.

At times he was felt to cause difficulties in mining conferences by the high moral tone of his polemical remarks. But Straker was never a bigot, and Ebby Edwards used to tell how when, as a youthful Marxist and atheist he was getting into hot water among the Northumbrian Lib-Labs and Methodists, it was Straker from the chair who would come to his rescue and insist on tolerance. In the changes in his industrial and political attitudes Straker reflected the general views of the north-east coalfield. At the seventh international miners' conference at Aix-la-Chapelle, in 1896, he moved a destructive amendment to the resolution on the minimum wage moved by the MFGB. Only Northumberland voted for the amendment; even the Durham delegates abstained. But Straker's ideas, like so many of his fellow miners, began to shift away from the Lib-Labism of the 1890s after 1900. In 1912 he was a member of the sub-committee of the MFGB which was given the task of drafting a parliamentary bill on nationalisation of the coalmines. The other members were William Adamson MP and Vernon Hartshorn. They were assisted by H. H. Slesser, at the time draftsman to the Parliamentary Labour Party. The Bill was never, in fact, brought before the Commons [Arnot (1953) 132–3]. In 1919 Straker, on behalf of the MFGB, presented the detailed plans before the Sankey Commission for the control of the mining industry under nationalisation; and in the early 1930s he was a member of the Northumberland Investigations Committee under the Mines Act of 1930.

Like most active trade unionists in the mining areas, Straker was also much involved in local affairs. He was a member of the Northumberland Education Committee for thirty-two years; a member of the council of Armstrong College during the inter-war period; a member of the house committee of the Newcastle Royal Infirmary. He was for some years a Commissioner of the Inland Revenue, and for over twenty years a working director of the Co-operative Printing Society. His religion was Primitive Methodism and for many years he was a local preacher. In 1930 he was awarded the OBE.

He married Margaret Ann Sinclair in 1881 and there were two sons and five daughters of the marriage. His wife died in 1933, and he himself at the age of eighty-six on 31 December 1941. He left effects valued at £273.

Writings: Straker was editor of the *Monthly Circular* of the NMA for about twenty years, and he made the *Circular* very much a reflection of his own strong personality. He also wrote many newspaper articles, mostly in his own region.

Sources: *WWW* (1941–50); E. Welbourne, *The Miners' Union of Northumberland and Durham* (Cambridge, 1923); R. Page Arnot, *The Miners*, vols 1 and 2 (1949 and 1953); R. F. Wearmouth, *The Social and Political Influence of Methodism in the Twentieth Century* (1957); W. R. Garside, *The Durham Miners, 1919–1960* (1971); biographical information: Dr R. Page Arnot; Dr A. Mason. OBIT. *Newcastle J.*, 1 Jan 1942; NMA, *Monthly Circular* (1942).

JOHN SAVILLE

See also: †Thomas ASHTON, for Mining Trade Unionism, 1900–14; †Thomas BURT; †Thomas Henry CANN; *Arthur James COOK, for Mining Trade Unionism, 1915–1926; †Charles FENWICK; Peter LEE, for Mining Trade Unionism, 1927–44; †Benjamin PICKARD, for Mining Trade Unionism, 1880–99.

SULLIVAN, Joseph (1866–1935)
MINERS' LEADER AND LABOUR MP

Born on 8 September 1866 at Cambuslang, near Glasgow, the son of Bernard Sullivan, an Irish miner, Joseph was educated at Bellshill and Newton elementary schools, and started work in the pits before his thirteenth birthday. From his early youth he was active in trade unionism, and at the age of twenty-one he was elected a checkweighman. In his early thirties he became an agent for the Lanarkshire Miners' Union and much later, in 1921, he represented the Scottish miners on the MFGB.

He joined the ILP before 1914, and contested several parliamentary elections before entering Westminster as Labour MP for North Lanark in 1922. Defeated at the general election of 1924, he was successful in March 1926 at a by-election for the Bothwell division caused by the death of John Robertson, a Labour Whip and formerly chairman of the Lanarkshire Miners' Union. Sullivan retained the seat in 1929 but was defeated in 1931. Like Hugh Murnin, another mining colleague in the Commons, Sullivan was a Roman Catholic, and their election represents, at least to some extent, a decline in religious sectarianism among the Scottish mining communities. But this was to be offset still later by an increase of the influence of the newly formed

Catholic Action amongst the Lanarkshire miners which was not unconnected with the previous bitter struggle of Orange and Green, among the families of Irish descent.

Apart from his work for the miners, he was also active in local affairs. He had extensive experience of local government from parish council (twelve years) to county council (nine years); was a JP for Lanarkshire; had served on a school board for nine years and the education authority for three. He was prominent also in the friendly society and co-operative movements. Much of his public work related to housing and unemployment problems and he was always vigorously advocating the making of poor relief a national rather than a local charge; he was awarded the MBE for his public services.

He was twice married; first in 1888 to the daughter of Thomas Winter, who died in 1923, and secondly in 1929 to Anne, daughter of Michael and Elizabeth Dickson Murphy. He had a family of four daughters. He died on 13 February 1935 at his Mossend, Bellshill, home and was survived by his wife and grown-up family. At the time of his death he was Labour candidate for the Bothwell division. Following a service in Holy Family Chapel, Mossend, he was buried in Bothwell Park Cemetery, Bellshill (lair no. 138). He left estate valued at £467.

Sources: S. V. Bracher, *The Herald Book of Labour Members* (1923) [with photograph]; *Labour Who's Who* (1927); *Times, House of Commons* (1929); Anon., *The Scottish Socialists* (1931); *Dod* (1931); *Kelly* (1932); *WWW* (1929–40). OBIT. *Times*, 15 Feb 1935; *Hamilton Advertiser*, 16 Feb 1935.

JOYCE BELLAMY

See also: Hugh MURNIN; *Robert SMILLIE, for Scottish Mining Trade Unionism.

SWIFT, Fred (1874–1959)
MINERS' LEADER AND LABOUR ALDERMAN

Fred Swift was born on 19 May 1874 at Green Parlour, Writhlington, Somerset, the son of William Swift, a coalminer and his wife Bertha (née Treasure). It was at the Junior and Church schools of Writhlington and Radstock that young Fred received his early education, and he was also a member of the choir of St Mary Magdalene, the parish church of Writhlington, where he became a tenor soloist. Fred's working life began at the age of ten with stone-breaking for the Frome RDC, and this was followed a year later by sheep-minding at a local farm for 3s a week. He started at the Writhlington Pit when he was twelve, and so began a lifelong association with the North Somerset coalfield.

The local rector, the Rev. Alexander Ramsay, encouraged Fred to extend his education and allowed him the use of his library. In his youth Fred became a close friend of the vicar's sons Geoffrey and Ronald. He visited them during their undergraduate days at Cambridge, and Geoffrey, who succeeded his father in the living, and became a CWS director in the 1920s, remained a close friend and helped Fred for many years with his more important letters and speeches. Ronald, who also entered the Church, later became Bishop of Malmesbury. Fred himself remained a practising Anglican all his life.

He became involved in trade union affairs early in his working career, and already at the age of twenty was representing the carting boys of Lower Writhlington. In 1899 he was chosen as delegate from his own colliery to the meetings of the Somerset Miners' Association; and in 1904 was appointed financial secretary, a position he held until 1917, when he succeeded S. H. Whitehouse as miners' agent for the SMA. Swift retired in 1945. Although the SMA was among the smallest unions affiliated to the MFGB, he won national recognition for his abilities and for seven years between 1917 and 1941 served on the MFGB executive. He represented British miners at a number of international conferences, and in 1945 was awarded the MBE for his services to the mining community.

Among the miners' leaders of the 1920s Swift counted as a moderate. Right from the beginning of the miners' strike in 1926 he had doubts about the course of action proposed by the militants, and throughout the later negotiations he seems to have advocated an earlier rather than a later settlement of the dispute. Apart from his onerous day-to-day work as a county union secretary, his main contribution to the welfare of miners was in the field of compensation; and he is especially remembered for the part he played in publicising the incidence of silicosis. In the early 1920s he had become increasingly concerned with the health hazards of mining in his own area, and with the assistance of two local doctors (Dr Euston of Peasedown and Dr Jones of Coleford) he obtained a post-mortem on a deceased miner. This revealed that an illness diagnosed as bronchial catarrh had, in fact been caused by a silicious deposit on the lungs, and it therefore ought to qualify as an industrial disease. Swift collected further evidence, some of which was used in an interview which the executive committee of the MFGB had with the Home Secretary, Sir William Joynson-Hicks, in February 1926; and this led to the enactment of The Various Industries (Silicosis) Scheme in 1928. Fred Swift's efforts were officially recognised in 1931 when J. S. Haldane read a paper to the Institution of Mining Engineers, in which he said:

The consequences were first detected in the small Somerset Coalfield, through the efforts of Mr Swift, the much respected local Miners' Agent, who collected and sent to the Mines Department the details of several cases, which on further investigation were found to be typical cases of silicosis or miners' phthisis. These were due, apparently, to driving roads in a stone known locally as 'greys'.

Haldane sent a copy of his paper to Fred Swift, with a covering letter:

. . . You will see the reference in it to your own very important work on the subject, and I think it will be a satisfaction to you to know that this work, which must have cost you much trouble and thought, is widely appreciated.

The 1928 Scheme had restrictions which prejudiced the claims of coalminers because it dealt specifically with silicosis, a disease caused by some rock-dusts. It was not realised at that time that large numbers of coalminers were suffering from lung disease caused by fine coal dust, coal-workers' pneumoconiosis. However, Fred Swift lived to see these men obtaining compensation too, under the Workmen's Compensation Act of 1943.

In addition to his involvement with trade unionism, Fred Swift took an active part in politics for most of his life. In 1907, together with the Rev. Geoffrey Ramsay and a few other pioneers, he founded a Radstock branch of the ILP, and travelled around Somerset holding meetings at street corners, in marketplaces and public houses. When Fred Swift died, a memory of these early days was recalled in a letter from Mark Starr, a former Central Labour College lecturer, who emigrated to America in the late 1920s, and eventually became director of education for the International Ladies Garment Workers. Starr had been a carting boy at the same colliery where Swift was a hewer. He wrote [*Somerset Guardian*, 22 Jan 1960]:

When I became a carting boy years ago, Fred Swift and Charley Bartlett were the hewers whose coal we loaded. At that time the carting boys in the Writhlington pit wore 'the gus and crook'. This is now unknown, as it should be, and I hope in an appropriate museum. Anyway, I had a chance of benefiting from the good sense and fellowship of Fred Swift when he was working at the coalface. Those cycling trips to Wells, Glastonbury and to Street, as well as the ILP meetings in the Square at Radstock, left a lasting impression upon those of us who participated in them. Fred Gould, George and Walter Beard and the Rev. Geoffrey Ramsay were among Fred Swift's comrades in the old ILP days. They showed the way forward. Later, when Fred became the miners' agent for the Somerset miners, I, with other coal-diggers, benefited from his wise leadership . . . I am sure that Fred thought that some of us youngsters had Left-wing ideas, but his faith in us and his constant encouragement were typical of his understanding.

In 1914 he was elected as first chairman of the Radstock Trades Council and in 1918 became the first chairman of the Trades and Labour Council. On 20 March of the latter year he was elected to the presidency of the newly formed Frome Divisional Labour Party and served in this capacity continuously until January 1938, when he was appointed honorary vice-president. In 1919 he became the first Labour member to be elected to the Somerset County Council, on which he served continuously until ill-health forced him to retire in 1958. From 1946 until his retirement he was a member of the aldermanic bench, and from 1930 was a JP for the county. He inspired others with his philanthropic zeal and one of these was Stanley Whittock, a fellow-member of the County Council and an employee of the Radstock and District Co-operative and Industrial Society whose father had been a miner and had suffered from wearing the 'gus and crook' when he was a carting boy. In a tribute after Swift's death, Whittock, who had worked with him for forty years, wrote:

Second only to his devotion and loyalty to his comrades of the coalfields, were his services in the cause of mental and physical health. For his services to Cambrook House, on the Board of Guardians and since, his name is enshrined over the newly-erected wards on the ground floor. We served together on several hospital, infirmary, mental homes, occupation centres, nursery, boys' and girls' homes, welfare centres, and other committees, in addition to school governors. A very high moral code, and the Ten Commandments governed all his conduct, and his only aggressions were levelled against injustices [Somerset Guardian, 4 Dec 1959].

A keen sportsman, Fred Swift played football for his County during four seasons, and regularly for the local Radstock team; he was also a cricketer and a bowler of some repute. He had married, in 1899, Nellie Wilcox, by whom he had a daughter and two sons. The daughter, Evelyn, was employed by the Radstock Co-operative Society before her marriage; the eldest son, Norman Leslie, was employed by the Shell Company in Venezuela, but on his return to England was appointed an official of the Royal Household, and retired from the position of Registrar of the Central Chancery of the Orders of Knighthood in 1959. The younger son, Clarence Fred, spent the whole of his career in the RAF Regiment and attained the rank of Squadron Leader. Fred Swift was a devoted and understanding husband and father, and he and his wife had celebrated their diamond wedding anniversary only a few weeks before he died at his Radstock home on 24 November 1959. After a service at the Writhlington Parish Church, where he had worshipped regularly, he was buried in the local cemetery. His wife and family survived him, and he left an estate valued at £2589.

Sources: R.C. on Mines vol. 1 1907 Cd 3548 XIV; MFGB, Memorandum on Silicosis among Coalminers (1930); J. S. Haldane, 'Silicosis and Coal-mining', Trans of the Institution of Mining Engineers, 80, pt 5 (1930–1) 415–51; R. Page Arnot, vol. 2, The Miners: years of struggle (1953); idem, vol. 3, The Miners in Crisis and War (1961); W. W. Craik, The Central Labour College 1909–29 (1964); A. R. Griffin, Mining in the East Midlands 1550–1947 (1971); personal information: N. L. Swift, Bath, son; S. Whittock, Radstock. We are also much indebted to Mr John Foster, of the Safety in Mines Research Establishment, Sheffield, for technical information incorporated in the text. OBIT. Bristol Evening Post and Bristol Evening World, 25 Nov 1959; Somerset Guardian, 27 Nov 1959; Writhlington J. (parish magazine of St Mary Magdalene, Writhlington), Dec 1959; Somerset Guardian, 4 Dec 1959, Somerset Guardian, 8 and 22 Jan 1960.

JOYCE BELLAMY
JOHN SAVILLE

See also: †Thomas ASHTON, for Mining

Trade Unionism, 1900–14; *Arthur James Cook, for Mining Trade Unionism, 1915–1926; Peter Lee, for Mining Trade Unionism, 1927–45; *Samuel Henry Whitehouse.

THICKETT, Joseph (1865–1938)
TRADE UNIONIST

Born on 14 July 1865 at Wolverhampton, Joseph Thickett was the son of Job Thickett, a journeyman edge-tool maker, and Maria Thickett (née Pittaway). While he was still a baby the family moved to Wood Green, between Wednesbury and Walsall, and Thickett grew up in this area. His father died when Joseph was eleven, by which time the boy was working as a part-timer at Elwell's Forge, Wednesbury, earning 3s per week for a seven-hour morning shift and attending Wednesbury Church School in the afternoon. The depressed condition of the Black Country metal trades and the consequent irregularity of employment led him, as a young man, to seek a more secure job, and at the age of twenty-two he started work on the railway. He began as a porter at Bescot (Walsall) station, earning 17s 6d per week for a twelve-hour day, and eventually became a signalman at Pleck Junction signal box (Walsall), on the former London and North Western Railway.

Thickett quickly involved himself in the activities of the Walsall No. 2 branch of the Amalgamated Society of Railway Servants, and in 1905 he served on the national executive committee of the Society. Always an advocate of direct parliamentary representation of labour, and of industrial unionism, Thickett welcomed the formation in 1913 of the National Union of Railwaymen by the amalgamation of the Amalgamated Society of Railway Servants with the General Railway Workers' Union and the United Pointsmen and Signalmen's Society. He never again achieved national office, but he did become president of the Walsall branch of the NUR and retained an active interest in its affairs until his death. As the railwaymen's delegate to the Walsall Trades Council for many years Thickett was one of the pioneers of trade unionism in the town. He became vice-president of the Trades Coun-

cil in 1900 and in 1906 was elected the first president of the newly constituted Walsall Trades and Labour Representation Council. In this capacity he played a leading part in the great Black Country strike of 1913. This began as a series of relatively small unconnected disputes and developed quickly into a concerted mass movement. Originating from the largely successful attempt by the Workers' Union to establish a 23s per week minimum wage at major engineering firms in Birmingham, Smethwick and West Bromwich, the strike spread across the Black Country, and for about six weeks in late spring and early summer some 40,000 workers were affected. In Walsall Thickett's influence was a major factor in bringing the strike to a successful conclusion, obtaining increases of around 5s per week for thousands of Black Country labourers, and establishing the Workers' Union as a major industrial force [Hyman (1971) 51ff].

Also in 1913, after three unsuccessful attempts, Thickett was elected to Walsall Town Council to fill a vacancy in Pleck ward, which he then continued to represent until his death. He was the first Labour Party member of the Council, the two previous Labour representatives, Benjamin Dean and William Millerchip both being Lib-Labs. During his twenty-five years on Walsall Council Thickett made an important contribution to the civic life of the town, especially as chairman of the Corporation Transport Committee and the Electricity Supply Committee. He became the first Labour Party mayor of Walsall in 1923, and an alderman in 1928, retaining this latter office until his death. He also earned a considerable reputation, which spread far beyond Walsall, as an eloquent and witty public speaker. This talent was the chief strength of his campaign as Walsall's first Labour Candidate at the parliamentary election of 1918. Despite an almost non-existent party organisation Thickett polled 8336 votes, pushed the Liberal candidate into third place, and effectively established the Labour Party as a viable organisation in Walsall. In the same year he became a magistrate.

On his retirement from signal box duty in

1930, after forty-three years as a railwayman, Thickett became for a short time licensee of the Vine Inn, Walsall, before finally retiring altogether. He died suddenly at his home, 13 Goodall Street, Walsall, on 7 November 1938, and was survived by his wife and four sons. Following a service at St Peter's Church he was buried in Ryecroft Cemetery, Walsall, six railwaymen acting as pall bearers. Of Thickett's four sons the eldest, Benjamin, became a printer, while another two trained as tailors, though only Harold finally followed the trade. The other, Ernest, became a publican, and was licensee of the Bridge Inn, Walsall, for twenty-five years. Frederick, the third son, trained as a press tool maker, but being unable to find a job on the completion of his apprenticeship he joined the RAF for three years. On his discharge in 1926 he was still unable to find a job in his trade, so he became a labourer at Walsall Gas Works. He was promoted to foreman in 1937, and in 1940 was awarded the BEM for devotion to duty at the Gas Works during an air raid. He became an active member of the General and Municipal Workers' Union, and from 1946 to 1950 was president of Walsall Labour Party. In 1950 he was elected to Walsall Town Council, for Pleck ward, and served for thirteen years before resigning on account of ill-health. In 1950 also he became a JP, and in 1969 was appointed chairman of the Walsall bench, from which he retired in 1972. Since July 1967 he has been living in retirement in Walsall. Benjamin, Harold and Ernest are all now dead. No will was located at Somerset House.

Sources: Reports of Walsall Town Council meetings, Trades Council, ASRS and NUR activities in *Walsall Advertiser*, 1892–1914; *Walsall Free Press*, 1892–1903; *Walsall Observer*, 1892–1938; *Walsall Times*, 1925–1938; *Walsall Red Book* [photographs in editions of 1914, 1924 and 1929]; P. S. Gupta, 'History of the Amalgamated Society of Railway Servants 1871–1913' (Oxford DPhil., 1960); P. S. Bagwell, *The Railwaymen* (1963); K. J. Dean, 'Parliamentary Elections and Party Organisations in Walsall 1906–45' (Birmingham MA,

1969); R. Hyman, *The Workers' Union* (Oxford, 1971); K. J. Dean, *Town and Westminster: a political history of Walsall from 1906–1945* (Walsall, 1972); personal information: F. Thickett, Walsall, son. OBIT. *Wolverhampton Express and Star*, 7 Nov 1938; *Walsall Observer* and *Walsall Times*, 12 Nov 1938 [photographs].

ERIC TAYLOR

See also: Richard BELL; †Benjamin DEAN; Henry HUCKER; †William MILLERCHIP.

TOOTILL, Robert (1850–1934)
TRADE UNION LEADER AND LABOUR MP

Though in later life he spelt his surname Tootill, at birth he was registered as Robert Tootell. He was born into a humble home on 22 October 1850, the son of James Tootell, a weaver, of Albion Street, Chorley, and his wife, Margaret (née Halliday). His life in youth was monotonous and he had no formal education; at the age of seven he began work at the Birkacre Printing works in Chorley, and a year later he took a job in Lawrence and Son's cotton spinning mills as a little piecer. When he was twenty-four he moved to Bolton, where he became a side piecer at Haslam's Victory mill. He continued to work in the cotton trade for several years, being employed as a minder at Shappie's mill and then at the Bolton Union Spinning Company's mill.

In 1887 Tootill rose to prominence in local labour politics as a leading supporter of the engineers' strike that had broken out. The authorities had responded to the strike by sending extra police into Bolton, and Tootill voiced the indignation felt by many workers at this action. He was the principal speaker at a mass meeting held in the Temperance Hall; this led to his being appointed as a member of a deputation to the Home Secretary which expressed disquiet over the way in which order had been restored.

A year later Tootill contested West Ward as a Labour candidate and was elected to the Bolton town council, upon which, except for one year (1901–2), he served continuously for twenty-six years, until 1914.

During the years before the First World War he was a leading figure in local trade unionism. He was a strenuous advocate of the principle of trade union organisation. He was secretary of the Bolton Trades Council for some twenty years and in 1909 a presentation of silver plate was made to him in recognition of his thirty years' service as a delegate to the Council. He was also secretary of the Machine and Labourers' Union and helped in the formation of unions for shop assistants, carters and lorrymen, labourers, warehousemen and clerks, and for several sections of Corporation employees; more than once he attempted to establish a union for piecers, who, because of the peculiar occupational structure of the cotton trade, were poorly paid and difficult to organise. After some years of factory work, he found employment for a time as a commercial traveller and also as a registrar of births and deaths (the exact dates when he held these posts have not been established). He acted, too, as a labour correspondent for the Board of Trade; but throughout these years he continued as general secretary of the Machine and Labourers' Union.

After the death in August 1914 of A. H. Gill, who had sat as Labour MP for Bolton since 1906, Tootill was elected by the Bolton Labour Party as parliamentary candidate for the borough. The wartime electoral truce was in operation, and he was returned unopposed in September 1914. Along with a majority of the Labour Party, Tootill supported the war. In May 1916 he was one of several Labour MPs who became vice-presidents of the British Workers' League (*Times*, 15 May 1916). He remained a supporter of this ultra-patriotic body until it began to emerge as a rival to the Labour Party; pressure was then put on him to resign, and at the Labour Party conference held at Nottingham in January 1918 it was announced that Tootill, along with William Abraham and Will Crooks, had left the BWL. He was also a member of the National War Aims Committee, and visited Flanders in September 1915 to observe the situation at the front. On his return he undertook strenuous propaganda work on behalf of the Ministry of Munitions.

It was estimated that he addressed over a million and a half workers during the war, a contribution to the war effort that was acknowledged in 1918 by his appointment as a CBE. He was returned unopposed to the House of Commons in December 1918, but did not stand for re-election in 1922.

On his retirement Tootill went to live in Blackpool, where he also became known in public life. He had been appointed a JP for Bolton in 1905 and was transferred to the borough bench at Blackpool. One of his main interests was the local branch of the League of Nations Union; he became its chairman and worked hard to strengthen it. In recognition of his efforts, on his seventy-ninth birthday J. R. Clynes presented Tootill with a gold watch at a meeting held in the Blackpool Tower and attended by nearly 4000 people. In 1925 he had joined the West Lancashire Century Freemason's Lodge, no. 2349 and remained a member until his death.

In religion a Methodist, he was an active lay preacher and in 1910 the National Sunday School Union awarded him a diploma of honour for forty years' continuous service to Sunday Schools, in particular the Albert Place United Methodist Sunday School, Bolton. Tootill died at his home in Blackpool on 2 July 1934, aged eighty-three. He was buried at Lytham St Annes Park Cemetery on 5 July after a service at the Central Methodist Church. In his will he left effects to the value of £5517, and made £50 bequests to the Victoria Hospital, Blackpool and the Royal Bolton Infirmary. He had married Jane, a daughter of James Smith, in 1875; his wife, a daughter and a son survived him.

Sources: *Dod* (1915–22); C. A. Clarke, *Moorlands and Memories* (3rd ed., Blackpool and London, 1924); *WWW* (1929–40); *Kelly* (1932); R. Douglas, 'The National Democratic Party and the British Workers' League', *Hist. J. 15* (Sep 1972) 533–52; biographical information: Grand United Lodge of England, and Province of West Lancashire [Freemasons]. Obit. *Bolton Evening News*, 2 July 1934; *Blackpool Gazette &*

Herald, Fylde News and Advertiser, 7 July 1934.

DAVID E. MARTIN

See also: †Arthur HENDERSON, for British Labour Party, 1914–31.

TORKINGTON, James (1811–67)
CHARTIST

James Torkington was born in Stockport, Cheshire, in 1811. He was a calico weaver by trade. Nothing is known of his early life, and there is no record of his being active in the working-class movement before 1840. By December of that year he was apparently well known among the local Chartists, who were engaged in a campaign for the return of the exiled Welsh Chartists, Frost, Williams and Jones. The Stockport committee recommended Torkington and three colleagues as honorary members of the Birmingham Restoration Committee. Torkington also took up the cause of the Chartist prisoners from Stockport, namely James Mitchell and Charles Davies, who in August 1839 had been sentenced at Chester to eighteen months' imprisonment, and their friends Isaac Armitage, James Burton, George Wareham, Isaac Johnson and Thomas Howarth, who had received twelve months' imprisonment at the Chester Assizes in April 1840. All these men were still serving their sentences in Chester Castle.

Torkington was elected as Stockport representative to the Chartist National Delegate Meeting, which was held in Tib Street, Manchester, in February 1841. He thus helped to plan the organisation of the National Charter Association. When in accordance with the new scheme, nominations were submitted for the National Council, Torkington was selected as a committee member for Stockport's Bamford Street branch. In February 1842 he visited Hazel Grove, to deliver a lecture on the 'fallacies of the Anti-Corn Law Plaguers'. A month later O'Connor visited Stockport, and Torkington used the occasion to revive the campaign for the return of Frost, Williams and Jones. Not that the Anti-Corn Law League had been forgotten: when the League sent its own delegates to London that summer, as self-styled representatives of the distressed inhabitants of Stockport, a Chartist meeting, presided over by Torkington, sent a protest to Sir Robert Peel's Government.

With the decline in Chartist activity in the middle years of the decade, Torkington turned in 1846 to the campaign against the Municipal Improvement Bill, whose principal advocate was the Whig Town Clerk. Many of the Bill's clauses provided for improvements in the town which the Chartists agreed would be beneficial: roads and bridges were to be built and other roads widened, widths of streets and heights of houses were to be regulated. But here the Chartist's approval ended. The fourth clause of the Bill provided that any sum not exceeding £100,000 might be borrowed on the security of the rates. The existing Improvement Act had stipulated that no sum greater than £200 could be spent by the Council without the agreement of a meeting of ratepayers; this was now repealed by the 29th clause of the new Bill. By opponents of the Whig Corporation this was seen as an attempt to divest the ratepayers of their control over financial affairs. Some clauses dealing with public health were also objected to, not on the grounds that such improvements were unnecessary but because the onus for their execution was placed upon poorer tenants rather than upon landlords and the wealthier section of the inhabitants. For example, houses were to be whitewashed and purified by the occupiers, or a 5s penalty paid for every day's neglect after certain orders had been given. The Chartists naturally believed that such neglect of houses was the responsibility of the landlord, who should be fined 10s in such cases. Thus the Chartists saw the Improvement Bill as an attempt by the Whigs to develop the town in the interests of the middle classes, at the expense of the poorer ratepayers.

The opposition to the Improvement Bill took the form of a Chartist/Tory alliance. James Williams, later executive member of the 1854 Labour Parliament, became secretary to the Stockport Improvement Bill Committee; Torkington, Abraham Docker and George Bradburn were also active. The organisation sought the assistance of Thomas Slingsby Duncombe MP, who recommended them to petition Parliament. The petition, moved by Torkington at a public meeting in June 1846, asked that the 29th clause should be expunged from the Bill and replaced by a clause restoring to the ratepayers control over expenditure in excess of £2000 p.a., such a sum being considered sufficient to complete the contemplated improvements. The petition received 4000 signatures before Duncombe presented it to the Commons in July. The result of such efforts was a fortnight's adjournment of the Third Reading, at which the Bill was eventually lost. The likelihood that a new Bill would be introduced led to the formation by its opponents of a Ratepayers' Association, later known as the Working Men's Ratepayers' Association, of which Torkington again became a member. But the organisation failed to prevent the passing of the new Stockport Manorial Tolls and Bridges Bill, which became law in October 1847. When the Association then organised a public meeting in order to consider their future policy, Torkington was elected to the chair.

By November 1847, however, his activities were again turning towards the cause of Chartism. He took the chair at a public meeting called to revive the movement in the town and addressed by Thomas Clark and Philip M'Grath of the executive. When depression in the cotton trade again affected Stockport in 1847, Torkington took part in a plan to stage a one-month strike, in order to force employers to provide assistance for the operatives – a scheme which was wholly impractical and was never implemented. In March 1848 Torkington was again busy with Chartist activities. In the following month he was chairman of a meeting called to protest against the 'Gagging Bill', but on this occasion he urged the large crowd to be peaceable, stressing the case for moral force.

Torkington was also an advocate of the Chartist Land Scheme. In October 1848 he travelled to Birmingham as Stockport delegate to the National Land Company Conference. Although the Company was by now in grave financial difficulties, he discussed the best time to place allottees on the land, and noted with pleasure the support given by Company members to the Charter. In 1850, when the local Land Society Committee had apparently ceased to function, Torkington was one of the remaining members who called a meeting at which they declared continuing faith in O'Connor. This was the last recorded event in his public life. He died on 27 September 1867 in Stockport Workhouse, and was buried on 1 October. He left a widow, Mary, and three sons. No will has been located.

Sources: (1) MSS: 1851 Census, Stockport, PRO: H.O. 107/2157; 1861 Census, Stockport, PRO: R.G.9 2570; Stockport Cemetery records; (2) Other: *Northern Star*, 1840–50; *Stockport Advertiser*, 1842–8; R. G. Gammage, *History of the Chartist Movement 1837–54* (1894: repr. with an Introduction by John Saville, New York, 1969); A. R. Schoyen, *The Chartist Challenge* (1958); *Chartist Studies*, ed. Asa Briggs (1959).

NAOMI REID
T. D. W. REID

See also: John ALLINSON; George BRADBURN; Joseph CARTER; Abraham DOCKER; *Feargus O'CONNOR.

TOYN, Joseph (1838–1924)
MINERS' LEADER AND CO-OPERATOR

Born on 28 September 1938 at Tattershall in Lincolnshire, Toyn began work on a farm when he was six years old, earning threepence a day by scaring birds; he continued in farm work until he was fourteen, when he was earning 3s 6d for a full six-day week. In the following three-and-a-half years he worked on a canal barge sailing between Lincolnshire and Barnsley. He subsequently entered the Cleveland ironstone mines, and after working through all grades became an overman. He held this position for a year before resigning to work at the face. At that stage in his career he became interested in trade union affairs. The Cleveland Miners' Association was formed in 1872; Toyn was at first a delegate, and then in

1875 he was made president; this was an unpaid position, but in June 1876 he was also appointed agent of the Association, and ceased to work in the mine. As one of the representatives of the Miners' National Union Toyn attended the Trades Union Congress at Aberdeen in 1884 and the Southport TUC in 1885. In 1889 he attended the Dundee TUC as a representative of the North Yorkshire and Cleveland Miners' Association (which claimed 5497 members at the Liverpool TUC of 1890). In 1892 Toyn attended the Glasgow TUC as a representative of the Miners' National Union.

For many years he was a member of the central board of the Miners' National Union and he was present at the famous January 1889 conference of the MNU at Leeds which preceded the formation of the MFGB later in the same year. Toyn was a staunch advocate of the principle of a legal eight-hour day for the miners, and it was on this issue in particular that in 1892 he persuaded the Cleveland miners to leave the MNU and join the MFGB. He served on the executive of the latter in 1896. His leadership as president and agent of the Cleveland miners continued for thirty-five years, until 1911, and it was largely his influence that led to the introduction of conciliation board procedures as a result of which there was no strike in the local ironstone industry during his whole period as agent. He attended a number of international miners' conferences, and was a witness on behalf of the miners before a number of Government committees and inquiries.

Like many of the northern miners' leaders, Toyn was an ardent Primitive Methodist, a lay preacher and class leader whose abilities for public speaking were also harnessed to the cause of political reform. He was a member of a delegation to Gladstone on the county franchise question, and was one of a group of working men chosen to visit Ireland in 1881 and report on the condition of the Irish people. As a strong believer in direct Labour representation in Parliament he lectured on this subject in the 1880s but he did not favour independent Labour representation divorced from

the Liberal Party. In the early 1890s he belonged to the Labour Electoral Association, a radical organisation supporting close links with the advanced wing of the Liberal Party, and in 1902 was included in a list of Liberal candidates for a parliamentary vacancy in Cleveland. The Cleveland Iron Miners' Union, however, was affiliated to the Labour Representation Committee, formed in 1900 to support independent Labour candidates, and Keir Hardie had hopes of running an LRC candidate at the by-election. The inclusion by the Liberals of Toyn among their candidates made the local Labour group reluctant to propose an independent labour man; but in the end Toyn declined to contest the seat in the Lib-Lab interest and a Liberal candidate, Herbert Samuel, was elected [Bealey and Pelling (1958) 138]. Toyn had other invitations to contest parliamentary seats but did not accept any of them.

He also played an active part in local affairs in North Yorkshire. For nineteen years he represented Brotton on the Cleveland Board of Guardians, was a JP for the North Riding from 1906 – the first Labour leader to be a Cleveland magistrate – and in 1911 was one of the original members of the Advisory Council for Cleveland.

Hallam wrote in 1894 that Toyn had 'a firm belief in the possibility of almost indefinite elevation and improvement of the working classes', and that trade unionism and co-operation were 'the two best levers to achieve that end'. As would be expected of him, Toyn was among the pioneers of co-operation in Cleveland, and in the early days of the movement he helped to serve behind the counter of the first co-operative store in Skelton.

He died at Saltburn on 27 January 1924, aged eighty-five. A son, who had entered the Primitive Methodist ministry, and a daughter, survived him.

Sources: Evidence before the following Government inquiries: R.C. on Accidents 1881 XXVI Qs 13168–263; S.C. on Employers Liability Act (1880) Amendment Bill 1886 VIII Qs 2183–287; R.C. on Mining Royalties 1890–1 XLI Qs 15989–16101;

R.C. on Labour 1892 XXXIV Qs 693–1191; R.C. on Mines vol. III 1908 XX Qs 28857–9279; Labour Electoral Congress Reports (1893) and (1895): LSE; W. Hallam, *Miners' Leaders* (1894) [photograph]; A. W. Humphrey, *A History of Labour Representation* (1912); R. F. Wearmouth, *Methodism and the Struggle of the Working Classes 1850–1900* (Leicester, 1954); idem, *The Social and Political Influence of Methodism in the Twentieth Century* (1957); F. Bealey and H. Pelling, *Labour and Politics 1900–1906* (1958); E. J. Hobsbawm, *Primitive Rebels* (Manchester, 1959). OBIT. *North-Eastern Gazette*, 28 Jan 1924; *Times*, 29 Jan 1924; *Aldersgate Mag. 106* (Jan 1925) 66–7.

JOYCE BELLAMY

See also: †Thomas ASHTON, for Mining Trade Unionism, 1900–14; †Alexander MACDONALD, for Mining Trade Unionism, 1850–79; †Benjamin PICKARD, for Mining Trade Unionism, 1880–99.

TWIST, Henry (Harry) (1870–1934)
MINERS' LEADER AND LABOUR MP

Harry Twist was born on 30 January 1870 at Platt Bridge, two miles south-east of Wigan, Lancashire, the son of a miner who died when Harry was only three months old. His mother died when he was eight. Up to the age of ten he was educated at the Wesleyan Day School, Platt Bridge, but soon after reaching his eleventh birthday he began work at a local colliery, first on the surface and then, later, below ground as a door-tender. In his life as a miner he worked at every job up to hewer, and at the age of thirty he was made checkweighman at the Mains Pit of the Bamfurlong collieries. He had become involved as a young man in the trade union movement, and in 1902 he was elected president of the Lancashire and Cheshire Miners' Federation. Four years later, in 1906, he succeeded Sam Woods as agent for the Ashton-in-Makerfield district and he held this position for twenty-eight years until his death. He represented Lancashire on the executive of the MFGB in 1908, 1917, 1927 and 1931; and in 1918 he was a candidate for the post of general

secretary of the MFGB when Frank Hodges was elected.

Twist, according to his own testimony, had been a member of the ILP from its earliest days. He provided a long statement of his beliefs in an interview for the *Christian Commonwealth* (15 June 1910), an extract from which is given below:

I became a Socialist before I joined the Labour movement, and I should say equally as much because of my belief in Christian principles, and because of my faith in the social side of Christ's Gospel, as because of my study of the writings of Socialist leaders in economics. The ethical appealed to me equally with the economic. The rivalry arising out of competition always seemed to me to be incompatible with the teachings of Christ as well as destructive of economic freedom. Believing, as I do, that the complete redemption of man must be by the double remedy – the change of environment and the regeneration of the individual from within – I remain a Socialist for exactly the same reasons that I first became a Socialist.

There was a strong tradition of working-class Conservatism in Lancashire, and the politics of the mining community, which reflected this tradition, are a complicated story. Lancashire was also an old coalfield with poor working conditions; hours were long and earnings were low [Gregory (1968) Ch. 4]. Twist's early conversion to Christian Socialism was unusual for any mining community, although the ILP was to build a vigorous movement in Wigan. The town had returned a Conservative to Parliament in every election between 1885 and 1906 although in the latter year the defeat of the Liberal candidate (a Catholic) was due to the intervention of an independent Women's Suffrage candidate, who won a large proportion of the regular chapel and temperance vote. Twist was nominated by the Lancashire and Cheshire miners as Labour candidate for Wigan in 1908; and in the general election of January 1910 he gained a sensational victory, in a straight fight, over the Conservative candidate. He lost the seat, however, at the second election of 1910, held in December; and resigned as candidate for Wigan in 1916. He was later elected as Labour MP for Leigh in the general election of 1922, resigning on grounds of ill-health just before the election of December 1923, when he was succeeded by another miners' leader, J. Tinker.

For the last ten years of his life Twist suffered from increasing ill-health, but he continued his many activities. He had been a local councillor on the Abram Urban District Council for three years between 1905 and 1908; was appointed a magistrate in the latter year and served until his death; and retained, also until his last days, an active interest in both the local co-operative movement and the Congregational Church. In his younger days he had been well known as a lay preacher. He died 16 May 1934 leaving a widow, three married sons and a married daughter; he left effects valued at £486.

Sources: 'Miners as Pioneer Reformers: interview with Mr H. Twist MP', *Christian Commonwealth*, 15 June 1910; *Dod* (1923); S. V. Bracher, *The Herald Book of Labour Members* (1923); *WWW* (1929–40); R. Page Arnot, *The Miners: years of struggle* (1953); H. Pelling, *Social Geography of British Elections 1885–1910* (1967); R. Gregory, *The Miners and British Politics, 1906–1914* (Oxford, 1968); R. Challinor, *The Lancashire and Cheshire Miners* (Newcastle, 1972). OBIT. *Times*, 18 May 1934; *Wigan Observer and District Advertiser*, 19 May 1934; *Labour Party Report* (1934).

JOHN SAVILLE

See also: †Thomas ASPINWALL; †Thomas ASHTON, for Mining Trade Unionism, 1900–1914; *Arthur James COOK, for Mining Trade Unionism, 1915–26; *Stephen WALSH.

VARLEY, Frank Bradley (1885–1929)
MINERS' LEADER AND LABOUR MP

Frank Varley was born on 18 June 1885 in the hamlet of Greenhill Lane, north-west of the town of Riddings in the parish of Alfreton, Derbyshire, the son of Thomas Henry Varley, a miner, and his wife, Susannah (née Bradley). Frank was one of fifteen children and was educated at an elementary school which he left at eleven years of age to earn his living as a draper's errand boy. A year later he entered Pye Hill Colliery as a pit boy, but continued to extend his education by evening classes, and at nineteen won a three-year scholarship to Sheffield University to study mining part-time. At the end of the course, in 1906, he was awarded a colliery manager's first class certificate of competency. Varley was then offered a place at Ruskin College, but for financial reasons was unable to accept. He returned to Pye Hill Colliery, and in 1910 the miners' lodge there appointed him as their delegate to the council of the Nottingham Miners' Association, founded in 1880, which by the end of 1910 had 31,252 members organised in fifty-one branches.

After the Coal Mines (Minimum Wage) Act of 1912 (passed on 29 March 1912 during the first national miners' strike) Joint District Boards were set up in a score of coalfields to settle minimum rates of wages and district rules. Varley, at the age of twenty-seven, was chosen to serve on the Nottinghamshire JDB. The rates originally demanded varied from 6s in the smaller districts to 8s 3d in Nottinghamshire, which was the highest; but in the modified demand of 6 February 1912 they varied from 4s 11d in Somerset to 7s 6d in Nottinghamshire. In the latter county the new Joint District Board failed to settle within the prescribed period of seven weeks, whereupon the independent chairman gave an award of 7s on 24 June 1912. In 1913 Varley was elected vice-president of the Nottingham Miners' Association, becoming president in 1918. In the meantime, in 1915, he had moved to Welbeck Colliery at Warsop near Mansfield, and early in 1917 became the Colliery's first checkweighman. The union recognised his organising ability when they appointed him a full-time official in May 1919 and financial secretary in 1921. In the latter year the Wages Board for the Eastern Area was inaugurated and Varley became a member, subsequently attending many deputations to the Government. He served on the R.C.

on Mining Subsidence appointed in 1923, and on the Departmental Committee on Rescue Regulations appointed in the same year, and he was also a member of the Departmental Committee on Co-operative Selling in the Coal Mining Industry in 1926. In 1920 and from 1922 to 1926 he represented the Nottinghamshire miners on the MFGB executive, but he was not re-elected to the national executive by his own association in 1927, although in the following year he was elected to represent Group 5 (Nottinghamshire and South Derbyshire) on the national executive.

Varley's career from the time of the First World War parallels that of George Spencer, although he was a good deal younger than Spencer, and he died at the early age of forty-four. But during the First World War Varley became almost as well known in the Nottinghamshire coalfield as Spencer himself, and both men, with their considerable ability and great energy were in sharp contrast with the leading figure in the coalfield, the rather colourless J. G. Hancock, Lib-Lab MP for Belper. It was when Hancock was 'downgraded' from secretary to agent in 1921 that Spencer took his place as general secretary, Varley becoming financial secretary. Both Spencer and Varley at this time were moderate men of the centre; and both were to move to the right in their political and industrial attitudes in the years which followed. Varley, who was an efficient financial secretary, was in general agreement with Spencer both inside the Nottinghamshire coalfield and at national discussions. In 1925 he presented the MFGB evidence on wages to the Samuel Commission; but his moderate and compromising approach to the industrial struggles of 1926 brought him severe condemnation from many sections of the miners' movement. Varley did not go with Spencer when the latter organised the break-away Industrial Union. Spencer did not, it should be emphasised, initiate the break-away. This was done by Harry Willett, Joe Birkin and others, who had formerly been associated with the British Workers' League; and Spencer did not join the break-away until after his expulsion from the MFGB.

It has been suggested [Arnot (1961) 201] that there was bitter personal animosity between Spencer and Varley before the Industrial Union was established. Varley's family denies this story (1972); A. R. Griffin, the historian of the Nottinghamshire coalfield, has found no evidence to support the thesis, and Herbert Booth, a militant of 1926, also believes it to be untrue (1972). After Spencer's break-away, the situation was very different, and Varley certainly refused to have further dealings with Spencer. Varley remained as financial secretary to the Notts Miners' Association, and achieved a minor success in 1928 in obtaining a revision of the legal minimum rates. The Association was, however, working under very considerable difficulties, as many colliery companies dealt only with Spencer's Union. Varley continued to play some part in union affairs at national level, and in 1928 he was a member of the three-man committee set up by the MFGB executive to inquire into certain actions of A. J. Cook during the General Strike. (The other two members were Ebby Edwards and Harry Hicken, the latter absenting himself from most of the meetings [Griffin (1962), Ch. 13].)

Varley was a vigorous personality and an excellent speaker. Herbert Booth (a local Nottinghamshire militant) said that he was the only one of the Nottinghamshire officials able to hold his own with A. J. Cook in the Mansfield district during the 1926 lock-out; Mansfield being the most militant of the Nottinghamshire districts. Like so many personalities in the coalfields, Varley began early to be involved in local political affairs. He was elected to the Derbyshire CC in 1913 and served until 1919. He was active during these years within the local Labour movement, and he was elected to the Labour Party's national executive for 1921–2. In December 1923 he easily won the Mansfield seat for Labour (W. Carter having lost it in the previous year), and he retained the seat at the general election of 1924 and sat in the Commons until his death. He developed serious heart trouble in the last months of his life and died on 17 March 1929 at his Nottingham home. His funeral was at

Riddings, his birth place in Derbyshire, and he was survived by his wife, two sons and a daughter. He left effects valued at £2164.

Writings: Evidence before the R.C. on the Coal Industry [Samuel Commission] 1926 XIV, vol. 2 pt A Qs 7358–837; 'What the Owners' Terms mean to the Miner', *Soc. Rev.*, 2nd ser., no. 1 (Feb 1926) 47–50; and 'The Text of the Miners' Evidence', [Miners' plan for nationalising coal], ibid., 51–8.

Sources: *Labour Who's Who* (1927); *Dod* (1929); *WWW* (1929–40); R. Page Arnot, *The Miners: years of struggle* (1953); A. R. Griffin, *The Miners of Nottinghamshire* 2 vols: 1881–1914 (Nottingham, 1956) and 1914–1944 (1962); R. Page Arnot, *The Miners in Crisis and War* (1961); A. R. Griffin, *Mining in the East Midlands 1550–1947* (1971); biographical information: Dr A. R. Griffin; personal information: B. F. Varley, West Bridgford, Nottingham, son. Obit. *Nottingham Guardian, Nottingham J.*, and *Times*, 18 Mar 1929.

JOYCE BELLAMY
JOHN SAVILLE

See also: *Arthur James COOK, for Mining Trade Unionism, 1915–26; †George Alfred SPENCER; †William CARTER.

WARDLE, George James (1865–1947)
JOURNALIST AND LABOUR MP

George James Wardle was born on 15 May 1865 at Newhall in Derbyshire and three-and-a-half miles to the south-east of Burton-upon-Trent, the second of eight children of George Wardle, a collier (later a railway horsekeeper). He first attended a private school at Wisbech, where he received what he later described as 'a really good all round education' for 2d a week. When he was eight years old the family moved to Keighley, where Wardle served for five years as a half-timer and two years as a full-time worker in a woollen factory. He continued his education at the Wesleyan Day School in the town and on three occasions was awarded a scholarship but was unable to take advantage of the offer because his factory earnings were needed to augment the family income. Between the ages of fifteen and thirty he was employed as a clerk on the Midland Railway in Keighley. On 26 December 1889 he married Miss Atla Matilda Terry of Keighley at the Temple Street Wesleyan Chapel in the town. There were two children of the marriage, one son and one daughter. In his early manhood Wardle was a Sunday School teacher and lay preacher, but he was later 'assailed by religious doubts' and abandoned all formal connections with Methodism. He was a widely read man, being influenced in his younger days by George Dawson, Charles Kingsley and George Macdonald, and by Carlyle and Ruskin when he began to take an interest in social and labour questions.

At Keighley Wardle became one of the first railway clerks to join the local ASRS branch. He was active also in the co-operative movement, in 1897 seconding a proposal to contribute £1000 of the local society's money to the national strike fund of the engineers. From 1893 to 1897 he edited the *Keighley Labour Journal*. When the editor of the *Railway Review*, F. Maddison, resigned in December 1897, Wardle was chosen from among twenty applicants to succeed him, at a starting salary of £3 10s a week. For many years the paper flourished under his leadership. The circulation reached 40,000 copies a week, and for the first time in its history receipts from sales more than covered costs of production. As editor he gave every encouragement to the discussion in the correspondence columns of the case for independent labour representation in Parliament. At the conference of trade union and socialist bodies held in the Memorial Hall, Farringdon Street, London on 27 February 1900 he seconded Keir Hardie's amendment in favour of the establishment of 'a distinct Labour Group in Parliament'.

In May 1903 Wardle was adopted as prospective Labour Parliamentary candidate for the two-member constituency of Stockport. His selection may well have been helped by the fact that the chairman of the local Trades Council, P. J. Tevenan, was a fellow member of the ASRS. In an interview soon after his election, Wardle was insistent on the need for an independent Labour position in the new House of Commons:

What are your relations with the Liberal Party? – We shall stand by ourselves. If Liberals wish to help us we shall make no objection, provided they don't ask for any alliance. We do not intend to be swallowed up. We intend to be a distinct party, and whether hostile or friendly depends on how we are met.

Then you won't be the lamb to the Radical wolf? – Certainly not; we shall assert our independence, and uphold our principles [*Stockport Advertiser*, 29 May 1903].

In his adoption speech he advocated old age pensions, the right to work, housing reform, unsectarian education, the state control of the liquor trade, the taxation of land values and the nationalisation of the land, the mines and the railways. In the general election of January 1906 Wardle headed the poll, the only Liberal candidate being the other member returned. Wardle's victory was due partly to the large number of 'plumper' votes as well as to many votes which were split with the Conservative candidate – 'clear evidence of the presence of a number of Conservative working men' [Pelling (1967) 255].

In the Parliament of 1906–10 Wardle crossed swords with his union's general secretary, Richard Bell, who pursued an independent line often contrary to his executive's decisions. On 6 March 1907, for example, Bell voted in the opposite lobby to his two colleagues, Hudson and Wardle. On this occasion Wardle had moved an amendment to give the Board of Trade more effective power to deal with the excessive hours of labour on the railways. Bell, however, acted as one of the tellers in the Government lobby while Hudson and Wardle were tellers for the Opposition. Bell's action was designed to please the railway interest in Parliament, as his objective was to secure union recognition from the companies. On another occasion when the Great Northern, Great Central and Great Eastern Railways Bill (for an amalgamation of these companies) was presented on 31 March and 5 April 1909, the division lists show Bell voting in the opposite lobby to that of his colleagues. Bell favoured a compromise settlement with the railway directors and the Government, to safeguard the interests of the company's employees, while Wardle and the third ASRS MP Walter Hudson adhered to the union's policy of 'blocking' all railway bills until the eight-hour day had been conceded. On questions affecting the railways before 1914, Wardle always seems to have taken up a fairly advanced position. He was an early advocate of nationalisation, publishing a pamphlet on the subject in 1908; and in evidence before the S.C. on Railway Agreements and Amalgamations, Wardle used the published accounts of fourteen of the principal railway companies to show that pressure to work harder was intensified after amalgamations had taken place, and that the proportion of receipts spent on wages was decreased (27 Apr 1910). On other issues, however, Wardle soon became identified with the moderate wing of the Parliamentary Labour Party. This caused a growing opposition to him in his own constituency. Although he was once more returned at the head of the poll in Stockport in January 1910, in the election of December in the same year he yielded first place to the Liberal. By 1913 the Stockport Labour Party was seriously split over Wardle's candidature at the next general election. The BSP was taking the lead in opposing him, and as a spokesman explained to the *Stockport Advertiser* (8 Aug 1913):

We are thoroughly dissatisfied with his action over the Insurance Act, Labour Exchanges, the Bill for the Feeble-minded, and his support of the Government's action in using the military during strikes.

When the war began in August 1914 Wardle immediately adopted a patriotic attitude. In a speech at Stockport on 8 September 1914 he emphasised that the war was one for 'freedom, honour, justice, and truth'; but he went on to insist that the working class must not be alone in being called upon to make sacrifices. He associated himself with the manifesto of the Parliamentary Committee of the TUC which asked the Government 'to see to it that our future Balaclava heroes should not linger in the Work-house or doss-house, or have to hide themselves in the slums of this country'. Wardle campaigned vigorously for army recruitment, and a visit to France in 1915 only increased his ardour. He voted against the first reading of the Military Service Bill in January 1916 (which introduced conscription) and then abstained on the second reading, but his general attitude to the war was not affected, and in 1917 he was made a Companion of Honour for his recruiting services. From 1913 to 1919 he served on the executive of the Labour Party, and from 1916 he was its acting chairman. In the summer of 1917 he went to Paris with Arthur Henderson and Ramsay MacDonald, to discuss the war situation with French and Russian Socialists, and soon afterwards he was appointed parliamentary secretary to the Board of Trade. This official position in the Government led him to relinquish temporarily the editorship of the *Railway Review*, but resigned from the *Review* editorship on 31 March 1918.

When the war ended, a special conference of the Labour Party (14 Nov 1918) resolved to end all co-operation with the War Cabinet, and advised all the Party's MPs who held government office to resign. Wardle refused to comply, in company with G. N. Barnes, G. H. Roberts and James Parker. Wardle stood as a Coalition Labour candidate in the general election of December 1918, and together with the Liberal Coalition candidate was returned unopposed. When the Government was reorganised after the Coalition election victory, Wardle was appointed parliamentary secretary to the Ministry of Labour. In January 1920 the Hornsey branch of the NUR, to which he belonged, demanded his expulsion from the union for refusing to leave the Coalition Government; but the national executive refused to comply, on the grounds that he had 'ceased to exercise any influence either for or against the interest of the members'.

After the war ended Wardle gave full support to Lloyd George's National Industrial Conference, which first met on 27 February 1919. On 1 June 1919 Wardle told a Brotherhood Conference in London that he wished to see industrial unity in place of the current industrial strife. Deploring the wave of strikes then affecting Britain he warned that this would prove to be 'a blind Samson who pulls down the pillars of society'. In September of the same year he denounced the railway strike as revealing the effects of the poison of 'Bolshevism in the industrial system'.

It was not long before the strain of the war years and the immediate post-war struggles took their toll of his health. In March 1920 he resigned both his office and his seat in Parliament. In 1922 he retired to Hove where he spent the last twenty-five years of his life, taking an active part in social affairs and charities in the locality, but playing no further part in national politics. The break with his old union, the NUR, was so complete that his death, on 16 June 1947, went unnoticed in the *Railway Review*, the paper he had edited for twenty-one years. He left an estate valued at £13,995, divided between his son Reginald and his daughter Ella.

Writings: *Problems of the Age and other Poems* (1897); *The Principles of Association* (1904); *A Railway Garland* [Poems] (ed. & arranged 1904); *Railway Nationalisation* (1908); Evidence before S.C. on Railway Agreements and Amalgamations 1911 XXIX Qs 16543–914; 'The Way to Industrial Unity' in *The Industrial Future in the Light of the Brotherhood Ideal* ed. S. M. Watts (1919).

Sources: (1) MSS: Labour Party archives: LRC; (2) Other: *Railway Rev.* (1897–1918); *Cheshire County News*, 22 and 29 May 1903; *Stockport Advertiser*, 29 May 1903; 'How I got on', *Pearson's Weekly*, 22 Feb 1906; *Hansard*, 1907, 170, cols 885–923; *Hansard*, 1909, cols 441–6, 808, 843, 845–8; W. Ward, *Brotherhood and Democracy* [1910]; *Stockport Advertiser*, 8 Aug 1913; *Cheshire Daily Echo*, 8 Aug 1913; *Times*, 12 June and 25,

Aug 1917 and 28 Sep 1918; *Stockport Advertiser*, 24 Aug 1917; *WW* (1918); *Stockport Advertiser*, 20 Mar 1920; G. Alcock, *Fifty Years of Railway Trade Unionism* (1922) 297, 557, 621; G. D. H. Cole, *A History of the Labour Party from 1914* (1948); H. Pelling, *Social Geography of British Elections 1885–1910* (1967). OBIT. *Times*, 20 June 1947; *Brighton and Hove Herald*, 21 June 1947.

PHILIP BAGWELL

See also: RICHARD BELL; Walter HUDSON.

WEBB, Beatrice (1858–1943) and
WEBB, Sidney James (1859–1947)
(1st **Baron Passfield of Passfield Corner**)
WRITERS, HISTORIANS AND RESEARCH
WORKERS, SOCIOLOGISTS AND LABOUR
PROPAGANDISTS AND POLITICIANS

Although the 'Webb Partnership' did not come into being until both partners were over thirty, and when each partner had already completed a fair stint of memorable work, the change in quality of both of them after their marriage is so remarkable – as remarkable as their immense joint achievement – that it would be waste of space to try to write of them separately. 'One and one,' Sidney is reported as saying during the period of his courtship, 'when placed in a sufficiently integrated relationship, make not two but eleven', and this was if anything an understatement. There have been other notable partnerships, such as that of the Curies in physical science; but in the field of the social services and social history there has been none so long-lasting, so productive, and so influential, as that of the Webbs. It is remarkable, too, in that, though the partners were both convinced Socialists, informed continuously during their partnership by a social-democratic theory of society, their influence derived much less from any theoretical work of theirs than from its practical expression in the institutions they founded, the specific reforms they advocated and in some cases secured, and in their methods of working and securing support. The story of the Webbs is thus a large part of the social history of the Britain of their times.

The first notable fact in that story is that the two of them came from widely differing social strata. Beatrice, the senior by a year and a half, was born Beatrice Potter on 22 January 1858, at Standish House in Gloucestershire, the eighth daughter of Richard Potter and his wife Laurencina Heyworth, the daughter of a small Lancashire manufacturer who had gone up in the world. Richard Potter was himself the son of 'Radical Dick' of Tadcaster, one of a pair of brothers who had been very active in the cause of parliamentary reform; but the younger Richard had been brought up to be a gentleman of leisure, until the crisis of 1847–8 removed much of his unearned income and forced him to become an entrepreneur on an increasing scale. He made a good deal of money in the timber trade (partly by building huts for the Army during the Crimean War); he became president of the GWR and of the Grand Trunk Railway of Canada, and had his finger in many other business pies – about which Beatrice learned much when she became assistant to him. In his personal views he retained liberal leanings all his life, giving his daughters as much freedom as he would have given to his sons – no small matter at that date – and entertaining in his own home persons of very varied views and experience, a practice which proved of great value to his eighth daughter. Beatrice was a lonely, sickly and introspective child. Her mother, who, according to her daughter's account in *My Apprenticeship* 'disliked women and was destined to bear nine daughters and to lose her only son' (the ninth child, who died at three years old), had comparatively little affection for Beatrice and even less appreciation of her gifts. Beatrice, therefore, subject to frequent illnesses and insomnia – to which subsequent generations owe an immense debt for that astonishing production, *Beatrice Webb's Diaries*, which she began to keep before she was fifteen – had scarcely any formal education. She shared intermittently in her sisters' various governesses, and was for a brief while a 'parlour boarder' at a fashionable girls' school: but for the rest she was largely, in the Victorian phrase, 'brought up by servants'.

For several reasons, however, this régime was far from being the handicap it might appear. Chief among the 'servants' was her nurse, Martha Jackson (Mrs Mills, known as 'Dada'), who was a distant relative of Laurencina Heyworth on the side that had not gone up in the world. 'Dada', with her cool commonsense, was Beatrice's protector and confidante, half taking the place of a mother to her, and introducing her, as 'Miss Jones from Wales', to the social group in Lancashire from which the Heyworths sprang. The second modification was meeting and talking with the intelligent and in- quiring minds of those who came as visitors to the Potter home, and of these much the most important, in those early years, was Herbert Spencer. This crabbed and cranky philosopher really enjoyed talking with the Potter girls, Beatrice in particular; and though she came to reject his Comtist philo- sophy (though towards the end of her days she somewhat surprisingly thought she had found a new Comtist commonwealth in the U.S.S.R.), she owed a very great deal to his continued friendly interest, and in *My Apprenticeship* paid grateful tribute to how much he had taught her in the way of per- sistently seeking out and sorting facts, and still more of continuous application to a self- imposed task without care for physical dis- comforts.

In 1882 her mother died rather unex- pectedly, and as all her sisters except the youngest were married or about to be married to distinguished men she became practically head of the domestic side of the household and part-assistant to her father in some of his business dealings: when to- wards the end of 1885 he had a serious stroke her responsibilities greatly increased for the remaining four years of his life. To her widening knowledge of the world of capitalist enterprise and of London 'Society' – of which, thirty years later, she published a vivid and mordant account – there was added, simultaneously, a widening of experi- ence of quite another kind. Towards the end of 1883 she went with Martha Jackson to explore in Bacup the social life of her for- gotten relatives, and was fascinated by the life of the 'respectable working-men'

(mostly mill-hands) and by the institutions such as the chapels and co-operative societies which they had created for themselves. A few months earlier she had met for the first time Joseph Chamberlain, then at the height of his reputation as a radical social reformer – and looking for a third wife. The ambitions which he disclosed to her at many meetings from early 1884 chimed in so well with her Lancashire discoveries that she was fascin- ated, and fell deeply in love. It was generally expected that they would marry, and it was some time before Beatrice realised pain- fully that the other side of Chamberlain, particularly his desire for personal domin- ation, would be a fatal obstacle, and with- drew; but the wound went deep.

She consoled herself, in part, by looking elsewhere for a role in life, and her Bacup experiences, about which she wrote long des- criptive and reflective letters to her father, ensured that this role should be one of social investigator. At first she tried working as a visitor for the Charity Organisation Society and as rent-collector for a block of working- class flats in London dockland; but these well-meaning but piecemeal attempts at salving a few of the mass of sores created by poverty gave her little satisfaction, and in the summer of 1886 she gladly acceded to the request of her cousin, the philanthropic shipowner Charles Booth, that she should assist him in his monumental inquiry into life and labour in London. In the spring of the following year she started this work, living in an hotel in Bishopsgate while her sisters relieved her from time to time in attendance upon her father; and prepared studies of the life of dockers and their families in East London, and of sweated labour in the tailoring trade. To get material for the second of these she took (anony- mously) a series of jobs as 'a plain trouser- hand', as a result of which she was called upon to give evidence, publicly, to the House of Lords Committee on the Sweating System. By this time (1888–9), she was beginning to be convinced that the real cause of sweating and other symptoms of poverty lay in the existing economic system and was finding, in the co-operative move- ment as she had seen it first in Lancashire, some suggestion of an alternative principle. Accordingly, rejecting an adjuration by the distinguished economist Alfred Marshall that she should make herself an expert on women's labour, she began, in the spring of 1889, a task of investigation which after two years of hard and often depressing labour resulted in the publication of a little book, entitled *The Co-operative Movement in Great Britain*, by Beatrice Potter. Before then, however, two things had happened to the author. She had read a volume called *Fabian Essays in Socialism*, which introduced her to a full-blown and thought-out theory of social development; and when trying vainly to find out something about the history of working-class organisation in the past had been introduced through a friend to one of the seven Essayists, a little man 'who literally pours out information'. This was Sidney Webb.

Sidney James Webb was born on 13 July 1859 in Cranbourn Street, Leicester Square, the second son of Charles Webb, a 'public accountant', himself son of a Kentish publican of radical views, and his wife Elizabeth Mary (née Stacey), who ran a small ladies' dressmaking and hairdressing business. There were three children in all, and the family was definitely lower middle-class: Beatrice, when she first visited them, was obviously surprised by their modest standard of living and the absence of ambition or emulation. The elder Webb was one of the committee-men for John Stuart Mill; and this may have played its part in deciding the political opinions of the son, for it is only a short step from the ideas of Mill in his later years to the Fabian Socialism which, combined with an almost romantic love of London, as a city, became the moving force of Webb's life.

After elementary school, the boy finished his education at the City of London School and the Birkbeck Institute, supplementing this with some study abroad in Switzerland and Mecklenburg-Schwerin; but in 1875 he had to go to work as a clerk in the City office of a firm of colonial brokers. Attending evening classes meanwhile, in 1878 he sat the open examination for the civil service, which his phenomenal memory enabled him

to pass with ease; and having entered the service as a second division clerk in the War Office, he rose rapidly until in 1881 he reached the Colonial Office as a first division clerk. But he did not intend to devote his life to bureaucracy; he read for the Bar in Grays Inn, becoming in 1885 an LL.B of the University of London, saved money from his salary and from slow-growing journalistic earnings, and had already left the civil service the year before his marriage to a lady with £1000 a year of her own made it unnecessary to seek other paid employment. Long before that, however – in 1879 – he had met, in a debating club in Central London calling itself the Zetetical Society, a struggling young red-bearded journalist named Bernard Shaw.

Shaw, who had joined the Zetetical Society in order to get practice in public speaking – he was already on the fringe of several anarchist and semi-socialist groupings – very quickly realised the great potential value to him and other propagandists of Webb's remarkably exact memory for facts and his gift for tearing the relevant heart out of any document presented to him. According to his own statement (*Sixteen Self-Sketches*, p. 65), 'Quite the wisest thing I ever did was to force my friendship on him . . . for the difference between Shaw with Webb's brains, knowledge, and official experience and Shaw by himself was enormous'. They became firm friends, going on several holidays together; and in the early eighties Shaw took his friend along to a meeting of the little newly-formed Fabian Society which he himself had joined at its third meeting. By 1885 the two of them were members of the Society's tiny executive committee; and two years later Webb produced his first (unsigned) Fabian pamphlet, *Facts for Socialists*. The combination of Shaw's command of the English language with Webb's extraordinary memory for facts and instinct for organisation can scarcely be overstressed; it accounts in great part for the influence of the Fabian Society, in the first half of its life, on English society. The practical bent of Webb's mind can be observed in the Fabian Tract, *How to Deal With Unemployment*, which he and Frank

Podmore (the biographer of Robert Owen) persuaded the Society to publish in 1886, and in the various lists which the Society brought out of pertinent questions for Fabians to put to persons seeking election to local governing bodies of all kinds; but no great publicity reached them until in 1889 a set of lectures given at the end of the previous year by seven members of the Society was published under the title *Fabian Essays in Socialism* – and immediately became a best-seller. Shaw wrote two of the essays as well as the preface, and tidied up those of some of his fellow-essayists. Webb's contribution was called *Historic*; it is a fairly straightforward exposition, in non-Marxist language, of how the development of society at this stage of history demands its organisation on Socialist lines, and how, in fact, this is happening in many quarters in a piecemeal sort of fashion.

It was a year later that Webb, who had read with interest the first volume of Charles Booth's *Survey* and had noted in his review of it that 'the only contributor with any literary talent is Miss Beatrice Potter', found his assistance solicited by that same contributor, and responded at their first meeting with 'a list of sources swiftly drafted, then and there, in a faultless handwriting'. He continued with eager correspondence, which before very long turned into definite courtship; but it was a long time before Beatrice could get over the disappointment of her former love sufficiently to realise that in the scruffy little person, with the large head and tiny feet, the spectacles and the shiny suits, she had met the man whose gifts of patience, meticulous accuracy, imperturbable intellectual conviction and deep unwavering love were exactly what she needed to complement her own qualities and allay her internal doubts. They had met first in January of 1890: in the Whitsun following, at a Co-operative Congress in Glasgow, 'two Socialists came to a working compact'. But though they corresponded and collaborated a good deal, it was not until the summer of the following year that they became definitely engaged, and even then it had to be kept a secret, except from close friends, as long as Richard

Potter lived. He died on New Year's Day, 1892; and the August issue of *Fabian News* came out with the laconic announcement that 'Sidney Webb was married on 23rd ult. to Beatrice Potter'. For their honeymoon they decided to go to Glasgow and Dublin to study early trade union organisation.

On their return, after a short interval, they set up house on the Westminster Embankment in 41 Grosvenor Road (later Millbank), the house which H. G. Wells was to make so famous or infamous in *The New Machiavelli* – the site is now occupied by the tall building of Millbank Towers. The routine of their joint lives was quickly established. In the mornings they worked together on their research and writing-up of the material for the history and nature of British Trade Unionism, the first fruits being the two great books, *The History of Trade Unionism* (1894), and *Industrial Democracy* (1897), in which, it was said, they not only studied but all but invented the characteristic organs of the British working class. In the afternoons Beatrice rested, and Sidney occupied himself partly with executive committee duties with the Fabian Society – in which Beatrice, though a self-confessed Socialist since the beginning of 1890, was for some years a comparatively passive member – but much more with the London County Council, to which he had been elected, in the year of his marriage, as Progressive member for Deptford, after a campaign in which much of the ammunition had been provided by leaflets and pamphlets issued by the Fabian Society and prepared, according to Edward Pease, its part-time secretary, largely by Webb himself.

Webb held his LCC seat until March 1910, when he 'quietly stepped out', having survived the 1907 débâcle of the Progressive Party. But though he did general duty by serving on over a dozen committees and helping to beat off the end-of-the-century endeavour of the Conservative Party to destroy the LCC and divide up its area into a number of large boroughs, his main effort in public life was devoted not, as might well have been expected, to the extension of municipal enterprise and muncipal trading, but to the service of education. Immediately after his election he was made chairman of the Technical Education Board, which had in its charge, *inter alia*, the spending of the 'whiskey money' which had accrued three years earlier to the newly-created County Councils. These funds he persuaded the LCC to use for the promotion of post-elementary education in London – elementary education, until the Act of 1903, being still in the hands of the London School Board. This was accomplished largely by the method of 'pump-priming', under which the chairman of the Board, ably assisted by brilliant subordinates like William (later Sir William) Garnett and W. R. Lethaby and (outside the LCC Service) by Sir Arthur Acland and Hubert Llewellyn Smith, used its modest funds to support and influence the work of existing institutions, secondary schools, technical colleges etc., in preference to the much more expensive policy of setting up rival bodies of its own. The most important of these subventions was the small grant given to the Polytechnic in Regent Street, put through by the joint efforts of Webb and his Moderate (i.e. Conservative) colleague on the Council, Quintin Hogg the Polytechnic's founder – though, it should be remembered, the grant was fiercely opposed by John Burns, who thought that the directors of City companies who sat on the Polytechnic's Board could well finance whatever was required by cutting down their own banqueting expenses. The grant, however, survived, was extended to other Polytechnics and 'aided' institutions, and grew gradually to the millions of pounds which in the London of today finance the non-university institutions of higher education. When, under the 1903 Education Act, the County Council became the sole education authority for London, under the national scheme foreshadowed by Webb in a Fabian Tract, *The Education Muddle and the Way Out*, the Technical Education Board became the Technical Education Committee, and Webb continued his efforts. An intensive scholarship scheme was instituted; and to accommodate the scholars 'maintained' county grammar schools were established in addition to the 'aided' ones – a provision which produced considerable difficulties

sixty and seventy years later, when a Labour controlled County Council was endeavouring to put into effect its comprehensive school policy. But at the time the sharp differences which developed between Webb and some of his colleagues, notably Graham Wallas, were not over that, but over the abolition of the *ad hoc* London School Board with its impressive record of achievement and, more fundamentally, over the decision on a national scale to prop up the denominational schools, Anglican and Roman Catholic particularly, with hand-outs of ratepayers' money. Webb answered the arguments against this policy by saying that as it was clearly impracticable for the public authorities to take over and run the hundreds of schools in that category, a refusal of aid could only mean that thousands of children would have to continue to attend grossly inferior schools: his stand nevertheless lost him the support of the Nonconformists in the Progressive Party.

His interest in higher education had not stopped at the grants to the Polytechnics. He had joined, round about the turn of the century, with R. B. Haldane, Q.C., in the agitation which transformed the University of London from a mainly examining body into a real educational institution, a federation of colleges and schools of the university; but his greatest single contribution was the foundation of the London School of Economics and Political Science, modelled in part on the famous Écoles Polytechniques of Paris. The means for this came to his hand in 1894 when an eccentric Fabian, Henry Hutchinson, died leaving the bulk of his estate, amounting to ten thousand pounds, to trustees, including Webb himself, for the purpose of furthering the objects of the Fabian Society. This information came to Webb while on holiday with Graham Wallas and Bernard Shaw; and he and his wife quickly decided that it would be folly to give to the Society itself the money to play with; but that half the sum should be devoted to setting up an institution of university standard aimed at 'curing the economic ignorance of the capital', the rest going to pay salaries and expenses of travelling lecturers on Fabian Socialism. When this decision – not the text of the will itself – was communicated to the Fabian executive, that body raised no objection, though Bernard Shaw in the following year wrote an angry private letter of protest, and Ramsay Mac-Donald did his best, subsequently, to sabotage the activities through his position on the LCC. Webb, however, took no notice except privately to 'take counsel's opinion' on whether his actions were legally justifiable. Counsel – R. B. Haldane – inquired whether he really believed that his actions would forward the course of Fabian Socialism, and being assured on that point advised him to go ahead, which he did; that he was not too confident about the possible attitude of the world at large may be gathered from the fact that he persuaded his fellow-trustees to vote that minutes and records of the proceedings of the Hutchinson Trust should be kept secret until all the original trustees were dead. This condition was not fulfilled until Edward Pease died in 1955; and it was only in 1963 that Sir Sydney Caine studied the opened archives and produced his brief *History of the Foundation of the London School of Economics*, which informed its readers in full detail of the remarkable, not to say Machiavellian series of manoeuvres and expedients which Webb used to get the School going and to help it over its early years – they included, for example, the appointment of a Tory (afterwards to be Chamberlain's assistant in the Tariff Reform campaign) as its first Director, the securing of recognition from the reformed London University and of a cheap site from the LCC during the development of the Kingsway/ Aldwych area, the discovery of a legal loophole which enabled the School to escape the payment of rates, the recruitment of classes from the Chamber of Commerce and the railway companies as well as direct subventions from the Technical Education Board and individual subscriptions from sympathisers such as the rich Irishwoman who became Mrs Bernard Shaw – and a host of others.

Webb himself was chairman of the governors, and so remained until in 1912, perceiving that a speech he had made advocating nationalisation of railways was having an adverse effect on the attitude of the railway companies, he resigned and thereafter held only the post of Professor of Public Administration (unpaid) which he retained until 1927. On the whole story it may be observed (1) that the LSE is the only institution of university standing in the country which was built up from scratch without any initial capital endowment whatsoever; (2) that this would have been quite impossible had the Fabian Society, or even the word Fabian, been openly associated with it; and (3) that nevertheless, and notwithstanding the fact that only a few of the lecturers employed by it have been convinced Socialists, it seems to have produced from its student body a larger proportion of Socialists than any other comparable college. So far was Webb's confident pledge to Haldane justified; with the result that though the Webbs never interfered with the running of the School even on occasions when they disagreed with its policy, it remained, as Lord Beveridge frequently observed, their favourite child.

Alongside all these activities, the Partnership proper was completing its study of trade unions, and moving on to that much vaster enterprise, the history and anatomy of local government in England from 1688 onwards. They started work on this in 1899, preceding it with a 'voyage of discovery' – on which they were accompanied by the young Charles Trevelyan – through the major cities of the United States, going on to visit also Australia and New Zealand. (The Diaries of these expeditions were published in separate volumes after their deaths.) On their return they followed this by short intensive fact-finding and interviewing tours in various parts of England and Wales; and the task proved so large that it was six years before the first book, on *The Parish and the County* appeared, to be followed two years later by the two volumes of *The Manor and the Borough*. By this time the Poor Law Commission and the battle with H. G. Wells in the Fabian Society, both of which are chronicled below, were in full swing; and the work on local government therefore slowed down; but it never ceased altogether. Book after book came out to join the corpus, one of the most seminal being *Statutory Authorities for Special Purposes*, which under an unappetising title described some of the most historically important institutions, hitherto almost unknown to historians, which had grown up in the century before the Reform Act.

This shift of emphasis marked the end for the time being of the close connections with the institutions of the working class – trade unions and co-operative societies and their members and officials – which Beatrice had made with such pleasure in the years before her marriage, and which had been kept up while they were at work on their first two books. Beatrice had confided to her diary a thought that the Webbs might perhaps come to be 'clerks to Labour'; but that consummation proved to be a long way off. For political Labour – such as there was then – they, particularly Beatrice, had little use; she was highly critical of John Burns, the most prominent among the leaders, and she had little but scorn for the vocal Socialists like Keir Hardie, MacDonald, and H. M. Hyndman. When the Labour Representation Committee was formed in 1900, Sidney sent the faithful Pease to represent the Fabian Society in its deliberations; the Webbs scarcely seemed to know it was there. At the same time, they found themselves having little in common with the radical wing of the Liberal Party: they thought nothing of Campbell-Bannerman, and never got on terms with either Lloyd George or Asquith – Beatrice having a strong personal dislike for Margot; their choice among Liberal politicians was the group of the 'Limps', notably Haldane and Edward Grey, and Beatrice had most pleasure in meetings with an old friend of hers, the Tory Arthur Balfour. So, about the turn of the century and in the few years following, the Webbs moved in the direction of middle- and upper-class society of the kind she had known in her girlhood, and discussed in small select dinner-parties the policy of a 'consensus approach' to questions of social and political reform, under which (so ran Beatrice's unspoken assumption) the leaders of either party would be judiciously guided by Fabians or Fabian sympathisers sitting at

their right hands. This policy, which is most nearly exemplified in the story of the 1902-3 Education Acts, came to be known as 'permeation'. Whatever its abstract merits, it is clearly not practicable where emotional issues are at stake, as was made plain at the time of the South African war: the Webbs were bored with the propaganda and agreed with the Fabian Society's decision to say nothing publicly either way – though Beatrice did presciently remark to her diary that neither side in the battle cared twopence about the natives of South Africa, she never seems to have followed up the thought.

But the 'permeaters' were wrong. They failed altogether to observe the tide of radicalism that was rising in the country as a whole, and they were taken aback when the election of January 1906 overwhelmed Tories and 'Limps' alike – and affronted when a ripple in that tide, in the person of H. G. Wells with a supporting cast of new members, appeared in the Fabian Society and threatened the Old Guard. This was a particular disappointment for the Webbs, because they themselves had personally recruited Wells in 1902, when he was newly turned from a popular novelist and writer of science fiction to a social reformer and prophet of Utopia. Beatrice was especially intrigued with the book of essays on future developments which he called *Anticipations*, and with his suggestions for drastic reform of English local government – he had just had an acrimonious dispute with his local borough council. She also enjoyed discussing with him theories of society, a pastime which left her husband cold: Sidney, having once and for all decided the main tenets of his own belief, viz. that the goal was the Benthamite one of the greatest happiness of the greatest number, that this goal could be achieved by the reorganisation of society on Socialist, non-profit making lines, and, further, that the world is in fact moving in the direction of Socialism – all this is contained in his contribution to *Fabian Essays* – felt no need to go on discussing philosophic problems; it was mostly waste of time and energy. All that was needed, since the *Zeitgeist* was on the side of the Fabians, was to assist the *Zeitgeist* by reiterating in plain language the merits of Socialism, by devising intelligent plans for speeding up transition, and above all by collecting and publishing the established *facts* about the existing system, which could scarcely fail, once they were clearly set out, to convince any ordinary intelligent person of the necessity for change. *Facts for Socialists*, the Fabian Tract which Sidney Webb completed in 1887, and which was many times revised and reissued thereafter, is the first and clearest example of this technique.

Wells, however, was not long to remain contented as a disciple of the Webbs. He did not find their style of life, which might perhaps be described as dedicated semi-austerity, attractive; still less did he like their conviction of rightness when it manifested itself in the organisation and instruction, not always too tactfully, of other people. Moreover, sharing in the flush of radicalism and adventure which was producing the great new Liberal majority, he found the Fabian Society not inspiring, but shabby, depressing, and mean-spirited. In 1906, at a private meeting of members, he came out with a vigorous diatribe which he called *The Faults of the Fabian*, in which he made all these accusations, and demanded that the Society should cease to ignore the great and vivid world in which it lived, should use its imagination, open out on a large scale, publish exciting books and pamphlets, and generally make a splash in society. His specific proposals were largely impracticable for a small organisation with no large revenue resources and after a struggle lasting about a year and a half he was finally defeated, largely, as he much later admitted to his own *Experiment in Autobiography*, through his own fault. He lacked altogether the competence of Shaw and Webb in debate; nor had he the patience or perseverance needed in order to organise into effective rebellion the very large support and sympathy he commanded among members of the Society itself, particularly those who joined from the left-wing ranks of the Liberals. When he resigned, the limit of his success, apart from some minor administrative changes, was in forcing the Fabian Society openly to declare itself in favour of

equal rights for women. This came about when Shaw reported to the executive that the members of the Women's Group were going to vote for Wells's proposals in a body if it were not done, and the executive hurriedly gave way; it is ironical that this victory more or less coincided with Wells's making a 'dishonest woman' of the young daughter of a prominent Fabian who was also a personal friend of the Webbs. This episode, described fictionally by its leading character in the novel *Ann Veronica*, hardly endeared Wells to the Webbs: but he was much more resentful of his defeat, and revenged himself in 1911 in that rather long-winded political novel *The New Machiavelli*, which contains a savage caricature of Beatrice and Sidney (under the name of Bailey) in their 'hard little house on the Embankment', weaving spiders' webs for the spiritual destruction of rising young politicians. The picture was manifestly unfair; but it expressed a good part of the impression of the Webbs which the Wells episode had left in the minds of the young, and contributed to some of the difficulties they encountered in the years just before the war. But for the moment they had other interests to distract them.

The distraction was the Poor Law Commission, and the subsequent campaign. Late in 1905, the Tory Government, as almost its last act, had decided to appoint a Royal Commission with the purpose of bringing some order into the administration of the Poor Laws, which had got into a sad state of chaos, as social changes – including the growth of humanitarianism – induced various Boards of Guardians to depart in different ways from the stern principles laid down in Chadwick's Act of seventy years before. It was not very surprising that Balfour invited his old friend Mrs Sidney Webb, in view of the work she had been so deeply engaged in during the past few years, to serve on the Commission; and it was possibly natural that Mr James Davy, the recently-appointed head of the Poor Law division of the Local Government Board, should confide to the society lady his plans to induce the Commission, by means of a stream of witnesses provided from his own staff, to recommend a definite nation-wide return to 'the principles of 1834', of which the chief was the insistence that the lot of the pauper should invariably be harsher than that of the worst-off person not in receipt of relief. This fortunate indiscretion enabled Beatrice to make her own plans. She aimed at forcing the Commission to set up its own inquiries, call its own evidence, and produce a revolutionary report calling for an entirely new treatment of the problem of poverty leading to destitution, based on the principle of prevention at root and the establishment of what she and Sidney called a National Standard of Civilised Life.

She had some initial success, in that the Commission did agree to cast its net a good deal wider, and to work its members a great deal harder than they can have anticipated; they heard much evidence and studied many memoranda, some of them provided or instigated by Beatrice herself, employing secretarial assistance partly paid for by Charlotte Shaw. But in her major purpose she failed; and by the end of 1907 she had realised that for all her efforts and machinations – of which *Our Partnership* gives long and lively accounts – she was not going to induce a Commission composed largely of administrators of the existing laws and of members of the Charity Organisation Society like C. S. Loch its secretary, and Octavia Hill, one of its founders, to support so large a dose of 'collectivism' as she was suggesting. Accordingly, she set out to draft a Minority Report which was signed eventually by herself, George Lansbury, the Reverend Russell Wakefield, and Francis Chandler of the Carpenters' Union. This Report, putting the responsibility for destitution and unemployment squarely upon the shoulders of the nation as a whole, and formulating a full and detailed scheme of 'social security' which anticipated by a quarter of a century the Beveridge Report, and in some ways went beyond it, was separately published in cheap form by the Fabian Society (after a brush about copyright law in which Webb and Haldane successfully challenged the Treasury), and immediately became front-page news. The Reports, Majority and Minority, came out in February 1909; but

by the summer Beatrice was presiding over a tearing propaganda campaign, run by a body later known as the National Committee for the Prevention of Destitution, in which persons of all parties played active parts, to force the Government to adopt the Minority Report. Beatrice, plunging at fifty-one years old into directing and organising on a wide scale, enjoyed it immensely – for fuller details see *Our Partnership* and Joan Simeon Clarke's chapter in *The Webbs and their Work*; and notwithstanding the opposition of John Burns at the Local Government Board the agitation looked very formidable until Lloyd George, learning from German experience, succeeded in passing the Insurance Acts of 1911 through Parliament. At once the Liberals and Tories who had supported the NCPD found their views satisfied with this offer of 'contributory' insurance, and, as Beatrice admitted, 'all the steam went out' of the campaign. 'Permeation' on a national scale had failed; and the Webbs, who never cried over spilt milk, shut down the campaign and went on a world tour, beginning to meditate on the possibility of permeating the Labour Party – 'a poor thing, but our own' – mainly by means of the Fabian Society.

On returning from their tour, however, the Webbs found the Society much less of an amenable tool than they had thought. As Shaw had warned Beatrice, the spirit of Wellsian radicalism and the general 'unrest' of those years was very manifest among its members, and there was more than one 'revolt', the last of which, the Guild Socialist movement led by G. D. H. Cole and William Mellor of the Oxford Fabian Society and joined by many other young university Socialists and others – its theory was first developed by S. G. Hobson and A. R. Orage in the *New Age* – came within an ace of capturing the Society and might well have done so but for the outbreak of war. The Webbs had set up a Fabian Research Committee, whose purpose, according to their idea, was to work out a detailed programme for the Labour Party to adopt, and incidentally to dispose of the Syndicalism which was gaining so much ground among the articulate members of the working class and of intellectuals in revolt against the 'soulless bureaucracy' of Fabian Collectivist thought. Guild Socialism, which sought to combine social ownership of capital resources with control by the organised workers of their day-to-day working, made a strong appeal, which became much stronger as the necessities of wartime increased so enormously the effective power of the working classes, of their unions and their committees of shop stewards; Guild Socialists took over and manned the Research Committee, which eventually hived itself off as the independent Labour Research Department.

The Webbs were distressed, not to say cross, at this development; but they were not concerned seriously to oppose it. *Revanche* was never their policy; and they had other fish to be frying. A year before the war they had succeeded in founding an independent weekly journal, the *New Statesman*, to which they appointed as editor Clifford Sharp, their lieutenant in the Poor Law campaign; and in the remarkable series of *New Statesman Supplements* they caused to be published studies by themselves and others of the problems of the day. Their own contributions included one on *State and Municipal Enterprise* and two on *Co-operative Production* and *The Co-operative Movement*: in two others they hired Leonard Woolf to work out one of the first blueprints for a League of Nations. The *New Statesman*, greatly as its character has changed over the years, has proved one of the most lasting of the Webbs' creations: outside it Sidney, in the book *How to Pay for the War* (1916) set out a comprehensive programme of collectivisation almost all of which has since been put into effect.

Meantime, they were becoming 'clerks to Labour' in more ways than one. Two days after the declaration of war, Sidney was made an adviser to the vast coalition of all the main working-class bodies (including the National Union of Teachers) which was known by the clumsy title of 'War Emergency Workers' National Committee'; and a year later, as Fabian representative on the Labour Party Executive, he became officially part of the Committee itself and so was

brought into continuous collaboration with Arthur Henderson, leader of the party during MacDonald's temporary eclipse. The original aim of the Committee was to protect the working class against war inroads upon its standard of living, and within a week of its formation Webb had prepared for it a pamphlet, *The War and the Workers*, which anonymously gave advice and instructions to local committees all over the country; and as the war went on and the immediate problems grew both in number and intensity he consolidated his position among his colleagues by a stream of memoranda, recommendations, and other behind-the-scenes activity until such event as the curt dismissal of Henderson from the War Cabinet and the revolution in Russia had convinced Henderson that Labour must take the field as a serious Party on its own instead of working mainly as a pressure group. In 1917–18 Webb was called upon to assist in drawing up a new constitution for the Party – operative, with only minor alterations, for the next fifty-five years, to help draft the statement of 'Labour's War Aims', and to write, single-handed, the first and by far the most definite statement of Labour policy in general, adopted under the title *Labour and the New Social Order*. In all this, Beatrice played no part but that of hostess and helpmate, feeling from time to time slightly resentful of the way in which the Labour men appeared to take all Sidney's work for granted. She was more affected than he was by the slaughter, which engulfed some of the sons of her sisters and her friends; but recovering after a short breakdown, she served upon some of the committees generated by the vast and ill-fated Ministry of Reconstruction, and also on the War Cabinet committee on Women in Industry – deriving from the last-named information sufficient to produce another minority report, published in book form as *The Wages of Men and Women – Should They Be Equal?* It is still a minor classic. Sidney, for his part, was serving on the government committee on Trusts and Profiteering.

By the time the war ended, Sidney was high in the counsels of the Labour Party, and in the 1918 election actually stood as

Labour candidate for the University of London, where energetic electioneering work obtained for him a very respectable vote, until a last-minute effort by alarmed Tories brought about his defeat, rather to his own, and greatly to his wife's relief. His great public triumph, however, came a few months later, after the appointment of the Royal Commission on the Coal Mines, presided over by Mr Justice Sankey. Webb had been selected by the Miners' Federation as one of their three outside experts (the others were R. H. Tawney and Sir Leo Chiozza Money); and on the impressive stage of the Chamber of the House of Lords he made hay with the statistics and economic arguments of the mineowners and their experts. The Sankey Commission, with its penetrating cross-examinations and its disclosures about the social conditions in the industry, created enormous excitement, especially when a majority of the Commission declared itself in favour of nationalisation, and it was recalled that Bonar Law, the Leader of the House, had undertaken to carry out the recommendations of the Commission 'in the spirit and to the letter'. The miners were very grateful to their champions; and in Webb's case showed it by helping to put him at the head of the poll for the Labour Party's Executive in 1919; and then by inviting him to stand for Parliament as one of their sponsored candidates. After some hesitation, he agreed, and in the election of 1922 was returned by an immense majority for Seaham Harbour in Durham, which he held without difficulty in the two subsequent elections. He, and still more Beatrice, were delighted with their constituency and their constituents: he had written for them in 1921 a brief *History of the Durham Miners*, while she ran classes for the miners and their wives – which she called to their great pleasure 'The University of Seaham' – sent them a whole library of books and entertained them on visits to London. For several years she thus revived the direct contacts with individual working men and women which she had known in the long-ago years before and after her marriage: it was an altogether happier experiment than her London 'Half-Circle Club' in which she endeavoured, with the best intentions but with a certain amount of rather heavy-handed tactlessness, to 'groom' the wives of leading trade unionists and rising Labour politicians to fit them to hold their own in middle-class society. By 1923 the Webb prestige and influence stood high; and it was in that year when they were negotiating for the house in Hampshire – Passfield Corner – which became their home in the years of retirement, that Sidney, as chairman of the Labour Party, delivered to its annual conference the presidential address which contained the famous phrase, 'the inevitability of gradualness'.

It is difficult, fifty years later, to see quite why this speech caused such a furore. Ever since the early catastrophic revolutionism of Owenite trade unionism and the physical-force Chartists had gone down to destruction, the mood and practice of the British working class and of the unions which were the main support of the Labour Party had been 'gradualist' to a degree; and Webb, in pointing out that 'for Labour, Socialism is rooted in political Democracy, which necessarily compels us to recognise that every step towards our goal is dependent upon gaining the assent and support of at least a numerical majority of the whole people', must have thought he was merely stating the obvious. 'Why', he asked almost plaintively, 'because we are idealists, should we be supposed to be idiots?' It was as simple as that: but though the post-war boom had broken, the realities of depression and unemployment had not yet bitten so hard into the consciousness of organised labour as to darken its high hopes, and Webb's words came as a cold shock, were ill received and long quoted against him.

This episode is indicative of the fact that the peak of the achievements of the Partnership was reached in 1923. At the time, and even for some while afterwards, this would have seemed a curious judgement. Without taking account of the Labour governments still to come, the world would have observed that the Webbs had managed to combine much serious writing with their political activities. They had continued their series on local government; in 1920 they had published a revised edition of *The History of*

Trade Unionism which made some concessions to their Guild Socialist critics, and in the following year a large descriptive and critical study of *The Consumers' Co-operative Movement* (to which the co-operative movement paid practically no attention). In 1920, also, in *A Constitution for the Socialist Commonwealth of Great Britain*, they had produced their only contribution to utopia-building – a remarkably dry collection of administrative schematics; and in 1923 a much more lively and well-written indictment of the existing system which, under the title *The Decay of Capitalist Civilisation*, was largely a plea to their countrymen to 'choose equality and flee greed'. But disillusionment was beginning.

Partly, their disillusionment was with Parliament and the Labour movement. They did not find the Labour MPs admirable at close quarters; Sidney's attendances in Parliament broke up the pattern of life and work which had existed since their marriage, and at over sixty they were too old to relish change. Sidney was not a success in debate, nor as a minister. As President of the Board of Trade in 1924, he performed adequately a somewhat routine job, combining it with other oddments which he described in a long private memorandum on the first Labour Government printed in the *Political Quarterly* for January 1961. But as Colonial Secretary (see below) he distinguished himself less. Outside Parliament, they sympathised not at all with the General Strike of 1926 and the attitude of the miners' leaders – this eventually cost Sidney his seat on the Labour executive – and Beatrice observed the growth of what she called 'creed-autocracies' in Russia and Italy, and contrasted them with the absence of fervour and dedicated leadership in the Labour ranks. Sidney gave up his candidature for Seaham; and they had all but decided to retire from political life when the Labour victory of 1929 caused MacDonald to ask Sidney to go to the House of Lords and from there run the Colonial Office. There he was not a success, as he himself admitted. He took some useful decisions – set out in Sir Drummond Shiels' contribution to *The Webbs and Their Work*, and laid the foundations for the 1931

Statute of Westminster; but in dealing with the coloured populations of the Empire, particularly in East Africa, he relied too much upon the advice of 'experienced' civil servants, and showed little understanding of the emotional libertarianism of either the native leaders or their English champions like Roden Buxton and Norman Leys. In Palestine, however, where trouble began right from the start with the riots at the Wailing Wall, he bears responsibility less than the terms of the Mandate itself and the attitude of the Foreign Office and the military authorities thereto. Late in 1930 Palestinian affairs were taken out of the control of the Colonial Secretary; Webb might well have resigned, but decided to stand by the Government.

In the mid-twenties, Beatrice's energies were deeply occupied, first with the unique opening volume of autobiography which she called *My Apprenticeship* and then with the preparation of the three books on the Poor Law which concluded the local government series. After that she had little to do which she counted worth while, and her attention was attracted more and more to events in Soviet Russia. She became friendly with Sokolnikov, the ambassador, and his wife, who prescribed and lent her reading matter, and in response to the questions she asked urged her continually to go and see for herself. After the fall of the Labour Government and the subsequent election, both of which they received sadly but without much surprise, the Webbs yielded to this urging and their own impulses and, having completed their book on *Methods of Social Study*, they arrived in Leningrad in May 1932, to be received, as Sidney noticed with some surprise, as 'a kind of minor royalty'. They were both over seventy years old.

They stayed for some months in the U.S.S.R.; and three years later, after Sidney had made a further 'checking-up' visit, they published, in *Soviet Communism: a new civilisation?*, the most immense political guidebook in the world.

Their verdict was almost entirely favourable, as G. D. H. Cole had predicted, though he did not then know that, long before they had even left their own country, Beatrice had confided to her diary a forecast of what their findings would be – that the framework of society in post-revolutionary Russia bore a close resemblance to that which in their *Constitution* they had advocated for Britain, informed, however, by 'the religion of Humanity' and directed by 'a religious order, the Communist Party with its strict disciplines, its vows of obedience and poverty'. Substantially, these were the views expressed in the book when it appeared, with the addition of a belief, confidently stated, that the features of Soviet society which they criticised, such as the suppression of adverse opinion, would disappear in time. They made efforts, as everyone who has read their book through will realise, to check their information, and to study the statements of opponents of the régime; and the book was very far from being a straight encomium. But the conclusions were settled in advance: the Webbs, as they themselves freely admitted, 'fell in love with the Soviet Union', and to those who visited Passfield Corner in the years following their return it sometimes seemed as though that country meant more to them than anything else in the world.

This was not quite the case. They were in retirement from politics: in Sidney's case this was made definite by a stroke which he suffered in March 1938, from which he never altogether recovered. But they continued to feel and to express a lively and continuing interest in current affairs and in the personalities of the Labour movement. Beatrice wrote in her diary more voluminously, and completed the preparation of *Our Partnership*, the autobiographical volume published after her death; she broadcast with effect, and in 1939 accepted the presidency of a Fabian Society revived and reconstituted under the leadership of G. D. H. Cole and a number of other Socialists, including both former Guildsmen and members of future Labour administrations. They sought and received many visitors. Passfield Corner became a place of resort and pilgrimage for inquirers and admirers from many countries as well as for their own relatives and personal friends, who enjoyed the long hours of political conversation and reminiscence.

Beatrice died, after a short illness, on 30 April 1943 and her ashes were buried in the wood at Passfield Corner. After her death, the Order of Merit was conferred upon Lord Passfield in specific recognition of the work of the Partnership. He died on 13 October 1947, and in December of that year, after a campaign led by Bernard Shaw, the ashes of both Partners were reinterred beneath the flags of Westminster Abbey.

The Webbs, as already mentioned, formed a partnership nearly unique, in its combination of serious research with practical action. On the research side, their work was careful and thorough; and with the notable exception of *Soviet Communism*, none of their big books show signs of *a priori* thinking: they explored regions of social institutions such as trade unionism which had never before their time been thought worthy of serious study. As a consequence, though the books they produced have naturally dated as later writers followed their pioneers, they have never lost their status as classics indispensable to social historians. In the realm of institutions, their work has proved even more lasting, the London School of Economics being only the largest of their surviving 'children'; even where the institution has changed a good deal from its original form, the stamp of the Webbs has remained on it – largely if paradoxically owing to the fact that they never tried seriously to stand in the way of its development.

On abstract political theory they wrote little, and even on planning for a Socialist society their views must, apart from one book which stands alone [*A Constitution for the Socialist Commonwealth of Great Britain* (1920)], be sought in such *parerga* as Beatrice's *Minority Report* (largely drafted, in fact, by Sidney) and the anonymous pamphlet *Labour and the New Social Order*. But those views, and the actions which they recommended to all thinking persons of their day, are clearly apparent in a whole host of lesser publications, signed or unsigned, and strengthened on their first appearance by the known personality of the Partnership. For Sidney and Beatrice Webb were not dim or cloistered creatures: their chosen pattern of life, their personal values, their preferences in 'leisure-time' occupation and spending, even their social manners – these were as well-known as their opinions, and as such find constant reference in memoirs and histories of the period. Admiration and dislike are both to be found in these accounts; but on one thing at least there is general agreement. The Webbs were among the most generous of social thinkers; they showed no rancour towards those who had opposed or frustrated them; they never claimed credit for what they had not done or denied it to others; and they were perennially interested in and helpful to the efforts and progress of their successors in the field. This fact, in addition to their own achievements, has helped to keep their memory alive and ever controversial forty years after their active career ended.

The Webbs had no children. This was a deliberate decision, reached partly out of consideration for Beatrice's health. It will be remembered that childbed was in 1892 a much more risky place than it subsequently became; but in later life Beatrice, watching with some envy the progress of the very numerous progeny of her eight sisters, occasionally wondered whether it had been a right decision. Their estate, proved at £59,419 on the death of Sidney Webb, was left to a trust for the promotion of social research, the Fabian Society and the London School of Economics both being referred to by name. A Memorial Fund for Beatrice Webb, raised immediately after her death, was eventually spent on purchasing a residential centre for weekend and summer schools, etc., on the Surrey hills near Dorking, called Beatrice Webb House.

MARGARET COLE

Writings: A comprehensive record of the writings of Beatrice and Sidney Webb is available in the Webb Coll., British Library of Political and Economic Science, LSE, and the BLPES are planning to publish *An Interim Check-list of the Publications of Sidney Webb, Baron Passfield and Beatrice Webb, formerly Potter*. The lists which follow indicate their major works, separately and then jointly, together with a selection of their periodical publications. It must be emphasised that the bibliography set out below makes no claim to completeness. It excludes: (1) the Fabian Tracts, of which Sidney wrote forty-five and Beatrice three; (2) a large selection of their writings for the *New Statesman, Fabian News* and other journals; (3) ephemera such as leaflets; (4) anonymous contributions to the *New Statesman* and other journals; (5) newspaper articles, which in some matters are often more revealing than the longer articles in periodical publications. A. M. McBriar, *Fabian Socialism and English Politics 1884–1918* (Cambridge, 1962) provides a very useful bibliographical introduction to their writings, including a nearly complete list of Fabian Tracts, together with a lengthy guide to secondary sources. For a comprehensive account of both writings and sources, the forthcoming biography of the Webbs by Professor Royden Harrison will be indispensable.

BEATRICE WEBB

(1) **Books** (incl. some pamphlets): *The Co-operative Movement in Great Britain* (1891, repr. with additional preface, 1930 and with a new Introduction by M. Cole, a forthcoming LSE publication); *Committee of Inquiry on the Control of Industry* (Letchworth [189–?]) 12 pp.; Editor of *The Case for the Factory Acts* (1901); Edited and with a Preface by B. Webb, *The Case for the National Minimum* (1913); *The Wages of Men and Women: should they be equal?* (1919); *My Apprenticeship* (1926); *The Discovery of the Consumer* (Self and Society Ser., no. 3: 1928) 32 pp.; *The English Poor Law: will it endure?* (Barnett House Papers, no. 11: 1928) 32 pp.; *Our Partnership*, ed. B. Drake and M. I. Cole (1948, repr. with an Introduction by G. Feaver, a forthcoming LSE publication); *Beatrice Webb's Diaries 1912–1924*, ed. M. I. Cole (1952); *Beatrice Webb's Diaries 1924–1932*, ed. and with an Introduction by M. Cole (1956); *Beatrice Webb's American Diary 1898*, ed. D. A. Shannon (Univ. of Wisconsin Press, 1963).

(2) **Articles:** 'The Dock Life of East London', *19th C. 22* (Oct 1887) 483–99; 'East London Labour', ibid., *24* (Aug 1888) 161–183; 'Pages from a Work-Girl's Diary', ibid., *24* (Sep 1888) 301–14; three articles in *Life and Labour 1: East London*, ed. C. Booth (1889): 'The Docks', pp. 184–208, 'The Tailoring Trade', pp. 209–40 and 'The Jewish Community', pp. 564–90; 'The Lords and the Sweating System', *19th C. 27* (June 1890) 885–905; *The Relationship between Co-operation and Trade Unionism* (paper read at conference of trade union officials and co-operators at Tynemouth, 12 Aug 1892) 16 pp.; *How best to do away with the Sweating System* (paper at Co-op. Congress, 1892) 16 pp.; and in S. & B. Webb, *Problems of Modern Industry* (1898) 139–55; 'The Failure of the Labour Commission', *19th C. 36* (July 1894) 2–22; (with others), 'Law and the Laundry, no. 1: Commercial Laundries', ibid., *41* (Feb 1897) 224–31; 'The Diary of an Investigator' and 'The Jews of East London' in S. & B. Webb, op. cit., 1–19 and 20–45; 'Methods of Social Investigation' [an address], *Sociological Papers 3* (1907) 345–54; 'The Economics of Factory Legislation', in *Socialism and the National Minimum* (Fabian Socialist Ser., no. 6: 1909) 5–49; 'Voteless Women and Social Revolution', *New Statesman 2*, 14 Feb 1914, 584–5; Introduction to Special Supplements on *The Awakening of Women*, ibid., 1 Nov 1913 and 21 Feb 1914; 'Motherhood and Citizenship', in *Supplement on Motherhood*, ibid., *3*, 16 May 1914; 'Personal Rights and the Women's Movement: 1. The Individual, Other Individuals and the Community', ibid., *3*, 4 July 1914, 395–7, '2. The Falling Birthrate', ibid., 11 July 1914, 428–30, '3. Maternity under Free Conditions', ibid., 18 July 1914, 461–3, '4. The Rights of the Women to Free Entry into All Occupations', ibid., 25 July 1914, 493–4, '5. Equal Remuneration for Men and Women', ibid., 1 Aug 1914, 525–7; 'The Co-operative Movement of Great Britain and its Recent Developments', *Int. Lab. Rev. 4* (Nov 1921) 227–56; 'Reminiscences: 2. The Consumers' Co-operative Movement', *St Martin's Rev.*, no. *453* (Nov 1928) 573–80; 'A Reform Bill for 1932', *Pol. Q. 2* (Jan.

1931) 1–22; 'Wanted: a new reform bill' [letter to Editor], *Spec. 146*, 7 Mar 1931, 346–7; 'Views on Russia' [Interview with B. Webb], *Rev. of Revs. 82* (Nov 1932) 36–9; 'The Trade Unions in Russia', [Interview], *Labour Mag. 11* (Sep 1932) 195–7; 'Famine in Russia' [letter to Editor], *New Statesman and Nation 9*, 23 Mar 1935, 415; (with W. H. Auden, Pearl Buck et al.), *I believe: the personal philosophies of twenty-three eminent men and women of our time* (1940) 325–48.

(3) **Evidence before and Membership of principal Government Commissions, Committees etc.**

1888: Evidence before S.C. of the House of Lords on the Sweating System 1888 XX Qs 3246–415.

1905–9: R.C. on Poor Law and Relief of Distress 1909 XXXVII Cd 4499 [Signatory of the Minority Report with F. Chandler, G. Lansbury and Rev. R. Wakefield].

1914–15: Sub-committee for London of the Local Government Board Committee on the Prevention and Relief of Distress arising out of the War 1914 LXXI Cd 7603; also member of the sub-committee on Urban Housing Questions set up by the same committee in August 1914.

1916–17: Statutory Committee on War Pensions 1917–18 XVII Cd 8750.

1917–18: Ministry of Reconstruction Committee and also on its Local Government Committee and the Advisory Housing Panel, 1917–18 XXXVIII Cd 8916; 1917–18 XVIII Cd 8917 and 1918 XIII Cd 9231.

1918–19: Committee on the Machinery of Government 1918 XII Cmd 9230 and War Cabinet Committee on Women in Industry 1919 XXXI Cmd 135.

1919–20: Lord Chancellor's Advisory Committee for Women Justices.

1931: Evidence before the R.C. on Unemployment Insurance 1931 non-parl, Qs 10504–710 and memorandum paper no. 100.

SIDNEY WEBB

(1) **Books** (incl. some pamphlets): *What Socialism means; a Call to the Unconverted* (4th ed., 1888) 7 pp.; *Wanted, a Programme: an appeal to the Liberal Party* (private circulation, [1888]) 16 pp.; *Socialism in England* (first published in *American Econ. Association Publications 4*, no. 2 (1889); repr. separately in 1890 and repr. with an Introduction by H. B. Acton, a forthcoming LSE publication); *The Best Method of bringing Co-operation within the Reach of the Poorest of the Population* (Manchester, [1891]) 12 pp.; (with H. Cox), *The Eight Hours Day* (1891); *The London Programme* (1891, new ed. 1895); *London Education* (1904); *Grants in Aid* (1911, rev. ed. 1920); (Edited with A. Freeman), *Seasonal Trades* (1912); *Towards Social Democracy?* (first published in *Cambridge Modern History 12* (1910) Ch. 23 and repr. separately, [1916]) 48 pp.; *How to pay for the War* (1916, rev. 1917); (with A. Freeman), *Great Britain after the War* (1916); *The Works Manager Today* (1917); *The Restoration of Trade Union Conditions* (1917); *The Story of the Durham Miners 1662-1921* (1921); *The Constitutional Problems of a Co-operative Society* (1923) 24 pp.

(2) **Articles:** 'The Rate of Interest and the Laws of Distribution', *QJE 2* (1888) 188–208; 'The Rate of Interest', ibid., *2* (1888) 469–72; 'The Historic Basis of Socialism', in G. B. Shaw et al., *Fabian Essays in Socialism* (1889, 6th ed. with a new Introduction by A. Briggs, 1962); 'The Limitation of the Hours of Labour', *Cont. Rev. 56* (Nov 1889) 859–83; 'The Reform of the Poor Law', ibid., *58* (July 1890) 95–120; 'An English Poor Law Reform Association', *QJE 5* (1891) 370–2; 'The Difficulties of Individualism', *Econ. J. 1.* (June 1891) 360–381; 'The Alleged Differences in the Wages paid to Men and Women for Similar Work', ibid., *1* (Dec 1891) 635–62; 'Women Compositors', *Econ. Rev. 2* (Jan 1892) 42–5; 'The Moral of the Elections', *Cont. Rev. 62* (Aug 1892) 272–87; 'What Mr Gladstone ought to do', *Fortn. Rev. 53* n.s. (Feb 1893) 281–7; (with G. B. Shaw), 'To your Tents, Oh Israel!', ibid., *54* n.s. (Nov 1893) 569–89;

'The Condition of the Working Class in Great Britain in 1842 and 1892', *Co-op. Annual* (1893) 537–54; 'The Work of the London County Council', *Cont. Rev. 67* (Jan 1895) 130–52; 'Some Facts and Considerations about Municipal Socialism', *Co-op. Annual* (1896) 286–322; 'La Fabian Society et la Mouvement Socialiste en Angleterre', *Revue de Paris* (Mar 1896) 112–37; 'The Function of the Public Library in Respect of Political Science; with some Particulars of the British Library of Political Science', *Library 9* (1897) 230–8; 'Lord Rosebery's Escape from Houndsditch', *19th C. 50* (Sep 1901) 366–86; 'London University: a policy and a forecast', *19th C. 51* (June 1902) 914–31; 'The Making of a New University', *Cornhill Mag. 14* (1903) 530–40; 'London Education', *19th C. 54* (Oct 1903) 561–80; 'The Policy of the National Minimum', *Ind. Rev. 3* (July 1904) 161–78; 'Physical Degeneracy or Race Suicide', *Popular Science Mon. 69* (1906) 512–29; 'The Necessary Basis of Society', *Cont. Rev. 93* (June 1908) 658–68; 'The Problem of Unemployment in the United Kingdom with a Remedy by Organisation and Training', *Annals of the American Academy of Political and Social Science 33* (Mar 1909) 196–215; 'Economic Aspects of Poor Law Reform', *Engl. Rev. 3* (Oct 1909) 501–16; 'The Osborne Revolution', ibid., *7* (Jan 1911) 380–93; 'The Economic Theory of a Legal Minimum Wage', *JPE 20* (Dec 1912) 973–98; 'The Coming Educational Revolution: 1. Half-time for Adolescents', *Cont. Rev. 110* (Nov 1916) 584–93 and '2. Health and Employment', ibid., *110* (Dec 1916) 724–33; 'British Labor under War Pressure', *North American Rev. 205* (June 1917) 874–85; 'The Future of International Trade', *Soc. Rev. 16* (Jan-Mar 1919) 68–81; 'Facts of the Strike', *New Statesman 14*, 4 Oct 1919, 4–6; 'The Process of Amalgamation in British Trade Unionism', *Int. Lab. Rev. 1* (Jan 1921) 45–60; 'The Party Today', *Labour Mag. 1* (Aug 1922) 150–1; 'Labour and Local Government', ibid., *1* (Feb 1923) 463–4; 'The British Labour Movement and the Industrial Depression', *Int. Lab. Rev. 7* (Feb–Mar 1923) 209–29; 'Craft or Industrial Unionism', *Labour Mag. 2* (Sep 1923)

220–2; 'The Crisis in British Industry', *Current History 23* (Oct 1925) 12–19; 'Problems of Trade Unionism', *Soc. Rev.* no. *16* ser. 2 (May 1927) 1–6; 'Towards Industrial Conscription', *Labour Mag. 6* (May 1927) 6–8; 'Britain's New Industrial and Political Crisis', *Current History 26* (July 1927) 575–80; 'Reminiscences: 1. Trade Unionism', *St Martin's Rev.* no. *452* (Oct 1928) 478–81 and 'Reminiscences: 3. The London County Council', ibid., no. *454* (Dec 1928) 621–6; 'Fabianism', in *Encyclopaedia of the Labour Movement* ed. H. B. Lees-Smith (1928) 266–70; 'What happened in 1931: a record', *Pol. Q. 3* (Jan–Mar 1932) 1–17; 'British Labour's Reaction to Defeat', *Current History 35* (Jan 1932) 537–43; 'Business Life in Soviet Russia', ibid., *37* (Nov 1932) 147–54; 'The Worker in Soviet Russia', ibid., (Dec 1932) 273–80; 'Freedom under Soviet Rule', ibid., (Jan 1933) 399–407; 'Freedom in Soviet Russia', *Cont. Rev. 143* (Jan 1933) 11–21; 'The Wage-Earner in Soviet Russia', *Labour Mag. 11* (Jan 1933) 390–4; 'On the Emergence of a New World-Religion', *Int. J. Ethics 43* (Jan 1933) 167–182; 'The Steel Frame of Soviet Society', *Pol. Q. 4* (Jan 1933) 1–15; 'Is Soviet Russia a Democracy?', *Current History* (Feb 1933) 532–8; 'State Publishing in Soviet Russia', *Bookman 83* and *84* (Mar–Apr 1933) 490–2 and 16–17; 'The Family in Soviet Russia', *Current History* (Apr 1933) 52–60; 'Soviet Russia as a Federal State', *Pol. Q. 4* (Apr 1933) 182–200; 'Soviet Communism: its present position and prospects', *Int. Affairs 15* (May–June 1936) 395–413; 'A Basis for Political Science?', *Politica* (Sep 1937) 480–494; Foreword to *Warwick County Records 4 Quarter Sessions Order Book 1657–1665* ed. S. C. Ratcliff and H. C. Johnson (Warwick, 1938); 'The First Labour Government', *Pol. Q. 32* (Jan 1961) 6–44 [a previously unpublished memorandum].

(3) **Evidence before and Membership of principal Government Commissions, Committees etc.**

1892: Evidence before R.C. on Labour 1893–4 XXXIX Qs 3578–877.

1895: Evidence [with Dr W. Garnett] before the R.C. on Secondary Education 1895 XLIV Qs 2537–858.

1903–6: R.C. on Trade Disputes and Trade Combinations 1906 LVI Cd 2825.

1904–5: Departmental Committee on Royal College of Science, reports: 1905 LXI Cd 2610 and 1906 XXXI Cd 2872.

1905–6: Departmental Committee on Agricultural Settlements in British Colonies 1906 LXXVI Cd 2978 and Cd 2979.

1910–22: Development Commission 1911 XV First report May 1910–Mar 1911; eleventh report, 1921.

1918–20: Committee on Trusts 1918 XIII Cd 9236.

1919: R.C. on the Coal Industry (Sankey Commission) 1919 XI Cmd 359.

1919–20: Central Committee on the Investigation of Prices (under Profiteering Act, 1919). In addition S. Webb was chairman of two of the sub-committees: on Road Transport Rates 1920 XXIII Cmd 549 and on the Tobacco Industry 1920 XXIII Cmd 558.

SIDNEY AND BEATRICE WEBB:

(1) **Books** (inc. some pamphlets): *The History of Trade Unionism* (1894, rev. ed 1920, repr. 1926 and 1950); *Principles of the Labour Party* [189–?] 4 pp.; *Industrial Democracy*, 2 vols (1897, further eds 1902 and 1920); *Problems of Modern Industry* (1898, further eds 1902 and 1920); *English Local Government: The History of Liquor Licensing in England* (1903, repr. 1963), *The Parish and the County* (1906, repr. with a new Introduction by B. Keith-Lucas, 1963), *The Manor and the Borough* (1908, repr. with a new Introduction by B. Keith-Lucas, 1963), *The Story of the King's Highway* (1913, repr. with a new Introduction by G. J. Ponsonby, 1963), *Statutory Authorities for Special Purposes* (1922, repr. with a new Introduction by B. Keith-Lucas, 1963), *English Prisons under Local Government* (1922, repr. with a new Introduction by L. Radzinowicz, 1963), *English Poor Law History*, pt *1* (1927 and pt 2, 1930, repr. with a new Introduction by W. A. Robson, 1963);

Bibliography of Road Making and Maintenance in Great Britain (1906) 34 pp.; *The Break-up of the Poor Law* (pt 1 of the Minority Report of the Poor Law Commission, ed. with Introduction by S. & B. Webb, 1909); *The Public Organisation of the Labour Market* (pt 2 of the Minority Report of the Poor Law Commission, ed. with Introduction by S. & B. Webb, 1909); *English Poor Law Policy* (1910, repr. with a new Introduction by W. A. Robson, 1963); *The State and the Doctor* (1910); *The Prevention of Destitution* (1911, repr. with a new Introduction, 1920); *A Constitution for the Socialist Commonwealth of Great Britain* (1920); *The Consumers' Co-operative Movement* (1921); *The Decay of Capitalist Civilisation* (1923, 2nd ed., 1923); *Methods of Social Study* (1932); *Soviet Communism: a new civilisation?* 2 vols (1935, 2nd ed. 1937; repr. with a new Introduction, 1941); *Is Soviet Communism a New Civilisation?* (1936) 30 pp.; *Soviet Communism: dictatorship or democracy?* (1936) 32 pp.; *The Truth about Soviet Russia* (1942, 2nd ed. 1944); *Visit to New Zealand in 1898: Beatrice Webb's diary with entries by Sidney Webb* (Wellington, 1959); *The Webbs' Australian Diary 1898*, ed. A. G. Austin (1965).

(2) **Articles:** 'The Method of Collective Bargaining', *Econ. J. 6* (Mar 1896) 1–29; 'Are Trade Unions Benefit Societies?', *Econ. Rev. 6* (July 1896) 441–55; 'The Standard Rate', *Econ. J. 6* (Sep 1896) 356–388; 'Primitive Democracy in British Trade Unionism', *Pol. Sc. Q. 11* (Sep 1896) 397–432; 'Arbitration in Labour Disputes', *19th C. 40* (Nov 1896) 743–58; 'Representative Institutions in British Trade-Unionism', *Pol. Sc. Q. 11* (Dec 1896) 640–71; 'What happened to the English Parish?', ibid., *17* (June 1902) 223–46 and (Sep 1902) 438–59; 'The Assize of Bread', *Econ. J. 14* (June 1904) 196–218; 'A National Crusade against Destitution', *Co-op. Annual* (1910) 143–68; 'China in Revolution', *Crusade against Destitution 3* (Mar 1912) 43–4; *What Syndicalism means* (supplement to *Crusade against Destitution 3*, no. 8: 1912) 19 pp.; *Co-operative Production and Profit-sharing*

(supplement to *New Statesman 2*, 14 Feb 1914) 31 pp., *The Co-operative Movement* (supplement to *New Statesman 3*, 30 May 1914) 36 pp.; *State and Municipal Enterprise* (supplement to *New Statesman 5*, 8 May 1915) 32 pp.; *English Teachers and their Professional Organisation* (supplements to *New Statesman*, 2 pts, 5, 25 Sep 1915, 22 pp. and 2 Oct 1915, 24 pp.); *Professional Associations* (supplement to *New Statesman 9*, no. 211, 21–28 Apr 1917) 48 pp.

Sources: (1) **MSS:** The major source is the Webb Coll., LSE but other material will be found in: Asquith papers, Bodleian Library, Oxford; Samuel papers, House of Lords Record Office; Sir Horace Curzon Plunkett papers, Plunkett foundation for Co-operative Studies Library, Oxford; letters to Hubert Hall, Kent Archives Office and LSE; letters to W. A. S. Hewins, Sheffield University Library; Labour Party archives, Transport House, London especially files on the War Emergency Workers' National Committee (WNC and WNC/ADD) and on the Party's Special Sub-committee on the Liquor Traffic 1923. The Middleton papers, also at Transport House, include a Webb file (JSM/WEB) with six letters from Sidney and two from Beatrice and there is also a file of the Seaham Division Labour Party, Co. Durham containing Beatrice's duplicated letters to the Women's Sections of the Party between Dec 1922 and Dec 1926. Other material will be found in the Fabian Society archives and the Cole Coll., both of which are at Nuffield College, Oxford. This list cannot be regarded as complete. It omits collections in countries outside the U.K. for which reference should be made to the forthcoming book by Professor Royden Harrison; and reference should also be made to the *see also* entries at the end of this bibliography.
(2) **Theses:** R. D. Howland, 'Fabian Thought and Social Change in England from 1884–1914' (London PhD, 1942); E. Hobsbawm, 'Fabianism and the Fabians, 1884–1914' (Cambridge PhD, 1950); A. M. McBriar, 'Fabian Socialist Doctrine and its Influence in English Politics, 1884–1918' (Oxford

PhD, 1950); E. J. T. Brennan, 'The Influence of Sidney and Beatrice Webb on English Education, 1892–1903' (Sheffield MA, 1959); W. P. McCann, 'Trade Unionist, Co-operative and Socialist Organisations in Relation to Popular Education 1870–1902' (Manchester PhD, 1960); J. Schofield, 'The Labour Movement and Educational Policy, 1900–1931' (Manchester, MEd, 1964); M. Warner, 'The Webbs – a Study of the Influence of Intellectuals in Politics (largely between 1889–1918)' (Cambridge PhD, 1967); R. S. Barker, 'The Educational Policies of the Labour Party, 1900–1961' (London PhD, 1968) and see also bibliographies of the British Labour Party: for 1900–13 in this volume under George Lansbury and for 1914–31 in *DLB 1* (1972) under Arthur Henderson.

(3) **Biographical Works:** G. Meinertzhagen, *From Ploughshare to Parliament: a short memoir of the Potters of Tadcaster* (1908); R. Berkeley MP., 'Three Leaders of Labour', *Spec. 132*, 26 Jan 1924, 117–18; 'Rt Hon. Sidney Webb MP. Labour's First President of the Board of Trade', in *The Book of the Labour Party 3* ed. H. Tracey [1925] 190–205; M. A. Hamilton, *Sidney and Beatrice Webb: a study in contemporary biography* [1933]; 'The Webbs and the New Statesman', *New Statesman and Nation 7*, 14 Apr 1934, 547–8; H. J. Laski and M. Cole, 'Mrs Webb's 80th Birthday', *New Statesman and Nation 15*, 22 Jan 1938, 116; H. G. Wells, 'Mrs Webb's Birthday', ibid. 22 Jan 1938, 110; G. B. Shaw, 'Beatrice Webb, Octogenarian', *Spec. 160*. 21 Jan 1938, 79; 'America sends Greetings, Mrs Webb', *Social Service Rev.* 12 Mar 1938, 123–4; *DNB* (1941–50) [by M. A. Hamilton]; R. H. Tawney, *The Webbs and their Work* (Webb Memorial Lect: 11 May 1945) 16 pp.; Bernard Shaw, 'The History of a Happy Marriage', *Times Literary Supplement*, 20 Oct 1945, 493–4; M. Cole, *The Social Services and the Webb Tradition* (Webb Memorial Lect: 23 May 1946) 12 pp.; M. I. Cole, *Beatrice Webb* (1946); H. J. Laski, *The Webbs and Soviet Communism* (Webb Memorial Lect: 4 June 1947) 20 pp.; 'Sidney Webb (1859–1947)' in M. Cole, *Makers of the Labour Movement* (1948) 227–47; H. Tracey, 'Sidney and

Beatrice Webb' in *The British Labour Party 3* (1948) 171–6; 'Fruitful Friendships' in G. B. Shaw, *Sixteen Self-Sketches* (1949) 65–68; *The Webbs and their Work*, ed. M. Cole (1949, repr. Brighton, 1974); Sir W. K. Hancock, *The History of our Times* (Webb Memorial Lect: 21 Nov 1950) 22 pp.; R. H. Tawney, *The Webbs in Perspective* (Webb Memorial Lect: 9 Dec 1952) 21 pp.; M. Cole, *Beatrice and Sidney Webb* (Fabian Tract no. 297: 1956) 47 pp.; J. Strachey, 'Sidney and Beatrice Webb', *Listener*, 13 Oct 1960, 617–19; M. Cole, 'The Webbs and Social Theory', *British J. of Sociology, 12* (June 1961) 93–105; T. S. Simey, 'The Contribution of Sidney and Beatrice Webb to Sociology', ibid., *12* (June 1961) 106–23; V. L. Allen, 'Valuations and Historical Interpretation: a case study', ibid., *14*, no. 1 (Mar 1963) 48–58; M. Warner, 'Sidney and Beatrice Webb', *Tribune*, 21 Aug 1964; 'Beatrice Webb: science and the apotheosis of politics', in S. R. Letwin, *The Pursuit of Certainty* (Cambridge, 1965) 321–78; R. Adam and K. Muggeridge, *Beatrice Webb: a life, 1858–1943* (1967).

(4) **The most important secondary works are:** E. R. Pease, *History of the Fabian Society* (1916, 2nd ed. 1925; repr. with a new Introduction by M. Cole, 1963); R. B. Haldane, *An Autobiography* (1929); G. D. H. Cole, *A History of the Labour Party from 1914* (1948); M. I. Cole, *Growing up into Revolution* (1949); H. Pelling, *The Origins of the Labour Party 1880–1900* (1954, 2nd ed. rev. Oxford, 1965); G. D. H. Cole, *A History of Socialist Thought 3* pts 1 and 2: *The Second International* (1956, 3rd repr. 1967); idem, *A History of Socialist Thought 4* pts 1 and 2: *Communism and Social Democracy* (1958–60, 3rd repr. 1969); B. Semmel, *Imperialism and Social Reform* (1960); M. Liebman, 'Fabianisme et Communisme: les Webb et l'Union Soviétique', 2 pts, *Int. Rev. Social Hist. 5* (1960) 400–23 and *6* (1961) 49–73; M. Cole, *The Story of Fabian Socialism* (1961); A. M. McBriar, *Fabian Socialism and English Politics 1884–1918* (1962) [with a comprehensive bibliography]; B. Simon, *Education and the Labour Movement 1870–1920* (1965); Dan H. Laurence, *Collected Letters of Bernard Shaw 1;*

1874–1897 (1965); P. Thompson, *Socialists, Liberals and Labour: the struggle for London 1885–1914* (1967); Dan H. Laurence, *Collected Letters of Bernard Shaw 2: 1898–1910* (1972).

See also: M. G. Fawcett, 'Mr Sidney Webb's Article on Women's Wages', *Econ. J. 2* (Mar 1892) 173–6; G. Drage, 'Mrs Sidney Webb's Attack on the Labour Commission', *19th C. 36* (Sep 1894) 452–67; H. G. Wells, *The Faults of the Fabian* (Fabian Society, 1906) [for members only] 16 pp.; idem, *The New Machiavelli* (1911); M. Beer, *A History of British Socialism* (1920, repr. 1948); R. W. Lyman, *The First Labour Government* [1957]; A. E. Davies, *The Story of the London County Council* (1925); E. Halévy, *A History of the English People 5: Imperialism and the rise of Labour 1895–1905* (1926, 2nd ed. 1952); E. Abbott, 'The Webbs on the English Poor Law', *Social Service Rev. 3* (June 1929) 252–69; E. Wertheimer, *Portrait of the Labour Party* (1929); E. Halévy, *A History of the English People 6: the rule of democracy (1905–1914)* (1932: paperback 1961); H. G. Wells, *Experiment in Autobiography* (1934); M. A. Hamilton, *Arthur Henderson: a biography* (1938); S. G. Hobson, *Pilgrim to the Left: memoirs of a modern revolutionist* (1938); F. Brockway, *Inside the Left* (1942); M. A. Hamilton, *Remembering my Good Friends* (1944); H. Samuel, *Memoirs* (1945); A. B. Ulam, *Philosophical Foundations of English Socialism* (Harvard, 1951); G. K. Lewis, 'Fabian Socialism; some Aspects of Theory and Practice', *J. of Politics 14*, no. 3 (Aug 1952) 442–70; L. S. Amery, *My Political Life* vols 1 and 2 (1953); C. L. Mowat, *Britain between the Wars* (1955); B. Russell, *Portraits from Memory and Other Essays* (1956); F. Bealey and H. Pelling, *Labour and Politics 1900–1906* (1958); P. P. Poirier, *The Advent of the Labour Party* (1958); H. Pelling, *A Short History of the Labour Party* (1961); S. Caine, *The History of the Foundation of the London School of Economics and Political Science* [1963]; K. Sinclair, *William Pember Reeves: New Zealand Fabian* (Oxford, 1965); R. Skidelsky, *Politicians and the Slump: the Labour Govern-*

ment of 1929–1931 (1967); W. S. Smith, *The London Heretics 1870–1914* (1967); M. Cowling, *The Impact of Labour 1920–24* (1971); R. Harrison, 'The War Emergency Workers' National Committee' in *Essays in Labour History 1886–1923* ed. A. Briggs and J. Saville (1971) 211–59; M. Swartz, *The Union of Democratic Control in British Politics during the First World War* (1971); R. Barker, *Education and Politics, 1900–1951: a study of the Labour Party* (Oxford, 1972).

OBIT. **Beatrice Webb:** *Daily Express, Daily Herald, Daily Mail, Daily Telegraph, Daily Worker, Glasgow Herald, Manchester Guardian, News Chronicle, Times* and *Yorkshire Post,* 1 May 1943; *Observer* and *Reynolds News,* 2 May 1943; *Manchester Guardian,* 4 May 1943; *Spec. 170,* 7 May 1943, 423 [by M. A. Hamilton]; *New Statesman and Nation 25,* 8 May 1943 [by Kingsley Martin] 302–3 and [M. Cole, 'Webb Partnership'] 303; *Labour Mon. 25* (June 1943) 189 [by R. Page Arnot]; *Social Service Rev. 17* (Sep 1943) 377–8; R. H. Tawney, 'Beatrice Webb 1858–1943', *Proc. British Academy 29* (1943) 285–311; L. Woolf, 'Beatrice Webb (1858–1943)' *Econ. J. 53* (June–Sep 1943) 284–90; G. D. H. Cole, 'Beatrice Webb as an Economist', ibid., *53* (Dec 1943) 422–37. **Sidney Webb:** *Daily Herald, Daily Telegraph, Daily Worker, Manchester Guardian, News Chronicle, Scotsman,* and *Times,* 14 Oct 1947; *Glasgow Herald* and *Times,* 15 Oct 1947; *New Statesman and Nation 34,* 18 Oct 1947, 306 [by Kingsley Martin]; *Reynolds News,* 19 Oct 1947; *Illustrated London News 211,* 25 Oct 1947, 461; *New Statesman and Nation 34,* 25 Oct 1947, 331 [by S. K. Ratcliffe]; *Labour Mon. 29* (Nov 1947) 344–6 [by R. P. Dutt]; R. H. Tawney, 'In Memory of Sidney Webb', *Economica 14* n.s., no. 56 (Nov 1947) 245–253; Lord Beveridge, 'Sidney Webb (Lord Passfield) (1859–1947)' *Econ. J. 58* (Sep 1948) 428–34.

The famous picture of the Webbs by Sir William Nicholson is in the Founders' Room at LSE. Photographs of the Webbs are published in a number of the biographical works already listed and there are also books, mementos etc. at Beatrice Webb House, near Dorking.

See also: †William Henry Brown, for Retail Co-operation, 1900–45; *George Douglas Howard Cole; †Arthur Henderson, for British Labour Party, 1914–31; †George Jacob Holyoake, for Retail Co-operation, Nineteenth Century; †Benjamin Jones for Co-operative Production; George Lansbury, for British Labour Party, 1900–13; †James Ramsay MacDonald; Edward Reynolds Pease; William Pember Reeves; *Richard Henry Tawney.

WEBB, Catherine (1859–1947)
CO-OPERATOR AND AUTHOR

Catherine Webb was born on 4 May 1859 in Battersea, the daughter of Thomas Edward Burgess Webb, a journeyman coppersmith and co-operative pioneer who later became a CWS director. Thomas Webb imbued his children with his own belief in co-operation and gave them a detailed knowledge of the organisation of the movement. Catherine's mother had studied astronomy and polar exploration, unusual interests which she maintained throughout her long life of over ninety years.

Catherine Webb was among the earliest members of the Women's Co-operative Guild, which was established in 1884. She was chairman of the first Guild conference, held in London in April 1886, and was also founder and first secretary of the Battersea Branch of the Guild. She became a close friend and colleague of Margaret Llewelyn Davies, served on the Guild's central committee from 1885 to 1888 and again from 1892 to 1893, and read papers at several Guild congresses. She also wrote a short history of the first ten years of the Guild, and later extended this in *The Woman with the Basket* to cover the Guild's history from 1884 to 1927. In the early days of the Guild she had argued that women should undertake public speaking for the movement although this was opposed by Mrs Alice (later Lady) Acland on the ground that it would arouse public hostility.

The 1884 meeting decided that there

should be 'no platform speaking . . . no going out of our woman's place'; but Catherine Webb did not conform. Her concern with social problems was strengthened by contact with Graham Wallas, who in 1892–3 conducted a university extension course on 'The English Citizen', followed by one on 'The Making of the English Constitution', both at Morley College, London. He repeated the lectures at the CWS headquarters, Leman Street, where Catherine attended them and was thus introduced to the study of the social sciences. Wallas also encouraged her to undertake some lecturing. As she later wrote in a History of Morley College: 'My reaction to his encouragement was to start out on a month's tour of certain Midland and Northern towns, repeating to the best of my untrained ability the story of 'The English Citizen' with local applications.' Starting in October 1894, she made her headquarters at Nottingham and gave a lecture each week at Hucknall Torkard, Langley Mill, Long Eaton, Nottingham and Sutton and three lectures at Leicester, making twenty-three in the month. Her second course covered Newcastle, Walker, Wallsend and Willington Quay. None of the co-operative societies had previously attempted such a series of lectures, and attendances were very satisfactory.

In the wider movement she was a delegate, from Battersea and Wandsworth, to several Co-operative Congresses in the 1890s. At the 22nd Congress in Glasgow she expressed regret at the formation of a separate Women's Guild movement in Scotland and appealed for unity between the English and Scottish organisations. She read a paper on 'The Guild and Store Life' at a festival held in Manchester in July 1892 to celebrate the formation of the hundredth branch of the Guild and, at the Sunderland Congress in 1894, she appealed for more participation by women in the committees of the co-operative movement. She was also advocating at this time the more thorough education of both managers and their employees in the principles of co-operation, and she strongly urged the importance of the 'missionary' aspect of the movement. From 1895 to 1902 she represented the southern board on the central board of the Co-operative Union. She wrote many articles for the early 'Women's Corner' in the *Co-operative News* and for some time edited this feature. In 1904, *Industrial Co-operation* was published under her editorship, and this served as a standard textbook for co-operative educators for many years, a twelfth edition being printed in 1929. Catherine Webb was a regular attender at the annual educational conventions of the Co-operative Union and during the First World War was actively associated with the Southern Educational Association.

She was a woman of integrity with a kind and generous personality and her name is especially linked with the Guild Convalescent Fund instituted in 1894 as a memorial to Mrs Benjamin Jones, one of the first presidents of the Guild. At the Sheffield Guild Congress in 1905, Catherine Webb was elected the honorary secretary of the Fund, a position which she held until 1930 and which she described in 1927 as 'my happiest service till now'. In 1930 the Raynes Park Guild conferred upon her the 'freedom of the branch' in recognition of her twenty-five years' secretaryship of the Fund, and it was with deep regret that the Annual Guild Congress accepted her resignation from office in the same year. She was also one of the founders of the Southern Sectional Convalescent Fund, served as its secretary from its commencement in 1904 until 1934, and was its honorary secretary thereafter until her death. At its thirtieth annual meeting, in 1935, she read a paper in which she traced the history of the Fund.

Among her other early interests was the work of the Women's Industrial Council. In 1894, the Women's Trade Union Association called a conference with the object of forming a central body of affiliated women's societies to investigate and report on questions affecting women, and Miss Webb was one of two representatives from the Women's Co-operative Guild. The Women's Industrial Council was formed after this meeting, with Miss Amy Hicks as the first

secretary; on the latter's marriage in 1895, Miss Webb succeeded her and continued to hold this office until 1902. Her earlier lecturing experience proved useful in this connection, and her name appeared among the list of the Council's lecturers in its second annual report published in 1896. One of the earliest publications of the Council was in the following year and related to home industries for women in 1897. In the first decade of the twentieth century the Council reported on technical education for women and girls at home and abroad, and in 1915 it published the report of an inquiry into the work of married women.

Although she probably counted herself as a Liberal, Catherine Webb was not active in politics. She regarded the co-operative movement as an entity in itself, within which members were entitled to hold differing political opinions. In the later decades of her life she was closely associated with the work of Morley College, which was opened in 1889 and whose origins dated back to 1880 when Emma Cons took over the Royal Victoria Theatre to provide a recreational centre for the working classes. By the mid-1890s the work of the College was extended to include a variety of technical and commercial classes as well as those catering for more recreational pursuits. From 1909 it was a centre for WEA tutorial classes and in addition, under the guidance of Gustav Holst, became well known for its musical activities. Miss Webb concerned herself with many aspects of its work and was on its panel of lecturers during the First World War. In 1915 she was elected to the College Council as a representative of the City Parochial Foundation, and served continuously until her death. A vice-chairman of the Council for many years, she was made a vice-president of the College in 1946. Towards the end of her life her eyesight began to fail, but she continued to work, and shortly before her death she completed a history of the College in which she wrote that, following her election to the Council, 'Morley College became a part of my life's greater interests'.

She spent the last years of her life at the home of her brother and his family in

Wimbledon where she continued her writing and her other activities, assisted during the Second World War by her niece, Miss Gwynneth Webb. At this period it was with reluctance that she consented to live in the country to avoid the air raids on London. After the war she returned to Wimbledon, where she died on 29 July 1947 in her eighty-ninth year. Her funeral took place at Streatham Vale Crematorium on 1 August, and she left effects valued at £783.

Writings: *The Central Board: its use, work and cost* (1885) 16 pp.; 'Guild Dividends', paper read at WCG conference (1887); 'Co-operation and Domestic Life', paper read at WCG conference (1893); *Should Co-operative Employees understand the Principles of the Movement and, if so, how are they to be taught?* (Manchester, 1894) 24 pp.; 'Short History of the Guild 1883–1894' in *Guild Annual Meeting Handbook* (1894); *The Machinery of the Co-operative Movement* (Manchester, 1896) 18 pp.; *High Dividends: what they mean* (Kirkby Lonsdale, 1897) n.p.; *Industrial Co-operation: the story of a peaceful revolution* (Manchester, 1904; twelfth ed. Manchester, 1929); *The Southern Co-operative Convalescent Fund: a co-operative road to health* (April 1909) 10 pp.; *All Societies should join the Co-operative Union* (1910) 4 pp.; *Lives of Great Men and Women: short biographies of some heroes and friends of co-operation* (Manchester, 1911; rev. ed. Manchester, 1933); *The Women's Guild and the Co-operative Union* (1915) 8 pp.; 'A Short Record of Co-operation in London', in W. T. Davis, *The History of the Royal Arsenal Co-operative Society Ltd 1868–1918* (Woolwich, [1922]); *The Woman with the Basket: the history of the Women's Co-operative Guild 1883–1927* (Manchester, 1927); *The Story of Thirty Years' Work 1904–1934: The Southern Co-operative Convalescent Fund* (Reading, 1935) 15 pp.; History of Morley College for Working Men and Women in Lambeth, London [1947] [typescript copies at Morley College and the Co-operative College, Loughborough].

Sources: (in addition to her own publica-

tions cited above): *Co-op. Congress Reports* for 1890, 1894, 1902; M. L. Davies, *The Women's Co-operative Guild 1883–1904* (Kirkby Lonsdale, 1904); L. Baylis, 'Emma Cons: the founder of the Vic', in C. Hamilton and L. Baylis, *The Old Vic* (1926) 249–285; G. D. H. Cole, *A Century of Co-operation* (Manchester, [1945?]); D. Richards, *Offspring of the Vic: a history of Morley College* (1958); T. Kelly, *A History of Adult Education in Great Britain* (Liverpool, 1962); M. T. Wiener, *Between Two Worlds: The Political Thought of Graham Wallas* (Oxford, 1970); biographical information: G. T. Cottrell, secretary, and Miss M. M. Green, librarian, Morley College; Merton Borough Library; personal information: Miss G. Webb, JP, London, niece. OBIT. *Co-op. News,* 9 Aug 1947; *Morley Mag.* (Sep 1947).
JOYCE BELLAMY
H. F. BING

See also: †Alice Sophia ACLAND; †Margaret Llewelyn DAVIES; †Thomas Edward WEBB.

WEBB, Sidney James (1st Baron Passfield of Passfield Corner) *see* **Webb,** Beatrice.

WEIR, William (1868–1926)
MINERS' LEADER

Born on 28 May 1868 at the colliery village of Mickley Square, just west of Prudhoe, Northumberland, he was the son of a colliery fitter at Mickley Colliery. William Weir was educated at Prudhoe Colliery school, and after the family moved to West Wylam he began work as a trapper boy in West Wylam Pit, owned with three other mines by the Mickley Coal Co. Ltd. Weir worked his way through all the grades underground and remained a hewer at the coal face until in 1914 he was made president of the Northumberland Miners' Mutual Confident Association, which became a constituent part – known as the Northumberland Area – of the National Union of Mineworkers in 1945.

Weir had the typical career of a miners' leader. He attended his first delegate meeting in 1900; was president of the West Wylam lodge between 1905 and 1914; became a trustee of the NMCA in May 1911 and a member of its executive committee in 1914; and was elected president and compensation agent in 1914, positions he continued to hold until his death. He was a member of the British delegation to the Miners' International Conference at Carlsbad, Austria, in 1913, and among his other interests was a lifelong concern for the Northumberland Aged Mineworkers' Homes Association, of which he was a governor for many years.

His activities extended to local affairs. He played an active part in local government, being a member of the local parish council for nine years; a member of the Prudhoe Urban District Council before 1914; and a member of the Northumberland County Council, being made an alderman in March 1925. His special interest as a county councillor was in education and for a long period he sat on the County Education Committee, taking a full part in the work of its subcommittees. He was made a JP in 1909, and for eleven years served on the Hexham Board of Guardians. Among his charitable interests was a close concern in the welfare of the Royal Victoria Infirmary, Newcastle, and Weir served on its house committee for a number of years before his death. In politics he was a Liberal but accepted the miners' changeover to the Labour Party in the years before 1914; and in 1918 he stood, unsuccessfully, as Labour Party candidate for Hexham, where top of the poll was Captain Clifton Brown, a Coalition Liberal, who much later became Speaker of the House of Commons. This was Weir's only attempt to enter national politics.

He was a Primitive Methodist in religion; secretary and trustee of the West Wylam chapel for many years; and a Sunday school teacher until he moved to Newcastle in 1914. He was married twice: first to Jane Hodgson, who died in 1906, and there was a son and a daughter of the marriage; and then to Eliza Hannah Emmerson, and they had a daughter. Weir died on 9 December 1926, and was survived by his wife. He left effects worth £869.

Sources: E. Welbourne, *The Miners' Unions of Northumberland and Durham* (Cambridge, 1923); R. Page Arnot, *The Miners* (1949); R. F. Wearmouth, *Social and Political Influence of Methodism in the Twentieth Century* (1957). OBIT. *Newcastle J.*, 10 Dec 1926; *Newcastle Weekly Chronicle*, 11 Dec 1926; NMA, *Monthly Circular* (1927).

ANTHONY MASON
JOHN SAVILLE

See also: †Thomas ASHTON, for Mining Trade Unionism, 1900–14.

WELSH, James C. (1880–1954)
MINERS' LEADER, LABOUR MP AND AUTHOR

Born on 2 June 1880 in the *quoad sacra* parish and mining village of Haywood, in the Upper Ward of Lanarkshire, James Welsh was the son of William Welsh, a miner, and his wife, Helen Yuille. He was the fourth child in a family of twelve children. Years later Robert Smillie gave a vivid description of the housing conditions of the Haywood miners:

The houses in which miners lived at Haywood were owned by the colliery company, and it would not be too much to say that they were under the average in comfort and accommodation. To anyone who knows the housing conditions of the Scottish miners that statement is sufficient. The houses at the Colliery Row at Haywood were usually a single apartment about 14 ft. square, 9 in. brick walls, with two set-in beds along one side of the house. The supply of family coal was either left in a heap opposite the door or was carefully stored underneath one of the beds. The water for the use of the household had usually to be carried from a pipe which was common to the whole village, and a considerable distance from some of the homes, and this when conveyed in stoups or tin pans was kept usually in a little recess under the end of one of the beds, and behind the door. The family washing was done in this single apartment, the clothes being boiled either over the kitchen fire or in a pot set up on a few bricks opposite the door. A filthy common necessity served the whole of the families,

18 or 20 in one row, the common ashpit being an open one, emptied, it might be, once in three or four months. The window of the house was a fixture, and the door was generally wide open during the day for ventilation, and when it was shut at night it was usually so badly fitting that a considerable current of fresh air could pass inward. The pit clothes were stowed under one of the beds, and were spread around the fire at night to be dried. This was the kind of home in which James Welsh first opened his eyes or raised his melodious voice [*Forward*, 9 June 1917].

His mother was famed throughout the local countryside for her singing of old Scottish songs, and her influence no doubt contributed to the feeling for poetry which James showed from an early age. His father was killed in a colliery accident while James was still a boy. He began attending Haywood Public School when he was five years old, and began work at the pithead when he was eleven. A year later he was working a twelve-hour shift, for which he was paid 1s 3d a day. Welsh had begun to write poetry and prose when he was thirteen and his first publications were some short stories on Upper Ward life. When he was eighteen the family moved to Ponfeigh, also in the Upper Ward of Lanarkshire, and it was there as a young man that he began to take an active part in trade union affairs and in radical politics. He joined the ILP and became a lively propagandist. In 1906 Welsh went to New Zealand but after fifteen months homesickness caused him to return to Scotland. He obtained work at Douglas Castle Colliery, Douglas Water, and was made president of the local branch of the Lanarkshire Miners' Union at the early age of twenty-seven. Later, in 1914, he became checkweighman at the same colliery. In 1917 his first major literary work was published, *Songs of a Miner*, of which 5000 copies were sold. Although mining as such entered only slightly into his poems, his novel, *The Underworld* (1920), was based on the life of a miner. By April 1920 about 50,000 copies had been sold, and it was translated into several languages.

In 1919 Welsh was appointed a full-time agent and vice-president of the union, and in 1923 he represented the Scottish miners on the MFGB executive. In these years he was a close friend of Robert Smillie, whom Welsh always acknowledged as the most powerful influence in his life.

Welsh fought his first parliamentary election in 1918, in South Lanarkshire, where he was defeated by a two-to-one majority by the Coalition Unionist candidate, Captain Walter Elliott, a former president of the Socialist Club in Glasgow University, and one day to be Conservative Secretary of State for Scotland. Welsh stood for Coatbridge in 1922, and he held the seat at all subsequent elections until 1931. His maiden speech (15 Feb 1923) was reprinted by the ILP as a pamphlet with the title *The King and the Miner: a contrast*. In 1924 he was a member of the Empire Parliamentary Association's delegation to South Africa. During the second Labour Government he became, for a few months in 1931, parliamentary private secretary to the Rt Hon. William Adamson, at the time Secretary of State for Scotland. Like so many of his Labour colleagues, Welsh lost his seat in the general election of 1931, but he re-entered the Commons in 1935 as MP for the Bothwell division, having succeeded Joseph Sullivan as the Labour candidate a few months earlier. He did not stand again in 1945, having been in poor health for several years.

Apart from his trade union and political activities, Welsh was an active co-operator for most of his life; he was a director of the Douglas Water Co-operative Society, and a regular attender at co-operative conferences.

Welsh's political ideas seem to have shifted steadily to the Right over the half-century of his active life. He accepted Smillie's leadership for many years, but an article that Welsh wrote in the *Socialist Review* (Jan 1918) already indicated a cautious reformist attitude. After underlining the urgent need for 'total reorganisation' in Scottish mining trade unionism, in order to eliminate the 'autocracy' which then existed, he continued:

Hence the desire for reform, but it is imperative that a coming together of those who seek reform should be arranged, for wild schemes are being enunciated as well as sane ones, and a revolutionary attitude does not always betoken a sensible grappling with responsibilities. Much revolutionary ardour is at present being displayed among certain of the discontented sections, and they are putting forward schemes which have absolutely neither balance nor sanity about them. Wild cries of 'control of industry' are heard, and the throwing over of ownership by the State, and a revolutionary industrialism is being preached which shall have very serious dangers unless a soberer outlook finds a readier expression. Industrial Unionism we must have, but we must beware lest in upsetting one tyrant we do not plant another more firmly upon the lives of the workers. Control of industry we must have also, but a control based upon the larger consideration of the common weal, and not a bastard syndicalism.

In 1924 his novel *The Morlocks* was a thinly disguised attack on the Miners' Minority Movement; and his acceptance of the post of PPS to Willie Adamson was a clear indication that he took the latter's side in the bitter controversies which ravaged Scottish mining trade unionism in the years from 1927-8 [Arnot (1955) 182 ff.]. After 1931, from the evidence of some twenty letters still (1973) in the keeping of the family, Welsh remained on fairly close personal terms with Ramsay MacDonald, a somewhat unusual relationship given the political circumstances of the time. From his fairly infrequent speeches and questions in the House of Commons, Welsh would seem to have been an ordinary Labour backbencher. He seconded a motion, proposed by Emanuel Shinwell, on the distressed areas in December 1935; spoke several times on mining matters; and was especially concerned with housing questions, particularly those of Scotland (see his speech of 22 Nov 1938) about which it is clear that he felt deeply.

He had married in 1905 Elizabeth, daughter of John Hunter JP, of Ponfeigh, and they had a son and three daughters (two of whom were adopted). He died on 4 November 1954 in a Lanarkshire hospital, and his funeral was conducted by Tom Fraser MP at the Glasgow Crematorium. His wife had predeceased him by three years, but he was survived by his family, and left an estate valued at £399. He also left a considerable amount of unpublished material, now in the possession of the family, which has been catalogued by the National Register of Archives (Scotland). When he started writing he added C to his name as a middle initial and continued to use it during his subsequent parliamentary career, probably because there was another Scottish Labour MP of the same name.

Writings: *Songs of a Miner* [poems] (1917); 'The Scottish Miners and their Union', *Soc. Rev. 15* (Jan 1918) 78-81; 'In a Moorland Pass' [poem] *Soc. Rev. 16* (Apr-June 1919) 124; 'The Price of Empire' [poem], *Soc. Rev. 16* (July-Aug 1919) 223-4; *The Underworld: the story of Robert Sinclair, miner* (1920); *The King and the Miner* [1923] 8 pp.; Introduction to *Shopmates* [short stories] (Labour Publishing Co., 1924); *The Morlocks* [a novel] (1924); *Norman Dale MP* [a novel] (1928).

Sources: (1) MSS: personal papers: inquiries to National Register of Archives (Scotland); (2) Other: R. Smillie, 'Rebel, Poet and Miner: James C. Welsh', *Forward*, 9 June 1917; *Edinburgh Evening News*, 12 Apr 1920; S. V. Bracher, *The Herald Book of Labour Members* (1923) [photograph]; *Evening Times* [Glasgow], 16 Apr 1924; *Labour Who's Who* (1927); *Dod* (1928); *Times, House of Commons* (1929) and (1935); Anon., *The Scottish Socialists* (1931); *WW* (1932) and (1954); *Kelly* (1949); R. Page Arnot, *A History of the Scottish Miners* (1955); personal information: Mrs J. L. Irvine, Hamilton, daughter. OBIT. *Times*, 5 Nov 1954; *Hamilton Advertiser*, 6 Nov 1954 [photograph]; *Labour Party Report* (1955).

JOYCE BELLAMY
JOHN SAVILLE

See also: *William ADAMSON; †Thomas ASHTON, for Mining Trade Unionism, 1900–1914; *Arthur James COOK, for Mining Trade Unionism, 1915–26; Peter LEE, for Mining Trade Unionism, 1927–44; †James Ramsay MACDONALD; *Robert SMILLIE, for Scottish Mining Trade Unionism.

WESTWOOD, Joseph (1884–1948)
MINERS' LEADER AND LABOUR MINISTER

Born on 11 February 1884 at Wollescote near Stourbridge, Joseph was the son of Solomon Westwood, a coalminer, and his wife Harriet (née Sidaway). His father moved to Fife in 1887 and Joseph was educated at the Buckhaven Secondary School, Fife. After leaving school at thirteen he worked first as a draper's apprentice but entered mining a year later, and he continued to work as a miner until, in 1916, the Fife miners appointed him as their industrial organiser. Two years later he became political organiser for the Scottish Miners' Union, a position he held until 1929. It is presumed that he followed William Adamson in the bitter controversy that developed within the Fife area during 1928–9 [Arnot (1955) 190 ff.].

He entered national politics in 1922 when he was elected Labour MP for Peebles and South Midlothian and retained his seat until 1931. He served William Adamson as his parliamentary private secretary in 1929 during the second Labour Government and in 1931 he was Under-Secretary of State for Scotland but lost his seat at the general election of that year. He returned to Parliament in 1935 as Labour MP for Stirling and Falkirk, a seat which had been held by Hugh Murnin in 1922 and from 1924 to 1931. In the wartime Coalition Government he served once more as Under-Secretary of State for Scotland and at the general election of 1945 retained his parliamentary seat. In the Attlee Government he was Scottish Secretary of State from 1945 to 1947. He retired in the early autumn of 1947 as part of a general reshuffle of ministerial posts, the main purpose of which was to promote younger men.

Apart from his work for the miners and

for Scotland generally, he was also keenly interested in local government administration. He was a JP for Kirkcaldy, convenor of the housing committee of the town council and had a passionate interest in education, serving for many years on the Fife Education Committee, and playing an important role in the passing of the Scottish Education Act of 1945. He was also a member of the Educational Endowments (Scotland) Commission, the National Committee on Scottish Health Services, and was chairman of the Scottish Housing Advisory Committee, apart from other local activities. He was made a PC in 1943 and in recognition of his services to Kirkcaldy and Stirling was given the freedom of both cities. Both he and his wife (the latter especially) were active members of the Salvation Army in Kirkcaldy.

He had married in 1906 Frances, daughter of James Scarlett and Frances Harvey, and had three sons and five daughters. He and his wife were killed in a car accident on 17 July 1948 at Strathmiglo, Fife, and were buried in Dysart Cemetery, Kirkcaldy, their three sons being among the pallbearers. The funeral service would have been held in the local Salvation Army Hall but there were too many mourners and the Sinclairtown Parish Church was used; the service was conducted by the general secretary of the Scottish Salvation Army, Colonel Edwin Calvert, assisted by local church ministers. A London memorial service at the Crown Court Church, Russell Street, Bloomsbury, was held on the 28 July. Westwood left an estate valued at £5159. He was succeeded as Labour MP for Stirling and Falkirk by Malcolm MacPherson.

Sources: Labour Who's Who (1927); Anon., The Scottish Socialists: a gallery of contemporary portraits (1931); Dod (1947); WWW (1941–50); R. Page Arnot, A History of the Scottish Miners (1955); biographical information: Col. E. Anderson, general secretary, Salvation Army, Scotland. OBIT. Times, 19 July 1948; Stirling J. and Advertiser, 22 July 1948; Labour Party Report (1949).

JOYCE BELLAMY

See also: *William ADAMSON; *Robert SMIL-
LIE, for Scottish Mining Trade Unionism.

WHITEFIELD, William (1850–1926)
MINERS' LEADER

Born on 4 January 1850 in a small mining
village near Newcastle upon Tyne, William
Whitefield began work in the mines as a
door boy at the age of ten. He earned ten
pence for a twelve-hour day. He later joined
the 98th Regiment of the Foot, from which
he was bought out by an aunt, and then
worked for a time in the South Shields
Police Force before returning to work at the
coal face as a hewer. He had received but a
scanty education as a child but he remedied
this in early adult life by assiduous attendance and diligent study at various evening
schools and classes. By these means he succeeded in winning no fewer than four South
Kensington certificates for the subjects of
electricity and magnetism, acoustics, light
and heat, and physiography. He became involved in trade union affairs in early adult
life and in due course was elected to the
position of checkweighman which he held
for seven years before becoming a deputy.
He was a strong vigorous speaker and together with Charles Fenwick represented
the Northumberland miners at the conference of the Miners' National Union early in
1889; but next year at the Liverpool Trades
Union Congress he was one of five listed
from the MFGB.

By this time Whitefield had become agent
for the Bristol Miners' Association which
had been formed in the later 1880s and registered as a union in 1887. The Association
covered the pits in and around Bristol,
including Kingswood Chase, where John
Wesley had preached to the colliers in the
eighteenth century. In 1889 the Association
was looking for an agent and invited Whitefield to seek nomination. He delivered six
addresses on labour questions, and was
elected. At the end of his first year in office
he published his first annual report, in which
he recalled the conditions under which he
had accepted the nomination of agent –
these being that there should be a central
executive committee, that branch funds

should be centralised and that contributions
were to be increased from a penny to threepence per week. He further noted that membership had increased from 700 to 3300
and funds from £70 to 'upwards of £2000'.

Whitefield was a member of the first executive committee elected at the founding conference of the MFGB at Newport in November 1889; and he was re-elected at the first
annual conference in January 1890. He
served further terms on the executive in
1894, 1898 and 1904. Two weeks after the
January 1890 Conference, together with
Ned Cowey of Yorkshire, he was appointed
to conduct an inquiry into the Llanerch
Colliery explosion in which 176 men had
been killed. Their report, which was sharply
critical of a number of serious infringements
of mine safety regulations – especially the
use of naked lights – became a model for
many subsequent reports on colliery disasters.

Whitefield attended the first Miners'
International Conference at Jolimont in
1890 and the second at Paris in 1891,
and many thereafter. Together with Harry
Gosling he represented the TUC at the
Baltimore Convention of the American
Federation of Labor in 1916. He retired from
his post as agent in 1921.

In addition to his work for the miners,
Whitefield was active in local affairs from
the time of his arrival in Bristol. After not
much more than a year in the town, he was
nominated as Labour candidate at a by-
election in Bristol East in 1890; but he withdrew, allegedly for reasons of health, but
really because he saw no chance of winning
the seat. He also said that he did not want to
waste the miners' money. He served on the
Bristol School Board in 1892–3 and again
from 1901 to 1903; one of his main aims was
to see that Bristol schools burnt Bristol coal.
Whitefield's political career well illustrated
the transition of a trade union leader from
Liberal to Labour. He supported the ILP
candidate at a by-election in Bristol East in
1895, but then at the general election a few
months later he returned to the Liberal fold
and condemned the ILP for interfering: he
still regarded the election of a Liberal
Government (from which he hoped for a

Coal Mines Eight Hours Act) as of paramount importance. Yet by the early twentieth century he had definitely cast in his lot with Labour, being elected to the City Council for St George's East. Whitefield may even have been a member of the ILP at this time. The *Labour Leader* referred to him as such in 1906 and 1912 when reporting his election successes in St George's East, and the Bristol ILP Branch Minutes for 19 January 1908 refer to him as being on a list of ILP speakers. He certainly worked with the Bristol ILP, and sometimes spoke for them on the City Council. He retained his Council seat until 1919, when he became an alderman – only the third Labour alderman to be elected. He was also a JP for Bristol.

During the First World War Whitefield was an extreme jingo in politics, and he also became increasingly involved with spiritualism, which had interested him for many years. In his union work, in his last years, he lost the respect of the miners' national leaders – not least, it should be added, for his extraordinary conceit. He died at his Bristol home on 20 October 1926. The funeral was conducted by the president of the First Spiritual Church, and Whitefield was buried on 25 October at Avon View Cemetery, St George. He had married young, while still in the Army, and there were at least two daughters of the marriage, one of whom predeceased him. He left effects worth £431.

Sources: W. Hallam, *Miners' Leaders* (1894) [photograph]; S. Bryher, *An Account of the Labour and Socialist Movement in Bristol describing its early beginnings, struggles and growth* (Bristol, 1929); R. Page Arnot, *The Miners* (1949); idem, *The Miners: years of struggle* (1953); B. J. Atkinson, 'The 'Bristol Labour Movement 1868 to 1906' (Oxford DPhil., 1969); biographical information: Dr B. J. Atkinson, Univ. of Kent; NUM (S. Wales). Obit. *Bristol Evening News*, 20 Oct 1926; *Clifton Chronicle* and *Western Daily Press*, 21 Oct 1926; *Western Daily Press*, 26 Oct 1926.

R. Page Arnot
John Saville

See also: †Thomas Ashton, for Mining

Trade Unionism, 1900–14; †Benjamin Pickard, for Mining Trade Unionism, 1880–99.

WILLIAMS, Ronald Watkins (1907–58)
LABOUR MP

Williams was born on 18 July 1907 at Michaelstone Lower, Cwmavon, Glamorgan, the son of Thomas Jenkin Watkins a coalminer and his wife Mary Ellen (née Evans), and on his birth certificate his name was registered as Ronald Baily Watkins. When he was three his mother died and an uncle, Isaac Williams, a tobacconist, adopted him. After being educated at a Britton Ferry elementary school, he attended commercial school until he started work at the age of fifteen as a junior clerk in the office of a Swansea solicitor. He was articled in 1925 and after qualifying as a solicitor five years later he went into practice and was in partnership for six years in Swansea and Britton Ferry.

Williams first became active in the labour movement in 1936 when he applied for the post of solicitor to the Durham Miners' Association, (to which he was appointed out of about 200 applicants), and joined the Labour Party. He lived in Durham from 1936 to 1945, and during the Second World War he acted as the assistant county controller for Durham. In 1945 he moved to London as legal adviser to the National Union of Mineworkers, a post which he held full time until 1948. After the death of William Foster, Labour MP for Wigan, Williams was returned for that borough in a by-election in March 1948. In the general elections of 1950, 1951 and 1955 he was returned for the constituency with large majorities. Williams, who continued to advise the NUM, took with him to Parliament a highly specialised knowledge of the law as it related to such measures as workmen's compensation, industrial injury and social insurance. In 1939 and 1940 he had given evidence on behalf of the MFGB to the Royal Commission on Workmen's Compensation, and as the representative of a constituency in which coalmining was an important industry he continued to be active in these fields. He was a member of the Fabian Society, also for a time chairman of the Nationalised Industries group of the PLP, and he lectured at trade union and NCLC schools. At the time of his death he was a member of the standing committee on the Opencast Coal Bill.

Williams was active in other directions too. In 1949 he went with the Inter-Parliamentary Union delegations to Nice and Stockholm; he paid a visit to Malaya in 1950 as a member of the Commission of Parliamentary Delegates, and in 1951 he attended the Council of Europe at Strasbourg. He became especially interested in African affairs, and was a member of the Commission of Inquiry into the disorders in Nigeria in 1949. Williams was admitted to the Northern Rhodesian Bar in January 1953 when he represented the Northern Rhodesian African Mineworkers' Union in their claim for increased basic wages; the arbitrator in this dispute was C. W. Guillebaud, with Sir Hartley Shawcross (formerly Attorney-General 1945–51) acting as counsel for the mining companies. Two years later Williams again visited Northern Rhodesia to advise African miners who were on strike. On this occasion he went on behalf of the International Miners' Federation, and although the strikers had to accept a return to work without gaining any concessions, for the most part observers were impressed by his role in the negotiations. However, on reporting back to Labour Party colleagues he was subject to some criticism from the Movement for Colonial Freedom on the ground that the settlement was too much of a compromise. He had been one of the three Opposition members of a six-man Parliamentary Delegation to visit the troubled areas of Kenya in January 1954, during the Mau Mau period, and in 1956 he travelled to Kenya again, as a member of the Commonwealth Parliamentary Association delegation.

Williams died on 14 March 1958 at his home in Sanderstead, Surrey. At an inquest, after evidence that death was due to barbiturate poisoning aggravated by alcohol, the Coroner concluded that the cause was accidental, and recorded a verdict of misadventure. The funeral took place at the South London Crematorium, Streatham Vale, on 20 March, when James Griffiths MP, and Ernest Jones, president of the NUM, gave addresses. Hugh Gaitskell was among a number of MPs present. In 1934 Williams had married Miss Olive Bazzard, who survived him. There were no children of the marriage. Outside his political activities he was interested in singing and music. He was not a member of any religious denomination. In his will he left effects amounting to £6943.

In a tribute, Tom Brown, MP for Ince, wrote of Williams as one 'who was destined to make his mark in the realm of politics. He had the ability, he had legal training, a charming personality, a kindly nature, possessed of patience, and many other sterling qualities. ... He always impressed me when considering intricate and complicated matters arising from the many acts of Parliament. Understanding, of sterling honesty and determination, he was very conscientious and possessed a profound humanitarianism; he was courageous and never hesitated to express his opinions according to his connections, yet he bore no malice' [*Wigan Observer*, 21 Mar 1958].

Some years later, Lord Robens recorded an equally warm tribute to Williams's work in Parliament:

He was more than a member of the Standing Committee on the Opencast Coal Bill; he was heavily engaged in all the meetings dealing with the Labour Opposition's careful scrutiny of the Bill, and drafted every single amendment that we put down. This he did unaided; his legal abilities made him an ideal parliamentary draughtsman. I was leading for the Opposition in the Committee and leaned heavily upon him. He never grumbled, although I knew that this added burden added considerably to the pressure of his parliamentary duties. On the day of the evening he died, we discussed together another batch of amendments that would need to be drafted. They were a formidable assortment and time was short. His last words to me were 'Don't worry, Alf, I'll have them all done for Monday', in his usual cheery smiling way. That was a Sunday afternoon. He died during that night, and the labour movement lost a great figure and we who were his friends lost a man for whom we had the greatest affection [private letter of 29 Oct 1971].

Sources: Evidence before the R.C. on Workmen's Compensation [examined with several other witnesses] 1939-40 Non-Parl. Qs 6822-7537; Colonial Office Enquiry into the Disorders in the Eastern Provinces of Nigeria, *Proceedings of the Commission* (2 vols., HMSO); *Report of Commission of Enquiry* (Colonial No. 256, 1950); *Report to the Secretary of State for the Colonies by the Parliamentary Delegation to Kenya, January 1954, 1953–54* Cmd 9081 XI; *Times*, 3 Mar 1955; *Dod* (1957); *Labour Party Report* (1958); *WWW* (1951–60); personal information: Mrs Olive M. Williams, Sanderstead, widow; Lord Brockway; Lord Robens. OBIT. *Times*, 15 Mar 1958; *Wigan Examiner* and *Wigan Observer*, 21 Mar 1958.

DAVID E. MARTIN

See also: *Clement Richard ATTLEE, for British Labour Party, 1931–51.

WILLIAMS, Thomas (Tom)
(Lord Williams of Barnburgh)
(1888–1967)
MINERS' LEADER AND LABOUR POLITICIAN

Born on 18 March 1888 at Blackwell in Derbyshire, Tom Williams was the seventh son and tenth child in a family of fourteen of a Derbyshire miner. When he was two years old his father moved to Yorkshire and Tom received his early education at an elementary school in Swinton. His first earnings were from newspaper selling, and as neither of his parents could read or write he used to read to them frequently. He started as a full-time worker at Thrybergh Hall Colliery on the river Don when he was eleven and earned 7s 6d for a forty-hour week, and subsequently worked at other mines in the area, becoming an active trade unionist. While working at Wath Main

Colliery he was elected to the branch committee when he was only twenty and served for two years. He was also a delegate to the Mexborough Trades and Labour Council where he learned to prepare and deliver reports. After a period of unemployment following victimisation he and his wife, although abstainers, became steward and stewardess of the Wath Working Men's Club in 1912 where they remained for two years. While at the club, Williams extended his early education through a correspondence course and private study and qualified as a mining deputy, but more important was the general widening of his intellectual horizons which came from mixing with the club's customers. Exactly when Williams became a convinced Socialist is not quite clear, but it was probably during the years of the First World War. He became a member of both the ILP and the BSP: 'for variety as much as anything else', he noted in his autobiography, and the books that seem to have made most impression on him were Blatchford's *Merrie England* (1894), Jack London's *Iron Heel* (1907) and R. B. Suthers' *Mind Your Own Business* (1905).

Williams retired from the Working Men's Club in 1914 and returned to the pits. After working for a short time at Elsecar, he went to the newly opened colliery of Barnburgh Main where, at the end of 1915, he was elected checkweighman. He was also elected secretary of the branch committee but after a few years withdrew from this when he became delegate to the Yorkshire Miners' Association. He obtained further local prominence in 1918 when he was chosen to serve on the Doncaster Board of Guardians and was chairman of the Labour group on the Board for most of his five years' membership. In 1919 he was elected to the Bolton-on-Dearne Urban District Council when the Labour Party first took control of the Council and later served as chairman of the Council's housing committee.

He was chosen by the Yorkshire Miners' Association as one of their nominees for Parliament and at the 1922 general election he entered the Commons as Labour MP for the Don Valley constituency, a seat he held continuously for thirty-seven years and from which he retired on health grounds in 1959. In the Labour Government of 1924, he was parliamentary private secretary to the Minister of Agriculture and in the second Labour Government of 1929 to 1931 held the same position to the Minister of Labour (Margaret Bondfield). It was, however, in agriculture that he developed a specialist interest and in the wartime Coalition of 1940 to 1945 he served as parliamentary secretary to the Minister of Agriculture. With the Labour Party victory in the summer of 1945 Williams was the obvious choice for Minister of Agriculture. During the war and post-war years British agriculture was revitalised and Williams was primarily responsible for the Agriculture Act of 1947 which for more than two decades shaped post-war agricultural policy. When Labour went out of office in 1951 he remained the chief Opposition spokesman on agriculture until he left the Commons. Williams was a popular Minister (with the Parliamentary Opposition as well as with the farming community) and with the change of Government in 1951 and his departure from office, the affection with which he was held was demonstrated when about a hundred of the permanent officials in his Ministry inscribed an album to 'Dear Tom'. He was succeeded as MP for the Don Valley by Richard Kelley.

A Privy Councillor in 1941, he was given a life peerage in 1961 and adopted the title of Lord Williams of Barnburgh, the village in which he had worked as a miner. Other honours included the award of the gold badge of the National Union of Agricultural Workers; he was the first non-member of the Union to receive it. In 1961 he became one of three members of the Political Honours Committee and in 1962 received the Freedom of Doncaster. Honorary LL.D degrees were conferred on him by Cambridge in 1951 and Nottingham in 1955; and in 1965 he published his autobiography, *Digging for Britain*.

In his younger days, he was secretary of the Wath football team and later became a loyal supporter of Doncaster Rovers. He had married in 1910 Elizabeth Ann, daughter of Thomas Andrews and they had a son and daughter. In the last years of his life he suffered increasingly from rheumatoid arthritis and died at his Doncaster home on 29 March 1967. He was cremated at Rose Hill on 1 April 1967 and was survived by his wife and family; he left an estate valued at £9472.

Writings: *Digging for Britain* (1965).

Sources: S. V. Bracher, *The Herald Book of Labour Members* (1923); *Labour Who's Who* (1927); *Dod* (1948) and (1966); *Kelly* (1955); C. L. Mowat, *Britain between the Wars* (1955); G. D. H. Cole, *The Post-war Condition of Britain* (1956). OBIT. *Doncaster Gazette, Times* and *Yorkshire Post*, 31 Mar 1967; *Labour Party Report* (1967).

JOYCE BELLAMY
JOHN SAVILLE

See also: *Clement Richard ATTLEE, for British Labour Party, 1931–51; *Arthur James COOK, for Mining Trade Unionism, 1915–26; †Arthur HENDERSON, for British Labour Party, 1914–31.

WILLIS, Frederick Ebenezer (1869–1953)
TRADE UNIONIST

Willis's origins remain somewhat obscure. He was born in Birmingham on 5 May 1869 of unknown parents; one account states that he was put out to foster-parents until the age of nine. He then spent the next few years in Leicester with relatives of his foster-father (who had abandoned him), until he ran away to Birmingham at fourteen years of age [*Railway Services J.*, 15 Aug 1919]. One consequence of this unhappy and unsettled childhood was that Fred had only an elementary education, and in later life was largely self-taught.

In Birmingham he joined the Lawley Street Goods depot of the Midland Railway as a lorry boy. At the age of nineteen he took a better-paid job at a builder's, where he remained for about eighteen months before returning to the Midland as a porter. At this time he was struggling to improve his education, and after studying for a clerkship he was placed on the salaried staff of the railway in 1893. Two years later he became a bonded clerk at Birmingham Central station, and eventually rose to manager of the bonded stores, a post he held until his retirement in 1931.

As a young man in his early twenties he joined the Britannia Lodge No. 1345 of the Birmingham district of the Grand United Order of Oddfellows; and for the next two decades most of his leisure time seems to have been given to the Order. In 1892 he became Noble Grand of his Lodge and in 1899 was appointed District Master. At Glossop, in 1903, he attended his first Annual Movable Conference and was elected a member of the Board of Directors. In 1906 at the Oldham Conference he was appointed Deputy Grand Master, by a very large vote, and the next year he was unanimously elected Grand Master of the Order. For many years he was an influential figure in the friendly society movement in the Midlands, being a founder-member of the Birmingham and District Friendly Society Council. In addition to his gifts as a speaker, these activities served as qualification for his appointment in 1911 as a State lecturer on the National Health Insurance Act, after the passing of which he sat on the Old Age Pensions regional sub-committee.

Down to the years of the First World War, Willis does not seem to have taken any part in the trade union movement. All that is known of his general ideas, apart from his devoted commitment to the Oddfellows, is that he was a convinced rationalist in the tradition of Holyoake and Bradlaugh, and some accounts state that he was an active propagandist for the secularist movement. In April 1915, however – one month before reaching the age of forty-six – he joined the Railway Clerks' Association, and quickly rose to prominence. He was a delegate of the Birmingham No. 1 branch to the RCA annual conference at Cardiff in 1916, and was commended by his own union members for the part he played in the 1917 RCA conference at Chester. In 1919 he was elected to the executive council of the RCA, upon which he served until 1931. From 1931 to 1950 he was a trustee of the Association, so that his connection with it lasted altogether for some thirty-five years. At a local level he was also active in Labour politics. A railway clerks' delegate to the Birmingham Trades Council, he was elected its president in 1919, and his long service to the Council was later recognised when he was made a life member.

Among his other interests was working-class education. He helped to establish the Polytechnic Bursary scholarships for Birmingham University, and in 1920 he was made a life governor of the University. In the same year he was appointed a magistrate, serving as chairman of the Birmingham Licensing Justices from 1944 to 1948.

After two years of poor health, Willis died at his home in Church Road, Birmingham, on 28 February 1953, aged eighty-three, and was cremated at Yardley on 3 March. He was twice married and had three daughters. His second wife, Lizzie Maud, survived him, and he left effects of £2784 in his will.

Sources: *Railway Services J.*, 15 Aug 1919 [photograph] and Aug 1931; *Cornish's Birmingham Year Book* (1937–8); *Birmingham Post Year Book* (1952–3); J. Corbett, *The Birmingham Trades Council 1866–1966* (1966); biographical information: Grand United Order of Oddfellows Friendly Society; TSSA. OBIT. *Birmingham Mail*, 28 Feb 1953; *Birmingham Post*, 2 Mar 1953; *Transport Salaried Staff J.* (Apr 1953) 164.

DAVID E. MARTIN
JOHN SAVILLE

See also: John Arthur FALLOWS; †George Leydon PERKINS; John Valentine STEVENS,

WILSON, John (1856–1918)
MINER

John Wilson was born on 25 December 1856 in the parish of Doddington near the river Till, which runs into the Tweed, three miles north of Wooler, in the northern part of Northumberland. He was educated, for a short time only, at the village school of Lowick. At the age of eight he began work at Bideabout in a small landsale pit (one where the coal was sold at the mouth of the pit and taken away in carts), although it was illegal to work underground at that age. He left the area in his teens and went to work at Shilbottle Colliery three miles south of Alnwick, and then moved to pits further south. Between 1878 and 1884 he worked at Cambois Colliery, north of Blyth, but left the pit in the latter year owing to poor health, and he became an insurance agent in the Bishop Auckland area of Durham. In 1888 he helped William House, the president of the Durham Miners' Association to fight an electoral contest for the newly created Durham County Council, and his insurance business suffered from the publicity surrounding the election. His health, however, had improved and he returned in the same year to Cambois and the mines. In 1895 he was elected delegate to the NMA Council and he became a member of the Conciliation Board in 1900. In the same year the Northumberland Aged Mineworkers' Homes Association was established and Wilson was appointed its first secretary. For the first three or four years he received no salary but out-of-pocket expenses and the equivalent of lost wages. The number of days he had to take off for the work of the Association brought him into increasing conflict with the local colliery manager – Wilson was living in a colliery house – and in 1906 it was decided to pay him a weekly part-time salary of twenty-five shillings, with freedom to take other part-time work. Wilson then moved to Blyth and in 1910 became full-time paid secretary of the Association and moved again to Gosforth, just north of Newcastle, where he remained until his death. By that time the Association had built twenty groups of cottages for aged miners. The president of the Association from 1900 to 1923 was John Cairns.

Wilson, like so many other miners, played an important part in local affairs. He was a school manager at Cambois and a member of the Bedlington District Evening Class committee. From 1899 until he moved to Blyth he was on the Morpeth Board of Guardians. He became an active member of Blyth and District Trades Council and was the Labour and Trades Council member for Cowpen Quay on the Tynemouth Board of Guardians. For most of his life he was a Liberal and in 1900 was treasurer of the Morpeth Liberal Association, since he was a close personal friend of Thomas Burt, who had represented the borough from 1874. Wilson did, however, transfer his political allegiance to the Labour Party in the years before the First World War. Like many miners, too, he was a staunch co-operator and for years was a member of the Cambois Co-operative Society. In religion he was a Primitive Methodist, having been converted in his youth during a revivalist movement in the Lowick area; and he was a Sunday school teacher and a lay preacher. He helped start the Christian Endeavour movement at Cambois, and was an early president of the Bedlington and District Free Church Council.

He married Mary Hunter of Cambois in 1881 and their only child became head teacher of the Prudhoe County Council schools. Wilson suffered a nervous breakdown in 1914 and never fully recovered. He died 17 September 1918 at his Gosforth home. No record of a will has been located.

Sources: A. Watson, *A Great Labour Leader* (1908); B. Welbourne, *The Miners' Unions of Northumberland and Durham* (Cambridge, 1923); T. Burt, *Autobiography* (1924); *Jubilee Souvenir of the Northumberland Aged Mineworkers' Homes Association from 1900 to 1950* [1950]; R. F. Wearmouth, *Social and Political Influence of Methodism in the Twentieth Century* (1957); biographical information: Dr R. Page Arnot. OBIT. *Newcastle J.* 18 Sep 1918; NMA, *Monthly Circular* (1918).

ANTHONY MASON
JOHN SAVILLE

See also: †Thomas ASHTON, for Mining Trade Unionism, 1900–14; John CAIRNS; †Charles FENWICK; George Edward MIDDLETON; William STRAKER.

WINWOOD, Benjamin (1844–1913)
MINERS' LEADER

Winwood was born on 8 March 1844 at Bayton, a small village near Bewdley, in

Worcestershire. When he was only twelve months old his parents moved to Blackheath in South Staffordshire, and Winwood spent nearly all his life in this corner of the Black Country. He started work at the age of six, blowing bellows in a rivet-maker's shop. Subsequently he worked in a brickyard, carrying clay for the brickmakers, and then, at the age of ten, joined his father in the mines. His very first day underground almost proved fatal. Only his father's presence of mind in snatching the boy away prevented his being killed or seriously injured by a fall of the heavy balancing chains used to lower the skip.

Incidents such as this were common in the South Staffordshire coalfield during the middle years of the nineteenth century. As well as being among the most productive coalfields in the country (in 1866 output reached 10.3 million tons, more than one-tenth of the total for the whole of Great Britain), it also had the highest death rate. This was due to a number of factors: the constant inundation of the mines by water, the pillar and stall method of working the unique and magnificent 'ten yard coal' seam, and the organisation of production on the sub-contract or 'butty' system. Under this system, the organisation of production was based on a threefold division of function between landlord, tenant and charter-master or butty. The landlord leased to the tenant for a royalty, usually based on the selling price of coal. The tenant, who was usually an ironmaster, was responsible for providing most of the fixed capital in the pit – the engine-house, steam-engine and pithead gear. The tenant was also responsible for maintaining the rails in the pit and ensuring its dryness. The butty was the contractor of the tenant and it was he who actually drew the coal. He provided the rest of the fixed capital and the circulating capital – tools, skips, horses, etc., and he paid the colliers' wages. For this the butty was paid an agreed price per ton of coal raised. His income thus depended on his success in keeping costs down while raising the maximum amount of coal, and this frequently resulted in the abuse and disregard of safety regulations.

As a young man Winwood frequently acted as spokesman for his fellow miners in their attempts to obtain better wages and conditions. He was consequently victimised and blacklisted in South Staffordshire, and in 1867 was forced to leave the district altogether. After working for about twelve months in the north of the county, he returned to South Staffordshire, and in 1870 took part in establishing the Old Hill Miners' Association. Over the next years, in spite of continuing persecution by the coal-owners, he played a leading role in the Association's agitations, and in 1883 was elected full-time agent in succession to William Breakwell.

By this time a sharp division in temper had appeared among the Black Country miners. The Black Country is effectively divided into two sections by a limestone ridge running from north-west to south-east across the area. North-east of this line (usually referred to as 'east of Dudley') union attitudes tended to be, on the whole, co-operative and conciliatory. In the south-west sector ('west of Dudley') they tended to be belligerent, suspicious and un-cooperative. The reasons for this have not yet been authoritatively established, but an explanation can be attempted in terms of three factors producing a different group psychology in the miners of the two sectors. These factors were the greater vulnerability of the miners, *vis-à-vis* the owners, in the north-east sector, arising from the fact that from the middle 1860s mining in this sector was declining, while west of Dudley it was still expanding; a different pattern of immigration into the two sectors; and the differences in the structure of industry between the two sectors. The iron industry was heavily concentrated in the north-east sector and from 1872 industrial relations in this industry were based on a system of conciliation and sliding scales, operated through a succession of wages boards. On the other hand, by 1860 and increasingly thereafter, the two main domestic trades of the Black Country, nail- and chain-making, were concentrated in the small towns and villages west of Dudley. The main industrial weapon of the operatives in these industries was the restriction-of-output strike. These contrasting approaches to the problem of wage settlement among their fellow working men could have been the third contributory factor to the differing attitudes of miners east and west of Dudley. By the time Winwood succeeded to the agency the Old Hill Association was firmly rooted in the militant 'west of Dudley' tradition, and under his leadership this was maintained and further developed.

Significantly, in the light of the hypothesis outlined above, ironworkers never formed a numerous group in this district, and it was one of the last strongholds of the domestic trades. Similarly the Old Hill part of the South Staffordshire coalfield was among the last to be worked, so that it was still expanding while surrounding districts were in accelerating decline. Winwood's election to the Old Hill agency coincided with the establishment of the first South Staffordshire and East Worcestershire Miners' Wages Board, which was committed to the principles of sliding scales and arbitration. The Old Hill Association resolved to take no part in its proceedings, identifying itself instead with the growing national movement towards policies of restricting output and limiting hours. The Wages Board was effectively destroyed within a year by the third of the great Black Country coal strikes in 1884. The men's representatives on the Board pledged them to accept a reduction in wages from 3s 8d to 3s 4d per day, but in defiance of this the miners came out. A four-month strike ensued, at the end of which the reduction was enforced. Winwood's strenuous advocacy of a 3s 8d per day minimum wage, and the revealed inadequacy of the Wages Board, considerably enhanced his prestige among the Black Country miners and heightened the owners' hatred of him. The failure of the strike strengthened Winwood's conviction, grounded in his experience of the previous unsuccessful strikes of 1864 and 1874, that isolated strikes could never succeed, and that effective action required broadly-based support. In pursuit of this policy he took the Old Hill miners into the Midland Counties Trades Federation (for which see Richard Juggins [DLB 1 (1972) 206–8]) until the establishment of the Miners' Federation of Great Britain provided a more suitable form of alliance.

The three years between the formation of the Midland Counties Trades Federation and the establishment of the MFGB saw two important developments in mining unionism in the Black Country. Late in 1886 the second Midland Miners' Federation was formed, and control of policy was quickly established in the hands of anti-sliding-scale leaders, such as Enoch Edwards and Ben Dean. Though all the Black Country unions remained members of the Midland Federation until this body joined the MFGB in 1889, except for the Old Hill Association their participation was purely nominal, and in the autumn of 1888 the great body of Black Country miners formally set themselves apart from the Midland Federation and all it represented, with the establishment of the second South Staffordshire and East Worcestershire Wages Board. Once again Winwood declared the Old Hill Association's intention of standing apart from the Board. Since, however, most of the pits in his district were owned by masters who had collieries elsewhere in the Black Country and were organised by leaders committed to the sliding scales of the Wages Board, this intention was difficult to carry into practice. Accordingly, Winwood became vice-chairman of the Wages Board and the Old Hill Association a reluctant partner in its deliberations.

When the MFGB was established, Winwood's support for its proposed policy of restriction of output contrasted sharply with the refusal of the other miners' representatives on the Board to commit themselves to abide by Rule 20 of the Federation. This was the famous militancy rule, empowering the Federation to call a general strike if any constituent county, federation or district should be attacked on the wages question or on any action endorsed by a general conference, and acceptance of it was clearly incompatible with adherence to sliding scales. So, less than a year after accepting the position, Winwood resigned as vice-chairman of the Wages Board, and took the

Old Hill Association into the MFGB, while the rest of the Black Country unions, now dominated by the West Bromwich Association, remained outside. Thus there were now some 8000 to 9000 miners who recognised the authority of the Wages Board, while about 3000 stood apart from it, paying no levies, but none the less having their wages regulated by it. Consequently to the owners' hostility towards Winwood was now added the suspicion of other Black Country miners' leaders.

Having committed himself and his Association to the MFGB Winwood remained unswervingly loyal to it despite many bitter attacks on him by those who remained outside the Federation, and through the 1890s the logic of allying with the national movement gradually permeated the rest of the Black Country districts. As the decade wore on, the sliding scale became increasingly inoperative and it became obvious that wage rates in the Black Country were effectively governed by those in the Federation districts. Thus during the Federation lock-out of 1893 the Black Country districts remained at work and were consequently inundated with orders, but the $7\frac{1}{2}$ per cent reduction imposed in the Federation districts in the year following the lock-out was also made effective in the Black Country. In these circumstances the Wages Board became merely a symbol, and with the election of Tom Mansell as secretary of the West Bromwich Association in 1894 the Black Country miners drew ever closer to the MFGB. Finally, in 1899, the West Bromwich Association, which had now absorbed all the other Black Country unions except Old Hill, rejoined the Midland Federation and hence affiliated to the MFGB, leaving the Wages Board to be reconstituted as a Conciliation Board, a form in which it continued for some years. Thus as the century ended, all organised Black Country miners were in the MFGB, and Mansell joined Winwood and Benjamin Dean on the committee of the Midland Miners' Federation.

Thus vindicated, his uncompromising militancy amply justified by events, Winwood assumed the position of elder statesman among the miners' agents in the Black Country. The obduracy he exhibited as a union leader contrasted strongly with his quiet and reserved nature. He did not belong to any religious sect, and he took little part in public life, except for service on the Halesowen Old Age Pensions Committee and the South Staffordshire Mining Compensation Fund Committee, and for a short time on Hill (Halesowen) Parish Council.

In his last years Winwood suffered from Bright's disease, and increasingly delegated the affairs of the Old Hill Association to the financial secretary, Samuel Edwards. By the time of the dispute over the individual minimum wage in 1912 he was a very sick man, but he stayed on to lead the Association through the national strike and the local dispute which followed, before retiring in July, to be succeeded by Edwards. During the period of his agency Winwood had seen miners' wages in the Black Country rise from 3s 4d per day to 6s 3d per day, and had been largely instrumental in building up the Association to almost 100 per cent membership of the 2500 miners in the Old Hill district. In February 1913, in the presence of thirty delegates representing all the South Staffordshire miners, he was presented with a purse of gold sovereigns in recognition of his services to trade unionism.

Winwood died at his home Clent View Cottages, Olive Lane, Halesowen, on 11 September 1913, survived by his wife, one son and four daughters. On 16 September he was buried in the churchyard of Blackheath Parish Church, after a service according to the rites of the Ancient Order of Foresters, of which he had been a member for many years. The pall-bearers were six working miners; at the end of the ceremony they clasped hands across the open grave in a last gesture of respect to the man whose integrity and single-mindedness had done so much for the cause of unionism and the welfare of miners. At the time of Winwood's death, his son Benjamin Southwick Winwood was a coal merchant. He later became a partner in a small engineering firm, Joseph Wyle and Co. of Blackheath. He was an active member of the Liberal Party, and from 1911 to 1920 he was a member of the former Oldbury Urban District Council. He died from injuries sustained in a road accident in March 1933, when he was sixty-three years old.

Sources: Reports of activities of Old Hill Miners' Association in *County Advertiser* [for Staffordshire and Worcestershire], *County Herald* [for Worcestershire and Staffordshire], *Dudley Herald, Stourbridge County Express,* especially 1883–1912 [copies of the *County Advertiser, Herald* and *Express* at offices of *County Express,* Stourbridge; *Dudley Herald:* Dudley Public Library]; *Labour Tribune,* 1886–1894; W. Hallam, *Miners' Leaders* (1894); T. E. Lones, *History of Mining in the Black Country* (Dudley, 1898); *Stourbridge County Express,* 17 Oct 1908 [interview with Winwood on 25th anniversary of his appointment as Old Hill agent]; *County Herald,* 9 Mar 1912 [photograph]; *County Herald,* 22 Feb 1913; G. C. Allen, *The Industrial Development of Birmingham and the Black Country 1860–1927* (1929, repr. 1966) [esp. pt 2, ch. 6 and pt 4, ch. 2 for the butty system]; R. Page Arnot, *The Miners* (1949); A. Fox, 'Industrial Relations in Birmingham and the Black Country 1860–1914' (Oxford BLitt., 1952); A. J. Taylor, 'The Sub-contract system in the British Coal Industry' in *Studies in the Industrial Revolution,* ed. L. S. Pressnell (1960). OBIT. *County Advertiser* [for Staffordshire and Worcestershire], *County Herald, Stourbridge County Express,* 13 Sep 1913; *County Advertiser* and *County Herald,* 20 Sep 1913.

ERIC TAYLOR

See also: †Benjamin DEAN; †Enoch EDWARDS; *Samuel EDWARDS; †Richard JUGGINS; *Thomas MANSELL; Henry RUST; *John TAYLOR.

WYLD, Albert (1888–1965)
CO-OPERATOR

Albert Wyld was born on 9 August 1888 at Kettleshulme, near Macclesfield, Cheshire, the son of James Thomas Wyld, a coalminer and his wife Mary (née Jackson). He was a pupil at the Kettleshulme village school but, although a good scholar, he was prevented by family circumstances from attending a secondary school. He was an Anglican by religion, and was organist at the local Church in his youth. While he was apprenticed to the Whaley Bridge and Buxton Co-operative Society he extended his education through evening classes and correspondence courses under Professor Fred Hall of the Co-operative College. From 1913 to 1924 he was general manager of the Dove Holes Co-operative Society and from 1924 to 1928 he served the Cinderford Co-operative Society, Gloucestershire as secretary-manager. From 1928 to 1932 he was the general manager of the Cainscross and Ebley Co-operative Society near Stroud, and from 1932 to 1936 general secretary of the Scunthorpe Co-operative Society. He then transferred to Reading, where from April 1936 until his retirement in April 1950 he was general manager of the local co-operative society. During his long service with the retail co-operative movement, he was a member of several of its regional and national organisations. From 1942 to 1943 he was president of the Southern Co-operative General and Grocery Managers' Association; he was a member of the Coal Merchants' Consultative Committee of London, and of the food committee and other committees in Reading during the Second World War, and from December 1947 to March 1950 he was chairman of the National Co-operative Coal Trade Association.

He was a member of the Co-operative and Labour Parties all his adult life and was always active in local affairs, serving on the Stroud Urban District Council for three years, as a JP for Berkshire from 1944 to 1951 and during 1947 to 1951 on the bench of the juvenile court. He retired to Bournemouth where his first wife died in 1952, and in the following year he married a family friend, Miss Elsie Clark, whose father had been an active co-operator in the Scunthorpe area, a trade unionist and a Labour Party worker [*DLB 1* (1972) 73–4]. After an unsuccessful attempt to become a magistrate at Bournemouth, a matter evidently of political or social prejudice, or perhaps both, Albert Wyld then undertook prison visiting at Dorchester Prison from 1954 to 1959. He

and his wife then decided to return to
Scunthorpe and within six months Wyld was
appointed to the Scunthorpe Bench, on
which he served from 1960 until 1963 when
he had reached the age limit of seventy-five.
Mr and Mrs Wyld then returned to Bournemouth where he died, after a short illness,
on 17 December 1965.

By his first wife, Miss Martha Rothwell,
whom he had married in 1913, he had a son,
Cecil Thomas, who became a pharma-
ceutical chemist. Albert Wyld was survived
by his second wife and his son and he left an
estate valued at £5690.

Sources: Minutes of Co-operative Coal
Trade Association: Co-operative Union,
Manchester; personal information: Mrs E.
Wyld, Yaddlethorpe, near Scunthorpe,
widow. OBIT. *Co-op. News*, 1 Jan 1966.

JOYCE BELLAMY

See also: †Fred CLARK; †Fred HALL, for Co-
operative Education.

Consolidated List of Names
Volumes I and II

ABBOTTS, William (1873–1930) I
ABRAHAM, William (Mabon)
  (1842–1922) I
ACLAND, Alice Sophia (1849–1935) I
ACLAND, Sir Arthur Herbert Dyke
  (1847–1926) I
ADAIR, John (1872–1950) II
ADAMS, John Jackson, 1st Baron Adams
  of Ennerdale (1890–1960) I
ADAMS, William Thomas (1884–1949) I
ALEXANDER, Albert Victor
  (Earl Alexander of Hillsborough)
  (1885–1965) I
ALLAN, William (1813–74) I
ALLEN, Reginald Clifford (Lord Allen
  of Hurtwood) (1889–1939) II
ALLEN, Robert (1827–77) I
ALLEN, Sir Thomas William
  (1864–1943) I
ALLINSON, John (1812/13–72) II
AMMON, Charles (Charlie) George
  (Lord Ammon of Camberwell)
  (1873–1960) I
ANDERSON, Frank (1889–1959) I
ANDERSON, William Crawford
  (1877–1919) II
APPLEGARTH, Robert (1834–1924) II
ARCH, Joseph (1826–1919) I
ARNOLD, Thomas George (1866–1944) I
ASHTON, Thomas (1844–1927) I
ASHWORTH, Samuel (1825–71) I
ASPINWALL, Thomas (1846–1901) I
AUCOTT, William (1830–1915) II

BAILEY, Sir John (Jack) (1898–1969) II
BAILEY, William (1851–96) II
BALLARD, William (1858–1928) I
BAMFORD, Samuel (1846–98) I
BARKER, George (1858–1936) I
BARNETT, William (1840–1909) I
BARTON, Eleanor (1872–1960) I

BATES, William (1833–1908) I
BATEY, John (1852–1925) I
BATEY, Joseph (1867–1949) II
BAYLEY, Thomas (1813–74) I
BEATON, Neil Scobie (1880–1960) I
BELL, George (1874–1930) II
BELL, Richard (1859–1930) II
BIRD, Thomas Richard (1877–1965) I
BLAIR, William Richard (1874–1932) I
BLAND, Thomas (1825–1908) I
BLANDFORD, Thomas (1861–99) I
BOND, Frederick (1865–1951) I
BONDFIELD, Margaret Grace
  (1873–1953) II
BONNER, Arnold (1904–66) I
BOYLE, Hugh (1850–1907) I
BOYNTON, Arthur John (1863–1922) I
BRACE, William (1865–1947) I
BRADBURN, George (1795–1862) II
BRAILSFORD, Henry Noel
  (1873–1958) II
BRANSON, Clive Ali Chimmo
  (1907–44) II
BROADHURST, Henry (1840–1911) II
BROWN, James (1862–1939) I
BROWN, Herbert Runham
  (1879–1949) II
BROWN, William Henry
  (1867/8–1950) I
BRUFF, Frank Herbert (1869–1931) II
BUGG, Frederick John (1830–1900) I
BURNETT, John (1842–1914) II
BURT, Thomas (1837–1922) I
BUTCHER, John (1833–1921) I
BUTCHER, John (1847–1936) I
BYRON, Anne Isabella, Lady Noel
  (1792–1860) II

CAIRNS, John (1859–1923) II
CAMPBELL, Alexander (1796–1870) I
CANN, Thomas Henry (1858–1924) I

CAPPER, James (1829–95) II
CARPENTER, Edward (1844–1929) II
CARTER, Joseph (1818–61) II
CARTER, William (1862–1932) I
CATCHPOLE, John (1843–1919) I
CHARTER, Walter Thomas (1871–1932) I
CHEETHAM, Thomas (1828–1901) I
CIAPPESSONI, Francis Antonio
  (1859–1912) I
CLARK, Fred (1878–1947) I
CLARKE, Andrew Bathgate
  (1868–1940) I
CLARKE, William (1852–1901) II
CLAY, Joseph (1826–1901) I
COCHRANE, William (1872–1924) I
COMBE, Abram (1785?–1827) II
COOK, Cecily Mary (1887/90?–1962) II
COOPER, George (1824–95) II
COOPER, Robert (1819–68) II
COOPER, William (1822–68) I
COULTHARD, Samuel (1853–1931) II
COURT, Sir Josiah (1841–1938) I
COWEN, Joseph (1829–1900) I
COWEY, Edward (Ned) (1839–1903) I
CRABTREE, James (1831–1917) I
CRAIG, Edward Thomas (1804–94) I
CRAWFORD, William (1833–90) I
CROOKS, William (1852–1921) II

DALLAWAY, William (1857–1939) I
DALY, James (?–1849) I
DARCH, Charles Thomas (1876–1934) I
DAVIES, Margaret Llewelyn
  (1861–1944) I
DAVISON, John (1846–1930) I
DEAKIN, Arthur (1890–1955) II
DEAN, Benjamin (1839–1910) I
DEAN, Frederick James (1868–1941) II
DEANS, James (1843/4?–1935) I
DEANS, Robert (1904–59) I
DENT, John James (1856–1936) I
DIXON, John (1828–76) I
DOCKER, Abraham (1788/91?–1857) II
DRAKE, Henry John (1878–1934) I
DUDLEY, Sir William Edward
  (1868–1938) I
DUNCAN, Andrew (1898–1965) II
DUNCAN, Charles (1865–1933) II
DUNNING, Thomas Joseph
  (1799–1873) II
DYE, Sidney (1900–58) I
DYSON, James (1822/3–1902) I

EADES, Arthur (1863–1933) II
EDWARDS, Enoch (1852–1912) I
EDWARDS, John Charles (1833–81) I
EDWARDS, Wyndham Ivor (1878–1938) I
ENFIELD, Alice Honora (1882–1935) I
EVANS, Isaac (1847?–97) I
EVANS, Jonah (1826–1907) I

FALLOWS, John Arthur (1864–1935) II
FENWICK, Charles (1850–1918) I
FINCH, John (1784–1857) I
FINNEY, Samuel (1857–1935) I
FISHWICK, Jonathan (1832–1908) I
FLEMING, Robert (1869–1939) I
FORMAN, John (1822/3–1900) I
FOSTER, William (1887–1947) I
FOULGER, Sydney (1863–1919) I
FOWE, Thomas (1832/3?–94) I
FOX, James Challinor (1837–77) I
FOX, Thomas (Tom) (1860–1934) II
FRITH, John (1837–1904) I

GALBRAITH, Samuel (1853–1936) I
GALLAGHER, Patrick (Paddy the Cope)
  (1871–1966) I
GANLEY, Caroline Selina (1879–1966) I
GIBBS, Charles (1843–1909) II
GILL, Alfred Henry (1856–1914) II
GLOVER, Thomas (1852–1913) I
GOLIGHTLY, Alfred William
  (1857–1948) I
GOODY, Joseph (1816/17–91) I
GRAHAM, Duncan MacGregor
  (1867–1942) I
GRAY, Jesse Clement (1854–1912) I
GREENALL, Thomas (1857–1937) I
GREENING, Edward Owen
  (1836–1923) I
GREENWOOD, Abraham (1824–1911) I
GREENWOOD, Joseph (1833–1924) I
GROVES, William Henry (1876–1933) II

HACKETT, Thomas (1869–1950) II
HADFIELD, Charles (1821–84) II
HALL, Frank (1861–1927) I
HALL, Fred (1855–1933) II
HALL, Fred (1878–1938) I
HALL, George Henry (1st Viscount Hall
  of Cynon Valley) (1881–1965) II
HALL, Joseph Arthur (Joe)
  (1887–1964) II
HALL, Thomas George (1858–1938) II

HALLAM, William (1856–1902) I
HALLAS, Eldred (1870–1926) II
HALSTEAD, Robert (1858–1930) II
HANCOCK, John George (1857–1940) II
HANDS, Thomas (1858–1938) II
HARDERN, Francis (Frank)
  (1846–1913) I
HARES, Edward Charles (1897–1966) I
HARRISON, Frederic (1831–1923) II
HARRISON, James (1899–1959) II
HARTSHORN, Vernon (1872–1931) I
HARVEY, William Edwin (1852–1914) I
HASLAM, James (1842–1913) I
HASLAM, James (1869–1937) I
HAWKINS, George (1844–1908) I
HAYHURST, George (1862–1936) I
HAYWARD, Sir Fred (1876–1944) I
HEADLAM, Stewart Duckworth
  (1847–1924) II
HENDERSON, Arthur (1863–1935) I
HETHERINGTON, Henry (1792–1849) I
HIBBERT, Charles (1828–1902) I
HICKEN, Henry (1882–1964) I
HILTON, James (1814–90) I
HINDEN, Rita (1909–71) II
HINES, George Lelly (1839–1914) I
HOBSON, John Atkinson (1858–1940) I
HOLE, James (1820–95) II
HOLYOAKE, Austin (1826–74) I
HOLYOAKE, George Jacob (1817–1906) I
HOOSON, Edward (1825–69) I
HOUSE, William (1854–1917) II
HOWARTH, Charles (1814–68) I
HOWELL, George (1833–1910) II
HUCKER, Henry (1871–1954) II
HUDSON, Walter (1852–1935) II
HUGHES, Edward (1856–1925) II
HUGHES, Hugh (1878–1932) I
HUTCHINGS, Harry (1864–1930) II

IRONSIDE, Isaac (1808–70) II

JACKSON, Henry (1840–1920) I
JARVIS, Henry (1839–1907) I
JENKINS, Hubert (1866–1943) I
JOHN, William (1878–1955) I
JOHNS, John Ernest (1855/6–1928) II
JOHNSON, Henry (1869–1939) II
JOHNSON, John (1850–1910) I
JOHNSON, William (1849–1919) II
JONES, Benjamin (1847–1942) I
JONES, Patrick Lloyd (1811–86) I

JUGGINS, Richard (1843–95) I

KELLEY, George Davy (1848–1911) II
KENYON, Barnet (1850–1930) I
KILLON, Thomas (1853–1931) I
KING, William (1786–1865) I

LANG, James (1870–1966) I
LANSBURY, George (1859–1940) II
LAWSON, John James (Lord Lawson of
  Beamish) (1881–1965) II
LEE, Frank (1867–1941) I
LEE, Peter (1864–1935) II
LEES, James (1806–91) I
LEWIS, Richard James (1900–66) I
LEWIS, Thomas (Tommy) (1873–1962) I
LIDDLE, Thomas (1863–1954) I
LINDGREN, George Samuel
  (Lord Lindgren of Welwyn Garden City)
  (1900–71) II
LOCKWOOD, Arthur (1883–1966) II
LONGDEN, Fred (1886–1952) II
LOVETT, Levi (1854–1929) II
LOWERY, Matthew Hedley
  (1858–1918) I
LUDLOW, John Malcolm Forbes
  (1821–1911) II
LUNN, William (Willie) (1872–1942) II

MACARTHUR, Mary (1880–1921) II
MACDONALD, Alexander (1821–81) I
MacDONALD, James Ramsay
  (1866–1937) I
McGHEE, Henry George (1898–1959) I
MANN, Amos (1855–1939) I
MARCROFT, William (1822–94) I
MARLOW, Arnold (1891–1939) I
MARTIN, James (1850–1933) I
MAXWELL, Sir William (1841–1929) I
MAY, Henry John (1867–1939) I
MERCER, Thomas William (1884–1947) I
MESSER, Sir Frederick (Fred)
  (1886–1971) II
MIDDLETON, George Edward
  (1866–1931) II
MILLERCHIP, William (1863–1939) I
MILLINGTON, Joseph (1866–1952) II
MITCHELL, John Thomas Whitehead
  (1828–95) I
MITCHISON, Gilbert Richard (Baron
  Mitchison of Carradale)
  (1890–1970) II

MOLESWORTH, William Nassau (1816–90) I

MOORHOUSE, Thomas Edwin (1854–1922) I

MORGAN, David (Dai o'r Nant) (1840–1900) I

MORGAN. David Watts (1867–1933) I

MORGAN, John Minter (1782–1854) I

MUDIE, George (1788?–?) I

MURNIN, Hugh (1865–1932) II

MURRAY, Robert (1869–1950) I

NEALE, Edward Vansittart (1810–92) I

NEWTON, William (1822–76) II

NOEL, Conrad le Despenser Roden (1869–1942) II

NORMANSELL, John (1830–75) I

NUTTALL, William (1835–1905) I

O'GRADY, Sir James (1866–1934) II

OLIVER, John (1861–1942) I

ONIONS, Alfred (1858–1921) I

PARE, William (1805–73) I

PARKER, James (1863–1948) II

PARKINSON, John Allen (1870–1941) II

PARKINSON, Tom Bamford (1865–1939) I

PARROTT, William (1843–1905) II

PASSFIELD, 1st Baron Passfield of Passfield Corner. See Webb, Sidney James II

PATTERSON, William Hammond (1847–96) I

PATTISON, Lewis (1873–1956) I

PEASE, Edward Reynolds (1857–1955) II

PEASE, Mary Gammell (Marjory) (1861–1950) II

PENNY, John (1870–1938) I

PERKINS, George Leydon (1885–1961) I

PICKARD, Benjamin (1842–1904) I

PICKARD, William (1821–87) I

PIGGOTT, Thomas (1836–87) II

PITMAN, Henry (1826–1909) I

POINTER, Joseph (1875–1914) II

POLLARD, William (1832/3?–1909) I

POSTGATE, Daisy (1892–1971) II

POSTGATE, Raymond William (1896–1971) II

POTTS, John Samuel (1861–1938) II

PRATT, Hodgson (1824–1907) I

PRINGLE, William Joseph Sommerville (1916–62) II

PRYDE, David Johnstone (1890–1959) II

PURCELL, Albert Arthur (1872–1935) I

RAE, William Robert (1858–1936) II

RAMSEY, Thomas (Tommy) (1810/11–1873) I

REDFERN, Percy (1875–1958) I

REEVES, Samuel (1862–1930) I

REEVES, William Pember (1857–1932) II

RICHARDS, Thomas (1859–1931) I

RICHARDSON, Robert (1862–1943) II

RITSON, Joshua (Josh) (1874–1955) II

ROBINSON, Richard (1879–1937) I

ROBSON, James (1860–1934) II

ROBSON, John (1862–1929) I

ROGERS, Frederick (1846–1915) I

ROWLINSON, George Henry (1852–1937) I

ROWSON, Guy (1883–1937) II

RUST, Henry (1831–1902) II

RUTHERFORD, John Hunter (1826–90) I

SAMUELSON, James (1829–1918) II

SCHOFIELD, Thomas (1825–79) II

SEDDON, James Andrew (1868–1939) II

SEWELL, William (1852–1948) I

SHACKLETON, Sir David James (1863–1938) II

SHALLARD, George (1877–1958) I

SHANN, George (1876–1919) II

SHARP, Andrew (1841–1919) I

SHILLITO, John (1832–1915) I

SHURMER, Percy Lionel Edward (1888–1959) II

SIMPSON, James (1826–95) I

SIMPSON, William Shaw (1829–83) II

SITCH, Charles Henry (1887–1960) II

SITCH, Thomas (1852–1923) I

SKEVINGTON, John (1801–50) I

SLOAN, Alexander (Sandy) (1879–1945) II

SMITH, Herbert (1862–1938) II

SMITHIES, James (1819–69) I

SPARKES, Malcolm (1881–1933) II

SPENCER, George Alfred (1873–1957) I

SPENCER, John Samuel (1868–1943) I

STANLEY, Albert (1862–1915) I

STANTON, Charles Butt (1873–1946) I

STEVENS, John Valentine (1852–1925) II

STEWART, Aaron (1845–1910) I
STRAKER, William (1855–1941) II
SULLIVAN, Joseph (1866–1935) II
SWIFT, Fred (1874–1959) II

TAYLOR, John Wilkinson
  (1855–1934) I
THICKETT, Joseph (1865–1938) II
THORNE, William James (1857–1946) I
THORPE, George (1854–1945) I
TOOTILL, Robert (1850–1934) II
TOPHAM, Edward (1894–1966) I
TORKINGTON, James (1811–67) II
TOYN, Joseph (1838–1924) II
TRAVIS, Henry (1807–84) I
TWEDDELL, Thomas (1839–1916) I
TWIGG, Herbert James Thomas
  (1900–57) I
TWIST, Henry (Harry) (1870–1934) II

VARLEY, Frank Bradley (1885–1929) II
VINCENT, Henry (1813–78) I
VIVIAN, Henry Harvey (1868–1930) I

WADSWORTH, John (1850–1921) I
WALKER, Benjamin (1803/4?–83) I
WALSHAM, Cornelius (1880–1958) I
WARDLE, George James (1865–1947) II
WATKINS, William Henry (1862–1924) I

WATTS, John (1818–87) I
WEBB, Beatrice (1858–1943) II
WEBB, Catherine (1859–1947) II
WEBB, Sidney James (1st Baron Passfield
  of Passfield Corner) (1859–1947) II
WEBB, Simeon (1864–1929) I
WEBB, Thomas Edward (1829–96) I
WEIR, John (1851–1908) I
WEIR, William (1868–1926) II
WELSH, James C. (1880–1954) II
WESTWOOD, Joseph (1884–1948) II
WHITEFIELD, William (1850–1926) II
WHITEHEAD, Alfred (1862–1945) I
WILLIAMS, Aneurin (1859–1924) I
WILLIAMS, John (1861–1922) I
WILLIAMS, Ronald Watkins
  (1907–58) II
WILLIAMS, Thomas (Tom) (Lord
  Williams of Barnburgh) (1888–1967) II
WILLIS, Frederick Ebenezer
  (1869–1953) II
WILSON, John (1837–1915) I
WILSON, John (1856–1918) II
WINSTONE, James (1863–1921) I
WINWOOD, Benjamin (1844–1913) II
WOODS, Samuel (1846–1915) I
WORLEY, Joseph James (1876–1944) I
WRIGHT, Oliver Walter (1886–1938) I
WYLD, Albert (1888–1965) II

General Index

Compiled by V. J. Morris and G. D. Weston
with the assistance of Margaret 'Espinasse and Joyce Bellamy

Numbers in bold type refer to biographical entries

Abbotsholme School, 89
Aberdare, 146, 147
Aberdare Cables Ltd, 147–8
Aberdeen, 11
Abraham, William, 366
Accrington Weavers' Association, 335
Acland, Lady Alice Sophia, 396
Acland, Sir Arthur Herbert Dyke, 380
Acts of Parliament: *see* Parliamentary Acts
Adair, John, **1**
Adams, Harry, 56
Adamson, Professor Robert, 47
Adamson, William, 269, 360, 400, 402
Adelphi Permanent Benefit Land, Building and Investment Society, 184–5, 191
Admiralty, 147
Adult Education, 155, 157–8. *See also* Education, working-class
Adult School Movement, 142, 209, 339
Adult Suffrage Society, 40
Afghan Wars (1879–80), 167
Agriculture, Ministry of, 407
Akroydon (Halifax), 184
Alexander, Albert Victor (*later* Earl Alexander of Hillsborough), 238
Allan, William, 16, 73, 129, 130, 188, 248, 270, 272, 273
Allen, Edith, 305
Allen, Marjory (Lady Allen of Hurtwood), **8**
Allen, Reginald Clifford (*later* Lord Allen of Hurtwood), **1–10**, 13, 41, 49, 69, 217, 240
Allen, Victor Leonard, 112
Alliance Cabinet-Makers' Society, 131–2
Allinson, John, **10–11**, 93
Allotments system, 77
Amalgamated Malleable Ironworkers of Great Britain (1868–87), 23, 24, 83, 84, 299, 300. *See also* Associated Iron and

Steel Workers of Great Britain (formerly National Amalgamated Association of Ironworkers)
Amalgamated Society of Carpenters and Joiners, 16, 17, 18, 19, 20, 21, 351, 384
Amalgamated Society of Engineers, 14, 16, 73, 113, 123–4, 129, 247, 248, 270, 271, 272, 273
Amalgamated Society of Lithographic Printers, 211, 213
Amalgamated Society of Railway Servants, 34, 35, 37, 40, 195, 197, 198, 199, 265, 364, 373, 374; All Grades Campaigns, 35, 37; Darlington Programme, 197
Amalgamated Society of Tailors, 73
Amalgamated Society of Woodworkers, 152
Amalgamated Tinplate Workers' Association, 356
Ambatielos, Mrs Betty, 241
American Civil War, 17, 102, 105, 129, 130, 165, 189, 248, 274
American Federation of Labor, 41, 139, 150, 337, 403
Amery, Leopold Charles Maurice Stennett, 217, 341
Anarchism, 204, 205
Anchorsmiths, Shackle and Shipping Tacklemakers Association, 345
Anderson, Mary (Mrs W. C. Anderson): *see* Macarthur, Mary Reid
Anderson, William Crawford, 2, **11–16**, 254, 256, 258, 259, 303
Angell, Sir Norman, 351
Anglo–Hellenic League, 318, 319
Anti-Aggression League, 167
Anti-Corn Law League, 10, 93, 106, 244, 367
Anti-Semitism, 7, 8
Anti-Slavery Association, 244